3rd Edition

COMMON CULTURE

Reading and Writing about American Popular Culture

Edited by

Michael Petracca
Madeleine Sorapure

University of California at Santa Barbara

Prentice
Hall

Upper Saddle River, New Jersey 07458

Library of Congress Cataloging-in-Publication Data

Common culture : reading and writing about American popular culture / edited by
Michael Petracca, Madeleine Sorapure. —3rd ed.
    p. cm.
  Includes bibliographical references (p.603) and index.
  ISBN 0-13-085098-5

   1. Popular culture—United States. 2. United States—Social life and customs—1971– I.
Petracca, Michael, (date). II. Sorapure, Madeleine.

E169.04.C65   2000
306'.0973—dc21   00–029796

Editorial Director: *Laura Pearson*
Editor-in-Chief: *Leah Jewell*
Acquisitions Editor: *Corey Good*
Assistant Editor: *Vivian Garcia*
Editorial Assistant: *Jennifer Collins*
Managing Editor: *Mary Rottino*
Production Liaison: *Fran Russello*
Project Manager: *Pine Tree Composition*
Prepress and Manufacturing Buyer: *Mary Ann Gloriande*
Art Director: *Jayne Conte*
Cover Designer: *Bruce Kenselaar*
Cover Art:
Director, Image Resource Center: *Melinda Lee Reo*
Manager, Rights & Permissions: *Kay Dellosa*
Image Specialist: *Beth Boyd*
Photo Researcher:
Marketing Manager: *Brandy Dawson*

Acknowledgments appear on pages 633–638, which constitute a continuation of the
copyright page.

This book was set in 10/12 Palatino by Pine Tree Composition, Inc., and was printed
and bound by Courier Companies, Inc. The cover was printed by Phoenix Color Corp.

© 2001, 1998, 1995 by Prentice-Hall, Inc.
A Division of Pearson Education
Upper Saddle River, New Jersey 07458

Printed in the United States of America
10 9 8 7 6 5 4 3 2 1

ISBN 0-13-085098-5

Prentice-Hall International (UK) Limited, *London*
Prentice-Hall of Australia Pty. Limited, *Sydney*
Prentice-Hall Canada Inc., *Toronto*
Prentice-Hall Hispanoamericana, S.A., *Mexico*
Prentice-Hall of India Private Limited, *New Delhi*
Prentice-Hall of Japan, Inc., *Tokyo*
Pearson Education Asia Pte. Ltd., *Singapore*
Editora Prentice-Hall do Brasil, Ltda., *Rio de Janeiro*

For my sister, brave explorer of nerve pathways,
healer of wounded neckbones, dedicated
connoisseuse *of the half-hour sitcom.*
—M.P.

For my mother, whose odd tastes I inherited,
and whose grace and courage I admire.
—M.S.

Contents

2 Advertising   36

5 Cyberculture   333

6 Sports   408

Preface

When we started teaching composition courses that examined television, pop music, movies, and other media-generated artifacts, we looked for a text that would cover a full range of topics in the field of popular culture from a variety of theoretical perspectives. We discovered that no satisfactory text existed, and therefore we began putting together assignments and reading materials to meet our needs. From this compilation *Common Culture* emerged.

The more we've taught writing courses based on popular culture, the more convinced we've become that such courses are especially appealing for students and effective in improving their critical thinking, reading, and writing skills. Students come into the writing classroom already immersed in the culture of Beavis and Butt-head, Benetton, Beastie Boys, and Barry Bonds. The advantage, then, is that we don't have to "sell" the subject matter of the course and can concentrate on the task at hand—namely, teaching students to think critically and to write clear and effective prose. Obviously, a course that panders to the lowest common denominator of students' taste would be a mindless, unproductive enterprise for all concerned. However, the underlying philosophy of a pop culture-based writing course is this: By reading, thinking, and writing about material they find inherently interesting, students develop their critical and analytical skills—skills which are, of course, crucial to their success in college.

Although students are already familiar with the many aspects of popular culture, few have directed sustained, critical thought to its influence or implications—that is, to what shopping malls might tell them about contemporary culture or to what they've actually learned from watching "The Jerry Springer Show." Because television shows, advertisements, and music videos, for example, are highly crafted artifacts, they are particularly susceptible to analysis; and because so much in contemporary culture is open to interpretation and controversy, students enjoy the opportunity to articulate and argue for their own interpretations of objects and institutions in the world around them.

Although popular culture is undeniably a sexy (or, at least, lively) subject, it has also, in the past decade, become accepted as a legitimate object of academic discourse. While some may contend that it's frivolous to write a dissertation on "The Brady Bunch," most scholars recognize the importance of studying the artifacts and institutions of contemporary life. Popular culture is a rich field of study, drawing in researchers from a variety of disciplines. Because it is also a very inviting field of study for students, a textbook that addresses this subject in a comprehensive and challenging way will be especially appealing both to them and to their writing teachers.

Common Culture, third edition, contains an introductory chapter that walks students through one assignment—in this case, focusing on the Barbie doll—with step-by-step instruction in reading carefully and writing effectively. The chapters that follow open with a relevant and catchy cultural artifact (for example, a cartoon, an ad, an album cover) that leads into a reader-friendly, informative introduction; a selection of engaging essays on an issue of current interest in the field of pop culture; carefully constructed reading and discussion questions; and writing assignments after each reading and at the end of the chapter.

Common Culture approaches the field of popular culture by dividing it into its constituent parts. The book contains chapters on advertising, television, music, cyberculture, sports, movies, and leisure. Most of the chapters are divided into two parts: the first presents essays that address the topic generally, while the second offers essays that explore a specific aspect of the topic in depth. For example, in the chapter on advertising, the essays in the first group discuss theories and strategies of advertising, while later essays explore images of women and men in ads.

We've purposely chosen readings that are accessible and thought-provoking, while avoiding those that are excessively theoretical or jargon-ridden. The readings in this book have the added advantage of serving as good models for students' own writing; they demonstrate a range of rhetorical approaches, such as exposition, analysis, and argumentation, and they offer varying levels of sophistication and difficulty in terms of content and style. Similarly, the suggested discussion and writing topics move from relatively basic concerns to tasks that require a greater degree of critical skill. Because of this range, instructors using *Common Culture* can easily adapt the book to meet the specific needs of their students.

Acknowledgments

As California instructors and therefore participants in the growth-and-awareness movement, we'd like first to thank each other for never straying from the path of psychic goodwill and harmony, and then to thank the universe for raining beneficence and light upon this project. And while on the subject of beneficence and light, we'd like to thank our current Editor-in-Chief, Leah Jewell, and our original editor, Nancy Perry, both of whom radiate these qualities and without whose wisdom, largesse, and good humor we would have fallen into deep despair. Thanks, furthermore, to Mark Gallaher, our development editor for the first edition; Harriett Prentiss, who helped us with the second; and our present editor Vivian Garcia, who patiently shepherded us through the third. We'd like to thank the following reviewers of the second edition: James Morrison, North Carolina State University; Brian K. Reed, Bethane-Cookman College; David D. Moser, Butler County Community College; Joe P. Wiggins, University of Idaho; Wendy Secrist, University of Idaho; and Susan A. Nash, Capital University.

We want to thank Muriel Zimmerman, former Director of the Writing Program at UCSB, for lending moral and intellectual support to the original project, and Judith Kirscht, our current director. Johanna Blakely and Bonnie Beedles suggested several of the readings we included here, while Evelyn Chiaverini and Rita Raley assisted in formulating endnotes and end-of-reading questions. Thanks also to Larry Behrens and Sheridan Blau for lending their expertise in the area of textbook publishing.

Michael Petracca
Madeleine Sorapure

1
Reading and Writing about American Popular Culture

Just do it!
Dilbert.
The Gap.
Caesar's Palace.
Tiger Woods.
"The Simpsons."
Yo Quiero Taco Bell.
Super Bowl.
Lilith Fair.
Y2K bug.

If any of these names and phrases sounds familiar—and it would be a great surprise if some didn't—it's because we spend our lives immersed in popular culture. There's no escaping it. Like hydrogen atoms and common-cold viruses, pop culture is everywhere. You absorb it at home watching television, listening to the stereo, or reading a magazine or newspaper; passing billboards or listening to the radio on the street; chatting over coffee at work or having a burger with friends; going out to movies and dance clubs, health spas, fast-food restaurants, shopping malls and sports arenas; even noticing the graffiti that glares out at you on building facades and highway overpasses.

In fact, unless you're isolated in a mountaintop cave, you can hardly avoid the influence of popular culture. Television, radio, newspapers, and magazines shape your ideas and behavior; like family, friends, and school, pop culture is part of your learning environment, supplying ready-made images, ideas, and patterns of behavior that you draw from, consciously or unconsciously, as you live your daily life. Exactly how you learn and just what you learn may not be all that certain, but it is undeniable that popular culture is one of your most powerful teachers.

One reason to study popular culture is that, by paying closer attention to this daily bombardment of information, you can think more critically about how it affects you and others. You may start by asking relatively simple questions—"Do I really need my breath to be 'Mentos fresh and full of life'?"—and work your way to far more significant ones—"How can we keep young women from starving themselves in their desire to conform to the images they see in advertisements?" Analyzing pop culture with a critical eye allows you to begin to free yourself from the manipulation of the media; it is an important step toward living an examined life.

WHAT IS POPULAR CULTURE?

What do we mean by popular culture? The term may at first seem contradictory. *Popular*, in its broadest sense, means "of the people," while we often associate *culture* with refinement and intellectual superiority, "the best which has been thought and said," as Matthew Arnold put it. We might ask how culture, traditionally reserved for the elite, the educated, and the upper class, can simultaneously belong to the common mass of humanity.

One way to resolve this seeming dilemma is to think of culture in an anthropological sense, as the distinct practices, artifacts, institutions, customs, and values of a particular social group. This is the way, for instance, that we distinguish the culture of the United States in the early twenty-first century from the culture of our great-grandparents or from that of societies in other times and places.

We can also define popular culture by distinguishing it from its counterparts: *high culture* and *folk culture.*

High culture consists of the artifacts traditionally considered worthy of study by university academics and other educated people: classical music by composers such as Beethoven and Brahms; "fine" art from the impressionists and expressionists; literature and philosophy written by the likes of Shakespeare and Sartre.

At the other end of the spectrum, folk culture refers to artifacts created by a specific community or ethnic group, usually a relatively isolated nontechnological society such as the pygmies of Africa's Ituri Forest or certain communities in our own Appalachian Mountains. While high culture is primarily preserved and studied in the academy, folk culture is generally transmitted through oral communication; both, however, place a high value on tradition, on artifacts produced in the past, and on the shared history of the community.

By contrast, popular culture encompasses the most immediate and contemporary elements in our lives—elements which are often subject to rapid changes in a highly technological world in which people are brought closer and closer by the ubiquitous mass media. Pop culture offers a common ground, as the most visible and pervasive level of culture in a given society. If the Metropolitan Opera House represents high culture, then Madison Square Garden represents pop. If the carefully crafted knives used in Asian cooking rely on a folk tradition, then the Veg-O-Matic is their pop counterpart.

Several other terms help us establish a working definition of popular culture. *Mass culture* refers to information we receive through print and electronic media. While mass culture is often denigrated as juvenile or "low," it has to be treated as an important component of popular culture by virtue of the immense size of its audience. The terms *subculture* and *counterculture,* on the other hand, suggest a desire to resist the pressures, implied or explicit, to conform to a common culture. Subcultures are specific segments of society outside the core of dominant culture. Minority groups in the United States might be called subcultures, just as certain groups such as artists, homosexuals, lawyers, or teenagers can be thought of as having cultural markers distinct from the broader culture. A counterculture, on the other hand, is a group or movement which defines itself specifically as opposing or subverting the dominant culture. Hippies of the 1960s and punk-rockers of the 1980s defined themselves as countercultural groups.

Although we may place ourselves in specific folk or high cultures, subcultures or countercultures, we are still aware of and immersed in the broader popular culture simply by virtue of living in society. As Edward Jay Whetmore notes,[1] "Popular culture represents a common denominator, something that cuts across most economic, social, and educational barriers." If the notion of culture reflects a certain degree of social stratification and differentiation, then popular culture represents the elements of everyday life, the artifacts and institutions shared by a society, and a body of common knowledge.

Another distinguishing characteristic of popular culture is its transitory nature. New images appear on our TV screens, replacing the popular images of years or seasons before; new phrases supersede former favorites in our popular lexicon; unknown entertainers become celebrities overnight, while others fade just as quickly from the spotlight. Madonna takes the place of Gidget; "Change of Heart" replaces "Studs," which replaced "Singled Out," which took over from "The Dating Game"; the expression "Just do it!" was for the 1990s what "Ring around the collar!" was for the 1970s.

Interestingly, if an icon of popular culture survives, it can often make the leap into high culture. For example, Wilkie Collins's nineteenth-century horror stories were read as avidly as Stephen King's novels are today. His works survive among today's elite audiences but are virtually unknown to most popular audiences. We might ask then, what of contemporary popular culture might survive beyond the immediate here and now and ultimately speak to future audiences at a higher, more specialized level?

What, then, is pop culture? Although it's notoriously difficult to define, some elements of a definition emerge from this discussion: pop culture is the shared knowledge and practices of a specific group at a specific time. Because of its commonality, pop culture both reflects and influences the people's way of life; because it is linked to a specific time and place, pop culture is transitory, subject to change, and often an initiator of change.

WHY STUDY POPULAR CULTURE?

Though pop culture is increasingly accepted as a legitimate object of academic inquiry, educators still debate whether it should be studied. Some critics contend that it would be more valuable to study the products of high culture—Shakespeare rather than Spielberg, Eliot rather than Elvis. Their arguments often center on the issue of *quality*, as they assert that pop culture, transitory and often trendy, lacks the

---

[1]Whetmore, Edward Jay. *Mediamerica: Form, Content, and Consequence of Mass Communication.* Belmont, CA: Wadsworth 1989.

lasting value and strong artistic merit of high culture. Further, they argue that, because pop appeals to a mass audience rather than an educated elite, it is necessarily of low quality, no better than average. Although few critics of pop culture deny its pervasive influence, many argue that this influence should be considered negative, and they point to the violence and sexual explicitness of song lyrics, television programs, and movies, as well as to the triviality and downright foolishness of many popular trends. Pop culture debases us, these critics contend, turning us into passive recipients of low-quality goods, distracting us from higher pursuits.

It's important to note that very few proponents of pop culture—pop cultists, as Marshall Fishwick[2] calls them—take a wholesale, uncritical approach and approve all things popular. Many, for example, accept the argument that products with mass appeal are often qualitatively inferior to those intended for an educated, elite audience. However, pop cultists remind us that the gap between the two isn't always so wide; that the same basic activities of creation, refinement, and reception are involved in both popular and high culture; and that, as we've noted, the "popular" works of one era can become the "classics" of another.

Moreover, pop cultists argue for the validity of studying MTV, *The National Enquirer*, video games, and the Miss America Pageant because such mass phenomena serve as a kind of mirror in which we can discern much about ourselves. George Lipsitz,[3] for instance, suggests that "perhaps the most important facts about people have always been encoded within the ordinary and the commonplace." And as Ray Browne,[4] a noted scholar of pop culture, puts it, "Popular culture is a very important segment of our society. The contemporary scene is holding us up to ourselves to see; it can tell us who we are, what we are, and why."

We see reflected in pop culture certain standards and commonly held beliefs about beauty, success, love, or justice. We also see reflected there important social contradictions and conflicts—the tension between races, genders, or generations, for example. To find out about ourselves, then, we can turn to our own popular products and pastimes.

---

[2]Browne, Ray B., and Marshall Fishwick. *Symbiosis: Popular Culture and Other Fields*. Bowling Green, OH: Bowling Green U.P., 1988.

[3]Lipsitz, George. *Time Passages: Collective Memory and American Popular Culture*. Minneapolis: Univ. of Minnesota Press, 1990.

[4]Browne, Ray B., and Marshall Fishwick. *Symbiosis: Popular Culture and Other Fields*. Bowling Green, OH: Bowling Green U.P., 1988.

Another argument for studying popular culture focuses on the important influence it exerts on us. The media and other pop culture components are part of the fund of ideas and images that inform our daily activities, sometimes exerting a more compelling influence than family or friends, school or work. When we play sports, we mimic the gestures and movements of professional athletes; we learn to dance from the videos on MTV; we even name our children after popular television characters. More importantly, we discover role models; we learn lessons about villainy and heroism, love and relationships, acceptable and unacceptable behavior; we see interactions with people from other cultures. Even if popular culture is merely low-quality amusement or a means of escaping the demands of the "real" world, it delivers important messages that we may internalize and later act on—for better or for worse. We should examine and analyze pop culture, then, in order to assess—and sometimes resist—its influences.

The readings and assignments in *Common Culture* give you the chance to explore these issues and determine for yourself the role of popular culture in shaping society and in shaping you as an individual. The book includes chapters on important components of popular culture: advertising, television, music, cyberculture, sports, movies, and leisure activities. You may already know quite a lot about some of these topics, and you may have relatively little interest in or exposure to others. Either way, as disinterested observer or engaged participant, you can bring your critical skills to bear on phenomena of the contemporary world. The readings and assignments encourage you to observe carefully, to question, and to construct and defend your own interpretations of some of the institutions and events, the beliefs and practices, the media and the messages in your everyday life.

Before beginning, we will look at methods of reading and writing that will help you participate fully and critically in reaching the goals of this book.

ACTIVE READING

We've discussed the importance of paying attention to the "common culture" that surrounds you in order to recognize its meanings and influences on your life. In this section, we present specific reading strategies that you can apply both to pop culture and to the essays in this book. Whether you're watching TV or reading an essay about TV, the habit of active, engaged interpretation will make the experience much more worthwhile. While you may have been encouraged to be an active reader of print material, the essays throughout this book also encourage you to be an active reader of the culture around you.

There's a crucial difference between passively receiving and actively reading. Passively ingesting information requires very little - effort or interest, and it gives very little in terms of reward or stimulation. Active reading demands more of your time, effort, and thought, but it is ultimately much more useful in helping you develop a better understanding of ideas.

Although reading is generally a solitary activity, it helps to think of active reading as a discussion or dialogue with another person. You listen carefully; you compare what the person tells you to what you already know; you question statements that strike you as complicated, confusing, or incorrect; you identify ideas that are particularly interesting and important to you; you respond with ideas of your own. As a result of your active participation, you come away with new insights and a clearer sense of your own position. You may even be stimulated to seek out more information from other sources in order to clarify your thoughts.

When you read actively—whether printed texts or products of popular culture—you use very similar strategies, questioning and responding and speculating about what you're reading. You are no longer a disinterested bystander simply "listening in"; rather you are a participant who is energetically engaged with an author's ideas or with the messages underlying a commercial or television program.

Strategies for Active Reading

There are a number of specific stages and strategies involved in active reading. In the **preparatory** stage you develop a general sense of what the essay will be about. In the **reading** stage, you begin the actual dialogue with the author by paying close attention to what he or she has written, identifying key points, responding to certain ideas, and asking questions. Next comes the **re-reading** stage, in which you go back through the essay to get a clear and firm understanding of what you've read. Finally, in the **reviewing** stage, you take time to draw conclusions, evaluate the author's position, and develop your own responses; often you'll want to go back to the essay and read certain sections even more carefully or to turn to other sources to help you formulate your response. In the actual practice of active reading, these four stages circle back on one another as well as spiral outward, prompting you to do further reading and exploration.

As you see, active reading is quite different from passively receiving or consuming information. By reading actively, you'll be able to clarify and develop your own ideas and your responses to the influences operating on you in your everyday life. You can become a more proficient and accomplished writer, increasing the range and precision of your vocabulary, using different options for constructing sentences and paragraphs, creating different stylistic effects, and, in general, improving your "feel" for written language.

An Active Reading Casebook: Three Selections about Barbie

This section includes three reading selections—a poem and two essays about the Barbie doll—that demonstrate the strategies of active reading and suggest the kind of reading you'll be doing in later chapters.

We've chosen to begin with a look at Barbie because of her longevity, popularity, and cultural significance. Since her "birth" in 1959, Barbie has achieved celebrity status in United States culture and, indeed, worldwide. More than 775 million Barbies have been sold in the last thirty-five years, and Barbie products continue to bring in hundreds of millions of dollars every year for Mattel Inc., her owner and America's biggest toy company. In 1994, Mattel estimated that 95 percent of girls aged three to eleven own at least one Barbie, while the average is seven. Barbie lives in nearly every United States and Canadian household that includes children and in more than sixty other countries as well. In addition to her extensive accessories and her many friends (among them, her boyfriend, Ken, and her African American pal, Shani), Barbie has her own magazine and fan club and her own corps of press agents, advertising executives, and "personal secretaries" to answer her fan mail. Yves St. Laurent and Bill Blass have designed clothes especially for her; Tiffany created a sterling silver version of Barbie; and New York City's Fifth Avenue became "Barbie Boulevard" to mark her twenty-fifth birthday.

For three decades, girls (and boys, too) have been playing with and learning from Barbie, and thus she serves as an important force in conveying cultural values and attitudes. Barbie's influence is undeniable, but opinions vary as to the quality of that influence on the children who play with her and on the adults they become. Barbie's critics argue that her influence has been largely detrimental, that her improbable measurements (36-18-33), her even more improbable hair, and her inexhaustible supply of clothes and accessories help perpetuate an inappropriate model of women's interests and lives. However, defenders argue that her influence has been positive, at least in part. They point out that Barbie has recently had careers such as corporate executive, airline pilot, medical doctor, animal rights activist, and even presidential candidate, offering girls a chance to envision themselves being successful in the working world. Although Barbie's wedding dress is one of her most popular outfits, she's never officially married Ken (or G.I. Joe), and she remains a single, independent career woman, providing, some observers say, an alternative to the view that women's primary roles are as wives and mothers.

You can see that Barbie has served as a symbolic reference point for broader debates about femininity and masculinity, about beauty and success, about consumerism and lifestyle in our culture. Barbie is a good example of the way elements of popular culture can be interpreted in order to reveal some fundamental aspects of our society.

While reading this background information on Barbie, you may be thinking of your own experience as a child playing with Barbie or with other dolls and toys, and speculating about their formative influence on you. If so, you've begun to prepare for reading, by orienting yourself to the topic, by exploring your own ideas and experiences, and by thinking about the issues at hand.

Preparing to Read   Let's turn now to our first selection, a poem about Barbie written by Hilary Tham. All the readings in this book are accompanied by headnotes, which briefly explain what the reading is about and give some background information on the author. In this sense, headnotes are like the front and back covers of many books, providing an overview of what will follow and serving as the place to begin thinking about the topic. Here is the headnote for the poem "Barbie's Shoes":

> Our first selection is a poem by Hilary Tham. Tham was born in Kelang, Malaysia, and currently lives in Virginia with her husband and three daughters. She teaches creative writing in high schools and has published several books of poetry, including *No Gods Today, Paper Boats, Bad Names for Women,* and *Tigerbone Wine.*

You can get an idea of what to expect from the poem both by reading the headnote and by recalling what you know about poetry in general. The headnote tells you that Hilary Tham is originally from Malaysia and now lives in the United States. You might conclude from this information that Tham brings a dual perspective to the Barbie doll and other features of United States pop culture. The headnote also points out that Tham has three daughters and teaches high school students. Before you read the poem, then, you might speculate on how being a mother and a teacher would influence Tham's thoughts about the Barbie doll.

Reading and Annotating   In the reading stage, one of the most useful strategies you can use is *annotating* the text. When you annotate you use a pencil or pen to mark key words and phrases in the text and to write questions and responses in the margins. You underline words that you need to look up in a dictionary and phrases that you find particularly interesting, forceful, important, questionable, or confusing.

You also record your reactions, thoughts, questions, and ideas in the margins. By annotating in this way, you keep track of what the author is saying and of what you're thinking as you read.

Here are one student's annotations of Tham's poem...but keep in mind that your annotation would probably identify different elements as particularly important.

Barbie's Shoes
HILARY THAM

I'm down in the (basement)   *Why the basement?*
sorting Barbie's shoes.
   sequin pumps, satin courts,
   western boots, Reebok sneakers,   *Different shoes show*
   glass slippers, ice-skates, thongs.   *Barbie's many activities*
All will fit the dainty, forever arched
feet of any one Barbie: Sweet Spring
   Glitter-Eyed, Peaches and Cream,
   a Brazilian, Russian, Swiss, Hong Kong
   Hispanic or Mexican, Nigerian
   or Black Barbie. All are cast   *Barbies are different*
in the (same) mold, (same) rubbery,   *but also the same*
impossible embodiment of male fantasy
with carefully measured
   doses of melanin to make
     a Caucasian Barbie,
      Polynesian Barbie
      African-American Barbie.
Everyone knows that she is the (same)   *Barbie =*
Barbie and worthy of the American Dream   *American Dream*
House, the Corvette, opera gloves, a
hundred pairs of shoes to step into. If only
the differently colored men and women we know
could be like Barbie, always smiling, eyes
wide with admiration, even when we yank
off an arm with a hard-to-take-off dress.
Barbie's shoes, so easily lost, mismatched,   *Simile: Barbie's shoes*
useless; they end up, like our prejudices,   *are like our prejudices—*
in the basement, forgotten as spiders   *forgotten, but still there,*
sticking webs in our darkest corners,   *in the basement, like*
we are amazed we have them still.   *spider webs.*

Re-reading   After you read and annotate the poem, your task is to fully understand it and formulate your own response to it. Many students close the book after just the first reading without realizing that the next two stages, re-reading and reviewing, are crucial to discovering the significance of what they have read.

In the re-reading stage, you go back through the poem and the annotations in order to develop a good understanding of the writer's ideas. Then you begin to articulate those ideas—in your own words. Here's an example drawn from the earlier annotation of "Barbie Shoes."

> I'm really drawn to the simile in the last few lines: that Barbie's shoes are "like our prejudices, / in the basement, forgotten as spiders / sticking webs in our darkest corners, / we are amazed we have them still." Tham is saying that Barbie's shoes are more than just tiny plastic footwear. They represent prejudices which we think we've thrown away but in fact still have in our "basements" (our subconscious thoughts?). And by comparing these prejudices to spiders' webs "in our darkest corners," perhaps Tham is suggesting that our prejudices still "catch" things; they still operate in our lives even if we've forgotten them or don't see them.

With ideas like these as a starting point, you can go back through the entire poem and begin to formulate a response to other key ideas and phrases: the list of Barbie's shoes; the list of different nationalities and ethnicities of Barbie dolls; the idea that all Barbies are in some way the same; the suggestion that Barbie represents the American Dream. Re-reading like this will surely provoke further questions about the poem. For instance, why does Tham make a point of mentioning the many different types of Barbies? In what ways are these differences only superficial and unrealistic? And what does Tham mean when she writes, "If only / the differently colored men and women we know / could be like Barbie, always smiling, even when we yank / off an arm...."? You know that Tham is being ironic since we don't generally yank arms off other people, but what point is she making in this comparison, and how does it relate to her ideas about prejudice?

These kinds of questions lead you to re-read the poem, clarifying your understanding and finding further meanings in it. After each essay in this book there are similar sorts of reading questions which will help you explore the ideas you've read about. We also encourage you to develop your own questions about what you read to focus your exploration on those points that you find most interesting, important, or controversial.

Reviewing   After re-reading, questioning, and exploring the writer's ideas in detail, you should take time to summarize what you've learned. Here is a student's summary of her analysis of "Barbie's Shoes."

1. Tham suggests that Barbie's shoes are like prejudices (forgotten, seemingly lost, down in the basement, "useless" and "mismatched"); why can't we just throw them out? why are they still in the basement?
2. Why does Barbie have so many shoes?! Perhaps Tham is implying that we have an equal number of seemingly insignificant prejudices, one for every occasion, even.
3. Tham points out that there are many different kinds of Barbie dolls (Caucasian, Polynesian, African American) but all are "worthy of the American Dream House." In this sense Barbies are all the same. So does Barbie influence us to overlook the real differences in women's lives? We're not dolls, after all, and although we're all worthy of success and accomplishment, we don't all get the same chances.
4. Tham describes Barbie as the "impossible embodiment of male fantasy." How is this observation related to the rest of the poem? Could she be saying that this fantasy is related to prejudice?

Such questions and tentative answers can help you begin to formulate your own interpretation of and complete response to what you've read.

Reading Pop Cultural Criticism   In the previous discussion we used Hilary Tham's poem as our example because poetry can pack so much meaning into the space of relatively few words. In the chapters that follow you'll be reading not poems but rather articles, essays, and chapters of books, most of which fall into one of two categories. The first we might call *pop cultural criticism* and includes the kind of pieces written for general audiences of popular magazines and mass market books. Typically these reflect a particular social perspective, whether traditionalist or cutting edge, conservative or liberal, pro- or anticapitalist, and often they are written in response to a particular issue or phenomenon reported in the media.

The following piece by John Leo is an example of pop cultural criticism. As you read, practice the strategies that we've discussed. Begin by considering the headnote and what it suggests about Leo's perspective and purpose, then underline important passages in the essay and jot down your thoughts, responses, and questions in the margins.

The Indignation of Barbie
JOHN LEO

John Leo's "The Indignation of Barbie" was first published in U.S. News & World Report *in 1992. Leo, a conservative journalist and social commentator, writes about the controversy surrounding the talking Barbie doll produced by Mattel in the early 1990s. Among Talking Barbie's repertoire of phrases was "Math class is tough," viewed by some feminists and professional women as discouraging girls from pursuing the subject. Here, Leo imagines a dialogue with Barbie, in which the talking doll defends herself against charges that she's a "prefeminist bimbo."*

Barbie will probably survive, but the truth is, she's in a lot of trouble. It seems that the new Teen Talk Barbie, the first talking Barbie in 20 years, has shocked many feminists with a loose-lipped comment about girls and math. Each $25 doll speaks four of 270 programmed one-liners. In one of those messages, Barbie says, "Math class is tough." This was a big error. She should have said, "Math is particularly easy if you're a girl, despite the heavy shackles of proven test bias and male patriarchal oppression." 1

Because of this lapse from correctness, the head of the American Association of University Women is severely peeved with Barbie, and you can no longer invite both of them to the same party. Other feminists and math teachers have weighed in with their own dudgeon. 2

Since this is Barbie's darkest hour, I placed a phone call out to Mattel, Inc. in California to see how the famous long-haired, long-legged forerunner of Ivana Trump was holding up. To my astonishment, they put me right through to Barbie herself. 3

"Barbie, it's me," I said. As the father of three girls, I have shopped for 35 to 40 Barbies over the years, including doctor Barbie, ballerina Barbie, television news reporter Barbie, African-American Barbie, animal-rights Barbie, and Barbie's shower, which takes two days to construct and makes the average father feel like a bumbling voyeur. So I figured that Barbie would know me. 4

Barbie spoke: "Do you want to go for a pizza? Let's go to the mall. Do you have a crush on anyone? Teaching kids is great. Computers make homework fun!" 5

In a flash I realized that Barbie was stonewalling. These were not spontaneous comments at all. They were just the prerecorded messages that she was forced to say, probably under pressure from those heartless, controlling patriarchs at Mattel. 6

Subtle rebuttal. At the same time, I began to appreciate Barbie's characteristic subtlety; by reminding me that she was recommending the educational use of computers to young girls, she was, in effect, stoutly rebutting the charge of antifeminist backlash among talking toys. I had to admit it was pretty effective. 7

So I pleaded with her to speak honestly and clear her name. I heard a telltale rustle of satin, and then she spoke. "You're the one who took three days to put my shower together. That was ugly." 8

"Two days," I said, gently correcting the world-famous plastic figurine. I asked her about the harsh words of Sharon Schuster, the awfully upset head of the AAUW. Schuster had said, "The message is a negative one for girls, telling them they can't do well in math, and that perpetuates a stereotype." 9

"That's a crock," Barbie replied. "Just because a course is tough or challenging doesn't mean my girls can't do it. Weren't your daughters a 10 little apprehensive about math?" I admitted that they were. "Well, how did they do?" "Top of the class," I replied brightly.

"Then tell Sharon Schuster to stop arguing with dolls and go get a 11 life." Her remark was an amazement. This was not roller-skating Barbie or perfume-wearing Barbie. It was the real thing: in-your-face tough-talking Barbie.

"The first time I open my mouth after 20 years, and what hap- 12 pens? I get squelched by a bunch of women." At this point, I mentioned that my friend M. G. Lord, the syndicated columnist who is doing a book on Barbie, is firmly on her side. M. G. told me: "Math class *is* tough, but it doesn't mean you have to drop out and go to cosmetology school. These people are projecting a lot of fears onto Barbie."

Barbie was grateful. "Thank M. G. and tell her I look forward to 13 her biography of me. And tell her that if she ever fails in life, she can always become head of the AAUW." That remark may have been a trifle sharp, I said. "Well," said Barbie, "I'm just tired of taking all this guff from women's groups. They're scapegoating the wrong girl. I'll match feminist credentials with any of them. I worked my way up from candy striper to doctor. I was a stewardess in the '60s, and now I'm a pilot. Ken is one of my flight attendants. You can buy me as Olympic athlete, astronaut and executive."

Barbie was on a roll now. I was writing furiously to keep up. "This 14 summer they put out a presidential candidate Barbie, and two days later, Ross Perot withdrew. Figure it out," she said. "As far back as 1984, my ad slogan was, 'We girls can do anything.' I've done more than any other doll to turn girls into achievers, and still they treat me as a prefeminist bimbo. What's wrong with the women's movement?"

I knew enough not to touch that one. Besides, it's a very short col- 15 umn. But I was struck by her comment that Ken was now employed as a flight attendant. "Didn't he used to be a corporate executive?" I asked. "We're not voting for Bush again," she replied bitterly.

Then I heard a muffled side comment: "Ken! Be careful with those 16 dishes." I said I felt bad about Ken's comedown, but Barbie brought me back to reality: "Remember," she said, "he's only an accessory." This was tough to take, but the issue was settled. Barbie is indeed a feminist. Over to you, Sharon Schuster.

As you first read Leo's essay, his technique of personifying the doll as an "in-your-face tough-talking Barbie" is most striking and allows him to humorously present a talking Barbie who seemingly speaks up for herself. In re-reading you can see even more clearly Leo's purpose: he uses Barbie's "voice" to offer his own defense of her influence and significance. Moreover, ultimately he is making fun of feminists "projecting a lot of fears onto Barbie," since she herself derisively asks, "What's wrong with the women's movement?" When Leo has Barbie "say" that she's "done more than any other doll to turn girls into achievers," it's clear that Leo himself agrees and feels that Barbie critics should lighten up.

As a reviewing activity, you might write down your thoughts about the following questions and discuss them with your group or class:

1. Do you agree that Barbie has "done more than any other doll to turn girls into achievers" (paragraph 14)?
2. Do you think Leo's use of humor contributes to the effect of his essay?
3. According to Leo, what is the relationship between Barbie and Ken? Do you agree with Leo's ideas?
4. If you could give speech to Barbie, what would you have her say?

Reading Academic Analyses   In addition to pop cultural criticism, this book provides essays on pop cultural phenomena written not for a general audience, but by academics primarily for other academics. Generally published in academic journals or in collections from scholarly presses, these essays often present the results of extensive research or provide a very close, detailed, and original analysis of the subject at hand. You may find them more difficult than the pieces of pop cultural criticism, but in many ways they are closer to the kind of writing that will be expected of you in many of your college courses.

Note that, while "objective" in tone, academic cultural analysis generally reflects a particular interpretive framework, which may be ideological (e.g., feminist or Marxist) or methodological (e.g., semiotic, structuralist, or quantitative) or some combination of the two. These frameworks will be discussed in more detail in the headnotes to individual readings.

The following excerpt from an essay by Marilyn Ferris Motz is an example of academic cultural analysis, written from a perspective that might be called "feminist-historical." As you read the headnote and the essay itself, apply the strategies we've discussed: familiarize yourself with Motz's view and with the topic as it's presented in the headnote; then read the essay carefully and make your own annotations in the text and in the margins.

"Seen Through Rose-Tinted Glasses":
The Barbie Doll in American Society
MARILYN FERRIS MOTZ

Originally published in a longer form in The Popular Culture Reader, *Marilyn Motz's "'Seen Through Rose-Tinted Glasses': The Barbie Doll in American Society," takes its title from a 1983 Barbie sticker album marketed by Mattel. "If you stay close to your friend Barbie, life will always be seen through rose-*

tinted glasses." In her essay, however, Motz suggests that Barbie has other messages for us and that the doll's influence is more problematic, especially for children. Pointing out that several generations of girls have learned cultural values and norms from playing with Barbie, Motz focuses on the fact that, although Barbie has changed through the years to keep up with changes in the "baby boom" generation, the doll and her accessories still convey an outdated image of women's circumstances and interests.

A 1983 Barbie sticker album copyrighted by Mattel describes Barbie: 1

As beautiful as any model, she is also an excellent sportswoman. In fact, Barbie is seen as a typical young lady of the twentieth century, who knows how to appreciate beautiful things and, at the same time, live life to the fullest. To most girls, she appears as the ideal elder sister who manages to do all those wonderful things that they can only dream of. With her fashionable wardrobe and constant journeys to exciting places all over the world, the adventures of Barbie offer a glimpse of what they might achieve one day. If Barbie has a message at all for us, it is to ignore the gloomy outlook of others and concentrate on all those carefree days of youth. Whatever lies in store will come sooner or later. If you stay close to your friend Barbie, life will always be seen through rose-tinted glasses.

    Most owners of Barbie dolls are girls between the ages of three   2
and eleven years of age. A Mattel survey shows that by the late 1960s, the median age for Barbie doll play had dropped from age ten to age six (Rakstis 30). Younger children find it difficult to manipulate the relatively small dolls, although Mattel created "My First Barbie," that ostensibly was easier for young children to handle and dress. Although some boys admit to playing with Ken, or even Barbie, Barbie doll play seems to be confined largely to girls.

    Like all small figures and models, Barbie, at 11½ inches high, has   3
the appeal of the miniature. Most people are fascinated with objects recreated on a smaller scale, whether they are model airplanes, electric trains, dollhouse furnishings, or doll clothes. Miniatures give us a sense of control over our environment, a factor that is particularly important for children, to whom the real world is several sizes too large. In playing with a Barbie doll, a girl can control the action, can be omnipotent in a miniature world of her own creation.

    When a girl plays with a baby doll, she becomes in her fantasy the   4
doll's mother. She talks directly to the doll, entering into the play as an actor in her own right. When playing with a Barbie doll, on the other hand, the girl usually "becomes" Barbie. She manipulates Barbie, Ken and the other dolls, speaking for them and moving them around a miniature environment in which she herself cannot participate. Through the Barbie doll, then, a pre-adolescent can engage in role-playing activities. She can imitate adult female behavior, dress and speech and can participate vicariously in dating and other social activities, thus allaying some of her anxieties by practicing the way she will act in various situations. In consultation with the friends with whom she plays, a girl can

establish the limits of acceptable behavior for a young woman and explore the possibilities and consequences of exceeding those limits.

The girl playing with a Barbie doll can envision herself with a mature female body. "Growing-Up Skipper," first produced in 1975, grew taller and developed small breasts when her arms were rotated, focusing attention on the bodily changes associated with puberty. Of course, until the end of puberty, girls do not know the ultimate size and shape their bodies will assume, factors they realize will affect the way others will view and treat them. Perhaps Barbie dolls assuage girls' curiosity over the appearance of the adult female body, of which many have only limited knowledge, and allay anxiety over their own impending bodily development.   5

Through Barbie's interaction with Ken, girls also can explore their anxieties about future relationships with men. Even the least attractive and least popular girl can achieve, by "becoming" Barbie, instant popularity in a fantasy world. No matter how clumsy or impoverished she is in real life, she can ride a horse or lounge by the side of the pool in a world undisturbed by the presence of parents or other authority figures. The creator of the Barbie doll, Ruth Handler, claims that "these dolls become an extension of the girls. Through the doll each child dreams of what she would like to be" (Zinsser, "Barbie" 73). If Barbie does enable a girl to dream "of what she would like to be," then what dreams and goals does the doll encourage? With this question, some of the negative aspects of the Barbie doll emerge.   6

The clothes and other objects in Barbie's world lead the girl playing with Barbie to stress Barbie's leisure activities and emphasize the importance of physical appearance. The shape of the doll, its clothes and the focus on dating activities present sexual attractiveness as a key to popularity and therefore to happiness. Finally, Barbie is a consumer. She demands product after product, and the packaging and advertising imply that Barbie, as well as her owner, can be made happy if only she wears the right clothes and owns the right products. Barbie conveys the message that, as the saying goes, a woman can never be too rich or too thin. The Barbie doll did not create these attitudes. Nor will the doll insidiously instill these values in girls whose total upbringing emphasizes other factors. An individual girl can, of course, create with her own doll any sort of behavior and activities she chooses. Still, the products available for the doll tend to direct play along certain lines. Barbie represents an image, and a rather unflattering one, of American women. It is the extent to which this image fits our existing cultural expectations that explains the popularity of the Barbie doll....   7

As an icon, Barbie not only reflects traditional, outdated roles for women; she and Ken also represent, in exaggerated form, characteristics of American society as a whole. Through playing with these dolls, children learn to act out in miniature the way they see adults behave in real life and in the media. The dolls themselves and the accessories provided for them direct this play, teaching children to consume and conform, to seek fun and popularity above all else.   8

Thorstein Veblen wrote in 1899 that America had become a nation   9
of "conspicuous consumers." We buy objects, he wrote, not because we
need them but because we want others to know we can afford them. We
want our consumption to be conspicuous or obvious to others. The more
useless the object, the more it reflects the excess wealth the owner can afford to waste. In the days before designer labels, Veblen wrote that
changing fashions represent an opportunity for the affluent to show that
they can afford to waste money by disposing of usable clothing and replacing it with new, faddish styles that will in turn be discarded after a
few years or even months of wear (Veblen 60–131).

Sociologist David Riesman wrote in 1950 that Americans have be-   10
come consumers whose social status is determined not only by what
they can afford to buy but also by the degree to which their taste in objects of consumption conforms to that of their peers. Taste, in other
words, becomes a matter of assessing the popularity of an item with others rather than judging on the basis of one's personal preference. Children, according to Riesman, undergo a process of "taste socialization,"
of learning to determine "with skill and sensitivity the probable tastes of
the others" and then to adopt these tastes as their own. Riesman writes
that "today the future occupation of all moppets is to be skilled consumers" (94, 96, 101). This skill lies not in selecting durable or useful
products but in selecting popular, socially acceptable products that indicate the owner's conformity to standards of taste and knowledge of current fashion.

The Barbie doll teaches a child to conform to fashion in her con-   11
sumption. She learns that each activity requires appropriate attire and
that outfits that may at first glance appear to be interchangeable are
slightly different from one another. In the real world, what seems to be a
vast array of merchandise actually is a large collection of similar products. The consumer must make marginal distinctions between nearly
identical products, many of which have different status values. The
child playing with a Barbie doll learns to detect these nuances. Barbie's
clothes, for instance, come in three lines: a budget line, a medium-priced
line, and a designer line. Consumption itself becomes an activity to be
practiced. From 1959 to 1964, Mattel produced a "Suburban Shopper"
outfit. In 1976 the "Fashion Plaza" appeared on the market. This store
consisted of four departments connected by a moving escalator. As
mass-produced clothing made fashion accessible to all classes of Americans, the Barbie doll was one of the means by which girls learned to
make the subtle fashion distinctions that would guarantee the proper
personal appearances.

Barbie must also keep pace with all the newest fashion and leisure   12
trends. Barbie's pony tail of 1959 gave way to a Jackie Kennedy style
"Bubble-cut" in the early 1960s and to long straight hair in the 1970s.
"Ken-A-Go-Go" of 1960s had a Beatle wig, guitar and microphone,
while the "Now Look Ken" of the 1970s had shoulder-length hair and
wore a leisure suit (Leavy 102). In the early 1970s Ken grew a detachable

beard. In 1971 Mattel provided Barbie and Ken with a motorized stage on which to dance in their fringed clothes, while Barbie's athletic activities, limited to skiing, skating, fishing, skydiving and tennis in the 1960s, expanded to include backpacking, jogging, bicycling, gymnastics and sailing in the 1970s. On the shelves in the early 1980s were Western outfits, designer jeans, and Rocker Barbie dressed in neon colors and playing an electric guitar. In 1991 Rollerblade Barbie was introduced.

Barbie clearly is, and always has been, a conspicuous consumer. 13 Aside from her lavish wardrobe, Barbie has several houses complete with furnishings, a Ferrari and a '57 Chevy. She has at various times owned a yacht and several other boats as well as a painted van called the "Beach Bus." Through Barbie, families who cannot afford such luxury items in real life can compete in miniature. In her early years, Barbie owned a genuine mink coat. In the ultimate display of uselessness, Barbie's dog once owned a corduroy velvet jacket, net tutu, hat, sunglasses and earmuffs. Barbie's creators deny that Barbie's life is devoted to consumption. "These things shouldn't be thought of as possessions," according to Ruth Handler. "They are props that enable a child to get into play situations" (Zinsser 73). Whether possessions or props, however, the objects furnished with the Barbie doll help create play situations, and those situations focus on consumption and leisure.

A perusal of the shelves of Barbie paraphernalia in the Midwest 14 Toys "R" Us store reveals not a single item of clothing suitable for an executive office. Mattel did produce a doctor's outfit (1973) and astronaut suit (1965 and 1986) for Barbie, but the clothes failed to sell. According to Mattel's marketing manager, "We only kept the doctor's uniform in the line as long as we did because public relations begged us to give them something they could point to as progress" in avoiding stereotyped roles for women (Leavy 102). In the 1960s, Mattel produced "all the elegant accessories" for the patio including a telephone, television, radio, fashion magazines and a photograph of Barbie and Ken (Zinsser 72). The "Busy Barbie," created in 1972, had hands that could grasp objects and came equipped with a telephone, television, record player, "soda set" with two glasses and a travel case. Apparently Barbie kept busy only with leisure activities; she seems unable to grasp a book or a pen. When Barbie went to college in the 1970s, her "campus" consisted only of a dormitory room, soda shop (with phone booth), football stadium and drive-in movie (Zinsser 72). In the 1980s, Barbie traveled in her camper, rode her horse, played with her dog and cat, swam in her pool and lounged in her bubble bath (both with real water).

The Barbie doll of the 1980s presents a curiously mixed message. 15 The astronaut Barbie wore a pink space suit with puffed sleeves. The executive Barbie wore a hot pink suit and a broad-brimmed straw hat, and she carried a pink briefcase in which to keep her gold credit card. Lest girls think Barbie is all work and no play, the jacket could be removed, the pink and white spectator pumps replaced with high-heeled sandals, and the skirt reversed to form a spangled and frilly evening dress. Barbie may try her hand at high-status occupations, but her appearance does not suggest competence and professionalism. In a story in *Barbie* magazine (Summer 1985) Barbie is a journalist reporting on lost treasure in the Yucatan. She spends her time "catching some rays" and listening to music, however, while her dog discovers the lost treasure. Barbie is appropriately rewarded with a guest spot on a television talk show! Although Barbie is shown in a professional occupation and even has her own computer, her success is attributed to good luck rather than her own (nonexistent) efforts. She reaps the rewards of success without having had to work for it; indeed, it is her passivity and pleasure-seeking (could we even say laziness) that allows her dog to discover the gold. Even at work, Barbie leads a life of leisure.

Veblen wrote that America, unlike Europe, lacked a hereditary   16
aristocracy of families that were able to live on the interest produced by inherited wealth. In America, Veblen wrote, even the wealthiest men were self-made capitalists who earned their own livings. Since these men were too busy to enjoy leisure and spend money themselves, they delegated these tasks to their wives and daughters. By supporting a wife and daughters who earned no money but spent lavishly, a man could prove his financial success to his neighbors. Therefore, according to Veblen, affluent women were forced into the role of consumers, establishing the social status of the family by the clothes and other items they bought and the leisure activities in which they engaged (Veblen 44–131).

Fashions of the time, such as long skirts, immobilized women,   17
making it difficult for them to perform physical labor, while ideals of beauty that included soft pale hands and faces precluded manual work or outdoor activities for upper-class women. To confer status, Veblen writes, clothing "should not only be expensive, but it should also make plain to all observers that the wearer is not engaged in any kind of productive employment." According to Veblen, "the dress of women goes even farther than that of men in the way of demonstrating the wearer's abstinence from productive labor." The high heel, he notes, "makes any, even the simplest and most necessary manual work extremely difficult," and thus is a constant reminder that the woman is "the economic dependent of the man—that, perhaps in a highly idealized sense, she still is the man's chattel" (Veblen 120–21, 129)....

Despite changes in the lives and expectations of real women, Bar-   18
bie remains essentially the woman described by Veblen in the 1890s, excluded from the world of work with its attendant sense of achievement, forced to live a life based on leisure activities, personal appearance, the accumulation of possessions and the search for popularity. While large numbers of women reject this role, Barbie embraces it. The Barbie doll serves as an icon that symbolically conveys to children and adults the measures of success in modern America: wealth, beauty, popularity and leisure.

Suggestions for Further Reading

Leavy, Jane. "Is There a Barbie Doll in Your Past?" *Ms.* Sept. 1979.

Riesman, David, Nathan Glazer, and Reual Denney. *The Lonely Crowd: A Study of the Changing American Character.* Garden City, NY: Double-day Anchor, 1950.

Rakstis, Ted. "Debate in the Doll House." *Today's Health* Dec. 1970.

Veblen, Thorstein. *The Theory of the Leisure Class.* 1899. New York: Mentor, 1953.

Zinsser, William K. "Barbie Is a Million Dollar Doll." *Saturday Evening Post* 12 Dec. 1964: 72–73.

As you can see from Motz's essay, academic cultural analysis can present you with much information and many ideas to digest. A useful re-reading activity is to go through the text and highlight its main points by writing a one- or two-page summary of it. Then in the reviewing stage, you can use your summary to draw your own conclusions and formulate your own responses to the writer's ideas. To do so with Motz's essay, you might use the following questions as starting points:

1. In what ways do you think fashion dolls like Barbie provide a different play experience for children than "baby dolls"? Do you think one type of doll is "healthier" or more appropriate than the other?
2. To what extent do you think Thorstein Veblen's comments on status and consumerism in American society (paragraph 9) still apply today? Do you agree with Motz that Barbie contributes to the promotion of "conspicuous consumption"?
3. If Motz is right that Barbie represents an outdated and potentially detrimental image of women's lives, why do you think the doll continues to sell more and more successfully every year?
4. To what extent do you think that the values represented by Barbie—"wealth, beauty, popularity and leisure" (18)—are still central to success in America?

Ultimately, your goal as a reader in this course will most likely be to prepare yourself to complete specific writing assignments. In the next section, we present the process one writing student went through in composing an essay requested in the following assignment:

What do you see as the significance of the Barbie doll in contemporary American culture? How are your ideas related to those of Tham, Leo, and Motz in the selections presented here?

THE WRITING PROCESS

Frequently, when an instructor gives a writing assignment—for example, "Write an essay exploring the significance of the Barbie doll in contemporary American culture"—students experience a type of minipanic: producing a focused, coherent, informative, and logically developed paper seems a monumental task. Some students may be overwhelmed by the many ideas swirling around in their heads, worrying they won't be able to put them into coherent order. Others may think they won't have enough to say about a given topic and complain, "How long does the paper have to be? How can I come up with four pages!"

However, there's really no reason to panic. Just as there are definable activities in the active process of reading, so the writing process can be broken down into four discrete stages: **prewriting, drafting, distancing,** and **revising.** Taking it a step at a time can make writing an essay a manageable and productive experience.

Prewriting

The first stage of the essay-writing process should be especially invigorating and stress-free, since at this point you don't have to worry about making your prose grammatically sound, logically organized, or convincing to a reader. All you have to do is write whatever comes into your head regarding your topic, so that you can discover the beginnings of ideas and phrasings that may be developed in the drafting stage and ultimately massaged into an acceptable form of academic writing.

There are a number of prewriting strategies writers use to generate ideas and happy turns of phrase. Experiment with all of these, in order to discover which of them "clicks" in terms of how you think and most productively get your ideas down on paper. Most writers rely more heavily on one or two of these prewriting strategies, depending on their own styles and dispositions; it's a matter of individual preference. If you're a spontaneous, organic sort of person, for example, you might spend more time freewriting. On the other hand, if you have a more logical, mathematical mind, you might gravitate naturally to outlining and do very little freewriting. There's no right or wrong way to prewrite; it comes down to whatever works best for you. But what's best usually involves some combination of the three following techniques.

Freewriting   This prewriting strategy lets your mind wander, as minds will, while you record whatever occurs to you. Just write, write, write, with no judgment about the validity, usefulness, grammatical correctness, or literary merit of the words you're putting down. The only requirement is that you write nonstop, either on paper or a word processor, for a manageable period of time: say, fifteen minutes without a break.

Your freewriting can be open—that is, it can be pure, stream-of-consciousness writing in which you "stay in the present moment" and record every thought, sense impression, disturbing sound—or it can be focused on a specific topic, such as Barbie dolls. When freewriting in preparation for writing an essay, it's frequently helpful to keep in mind a central question, either one from your instructor's original topic assignment or one sparked by your own curiosity, so that your freewritten material will be useful when you start composing your actual essay. Here is a typical focused freewrite on the subject of Barbie dolls written by a student in response to the writing assignment quoted earlier:

> *Toys: what did you want as a child vs. what you were given? I don't know, but I wanted cars and ended up with Barbie Corvette. Brother got G.I. Joe, Tonka trucks, I got talking Barbie, Barbie play house, Corvette.*
>
> *B. served as model for ideal female figure, and now that ideal is depicted in magazines. I guess that represents a kind of perpetuation of this image: girls raised on Barbie → cycle continues w/images in the media. The I = ideal image of women in America seems to be let's see: white, flawless, flat nose, wide eyes, that kind of thing. Whatever, it's clear that Barbie creates unreal expectations for women.*
>
> *Yeah! her figure would be inhuman if a real person had it—they would probably die! If she puts on jogging shoes, Barbie stands sloped because she's designed for high heels...so it seems as though Barbie is clearly designed for display rather than real activity, let alone profession. Display.*
>
> *literature (written stuff) on Barbie packages—she's not interested in doctoring nurse, etc.; just having money, cars, looking good, taking trips etc. Re: tech—women think computers are "fun." Re: math—women supposedly aren't good at it. Barbie reinforces these stereotypes—and lots more—in girls*
>
> *Changes in society? discuss for concl.?*

Clustering Clustering is especially useful for discovering relationships between ideas, impressions, and facts. As a prewriting activity, it falls between freewriting and outlining, in that it's usually more focused than freewriting but less logically structured than an outline.

To prewrite by clustering, begin by writing a word or central phrase down in the center of a clean sheet of paper. In the case of the Barbie doll assignment, for example, you would probably start by writing "Barbie" in the middle of the page, and then drawing a circle around it. Having written and circled this central word or phrase, you can then jot down relevant facts, concrete examples, interesting ideas, and so on. Cluster these around the circled word, like this:

Frequently, one or more of your random jottings will serve as a new central word—as a jumping-off point for a new cluster of ideas. Later on, when you're drafting, you can use these clustered "nodes" as the basis for supporting paragraphs in the body of your essay.

Outlining   If you have a rough idea of what the main points of your paper will be, outlining is an extremely useful prewriting technique, in that it helps you plan the overall structure for your paper and often generates new ideas about your topic. There are several different types of outlines, most notably scratch, sentence, and topic outlines.

For a *scratch outline* you list your intended points in a very tentative order, one that may only reflect the fact that you don't yet know in what order you want to put your supporting ideas. A scratch outline might not even suggest which subordinating points are most important to developing your thesis. For this reason, scratch outlines are most useful early in the prewriting phase, as a means of generating ideas as well as beginning to organize your thoughts logically. In fact, if you have not yet arrived at a thesis for your paper, one may emerge in the process of listing all your main and subordinate points and then reviewing that list to discover which of those ideas is the most central and important.

As you think more about your essay and come up with new ideas and supporting evidence, you will almost certainly revise your scratch outline to make it more detailed and conventionally formatted with numbered and lettered headings and subheads. *A topic outline* presents items in key words or brief phrases, rather than sentences, and frequently features no indentation. A *sentence outline* is even more developed than a topic outline, in that it describes the listed items in complete sentences, each of which is essentially a subtopic for a supporting paragraph. In fact, sentence outlines, when fully developed, can contain most of the supporting information you're going to present in your essay, and can therefore be extremely useful tools during the prewriting process.

Developing her freewritten material about Barbie into an outline, our student writer sketched out the following:

I. *Introduction*
   A. *Discuss my own experience with toys while growing up: parents "let" me play with Tonka trucks, but they gave me a Barbie Corvette when I wanted a race car.*
   B. *Discuss social shaping of gender roles generally.*
   C. *Working Thesis: Significance of Barbie in American society is that although people say women have "come a long way" and that there are new expectations, this is not really true. If it were, Barbie, depicted as mere sexual, leisure-seeking consumer, could not be accepted.*

II. *The media see that people—especially young ones—need role models, and manufacture products to fill the following needs.*
   A. *Childhood: Barbie.*
      1. *Barbie presents a totally unrealistic female body as a role model for young women.*
      2. *This role-modeling is crucial in young women's psychological development, because little girls role-play with Barbie, taking her actions as their own.*
   B. *Pre-teen: Models in Seventeen magazine.*
   C. *Teen: Vogue and Mademoiselle.*
   D. *Adult: Cosmopolitan, Victoria's Secret lingerie models, advertisements in mainstream magazines.*

III. *The popularity of Barbie depicts the entrenched nature of traditional female roles.*
   A. *The change toward women's equality is not something that is deemed beneficial by everyone, such as the religious ultra-right.*
   B. *People purchasing Barbie either:*
      1. *don't see the image that's being perpetuated; or*
      2. *respect those values and want to pass them on to their children.*
   C. *Significance in popular culture of Barbie is that she illustrates inconsistencies between changing social roles (women and minorities) and the concepts we are teaching youngsters.*
   D. *Although the makers of Barbie make a superficial attempt at updating her, Barbie depicts traditional women absorbed in leisure, consumption, and beauty.*
      1. *Barbie completely reinforces old role expectations.*
      2. *Barbie in the '90s can have a career (she has some doctor outfits, I think), but she isn't ever functional in that career. The emphasis is still on leisure.*

IV. *The Racial Issue*
   A. *Barbie illustrates the assimilation of minorities; they lose part of their culture, because Americans are supposed to belong to the "same mold."*

    B. *In the '90s we say that we aren't prejudiced and that everyone should be ac-*
       cepted for who they are, but since the dominant culture is white, white men
       and women unconsciously (or in some cases consciously, I'm afraid) as-
       sume that others must take on white norms.

V. *Conclusion*
    A. *Bring it back around to my childhood play time and the necessity for par-*
       ents to think about the sorts of toys they are giving their children, so that
       they don't reinforce and perpetuate these old patterns.

You'll discover that this outline, while detailed, doesn't contain some of the points raised in the final essay's supporting paragraphs and that it includes a good deal of material that was not used in the final essay. The reason for this discrepancy is simple and illustrates a key point for you to remember about the writing process. As this writer began her essay, she discovered new points which she thought relevant to her thesis. At the same time, she realized that some of her outlined points were tangential and digressive rather than helpful in supporting her main point. She therefore cut some of those points, even though she thought they were valid and interesting ideas. That's one of the most painful but absolutely necessary tasks of the writer: getting rid of material which took some work to create and seems interesting and well written. If cutting some of your previously written material makes the final result better, then it's worth the sacrifice!

Drafting

Having generated a good amount of prewritten material and perhaps developed it into a detailed outline, your next task is to transform that material into an actual essay. Before proceeding with the drafting of your essay, however, it's a good idea first to consider your audience—your instructor only? Your instructor *and* your classmates? An imaginary editor or publisher? A third-grade student? Consider, too, the point you want to make about your topic to that audience. Unlike freewriting, which is by its nature often rambling and disjointed, essays succeed to the degree that they focus on a specific point and develop that point with illustrations and examples.

Thesis and Thesis Statement   The main point, the central assertion of your essay, is called a *thesis*. It helps to have a clear sense of your thesis before writing a paper. However, keep in mind that this isn't always necessary: some people use writing as a discovery process, and don't arrive at their thesis until they've completed a first draft. Generally, however, the process is easier if you have a thesis in

mind—even one that's not yet fully formed or that's likely to change—
before you begin drafting.

While the form of thesis statements may vary considerably, there
are some qualities that separate effective thesis statements from vague
or weak ones. First of all, your thesis statement should be inclusive but
focused: that is, it should be broad enough to encompass your paper's
main supporting ideas, but narrow enough to represent a concise explanation of your paper's main point that won't require you to write
fifty pages to cover the topic adequately. Furthermore, you want your
thesis statement to be a forceful assertion rather than a question or an
ambiguous statement of purpose such as, "In this paper I am going to
talk about Barbie dolls and their effect on society."

Much more effective, as you will see in the sample student paper
that concludes this chapter, is a statement which takes a stand:

> This is certainly one of the more dangerous consequences of Barbie's
> popularity in our society: a seemingly innocent toy defines for young
> girls the sorts of career choices, clothing, and relationships that will be
> "proper" for them as grown-up women.

Notice how this statement gives an excellent sense of the
thematic direction the paper will take: clearly, it will examine the relationship between Barbie dolls and gender role identification in contemporary America.

Opening Paragraphs   In most academic writing, you want to arrive at your thesis statement as quickly as possible, so that your reader
will have a clear sense of your essay's purpose from the start. Many
readers expect to find a thesis statement at the end of the introduction—
generally the final sentence of the first or second paragraph. Effective introductions are often structured so as to lead up to the thesis statement:
they draw the reader in by opening with an interesting specific point or
question, a quotation, a brief anecdote, a controversial assertion—which
serves to introduce the topic generally; a general overview then leads up
to the specific statement of the thesis in the last sentence.

In the student essay on page 33, for example, observe how the
writer begins with a personal reflection about Barbie. Her anecdote may
strike a familiar chord with readers and therefore draw them into the
topic. Having made the attempt to arouse her readers' interest in her
opening paragraph, the writer moves more pointedly into the general
topic, discussing briefly the possible social and psychological implications of her parents' gift choices. This discussion leads into her thesis
statement, a focused assertion that concludes her second paragraph.

Keep in mind that many writers wait until they have written a
first draft before they worry about an introduction. They simply lead

off with a tentative thesis statement, then go back later to look for effective ways to lead up to that statement.

Supporting Paragraphs   As you draft the body of your paper, keep two main goals in mind. First, try to make sure that all your supporting paragraphs are aimed at developing your thesis, so that you maintain your focus and don't ramble off the topic. Second, work toward presenting your supporting ideas in logical order, and try to provide smooth transitions between points.

The order in which you choose to present your ideas depends in large part on your topic and purpose. When you are arguing for a particular position, you might begin with less important ideas and work toward a final, crucial point. In this way you can build a case that you "clinch" with your strongest piece of evidence. Other kinds of essays call for different structures. For example, an essay tracing the history of the Barbie doll and its effect on American culture would probably be structured chronologically, from the introduction of the toy to its present-day incarnations, since that would be the most natural way to develop the discussion.

The student essay at the end of this chapter moves from a personal reflection on the topic of Barbie (paragraph 1); to a thesis statement that asserts the point of the paper (2); to a transitional paragraph moving from the writer's childhood experiences and a more general discussion of Barbie's role in reinforcing gender-role stereotypes in other young girls (3); to an overview of how sociologists and historians critique the Barbie phenomenon (4); to an examination of whether Barbie has changed in response to evolving attitudes regarding women in society (5–7), the heart of the writer's argument; to a conclusion that frames the essay by returning to the original, personal example (8). Each new discussion seems to flow naturally into the next because the writer uses a transitional phrase or parallel language to link the first sentence in each paragraph to the end of the preceding paragraph.

Evidence   Using evidence effectively is the critical task in composing body paragraphs, because your essay will be convincing only to the degree that you make your arguments credible. Evidence can take many forms, from facts and figures you collect from library research to experiences you learn about in conversations with friends. While library research isn't necessary for every paper, it helps to include at least some "hard" facts and figures gathered from outside sources—journals, newspapers, textbooks—even if you're not writing a full-blown research paper. Frequently, gathering your evidence doesn't require scrolling through computer screens in your school's library; it could be accomplished by watching the six o'clock newscast or while reading the paper over breakfast.

Quotations from secondary sources are another common way of developing and supporting a point in a paragraph. Using another person's spoken or written words will lend your arguments a note of authenticity, especially when your source is a recognized authority in the field about which you're writing. A few points to remember when using quotations:

1. Generally, don't begin or end a supporting paragraph with a quotation. Articulate your point *in your own words* in the first sentence or two of the paragraph; *then* provide the quotation as a way of supporting your point. After the quotation, you might include another focusing sentence or two that analyzes the quotation and suggests how it relates to your point.
2. Keep your quotations brief. Overly lengthy quotations can make a paper difficult to read. You've probably read texts that nearly put you to sleep because of their overuse of quotations. As a general rule, quote source material only when the precise phrasing is necessary to support your abstract points. Be careful not to allow cited passages to overpower your own assertions.
3. Remember that all of your secondary material—whether quoted or paraphrased—needs to be accurately attributed. Make sure to mention the source's name and include other information (such as the publication date or page number) as required by your instructor.

While quotations, facts, and figures are the most common ways of developing your supporting paragraphs with evidence, you can also use your imagination to come up with other means of substantiating your points. Design a questionnaire, hand it out to your friends and compile the resulting data as evidence. Interview a local authority on your topic, make notes about the conversation, and draw upon these as evidence. Finally, be your own authority: use your own powers of reasoning to come up with logical arguments that convince your readers of the validity of your assertions.

This body paragraph from the student essay on Barbie provides a good example of a writer using evidence to support her points:

> As Motz observes later in her article, Barbie has changed to adjust to the transforming attitudes of society over time. Both her facial expressions and wardrobe have undergone subtle alterations: "The newer Barbie has a more friendly, open expression, with a hint of a smile, and her lip and eye make-up is muted" (226), and in recent years Barbie's wardrobe has expanded to include some career clothing in addition to her massive volume of recreational attire. This transition appears to represent a conscious effort on the part of Barbie's manufacturers to integrate the concept of women as important members of the work force, with traditional ideals already depicted by Barbie.

The paragraph begins with an assertion of the general point that Barbie has changed in some ways over the years to reflect changes in societal attitudes toward women. This point is then supported with a quotation from an expert, and the page number of the original source is noted parenthetically. (Note that page references in this student essay are from the complete original essay by Motz, published in *The Popular Culture Reader*, not from the excerpt of the Motz essay earlier in this chapter.) The point is further developed with evidence presented in the writer's own words. The paragraph concludes with a final sentence that summarizes the main point of the evidence presented in the previous sentences, keeps the paragraph focused on the essay's thesis that Barbie perpetuates gender stereotypes, and sets the reader up for a transition into the next subtopic.

Obviously, all supporting paragraphs won't take this exact form; essays would be deadly boring if every paragraph looked the same. You'll encounter body paragraphs in professional essays that begin with quotations or end with quotations, for example. Just keep in mind that you want to *support* whatever general point you're making, so each paragraph should include a measure of specific, concrete evidence. The more you practice writing the more ways you'll discover to develop body paragraphs with illustrations, examples, and evidence.

Conclusions You may have learned in high school English courses that an essay's conclusion should restate the main points made in the paper, so that the reader is left with a concise summary that leaves no doubt as to the paper's intention. This was an excellent suggestion for high school students, as it reinforced the notion of focusing an essay on a specific, concrete point. In college, however, you'll want to start developing a more sophisticated academic style. Conclusions to college-level essays should do more than merely repeat the paper's main points; they should leave the reader with something to think about.

Of course, what that *something* is depends on your topic, your audiences, and your purpose in writing. Sometimes it may be appropriate to move from an objective discussion of a topic to a more subjective reflection on it. For instance, in analyzing the social effects of Barbie dolls, you might end by reflecting on the doll's significance in your own life or by commenting ironically on feminist critics who in your view make too much of Barbie's influence. Other ways to conclude are providing a provocative quotation; offering a challenge for the future; asserting a forceful opinion; creating a striking image or memorable turn of phrase; or referring back to an image or idea in your introduction.

What you want to avoid is a bland and overly general conclusion along the lines of, "Thus, in conclusion, it would seem to this author that Barbie has had a great and wide-reaching impact on today's contemporary society." Note how the writer of the Barbie essay created a strong conclusion by first returning to the subject of her opening paragraph—her own childhood toys—and then leaving the reader with a relatively memorable final sentence offering a challenge for the future:

> Looking back at my childhood, I see my parents engaged in this same struggle. By surrounding me with toys that perpetuated both feminine and masculine roles, they achieved a kind of balance among the conflicting images in society. However, they also seemed to succumb to traditional social pressures by giving me that Barbie Corvette, when all I wanted was a radio-controlled formula-one racer, like the one Emerson Fittipaldi drives. In a time when most parents agree that young girls should be encouraged to pursue their goals regardless of gender boundaries, their actions do not always reflect these ideals. Only when we demand that toys like Barbie no longer perpetuate stereotypes will this reform be complete.

Distancing

Distancing is the easiest part of the writing process because it involves doing nothing more than putting your first draft aside and giving yourself some emotional and intellectual distance from it. Pursue your daily activities, go to work or complete assignments for other classes, take a hike, throw a frisbee, polish your shoes, do anything but read over your draft...ideally for a day or two.

The reason to take the time to distance yourself is simple: you've been working hard on your essay and therefore have a strong personal investment in it. In order to revise effectively, you need to be able to see your essay dispassionately, almost as though someone else had written it. Stepping away from it for a day or two gives you the opportunity to approach your essay as an editor who has no compunction about changing, reordering, or completely cutting passages that don't work.

Also, the process of distancing allows your mind to work on the essay subconsciously even while you're going about your other non-writing activities. Frequently, during this distancing period, you'll find yourself coming up with new ideas that you can use to supplement your thesis as you revise.

Finally, factoring the process of distancing into the writing process will help you avoid the dread disease of all students: procrastination. Since you have to allot yourself enough time to write a draft *and* let it sit for a couple of days, you'll avoid a last-minute scramble for ideas and supporting material, and you'll have time to do a thorough revision.

One note of warning: Don't get so distanced from your draft that you forget to come back to it. If you do forget, all your prewritings and drafting will have gone to waste.

Revising

Many professional writers believe that revision is the most important stage in the writing process. Writers view the revision stage as an opportunity to clarify their ideas, to rearrange text so that the logical flow of their work is enhanced, to add new phrases or delete ones that don't work, to modify their thesis and change editorial direction... or, in some extreme cases, to throw the whole thing out and start over!

Just as with prewriting and drafting, many students dread revision because all the different issues that need to be considered make it appear to be a forbidding task. Most find it helpful to have a clear set of criteria with which to approach their first drafts. Following is such a checklist of questions, addressing specific issues of content, organization, and stylistics/mechanics. If you find that your answer is "no" to any one of these questions, then you need to rework your essay for improvement in that specific area.

Revision Checklist

Introduction
✔ Does the paper begin in a way that draws the reader into the paper while introducing the topic?

✔ Does the introduction provide some general overview that leads up to the thesis?

✔ Does the introduction end with a focused, assertive thesis in the form of a statement (not a question)?

Supporting Paragraphs and Conclusion
✔ Do your supporting paragraphs relate back to your thesis, so that the paper has a clear focus?

✔ Do your body paragraphs connect logically, with smooth transitions between them?

✔ Do your supporting paragraphs have a good balance between general points and specific, concrete evidence?

✔ If you've used secondary sources for your evidence, do you attribute them adequately to avoid any suspicion of plagiarism?

✔ If you've used quotations extensively, have you made sure your quoted material doesn't overpower your own writing?

✔ Does your last paragraph give your readers something to think about rather than merely restate what you've already said elsewhere in the essay?

Style and Mechanics

✔ Have you chosen your words aptly and sometimes inventively, avoiding clichés and overused phrases?

✔ Have you varied your sentence lengths effectively, thus helping create a pleasing prose rhythm?

✔ Have you proofread carefully, to catch any grammatical problems or spelling errors?

Make the minor changes or major overhauls required in your first draft. Then type or print out a second draft, and read it *out loud* to yourself, to catch any awkward or unnatural sounding passages, wordy sentences, grammatical glitches and so on. Reading your prose out loud may seem weird—especially to your roommates who can't help overhearing—but doing so helps you gain some new perspective on the piece of writing you have been so close to, and frequently highlights minor, sentence-level problems that you might otherwise overlook.

Sample Student Essay

The following essay demonstrates one way of approaching the assignment we presented earlier. As you read, note the essay's introductory paragraphs and thesis statement, the way body paragraphs are developed with illustrations and examples, the way it concludes without simply restating the writer's points, the writer's effective use of words, and sentence structure.

Role-Model Barbie: Now and Forever?
CAROLYN MUHLSTEIN

During my early childhood, my parents avoided placing gender boundaries on my play time. My brother and I both had Tonka trucks, and these were driven by Barbie, Strawberry Shortcake, and GI Joe to my doll house, or to condos built with my brother's Erector Set. However, as I got older, the boundaries became more defined, and certain forms of play became "inappropriate." For example, I remember asking for a remote controlled car one Christmas, anticipating a powerful race car like the ones driven at De Anza Days, the local community fair. Christmas morning waiting for me under the tree was a bright yellow Barbie Corvette. It seemed as though my parents had decided that if I had to have a remote controlled car, at least it could be a feminine Barbie one!   1

Although I was too young to realize it at the time, this gift represented a subtle shift in my parents' attitudes toward my gender-role choices. Where before my folks seemed content to let me assume either   2 traditional "boy" or traditional "girl" roles in play, now they appeared to be subtly directing me toward traditional female role-playing. This is certainly one of the more dangerous consequences of Barbie's popularity in our society: a seemingly innocent toy defines for young girls the sorts of career choices, clothing, and relationships that will be "proper" for them as grown-up women.

Perhaps the Barbie Corvette was my parents' attempt to steer me   3
back toward more traditional feminine pursuits. Since her birth thirty-five years ago, Barbie has been used by many parents to illustrate the "appropriate" role of a woman in society. During earlier decades, when women were expected to remain at home, Barbie's lifestyle was extremely fitting. Marilyn Ferris Motz writes that Barbie "represents so well the widespread values of modern American society, devoting herself to the pursuit of happiness through leisure and material goods... teaching them [female children] the skills by which their future success will be measured" (212). Barbie, then, serves as a symbol of the woman's traditional role in our society, and she serves to reinforce those stereotypes in young girls.

Motz' opinion isn't an isolated one. In fact, the consensus among   4
sociologists, historians, and consumers is that Barbie represents a life of lazy leisure and wealth. Her "forever arched feet" and face "always smiling, eyes wide with admiration" (Tham 180) allow for little more than evenings on the town and strolls in the park. In addition, the accessories Barbie is equipped with are almost all related to pursuits of mere pleasure. According to a Barbie sticker album created by Mattel:

Barbie is seen as a typical young lady of the twentieth century, who knows how to appreciate beautiful things and, at the same time, live life to the fullest... with her fashionable wardrobe and constant journeys to exciting places all over the world, the adventures of Barbie offer a glimpse of what they [girls] might achieve one day. (qtd. in Motz 218)

In this packaging "literature"—and in the countless other advertisements and packaging materials that have emerged since Barbie's invention some thirty years ago—the manufacturers exalt Barbie's materialism, her appreciation of "beautiful things," fine clothing, and expensive trips as positive personality traits: qualities which all normal, healthy girls in this society should try to emulate, according to the traditional view.

As Motz observes later in her article, Barbie has changed to   5
adjust to the transforming attitudes of society over time. Both her facial expressions and wardrobe have undergone subtle alterations: "The newer Barbie has a more friendly, open expression, with a hint of a smile, and her lip and eye make-up is muted" (226), and in recent years Barbie's wardrobe has expanded to include some career clothing in addition to her massive volume of recreational attire. This transition appears to represent a conscious effort on the part of Barbie's manufacturers to integrate the concept of women as important

members of the work force, with traditional ideals already depicted by Barbie.

Unfortunately, a critical examination of today's Barbie doll reveals that this so-called integration is actually a cynical, half-hearted attempt to satisfy the concerns of some people—especially those concerned with feminist issues. Sure, Barbie now has office attire, a doctor outfit, a nurse outfit, and a few other pieces of "career" clothing, but her image continues to center on leisure. As Motz observes, "Barbie may try her hand at high-status occupations, but her appearance does not suggest competence and professionalism" (230). Quite the opposite, in fact: there are few, and in some cases, no accessories with which a young girl might imagine a world of professional competence for Barbie. There are no Barbie hospitals and no Barbie doctor offices; instead, she has only mansions, boats, and fast cars. Furthermore, Barbie's arched feet make it impossible for her to stand in anything but heels, so a career as a doctor, an astronaut—or anything else that requires standing up for more than twenty minutes on a fashion runway—would be nearly impossible! 6

From these examples, it's clear that Barbie's manufacturers have failed to reconcile the traditional image of women as sexual, leisure-seeking consumers with the view that women are assertive, career-oriented individuals, because their "revision" of the Barbie image is at best a token one. This failure to reconcile two opposing roles for Barbie parallels the same contradiction in contemporary society. By choice and necessity women are in the work force in large numbers, seeking equal pay and equal opportunities with men; yet the more traditional voices in our culture continue to perpetuate stereotyped images of women. If we believe that we are at a transitional point in the evolution toward real equality for women, then Barbie exemplifies this transitional stage perfectly. 7

Looking back at my childhood, I see my parents engaged in this same struggle. By surrounding me with toys that perpetuated both feminine and masculine roles, they achieved a kind of balance among the conflicting images in society. However, they also seemed to succumb to traditional social pressures by giving me that Barbie Corvette, when all I wanted was a radio-controlled formula-one racer, like the one Emerson Fittipaldi drives. In a time when most parents agree that young girls should be encouraged to pursue their goals regardless of gender boundaries, their actions do not always reflect these ideals. Only when we demand that toys like Barbie no longer perpetuate stereotypes will this reform be complete.

References

Motz, Marilyn Ferris. "Through Rose-Tinted Glasses," in *Popular Culture: An Introductory Text,*" eds. Jack Trachbar and Kevin Lause. Bowling Green, OH: Bowling Green U.P., 1992.

Tham, Hilary, "Barbie's Shoes," in *Mondo Barbie,* eds. Lucinda Ebersole and Richard Peabody. New York: St. Martin's Press, 1993.

2

Advertising

What you see above is a very simple advertisement for a Timex watch. A picture of the watch, a short statement, a tag with information about the watch and the familiar Timex slogan, some small print at the bottom: there doesn't seem to be much more to it than that. But appearances can be deceiving—and indeed, they often are in advertisements.

Let's take a closer look. The ad is centered on a simple statement: "If you think it's cool, it is." The longest word in the sentence is only five letters, reminding us of other familiar advertising slogans such as "Just do it," "Coke is it," and "I love what you do for me." In addition to their quite basic vocabulary, these slogans share a certain quality of vagueness: the "it" in "Just do it," like the "it" in "Coke is it" and the "what" in the Toyota slogan, are what semioticians might call "floating signifiers": their meaning is open and flexible, determined substantially by the reader of the ad. The same can be said for the "it" in this Timex ad: does "it" refer only to the watch? If so, why doesn't the statement say, "If you think *this watch* is cool, it is"? Clearly, an all-encompassing word like "it" allows the statement to be about more than just the watch.

Even more interesting in this ad is the word "cool": what exactly is "cool"? It's a word that we all define differently, and Timex invites us here to take our own definition of "cool" and associate it with the watch. Whatever each of us thinks of as "cool," that's what this watch is. While vagueness usually leads to poor communication, you can see how it's used effectively here by the advertiser: "cool" tells us virtually nothing about the watch, but makes us feel good about it nonetheless. And of course, "cool" appeals to a certain audience: precisely the young, upscale, Generation X types who might be reading *Icon*, the glossy and expensive new "thoughtstyle" magazine in which we found the ad. So, targeting a smaller audience, Timex can afford to be more specific than Coke can be when it claims to be "it." Still, the watch is "cool" rather than "groovy" (too old) or "the bomb" (too new) or "rad" (too California-surfer). In that one word alone and in the way it's used, we can see the ad hard at work trying to make its product appealing to potential customers.

When we look at the entire sentence, we can also see a degree of complexity behind its seeming simplicity. Even if we accept that the word "it" refers only to the watch, the sentence invites two different interpretations:

1. "If you think this watch is cool, well, you're right, because it is."
2. "If *you* think this watch is cool, then it is (because you say it is)."

This is a fine difference, but an important one. The first way of reading the sentence suggests that the watch is naturally, essentially cool, and so the reader is to be congratulated on being perceptive enough to see coolness when he or she comes across it. In the second reading, the watch isn't naturally cool at all; it's the reader who decides that the watch is cool. Either way, the reader of the ad gets a compliment and perhaps an ego-boost: either he or she is cool enough to recognize a cool watch, or he or she has the power to determine coolness. The first option might appeal to a more insecure sort of reader, someone who fears that he or she can't distinguish cool from uncool. The second reading confirms the confidence of a more secure reader, someone who knows perfectly well what's cool and what isn't. In other words, the statement appeals simultaneously to both the "wanna-be cools" and the "already cools" who might be reading *Icon*.

Now you may think that we're reading too much into so simple an advertisement, especially considering the fact that we haven't gotten past the statement yet to consider other elements in the ad: all that white space, the strange information presented on the label (why do we need to know the date of the original design?), the Timex slogan at the bottom of the label. It's true that we're spending far more time interpreting this ad than most readers spend on it as they thumb through *Icon* looking for an interesting article to read. But we're not spending nearly as much time on the ad as its designers did. The fact is that nothing in this ad—or in any ad—is there by mistake; every detail is carefully chosen, every word carefully selected, every photograph carefully arranged. Advertisers know that readers usually spend only a few seconds glancing at ads as they page through a magazine; we drive quickly past billboards and use TV commercial minutes to grab food from the fridge. In those seconds that the advertisers have our attention, they need to make as strong a pitch as possible. All that we're doing with the Timex ad is speculating about each of the choices that the designers of the ad made in creating their pitch. In several writing and discussion assignments in this chapter, you'll be asked to do the same kind of analysis with ads that you select, and in readings in this chapter you'll see more detailed and complete analyses of ads that can serve, along with this mini-analysis of the Timex ad, as models for your own interpretations.

Keep in mind, too, that advertising agencies spend a great deal of time and money trying to understand the complex psychodynamics of their target audiences and then tailoring ads to appeal to those audiences. Even their simplest and most seemingly direct advertisements still carry subtly powerful messages—about "coolness" as well as about appropriate modes of behavior, standards of beauty and success, gender roles, and a variety of other markers for normalcy and status. In tailoring ads to appeal both to basic human impulses and to more culturally conditioned attitudes, they also ultimately reinforce and even engender such impulses and attitudes. So although advertisements like the one above seem to be thoroughly innocuous and unimportant, the argument of many pop culture critics is that they have quite an influence—perhaps all the more so because we think they're so bland and harmless.

Several readings in this chapter explain in further detail the ways in which we can be manipulated by advertising. Jib Fowles, for example, points out a variety of strategies advertisements use to appeal to our emotions even though we may think we are making product choices using our intellect. The readings in the second section of the chapter look at how advertising works to manipulate our notions of masculinity and femininity. You'll probably find that many advertisements, especially the ones in gender-specific magazines like *GQ* and *Vogue,* attempt to sell products by connecting them, however tenuously, to idealized and highly desirable images of masculinity and femininity: put bluntly, it's "buy this cologne (perfume) and you'll be the man (woman) you've always dreamed of being." No one really believes that, of course…at least not consciously. But these kinds of ads must be working or else advertisers would find other, more effective strategies to make their products appealing to consumers.

Whatever your view of advertising, keep in mind as you read the following sections that everything in advertisements—from sexy models to simple black and white pictures of watches—exist solely for three well-calculated reasons: to sell, sell, and sell.

Approaches to Advertising

In the Shadow of the Image

Stuart and Elizabeth Ewen

We begin this chapter with a selection from Stuart and Elizabeth Ewen's book Channels of Desire *(1982), in which they point out the impact of mass produced images on our lives and on our sense of identity. As the title suggests, the Ewens see us as existing in the shadow of these mass produced images, confronting them, puzzling over them, responding to them, judging ourselves in terms of them—in short, being influenced by images, especially advertising images, in ways about which we may not be fully aware.*

In this introduction to their book, the Ewens present a number of different scenes—"Meaningless moments. Random incidents. Memory traces"—in which people respond to the mass media images that surround them. Although each incident is seemingly insignificant, the Ewens suggest that, viewed together as "an ensemble, an integrated panorama of social life, human activity, hope and despair, images and information, another tale unfolds from these vignettes." As you'll see, this is a tale about contemporary American culture, about how we understand ourselves and relate to one another, and about the subtle yet profound influence of advertising and the mass media on our lives.

To begin your reading, *think of some familiar images from television, magazine, and billboard advertisements. Consider the effect these images have on you as you read the Ewens' description of the effect of such images on other people. How much of yourself do you see in the Ewens' scenes?*

Maria Aguilar was born twenty-seven years ago near Mayagüez, on the island of Puerto Rico. Her family had lived off the land for generations. Today she sits in a rattling IRT subway car, speeding through the iron-and-rock guts of Manhattan. She sits on the train, her ears dazed by the loud outcry of wheels against tracks. Surrounded by a galaxy of unknown fellow strangers, she looks up at a long strip of colorful signboards placed high above the bobbing heads of the others. All the posters call for her attention. 1

Looking down at her, a blond-haired lady cabdriver leans out of her driver's side window. Here is the famed philosopher of this strange urban world, and a woman she can talk to. The tough-wise eyes of the cabby combined with a youthful beauty, speaking to Maria Aguilar directly: 2

Estoy sentada 12 horas al dia.
Lo último que necesito son hemorroides.
(I sit for twelve hours a day. The last thing I need are hemorrhoids.)

Under this candid testimonial lies a package of Preparation H   3
ointment, and the promise "Alivia dolores y picasonas. Y ayuda a re-
ducir la hinchazón." (Relieves pain and itching. And helps reduce
swelling.) As her mind's eye takes it all in, the train sweeps into
Maria's stop. She gets out; climbs the stairs to the street; walks to work
where she will spend her day sitting on a stool in a small garment factory, sewing hems on pretty dresses.

Every day, while Benny Doyle drives his Mustang to work along   4
State Road Number 20, he passes a giant billboard along the shoulder.
The billboard is selling whiskey and features a woman in a black vel-
vet dress stretching across its brilliant canvas.

As Benny Doyle downshifts by, the lounging beauty looks out to   5
him. Day after day he sees her here. The first time he wasn't sure, but
now he's convinced that her eyes are following him.

The morning sun shines on the red-tan forehead of Bill O'Conner   6
as he drinks espresso on his sun deck, alongside the ocean cliffs of La
Jolla, California. Turning through the daily paper, he reads a story
about Zimbabwe.

"Rhodesia," he thinks to himself.   7

The story argues that a large number of Africans in Zimbabwe   8
are fearful about black majority rule, and are concerned over a white
exodus. Two black hotel workers are quoted by the article. Bill puts
this, as a fact, into his mind.

Later that day, over a business lunch, he repeats the story to five   9
white business associates, sitting at the restaurant table. They share a superior laugh over the ineptitude of black African political rule. Three
more tellings, children of the first, take place over the next four days.
These are spoken by two of Bill O'Conner's luncheon companions;
passed on to still others in the supposed voice of political wisdom.

Barbara and John Marsh get into their seven-year-old Dodge   10
pickup and drive twenty-three miles to the nearest Sears in Cedar
Rapids. After years of breakdowns and months of hesitation they've
decided to buy a new washing machine. They come to Sears because it
is there, and because they believe that their new Sears machine will be
steady and reliable. The Marshes will pay for their purchase for the
next year or so.

Barbara's great-grandfather, Elijah Simmons, had purchased a   11
cream-separator from Sears, Roebuck in 1897 and he swore by it.

When the clock-radio sprang the morning affront upon him,   12
Archie Bishop rolled resentfully out of his crumpled bed and trudged
slowly to the john. A few moments later he was unconsciously squeez-
ing toothpaste out of a mess of red and white Colgate packaging. A
dozen scrubs of the mouth and he expectorated a white, minty glob
into the basin.

Still groggy, he turned on the hot water, slapping occasional   13
palmfuls onto his gray face.

A can of Noxzema shave cream sat on the edge of the sink, a film   14
of crud and whiskers across its once neat label. Archie reached for the
bomb and filled his left hand with a white creamy mound, then spread
it over his beard. He shaved, then looked with resignation at the regular collection of cuts on his neck.

Stepping into a shower, he soaped up with a soap that promised   15
to wake him up. Groggily, he then grabbed a bottle of Clairol Herbal
Essence Shampoo. He turned the tablet-shaped bottle to its back label,
carefully reading the "Directions."

"Wet hair."   16

He wet his hair.   17

"Lather."   18

He lathered.   19

"Rinse."   20

He rinsed.   21

"Repeat if necessary."   22

Not sure whether it was altogether necessary, he repeated the   23
process according to the directions.

Late in the evening, Maria Aguilar stepped back in the subway   24
train, heading home to the Bronx after a long and tiring day. This time,
a poster told her that "The Pain Stops Here!"

She barely noticed, but later she would swallow two New Extra   25
Strength Bufferin tablets with a glass of water from a rusty tap.

Two cockroaches in cartoon form leer out onto the street from a   26
wall advertisement. The man cockroach is drawn like a hipster, wearing shades and a cockroach zoot-suit. He strolls hand-in-hand with a
lady cockroach, who is dressed like a floozy and blushing beet-red.
Caught in the midst of their cockroach-rendezvous, they step sinfully
into a Black Flag Roach Motel. Beneath them in Spanish, the words:

> Las Cucarachas entran...pero non pueden salir.
> (In the English version: Cockroaches check in...but they don't check out.)

The roaches are trapped; sin is punished. Salvation is gauged by   27
one's ability to live roach-free. The sinners of the earth shall be inun-

dated by roaches. Moral tales and insects encourage passersby to rid their houses of sin. In their homes, sometimes, people wonder whether God has forsaken them.

Beverly Jackson sits at a metal and tan Formica table and looks   28
through the *New York Post*. She is bombarded by a catalog of horror. Children are mutilated...subway riders attacked....Fanatics are marauding and noble despots lie in bloody heaps. Occasionally someone steps off the crime-infested streets to claim a million dollars in lottery winnings.

Beverly Jackson's skin crawls; she feels a knot encircling her   29
lungs. She is beset by immobility, hopelessness, depression.

Slowly she walks over to her sixth-floor window, gazing out into   30
the sooty afternoon. From the empty street below, Beverly Jackson imagines a crowd yelling "Jump!...Jump!"

Between 1957 and 1966 Frank Miller saw a dozen John Wayne   31
movies, countless other westerns and war dramas. In 1969 he led a charge up a hill without a name in Southeast Asia. No one followed; he took a bullet in the chest.

Today he sits in a chair and doesn't get up. He feels that images   32
betrayed him, and now he camps out across from the White House while another movie star cuts benefits for veterans. In the morning newspaper he reads of a massive weapons buildup taking place.

Gina Concepcion now comes to school wearing the Jordache   33
look. All this has been made possible by weeks and weeks of after-school employment at a supermarket checkout counter. Now, each morning, she tugs the decorative denim over her young legs, sucking in her lean belly to close the snaps.

These pants are expensive compared to the "no-name" brands,   34
but they're worth it, she reasons. They fit better, and she fits better.

The theater marquee, stretching out over a crumbling, garbage-   35
strewn sidewalk, announced "The Decline of Western Civilization." At the ticket window a smaller sign read "All seats $5.00."

It was ten in the morning and Joyce Hopkins stood before a mirror   36
next to her bed. Her interview at General Public Utilities, Nuclear Division was only four hours away and all she could think was "What to wear?"

A half hour later Joyce stood again before the mirror, wearing a   37
slip and stockings. On the bed, next to her, lay a two-foot-mountain of discarded options. Mocking the title of a recent bestseller, which she hadn't read, she said aloud to herself, "Dress for Success....What *do* they like?"

At one o'clock she walked out the door wearing a brownish tweed   38
jacket; a cream-colored Qiana blouse, full-cut with a tied collar; a dark
beige skirt, fairly straight and hemmed (by Maria Aguilar) two inches
below the knee; shear fawn stockings, and simple but elegant reddish-
brown pumps on her feet. Her hair was to the shoulder, her look tawny.

When she got the job she thanked her friend Millie, a middle   39
manager, for the tip not to wear pants.

Joe Davis stood at the endless conveyor, placing caps on a   40
round-the-clock parade of automobile radiators. His nose and eyes
burned. His ears buzzed in the din. In a furtive moment he looked up
and to the right. On the plant wall was a large yellow sign with
THINK! printed on it in bold type. Joe turned back quickly to the ra-
diator caps.

Fifty years earlier in another factory, in another state, Joe's   41
grandfather, Nat Davis, had looked up and seen another sign:

A Clean Machine Runs Better.
Your Body Is a Machine.
KEEP IT CLEAN.

Though he tried and tried, Joe Davis' grandfather was never able   42
to get the dirt out from under his nails. Neither could his great-grandfather, who couldn't read.

In 1952 Mary Bird left her family in Charleston to earn money as   43
a maid in a Philadelphia suburb. She earned thirty-five dollars a week,
plus room and board, in a dingy retreat of a ranch-style tract house.

Twenty-eight years later she sits on a bus, heading toward her   44
small room in north Philly. Across from her, on an advertising poster,
a sumptuous meal is displayed. Golden fried chicken, green beans
glistening with butter and flecked by pimento, and a fluffy cloud of
rice fill the greater part of a calico-patterned dinner plate. Next to the
plate sits a steaming boat of gravy, and an icy drink in an amber tum-
bler. The plate is on a quilted blue placemat, flanked by a thick linen
napkin and colonial silverware.

As Mary Bird's hungers are aroused, the wording on the placard   45
instructs her: *"Come home to Carolina."*

Shopping List   46

paper towels
milk
eggs
rice crispies
chicken

snacks for kids (twinkies, chips, etc.)
potatoes
coke, ginger ale, plain soda
cheer
brillo
peanut butter
bread
ragu (2 jars)
spaghetti
saran wrap
salad
get cleaning, bank, *must pay electric!!!*

On his way to Nina's house, Sidney passed an ad for Smirnoff   47
vodka. A sultry beauty with wet hair and beads of moisture on her
smooth, tanned face looked out at him. *"Try a Main Squeeze."* For a
teenage boy the invitation transcended the arena of drink; he felt a
quick throb-pulse at the base of his belly and his step quickened.

In October of 1957, at the age of two and a half, Aaron Stone was   48
watching television. Suddenly, from the black screen, there leaped a
circus clown, selling children's vitamins, and yelling "Hi! boys and
girls!" He ran, terrified, from the room, screaming.

For years after, Aaron watched television in perpetual fear that   49
the vitamin clown would reappear. Slowly his family assured him that
the television was just a mechanical box and couldn't really hurt him,
that the vitamin clown was harmless.

Today, as an adult, Aaron Stone takes vitamins, is ambivalent   50
about clowns, and watches television, although there are occasional
moments of anxiety.

These are some of the facts of our lives; disparate moments, dis-   51
connected, dissociated. Meaningless moments. Random incidents.
Memory traces. Each is an unplanned encounter, part of day-to-day
existence. Viewed alone, each by itself, such spaces of our lives seem
insignificant, trivial. They are the decisions and reveries of survival;
the stuff of small talk; the chance preoccupations of our eyes and
minds in a world of images—soon forgotten.

Viewed together, however, as an ensemble, an integrated   52
panorama of social life, human activity, hope and despair, images and
information, another tale unfolds from these vignettes. They reveal a
pattern of life, the structures of perception.

As familiar moments in American life, all of these events bear the   53
footprints of a history that weighs upon us, but is largely untold. We
live and breathe an atmosphere where mass images are everywhere in
evidence; mass produced, mass distributed. In the streets, in our

homes, among a crowd, or alone, they speak to us, overwhelm our vision. Their presence, their messages are given; unavoidable. Though their history is still relatively short, their prehistory is, for the most part, forgotten, unimaginable.

The history that unites the seemingly random routines of daily   54
life is one that embraces the rise of an industrial consumer society. It involves explosive interactions between modernity and old ways of life. It includes the proliferation, over days and decades, of a wide, repeatable vernacular of commercial images and ideas. This history spells new patterns of social, productive, and political life.

Examining the Text

1. What is the effect of the Ewens' strategy in this essay of presenting a number of brief, disconnected episodes in the lives of different people? Do you think it would have been more effective to include more commentary connecting the scenes? Why or why not?

2. What connections do you see among the episodes presented here? What thematic unities are there among the stories?

3. In their conclusion, the Ewens suggest that the moments they describe portray "explosive interactions between modernity and old ways of life" and spell "new patterns of social, productive, and political life" (paragraph 54). In your own words, what do you think the authors are suggesting here? Do you find their point persuasive?

For Group Discussion

Choose one of the scenes presented and, after re-reading and reflecting on your understanding, discuss as a group the similarities and differences in your individual responses to this scene.

Writing Suggestion

Add to the Ewens' essay an experience of your own in which you or someone you know is "in the shadow of an image." You might consider influential images in advertisements, TV shows, music videos, or movies.

Masters of Desire

Jack Solomon

This selection is taken from the book The Signs of Our Time *(1988), in which Jack Solomon uses semiology, the study of signs, in analyzing contemporary American culture. In this excerpt, Solomon interprets advertising from a semiological perspective, noting the signs and symbols at work in specific ads and suggesting what they mean and why they appeal to the American consumer.*

Solomon asserts that "the American dream breeds desire, a longing for a greater share of the pie," and that in order to sell us products advertisements exploit this and other desires, fears, and guilts we share. Specifically, ads present signs that encourage us to think that particular products can satisfy our desires (for social status, or belonging, or sexual attractiveness), alleviate our fears, and calm our guilt. On a conscious level, we know that most products can't do these things and that we shouldn't be swayed by such promises of beauty, popularity, and success. But the companies that spend millions of dollars on advertising are obviously betting that subconsciously we're more susceptible than we like to admit.

As you read, pay attention to the way Solomon interprets specific ads, identifying the signs they contain and the reasons these signs are effective. After you finish the essay, you'll have a chance to develop your own semiotic interpretation of an ad of your choice.

Amongst democratic nations, men easily attain a certain equality of condition; but they can never attain as much as they desire.

Alexis De Tocqueville

On May 10, 1831, a young French aristocrat named Alexis de Tocqueville arrived in New York City at the start of what would become one of the most famous visits to America in our history. He had come to observe firsthand the institutions of the freest, most egalitarian society of the age, but what he found was a paradox. For behind America's mythic promise of equal opportunity, Tocqueville discovered a desire for *unequal* social rewards, a ferocious competition for privilege and distinction. As he wrote in his monumental study, *Democracy in America:*

> When all privilege of birth and fortune are abolished, when all professions are accessible to all, and a man's own energies may place him at the top of any one of them, an easy and unbounded career seems open to his ambition.... But this is an erroneous notion, which is corrected by daily experience. [For when] men are nearly alike, and all follow the same track, it is very difficult for any one individual to walk quick and cleave a way through the same throng which surrounds and presses him.

Yet walking quick and cleaving a way is precisely what Americans dream of. We Americans dream of rising above the crowd, of attaining a social summit beyond the reach of ordinary citizens. And therein lies the paradox.

The American dream, in other words, has two faces: the one   3
communally egalitarian and the other competitively elitist. This contradiction is no accident; it is fundamental to the structure of American
society. Even as America's great myth of equality celebrates the
virtues of mom, apple pie, and the girl or boy next door, it also lures
us to achieve social distinction, to rise above the crowd and bask alone
in the glory. This land is your land and this land is my land, Woody
Guthrie's populist anthem tells us, but we keep trying to increase the
"my" at the expense of the "your." Rather than fostering contentment,
the American dream breeds desire, a longing for a greater share of the
pie. It is as if our society were a vast high-school football game, with
the bulk of the participants noisily rooting in the stands while, deep
down, each of them is wishing he or she could be the star quarterback
or head cheerleader.

For the semiotician, the contradictory nature of the American   4
myth of equality is nowhere written so clearly as in the signs that
American advertisers use to manipulate us into buying their wares.
"Manipulate" is the word here, not "persuade"; for advertising campaigns are not sources of product information, they are exercises in behavior modification. Appealing to our subconscious emotions rather
than to our conscious intellects, advertisements are designed to exploit
the discontentments fostered by the American dream, the constant desire for social success and the material rewards that accompany it.
America's consumer economy runs on desire, and advertising stokes
the engines by transforming common objects—from peanut butter to
political candidates—into signs of all the things that Americans covet
most.

But by semiotically reading the signs that advertising agencies   5
manufacture to stimulate consumption, we can plot the precise state of
desire in the audiences to which they are addressed. In this [essay],
we'll look at a representative sample of ads and what they say about
the emotional climate of the country and the fast-changing trends of
American life. Because ours is a highly diverse, pluralistic society, various advertisements may say different things depending on their intended audiences, but in every case they say something about
America, about the status of our hopes, fears, desires, and beliefs.

Let's begin with two ad campaigns conducted by the same com-   6
pany that bear out Alexis de Tocqueville's observations about the contradictory nature of American society: General Motors' campaigns for
its Cadillac and Chevrolet lines. First, consider an early magazine ad
for the Cadillac Allanté. Appearing as a full-color, four-page insert in
Time, the ad seems to say "I'm special—and so is this car" even before
we've begun to read it. Rather than being printed on the ordinary,
flimsy pages of the magazine, the Allanté spread appears on glossy

coated stock. The unwritten message here is that an extraordinary car deserves an extraordinary advertisement, and that both car and ad are aimed at an extraordinary consumer, or at least one who wishes to appear extraordinary compared to his more ordinary fellow citizens.

Ads of this kind work by creating symbolic associations between their product and what is most coveted by the consumers to whom they are addressed. It is significant, then, that this ad insists that the Allanté is virtually an Italian rather than an American car, an automobile, as its copy runs, "Conceived and Commissioned by America's Luxury Car Leader—Cadillac" but "Designed and Handcrafted by Europe's Renowned Design Leader—Pininfarina, SpA, of Turin, Italy." This is not simply a piece of product information, it's a sign of the prestige that European luxury cars enjoy in today's automotive marketplace. Once the luxury car of choice for America's status drivers, Cadillac has fallen far behind its European competitors in the race for the prestige market. So the Allanté essentially represents Cadillac's decision, after years of resisting the trend toward European cars, to introduce its own European import—whose high cost is clearly printed on the last page of the ad. Although $54,700 is a lot of money to pay for a Cadillac, it's about what you'd expect to pay for a top-of-the-line Mercedes-Benz. That's precisely the point the ad is trying to make: the Allanté is no mere car. It's a potent status symbol you can associate with the other major status symbols of the 1980s. 7

American companies manufacture status symbols because American consumers want them. As Alexis de Tocqueville recognized a century and a half ago, the competitive nature of democratic societies breeds a desire for social distinction, a yearning to rise above the crowd. But given the fact that those who do make it to the top in socially mobile societies have often risen from the lower ranks, they still look like everyone else. In the socially immobile societies of aristocratic Europe, generations of fixed social conditions produced subtle class signals. The accent of one's voice, the shape of one's nose, or even the set of one's chin, immediately communicated social status. Aside from the nasal bray and uptilted head of the Boston Brahmin, Americans do not have any native sets of personal status signals. If it weren't for his Mercedes-Benz and Manhattan townhouse, the parvenu Wall Street millionaire often couldn't be distinguished from the man who tailors his suits. Hence, the demand for status symbols, for the objects that mark one off as a social success, is particularly strong in democratic nations—stronger even than in aristocratic societies, where the aristocrat so often looks and sounds different from everyone else. 8

Status symbols, then, are signs that identify their possessor's place in a social hierarchy, markers of rank and prestige. We can all think of any number of status symbols—Rolls-Royces, Beverly Hills mansions, 9 even Shar Pei puppies (whose rareness and expense has rocketed them beyond Russian wolfhounds as status pets and has even inspired whole lines of wrinkle-faced stuffed toys)—but how do we know that something *is* a status symbol? The explanation is quite simple: when an object (or puppy!) either costs a lot of money or requires influential connections to possess, anyone who possesses it must also possess the necessary means and influence to acquire it. The object itself really doesn't matter, since it ultimately disappears behind the presumed social potency of its owner. Semiotically, what matters is the signal it sends, its value as a sign of power. One traditional sign of social distinction is owning a country estate and enjoying the peace and privacy that attend it. Advertisements for Mercedes-Benz, Jaguar, and Audi automobiles thus frequently feature drivers motoring quietly along a country road, presumably on their way to or from their country houses.

Advertisers have been quick to exploit the status signals that belong to body language as well. As Hegel observed in the early nineteenth century, it is an ancient aristocratic prerogative to be seen by the lower orders without having to look at them in return. Tilting his chin high in the air and gazing down at the world under hooded eyelids, the aristocrat invites observation while refusing to look back. We can find such a pose exploited in an advertisement for Cadillac Seville in which we see an elegantly dressed woman out for a drive with her husband in their new Cadillac. If we look closely at the woman's body language, we can see her glance inwardly with a satisfied smile on her face but not outward toward the camera that represents our gaze. She is glad to be seen by us in her Seville, but she isn't interested in looking at *us!*

Ads that are aimed at a broader market take the opposite approach. If the American dream encourages the desire to "arrive," to vault above the mass, it also fosters a desire to be popular, to "belong." Populist commercials accordingly transform products into signs of belonging, utilizing such common icons as country music, small-town life, family picnics, and farmyards. All of these icons are incorporated in GM's "Heartbeat of America" campaign for its Chevrolet line. Unlike the Seville commercial, the faces in the Chevy ads look straight at us and smile. Dress is casual; the mood upbeat. Quick camera cuts take us from rustic to suburban to urban scenes, creating an American montage filmed from sea to shining sea. We all "belong" in a Chevy.

Where price alone doesn't determine the market for a product, advertisers can go either way. Both Johnnie Walker and Jack Daniel's are better-grade whiskies, but where a Johnnie Walker ad appeals to the buyer who wants a mark of aristocratic distinction in his liquor, a Jack Daniel's ad emphasizes the down-home, egalitarian folksiness of its product. Johnnie Walker associates itself with such conventional status symbols as sable coats, Rolls-Royces, and black gold; Jack Daniel's gives us a Good Ol' Boy in overalls. In fact, Jack Daniel's Good Ol' Boy is an icon of backwoods independence, recalling the days of the moonshiner and the Whisky Rebellion of 1794. Evoking emotions quite at odds with those stimulated in Johnnie Walker ads, the advertisers of Jack Daniel's have chosen to transform their product into a sign of America's populist tradition. The fact that both ads successfully sell whisky is itself a sign of the dual nature of the American dream.

Beer is also pitched on two levels. Consider the difference be-   13 tween the ways Budweiser and Michelob market their light beers. Bud Light and Michelob Light cost and taste about the same, but Budweiser tends to target the working class while Michelob has gone after the upscale market. Bud commercials are set in working-class bars that contrast with the sophisticated nightclubs and yuppie watering holes of the Michelob campaign. "You're one of the guys," Budweiser assures the assembly-line worker and the truck driver, "this Bud's for you." Michelob, on the other hand, makes no such appeal to the democratic instinct of sharing and belonging. You don't share, you take, grabbing what you can in a competitive dash to "have it all."

Populist advertising is particularly effective in the face of foreign   14 competition. When Americans feel threatened from the outside, they tend to circle the wagons and temporarily forget their class differences. In the face of the Japanese automotive "invasion," Chrysler runs populist commercials in which Lee Iacocca joins the simple folk who buy his cars as the jingle "Born in America" blares in the background. Seeking to capitalize on the popularity of Bruce Springsteen's *Born in the USA* album, these ads gloss over Springsteen's ironic lyrics in a vast display of flag-waving. Chevrolet's "Heartbeat of America" campaign similarly attempts to woo American motorists away from Japanese automobiles by appealing to their patriotic sentiments.

The patriotic iconography of these campaigns also reflects the gen-   15 eral cultural mood of the early-to-mid–1980s. After a period of national anguish in the wake of the Vietnam War and the Iran hostage crisis, America went on a patriotic binge. American athletic triumphs in the Lake Placid and Los Angeles Olympics introduced a sporting tone into the national celebration, often making international affairs appear like one great Olympiad in which America was always going for the gold. In response, advertisers began to do their own flag-waving.

The mood of advertising during this period was definitely up-   16 beat. Even deodorant commercials, which traditionally work on our self-doubts and fears of social rejection, jumped on the bandwagon. In the guilty sixties, we had ads like the "Ice Blue Secret" campaign with its connotations of guilt and shame. In the feel-good Reagan eighties, "Sure" deodorant commercials featured images of triumphant Americans throwing up their arms in victory to reveal—no wet marks! Deodorant commercials once had the moral echo of Nathaniel Hawthorne's guilt-ridden *The Scarlet Letter*. In the early eighties, they had all the moral subtlety of *Rocky IV*, reflecting the emotions of a Vietnam-weary nation eager to embrace the imagery of America Triumphant.

The commercials for Worlds of Wonder's Lazer Tag game featured   17
the futuristic finals of some Soviet-American Lazer Tag shootout ("Practice hard, America!") and carried the emotions of patriotism into an even more aggressive arena. Exploiting the hoopla that surrounded the victory over the Soviets in the hockey finals of the 1980 Olympics, the Lazer Tag ads pandered to an American desire for the sort of clear-cut nationalistic triumphs that the nuclear age has rendered almost impossible. Creating a fantasy setting where patriotic dreams are substituted for complicated realities, the Lazer Tag commercials sought to capture the imaginations of children caught up in the patriotic fervor of the early 1980s.

LIVE THE FANTASY

By reading the signs of American advertising, we can conclude   18
that America is a nation of fantasizers, often preferring the sign to the substance and easily enthralled by a veritable Fantasy Island of commercial illusions. Critics of Madison Avenue often complain that advertisers create consumer desire, but semioticians don't think the situation is that simple. Advertisers may give shape to consumer fantasies, but they need raw material to work with, the subconscious dreams and desires of the marketplace. As long as these desires remain unconscious, advertisers will be able to exploit them. But by bringing the fantasies to the surface, you can free yourself from advertising's often hypnotic grasp.

I can think of no company that has more successfully seized   19
upon the subconscious fantasies of the American marketplace—indeed the world marketplace—than McDonald's. By no means the first nor the only hamburger chain in the United States, McDonald's emerged victorious in the "burger wars" by transforming hamburgers into signs of all that was desirable in American life. Other chains like Wendy's, Burger King, and Jack-In-The-Box continue to advertise and sell widely, but no company approaches McDonald's transformation of itself into a symbol of American culture.

McDonald's success can be traced to the precision of its advertis-   20
ing. Instead of broadcasting a single "one-size-fits-all" campaign at a time, McDonald's pitches its burgers simultaneously at different age groups, different classes, even different races (Budweiser beer, incidentally, has succeeded in the same way). For children, there is the Ronald McDonald campaign, which presents a fantasy world that has little to do with hamburgers in any rational sense but a great deal to do with the emotional desires of kids. Ronald McDonald and his friends are signs

that recall the Muppets, *Sesame Street*, the circus, toys, storybook illustrations, even *Alice in Wonderland*. Such signs do not signify hamburgers. Rather, they are displayed in order to prompt in the child's mind an automatic association of fantasy, fun, and McDonald's.

The same approach is taken in ads aimed at older audiences—   21
teens, adults, and senior citizens. In the teen-oriented ads we may catch a fleeting glimpse of a hamburger or two, but what we are really shown is a teenage fantasy: groups of hip and happy adolescents singing, dancing, and cavorting together. Fearing loneliness more than anything else, adolescents quickly respond to the group appeal of such commercials. "Eat a Big Mac," these ads say, "and you won't be stuck home alone on Saturday night."

To appeal to an older and more sophisticated audience no longer   22
so afraid of not belonging and more concerned with finding a place to go out to at night, McDonald's has designed the elaborate "Mac Tonight" commercials, which have for their backdrop a nightlit urban skyline and at their center a cabaret pianist with a moon-shaped head, a glad manner, and Blues Brothers shades. Such signs prompt an association of McDonald's with nightclubs and urban sophistication, persuading us that McDonald's is a place not only for breakfast or lunch but for dinner too, as if it were a popular off-Broadway nightspot, a place to see and be seen. Even the parody of Kurt Weill's "Mack the Knife" theme song that Mac the Pianist performs is a sign, a subtle signal to the sophisticated hamburger eater able to recognize the origin of the tune in Bertolt Brecht's *Threepenny Opera*.

For yet older customers, McDonald's has designed a commercial   23
around the fact that it employs a large number of retirees and seniors. In one such ad, we see an elderly man leaving his pretty little cottage early in the morning to start work as "the new kid" at McDonald's, and then we watch him during his first day on the job. Of course he is a great success, outdoing everyone else with his energy and efficiency, and he returns home in the evening to a loving wife and happy home. One would almost think that the ad was a kind of moving "help wanted" sign (indeed, McDonald's *was* hiring elderly employees at the time), but it's really just directed at consumers. Older viewers can see themselves wanted and appreciated in the ad—and perhaps be distracted from the rationally uncomfortable fact that many senior citizens take such jobs because of financial need and thus may be unlikely to own the sort of home that one sees in the commercial. But realism isn't the point here. This is fantasyland, a dream world promising instant gratification no matter what the facts of the matter may be.

Practically the only fantasy that McDonald's doesn't exploit is   24
the fantasy of sex. This is understandable, given McDonald's desire to present itself as a family restaurant. But everywhere else, sexual fantasies, which have always had an important place in American adver-

tising, are beginning to dominate the advertising scene. You expect sexual come-ons in ads for perfume or cosmetics or jewelry—after all, that's what they're selling—but for room deodorizers? In a magazine ad for Claire Burke home fragrances, for example, we see a well-dressed couple cavorting about their bedroom in what looks like a cheery preparation for sadomasochistic exercises. Jordache and Calvin Klein pitch blue jeans as props for teenage sexuality. The phallic appeal of automobiles, traditionally an implicit feature in automotive advertising, becomes quite explicit in a Dodge commercial that shifts back and forth from shots of a young man in an automobile to teasing glimpses of a woman—his date—as she dresses in her apartment.

The very language of today's advertisements is charged with   25
sexuality. Products in the more innocent fifties were "new and improved," but everything in the eighties is "hot!"—as in "hot woman," or sexual heat. Cars are "hot." Movies are "hot." An ad for Valvoline pulses to the rhythm of a "heat wave, burning in my car." Sneakers get red hot in a magazine ad for Travel Fox athletic shoes in which we see male and female figures, clad only in Travel Fox shoes, apparently in the act of copulation—an ad that earned one of *Adweek*'s annual "bad-vertising" awards for shoddy advertising.

The sexual explicitness of contemporary advertising is a sign not   26
so much of American sexual fantasies as of the lengths to which advertisers will go to get attention. Sex never fails as an attention-getter, and in a particularly competitive, and expensive, era for American marketing, advertisers like to bet on a sure thing. Ad people refer to the proliferation of TV, radio, newspaper, magazine, and billboard ads as "clutter," and nothing cuts through the clutter like sex.

By showing the flesh, advertisers work on the deepest, most coer-   27
cive human emotions of all. Much sexual coercion in advertising, however, is a sign of a desperate need to make certain that clients are getting their money's worth. The appearance of advertisements that refer directly to the prefabricated fantasies of Hollywood is a sign of a different sort of desperation: a desperation for ideas. With the rapid turnover of advertising campaigns mandated by the need to cut through the "clutter," advertisers may be hard pressed for new ad concepts, and so they are more and more frequently turning to already-established models. In the early 1980s, for instance, Pepsi-Cola ran a series of ads broadly alluding to Steven Spielberg's *E.T.* In one such ad, we see a young boy who, like the hero of *E.T.*, witnesses an extraterrestrial visit. The boy is led to a soft-drink machine where he pauses to drink a can of Pepsi as the spaceship he's spotted flies off into the universe. The relationship between the ad and the movie, accordingly, is a parasitical one, with the ad taking its life from the creative body of the film.

Pepsi did something similar in 1987 when it arranged with the   28
producers of the movie *Top Gun* to promote the film's video release in

Pepsi ad to the video itself. This time, however, the parasitical relationship between ad and film was made explicit. Pepsi sales benefited
from the video, and the video's sales benefited from Pepsi. It was a
marriage made in corporate heaven.

The fact that Pepsi believed that it could stimulate consumption   29
by appealing to the militaristic fantasies dramatized in *Top Gun* reflects similar fantasies in the "Pepsi generation." Earlier generations
saw Pepsi associated with high-school courtship rituals, with couples
sipping sodas together at the corner drugstore. When the draft was on,
young men fantasized about Peggy Sue, not Air Force Flight School.
Military service was all too real a possibility to fantasize about. But in
an era when military service is not a reality for most young Americans, Pepsi commercials featuring hotshot fly-boys drinking Pepsi
while streaking about in their Air Force jets contribute to a youth culture that has forgotten what military service means. It all looks like
such fun in the Pepsi ads, but what they conceal is the fact that military jets are weapons, not high-tech recreational vehicles.

For less militaristic dreamers, Madison Avenue has framed ad   30
campaigns around the cultural prestige of high-tech machinery in its
own right. This is especially the case with sports cars, whose hi-tech
appeal is so powerful that some people apparently fantasize about
being sports cars. At least, this is the conclusion one might draw from a
Porsche commercial that asked its audience, "If you were a car, what
kind of car would you be?" As a candy-red Porsche speeds along a
rain-slick forest road, the ad's voice-over describes all the specifica-
tions you'd want to have if you *were* a sports car. "If you were a car,"
the commercial concludes, "you'd be a Porsche."

In his essay "Car Commercials and *Miami Vice*," Tod Gitlin ex-   31
plains the semiotic appeal of such ads as those in the Porsche campaign. Aired at the height of what may be called America's "myth of
the entrepreneur," these commercials were aimed at young corporate
managers who imaginatively identified with the "lone wolf" image of
a Porsche speeding through the woods. Gitlin points out that such images cater to the fantasies of faceless corporate men who dream of entrepreneurial glory, of striking out on their own like John DeLorean
and telling the boss to take his job and shove it. But as DeLorean's
spectacular failure demonstrates, the life of the entrepreneur can be
extremely risky. So rather than having to go it alone and take the risks
that accompany entrepreneurial independence, the young executive
can substitute fantasy for reality by climbing into his Porsche—or at
least that's what Porsche's advertisers wanted him to believe.

But there is more at work in the Porsche ads than the fantasies of   32
corporate America. Ever since Arthur C. Clarke and Stanley Kubrick
teamed up to present us with HAL 9000, the demented computer of
2001: A Space Odyssey, the American imagination has been obsessed

with the melding of man and machine. First there was television's *Six Million Dollar Man,* and then movieland's *Star Wars, Blade Runner,* and *Robocop,* fantasy visions of a future dominated by machines. Androids haunt our imaginations as machines seize the initiative. *Time* magazine's "Man of the Year" for 1982 was a computer. Robot-built automobiles appeal to drivers who spend their days in front of computer screens—perhaps designing robots. When so much power and prestige is being given to high-tech machines, wouldn't you rather be a Porsche?

In short, the Porsche campaign is a sign of a new mythology that   33
is emerging before our eyes, a myth of the machine, which is replacing the myth of the human. The iconic figure of the little tramp caught up in the cogs of industrial production in Charlie Chaplin's *Modern Times* signified a humanistic revulsion to the age of the machine. Human beings, such icons said, were superior to machines. Human values should come first in the moral order of things. But as Edith Milton suggests in her essay, "The Track of the Mutant," we are now coming to believe that machines are superior to human beings, that mechanical nature is superior to human nature. Rather than being threatened by machines, we long to merge with them. *The Six Million Dollar Man* is one iconic figure in the new mythology; Harrison Ford's sexual coupling with an android is another. In such an age it should come as little wonder that computer-synthesized Max Headroom should be a commercial spokesman for Coca-Cola, or that Federal Express should design a series of TV ads featuring mechanical-looking human beings revolving around strange and powerful machines.

FEAR AND TREMBLING IN THE MARKETPLACE

While advertisers play on and reflect back at us our fantasies   34
about everything from fighter pilots to robots, they also play on darker imaginings. If dream and desire can be exploited in the quest for sales, so can nightmare and fear.

The nightmare equivalent of America's populist desire to "be-   35
long," for example, is the fear of not belonging, of social rejection, of being different. Advertisements for dandruff shampoos, mouthwashes, deodorants, and laundry detergents ("Ring Around the Collar!") accordingly exploit such fears, bullying us into consumption. Although ads of this type are still around in the 1980s, they were particularly common in the fifties and early sixties, reflecting a society still reeling from the witch-hunts of the McCarthy years. When any sort of social eccentricity or difference could result in a public denunciation and the loss of one's job or even liberty, Americans were keen to con-

form and be like everyone else. No one wanted to be "guilty" of smelling bad or of having a dirty collar.

"Guilt" ads characteristically work by creating narrative situa- 36 tions in which someone is "accused" of some social "transgression," pronounced guilty, and then offered the sponsor's product as a means of returning to "innocence." Such ads, in essence, are parodies of ancient religious rituals of guilt and atonement, whereby sinning humanity is offered salvation through the agency of priest and church. In the world of advertising, a product takes the place of the priest, but the logic of the situation is quite similar.

In commercials for Wisk detergent, for example, we witness the 37 drama of a hapless housewife and her husband as they are mocked by the jeering voices of children shouting "Ring Around the Collar!" "Oh, those dirty rings!" the housewife groans in despair. It's as if she and her husband were being stoned by an angry crowd. But there's hope, there's help, there's Wisk. Cleansing her soul of sin as well as her husband's, the housewife launders his shirts with Wisk, and behold, his collars are clean. Product salvation is only as far as the supermarket.

The recent appearance of advertisements for hospitals treating 38 drug and alcohol addiction have raised the old genre of the guilt ad to new heights (or lows, depending on your perspective). In such ads, we see wives on the verge of leaving their husbands if they don't do something about their drinking, and salesmen about to lose their jobs. The man is guilty; he has sinned. But he upholds the ritual of guilt and atonement by "confessing" to his wife or boss and agreeing to go to the hospital the ad is pitching.

If guilt looks backward in time to past transgressions, fear, like 39 desire, faces forward, trembling before the future. In the late 1980s, a new kind of fear commercial appeared, one whose narrative played on the worries of young corporate managers struggling up the ladder of success. Representing the nightmare equivalent of the elitist desire to "arrive," ads of this sort created images of failure, storylines of corporate defeat. In one ad for Apple computers, for example, a group of junior executives sits around a table with the boss as he asks each executive how long it will take his or her department to complete some publishing jobs. "Two or three days," answers one nervous executive. "A week, on overtime," a tight-lipped woman responds. But one young up-and-comer can have everything ready tomorrow, today, or yesterday, because his department uses a Macintosh desktop publishing system. Guess who'll get the next promotion?

Fear stalks an ad for AT&T computer systems too. A boss and 40 four junior executives are dining in a posh restaurant. Icons of corporate power and prestige flood the screen—from the executives' formal evening wear to the fancy table setting—but there's tension in the air.

It seems that the junior managers have chosen a computer system that's incompatible with the firm's sales and marketing departments. A whole new system will have to be purchased, but the tone of the meeting suggests that it will be handled by a new group of managers. These guys are on the way out. They no longer "belong." Indeed, it's probably no accident that the ad takes place in a restaurant, given the joke that went around in the aftermath of the 1987 market crash. "What do you call a yuppie stockbroker?" the joke ran. "Hey, waiter!" Is the ad trying subtly to suggest that junior executives who choose the wrong computer systems are doomed to suffer the same fate?

For other markets, there are other fears. If McDonald's presents   41
senior citizens with bright fantasies of being useful and appreciated beyond retirement, companies like Secure Horizons dramatize senior citizens' fears of being caught short by a major illness. Running its ads in the wake of budgetary cuts in the Medicare system, Secure Horizons designed a series of commercials featuring a pleasant old man named Harry—who looks and sounds rather like Carroll O'Connor— who tells the story of the scare he got during his wife's recent illness. Fearing that next time Medicare won't cover the bills, he has purchased supplemental health insurance from Secure Horizons and now securely tends his rooftop garden.

Among all the fears advertisers have exploited over the years, I   42
find the fear of not having a posh enough burial site the most arresting. Advertisers usually avoid any mention of death—who wants to associate a product with the grave?—but mortuary advertisers haven't much choice. Generally, they solve their problem by framing cemeteries as timeless parks presided over by priestly morticians, appealing to our desires for dignity and comfort in the face of bereavement. But in one television commercial for Forest Lawn we find a different approach. In this ad we are presented with the ghost of an old man telling us how he might have found a much nicer resting place than the run-down cemetery in which we find him had his wife only known that Forest Lawn was so "affordable." I presume the ad was supposed to be funny, but it's been pulled off the air. There are some fears that just won't bear joking about, some nightmares too dark to dramatize.

THE FUTURE OF AN ILLUSION

There are some signs in the advertising world that Americans are   43
getting fed up with fantasy advertisements and want to hear some straight talk. Weary of extravagant product claims and irrelevant associations, consumers trained by years of advertising to distrust what they hear seem to be developing an immunity to commercials. At least, this is the semiotic message I read in the "new realism" advertisements of the eight-

ies, ads that attempt to convince you that what you're seeing is the real
thing, that the ad is giving you the straight dope, not advertising hype.

You can recognize the "new realism" by its camera techniques.   44
The lighting is usually subdued to give the ad the effect of being
filmed while blinds were drawn. The camera shots are jerky and off-
angle, often zooming in for sudden unflattering close-ups, as if the
cameraman was an amateur with a home video recorder. In a "realistic" ad for AT&T, for example, we are treated to a monologue by a
plump stockbroker—his plumpness intended as a sign that he's for
real and not just another actor—who tells us about the problems he's
had with his phone system (not AT&T's) as the camera jerks around,
generally filming him from below as if the cameraman couldn't quite
fit his equipment into the crammed office and had to film the scene on
his knees. "This is no fancy advertisement," the ad tries to convince us,
"this is sincere."

An ad for Miller draft beer tries the same approach, recreating   45
the effect of an amateur videotape of a wedding celebration. Camera
shots shift suddenly from group to group. The picture jumps. Bodies
are poorly framed. The color is washed out. Like the beer it is pushing,
the ad is supposed to strike us as being "as real as it gets."

Such ads reflect a desire for reality in the marketplace, a weari-   46
ness with Madison Avenue illusions. But there's no illusion like the illusion of reality. Every special technique that advertisers use to create
their "reality effects" is, in fact, more unrealistic than the techniques of
"illusory" ads. The world, in reality, doesn't jump around when you
look at it. It doesn't appear in subdued gray tones. Our eyes don't
have zoom lenses, and we don't look at things with our heads cocked
to one side. The irony of the "new realism" is that it is more unrealistic, more artificial, than the ordinary run of television advertising.

But don't expect any truly realistic ads in the future, because a re-   47
alistic advertisement is a contradiction in terms. The logic of advertising
is entirely semiotic: it substitutes signs for things, framed visions of consumer desire for the thing itself. The success of modern advertising, its
penetration into every corner of American life, reflects a culture that has
itself chosen illusion over reality. At a time when political candidates all
have professional image-makers attached to their staffs, and the President of the United States is an actor who once sold shirt collars, all the
cultural signs are pointing to more illusions in our lives rather than
fewer—a fecund breeding ground for the world of the advertiser.

Examining the Text

1. What does Solomon see as the basic contradiction or conflict inherent in the American Dream? How does advertising exploit this contra-

diction? Think of specific ads you've seen recently that are manipulative or exploitative in the way that Solomon describes.

2. Solomon points out that advertisers manipulate consumers, using our dreams and desires as the "raw material" (paragraph 18). How does he propose we defend ourselves against this manipulation? What do you think of his solution?

3. Solomon offers short interpretations of some specific advertising campaigns—Pepsi, Porsche, McDonald's, and Cadillac, among others. For one example that you found particularly interesting, restate Solomon's interpretation. What would you add to make this interpretation stronger?

For Group Discussion

According to Solomon, advertisers usually appeal either to our dreams and desires or to our guilt and fear. Recall some ads that you think are particularly effective. Were they manipulating our fantasies or our nightmares or did they use other strategies discussed by Solomon? Discuss which strategies you think work best, and why.

Writing Suggestion

In this essay, Solomon takes a semiotic approach to advertising, because, as he explains, "The logic of advertising is entirely semiotic: it substitutes signs for things, framed visions of consumer desire for the thing itself" (47). List the signs you find in a recent magazine ad that interests you and explore in writing the meaning and the appeal of each of them. What overall conclusions about the ad can you draw from your own semiological analysis?

Advertising's Fifteen Basic Appeals

Jib Fowles

In the following essay, Jib Fowles looks at how advertisements work by examining the emotional, subrational appeals that they employ. We are confronted daily by hundreds of ads, only a few of which actually attract our attention. These few do so, according to Fowles, through "something primary and primitive, an emotional appeal, that in effect is the thin edge of the wedge, trying to find its way into a mind." Drawing on research done by the psychologist Henry A. Murray, Fowles describes fifteen emotional appeals or wedges that advertisements exploit.

Underlying Fowles's psychological analysis of advertising is the assumption that advertisers try to circumvent the logical, cautious, skeptical powers we develop as consumers, to reach, instead, the "unfulfilled urges and motives swirling in the bottom half of [our] minds." In Fowles's view, consumers are well advised to pay attention to these underlying appeals in order to avoid responding unthinkingly.

As you read, note which of Fowles's fifteen appeals seem most familiar to you. Do you recognize these appeals in ads you can recall? How have you responded?

EMOTIONAL APPEALS

The nature of effective advertisements was recognized full well   1
by the late media philosopher Marshall McLuhan. In his *Understanding Media,* the first sentence of the section on advertising reads, "The continuous pressure is to create ads more and more in the image of audience motives and desires."

By giving form to people's deep-lying desires, and picturing   2
states of being that individuals privately yearn for, advertisers have the best chance of arresting attention and affecting communication. And that is the immediate goal of advertising: to tug at our psychological shirt sleeves and slow us down long enough for a word or two about whatever is being sold. We glance at a picture of a solitary rancher at work, and "Marlboro" slips into our minds.

Advertisers (I'm using the term as a shorthand for both the prod-   3
ucts' manufacturers, who bring the ambition and money to the process, and the advertising agencies, who supply the know-how) are ever more compelled to invoke consumers' drives and longings; this is the "continuous pressure" McLuhan refers to. Over the past century, the American marketplace has grown increasingly congested as more and more products have entered into the frenzied competition after the public's dollars. The economies of other nations are quieter than ours since the volume of goods being hawked does not so greatly exceed demand. In some economies, consumer wares are scarce enough that no advertising at all is necessary. But in the United States, we go to the other extreme. In order to stay in business, an advertiser must strive to cut through the considerable commercial hub-bub by any means available—including the emotional appeals that some observers have held to be abhorrent and underhanded.

The use of subconscious appeals is a comment not only on condi-   4
tions among sellers. As time has gone by, buyers have become stoutly resistant to advertisements. We live in a blizzard of these messages

and have learned to turn up our collars and ward off most of them. A study done a few years ago at Harvard University's Graduate School of Business Administration ventured that the average American is exposed to some 500 ads daily from television, newspapers, magazines, radio, billboards, direct mail, and so on. If for no other reason than to preserve one's sanity, a filter must be developed in every mind to lower the number of ads a person is actually aware of—a number this particular study estimated at about seventy-five ads per day. (Of these, only twelve typically produced a reaction—nine positive and three negative, on the average.) To be among the few messages that do manage to gain access to minds, advertisers must be strategic, perhaps even a little underhanded at times.

There are assumptions about personality underlying advertisers' efforts to communicate via emotional appeals, and while these assumptions have stood the test of time, they still deserve to be aired. Human beings, it is presumed, walk around with a variety of unfulfilled urges and motives swirling in the bottom half of their minds. Lusts, ambitions, tendernesses, vulnerabilities—they are constantly bubbling up, seeking resolution. These mental forces energize people, but they are too crude and irregular to be given excessive play in the real world. They must be capped with the competent, sensible behavior that permits individuals to get along well in society. However, this upper layer of mental activity, shot through with caution and rationality, is not receptive to advertising's pitches. Advertisers want to circumvent this shell of consciousness if they can, and latch on to one of the lurching, subconscious drives.

In effect, advertisers over the years have blindly felt their way around the underside of the American psyche, and by trial and error have discovered the softest points of entree, the places where their messages have the greatest likelihood of getting by consumers' defenses. As McLuhan says elsewhere, "Gouging away at the surface of public sales resistance, the ad men are constantly breaking through into the *Alice in Wonderland* territory behind the looking glass, which is the world of subrational impulses and appetites."

An advertisement communicates by making use of a specially selected image (of a supine female, say, or a curly-haired child, or a celebrity) which is designed to stimulate "subrational impulses and desires" even when they are at ebb, even if they are unacknowledged by their possessor. Some few ads have their emotional appeal in the text, but for the greater number by far the appeal is contained in the artwork. This makes sense, since visual communication better suits more primal levels of the brain. If the viewer of an advertisement actually has the importuned motive, and if the appeal is sufficiently well fashioned to call it up, then the person can be hooked. The product in the ad may then appear to take on the semblance of gratification for the summoned motive. Many ads seem to be saying, "If you have this need, then this product will help satisfy it." It is a primitive equation, but not an ineffective one for selling.

Thus, most advertisements appearing in national media can be understood as having two orders of content. The first is the appeal to deep-running drives in the minds of consumers. The second is information regarding the good[s] or service being sold: its name, its manufacturer, its picture, its packaging, its objective attributes, its functions. For example, the reader of a brassiere advertisement sees a partially undraped but blandly unperturbed woman standing in an otherwise commonplace public setting, and may experience certain sensations; the reader also sees the name "Maidenform," a particular brassiere style, and, in tiny print, words about the material, colors, price. Or, the viewer of a television commercial sees a demonstration with four small boxes labelled 650, 650, 650, and 800; something in the viewer's mind catches hold of this, as trivial as thoughtful consideration might reveal it to be. The viewer is also exposed to the name "Anacin," its bottle, and its purpose.

Sometimes there is an apparently logical link between an ad's emotional appeal and its product information. It does not violate common sense that Cadillac automobiles be photographed at country clubs, or that Japan Air Lines be associated with Orientalia. But there is no real need for the linkage to have a bit of reason behind it. Is there anything inherent to the connection between Salem cigarettes and mountains, Coke and a smile, Miller Beer and comradeship? The link being forged in minds between product and appeal is a pre-logical one.

People involved in the advertising industry do not necessarily talk in the terms being used here. They are stationed at the sending end of this communications channel, and may think they are up to any number of things—Unique Selling Propositions, explosive copywriting, the optimal use of demographics or psychographics, ideal media buys, high recall ratings, or whatever. But when attention shifts to the receiving end of the channel, and focuses on the instant of reception, then commentary becomes much more elemental: an advertising message contains something primary and primitive, an emotional appeal, that in effect is the thin end of the wedge, trying to find its way into a mind. Should this occur, the product information comes along behind.

When enough advertisements are examined in this light, it becomes clear that the emotional appeals fall into several distinguishable categories, and that every ad is a variation on one of a limited number of basic appeals. While there may be several ways of classifying these appeals, one particular list of fifteen has proven to be especially valuable. Advertisements can appeal to:

1. The need for sex
2. The need for affiliation

3. The need to nurture
4. The need for guidance
5. The need to aggress
6. The need to achieve
7. The need to dominate
8. The need for prominence
9. The need for attention
10. The need for autonomy
11. The need to escape
12. The need to feel safe
13. The need for aesthetic sensations
14. The need to satisfy curiosity
15. Physiological needs: food, drink, sleep, etc.

MURRAY'S LIST

Where does this list of advertising's fifteen basic appeals come   12
from? Several years ago, I was involved in a research project which
was to have as one segment an objective analysis of the changing appeals made in post–World War II American advertising. A sample of
magazine ads would have their appeals coded into the categories of
psychological needs they seemed aimed at. For this content analysis to
happen, a complete roster of human motives would have to be found.

The first thing that came to mind was Abraham Maslow's fa-   13
mous four-part hierarchy of needs. But the briefest look at the range of
appeals made in advertising was enough to reveal that they are more
varied, and more profane, than Maslow had cared to account for. The
search led on to the work of psychologist Henry A. Murray, who together with his colleagues at the Harvard Psychological Clinic has
constructed a full taxonomy of needs. As described in *Explorations in
Personality*, Murray's team had conducted a lengthy series of in-depth
interviews with a number of subjects in order to derive from scratch
what they felt to be the essential variables of personality. Forty-four
variables were distinguished by the Harvard group, of which twenty
were motives. The need for achievement ("to overcome obstacles and
obtain a high standard") was one, for instance; the need to defer was
another; the need to aggress was a third; and so forth.

Murray's list had served as the groundwork for a number of sub-   14
sequent projects. Perhaps the best-known of these was David C. Mc-
Clelland's extensive study of the need for achievement, reported in his
The Achieving Society. In the process of demonstrating that a people's
high need for achievement is predictive of later economic growth, Mc-
Clelland coded achievement imagery and references out of a nation's
folklore, songs, legends, and children's tales.

Following McClelland, I too wanted to cull the motivational ap-   15
peals from a culture's imaginative product—in this case, advertising.
To develop categories expressly for this purpose, I took Murray's
twenty motives and added to them others he had mentioned in passing in *Explorations in Personality* but not included on the final list. The
extended list was tried out on a sample of advertisements, and motives which never seemed to be invoked were dropped. I ended up
with eighteen of Murrays' motives, into which 770 print ads were
coded. The resulting distribution is included in the 1976 book *Mass
Advertising as Social Forecast.*

Since that time, the list of appeals has undergone refinements as a   16
result of using it to analyze television commercials. A few more adjust-
ments stemmed from the efforts of students in my advertising classes to
decode appeals; tens of term papers surveying thousands of advertisements have caused some inconsistencies in the list to be hammered out.
Fundamentally, though, the list remains the creation of Henry Murray.
In developing a comprehensive, parsimonious inventory of human motives, he pinpointed the subsurface mental forces that are the least qui-
escent and most susceptible to advertising's entreaties.

FIFTEEN APPEALS

1. *Need for sex.* Let's start with sex, because this is the appeal   17
which seems to pop up first whenever the topic of advertising is
raised. Whole books have been written about this one alone, to find a
large audience of mildly titillated readers. Lately, due to campaigns to
sell blue jeans, concern with sex in ads has redoubled.

The fascinating thing is not how much sex there is in advertising,   18
but how little. Contrary to impressions, unambiguous sex is rare in these
messages. Some of this surprising observation may be a matter of definition: the Jordache ads with the lithe, blouse-less female astride a similarly clad male is clearly an appeal to the audience's sexual drives, but
the same cannot be said about Brooke Shields in the Calvin Klein commercials. Directed at young women and their credit-card carrying
mothers, the image of Miss Shields instead invokes the need to be
looked at. Buy Calvins and you'll be the center of much attention, just as
Brooke is, the ads imply; they do not primarily inveigle their target audience's need for sexual intercourse.

In the content analysis reported in *Mass Advertising as Social Fore-   19
cast* only two percent of ads were found to pander to this motive.
Even *Playboy* ads shy away from sexual appeals: a recent issue contained eighty-three full-page ads, and just four of them (or less than
five percent) could be said to have sex on their minds.

The reason this appeal is so little used is that it is too blaring and   20
tends to obliterate the product information. Nudity in advertising has
the effect of reducing brand recall. The people who do remember the
product may do so because they have been made indignant by the ad;
this is not the response most advertisers seek.

To the extent that sexual imagery is used, it conventionally works   21
better on men than women; typically a female figure is offered up to the
male reader. A Black Velvet liquor advertisement displays an attractive
woman wearing a tight black outfit, recumbent under the legend, "Feel
the Velvet." The figure does not have to be horizontal, however, for the
appeal to be present as National Airlines revealed in its "Fly me" campaign. Indeed, there does not even have to be a female in the ad; "Flick
my Bic" was sufficient to convey the idea to many.

As a rule, though, advertisers have found sex to be a tricky ap-   22
peal, to be used sparingly. Less controversial and equally fetching are
the appeals to our need for affectionate human contact.

2. *Need for affiliation.* American mythology upholds autonomous   23
individuals, and social statistics suggest that people are ever more going
it alone in their lives, yet the high frequency of affiliative appeals in ads
belies this. Or maybe it does not: maybe all the images of companionship
are compensation for what Americans privately lack. In any case, the
need to associate with others is widely invoked in advertising and is
probably the most prevalent appeal. All sorts of goods and services are
sold by linking them to our unfulfilled desires to be in good company.

According to Henry Murray, the need for affiliation consists of   24
desires "to draw near and enjoyably cooperate or reciprocate with another; to please and win affection of another; to adhere and remain
loyal to a friend." The manifestations of this motive can be segmented
into several different types of affiliation, beginning with romance.

Courtship may be swifter nowadays, but the desire for pair-   25
bonding is far from satiated. Ads reaching for this need commonly depict a youngish male and female engrossed in each other. The head of
the male is usually higher than the female's, even at this late date; she
may be sitting or leaning while he is standing. They are not touching
in the Smirnoff vodka ads, but obviously there is an intimacy, sometimes frolicsome, between them. The couple does touch for Martell Cognac when "The moment was Martell." For Wind Song perfume they
have touched, and "Your Wind Song stays on his mind."

Depending on the audience, the pair does not absolutely have to   26
be young—just together. He gives her a DeBeers diamond, and there is
a tear in her laugh lines. She takes Geritol and preserves herself for
him. And numbers of consumers, wanting affection too, follow suit.

Warm family feelings are fanned in ads when another generation   27
is added to the pair. Hallmark Cards brings grandparents into the pic-

ture, and Johnson and Johnson Baby Powder has Dad, Mom, and baby, all fresh from the bath, encircled in arms and emblazoned with "Share the Feeling." A talc has been fused to familial love.

Friendship is yet another form of affiliation pursued by advertis-   28
ers. Two women confide and drink Maxwell House coffee together; two men walk through the woods smoking Salem cigarettes. Miller Beer promises that afternoon "Miller Time" will be staffed with three or four good buddies. Drink Dr. Pepper, as Mickey Rooney is coaxed to do, and join in with all the other Peppers. Coca-Cola does not even need to portray the friendliness; it has reduced this appeal to "a Coke and a smile."

The warmth can be toned down and disguised, but it is the same   29
affiliative need that is being fished for. The blonde has a direct gaze and her friends are firm businessmen in appearance, but with a glass of Old Bushmill you can sit down and fit right in. Or, for something more upbeat, sing along with the Pontiac choirboys.

As well as presenting positive images, advertisers can play to the   30
need for affiliation in negative ways, by invoking the fear of rejection. If we don't use Scope, we'll have the "Ugh! Morning Breath" that causes the male and female models to avert their faces. Unless we apply Ultra Brite or Close-Up to our teeth, it's good-bye romance. Our family will be cursed with "House-a-tosis" if we don't take care. Without Dr. Scholl's antiperspirant foot spray, the bowling team will keel over. There go all the guests when the supply of Dorito's nacho cheese chips is exhausted. Still more rejection if our shirts have ring-around-the-collar, if our car needs to be Midasized. But make a few purchases, and we are back in the bosom of human contact.

As self-directed as Americans pretend to be, in the last analysis we   31
remain social animals, hungering for the positive, endorsing feelings that only those around us can supply. Advertisers respond, urging us to "Reach out and touch someone," in the hopes our monthly bills will rise.

3. *Need to nurture.* Akin to affiliative needs is the need to take   32
care of small, defenseless creatures—children and pets, largely. Reciprocity is of less consequence here, though; it is the giving that counts. Murray uses synonyms like "to feed, help, support, console, protect, comfort, nurse, heal." A strong need it is, woven deep into our genetic fabric, for if it did not exist we could not successfully raise up our replacements. When advertisers put forth the image of something diminutive and furry, something that elicits the word "cute" or "precious," then they are trying to trigger this motive. We listen to the childish voice singing the Oscar Mayer weiner song, and our next hot-dog purchase is prescribed. Aren't those darling kittens something, and how did this Meow Mix get into our shopping cart?

This pitch is often directed at women, as Mother Nature's chief   33
nurturers. "Make me some Kraft macaroni and cheese, please," says

the elfin preschooler just in from the snowstorm, and mothers' hearts go out, and Kraft's sales go up. "We're cold, wet, and hungry," whine the husband and kids, and the little woman gets the Manwiches ready. A facsimile of this need can be hit without children or pets: the husband is ill and sleepless in the television commercial, and the wife grudgingly fetches the NyQuil.

But it is not women alone who can be touched by this appeal. The father nurses his son Eddie through adolescence while the John Deere lawn tractor survives the years. Another father counts pennies with his young son as the subject of New York Life Insurance comes up. And all over America are businessmen who don't know why they dial Qantas Airlines when they have to take a trans-Pacific trip; the koala bear knows. 34

4. *Need for guidance.* The opposite of the need to nurture is the need to be nurtured: to be protected, shielded, guided. We may be loath to admit it, but the child lingers on inside every adult—and a good thing it does, or we would not be instructable in our advancing years. Who wants a nation of nothing but flinty personalities? 35

Parent-like figures can successfully call up this need. Robert Young recommends Sanka coffee, and since we have experienced him for twenty-five years as television father and doctor, we take his word for it. Florence Henderson as the expert mom knows a lot about the advantages of Wesson oil. 36

The parent-ness of the spokesperson need not be so salient; sometimes pure authoritativeness is better. When Orson Welles scowls and intones, "Paul Masson will sell no wine before its time," we may not know exactly what he means, but we still take direction from him. There is little maternal about Brenda Vaccaro when she speaks up for Tampax, but there is a certainty to her that many accept. 37

A celebrity is not a necessity in making a pitch to the need for guidance, since a fantasy figure can serve just as well. People accede to the Green Giant, or Betty Crocker, or Mr. Goodwrench. Some advertisers can get by with no figure at all: "When E.F. Hutton talks, people listen." 38

Often it is tradition or custom that advertisers point to and consumers take guidance from. Bits and pieces of American history are used to sell whiskeys like Old Crow, Southern Comfort, Jack Daniel's. We conform to traditional male/female roles and age-old social norms when we purchase Barclay cigarettes, which informs us "The pleasure is back." 39

The product itself, if it has been around for a long time, can constitute a tradition. All those old labels in the ad for Morton salt convince us that we should continue to buy it. Kool-Aid says "You loved it as a kid. You trust it as a mother," hoping to get yet more consumers to go along. 40

Even when the product has no history at all, our need to conform   41
to tradition and to be guided are strong enough that they can be invoked
through bogus nostalgia and older actors. Country-Time lemonade sells
because consumers want to believe it has a past they can defer to.

So far the needs and the ways they can be invoked which have   42
been looked at are largely warm and affiliative; they stand in contrast
to the next set of needs, which are much more egoistic and assertive.

5. *Need to aggress.*   The pressures of the real world create strong   43
retaliatory feelings in every functioning human being. Since these impulses can come forth as bursts of anger and violence, their display is
normally tabooed. Existing as harbored energy, aggressive drives present a large, tempting target for advertisers. It is not a target to be
aimed at thoughtlessly, though, for few manufacturers want their
products associated with destructive motives. There is always the danger that, as in the case of sex, if the appeal is too blatant, public opinion will turn against what is being sold.

Jack-in-the-Box sought to abruptly alter its marketing by going   44
after older customers and forgetting the younger ones. Their television
commercials had a seventy-ish lady command, "Waste him," and the
Jack-in-the-Box clown exploded before our eyes. So did public reaction
until the commercials were toned down. Print ads for Club cocktails
carried the faces of octogenarians under the headline, "Hit me with a
Club"; response was contrary enough to bring the campaign to a stop.

Better disguised aggressive appeals are less likely to backfire: Tri-   45
umph cigarettes has models making a lewd gesture with their uplifted
cigarettes, but the individuals are often laughing and usually in close
company of others. When Exxon said, "There's a Tiger in your tank," the
implausibility of it concealed the invocation of aggressive feelings.

Depicted arguments are a common way for advertisers to tap the   46
audience's needs to aggress. Don Rickles and Lynda Carter trade
gibes, and consumers take sides as the name of Seven-Up is stitched
on minds. The Parkay tub has a difference of opinion with the user;
who can forget it, or who (or what) got the last word in?

6. *Need to achieve.*   This is the drive that energizes people, caus-   47
ing them to strive in their lives and careers. According to Murray, the
need for achievement is signalled by the desires "to accomplish something difficult. To overcome obstacles and attain a high standard. To
excel one's self. To rival and surpass others." A prominent American
trait, it is one that advertisers like to hook on to because it identifies
their product with winning and success.

The Cutty Sark ad does not disclose that Ted Turner failed at his   48
latest attempt at yachting's America Cup; here he is represented as a
champion on the water as well as off in his television enterprises. If we
drink this whiskey, we will be victorious alongside Turner. We can

also succeed with O.J. Simpson by renting Hertz cars, or with Reggie Jackson by bringing home some Panasonic equipment. Cathy Rigby and Stayfree Maxipads will put people out front.

Sports heroes are the most convenient means to snare con- 49 sumers' needs to achieve, but they are not the only one. Role models can be established, ones which invite emulation, as with the profiles put forth by Dewar's scotch. Successful, tweedy individuals relate they have "graduated to the flavor of Myer's rum." Or the advertiser can establish a prize: two neighbors play one-on-one basketball for a Michelob beer in a television commercial, while in a print ad a bottle of Johnnie Walker Black Label has been gilded like a trophy.

Any product that advertises itself in superlatives—the best, the 50 first, the finest—is trying to make contact with our needs to succeed. For many consumers, sales and bargains belong in this category of appeals, too; the person who manages to buy something at fifty percent off is seizing an opportunity and coming out ahead of others.

7. *Need to dominate.* This fundamental need is the craving to be 51 powerful—perhaps omnipotent, as in the Xerox ad where Brother Dominic exhibits heavenly powers and creates miraculous copies. Most of us will settle for being just a regular potentate, though. We drink Budweiser because it is the King of Beers, and here comes the powerful Clydesdales to prove it. A taste of Wolfschmidt vodka and "The spirit of the Czar lives on."

The need to dominate and control one's environment is often 52 thought of as being masculine, but as close students of human nature advertisers know, it is not so circumscribed. Women's aspirations for control are suggested in the campaign theme, "I like my men in English Leather, or nothing at all." The females in the Chanel No. 19 ads are "outspoken" and wrestle their men around.

Male and female, what we long for is clout; what we get in its 53 place is Mastercard.

8. *Need for prominence.* Here comes the need to be admired and 54 respected, to enjoy prestige and high social status. These times, it appears, are not so egalitarian after all. Many ads picture the trappings of high position; the Oldsmobile stands before a manorial doorway, the Volvo is parked beside a steeplechase. A book-lined study is the setting for Dewar's 12, and Lenox China is displayed in a dining room chock full of antiques.

Beefeater gin represents itself as "The Crown Jewel of England" 55 and uses no illustrations of jewels or things British, for the words are sufficient indicators of distinction. Buy that gin and you will rise up the prestige hierarchy, or achieve the same effect on yourself with Seagram's 7 Crown, which ambiguously describes itself as "classy."

Being respected does not have to entail the usual accoutrements 56 of wealth: "Do you know who I am?" the commercials ask, and we learn that the prominent person is not so prominent without his American Express card.

9. *Need for attention.*   The previous need involved being *looked up*   57
to, while this is the need to be *looked at*. The desire to exhibit ourselves in such a way as to make others look at us is a primitive, insuppressible instinct. The clothing and cosmetic industries exist just to serve this need, and this is the way they pitch their wares. Some of this effort is aimed at males, as the ads for Hathaway shirts and Jockey underclothes. But the greater bulk of such appeals is targeted singlemindedly at women.

To come back to Brooke Shields: this is where she fits into Ameri-   58
can marketing. If I buy Calvin Klein jeans, consumers infer, I'll be the object of fascination. The desire for exhibition has been most strikingly played to in a print campaign of many years' duration, that of Maidenform lingerie.   The woman exposes herself, and sales surge. "Gentlemen prefer Hanes" the ads dissemble, and women who want eyes upon them know what they should do. Peggy Fleming flutters her legs for L'eggs, encouraging females who want to be the star in their own lives to purchase this product.

The same appeal works for cosmetics and lotions. For years, the   59
little girl with the exposed backside sold gobs of Coppertone, but now the company has picked up the pace a little: as a female, you are supposed to "Flash 'em a Coppertone tan." Food can be sold the same way, especially to the diet-conscious; Angie Dickinson poses for California avocados and says, "Would this body lie to you?" Our eyes are too fixed on her for us to think to ask if she got that way by eating mounds of guacomole.

10. *Need for autonomy.*   There are several ways to sell credit card   60
services, as has been noted: Mastercard appeals to the need to dominate, and American Express to the need for prominence. When Visa claims, "You can have it the way you want it," yet another primary motive is being beckoned forward—the need to endorse the self. The focus here is upon the independence and integrity of the individual; this need is the antithesis of the need for guidance and is unlike any of the social needs. "If running with the herd isn't your style, try ours," says Rotan-Mosle, and many Americans feel they have finally found the right brokerage firm.

The photo is of a red-coated Mountie on his horse, posed on a   61
snow-covered ledge; the copy reads, "Windsor—One Canadian stands alone." This epitome of the solitary and proud individual may work best with male customers, as may Winston's man in the red cap. But one-figure advertisements also strike the strong need for autonomy among American women. As Shelly Hack strides for Charlie perfume, females respond to her obvious pride and flair; she is her own person. The Virginia Slims tale is of people who have come a long way from subservience to independence. Cachet perfume feels it does not need a

solo figure to work this appeal, and uses three different faces in its ads; it insists, though, "It's different on every woman who wears it."

Like many psychological needs, this one can also be appealed to   62
in a negative fashion, by invoking the loss of independence or self-regard. Guilt and regrets can be stimulated: "Gee, I could have had a V-8." Next time, get one and be good to yourself.

11. *Need to escape.*   An appeal to the need for autonomy often co-   63
occurs with one for the need to escape, since the desire to duck out of our social obligations, to seek rest or adventure, frequently takes the form of one-person flight. The dashing image of a pilot, in fact, is a standard way of quickening this need to get away from it all.

Freedom is the pitch here, the freedom that every individual   64
yearns for whenever life becomes too oppressive. Many advertisers like appealing to the need for escape because the sensation of pleasure often accompanies escape, and what nicer emotional nimbus could there be for a product? "You deserve a break today," says McDonald's, and Stouffer's frozen foods chime in, "Set yourself free."

For decades men have imaginatively bonded themselves to the   65
Marlboro cowboy who dwells untarnished and unencumbered in Marlboro Country some distance from modern life; smokers' aching needs for autonomy and escape are personified by that cowpoke. Many women can identify with the lady ambling through the woods behind the words, "Benson and Hedges and mornings and me."

But escape does not have to be solitary. Other Benson and Hedges   66
ads, part of the same campaign, contain two strolling figures. In Salem cigarette advertisements, it can be several people who escape together into the mountaintops. A commercial for Levi's pictured a cloudbank above a city through which ran a whole chain of young people.

There are varieties of escape, some wistful like the Boeing "Some-   67
day" campaign of dream vacations, some kinetic like the play and parties in soft drink ads. But in every instance, the consumer exposed to the advertisement is invited to momentarily depart his everyday life for a more carefree experience, preferably with the product in hand.

12. *Need to feel safe.*   Nobody in their right mind wants to be in-   68
timidated, menaced, battered, poisoned. We naturally want to do whatever it takes to stave off threats to our well-being, and to our families'. It is the instinct of self-preservation that makes us responsive to the ad of the St. Bernard with the keg of Chivas Regal. We pay attention to the stern talk of Karl Malden and the plight of the vacationing couples who have lost all their funds in the American Express travelers cheques commercials. We want the omnipresent stag from Hartford Insurance to watch over us too.

In the interest of keeping failure and calamity from our lives, we   69
like to see the durability of products demonstrated. Can we ever forget

that Timex takes a licking and keeps on ticking? When the American Tourister suitcase bounces all over the highway and the egg inside doesn't break, the need to feel safe has been adroitly plucked.

We take precautions to diminish future threats. We buy Volks-   70 wagen Rabbits for the extraordinary mileage, and MONY insurance policies to avoid the tragedies depicted in their black-and-white ads of widows and orphans.

We are careful about our health. We consume Mazola margarine   71 because it has "corn goodness" backed by the natural food traditions of the American Indians. In the medicine cabinet is Alka-Seltzer, the "home remedy"; having it, we are snug in our little cottage.

We want to be safe and secure; buy these products, advertisers   72 are saying, and you'll be safer than you are without them.

13. *Need for aesthetic sensations.* There is an undeniable aes-   73 thetic component to virtually every ad run in the national media: the photography or filming or drawing is near-perfect, the type style is well chosen, the layout could scarcely be improved upon. Advertisers know there is little chance of good communication occurring if an ad is not visually pleasing. Consumers may not be aware of the extent of their own sensitivity to artwork, but it is undeniably large.

Sometimes the aesthetic element is expanded and made into an   74 ad's primary appeal. Charles Jordan shoes may or may not appear in the accompanying avant-grade photographs; Kohler plumbing fix-tures catch attention through the high style of their desert settings. Be-neath the slightly out of focus photograph, languid and sensuous in tone, General Electric feels called upon to explain, "This is an ad for the hair dryer."

This appeal is not limited to female consumers: J&B scotch says   75 "It whispers" and shows a bucolic scene of lake and castle.

14. *Need to satisfy curiosity.* It may seem odd to list a need for in-   76 formation among basic motives, but this need can be as primal and compelling as any of the others. Human beings are curious by nature, in-terested in the world around them, and intrigued by tidbits of knowl-edge and new developments. Trivia, percentages, observations counter to conventional wisdom—these items all help sell products. Any adver-tisement in a question-and-answer format is strumming this need.

A dog groomer has a question about long distance rates, and Bell   77 Telephone has a chart with all the figures. An ad for Porsche 911 is re-plete with diagrams and schematics, numbers and arrows. Lo and be-hold, Anacin pills have 150 more milligrams than its competitors; should we wonder if this is better or worse for us?

15. *Physiological needs.* To the extent that sex is solely a biologi-   78 cal need, we are now coming around full circle, back toward the start of the list. In this final category are clustered appeals to sleeping, eat-

ing, drinking. The art of photographing food and drink is so advanced, sometimes these temptations are wondrously caught in the camera's lens: the crab meat in the Red Lobster restaurant ads can start us salivating, the Quarterpounder can almost be smelled, the liquor in the glass glows invitingly. Imbibe, these ads scream.

STYLES

Some common ingredients of advertisements were not singled   79
out for separate mention in the list of fifteen because they are not appeals in and of themselves. They are stylistic features, influencing the way a basic appeal is presented. The use of humor is one, and the use of celebrities is another. A third is time imagery, past and future, which goes to several purposes.

For all of its employment in advertising, humor can be treacher-   80
ous, because it can get out of hand and smother the product information. Supposedly, this is what Alka-Seltzer discovered with its comic commercials of the late sixties; "I can't believe I ate the whole thing," the sad-faced husband lamented, and the audience cackled so much it forgot the antacid. Or, did not take it seriously.

But used carefully, humor can punctuate some of the softer ap-   81
peals and soften some of the harsher ones. When Emma says to the Fruit-of-the-Loom fruits, "Hi, cuties. Whatcha doing in my laundry basket?" we smile as our curiosity is assuaged along with hers. Bill Cosby gets consumers tickled about the children in his Jell-O commercials, and strokes the need to nurture.

An insurance company wants to invoke the need to feel safe, but   82
does not want to leave readers with an unpleasant aftertaste; cartoonist Rowland Wilson creates an avalanche about to crush a gentleman who is saying to another, "My insurance company? New England Life, of course. Why?" The same tactic of humor undercutting threat is used in the cartoon commercials for Safeco when the Pink Panther wanders from one disaster to another. Often humor masks aggression: comedian Bob Hope in the outfit of a boxer promises to knock out the knock-knocks with Texaco; Rodney Dangerfield, who "can't get no respect," invites aggression as the comic relief in Miller Lite commercials.

Roughly fifteen percent of all advertisements incorporate a   83
celebrity, almost always from the fields of entertainment or sports. The approach can also prove troublesome for advertisers, for celebrities are human beings too, and fully capable of the most remarkable behavior. If anything distasteful about them emerges, it is likely to reflect on the product. The advertisers making use of Anita Bryant and Billy Jean King suffered several anxious moments. An untimely death can also react poorly on a product. But advertisers are willing to take risks

because celebrities can be such a good link between producers and consumers, performing the social role of introducer.

There are several psychological needs these middlemen can play   84 upon. Let's take the product class of cameras and see how different celebrities can hit different needs. The need for guidance can be invoked by Michael Landon, who plays such a wonderful dad on "Little House on the Prairie"; when he says to buy Kodak equipment, many people listen. James Garner for Polaroid cameras is put in a similar authoritative role, so defined by a mocking spouse. The need to achieve is summoned up by Tracy Austin and other tennis stars for Canon AE-1; the advertiser first makes sure we see these athletes playing to win. When Cheryl Tiegs speaks up for Olympus cameras, it is the need for attention that is being targeted.

The past and future, being outside our grasp, are exploited by   85 advertisers as locales for the projection of needs. History can offer up heroes (and call up the need to achieve) or traditions (need for guidance) as well as art objects (need for aesthetic sensations). Nostalgia is a kindly version of personal history and is deployed by advertisers to rouse needs for affiliation and for guidance; the need to escape can come in here, too. The same need to escape is sometimes the point of futuristic appeals but picturing the avant-garde can also be a way to get at the need to achieve.

ANALYZING ADVERTISEMENTS

When analyzing ads yourself for their emotional appeals, it takes   86 a bit of practice to learn to ignore the product information (as well as one's own experience and feelings about the product). But that skill comes soon enough, as does the ability to quickly sort out from all the non-product aspects of an ad the chief element which is the most striking, the most likely to snag attention first and penetrate brains farthest. The key to the appeal, this element usually presents itself centrally and forwardly to the reader or viewer.

Another clue: the viewing angle which the audience has on the   87 ad's subjects is informative. If the subjects are photographed or filmed from below and thus are looking down at you much as the Green Giant does, then the need to be guided is a good candidate for the ad's emotional appeal. If, on the other hand, the subjects are shot from above and appear deferential, as is often the case with children or female models, then other needs are being appealed to.

To figure out an ad's emotional appeal, it is wise to know (or   88 have a good hunch about) who the targeted consumers are; this can often be inferred from the magazine or television show it appears in. This piece of information is a great help in determining the appeal and in deciding between two different interpretations. For example, if an ad features a partially undressed female, this would typically signal one appeal for readers of *Penthouse* (need for sex) and another for readers of *Cosmopolitan* (need for attention).

It would be convenient if every ad made just one appeal, were   89
aimed at just one need. Unfortunately, things are often not that simple. A cigarette ad with a couple at the edge of a polo field is trying to hit both the need for affiliation and the need for prominence; depending on the attitude of the male, dominance could also be an ingredient in this. An ad for Chimere perfume incorporates two photos: in the top one the lady is being commanding at a business luncheon (need to dominate), but in the lower one she is being bussed (need for affiliation). Better ads, however, seem to avoid being too diffused; in the study of post–World War II advertising described earlier, appeals grew more focused as the decades passed. As a rule of thumb, about sixty percent have two conspicuous appeals; the last twenty percent have three or more. Rather than looking for the greatest number of appeals, decoding ads is most productive when the loudest one or two appeals are discerned, since those are the appeals with the best chance of grabbing people's attention.

Finally, analyzing ads does not have to be a solo activity and prob-   90
ably should not be. The greater number of people there are involved, the better chance there is of transcending individual biases and discerning the essential emotional lure built into an advertisement.

DO THEY OR DON'T THEY?

Do the emotional appeals made in advertisements add up to the   91
sinister manipulation of consumers?

It is clear that these ads work. Attention is caught, communica-   92
tion occurs between producers and consumers, and sales result. It turns out to be difficult to detail the exact relationship between a specific ad and a specific purchase, or even between a campaign and subsequent sales figures, because advertising is only one of a host of influences upon consumption. Yet no one is fooled by this lack of perfect proof; everyone knows that advertising sells. If this were not the case, then tight-fisted American businesses would not spend a total of fifty billion dollars annually on these messages.

But before anyone despairs that advertisers have our number to   93
the extent that they can marshal us at will and march us like automatons to the check-out counters, we should recall the resiliency and obduracy of the American consumer. Advertisers may have uncovered the softest spots in minds, but that does not mean they have found truly gaping apertures. There is no evidence that advertising can get people to do things contrary to their self-interests. Despite all the finesse of adver-

tisements, and all the subtle emotional tugs, the public resists the vast majority of the petitions. According to the marketing division of the A.C. Nielsen Company, a whopping seventy-five percent of all new products die within a year in the marketplace, the victims of consumer disinterest which no amount of advertising could overcome. The appeals in advertising may be the most captivating there are to be had, but they are not enough to entrap the wiley consumer.

The key to understanding the discrepancy between, on the one hand, the fact that advertising truly works, and, on the other, the fact that it hardly works, is to take into account the enormous numbers of people exposed to an ad. Modern-day communications permit an ad to be displayed to millions upon millions of individuals; if the smallest fraction of that audience can be moved to buy the product, then the ad has been successful. When one percent of the people exposed to a television advertising campaign reach for their wallets, that could be one million sales, which may be enough to keep the product in production and the advertisements coming.   94

In arriving at an evenhanded judgment about advertisements and their emotional appeals, it is good to keep in mind that many of the purchases which might be credited to these ads are experienced as genuinely gratifying to the consumer. We sincerely like the goods or service we have bought, and we may even like some of the emotional drapery that an ad suggests comes with it. It has sometimes been noted that the most avid students of advertisements are the people who have just bought the product; they want to steep themselves in the associated imagery. This may be the reason that Americans, when polled, are not negative about advertising and do not disclose any sense of being misused. The volume of advertising may be an irritant, but the product information as well as the imaginative material in ads are partial compensation.   95

A productive understanding is that advertising messages involve costs and benefits at both ends of the communications channel. For those few ads which do make contact, the consumer surrenders a moment of time, has the lower brain curried, and receives notice of a product; the advertiser has given up money and has increased the chance of sales. In this sort of communications activity, neither party can be said to be the loser.   96

Examining the Text

1. Fowles's basic claim in this essay is that advertisers try to tap into basic human needs and emotions, rather than consumers' intellect. How does he go about proving this claim? What examples or other proof strike you as particularly persuasive? Where do you see weaknesses in Fowles's argument?

2. What do advertisers assume about the personality of the consumer, according to Fowles? How do these assumptions contribute to the way they sell products? Do you think that these assumptions about personality are correct? Why or why not?

3. Fowles's list of advertising's fifteen basic appeals is, as he explains, derived from Henry Murray's inventory of human motives. Which of these motives strike you as the most significant or powerful? What other motives would you add to the list?

For Group Discussion

In his discussion of the way advertising uses "the need for sex" and "the need to aggress," Fowles debunks the persistent complaints about the use of sex and violence in the mass media. What current examples support Fowles's point? Discuss your responses to his explanations.

Writing Suggestion

Working with Fowles's list of the fifteen appeals of advertising, survey a recent magazine, looking at all the ads and categorizing them based on their predominant appeal. In an essay, describe what your results tell you about the magazine and its readership. Based on your survey, would you amend Fowles's list? What additions or deletions would you make?

Minority Presence and Portrayal in Mainstream Magazine Advertising: An Update

Laurence Bowen and Jill Schmid

If advertising reflects our culture, shouldn't it also reflect our cultural diversity? This question is at the heart of the following study by Laurence Bowen, a professor at the University of Washington, and Jill Schmid, a professor at Willamette University. As they report, the 1990 Census shows that the population of the United States is 12.1% African-American, 2.9% Asian and Pacific Islander, and 9.0 percent Hispanic, with the population of all three of these groups growing at a faster rate than the population of Whites in the U.S. But Bowen and Schmid discovered in their research that ads in mainstream magazines reflect a "whiter" version of our society: of the nearly 2,000 advertisements they analyzed, Black models appeared in 10.6 percent,

Asians in 1.8 percent, and Hispanics in a surprisingly low 0.6 percent. Perhaps more significant is the fact that minority models seldom appear alone in ads; more than two-thirds of the ads in which minority models appeared were "mixed-ethnic ads." Bowen and Schmid also analyze the kinds of occupations the models portray, the interactions among the minority and White models, and other factors such as age and gender. Their conclusion is that minority models aren't getting "mainstream treatment" in mainstream magazines.

But why does this matter? Should advertisements be ethically (or legally?) obligated to present an accurate and unbiased reflection of our society? What responsibility do adverstising agencies have to portray members of minority groups (or women, or people with disabilities, or senior citizens) in a positive manner? Or put another way, must advertisements be "politically correct"? If all the ads in all the magazines you read pictured only young, upper-class, White models, would this pose a problem? In short, what influence does advertising have on the way we see ourselves as a society? These kinds of broad and important questions emerge from Bowen and Schmid's study. As you read, keep these questions in mind and note the perspective that Bowen and Schmid offer— usually implicitly rather than explicitly—on the responsiblities of advertisers.

INTRODUCTION

For most of its life as a nation, America has been referred to as the world's "melting pot." The emphasis has been on the "melt"—not what was in the pot. *E Pluribus Unum* was to be both motto and model, with acculturation and assimilation the keys to nation building. Institutional imperatives called for an "integrated" society where people of color could work together and live in harmony. Mass media, in general, and advertising, in particular, were seen as important windows on the melting pot, where progress, or the lack thereof, would be readily apparent. Television brought the window into America's living room, and a number of window gazers were quick to point out that the view was suburban, predominantly young, white, and middle class. 1

The NAACP and CORE were among the first to indict adverstising for its racial myopia and to challenge the media to provide "wider representation of Negroes in conventional middle-class settings...(such representation) will do much to erase the undesirable stereotypes of the Negro that exist in the white community."[1] The 1968 *Report on the National Advisory Commission on Civil Disorders* amplified, "Negro reporters and performers should appear more frequently...in news broadcasts, on weather shows, in documentaries and in advertisements...If what 2

---

[1]Peter Bart, "All Except Profits Are Big in Advertising," *New York Times*, 6 January 1964, sec. C, p. 88.

the white American reads in newspapers or sees on television conditions his expectations of what is ordinary and normal in the larger society, he will neither understand nor accept the black American."[2]

In the past decade, we've seen the "melting pot" metaphor challenged by multiculturalists calling for separate but equal approaches to life, liberty, and the pursuit of happiness.[3] It's likely that something like "peaceful coexistence" or "different strokes for different folks" may eventuate, but meanwhile, many are caught between the pot and those who would stir it. Not the least among them are those marketers and their advertising agencies who must serve up appealing images that are politically correct and racially sensitive, images that motivate us to buy.

How advertising uses race, age, and gender to promote the goods and services of a market society has been the subject of a long and continuing debate. Ad bashing has always been popular sport, but it's become a lifestyle for some racial coalitions, militant feminists, men's groups, and, more recently, the elderly. Industry sources are quick to point out that advertising's first obligation is client service—which translates roughly into compelling images that drive increased sales and profits. Critics contend, however, that in the process of creating those compelling images, advertising should reflect the broader society by fairly portraying its diversity. The thinking is that the "third-person effect" of such treatments will be a fuller, richer appreciation of our land and its peoples. The amount of cooperation and coordination required of such an effort escapes the critic who would simply have it done. As matters stand, any fuller and fairer representation rests with each ad maker, acting alone, guided solely by conscience.

Despite the absence of any industry-wide commitment to encourage and portray diversity, advertising has managed to chalk up modest gains in the inclusion of minorities in mainstream print media.[4] Begin-

---

[2]Kerner Commission, "Report of the National Advisory Commission on Civil Disorders" (Washington, DC: GPO, 1968).

[3]Felix F. Guitierrez, "Advertising and the Growth of Minority Markets and Media," *Journal of Communication Inquiry* 14 (winter 1990): 6–16.

[4]Keith K. Cox, "Social Effects of Integrated Advertising," *Journal of Advertising Research* 10 (April 1970): 41–44; David Colfax and Susan Frankel Sternberg, "The Perpetuation of Racial Stereotypes: Blacks in Mass Circulation Magazine Advertisements," *Public Opinion Quarterly* 36 (spring 1972): 8–18; James D. Culley and Rex Bennett, "Selling Women, Selling Blacks," *Journal of Communication* 26 (autumn 1976): 161–74; Paul J. Solomon, Ronald F. Bush, and Joseph F. Hair, "White and Black Consumer Sales Response to Black Models," *Journal of Marketing Research* 13 (November 1976): 431–34; Harold H. Kassarjian, "The Negro and American Advertising, 1946–1965," *Journal of Marketing Research* 6 (February 1969): 29–39; Ronald F. Bush, Alan J. Resnick, and Bruce L. Stern, "A Content Analysis of the Portrayal of Black Models in Magazine Advertising," in *Marketing in the 80's: Changes & Challenges*, ed. Richard P. Bagozzi, et al. (Chicago: American Marketing Association, 1980); Ronald Humphrey and Howard Schuman, "The Portrayal of Blacks in Magazine Advertisements: 1950–1982," *Public Opinion Quarterly* 48 (1984); 551–63.

ning at a scant .05% in 1953,[5] the numbers could not help but go up, reaching a high of 8.6% in a study of four mainstream magazines conducted in 1985.[6] Zinkhan studied five mainsteam magazines in 1986 and found an inclusion rate of only 4.4%.[7] More recent studies have focused on more specific questions such as minority portrayal in women's fashion magazines,[8] trade publications, or minority media, or as models for specific products.[9]

Portrayals are another issue. For those Black models pictured in mainstream advertising, the roles are often limited or demeaning.[10] They conform, for the most part, to the White "stereotype" of Black life which breaks along two major lines—those that entertain and those that serve. In those integrated ads where both minorities and Whites are featured, the settings and interactions are not social or intimate, but formal and professional.   6

Since Zinkhan's study, new specialty magazines have been created to serve advertiser demands for even more precise market segments. Mainstream magazines have responded by broadening their appeal to win new audiences and influence advertisers. Appealing to newly enfranchised and upwardly mobile minority groups is one tactic magazines are using to achieve a broader and more advertiser-attractive audience. These efforts are reinforced by the growth of minority agencies serving major corporate clients like Ford and McDonald's—a move that should improve the presence and portrayal of minorities in mainstream as well as minority media. These changes, coupled with the lack of recent research on minority portrayals, call for an update of minority representation in mainstream magazines. It seems appropriate to   7

---

[5]Audrey M. Shuey, "Stereotyping of Negroes and Whites: An Analysis of Magazine Pictures," *Public Opinion Quarterly* 17 (summer 1953); 281–87.

[6]Thomas H. Stevenson and William J. Stevenson, "A Longitudinal Study of Blacks in Magazine Advertising: 1970–1985," in *Proceedings of the Annual Meeting of the Southern Marketing Association* (Carbondale, IL: Southern Marketing Association, November 1988), 75–78.

[7]George M. Zinkhan, William J. Qualls, and Abhijit Biswas, "The Use of Blacks in Magazine and Television Advertising: 1946–1986," *Journalism Quarterly* 67 (autumn 1990): 547–53.

[8]Kelly S. Ervin and Linda A. Jackson, "The Frequency and Portrayal of Black Females in Fashion Advertisements," ERIC Document, ERIC, ED 315 483 (1990), 17.

[9]Thomas H. Stevenson, "A Content Analysis of the Portrayal of Blacks in Trade Publication Advertising," *Journal of Current Issues and Research in Advertising* 14 (1992): 67–74; Michael Leslie, "Slow Fade to ?: Advertising in *Ebony* Magazine, 1957–1989," *Journalism & Mass Communication Quarterly* 72 (summer 1995): 426–35; Leonard N. Reid, Karen Whitehall King, and Peggy J. Kreshel, "Black and White Models and Their Activities in Modern Cigarette and Alcohol Ads," *Journalism Quarterly* 71 (winter 1994): 873–86.

[10]Cox, "Social Effects," 41–44; Colfax and Sternberg, "Perpetuation of Racial," 8–18; Culley and Bennett, "Selling Women," 161–74; Humphrey and Schuman, "Portrayal of Blacks," 551–63; Shuey, "Stereotyping," 281–87.

broaden the definition of minority to include those groups that have been neglected in past research, i.e., Asians and Hispanics. The central question guiding this research is whether or not there has been any improvement in the presence, portrayal, and integration of minorities in mainstream magazine advertising.

METHOD

Sample Nine mass circulation magazines for the years 1987 and 8 1992 constituted the sample frame. These years were chosen so that research from the 1980s could be verified and then compared with more recent data. Where significant differences exist, the data from 1987 and 1992 are separated. Generally, though, the data are combined as there were very few significant differences between years, and the numbers of minority models—specifically Asian and Hispanic models—was so small that combining the data provides more stable categories.

The selected magazines were *Cosmopolitan, Esquire, Family Circle,* 9 *Fortune, Good Housekeeping, Life, New Yorker, Sports Illustrated,* and *Time.* The magazine audience is usually described as more literate (than the television audience), and higher education is often equated with higher income. Care was taken to ensure that the selected magazines represented a wide range of readership and demographic categories. The goal was to select magazines that, taken as a sample, would reflect what might be called "mainstream" America. Table 1 details the total audience, gender breakdown, median age, income, and minority readership of the selected magazines.[11] As expected, the sample skews toward slightly older, female, higher income, and a higher representation of minority readership than is present in the general population. The totals and averages compare favorably with 1990 census figures showing a 51%–49% female-gender split, a median age of 32.9, and a median household income of $35,225.

Four issues of each magazine for each year were selected for a 10 total of seventy-two issues, yielding 1,969 "populated" advertisements. No effort was made to control for regional editions or for ad duplication between magazines. All "populated" ads were counted and content analyzed.

Each ad was coded for minority presence, gender, age, occupa- 11 tion, and product category. When minorities and Whites appeared to-

---

[11]Percentages reported are for both Black and Hispanic readership, Simmons Market Research Bureau, *Simmons Study of Media and Markets, Publications: Total Audiences,* M-1 (Tampa, FL: Simmons Market Research Bureau, 1993), 30–31.

Table 1:   Total Audience, Gender, Median Age, Median Household Income, and
Minority Readership of Sampled Magazines

	Total Audience (000)	Gender		Median Age	Median HH Income	Minority Readers
		Male	Female			
Cosmopolitian	11,470	11%	89%	31.4	35,934	24.6%
Esquire	2,520	77	23	35.7	46,969	39.2
Family Circle	18,340	10	90	43.5	36,337	14.2
Fortune	3,850	69	31	39.1	58,638	12.4
Good Housekeeping	19,870	11	89	43.1	36,916	13.9
Life	11,650	53	47	35.6	37,029	18.5
New Yorker	2,580	47	53	43.6	56,061	10.7
Sports Illustrated	21,040	82	18	34.4	41,798	24.4
Time	24,410	55	45	38.0	44,086	19.9
Total/ Averages	115,730	46%	54%	38.2	43,752	19.7%

gether in the same ad, the relationship depicted was also coded. Minority was defined as any member of the Black, Asian, or Hispanic
population. Initial coding was performed by one of the authors; intercoder reliability was checked by having two colleagues code a smaller
but representative sample of the advertisements. The intercoder reliability coefficient was .95 for all coded categories.

Coded Categories Age was initially coded into eight groups: 12
0–2, 3–12, 13–18, 19–30, 31–54, 55+, mixed age group, and not determined. Given the small number of cases for the first three age groups,
they were collapsed to create an "18 or younger" group. Gender was
broken down into four groups: male, female, mixed gender group, and
not determined (infants and babies).

Occupation was broken down into eight classifications: white   13
collar/professional, middle class working, blue collar/laborer, family/
kids, other, celebrity, mixed occupation, and unknown. Product class
was originally coded into 23 categories and later collapsed into 15. The
categories included fashion/accessories, personal grooming aids, automobile, tobacco, alcohol, food/drink, retail stores, electronic/comput-
ers, home furnishings, travel, books/movies/music, public service
announcements, finance/insurance, and other.

In those ads that contained both minorities and Whites, the num-   14
ber of minority and White models was compared, the role or centrality

of the minority models was coded,[12] and the relationship between the two groups was coded according to interaction setting and level of interaction. Interaction setting was coded as formal (work), informal (social settings), and none (not determined or no specific setting).

The level of interaction was coded according to three categories: 15
(1) those situations in which there was no interaction between the two groups, e.g., there were separate pictures of the two racial groups; (2) limited interaction, e.g., the two groups were at the same party or office setting, but did not appear to be talking with each other; and (3) high interaction, e.g., the two groups were involved in the same activity and appeared to be in face-to-face contact.

Role or centrality of the minority model was coded into four cate-   16
gories: (1) major, e.g., the model was very important to the advertisement's layout; was shown in foreground and/or holding the product; (2) minor, e.g., the model was of average importance to the advertisement's layout; (3) background, e.g., the model is difficult to find and not important to the advertisement's layout; and (4) neutral, e.g., all models are treated in a neutral or similar fashion with no one model occupying a major role.

RESULTS

Presence   A total of 1,969 ads from 1987 and 1992 were analyzed   17
(1987: 1,039 ads; 1992: 930). Of the 1,969 ads, 143 featured a mixed-ethnic group in which a minority model was shown with White models (1987: 64; 1992: 79). Comparing the data from 1987 and 1992, Blacks were the only minority group that showed an increase in use in both the Black-race only category and in the Black mixed-ethnic category. The use of Hispanic and Asian models is extremely limited in 1987 and 1992 in both the mixed-ethnic and one-race-only categories (see Table 2).

Combining the figures for the one-race-only ads and the mixed-   18
ethnic ads, the use of Black models increased from 6.8% to 10.6%, which is signifigantly higher than the percentages reported in the Zinkhan study conducted in 1986. Doing the same for Asians and Hispanics, the use of Asians decreased from 2.5% to 1.8% and the use of Hispanics decreased from 1.5% to .6%.

Racial Composition   The tendency to feature minorities with   19
Whites reported in previous research is reaffirmed in this study.[13] Of

---

[12]Bush, Resnik, Stern, eds., "Content Analysis of the Portrayal of Black Models"; Robert E. Wilkes and Humberto Valencia, "Hispanics and Blacks in Television Commercials," *Journal of Advertising* 18 (1989): 19–25.

[13]Colfax and Sternberg, "Perpetuation of Racial," 8–18; Humphrey and Schuman, "Portrayal of Blacks," 551–63; Stevenson, "A Content Analysis," 67–74.

the 212 ads including minorities, more than two-thirds (67.5%) were mixed-ethnic ads. There is a significant difference in the number of Blacks shown in the mixed-ethnic ads vs. Black-only ads (see Table 2). The same pattern applies to Asian and Hispanic representation.

Of the 143 mixed-ethnic ads, 56.6% included only one minority,   20
24.5% included two minorities, 11.2% included three minorities, 6.3% included four minorities, and 1.4% included five or more minorities. The average number of models used in a mixed-ethnic ad was 5.5. Overall, the nature of the mixed-ethnic ads was one in which the minority model was outnumbered by White models. The ratio of White to Black models between the two years remained stable (1987: 2.89 to 1; 1992: 2.91 to 1). The ratio of White to Asian models was also stable (1987: 3.02 to 1; 1992: 3.00 to 1). The White to Hispanic models ratio changed slightly, but not significantly (1987: 4.46 to 1; 1992: 3.88 to 1).

Role Prominence   There were a number of ads in which each   21
minority was represented (one Black model, one Asian model, one Hispanic model, and one or more White models)—or some combination thereof. This type of ad was called "All-races-together" by Colfax and Sternberg.[14] In this study, the roles played in the "All-races-together" was coded "neutral." The neutral category is larger than

Table 2:   Racial Representation Percentages in Magazine Advertising by Year

	Year	
Race	1987	1992
White	91.0%	87.3%
Black	1.7	3.3
Hispanic	0.6	0.2
Asian	0.6	0.6
Mixed Ethnic[1]		
Black	5.1	7.3
Hispanic	0.9	0.4
Asian	1.9	1.2
Subtotal	6.2	8.6
Totals	100%	100%
	(1039)	(930)

[1]Mixed ethnic includes all ads with two or more races represented; there were 6.2% mixed ethnic ads in 1987 and 8.2% in 1992; the racial breakdown within the mixed-ethnic ads is shown above and does not total 100% because two or more races are represented.

$\chi^2=11.09$; d.f.=4; $p<.05$

---

[14]Colfax and Sternberg, "Perpetuation of Racial," 8–18.

other role categories for all three minority groups (see Table 3). Neutral ads typically featured a group of models in which all were presented in a similar manner, with no one model more prominent or more important than any other.

It is important to note that minority models were used promi-   22
nently in less than 25% of the ads. Minority models, with the exception of Hispanic models, were most often portrayed in minor or background roles, considered by some "token" positions.[15] Although Hispanic models did appear more often in major roles compared to Black or Asian models, this finding was based on only five ads (1987: 3 ads; 1992: 2 ads). However, because there were only four mixed-ethnic ads in 1992 in which Hispanic models appeared, it is interesting that two of those ads portrayed Hispanics in major roles.

Table 3 combines the data from 1987 and 1992 as there was only   23
one significant difference between the years. In the major category for Black models, there was an increase of 13.1% (13 advertisements). The Asian and Hispanic categories remained relatively stable, with any changes due to a general decrease in the number of ads in 1992.

Interaction Setting   The interaction setting for minority and   24
White models in the mixed-ethnic ads further defines the nature of the relationship. Except for Asian mixed-ethnic ads, the largest category was "formal" (work setting). This was especially pronounced for Hispanic mixed-ethnic ads (see Table 4). Overall, less than 2% of all ads showed minority and White models interacting in an informal setting.

Between 1987 and 1992 there were no significant changes for His-   25
panic mixed-ethnic and Asian mixed-ethnic ads, although in Hispanic mixed-ethnic ads, there was a drop in the formal setting category of six ads (again, a factor of the general drop in Hispanic mixed-ethnic ads). Comparing the 1987 and 1992 samples for Black mixed-ethnic

Table 3:   Mixed-Ethnic Ads by Role Prominence and Race (1987 and 1992 Ads Combined)

| | | Race | |
Role	Black	Asian	Hispanic
Major	20.9%	19.4%	38.5%
Minor	18.6	12.9	7.7
Background	20.9	22.6	7.7
Neutral	39.5	45.2	46.2
Totals	100%	100%	100%
	(129)	(31)	(13)

χ^2=4.3; d.f.=4; n.s.

---

[15]Colfax and Sternberg, "Perpetuation of Racial," 8–18.

Table 4:   Mixed-Ethnic Ads by Interaction Setting and Race (1987 and 1992 Ads Combined)

Role	Black	Race Asian	Hispanic
Formal	44.2%	45.2%	76.9%
Informal	17.1	9.7	15.4
None	38.8	45.2	7.7
Totals	100%	100%	100%
	(129)	(31)	(13)

χ^2=7.2; d.f.=4; n.s.

ads, there was a threefold increase in the number of informal settings (1987: 5 ads; 1992: 17 ads).

Level of Interaction   A final description of the relationship be-   26
tween minority and White models looked at level of interaction. As expected, interaction between White and minority models is quite limited with only a few ads depicting face-to-face interaction. Most depict either no or minimal contact (see Table 5).

For all three minority groups, "some interaction" was the largest   27
category, e.g., minority and White models are either pictured in the same setting but not interacting, or are pictured standing next to each other as part of a group in which no one is interacting—a "staged" photo, e.g., models posing in fall fashion layouts. For Black and Asian mixed-ethnic ads, the second-largest category is "no interaction," e.g., the models do not associate and often appear in separate pictures. It should be noted that although more Hispanic mixed-ethnic ads appear in the "high interaction" category when compared to the "no interaction" category, the real difference is only one ad (3 in high interaction, 2 in no interaction).

Few notable differences were found when comparing 1987 and   28
1992. For Black mixed-ethnic ads, all categories were relatively stable, with the largest increase in the "high interaction" category, 7.3%. For Asian mixed-ethnic ads, there appeared to be significant changes, but the numbers of actual ads is so small, conclusions are difficult. There was a 19.5% drop in the number of "some interaction" ads (1987: 13 ads; 1992: 5 ads), and a 22.3% increase in "high interaction" ads (1987: 1 ad; 1992: 3 ads). There were no notable differences in the Hispanic mixed-ethnic ads.

Overall, when comparing level of interaction with interaction   29
setting, less than one-half of 1% of the 1,969 advertisements showed minorities and Whites interacting face-to-face in a social setting.

Demographic Analysis   There were few minority-majority dif-   30
ferences in the demographic characteristics analyzed, with the gender

Table 5: Mixed-Ethnic Ads by Interaction Level and Race (1987 and 1992 Ads Combined)

		Race	
Level of Interaction	Black	Asian	Hispanic
High Interaction	19.4%	12.9%	23.1%
Some Interaction	42.6	58.1	61.5
No Interaction	38.0	29.0	15.4
Totals	100%	100%	100%
	(129)	(31)	(13)

χ^2=4.7; d.f.=4; n.s.

category showing the only significant changes. Combining all racial groups, more females appeared in advertisements than males (combination of the 1987 and 1992 data: 28.2% contained males only, 44.1% contained females only, 26.7% contained both males and females, and 1% were "unknown," pictures of infants and babies). Although the use of male models decreased from 1987 to 1992, the use of Black males increased 4.9% while the number of White males decreased 5.9% (χ^2=17.54; d.f.=4; p<.05).

Product Category Product class was also coded, but the large number of categories and the infrequent use of Asians and Hispanics made the differences in the use of minority models between product categories very small. One exception was public service ads where Black models had the highest presence. Combining 1987 and 1992 data, 12.5% of all public service advertisements featured Black models; when Black and mixed-ethnic public service ads are combined, the percentage jumps to 53.1%.

Other product categories in which Blacks were more likely to be represented included finance/insurance (nearly 21%), automobile (16.9%), and travel (18%). The travel category also had a higher than usual representation of Hispanic and Asian models (4.5% and 6.7% respectively).

Many of the finance/insurance advertisements were ones in which the company was advertising or promoting the company's involvement in the community. For example, State Farm Insurance placed many ads discussing their "Good Neighbor Awards" which were given to people who showed a special interest in helping those less fortunate or some kind of community-based program. In many cases, the minorities featured were the recipients of the aid.

In the travel category, especially those featuring Asian models, there was a logical "fit" with the use of the model and the service or product being advertised. United Airlines placed a number of ads promoting their flights to Taiwan or Japan. In these ads, Asian models appeared as flight attendants or Asian businessmen. L'eggs nylons promoted the "Look of the Orient" using real silk and an attractive Asian model to strengthen the "Oriental" connection.

Occupation Coding occupation proved difficult. For most races, 35 "unknown" was the largest category followed by "family/kids"—which was the largest category for Asian-only ads. The "other" category was largest for Blacks which included athletes and musicians, followed by "family/kids." There were no Asian-only "professional" ads and one Black-only ad which featured the minority as a "professional." There were three Hispanic-only ads (all from 1987) which featured the model as a "professional," not significant, but surprising considering the overall lack of use of Hispanic models.

DISCUSSION

Presence and Racial Composition The results indicate a steady 36 increase in the use of Blacks in mainstream magazine advertising, but the use of Asians and Hispanics remains low and shows signs of decline. Compared to census figures, all racial minorities are underrepresented as a percentage of the population. Blacks account for 12.1% of the U.S. population; Asian or Pacific Islanders account for 2.9% and Hispanics account for 9.0%.

When minority models were used, they tended to be used with 37 Whites in mixed-ethnic ads. The use of the minorities in single-race ads is still rare, especially for Asians and Hispanics. Whether this was due to a conscious decision on the part of the advertiser, the agency, or both is difficult to ascertain. One argument reported in previous research suggests it may reflect a reluctance on the part of some advertisers to have their product associated with minorities for fear of a "White backlash."[16]

---

[16]Arnold M. Barban and Edward W. Cundiff, "Negro and White Response to Advertising Stimuli," *Journal of Marketing Research* 1 (November 1964): 53–56; Arnold Barban, "The Dilemma of 'Integrated' Advertising," *Journal of Business* 42 (October 1969): 477–96; James Stafford, Al Birdwell, and Charles Van Tassel, "Integrated Advertising—White Backlash?," *Journal of Advertising Research* 10 (April 1970): 15–20; Lester Guest, "How Negro Models Affect Company Image," *Journal of Advertising Research* 10 (April 1970): 29–33; James W. Cagley and Richard N. Cardozo, "White Response to Integrated Advertising," *Journal of Advertising Research* 10 (April 1970): 35–39; William V. Muse, "Product-Related Response to Use of Black Models in Advertising," *Journal of Marketing Research* 8 (February 1971); 107–109; Carl E. Block, "White Backlash to Negro Ads: Fact or Fantasy," *Journalism Quarterly* 49 (summer 1972): 258–62; Mary Jane Schlinger and Joseph T. Plummer, "Advertising in Black and White," *Journal of Marketing Research* 19 (May 1972): 149–53; Ronald F. Bush, Robert F. Gwinner, and Paul J. Solomon, "White Consumer Sales Response to Black Models," *Journal of Marketing* 38 (April 1974): 25–29; Pravat K. Choudhury and Lawrence S. Schmid, "Black Models in Advertising to Blacks," *Journal of Advertising Research* 14 (June 1974): 19–22.

Some might argue that the small number of minorities featured   38
in mainstream magazine advertising may be due to a very deliberate
media strategy that successfully targets minorities in specialized and
minority media. However, each of the magazines analyzed does have
a minority readership and, in some cases, that readership is quite substantial. For example, according to *Simmons 1993 Study of Media and
Markets*, the Hispanic readership of *Life* is 9.9%, yet the inclusion of
Hispanics in *Life*'s advertisements was only .8%. *Cosmopolitan* has a
11.3% Black readership, yet only 4.3% of the advertisements included
Blacks; 13.3% of the magazines' readership is Hispanic and only .5% of
the advertisements use Hispanics.

Conversely, White readership was consistently lower than White   39
model representation (*Life:* 83.2% readership, 95.9% representation;
Cosmopolitan: 84.7% readership, 97.3% representation; *The New Yorker:*
88.5% readership, 98.8% representation). In only a few cases did the
use of minority models actually exceed readership figures (this was
never true in the case of Hispanics). For example, 10.6% of *Time*'s readers are Black and 14.9% of *Time*'s advertisements included Blacks;
17.1% of *Sports Illustrated*'s readers are Black and 20.8% of *SI*'s advertisements included Blacks. One might suggest that in the case of *SI*, the
difference has everything to do with the high use of Black athletes in
ads targeting sports-minded consumers.

It makes sense to market to your audience, and if that audience is   40
racially mixed, smart marketers are going to include minorities in their
advertising. Perhaps magazines need to do a better job of describing
the diversity of their circulations to potential advertisers and their
agency's media buyers.

Some advertisers mistakenly believe that if there is no special, "mi-   41
nority" media to reach minorities, then it is wasteful to use the mainstream media.[17] What many companies and advertising agencies don't
seem to realize is that they do not have to use minority media to reach
minorities. For advertisers to assume that minorities do not read mainstream magazines is naive, and from a marketing standpoint, economic
suicide given the size and financial resources of many minorities.

Minority populations make up a large percentage of the total   42
population, and they represent a significant proportion of society's
total purchasing power. Census data from 1990 show that the Black
population increased 13.2% from 1980, the Asian and Pacific Islander
population increased 107.8%, and the Hispanic population increased

---

[17]Cyndee Miller, "'Hot' Asian-American Market Not Starting Much of a Fire Yet," *Advertising Age,* 21 January 1991, 12; Guitierrez, "Advertising and the Growth of Minority
Markets," 6–16.

53.0%. By contrast, the White population increased 6.0%.[18] The U.S. Bureau of Labor Statistics for 1991 shows that Asian and Pacific Islanders have the highest family income levels with 73.2% earning more than $25,000; 55.1% of the Hispanic population and 43.5% of the Black population have family incomes above $25,000. The spending power of Blacks "represents a gross national product of $200 billion. Hispanics represent some $134 billion in purchasing power. And though the size of their population is much smaller, Asian Americans... wield some $61 billion in spending clout."[19]

Knowing the size and potential spending power of these minor-   43
ity groups, the question remains: If minorities do not ignore mainstream media, why should advertisers?

Demographic Analysis   Results obtained from analysis of the   44
gender category do not support earlier research indicating a reluctance to use adult minority males in advertisements, specifically Blacks. Despite the significant increase in the use of Black adult males in the ads analyzed, in many cases the portrayal of the Black male could be characterized as stereotypical. For example, Black males were included to signify strength or power or were shown as athletes. Along with well-known sports figures like Michael Jordan, Ken Griffey Jr., and Bo Jackson, there were also "unknown" athletes dressed as basketball, baseball, or football players. Often, these Black athletes were shown with White team members.

Occupation and Product Category   Previous research on the   45
use of Black athletes in advertisements suggests that White people believe "sports" are an "acceptable" profession for Blacks and that Blacks have native athletic abilities making them exceptional athletes. Similarly, music is seen as another "acceptable" occupation for Blacks.[20] Often, the overall theme of ads that included Black models was linked to music. An Olympus ad showed an older Black man playing a bass and the ad linked "New Orleans," "mood," and "soul," to the Olympus camera. A Hennessy Cognac ad showed a Black man playing a trumpet and said, "If you've ever been lost in a blue note you already know the feeling of Cognac Hennessy." And, a Gilby's

---

[18]U.S. Department of Commerce, *Statistical Abstract of the United States 1992,* 112th ed. (Washington, DC: Bureau of the Census, 1992).

[19]Frank DiGiacomo, "Doing the Right Thing," *Marketing and Media Decisions* 25 (June 1990): 27.

[20]Cox, "Social Effects," 41–44; Colfax and Sternberg, "Perpetuation of Racial," 8–18; Ellen Seiter, "Differenct Children, Different Dreams: Racial Representation in Advertising," *Journal of Communication Inquiry* 14 (winter 1990): 31–47.

Gin ad showed a Black man playing the drums and described the product as "The drink of the original beat generation."

On the face of it, there is nothing inherently wrong with portray- 46
ing Blacks as musicians or athletes. What it fails to do, however, is to recognize that minority groups have varied interests, skills, and talents. White models are portrayed in a variety of occupations and situations and the differences are used to amplify the product's versatility. Minorities deserve comparable consideration.

This study reinforces previous research findings that minorities 47
are used disproportionately in public service advertisements and government-sponsored ads.[21] Even traditional advertisers like Toyota and The Discover Card used minorities when they were making a "public service" appeal. In the State Farm Insurance "Good Neighbor Awards" campaign, minority groups were the beneficiaries of some sort of support or praise for performing "good works" around the country. In one State Farm ad, Hispanic, Asian, and Black inner-city youths were pictured cleaning up graffiti. Their teacher had been awarded a "Good Neighbor Award" for "helping students develop community spirit and math skills at the same time."

In a Discover Card ad, the company paid "Tribute to Young 48
America." Nine students were given scholarships; only one of the students was a minority—a Black male—and he was being given an athletic scholarship. In a Toyota ad, the company promoted its dedication to the environment and education by showing a picture of an inner-city Black boy holding a fish he caught. His teacher explained that this is the "first fish Jawan had seen that wasn't surrounded by French fries." The ad concludes: "Toyota: investing in the individual."

The inclusion of minorities in these ads does not seem to be based 49
on target marketing. Instead, they are being used to establish a company position or positive image. The consumer is led to believe that since the company cares about minorities and their problems we should feel good about the company and show our support by buying its products. At the same time, the message that minorities are in need of some assistance from the larger community is consistently reinforced.

Interaction Setting and Level of Interaction This study also 50
supports previous research showing a tendency to locate minority and White models in formal work settings.[22] On a more positive note, the use

---

[21]Colfax and Sternberg, "Perpetuation of Racial," 8–18.
[22]Bush, Resnik, and Stern, eds., "Content Analysis of the Portrayal of Black Models"; Humphrey and Schuman, "Portrayal of Blacks," 551–63; Stevenson, "A Content Analysis," 67–74.

of informal or social settings is increasing. This may indicate a more positive attitude toward social integration in magazine advertisements.
However, to understand the nature of this integration one must also
look at the level of interaction between White and minority models.

There were very few cases in which minority and White models   51
interacted, face to face, in social settings. Most ads continued to show
minorities and Whites interacting in work settings or not interacting at
all. In one Holiday Inn ad, a Black businessman and a White businessman held a meeting over lunch or breakfast. In another, four White
businessmen were interacting beside an indoor swimming pool; one
Black businessman was present, but he was slightly removed from the
group, sitting behind and to the far right of the rest of the group.

Overall, it is encouraging to note greater use of Blacks in main-   52
stream magazine advertising. Simple inclusion is a necessary first step,
but it does not equal integration or fair representation. Asians and
Hispanics are still woefully under-represented. Moreover, there are
few advertisements in which minorities appear alone and, when they
do appear, they are outnumbered by Whites. Minorities continue to be
used as "tokens" or as questionable links to some product attribute.

Although there have been some positive changes, this study   53
points out a number of areas in which there is room for improvement.
Richard deCordova summarizes some of the problems associated with
"integrating" advertising: "Eliminating a stereotypical character here
or adding a minority character to the background there can function as
a kind of quick fix, something that will not change the more latent
racist messages of advertisements but will diffuse criticism (especially
if that criticism is itself based on the notion of stereotypes and a simple
numerical count of minorities represented).[23]

While labeling advertising "racist" is perhaps too strong, deCor-   54
dova goes to the heart of the issue: It's easy for an advertiser to simply
add minority models to diffuse criticism; and, if one were to simply
count the number of times minoritites appear in adverstisements, the increase could be viewed as progress. However, it is not that simple, and
this analysis is very direct in pointing out that the actual number of times
minorities are included in advertisements in an equal fashion to White
models or as independent, potential consumers is really quite small.

Only a concerted effort from all sectors of the community can   55
correct that condition by beginning to portray all minority groups, not
just Blacks, in a variety of different occupations and social settings. Industry will need to assume a lead role. And like most change, enlight-

---

[23]Richard deCordova, "Notes on Stereotype Research: A Response to Ellen Seiter," *Journal of Communication Inquiry* 14 (winter 1990): 48–50.

ened self-interest will light the path. If companies are truly trying to reach minority markets, they must do a better job of not just including minorities in their mainstream advertising, but of also showing the minorities in various occupations, in meaningful roles, and in a variety of settings. Minorities read mainstream magazines and buy mainstream products. It's time they receive mainstream treatment.

Examining the Text

1. In analyzing ads that depict White and minority models together, Bowen and Schmid study interaction settings and levels of interaction. What do these categories mean? Why are they significant? What do Bowen and Schmid's findings suggest?

2. Choose one of the data tables in the article and write a three or four sentence summary of the major ideas represented in the table.

3. The "Results" section of the article is an objective report of Bowen and Schmid's findings, whereas the "Discussion" section presents their interpretation of these findings. What is your sense of Bowen and Schmid's opinion of their results in the Discussion section? Identify key sentences in which they express their views.

4. Toward the end of the article, Bowen and Schmid observe that simple inclusion is a necessary first step, but it does not equal integration or fair representation. Based on what they say in the article, what do you think the authors mean by equal integration and by fair representation?

5. Bowen and Schmid conclude by saying that minorities read mainstream magazines and buy mainstream products and it's time they received mainstream treatment. What do the authors mean by mainstream treatment? How would minority models be depicted if they were to be given mainstream treatment?

For Group Discussion

In the "Introduction" and "Discussion" sections Bowen and Schmid discuss the influence of advertising in our culture along with general issues involved in the representation of minorities in advertising. As a group, list and discuss the reasons Bowen and Schmid give for why advertising agencies should use more minority models in mainstream magazine advertising. Also list and discuss the reasons why ad agencies don't do so. Do you agree that changing the ethnic and racial make-up of mainstream advertisements would cause changes in society? Why or why not?

Writing Suggestion

Replicate part of Bowen and Schmid's research using more recent mainstream magazine advertisements. To do so, choose one of the magazines studied by Bowen and Schmid and analyze the ads in four recent issues, looking at one or two of the variables they discuss. For instance, you might count the number of Black, Asian, Hispanic, and White models who are represented alone or in prominent positions in the ads. Or you might count the number and percentage of ads in which White and minority models interact, and describe the kinds of interactions depicted. Or you might focus on one minority group and describe the kinds of occupations they're portrayed as having in the ads. Write a report of your findings.

Begin by discussing the significance of the variable you chose, referring to Bowen and Schmid's discussion and findings from the 1987 and 1992 magazines. Then present your results, perhaps including a table such as Bowen and Schmid do to show the numbers clearly. Finally, discuss the implications of your findings. Is there any improvement in the portrayal of minority models? If so (and if not), speculate on why this is so.

What's Wrong with Advertising?

David Ogilvy

The following passage is excerpted from a book written by one of the "fathers" of contemporary advertising theory and practice. In this chapter selection, David Ogilvy provides a bit of historical background for advertising in America, while defending his profession against critics who contend that advertising is a profoundly subversive force in American life. He argues that the majority of people in this country are not so gullible or so "brainwashed" by the media that advertisements are able to have an intellectually or morally destructive influence on them. In fact, he insists that with advertising, honesty is frequently the best policy. Americans, by and large, have a healthy critical intelligence and can see through misleading ads; therefore, if advertisers tell all the facts about a given product, the public will be much more enticed by it, and an advertising campaign will be successful.

On the other hand, Ogilvy is also careful to point out that advertising is not an entirely noble, selfless pursuit. In describing his own attitude toward the profession he helped create, Ogilvy takes a middle-of-the-road position, describing advertising as "no more and no less than a reasonably efficient way to sell." From this statement one can infer that Ogilvy believes advertising is neither a satanic force that's responsible for all of society's ills, nor the savior of humankind; it's simply a tool for achieving a particular end, namely, increased sales of a given product.

As you read this article, consider your own feelings about advertising: do you think it's a destructive force in our society or a valuable tool for disseminating information about the products of our mass culture? Further, consider the validity of Ogilvy's underlying assumptions: do advertisers actually avoid misleading consumers because truth sells products, as the author contends? Does the average American consumer have the critical awareness necessary to "see through" the manipulation of advertising copywriters?

In my *Confessions* I quoted the classic denunciations of advertis-   1
ing by Arnold Toynbee, John Kenneth Galbraith and a galaxy of earlier economists, and wheeled up Franklin Roosevelt and Winston
Churchill as witnesses for the defense.

Twenty years later the dons are still tilting at their old windmill.   2
Thus a professor at the New School of Social Research in New York
teaches his students that "advertising is a profoundly subversive force
in American life. It is intellectual and moral pollution. It trivializes,
manipulates, is insincere and vulgarizes. It is undermining our faith in
our nation and in ourselves."

Holy smoke, is *that* what I do for a living?   3

Some of the defenders of advertising are equally guilty of over-   4
stating their case. Said Leo Burnett, the great Chicago advertising
man: "Advertising is not the noblest creation of man's mind, as so
many of its advocates would like the public to think. It does not,
single-handedly, sustain the whole structure of capitalism and democracy and the Free World. It is just as nonsensical to suggest that we are
superhuman as to accept the indictment that we are subhman. We are
merely human, trying to do a necessary human job with dignity, with
decency and with competence."

My view is that advertising is no more and no less than a reason-   5
ably efficient way to sell. Procter & Gamble spends more than
$600,000,000 a year on advertising. Howard Morgens, their former
president, is quoted as saying, "We believe that advertising is the most
effective and efficient way to sell to the consumer. If we should ever
find better methods of selling our type of products to the consumer,
we'll leave advertising and turn to these other methods."

Few of us admen lie awake nights feeling guilty about the way   6
we earn our living. In Churchill's phrase, we just K.B.O.[1] We don't feel
"subversive" when we write advertisements for toothpaste. If we do it
well, children may not have to go to the dentist so often.

---

[1]Keep buggering on.

I did not feel "evil" when I wrote advertisements for Puerto Rico.   7
They helped attract industry and tourists to a country which had been
living on the edge of starvation for 400 years.

I do not think that I am "trivializing" when I write advertise-   8
ments for the World Wildlife Fund.

My children were grateful when I wrote an advertisement which   9
recovered their dog Teddy from dognappers.

Nobody suggests that the printing press is evil because it is used to   10
print pornography. It is also used to print the Bible. Advertising is only
evil when it advertises evil things. Nobody I know in advertising would
advertise a brothel, and some refuse to advertise booze or cigarettes.

Left-wing economists, ever eager to snatch the scourge from the   11
hand of God, hold that advertising tempts people to squander money
on things they don't need. Who are these elitists to decide what you
need? Do you *need* a dishwasher? Do you *need* a deodorant? Do you
need a trip to Rome? I feel no qualms of conscience about persuading
you that you do. What the Calvinistic dons don't seem to know is that
buying things can be one of life's more innocent pleasures, whether
you need them or not. Remember your euphoria when you bought
your first car? Most people enjoy window-shopping the ads, whether
for bargains or for luxuries. For 40 years I shopped the ads for country
houses, and finally saved up enough money to buy one.

It is not unknown for an advertisement in a newspaper to be   12
read by more people than any news item. When all the New York
newspapers went on strike for several weeks in 1963, research showed
that it was the advertisements which readers missed most.

If advertising were abolished, what would be done with the   13
money? Would it be spent on public works? Or distributed to stockholders in the form of extra dividends? Or given to the media to compensate them for the loss of their largest source of revenue? Perhaps it
could be used to reduce prices to the consumer—*by about 3 percent.*[2]

IS ADVERTISING A PACK OF LIES?

Introducing me at an Asian Advertising Congress in New Delhi   14
the other day, the Vice-President and former Chief Justice of India said
that I had "mastered what Stephen Leacock called the art of arresting
the human intelligence long enough to get money from it."

---

[2]Automobile manufacturers spend 1 percent of their revenue on advertising. Appliance
manufacturers 2 percent. Soft drinks 4 percent. Food manufacturers and brewers
5 percent.

If there are still any natural-born liars in advertising, we are   15
under control. Every advertisement we write is scrutinized by lawyers, by the National Association of Broadcasters and other such bodies. The Better Business Bureau and the National Advertising Review
Board (in Britain, the Advertising Standards Authority) review suspected violations of the various codes, and the Federal Trade Commission stands ready to prosecute us for deception. *Caveat emptor* has
given way to *caveat vendor*.

But how odd that the Commission does not monitor the advertis-   16
ing put out by departments of the U.S. Government. Writes Milton
Friedman, "Anyone who has bought government bonds over the past
decade has been taken to the cleaners. The amount he received on maturity would buy less in goods and services than the amount he paid
for the bond, and he has to pay taxes on the mislabeled 'interest.' Yet
the Treasury continues to advertise the bonds as 'building personal security,' and a 'gift that keeps on growing.'"[3]

"THE DIRGE OF OUR TIMES"

While very little advertising can be convicted of crimes against hu-   17
manity, exposure to 30,000 TV commercials every year—the average
dosage in American homes—suggests that Wilfrid Sheed had a point
when he wrote that "the sound of selling is the dirge of our times."
When I lived in New York, I did not notice it, either because I was too
busy to watch for more than half an hour a day (Walter Cronkite), or because I was corrupted by familiarity. But when I went to live in Europe,
I grew accustomed to smaller doses of advertising. Today, when I return
to the United States, I am enraged by the barrage to which I am subjected. And this does not apply only to television. On Sundays, the *New
York Times* often carries 350 pages of advertisements, and some of the
radio stations devote 40 minutes in every hour to commercials. I don't
know how all this clutter can ever be brought under control; the profit
motive is too strong in those who own the media.

In the average American home, the TV is turned on, if not   18
watched, for five hours a day, which adds up to 25 years in the average life. But don't blame the *commercials* for this addiction.

MANIPULATION?

You may have heard it said that advertising is "manipulation." I   19
know of only two examples, and neither of them actually happened. In

---

[3]*Free to Choose,* Harcourt Brace, 1980.

1957 a market researcher called James Vicary hypothesized that it might be possible to flash commands on television screens so fast that the viewer would not be conscious of seeing them, but his *unconscious* would see them—and obey them. He called this gimmick "subliminal" advertising, but he never even got around to testing it, and no advertiser has ever used it. Unfortunately word of his hypothesis found its way into the public prints, and provided grist for the mills of the anti-advertising brigade. The British Institute of Practitioners in Advertising solemnly banned the use of subliminal advertising—which did not exist.

My only other example of manipulation will make you shudder. 20
I myself once came near to doing something so diabolical that I hesitate to confess it even now, 30 years later. Suspecting that *hypnotism* might be an element in successful advertising, I engaged a professional hypnotist to make a commercial. When I saw it in the projection room, it was so powerful that I had visions of millions of suggestible consumers getting up from their armchairs and rushing like zombies through the traffic on their way to buy the product at the nearest store. Had I invented the *ultimate* advertisement? I burned it, and never told my client how close I had come to landing him in a national scandal.

One way and another, the odds against your being manipulated 21
by advertising are now very long indeed. Even if I wanted to manipulate you, I wouldn't know how to circumvent the legal regulations.

Hold your horses—I almost forgot. There is one category of ad- 22
vertising which is totally uncontrolled and flagrantly dishonest: the television commercials for candidates in Presidential elections.

POLITICAL CHICANERY

While statesmen in England, France and Persia have sometimes 23
consulted me, I have never taken political parties as clients of Ogilvy & Mather. First, because they would preoccupy the best brains of the agency, to the detriment of its permanent clients. Second, because they are bad credit risks. Third, because it would be unfair to those people in the agency who pray for the victory of the opposing party. And finally, because it would be difficult to avoid the chicanery which is endemic in all political campaigns.

The first politician to use television was Governor Dewey in his 24
1950 campaign for the governorship of New York. On one program, Happy Felton, the entertainer, interviewed passers-by under the marquee of the Astor Hotel on 7th Avenue. They would say what interested them in the campaign, and ask questions of the Governor. Dewey watched them on a monitor in the studio, and answered their questions. The day before, his staff had carefully *selected* the passers-by. They had *told* them what they were interested in, and rehearsed

their questions. On the last day of the campaign, Dewey was on television from 6 A.M. to midnight. People could telephone the studio. Four women on camera answered the calls and passed along the questions for Dewey to answer. A member of his staff was in a phone booth at the corner drugstore with a pile of nickels.

Dewey, the ex-District Attorney, the battler against corruption,   25
the Governor of the State, thought of himself as an honorable man. It never occurred to him that he was involved in deception. I doubt that it would occur to anyone, honorable or dishonorable, to pull such a play today, thirty years later. Times change.

Dewey was a *scientific* demagogue. Before speaking on major is-   26
sues, he used research to find out which policies had the widest popular support and then put them forward as if he believed in them.

In his book *The Duping of the American Voter*,[4] my colleague   27
Robert Spero analyzed the commercials used by Kennedy, Johnson, Nixon, Ford and Carter. He concluded that they were "the most deceptive, misleading, unfair and untruthful of all advertising...the sky is the limit with regard to what can be said, what can be promised, what accusations can be made, what lies can be told."

The nine Federal agencies which regulate advertising for prod-   28
ucts have no say in political advertising. The broadcasting networks, which turn down half the commercials for products submitted to them because they violate their codes, do not apply any code whatever to political commercials. Why not? Because political advertising is considered "protected speech" under the First Amendment of the U.S. Constitution. The networks are obliged to broadcast every political commercial submitted to them, however dishonest.

In 1964, Johnson's commercials disparaged Senator Goldwater   29
with a cynical dishonesty which would never be tolerated in commercials for toothpaste. They gave voters to understand that Goldwater was an irresponsible, trigger-happy ogre who would start nuclear wars at the drop of a hat. Johnson was presented as a dove of peace.

What had happened was this. Goldwater, one of the most decent   30
men in public life, had been asked by an interviewer to differentiate between the *reliability* and the *accuracy* of guided missiles. He had replied that they were accurate enough "to lob one into the men's room at the Kremlin." And he had told another interviewer that it would be *possible* to destroy the forests in North Vietnam by using low-yield atomic weapons. Goldwater did not *recommend* the use of atomic weapons, and Johnson knew this perfectly well.

---

[4]*The Duping of the American Voter.* Copyright © 1980 by Robert Spero. Harper & Row, NY.

Nixon's campaigns against Hubert Humphrey and George Mc-   31
Govern were less dishonest, but they too violated the network code for
product advertising.

Jimmy Carter's commercials pictured him as an innocent new-   32
comer to politics, with no political organization—a poor farmer with
no money. Nothing could have been further from the truth, but the
voting public swallowed it. Gerald Ford, his Republican opponent,
used commercials which were relatively honest—and lost the election.

The Kennedys and the Rockefellers have proved that it helps a   33
politician to be *rich*. In his campaign for election to a second term as Democratic Governor of West Virginia, Jay Rockefeller spent $11,000,000 of his
own money and defeated his Republican opponent, who spent only
$800,000. Rockefeller's commercials were unusually statesmanlike, and
a survey found that the people of West Virginia were not shocked by his
expenditure. Even his uncle Nelson Rockefeller had not spent so much
in his re-election campaign for Governor of New York.

In a period when television commercials are often the decisive   34
factor in deciding who shall be the next President of the United States,
dishonest advertising is as evil as stuffing the ballot box. Perhaps the
advertising people who have allowed their talents to be prostituted for
this villainy are too naïve to understand the complexity of the issues.

The United States is almost the only country which allows political   35
candidates to *buy* commercial time. In England, France and other democracies, the networks allot free time to serious discussion of the issues.

Could political commercials be banned in the United States? Not   36
without violating the U.S. Constitution. Could they be regulated, like
every other kind of advertising? That too would be illegal.

Can you imagine Abraham Lincoln hiring an agency to produce   37
30-second commercials about slavery?

DOWN WITH BILLBOARDS

Highways with billboards have three times as many accidents   38
as highways without billboards. President Eisenhower said, "I am
against those billboards that mar our scenery, but I don't know what I
can do about it." In California, Governor Pat Brown said, "When a
man throws an empty cigarette package from an automobile, he is liable to a fine of $50. When a man throws a billboard across a view, he
is richly rewarded."

Bob Moses, the illustrious Parks Commissioner of New York   39
State, said that "effrontery and impudence can go no further. The time
for compromise with these stubborn and ruthless people is over." But
the majority of legislators are still ready to compromise with them.
Here is how a State Senator explains it:

The billboard lobby shrewdly puts many legislators in its debt by giving them free space during election time. The lobby is savage against the legislator who dares oppose it by favoring anti-billboard laws. It subsidizes his opposition, foments political trouble in his home district, donates billboards to his opponents and sends agents to spread rumours among his constituents.

Says the *New York Times,* "the forces of uglification are rampant.   40
The Illinois Democrat and the Florida Republican are united in their determination to protect the financial welfare of the billboard industry at the expense of millions of ordinary tourists who would like to see some scenery as they drive."

The Highway Beautification Act actually states that it is the pur-   41
pose of Congress to *promote* outdoor advertising. Some departments of the Federal Government are *users* of billboards. The Internal Revenue Service once accepted the free gift of 4,000 empty billboards and used them to urge taxpayers to make honest returns.

One day Monty Spaght, then President of Shell, asked me, "We   42
get a lot of letters protesting against our use of billboards. Do we *need* billboards?" I replied, "If you give up billboards, you can still use newspapers and magazines and radio and television. That ought to be enough." Shell gave up billboards.

Billboards represent less than 2 percent of total advertising in the   43
United States. I cannot believe that the free-enterprise system would be irreparably damaged if they were abolished. Who is *in favor* of them? Only the people who make money out of them. What kind of people are they? When President Johnson sent the Highway Beautification Bill to Congress, the head of one billboard company protested that Johnson had "taken a stand in favor of an abstract concept—*beauty.* Some people like scenery and are interested in it. Others can take it or leave it. *There are times when most people would rather look at posters than scenery."*

The Roadside Business Association has said, "We do not believe   44
that everyone is for beauty in all things."

On a Sunday morning in 1958, vigilantes sawed down seven bill-   45
boards along a highway in New Mexico. Citizens of surrounding areas expressed support for them. One telephone call complained that the vigilantes had not cut down *enough* billboards, and another that they had frustrated the plan of a large group of citizens who had scheduled a mass burning of billboards for later in the month. The vigilantes were never arrested.

In 1961 the Quebec government sent hundreds of men with axes   46
to chop down billboards. In 1963 the head of the New York State Thruway Authority knocked down 53 billboards in a dawn raid; he was sick of legal bickering. But in June 1982, a judge in Oregon over-

turned an ordinance that required the removal of billboards on the ground that it was *a denial of free speech.* The battle goes on.

CAN ADVERTISING SELL BAD PRODUCTS?

It is often charged that advertising can persuade people to buy   47
inferior products. So it can—*once.* But the consumer perceives that the product is inferior and never buys it again. This causes grave financial loss to the manufacturer, whose profits come from *repeat* purchases.

The best way to increase the sale of a product is to *improve the*   48
product. This is particularly true of food products; the consumer is amazingly quick to notice an improvement in taste and buy the product more often. I have always been irritated by the lack of interest brand managers take in improving their products. One client warned me, "You are too prone to criticize our products. We could find it easier to accept criticism of our wives."

NOT ENOUGH INFORMATION

Do you think advertising gives you enough information about   49
products? I don't.

Recently, I smashed my car beyond repair and had to buy a new   50
one. For six months I read all the car ads in search of *information.* All I found was fatuous slogans and flatulent generalities. Car manufacturers assume that you are not interested in facts. Indeed, their advertising is not aimed at consumers. Its purpose is to win an ovation when it is projected on the screen at hoopla conventions of dealers. Show-biz commercials have that effect. Sober, factual advertising does not. If their engineering was as incompetent as their advertising, their cars would not run ten miles without a breakdown.

When I advertised Rolls-Royce, I gave the *facts*—no hot air, no   51
adjectives. Later, my partner Hank Bernhard used equally factual advertising for Mercedes. In every case sales went up dramatically—on peppercorn budgets.

I have written factual advertising for a bank, for gasoline, for a   52
stockbroker, margarine, foreign travel and many other products. It *always* sells better than empty advertising.

Before I started writing advertisements, I spent three years selling   53
ing Aga cooking stoves to Scottish housewives, door to door. All I did was give my customers the facts. It took me 40 minutes to make a sale; about 3,000 words. If the people who write Detroit advertising had

started *their* careers as door-to-door salesmen, you and I would be able to find the facts we need in their advertisements.

Examining the Text

1. In response to the social research professor's comment in the first paragraph, Ogilvy writes, "We don't feel 'subversive' when we write advertisements for toothpaste. If we do it well, children may not have to go to the dentist so often" (paragraph 6). What does this statement imply about advertisers' attitudes toward their profession? Furthermore, what does it suggest about the role of advertising in contemporary America? Do you agree or disagree with the philosophy expressed by Ogilvy in this passage?

2. Describing the pervasive influence of the media, Ogilvy offers, "I don't know how all this clutter can ever be brought under control; the profit motive is too strong in those who own the media" (17). What is his attitude toward the media, as suggested in his choice of words such as "clutter" and "dirge"? How does he manage to separate advertising from the media, so that he can conclude with the statement, "Don't blame the commercials for this addiction [to television]" (18)? Do you agree or disagree with the implication that televised advertising is worthwhile or at worst harmless, while television programming is potentially harmful because of its content and sheer volume?

3. In the Manipulation section of this reading (19–22), Ogilvy says, "There is one category of advertising which is totally uncontrolled and flagrantly dishonest: the television commercials for candidates in Presidential elections" (22). What specific factors, according to the author, make political ads so rampantly deceitful? In what ways is political advertising different (and, by Ogilvy's account, more insidious) than other kinds of advertising? Does the author offer suggestions for countering the effects of dishonest political advertising, which, he says, "is as evil as stuffing the ballot box"?

For Group Discussion

In this chapter, Ogilvy takes exception with the following statement, made by a professor at the New School of Social Research in New York: "...advertising is a profoundly subversive force in American life. It is intellectual and moral pollution. It trivializes, manipulates, is insincere and vulgarizes. It is undermining our faith in our nation and in ourselves" (2). Respond to each of the subassertions in this quote. Is advertising a subversive, anti-intellectual and antimoral force? Does it have the power to undercut our patriotism and feelings of self-worth? Provide examples that support or disprove Ogilvy's assertion that advertising does not have a negative social influence.

Writing Suggestion

Write an essay that agrees or disagrees with Ogilvy's contention that "advertising is no more and no less than a reasonably efficient way to sell" (5). This piece of writing should address the quotation on two levels: first, discuss whether or not you believe advertising works effectively toward its rhetorical end, namely, to sell things. Cite examples from your own life and the experiences of those around you to illustrate advertising's effectiveness or ineffectiveness as a motivator toward product consumption. Next, discuss the "no more no less" portion of Ogilvy's statement, which implies that advertising has, or should have, no social impact beyond the conveyance of product information. Aside from selling things, what other social influences might advertising have on the public?

Images of Women and Men in Advertising

Media Mirrors

Carol Moog

The following selection comes from Carol Moog's book, "Are They Selling Her Lips?": Advertising and Identity (1990), in which she examines advertising from two quite distinct perspectives: that of a psychologist interested in how ads influence our sense of who we are and who we want to be; and that of a consultant to ad agencies, who sees the decisions, sometimes illogical and arbitrary, made in designing an ad campaign.

In "Media Mirrors," Moog studies the evolution of Maidenform bra ad campaigns from the 1950s to the late 1980s, an era marked both by unprecedented success and unexpected controversy. Moog concludes that Maidenform, like most other companies, both reflects and responds to broader social changes in its attempt to touch the conscious and subconscious wishes of consumers. Because it sells to women, Maidenform, like other companies, has been compelled to stay current with the changes in women's lives and in their images of themselves, although they have not always been successful in this.

Moog focuses on lingerie advertising and so her essay raises questions about images of women in advertising. **Before you read,** *take a moment to reflect on some current ads for both women's products and men's products. How well do these ads reflect the lives and interests of men and women in the 1990s?*

Breasts.
Philip Roth yearned for them.
He built an empire on them.
But Maidenform made the fortune from them.

Sharon, the forty-seven-year-old wife of a dentist with two grown children, is telling me about the dream she had three nights before:

> Richard and I were in a restaurant. I think it was the Citadel, where we ate about a month ago—I don't know. But it was different. There were all these men around, and I felt uncomfortable. But they weren't alone. They were there with some old women—like their mothers or grandmothers or something. And I was very angry at Richard. I remember fighting with him there before too. He kept telling me to shut up, that I

was drinking too much. Suddenly, I realized I didn't have anything on and he was mad at me because everyone was staring. I thought, I've got to get out of here. I panicked. But I couldn't move. No one at the other tables seemed to pay any attention. And here's where it got really strange. I started to relax. I felt beautiful. And Richard smiled.

Sharon's dream has triggered a thought in my mind that starts to   2
crystallize into an image that helps me understand what she's thinking about. I'm imagining Bea Coleman and her mother, Ida Rosenthal, and the brilliant campaign they launched more than thirty years ago. A campaign so brilliant that it touched the most potent fantasies of a woman's dreams.

It was the Maidenform fantasy. The "I dreamed I was...in my   3
Maidenform bra" campaign ran for twenty years and made Bea Coleman and Ida Rosenthal rich beyond their wildest dreams.

The original Maidenform ads were created by the agency of Nor-   4
man, Craig and Kummel Advertising, and showed women acting out fantasies (frequently controversial fantasies), that fully displayed their Maidenform bras. Ads like the lady lawyer who "dreamed I swayed the jury in my Maidenform bra" unleashed and exposed the secret fantasizes of traditional women of the fifties and invited them to step brazenly into dreams of power and influence. What the ads had women "dream" was that they could go ahead and be exhibitionistic, but not just about their bodies; about their capabilities. Clearly, a psychological chord was struck with this campaign. Women sent scores of unsolicited photos of themselves in endless scenes of "I dreamed I was... in my Maidenform bra." In terms of how the campaign portrayed women, it was a real set-breaker. The campaign put the company on the map and gave cultural approval to powerful wishes women certainly harbored but rarely advertised.

What was going on in the women who responded so positively   5
to the Maidenform campaign? This was pre-women's lib, when gender roles were still plainly spelled out: Females were Devoted Housewives and males were Preoccupied Breadwinners. Then along comes Maidenform with full-color photos of poised, clear-eyed, confident women unabashedly exposing their fantasies along with their chests. They're not in the least self-conscious. They're relaxed and composed. The campaign offered a sensational subconscious release for the duty-bound women of that period. It was enormously gratifying to identify with the courage of the Maidenform woman daring to show herself as fully developed to anyone interested in looking. Interested persons included parents, husbands, clergymen, and teachers. The fifties woman got to vicariously thumb her nose at all the right people. She got to break out of the socially appropriate straitjacket she'd willingly

donned—ostensibly for the good of family and cultural stability—and try on a new identity.

Psychologically, that's what dreams are about anyway. They're   6
what the unconscious produces, busily fulfilling wishes that our rational selves have deemed too outrageous to express in real life. There's something else about dreams. They show us images of ourselves that we've already accepted internally but that we haven't risked trying out yet.

I see the "I dreamed..." campaign as a kind of emotional road map   7
for the women's lib activities that came to the surface in the seventies. Phyllis is the only woman I know who actually, ceremoniously, *burned* a bra—and if I told her that she could thank Maidenform for helping her get a picture of herself as an independent person, she'd have been furious. But like it or not, the campaign set the stage for Phyllis and the other women of her generation. Women interacted with the ads in spite of themselves because they were already gearing up for the kind of real-life dreams they made happen when the feminist movement took hold.

The "I dreamed I took the cue in my Maidenform bra" ad is a   8
prime example of the kind of ad that could get to Phyllis, regardless of her conscious protests. When a woman already fantasizing about being less inhibited reads the line "I dreamed I took the cue...," she's already projecting herself into the picture. She's already hooked into seeing herself taking charge in what was traditionally a male-dominated situation. Not only does she take the cue stick, but she proceeds to handle it in a deft behind-the-back maneuver, all without losing a trace of her sultry femininity. The fantasy was powerful but safe. Although Phyllis would never admit it, it was perfectly congruent with women's needs at that time to stay feminine while getting strong. At the same time, the campaign helped women picture having power and control far outside the domestic domain.

Here was a landmark campaign that came at precisely the right   9
time to rivet women's attention. A piece of anatomical support empowered their dreams, permitting them to become "Maidenform women," in control of themselves, their circumstances, and their future. The Maidenform campaign was a strong one, largely because it reflected one advertiser's personal convictions. Bea Coleman, Maidenform's dynamic CEO, always admired her entrepreneurial mother, Ida Rosenthal, who founded the company with her physician-husband, William. Ida was a powerhouse. Mother and daughter both dared to dream big and do more. The "I dreamed..." concept was turned down by another lingerie company but embraced by Maidenform, perhaps because it was consistent with both Bea's and Ida's perceptions of women. Bea seemed to use her mother as a positive role model, and Ida may have unintentionally modeled aspects of herself through the endless permutations of the dream campaign. She persuaded women

not just to buy $100 million worth of underwear, but to see themselves as more capable people.

But the dream campaign hit social forces beyond its control—and turned with the tide of change. By the late sixties, the younger women who should have been buying Maidenform bras had begun to associate "I dreamed..." images with their mothers—and bras themselves with the constraints of traditional female roles and functions. When young women started ditching their bras along with their mothers' ideas as they reached for autonomy, the advertiser responded to the psychological climate by ditching the "I dreamed..." campaign. (Interestingly, Bea Coleman's own story runs a close parallel to the course of the campaign—this was just about the time that she shocked the male-dominated intimate-apparel industry in 1968 by taking over the company as president after her husband's death.)   10

What happened? Like Bea Coleman herself, women weren't just acknowledging their dreams of power, they were out there making them happen. The dream campaign symbolized the exciting but frustrated longings of the past. These were fantasy ads meant for the women they were trying to escape in their mothers and in themselves. The ads no longer had their initial freeing effect. Instead, they waved a red flag. Women like my old friend Phyllis were burning their bras, not dreaming about showing them off.   11

The Maidenform woman was mothballed for eleven years. When she reappeared, she launched the greatest controversy in bra history. In a reincarnation created by the Daniel & Charles advertising agency, she was still depicted doing active, even aggressive things, like commuting to work, reading *The Wall Street Journal*, going to the theater, or being a lawyer. She was daringly clad in her matching bra and panties. But now *there were men in the picture!* They appeared disinterested, oblivious to the delectable spectacle of "The Maidenform Woman. You never know where she'll turn up." The men were shot slightly out of focus. They were deeply absorbed, eyes discreetly everywhere else but you-know-where.   12

Here was a real twist, and the campaign ended up generating the kind of hot attention that left feminists seething and Maidenform sales soaring. Completely unanticipated! Maidenform didn't intend (as many advertisers do) to create a potentially explosive campaign. The agency just thought it had a great new approach for a new age. Advertiser and agency were equally surprised when the campaign got scorching reviews from angered members of women's movements. It also put Maidenform in the painful position of having to reevaluate the "success" of a campaign that, without question, was a success in terms of sales.   13

What ticked off women when Maidenform tried to turn them on? As the advertiser sees it, the campaign was inadvertently suggesting   14 that the Maidenform woman had achieved her enviable position, such as tiger tamer, strictly on the basis of her sexuality rather than her actual competence. The most noteworthy clunker, the one that finally deep-sixed the "You never know where she'll turn up" campaign, was the white-coated lady doctor piece. Everyone (male or female) who had ever worn a white coat—nurses, lab technicians, beauticians, the American Medical Association—bombarded Maidenform with calls and letters of protest.

As the mail indicated, there were some obvious reasons why this   15
campaign caused the uproar it did. With a female doctor exposing herself in a patient's hospital room, women's lib took a giant step backward. "Strip off the professional cover," these ads seemed to be saying, "and what you'll find is just another sex object."

At the time this campaign got started, however, I thought it   16
would have upset people for an entirely different unconscious reason. I showed the ad to some of my colleagues and just asked their opinions of it. Mark, a Ph.D. psychologist who's been practicing about as long as I have, came up with what turned out to be the consensus:

"That's going to be one angry lady!"   17

"Okay," I asked, "why?"   18

Mark pointed to the two samples I'd shown him—the woman in   19
the tiger cage and the doctor ad—and noted, "Look at the men in the pictures. Here's a woman with her clothes off, and they aren't paying any attention to her at all."

Mark and the others confirmed my own sense of the underlying   20
problem. The most insulting thing about the ads was not that the woman had exposed herself—even in a professional role. That might have been intellectually offensive—yes, it could be demeaning to women who were rising in their professions—but it didn't explain the strength of the emotional reactions women had to the ads.

What was really most offensive were the self-indulgent, narcis-   21
sistic posturings of the *men* in the picture. For the woman wearing a Maidenform bra, the experience was no longer a good dream. It was a bad dream. It is humiliating on the deepest levels, where our feelings of self-worth are most fragile, for any of us to expose ourselves at our most naked and vulnerable...and make no impact whatsoever. Women can easily identify with the Maidenform image in the ads, put themselves in her position and feel the angry confusion of someone who dolls herself up but still gets ignored.

There's more. Despite being pictured in the trappings of power,   22
this Maidenform woman ended up looking weak and vulnerable. Look at the contrast between the unblinking confidence and forward-thrusting body posture of the lady pool-shark and check out the demure, downcast glance and tight-kneed toe-tipped stance of the tiger tamer. Maidenform tried to tell women that it was listening, that it re-

spected their hard-won accomplishments, but it sent some subtle messages that undercut the communication. Women bought the bras but were left with images of themselves as "sweet nothings"—ironically the name of one of Maidenform's best-selling lines.

After four years of profitable (although sometimes uncomfort- 23
able) campaigning, Maidenform pulled back from its big-strong-pretty-young-things-turning-up-half-naked-in-front-of-self-involved-men approach. Romance, Maidenform perceived, was coming back. It was time to turn from power to syrup. Women were beginning to gag on advertisers' endless portraits of them as superhuman jugglers of kids, career, hubby, and housework.

Stripped of any power cues, the next Maidenform Woman was 24
one who "Dares to Dream." And what are her daring dreams about now? Sitting around wearing underwear and a wistful, vacant expression, she boldly fantasizes about going out on a date. Here is a woman with no pretensions of being anything other than the lovely, compliant, and ever-so-feminine creature her mother modeled in the fifties. She's straight out of the whistle-clean Harlequin Romance series, right down to the quasi-book-jacket logo in the corner. And like these little stories, Maidenform declares that its "Delectables" will "make your life as soft and smooth as your dreams."

At this stage of the game, all of us, women especially, have got- 25
ten to be fairly sophisticated cynics. We know that advertisers run various images of us to see whether they can stir a ripple of salesworthy responses. The "Dares to Dream" campaign reached out to women who had been feeling like miserable failures for fantasizing about guys. While everybody else was out there self-actualizing into steel-plated CEOs, Maidenform gave the "new romantics" permission to go ahead and dream the dreams of adolescent girls if they wanted.

Sales proved that many women wanted just that. Enough battling 26
against male indifference and resistance. Maidenform was tired of trying to tickle the fancies of feminists; the campaign regressed to the lowest-risk imagery for the masses—woman as a glowworm for love.

While it clearly qualifies as a fluff piece, Wyse Advertising's 27
"Dares to Dream" campaign is surpassed in regressiveness by its next series of "lifestyle" ads. "The Maidenform Woman. Today she's playful," whisks our heroine backward in time until she's a prepubescent who gets kind of emotional, but that's okay, because Maidenform will "fit" her "every move and mood" so she can stay just as cute as she is now. She's not even old enough to think about guys—"frisky as a kitten," "Today she's playful."

Now, no angry letters spewed forth on the heels of "Today she's 28
playful." Whom *did* this appeal to? Well, there's Liz. She's very bright and possesses an MBA, which she sometimes waves over a conversation like a silk scarf—something to be admired but not used. She's sur-

rounded by working friends, but she's filled her life with tennis and shopping and lunches. I like Liz, and it's over one of these lunches that she says to me, "I feel like having a temper tantrum."

I can't help thinking about how Liz creates herself in the image of   29
the "Today she's playful" ad—defining herself not in terms of what she's accomplishing, but by her moods. Does Liz know what she's doing? I don't think so. Did the agency know what it was doing? I don't think so. Both are just creating what they hope are pretty pictures.

Where do you go with this? Unfortunately, Liz will probably just   30
continue to be the subject of her moods. Maidenform wasn't quite so stuck—it changed agencies.

Following this purely saccharine retreat from Maidenform's   31
gutsy heritage, the sixty-five-year-old lingerie company set out in pursuit of the Holy Grail of advertising—a new image. After a grueling selection process, Levine, Huntley, Schmidt & Beaver won the account—and the opportunity to sweat its way toward a singularly brilliant advertising idea.

What Levine, Huntley, Schmidt & Beaver created, and what the   32
advertiser had the courage to appreciate, is a radical departure for lingerie ads.

No women, no product—just male movie-star-types like Omar   33
Sharif, Michael York, and Corbin Bernsen. The campaign has been noticed by the media, by competitors, and apparently by women, who've written comments to the advertiser like "I don't normally watch commercials—however, your Michael York commercial is fantastic! So much so I've switched to Maidenform." "Your commercial will be shown at our annual meeting...as a prime example of excellent advertising. It appeals to women as adults, not children...keep up the good work." And "This is the type of commercial that instills a need in me to purchase your product."

Now just what is driving these ads? What happens when women   34
see someone like Omar Sharif shot in deep shadows, murmuring, "Lingerie says a lot about a woman. I listen as often as possible"? There's an edge of the forbidden, the dangerous, to Sharif's exotic, rakish seductiveness that is a psychological turn-on to the dainty dreamers of Maidenform's recent past. They can rebel against the sweet-young-thing image, and run away (in their fantasies) with a sexy devil. No one has to take the modesty of a woman publicly displayed in her underwear. Sharif's appeal is also clearly to a mature market; he's not exactly the current heartthrob of younger women. So the advertiser moved away from charming vignettes of moody little models and is effectively hooking grown-ups with male bait.

With Corbin Bernsen of L.A. Law, the psychological lure isn't just   35
juicy evil. Here's a recognizably competent lady-killer, who enters the mysterious realm of a lingerie department and finds it "a little embar-

rassing. A little intimidating." What a gift to the female ego! If Maidenform can give women a way to embarrass and intimidate the likes of Mr. Bernsen, even "a little," it's not just underwear anymore—it's personal power.

The story of women's relationship with Maidenform's images reflects the complex interactions we all have with advertising. Advertisers have to communicate with as large a group of us consumers as possible, but in reality, the communication is always one-to-one. Maidenform's first "I dreamed I . . ." campaign was a success because the fantasy it promoted matched the underlying aspirations of enough individuals to make up a mass market. The advertiser gave a big push to a hoop already rolling out the kitchen door of convention, but things changed when the fantasy of sexual power turned to the reality of political and social power.   36

Then Maidenform held up concrete images of strong women to try to keep up with all the changes. The trouble came when the advertiser unwittingly introduced doubts and insecurities with its "You never know where she'll turn up" series and women felt a bit as though they'd bought a measure of male indifference along with Maidenform's dream images. The advertiser responded by attempting to soothe its buyers with pictures of romantic security. And finally it courts its market with its latest put-yourself-in-the-picture invitations offered by dashing male sex objects.   37

The promise is still largely romance. But a woman isn't just faced with relating to an image of herself; now, she's asked to relate to her idea of a man's image of her. For this to work for Maidenform, a woman has to have enough self-confidence to imagine that she is the object of these lingerie lovers' underwear fantasies. It would work for Liz, but not for Ann. Ann's a nice woman who feels fat and unattractive and prefers to undress in the dark. These ads make her feel worse because she *can't* imagine herself in them. She flunks the fantasy test.   38

Maidenform's current strategy works for one other important reason—it sidesteps the question faced by all lingerie advertisers: How can you show a woman in her underwear without making her look either like an idiot or a slut? Most answers bomb. . . .   39

Advertisers don't deliberately insult the people they are trying to seduce; they're basically family-oriented, intelligent, profit-minded sorts who often take really lousy pictures that they think are great shots of their subject. Even more interesting is that we may like how we look in a picture at one point in our lives, and later on feel disgusted or embarrassed by the same photo. What we identified with in an ad five years ago may be completely out of sync with who we are now. And we form these conclusions almost immediately—not from logical deliberation, but by unconsciously weighing all the subtle verbal and nonverbal cues that make up an advertising message. If some   40 of the pieces don't fit, don't ring true—if we don't like how we see ourselves now or how we'd like to see ourselves in the future—we can end up feeling insulted, misunderstood, or confused....

The trouble with the advertising mirror is that we never really   41
see ourselves reflected; we only see reflections of what advertisers want us to think their products will do for us. If the image of who we might be if we used the advertiser's product resonates with where we secretly, or not so secretly, wish we were—then there we are, consciously or unconsciously, measuring up to Madison Avenue. Sometimes that's not such a bad thing, but sometimes whatever insecurities we have get exacerbated by advertisers' image-making and by our own intense desires to make it—to win first prize in Madison Avenue's perpetual lookalike contest.

Examining the Text

1. Briefly summarize Moog's descriptions of how the various Maidenform advertising campaigns appealed to several decades of consumers. Why does she think some campaigns were more successful than others? Does her analyses seem reasonable?

2. As a psychologist, Moog incorporates several references in this essay to the psychological effects of advertisements on specific people. What point do you think she is making with these references to the psychological impact of advertising? Can you think of any psychological impact that specific ads have had on you?

3. According to Moog, what role do consumers play in influencing advertising campaigns? How is Moog's view of consumer influence different from the view of other writers in this chapter? How do you account for this difference?

For Group Discussion

Moog concludes her essay by suggesting that "If the image of who we might be if we used the advertiser's product resonates with where we secretly, or not so secretly, wish we were—then there we are, consciously or unconsciously, measuring up to Madison Avenue" (paragraph 41). In your group, identify ad campaigns that "resonate" with where contemporary college students wish they were. Identify some characteristics these advertisements share that make them particularly appealing.

Writing Suggestion

Underlying Moog's essay is the presumption that advertisements reflect and respond to the social context in which they exist, and that they change with the times. Follow Moog's model and trace the development of advertising campaigns for a specific product, looking through magazines from the 1950s, 1960s, 1970s, 1980s and 1990s and studying the changes in that product's ads. What conclusions can you draw about how the ads respond to and reflect broader social changes?

A Gentleman and a Consumer
Diane Barthel

Diane Barthel's essay, taken from her book Putting On Appearances: Gender and Advertising *(1988), focuses on what ads have to say about men. As Barthel points out, advertising, like the culture in general, proposes certain notions of what it means to be masculine and what it means to be feminine. Whereas the feminine is stereotypically passive, narcissistic, and noncompetitive, masculinity is presented in terms of action, competitiveness, and power.*

In examining a number of ads designed for men—ads for cars as well as ads for what are typically considered "women's products" like moisturizers, haircare products, and cologne—Barthel focuses on the appeal to "power, performance, and precision" in images in which the male is in charge, decisive, and desirable. Barthel also points out a number of "homilies" or short sermons that we often see in advertising directed to a male audience. Like women, male consumers can be influenced by advertisements to accept certain standards of masculinity to which they must measure up. The question, as Barthel and others in this chapter have suggested, is whether we want to accept these conventional standards of masculinity and femininity.

Before you read, think about what the term "masculinity" means to you. What qualities are associated with being "masculine"? And how many of these qualities are also associated with the term "feminine"?

There are no men's beauty and glamour magazines with circula-   1
tions even approaching those of the women's magazines we have been examining here. The very idea of men's beauty magazines may strike one as odd. In our society men traditionally were supposed to make the right appearance, to be well groomed and neatly tailored. What they were *not* supposed to do was to be overly concerned with their appearance, much less vain about their beauty. That was to be effeminate, and not a "real man." Male beauty was associated with homosexuals, and "real men" had to show how red-blooded they were by maintaining a certain distance from fashion.

Perhaps the best-known male fashion magazine is *GQ* founded   2
in 1957 and with a circulation of 446,000 in 1986. More recently, we have seen the launching of *YMF* and *Young Black Male*, which in 1987

still have few advertising pages. *M* magazine, founded in 1983, attracts an audience "a cut above" that of *GQ*.

Esquire magazine, more venerable (founded in 1933), is classified   3
as a general interest magazine. Although it does attract many women readers, many of the columns and features and much of the advertising are definitely directed toward attracting the attention of the male readers, who still make up the overwhelming majority of the readership.

As mentioned in the introduction, the highest circulations for   4
men's magazines are for magazines specializing either in sex (*Playboy*, circulation 4.1 million; *Penthouse*, circulation nearly 3.8 million; and *Hustler*, circulation 1.5 million) or sports (*Sports Illustrated*, circulation 2.7 million). That these magazines share an emphasis on power—either power over women or over other men on the playing field—should not surprise. In fact, sociologist John Gagnon would argue that sex and sports now represent the major fields in which the male role, as defined by power, is played out, with physical power in work, and even in warfare, less important than it was before industrialization and technological advance.

If we are looking for comparative evidence as to how advertise-   5
ments define gender roles for men and women, we should not then see the male role as defined primarily through beauty and fashion. This seems an obvious point, but it is important to emphasize how different cultural attitudes toward both the social person and the physical body shape the gender roles of men and women. These cultural attitudes are changing, and advertisements are helping to legitimate the use of beauty products and an interest in fashion for men, as we shall see. As advertisements directed toward women are beginning to use male imagery, so too advertisements for men occasionally use imagery resembling that found in advertisements directed toward women. We are speaking of two *modes*, then. As Baudrillard writes, these modes "do not result from the differentiated nature of the two sexes, but from the differential logic of the system. The relationship of the Masculine and the Feminine to real men and women is relatively arbitrary." Increasingly today, men and women use both modes. The two great terms of opposition (Masculine and Feminine) still, however, structure the forms that consumption takes; they provide identities for products and consumers.

Baudrillard agrees that the feminine model encourages a woman   6
to please herself, to encourage a certain complacency and even narcissistic solicitude. But by pleasing herself, it is understood that she will also please others, and that she will be chosen. "She never enters into direct competition.... If she is beautiful, that is to say, if this woman is a woman, she will be chosen. If the man is a man, he will choose his woman as he would other objects/signs (HIS car, HIS woman, HIS eau de toilette).

Whereas the feminine model is based on passivity, complacency,   7
and narcissism, the masculine model is based on exactingness and choice.

> All of masculine advertising insists on rule, on choice, in terms of rigor
> and inflexible minutiae. He does not neglect a detail. . . . It is not a ques-
> tion of just letting things go, or of taking pleasure in something, but
> rather of distinguishing himself. To know how to choose, and not to fail
> at it, is here the equivalent of the military and puritanical virtues: intran-
> sigence, decision, "virtus."

This masculine model, these masculine virtues, are best reflected   8
in the many car advertisements. There, the keywords are masculine
terms: *power, performance, precision.* Sometimes the car is a woman, responding to the touch and will of her male driver, after attracting him
with her sexy body. "Pure shape, pure power, pure Z. It turns you
on." But, as the juxtaposition of shape and power in this advertisement suggest, the car is not simply other; it is also an extension of the
owner. As he turns it on, he turns himself on. Its power is his power;
through it, he will be able to overpower other men and impress and
seduce women.

> How well does it perform?
> How well can you drive? (Merkur XR4Ti)

> The 1987 Celica GT-S has the sweeping lines and aggressive stance that
> promise performance. And Celica keeps its word.

> Renault GTA:
> Zero to sixty to zero in 13.9 sec.

> It's the result of a performance philosophy where acceleration and brak-
> ing are equally important.
>   There's a new Renault sports sedan called GTA. Under its slick
> monochromatic skin is a road car with a total performance attitude. . . .
> It's our hot new pocket rocket.

In this last example, the car, like the driver, has a total perfor-   9
mance attitude. That is what works. The slick monochromatic skin,
like the Bond Street suit, makes a good first impression. But car, like
owner, must have what it takes, must be able to go the distance faster
and better than the competition. This point is explicitly made in advertisements in which the car becomes a means through which this masculine competition at work is extended in leisure. Some refer directly
to the manly sport of auto-racing: "The Mitsubishi Starion ESI-R. Patiently crafted to ignite your imagination. Leaving little else to say ex-

cept...gentlemen, start your engines." Others refer to competition in the business world: "To move ahead fast in this world, you've got to have connections. The totally new Cordolia FX 16 GT-S has the right ones." Or in life in general. "It doesn't take any [Japanese characters] from anyone. It won't stand for any guff from 300ZX. Or RX-7. Introducing Conquest Tsi, the new turbo sport coupe designed and built by Mitsubishi in Japan." Or Ferrari, which says simply, "We are the competition." In this competition between products, the owners become almost superfluous. But the advertisements, of course, suggest that the qualities of the car will reflect the qualities of the owner, as opposed to the purely abstract, a personal quality of money needed for purchase. Thus, like the would-be owner, the BMW also demonstrates a "relentless refusal to compromise." It is for "those who thrive on a maximum daily requirement of high performance." While the BMW has the business attitude of the old school ("aggression has never been expressed with such dignity"), a Beretta suggests what it takes to survive today in the shark-infested waters of Wall Street. In a glossy three-page cover foldout, a photograph of a shark's fin cutting through indigo waters is accompanied by the legend "Discover a new species from today's Chevrolet." The following two pages show a sleek black Beretta similarly cutting through water and, presumably, through the competition: "Not just a new car, but a new species...with a natural instinct for the road...Aggressive stance. And a bold tail lamp. See it on the road and you won't soon forget. Drive it, and you never will."

And as with men, so with cars. "Power corrupts. Absolute power 10 corrupts; absolutely" (Maserati). Not having the money to pay for a Maserati, to corrupt and be corrupted, is a source of embarrassment. Advertisements reassure the consumer that he need not lose face in this manly battle. Hyundai promises, "It's affordable. (But you'd never know it.)"

> On first impression, the new Hyundai Excel GLS Sedan might seem a trifle beyond most people's means. But that's entirely by design. Sleek European design, to be exact.

Many advertisements suggest sexual pleasure and escape, as in 11 "Pure shape, pure power, pure Z. It turns you on." Or "The all-new Chrysler Le Baron. Beauty...with a passion for driving." The Le Baron may initially suggest a beautiful female, with its "image of arresting beauty" and its passion "to drive. And drive it does!" But it *is* "Le Baron," not "La Baronness." And the advertisement continues to emphasize how it *attacks* [emphasis mine] the road with a high torque, 2.5 liter fuel-injected engine. And its turbo option can blur the surface of any passing lane." Thus the object of the pleasure hardly has to be female if it is beautiful or sleek. The car is an extension of the male that conquers and tames the (female) road: "Positive-response suspension will calm the most demanding roads." The car becomes the ultimate lover when, like the Honda Prelude, it promises to combine power, "muscle," with finesse. Automobile advertisements thus play with androgyny and sexuality; the pleasure is in the union and confusion of form and movement, sex and speed. As in any sexual union, there is ultimately a merging of identities, rather than rigid maintenance of their separation. Polymorphous perverse? Perhaps. But it sells.

Though power, performance, precision as a complex of traits find   12
their strongest emphasis in automobile advertisements, they also appear as selling points for products as diverse as shoes, stereos, and sunglasses. The car performs on the road, the driver performs for women, even in the parking lot, as Michelin suggests in its two-page spread showing a male from waist down resting on his car and chatting up a curvaceous female: "It performs great. And looks great. So, it not only stands out on the road. But in the parking lot. Which is one more place you're likely to discover how beautifully it can handle the curves" (!).

As media analyst Todd Gitlin points out, most of the drivers   13
shown in advertisements are young white males, loners who become empowered by the car that makes possible their escape from the everyday. Gitlin stresses the advertisements' "emphasis on surface, the blankness of the protagonist; his striving toward self-sufficiency, to the point of displacement from the recognizable world." Even the Chrysler advertisements that coopt Bruce Springsteen's "Born in the USA" for their "Born in America" campaign lose in the process the original political message, "ripping off Springsteen's angry anthem, smoothing it into a Chamber of Commerce ditty as shots of just plain productive-looking folks, black and white...whiz by in a montage-made community." As Gitlin comments, "None of Springsteen's losers need apply—or rather, if only they would roll up their sleeves and see what good company they're in, they wouldn't feel like losers any longer."

This is a world of patriarchal order in which the individual male   14
can and must challenge the father. He achieves identity by breaking loose of the structure and breaking free of the pack. In the process he recreates the order and reaffirms the myth of masculine independence. Above all, he demonstrates that he knows what he wants; he is critical, demanding, and free from the constraints of others. What he definitely does not want, and goes to some measure to avoid, is to appear less than masculine, in any way weak, frilly, feminine.

AVOIDING THE FEMININE

Advertisers trying to develop male markets for products previ-   15
ously associated primarily with women must overcome the taboo that only women wear moisturizer, face cream, hair spray, or perfume.

They do this by overt reference to masculine symbols, language, and imagery, and sometimes by confronting the problem head-on.

There is not so much of a problem in selling products to counter-   16 act balding—that traditionally has been recognized as a male problem (a bald woman is a sexual joke that is not particularly amusing to the elderly). But other hair products are another story, as the March 1987 *GQ* cover asks, "Are you man enough for mousse?" So the advertise-ments must make their products seem manly, as with S-Curl's "wave and curl kit" offering "The Manly Look" on its manly model dressed in business suit and carrying a hard hat (a nifty social class compro-mise), and as in college basketball sportscaster Al McGuire's testimo-nial for Consort hair spray:

> "Years ago, if someone had said to me, 'Hey Al, do you use hair spray?' I would have said, 'No way, baby!'"
> "That was before I tried Consort Pump."
> "Consort adds extra control to my hair without looking stiff or phony. Control that lasts clean into overtime and post-game interviews…"
> Grooming Gear for Real Guys. *Consort.*

Beside such "grooming gear" as perms and hair sprays, Real   17 Guys use "skin supplies" and "shaving resources." They adopt a "sur-vival strategy" to fight balding, and the "Fila philosophy"—"products with a singular purpose: performance"—for effective "bodycare." If they wear scent, it smells of anything *but* flowers: musk, woods, spices, citrus, and surf are all acceptable. And the names must be manly, whether symbolizing physical power ("Brut") or financial power ("Giorgio VIP Special Reserve," "The Baron. A distinctive fra-grance for men," "Halston—For the privileged few").

As power/precision/performance runs as a theme throughout   18 advertising to men, so too do references to the business world. Cars, as we have seen, promise to share their owner's professional attitude and aggressive drive to beat out the competition. Other products similarly reflect the centrality of business competition to the male gender role. And at the center of this competition itself, the business suit.

> At the onset of your business day, you choose the suit or sportcoat that will position you front and center…
> The Right Suit can't guarantee he'll see it your way. The wrong suit could mean not seeing him at all.

Along with the Right Suit, the right shirt, "You want it every time   19 you reach across the conference table, or trade on the floor, or just move about. You want a shirt that truly fits, that is long enough to stay put through the most active day, even for the taller gentleman." The businessman chooses the right cologne—Grey Flannel, or perhaps Quorum. He wears a Gucci "timepiece" as he conducts business on a cordless telephone from his poolside—or prefers the "dignity in styling" promised by Raymond Weil watches, "a beautiful way to dress for success."

Men's products connect status and success; the right products 20 show that you have the right stuff, that you're one of them. In the 1950s C. Wright Mills described what it took to get ahead, to become part of the "power elite":

> The fit survive, and fitness means, not formal competence...but conformity with the criteria of those who have already succeeded. To be compatible with the top men is to act like them, to look like them, to think like them: to be of and for them—or at least to display oneself to them in such a way as to create that impression. This, in fact, is what is meant by "creating"—a well-chosen word—"a good impression." This is what is meant—and nothing else—by being a "sound man," as sound as a dollar.

Today, having what it takes includes knowing "the difference be- 21 tween dressed, and well dressed" (Bally shoes). It is knowing that "what you carry says as much about you as what you put inside it" (Hartmann luggage). It is knowing enough to imitate Doug Fout, "member of one of the foremost equestrian families in the country."

> Because of our adherence to quality and the natural shoulder tradition, Southwick clothing was adopted by the Fout family years ago. Clearly, they have as much appreciation for good lines in a jacket as they do in a thoroughbred.

There it is, old money. There is no substitute for it, really, in busi- 22 ness or in advertising, where appeals to tradition form one of the mainstays guaranteeing men that their choices are not overly fashionable or feminine, not working class or cheap, but, rather, correct, in good form, above criticism. If, when, they achieve this status of gentlemanly perfection, then, the advertisement suggests, they may be invited to join the club.

When only the best of associations will do

Recognizing style as the requisite for membership, discerning men prefer the natural shoulder styling of Racquet Club. Meticulously tailored in pure wool, each suit and sportcoat is the ultimate expression of the clubman's classic good taste.

Ralph Lauren has his Polo University Club, and Rolex picks up on 23 the polo theme by sponsoring the Rolex Gold Cup held at the Palm Beach Polo and Country Club, where sixteen teams and sixty-four players competed for "the pure honor of winning, the true glory of victory":

It has added new lustre to a game so ancient, its history is lost in legend. Tamerlane is said to have been its patriarch. Darius's Persian cavalry, we're told, played it. It was the national sport of 16th-century India, Egypt, China, and Japan. The British rediscovered and named it in 1857.

The linking of polo and Rolex is uniquely appropriate. Both sponsor and sport personify rugged grace. Each is an arbiter of the art of thinking.

In the spring of 1987, there was another interesting club event— 24 or nonevent. The prestigious New York University Club was ordered to open its doors to women. This brought the expected protests about freedom of association—and of sanctuary. For that has been one of the points of the men's club. It wasn't open to women. Members knew women had their place, and everyone knew it was not there. In the advertisements, as in the world of reality, there is a place for women in men's lives, one that revolves around:

SEX AND SEDUCTION

As suggested earlier, the growing fascination with appearances, 25 encouraged by advertising, has led to a "feminization" of culture. We are all put in the classic role of the female: maniputable, submissive, seeing ourselves as objects. This "feminization of sexuality" is clearly seen in men's advertisements, where many of the promises made to women are now made to men. If women's advertisements cry, "Buy (this product) and he will notice you," men's advertisements similarly promise that female attention will follow immediately upon purchase, or shortly thereafter. "They can't stay away from Mr. J." "Master the Art of Attracting Attention." She says, "He's wearing my favorite Corbin again." Much as in the advertisements directed at women, the advertisements of men's products promise that they will do the talking for you. "For the look that says come closer." "All the French you'll ever need to know."

Although many advertisements show an admiring and/or de- 26 pendent female, others depict women in a more active role. "I love him—but life in the fast lane starts at 6 A.M.," says the attractive blonde trying on her jogging shoes, with the "him" in question very handsome and very asleep on the bed in the background. (Does this mean he's in the slow lane?) In another, the man slouches silhouetted against a wall; the woman leans aggressively toward him. He: "Do you always serve Tia Maria...or am I special? She: "Darling, if you weren't special...you wouldn't be here."

The masculine role of always being in charge is a tough one. The 27 blunt new honesty about sexually transmitted diseases such as AIDS appears in men's magazines as in women's, in the same "I enjoy sex, but

I'm not ready to die for it" condom advertisement. But this new fear is accompanied by old fears of sexual embarrassment and/or rejection. The cartoon shows a man cringing with embarrassment in a pharmacy as the pharmacist yells out, "Hey, there's a guy here wants some information on Trojans." ("Most men would like to know more about Trojan brand condoms. But they're seriously afraid of suffering a spectacular and terminal attack of embarrassment right in the middle of a well-lighted drugstore.") Compared with such agony and responsibility, advertisements promising that women will *want* whatever is on offer, and will even meet the male halfway, must come as blessed relief. Men can finally relax, leaving the courting to the product and seduction to the beguiled woman, which, surely, must seem nice for a change.

MASCULINE HOMILIES

A homily is a short sermon, discourse, or informal lecture, often   28
on a moral topic and suggesting a course of conduct. Some of the most intriguing advertisements offer just that, short statements and bits of advice on what masculinity is and on how real men should conduct themselves. As with many short sermons, many of the advertising homilies have a self-congratulatory air about them; after all, you do not want the consumer to feel bad about himself.

What is it, then, to be a man? It is to be *independent*. "There are   29
some things a man will not relinquish." Among them, says the advertisement, his Tretorn tennis shoes.

It is to *savor freedom*. "Dress easy, get away from it all and let Tom   30
Sawyer paint the fence," advises Alexander Julian, the men's designer. "Because man was meant to fly, we gave him wings" (even if only on his sunglasses).

It is to live a life of *adventure*. KL Homme cologne is "for the man   31
who lives on the edge." Prudential Life Insurance preaches, "If you can dream it, you can do it." New Man sportswear tells the reader, "Life is more adventurous when you feel like a New Man."

It is to *keep one's cool*. "J&B Scotch. A few individuals know how   32
to keep their heads, even when their necks are on the line."

And it is to stay one step *ahead of the competition*. "Altec Lansing.   33
Hear what others only imagine." Alexander Julian again: "Dress up a bit when you dress down. They'll think you know something they don't."

What is it, then, to be a woman? It is to be *dependent*. "A woman   34
needs a man," reads the copy in the Rigolletto advertisement showing a young man changing a tire for a grateful young woman.

The American cowboy as cultural model was not supposed to   35
care for or about appearances. He was what he was, hard-working

straightforward, and honest. He was authentic. Men who cared "too much" about how they looked did not fit this model; the dandy was effete, a European invention, insufficient in masculinity and not red-blooded enough to be a real American. The other cultural model, imported from England, was the gentleman. A gentleman did care about his appearance, in the proper measure and manifestation, attention to tailoring and to quality, understatement rather than exaggeration.

From the gray flannel suit of the 1950s to the "power look" of the   36
1980s, clothes made the man fit in with his company's image. Sex appeal and corporate correctness merged in a look that spelled success, that exuded confidence.

Whether or not a man presumed to care about his appearance, he   37
did care about having "the right stuff," as Tom Wolfe and *Esquire* call it, or "men's toys," as in a recent special issue of *M* magazine. Cars, motorcycles, stereos, sports equipment: these are part of the masculine appearance. They allow the man to demonstrate his taste, his special knowledge, his affluence: to extend his control. He can be and is demanding, for only the best will do.

He also wants to be loved, but he does not want to appear needy.   38
Advertisements suggest the magic ability of products ranging from cars to hair creams to attract female attention. With the right products a man can have it all, with no strings attached: no boring marital ties, hefty mortgages, corporate compromises.

According to sociologist Barbara Ehrenreich, *Playboy* magazine   39
did much to legitimate this image of male freedom. The old male ethos, up to the postwar period, required exchanging bachelor irresponsibility for married responsibility, which also symbolized entrance into social adulthood. The perennial bachelor, with his flashy cars and interchangeable women, was the object of both envy and derision; he had fun, but and because he was not fully grown up. There was something frivolous in his lack of purpose and application.

This old ethos has lost much of its legitimacy. Today's male can,   40
as Baudrillard suggests, operate in both modes: the feminine mode of indulging oneself and being indulged and the masculine mode of exigency and competition. With the right look and the right stuff, he can feel confident and manly in boardroom or suburban backyard. Consumer society thus invites both men and women to live in a world of appearances and to devote ever more attention to them.

Examining the Text
1. In your own words, restate Baudrillard's definition of the masculine and feminine modes in our culture (paragraphs 5–8). What do you

think of Barthel's conclusion that men today can operate in both modes? Do you think that women can also operate in both modes?

2. According to Barthel, what strategies do advertisers use in their efforts to sell men products that are associated primarily with women? Do you see evidence of this in contemporary advertising?

3. What do you think is the significance of the title of this essay? How, according to Barthel, is being a gentleman related to being a consumer?

For Group Discussion

Barthel's essay was written in 1988. Consider some of the more recent images of men in advertising—in ads for Obsession cologne or Guess clothing, for example. What new trends or strategies do they indicate in advertising to male consumers? What do you think lies behind these trends?

Writing Suggestion

Go through the ads in a men's magazine like *Esquire* or *Sports Illustrated*. Drawing on the list of "masculine homilies" (28–33) presented in Barthel's essay, write an explanation of ways in which the ads use these homilies. Create your own list of "short sermons" that the ads deliver to their male audience.

Getting Dirty

Mark Crispin Miller

Mark Crispin Miller's essay comes from his 1988 book Boxed In, *a study of the meaning and influence of television and advertising in contemporary American culture. In "Getting Dirty," Miller analyzes a television ad for Shield soap, paying close attention to seemingly neutral details and finding meanings that may surprise us. For instance, Miller suggests that the ad woos female viewers with a "fantasy of dominance," offering "a subtle and meticulous endorsement of castration," playing on certain "guilts and insecurities" of men and women. The way the commercial reverses stereotypical gender roles makes it an interesting and complex example of the ways images of men and women are used in advertising.*

To those who think he is reading too much into the ad, Miller counters that it is through the details, often unnoticed by viewers, that ads convey some of their most powerful—and questionable—messages.

*In this essay Miller is analytical but also is trying to persuade readers that his analysis of the advertisement is correct. **As you read,** note the strategies*

that Miller uses to construct a persuasive, well-supported analysis, and note as
well those moments where Miller does not persuade you of his interpretation.

We are outside a house, looking in the window, and this is what   1
we see: a young man, apparently nude and half-crazed with anxiety,
lunging toward the glass. "Gail!" he screams, as he throws the window open and leans outside, over a flowerbox full of geraniums: "The
most important shower of my life, and you switch deodorant soap!"
He is, we now see, only half-naked, wearing a towel around his waist;
and he shakes a packaged bar of soap—"Shield"—in one accusing
hand. Gail, wearing a blue man-tailored shirt, stands outside, below
the window, clipping a hedge. She handles this reproach with an ease
that suggests years of contempt. "Shield is better," she explains patiently, in a voice somewhat deeper than her husband's. "It's extra
strength." (Close-up of the package in the husband's hand. Gail's
efficient finger gliding along beneath the legend. THE EXTRA
STRENGTH DEODORANT SOAP.) "Yeah," whimpers Mr. Gail, "but
my first call on J.J. Siss [sic], the company's *toughest customer,* and *now*
this!" Gail nods with broad mock-sympathy, and stands firm: "Shield
fights odor better, so you'll feel *cleaner,"* she assures her husband, who
darts away with a jerk of panic, as Gail rolls her eyes heavenward and
gently shakes her head, as if to say, "What a half-wit!"

Cut to our hero, as he takes his important shower. No longer   2
frantic, he now grins down at himself, apparently delighted to be
caked with Shield, which, in its detergent state, has the consistency of
wet cement. He then goes out of focus, as if glimpsed through a
shower door. "Clinical tests prove," proclaims an eager baritone.
"Shield fights odor better than the *leading* deodorant soap!" A bar of
Shield (green) and a bar of that other soap (yellow) zip up the screen
with a festive toot, forming a sort of graph which demonstrates that
Shield does, indeed, "fight odor better, so you'll feel *cleaner!"*

This particular contest having been settled, we return to the   3
major one, which has yet to be resolved. Our hero reappears, almost
transformed: calmed down, dressed up, his voice at least an octave
lower. "I *do* feel cleaner!" he announces cheerily, leaning into the doorway of a room where Gail is arranging flowers. She pretends to be ecstatic at this news, and he comes toward her, setting himself up for a
profound humiliation by putting on a playful air of suave command.
Adjusting his tie like a real man of the world, he saunters over to his
wife and her flower bowl, where he plucks a dainty purple flower and
lifts it to his lapel: "And," he boasts throughout all this, trying to make
his voice sound even deeper, "with old J.J.'s business and my brains—"

"—you'll...*clean up again?*" Gail asks with suggestive irony, subverting his authoritative pose by leaning against him, draping one hand over his shoulder to dangle a big yellow daisy down his chest. Taken aback, he shoots her a distrustful look, and she titters at him.

Finally, the word SHIELD appears in extreme close-up and the   4
camera pulls back, showing two bars of the soap, one packaged and one not, on display amidst an array of steely bubbles. "Shield fights odor better, so you'll feel *cleaner!*" the baritone reminds us, and then our hero's face appears once more, in a little square over the unpackaged bar of soap: "I feel *cleaner* than *ever before!*" he insists, sounding faintly unconvinced.

Is all this as stupid as it seems at first? Or is there, just beneath   5
the surface of this moronic narrative, some noteworthy design, intended to appeal to (and to worsen) some of the anxieties of modern life? A serious look at this particular trifle might lead us to some strange discoveries.

We are struck, first of all, by the commercial's pseudofeminism, an   6
advertising ploy with a long history, and one ubiquitous on television nowadays. Although the whole subject deserves more extended treatment, this commercial offers us an especially rich example of the strategy. Typically, it woos its female viewers—i.e., those who choose the soap in most households—with a fantasy of dominance; and it does so by inverting the actualities of woman's lot through a number of imperceptible details. For instance, in this marriage it is the wife, and not the husband, who gets to keep her name; and Gail's name, moreover, is a potent one, because of its brevity and its homonymic connotation. (If this housewife were more delicately named, called "Lillian" or "Cecilia," it would lessen her illusory strength.) She is also equipped in more noticeable ways; she's the one who wears the button-down shirt in this family, she's the one who's competent both outdoors and in the house, and it is she, and only she, who wields the tool.

These visual details imply that Gail is quite a powerful housewife,   7
whereas her nameless mate is a figure of embarrassing impotence. This "man," in fact, is actually Gail's *wife;* he is utterly feminized, striking a posture and displaying attributes which men have long deplored in women. In other words, this commercial, which apparently takes the woman's side, is really the expression (and reflection) of misogyny. Gail's husband is dependent and hysterical, entirely without that self-possession which we expect from solid, manly types, like Gail. This is partly the result of his demeanor: in the opening scene, his voice sometimes cracks ludicrously, and he otherwise betrays the shrill desperation of a man who can't remember where he left his scrotum. The comic effect of this frenzy, moreover, is subtly enhanced by the mise-en-scène, which puts the man in a conventionally feminine position—in disha-

bille, looking down from a window. Thus we infer that he is sheltered and housebound, a modern Juliet calling for his/her Romeo; or—more appropriately—the image suggests a scene in some suburban red-light district, presenting this husband as an item on display, like the flowers just below his stomach, available for anyone's enjoyment, at a certain price. Although in one way contradictory, these implications are actually quite congruous, for they both serve to emasculate the husband, so that the wife might take his place, or play his part.

Such details, some might argue, need not have been the conscious 8 work of this commercial's makers. The authors, that is, might have worked by instinct rather than design, and so would have been no more aware of their work's psychosocial import than we ourselves: they just wanted to make the guy look like a wimp, merely for the purposes of domestic comedy. While such an argument certainly does apply to many ads, in this case it is unlikely. Advertising agencies do plenty of research, by which we can assume that they don't select their tactics arbitrarily. They take pains to analyze the culture which they help to sicken, and then, with much wit and cynicism, use their insights in devising their small dramas. This commercial is a subtle and meticulous endorsement of castration, meant to play on certain widespread guilts and insecurities; and all we need to do to demonstrate this fact is to subject the two main scenes to the kind of visual analysis which commercials, so brief and broad, tend to resist (understandably). The ad's visual implications are too carefully achieved to have been merely accidental or unconscious.

The crucial object in the opening shot is that flower box with its 9 bright geraniums, which is placed directly in front of the husband's groin. This clever stroke of composition has the immediate effect of equating our hero's manhood with a bunch of flowers. This is an exquisitely perverse suggestion, rather like using a cigar to represent the Eternal Feminine: flowers are frail, sweet, and largely ornamental, hardly an appropriate phallic symbol, but (of course) a venerable symbol of *maidenhood*. The geraniums stand, then, not for the husband's virility, but for its absence.

More than a clever instance of inversion, furthermore, these 10 phallic blossoms tell us something odd about this marital relationship. As Gail, clippers in hand, turns from the hedge to calm her agitated man, she appears entirely capable of calming him quite drastically, if she hasn't done so already (which might explain his hairless chest and high-pitched voice). She has the power, that is, to take away whatever slender potency he may possess, and uses the power repeatedly, trimming her husband (we infer) as diligently as she prunes her foliage. And, as she can snip his manhood, so too can she restore it, which is what the second scene implies. Now the flower bowl has replaced the flower box as the visual crux, dominating the bottom center of the frame with a crowd of blooms. As the husband, cleaned and dressed, comes to stand beside his wife, straining to affect a new authority, the flower bowl too appears directly at his lower center; so that Gail, briskly adding flowers to the bouquet, appears to be replenishing his vacant groin with extra stalks. He has a lot to thank her for, it seems: she is his helpmate, confidante, adviser, she keeps his house and grounds in order, and she is clearly the custodian of the family jewels.

Of course, her restoration of his potency cannot be complete, or   11
he might shatter her mastery by growing a bit too masterful himself. He could start choosing his own soap, or take her shears away, or— worst of all—walk out for good. Therefore, she punctures his momentary confidence by taunting him with that big limp daisy, countering his lordly gesture with the boutonniere by flaunting that symbol of his floral status. He can put on whatever airs he likes, but she still has his fragile vigor firmly in her hand.

Now what, precisely, motivates this sexless battle of the sexes?   12
That is, what really underlies this tense and hateful marriage, making the man so weak, the woman so contemptuously helpful? The script, seemingly nothing more than a series of inanities, contains the answer to these questions, conveying, as it does, a concern with cleanliness that amounts to an obsession: "Shield fights odor better, so you'll feel cleaner!" "I *do* feel cleaner!" "Shield fights odor better, so you'll feel *cleaner!*" "I feel *cleaner* than *ever before!*" Indeed, the commercial emphasizes the feeling of cleanliness even more pointedly than the name of the product, implying, by its very insistence, a feeling of dirtiness, an apprehension of deep filth.

And yet there is not a trace of dirt in the vivid world of this com-   13
mercial. Unlike many ads for other soaps, this one shows no sloppy children, no sweatsoaked workingmen with blackened hands, not even a bleary housewife in need of her morning shower. We never even glimpse the ground in Gail's world, nor is her husband even faintly smudged. In fact, the filth which Shield supposedly "fights" is not physical but psychological besmirchment: Gail's husband feels soiled because of what he has to do for a living, in order to keep Gail in that nice big house, happily supplied with shirts and shears

"My first call on J.J. Siss, the company's *toughest customer*, and   14
now *this!*" The man's anxiety is yet another feminizing trait, for it is generally women, and not men, who are consumed by doubts about the sweetness of their bodies, which must never be offensive to the guys who run the world. (This real anxiety is itself aggravated by commercials.) Gail's husband must play the female to the mighty J.J. Siss, a name whose oxymoronic character implies perversion: "J.J." is a stereotypic nickname for the potent boss, while "Sis" is a term of endearment, short for "sister" (and perhaps implying "sissy," too, in this case). Gail's husband must do his boyish best to please the voracious

J.J. Siss, just as a prostitute must satisfy a demanding trick, or "tough customer." It is therefore perfectly fitting that this employee refer to the encounter, not as a "meeting" or "appointment," but as a "call"; and his demeaning posture in the window—half dressed and bent over—conveys, we now see, a definitive implication.

Gail's job as the "understanding wife" is not to rescue her husband   15
from these sordid obligations, but to help him meet them successfully. She may seem coolly self-sufficient, but she actually depends on her husband's attractiveness, just as a pimp relies on the charm of his whore. And, also like a pimp, she has to keep her girl in line with occasional reminders of who's boss. When her husband starts getting uppity *après la douche,* she jars him from the very self-assurance which she had helped him to discover, piercing that "shield" which was her gift.

"And, with old J.J.'s business and my brains—" "—you'll...*clean*   16
up again?" He means, of course, that he'll work fiscal wonders with old J.J.'s account, but his fragmentary boast contains a deeper significance, upon which Gail plays with sadistic cleverness. "Old J.J.'s business and my brains" implies a feminine self-description, since it suggests a variation on the old commonplace of "brains vs. brawn": J.J.'s money, in the world of this commercial (as in ours), amounts to brute strength, which the flexible husband intends to complement with his mother wit. Gail's retort broadens this unconscious hint of homosexuality: "—you'll...*clean up again?*" Given the monetary nature of her husband's truncated remark, the retort must mean primarily, "You'll make a lot of money." If this were all it meant, however, it would not be a joke, nor would the husband find it so upsetting. Moreover, we have no evidence that Gail's husband ever "cleaned up"—i.e., made a sudden fortune—in the past. Rather, the ad's milieu and *dramatis personae* suggest upward mobility, gradual savings and a yearly raise, rather than one prior killing. What Gail is referring to, in fact, with the "again," is her husband's shower: she implies that what he'll have to do, after his "call" on J.J. Siss, is, quite literally, wash himself off. Like any other tidy hooker, this man will have to clean up after taking on a tough customer, so that he might be ready to take on someone else.

These suggestions of pederasty are intended, not as a literal char-   17
acterization of the husband's job, but as a metaphor for what it takes to get ahead: Gail's husband, like most white-collar workers, must debase himself to make a good impression, toadying to his superiors, offering himself, body and soul, to the corporation. Maybe, therefore, it isn't really Gail who has neutered him; it may be his way of life that has wrought the ugly change. How, then, are women represented here? The commercial does deliberately appeal to women, offering them a sad fantasy of control; but it also, perhaps inadvertently, illuminates the unhappiness which makes that fantasy attractive.

The husband's status, it would seem, should make Gail happy,   18
since it makes her physically comfortable, and yet Gail can't help
loathing her husband for the degradations which she helps him
undergo. For her part of the bargain is, ultimately, no less painful than
his. She has to do more than put up with him; she has to prepare him
for his world of affairs, and then must help him to conceal the shame.
Of course, it's all quite hopeless. She clearly despises the man whom
she would bolster; and the thing which she provides to help him "feel
cleaner than ever before" is precisely what has helped him do the job
that's always made him feel so dirty. "A little water clears us of this
deed" is her promise, which is false, for she is just as soiled as her
doomed husband, however fresh and well-ironed she may look.

Of course, the ad not only illuminates this mess, but helps per-   19
petuate it, by obliquely gratifying the guilts, terrors, and resentments
that underlie it and arise from it. The strategy is not meant to be noticed, but works through the apparent comedy, which must therefore
be studied carefully, not passively received. Thus, thirty seconds of ingenious advertising, which we can barely stand to watch, tell us something more than we might want to know about the souls of men and
women under corporate capitalism.

AFTERWORD

Advertising Age came back at this essay with an edifying two-   1
pronged put-down. In the issue for 7 June 1982, Fred Danzig (now the
magazine's editor) devoted his weekly column to the Shield analysis:
"The professor prunes a television trifle," ran the headline. After a
genial paraphrase of my argument, Danzig reported a few of the
things I'd told him in a telephone conversation, and then finally got
down to the necessary business of dismissive cluckling: "[Miller's]
confession that he had watched the Shield spot more than 15 times
quickly enabled me to diagnose his problem: Self-inflicted acute soap
storyboard sickness. This condition inevitably leads to a mind spasm,
to hallucination." The column featured the ad's crucial frames, over a
caption quoting an unnamed "Lever executive": "We can hardly wait
for Mr. Miller to get his hands on the Old Testament. His comments
merit no comment from us; the Shield commercial speaks for itself."

Leaving aside (with difficulty) that naive crack about the Bible, I   2
point here to the exemplary suppressiveness of his seeming "trifle" in
Advertising Age. Indeed, "the Shield commercial speaks for itself," but
the guardians of the spectacle try to talk over it, permitting it no significance beyond the superficial pitch: "—so you'll feel *cleaner!*"
Through managerial scorn ("no comment") and journalistic ridicule
("mind spasm...hallucination"), they would shut down all discussion.

(J. Walter Thompson later refused to send anyone to debate the matter with me on a radio program.) Thus was a divergent reading written off as the perversity of yet another cracked "professor"—when in fact it was the ad itself that was perverse.

Although that campaign did not appeal to its TV audience (J. Walter Thompson ultimately lost the Shield account), such belligerent "common sense" does have a most receptive public. While the admakers—and others—insist that "people today are adwise" in fact most Americans still perceive the media image as transparent, a sign that simply says what it means and means what it says. They therefore tend to dismiss any intensive explication as a case of "reading too much into it"—an objection that is philosophically dubious, albeit useful to the admakers and their allies. It is now, perhaps, one obligation of the academic humanists, empowered, as they are, by critical theory, to demonstrate at large the faultiness—and the dangers—of that objection.   3

A historical note on the Shield commercial's pseudofeminism. Since 1982, the contemptuous housewife has all but vanished from the antiseptic scene of advertising; Gail was among the last of an endangered species. By now, the housewife/mother is a despised figure—most despised by actual housewife/mothers, who make up 60% of the primetime audience. Since these viewers now prefer to see themselves represented as executives, or at least as mothers with beepers and attaché cases, the *hausfrau* of the past, whether beaming or sneering, has largely been obliterated by the advertisers. In 1985, Advertising to Women Inc., a New York advertising agency, found that, out of 250 current ads, only nine showed recognizable Moms.   4

This is a triumph not for women's liberation, but for advertising; for, now that Mom is missing from the ads, presumably off knocking heads together in the boardroom, it is the commodity that seems to warm her home and tuck her children in at night.   5

In any case, the Shield strategy itself has certainly outlasted the wry and/or perky Mommy-images of yesteryear. Indeed, because the sexes are now at war within the scene of advertising (and elsewhere), the nasty visual metaphors have become ubiquitous.   6

Examining the Text

1. Briefly define the term "pseudofeminism" (paragraph 6) in your own words. How, according to Miller, does the Shield advertisement display "pseudofeminism"? Is Miller justified in criticizing the ad in these terms?

2. Recalling that the title of this essay is "Getting Dirty," summarize Miller's points about cleanliness and dirt in the Shield advertisement.

What do you think of Miller's statement that "the filth which Shield supposedly 'fights' is not physical but psychological besmirchment" (13)?

3. Describe the strategic importance of Miller's eighth paragraph. What is Miller doing in this paragraph, and why does he place it here in the essay rather than earlier or later? Do you agree with Miller's ultimate conclusion that "the ad's visual implications are too carefully achieved to have been merely accidental or unconscious"?

4. How would you describe the tone of Miller's essay, particularly in the opening section in which he describes the Shield commercial? Why do you think Miller adopts this tone? Do you find it helps him convey his points? Why or why not?

5. What is Miller's main point in the Afterword? To what extent does the Afterword help make the essay itself more persuasive?

Group Discussion

Miller comments in the Afterword that "In fact most Americans still perceive the media image as transparent, a sign that simply says what it means and means what it says. They therefore tend to dismiss any intensive explication as a case of 'reading too much into it'" (3). How does this quote relate to your own response to Miller's essay? If you think Miller "reads too much into" the Shield ad, where in the essay does this occur? What could he do to make these parts of the essay more persuasive?

Writing Suggestion

Miller's analysis of the Shield advertisement focuses on its hidden misogyny. Reflect on other advertisements that also show some degree of misogyny, and write a description about how misogyny works in one specific ad. How does this ad, like the one for Shield, manage to appeal to female consumers even though its message is essentially derogatory toward women?

Sex, Lies and Advertising

Gloria Steinem

This chapter concludes with an essay by one of the most important and influential figures in the American feminist movement, Gloria Steinem. Steinem's essay, originally published in Ms. *magazine (which she cofounded), addresses some of the broader issues involving advertising and gender. As she demonstrates, we need to be aware not only of the* content *of advertisements, but also of how advertising agencies and their clients make demands that affect the entire content of magazines, women's magazines in particular.*

Steinem describes the difficulties Ms. *faced when soliciting advertisements for their new magazine in the 1970s. As a magazine with an entirely female readership,* Ms. *had first to convince advertisers that women were intelligent, active consumers. Then, the editors had to placate advertisers who demanded editorials and articles to promote their products. Steinem offers numerous examples of how companies try to influence the magazines they advertise in.*

Before you read, *look at a recent issue of a woman's magazine, such as* Ms. *or* Working Woman *or* Vogue *to notice what sort of advertisements and articles you find there. To what extent do you think these magazines represent the interests and needs of their female readership?*

About three years ago, as *glasnost* was beginning and *Ms.* seemed   1
to be ending, I was invited to a press lunch for a Soviet official. He entertained us with anecdotes about new problems of democracy in his country. Local Communist leaders were being criticized in their media for the first time, he explained, and they were angry.

"So I'll have to ask my American friends," he finished pointedly,   2
"how more *subtly* to control the press." In the silence that followed, I said, "Advertising."

The reporters laughed, but later, one of them took me aside: How   3
dare I suggest that freedom of the press was limited? How dare I imply that his newsweekly could be influenced by ads?

I explained that I was thinking of advertising's media-wide influ-   4
ence on most of what we read. Even newsmagazines use "soft" cover stories to sell ads, confuse readers with "advertorials,"[1] and occasionally self-censor on subjects known to be a problem with big advertisers.

But, I also explained, I was thinking especially of women's maga-   5
zines. There, it isn't just a little content that's devoted to attracting ads, it's almost all of it. That's why advertisers—not readers—have always been the problem for *Ms.* As the only women's magazine that didn't supply what the ad world euphemistically describes as "supportive editorial atmosphere" or "complementary copy" (for instance, articles that praise food/fashion/beauty subjects to "support" and "complement" food/fashion/beauty ads), *Ms.* could never attract enough advertising to break even.

"Oh, *women's* magazines," the journalist said with contempt.   6
"Everybody knows they're catalogs—but who cares? They have nothing to do with journalism."

---

[1]**"advertorial"** Advertisement designed to mimic the appearance of a feature article.—
EDS.

I can't tell you how many times I've had this argument in 25   7
years of working for many kinds of publications. Except as money-
making machines—"cash cows" as they are so elegantly called in
the trade—women's magazines are rarely taken seriously. Though
changes being made by women have been called more far-reaching
than the industrial revolution—and though many editors try hard to
reflect some of them in the few pages left to them after all the ad-
related subjects have been covered—the magazines serving the female
half of this country are still far below the journalistic and ethical standards of news and general interest publications. Most depressing of
all, this doesn't even rate an exposé.

If *Time* and *Newsweek* had to lavish praise on cars in general and   8
credit General Motors in particular to get GM ads, there would be a
scandal—maybe a criminal investigation. When women's magazines
from *Seventeen* to *Lear's* praise beauty products in general and credit
Revlon in particular to get ads, it's just business as usual.

When *Ms.* began, we didn't consider *not* taking ads. The most   9
important reason was keeping the price of a feminist magazine low
enough for most women to afford. But the second and almost equal
reason was providing a forum where women and advertisers could
talk to each other and improve advertising itself. After all, it was (and
still is) as potent a source of information in this country as news or TV
and movie dramas.

We decided to proceed in two stages. First, we would convince   10
makers of "people products" used by both men and women but advertised mostly to men—cars, credit cards, insurance, sound equipment, financial services, and the like—that their ads should be placed
in a women's magazine. Since they were accustomed to the division
between editorial[2] and advertising in news and general interest magazines, this would allow our editorial content to be free and diverse.
Second, we would add the best ads for whatever traditional "women's
products" (clothes, shampoo, fragrance, food, and so on) that surveys
showed *Ms.* readers used. But we would ask them to come in without
the usual quid pro quo of "complementary copy."

We knew the second step might be harder. Food advertisers have   11
always demanded that women's magazines publish recipes and articles on entertaining (preferably ones that name their products) in return for their ads; clothing advertisers expect to be surrounded by
fashion spreads (especially ones that credit their designers); and sham-

---

[2]**editorial** In the magazine industry, all nonadvertising content in a magazine, including
regular columns and feature articles.—EDS.

poo, fragrance, and beauty products in general usually insist on positive editorial coverage of beauty subjects, plus photo credits besides. That's why women's magazines look the way they do. But if we could break this link between ads and editorial content, then we wanted good ads for "women's products," too.

By playing their part in this unprecedented mix of *all* the things   12
our readers need and use, advertisers also would be rewarded: Ads for products like cars and mutual funds would find a new growth market; the best ads for women's products would no longer be lost in oceans of ads for the same category; and both would have access to a laboratory of smart and caring readers whose response would help create effective ads for other media as well.

I thought then that our main problem would be the imagery in   13
ads themselves. Car makers were still draping blondes in evening gowns over the hoods like ornaments. Authority figures were almost always male, even in ads for products that only women used. Sadistic, he-man campaigns even won industry praise. (For instance, *Advertising Age* had hailed the infamous Silva Thin cigarette theme, "How to Get a Woman's Attention: Ignore Her," as "brilliant.") Even in medical journals, tranquilizer ads showed depressed housewives standing beside piles of dirty dishes and promised to get them back to work.

Obviously, *Ms.* would have to avoid such ads and seek out the   14
best ones—but this didn't seem impossible. *The New Yorker* had been selecting ads for aesthetic reasons for years, a practice that only seemed to make advertisers more eager to be in its pages. *Ebony* and *Essence* were asking for ads with positive black images, and though their struggle was hard, they weren't being called unreasonable.

Clearly, what *Ms.* needed was a very special publisher and ad   15
sales staff. I could think of only one woman with experience on the business side of magazines—Patricia Carbine, who recently had become a vice president of *McCall's* as well as its editor in chief—and the reason I knew her name was a good omen. She had been managing editor at *Look* (really *the* editor, but its owner refused to put a female name at the top of his masthead) when I was writing a column there. After I did an early interview with Cesar Chavez, then just emerging as a leader of migrant labor, and the publisher turned it down because he was worried about ads from Sunkist, Pat was the one who intervened. As I learned later, she had told the publisher she would resign if the interview wasn't published. Mainly because *Look* couldn't afford to lose Pat, it *was* published (and the ads from Sunkist never arrived).

Though I barely knew this woman, she had done two things I al-   16
ways remembered; put her job on the line in a way that editors often talk about but rarely do, and been so loyal to her colleagues that she never told me or anyone outside *Look* that she had done so.

Fortunately, Pat did agree to leave *McCall's* and take a huge cut in   17
salary to become publisher of *Ms.* She became responsible for training
and inspiring generations of young women who joined the *Ms.* ad sales
force, many of whom went on to become "firsts" at the top of publishing.
When *Ms.* first started, however, there were so few women with experience selling space that Pat and I made the rounds of ad agencies ourselves. Later, the fact that *Ms.* was asking companies to do business in a
different way meant our saleswomen had to make many times the usual
number of calls—first to convince agencies and then client companies
besides—and to present endless amounts of research. I was often asked
to do a final ad presentation, or see some higher decision-maker, or
speak to women employees so executives could see the interest of
women they worked with. That's why I spent more time persuading advertisers than editing or writing for *Ms.* and why I ended up with an un-
sentimental education in the seamy underside of publishing that few
writers see (and even fewer magazines can publish).

Let me take you with us through some experiences, just as they   18
happened:

• Cheered on by early support from Volkswagen and one or two
other car companies, we scrape together time and money to put on a
major reception in Detroit. We know U.S. car-makers firmly believe
that women choose the upholstery, not the car, but we are armed with
statistics and reader mail to prove the contrary: A car is an important
purchase for women, one that symbolizes mobility and freedom.

But almost nobody comes. We are left with many pounds of   19
shrimp on the table, and quite a lot of egg on our face. We blame ourselves for not guessing that there would be a baseball pennant play-off
on the same day, but executives go out of their way to explain they
wouldn't have come anyway. Thus begins ten years of knocking on hostile doors, presenting endless documentation, and hiring a full-time
saleswoman in Detroit; all necessary before *Ms.* gets any real results.

This long saga has a semihappy ending: foreign and, later, do-   20
mestic car-makers eventually provided *Ms.* with enough advertising
to make cars one of our top sources of ad revenue. Slowly, Detroit
began to take the women's market seriously enough to put car ads in
other women's magazines, too, thus freeing a few pages from the hot-
house of fashion-beauty-food ads.

But long after figures showed a third, even a half, of many car   21
models being bought by women, U.S. makers continued to be uncomfortable addressing women. Unlike foreign car-makers, Detroit never
quite learned the secret of creating intelligent ads that exclude no one,
and then placing them in women's magazines to overcome past exclusion. (*Ms.* readers were so grateful for a routine Honda ad featuring
rack and pinion steering, for instance, that they sent fan mail.) Even

now, Detroit continues to ask, "Should we make special ads for women?" Perhaps that's why some foreign cars still have a disproportionate share of the U.S. women's market.

• In the *Ms.* Gazette, we do a brief report on a congressional   22
hearing into chemicals used in hair dyes that are absorbed through the skin and may be carcinogenic. Newspapers report this too, but Clairol, a Bristol-Myers subsidiary that makes dozens of products—a few of which have just begun to advertise in *Ms.*—is outraged. Not at newspapers or news magazines, just at us. It's bad enough that *Ms.* is the only women's magazine refusing to provide the usual "complementary" articles and beauty photos, but to criticize one of their categories—*that* is going too far.

We offer to publish a letter from Clairol telling its side of the   23
story. In an excess of solicitousness, we even put this letter in the Gazette, not in Letters to the Editors where it belongs. Nonetheless— and in spite of surveys that show *Ms.* readers are active women who use more of almost everything Clairol makes than do the readers of any other women's magazine—*Ms.* gets almost none of these ads for the rest of its natural life.

Meanwhile, Clairol changes its hair-coloring formula, apparently   24
in response to the hearings we reported.

• Our saleswomen set out early to attract ads for consumer elec-   25
tions: sound equipment, calculators, computers, VCRs, and the like. We know that our readers are determined to be included in the technological revolution. We know from reader surveys that *Ms.* readers are buying this stuff in numbers as high as those of magazines like *Playboy,* or "men 18 to 34," the prime targets of the consumer electronics industry. Moreover, unlike traditional women's products that our readers buy but don't need to read articles about, these are subjects they want covered in our pages. There actually *is* a supportive editorial atmosphere.

"But women don't understand technology," say executives at the   26
end of ad presentations. "Maybe now," we respond, "but neither do men, and we all buy it."

"If women *do* buy it," say the decision-makers, "they're asking   27
their husbands and boyfriends what to buy first." We produce letters from *Ms.* readers saying how turned off they are when salesmen say things like "Let me know when your husband can come in."

After several years of this, we get a few ads for compact sound   28
systems. Some of them come from JVC, whose vice president, Harry Elias, is trying to convince his Japanese bosses that there is something called a women's market. At his invitation, I find myself speaking at huge trade shows in Chicago and Las Vegas, trying to persuade JVC dealers that showrooms don't have to be locker rooms where women are made to feel unwelcome. But as it turns out, the shows themselves are part of the problem. In Las Vegas, the only women around the

technology displays are seminude models serving champagne. In Chicago, the big attraction is Marilyn Chambers, who followed Linda Lovelace of *Deep Throat* fame as Chuck Traynor's captive and/or employee. VCRs are being demonstrated with her porn videos.

In the end, we get ads for a car stereo now and then, but no VCRs; some IBM personal computers, but no Apple or Japanese ones. We notice that office magazines like *Working Woman* and *Savvy* don't benefit as much as they should from office equipment ads either. In the electronics world, women and technology seem mutually exclusive. It remains a decade behind even Detroit.   29

• Because we get letters from little girls who love toy trains, and who ask our help in changing ads and box-top photos that feature little boys only, we try to get toy-train ads from Lionel. It turns out that Lionel executives have been concerned about little girls. They made a pink train, and were surprised when it didn't sell.   30

Lionel bows to consumer pressure with a photograph of a boy *and* a girl—but only on some of their boxes. They fear that, if trains are associated with girls, they will be devalued in the minds of boys. Needless to say, *Ms.* gets no train ads, and little girls remain a mostly unexplored market. By 1986, Lionel is put up for sale.   31

But for different reasons, we haven't had much luck with other kinds of toys either. In spite of many articles on child-rearing; an annual listing of nonsexist, multiracial toys by Letty Cottin Pogrebin; Stories for Free Children, a regular feature also edited by Letty; and other prizewinning features for or about children, we get virtually no toy ads. Generations of *Ms.* saleswomen explain to toy manufacturers that a larger proportion of *Ms.* readers have preschool children than do the readers of other women's magazines, but this industry can't believe feminists have or care about children.   32

• When *Ms.* begins, the staff decides not to accept ads for feminine hygiene sprays or cigarettes: they are damaging and carry no appropriate health warnings. Though we don't think we should tell our readers what to do, we do think we should provide facts so they can decide for themselves. Since the antismoking lobby has been pressing for health warnings on cigarette ads, we decide to take them only as they comply.   33

Philip Morris is among the first to do so. One of its brands, Virginia Slims, is also sponsoring women's tennis and the first national polls of women's opinions. On the other hand, the Virginia Slims theme, "You've come a long way, baby," has more than a "baby" problem. It makes smoking a symbol of progress for women.   34

We explain to Philip Morris that this slogan won't do well in our pages, but they are convinced its success with some women means it will work with *all* women. Finally, we agree to publish an ad for a Virginia Slims calendar as a test. The letters from readers are critical—and smart. For instance: Would you show a black man picking cotton, the   35 same man in a Cardin suit, and symbolize the antislavery and civil rights movements by smoking? Of course not. But instead of honoring the test results, the Philip Morris people seem angry to be proven wrong. They take away ads for *all* their many brands.

This costs *Ms.* about $250,000 the first year. After five years, we   36
can no longer keep track. Occasionally, a new set of executives listens to *Ms.* saleswomen, but because we won't take Virginia Slims, not one Philip Morris product returns to our pages for the next 16 years.

Gradually, we also realize our naiveté in thinking we *could* decide   37
against taking cigarette ads. They became a disproportionate support of magazines the moment they were banned on television, and few magazines could compete and survive without them; certainly not *Ms.*, which lacks so many other categories. By the time statistics in the 1980s showed that women's rate of lung cancer was approaching men's, the necessity of taking cigarette ads has become a kind of prison.

• General Mills, Pillsbury, Carnation, DelMonte, Dole, Kraft,   38
Stouffer, Hormel, Nabisco: You name the food giant, we try it. But no matter how desirable the *Ms.* readership, our lack of recipes is lethal.

We explain to them that placing food ads *only* next to recipes as-   39
sociates food with work. For many women, it is a negative that works *against* the ads. Why not place food ads in diverse media without recipes (thus reaching more men, who are now a third of the shoppers in supermarkets anyway), and leave the recipes to specialty magazines like *Gourmet* (a third of whose readers are also men)?

These arguments elicit interest, but except for an occasional ad   40
for a convenience food, instant coffee, diet drinks, yogurt, or such extras as avocados and almonds, this mainstay of the publishing industry stays closed to us. Period.

• Traditionally, wines and liquors didn't advertise to women: 41
Men were thought to make the brand decisions, even if women did the buying. But after endless presentations, we begin to make a dent in this category. Thanks to the unconventional Michel Roux of Carillon Importers (distributors of Grand Marnier, Absolut Vodka, and others), who assumes that food and drink have no gender, some ads are leaving their men's club.

Beermakers are still selling masculinity. It takes *Ms.* fully eight   42
years to get its first beer ad (Michelob). In general, however, liquor ads are less stereotyped in their imagery—and far less controlling of the editorial around them—than are women's products. But given the underrepresentation of other categories, these very facts tend to create a disproportionate number of alcohol ads in the pages of *Ms.* This in turn dismays readers worried about women and alcoholism.

• We hear in 1980 that women in the Soviet Union have been   43
producing feminist *samizdat* (underground, self-published books) and circulating them throughout the country. As punishment, four of the

leaders have been exiled. Though we are operating on our usual shoestring, we solicit individual contributions to send Robin Morgan to interview these women in Vienna.

The result is an exclusive cover story that includes the first news   44
of a populist peace movement against the Afghanistan occupation, a
prediction of *glasnost* to come, and a grassroots, intimate view of Soviet women's lives. From the popular press to women's studies
courses, the response is great. The story wins a Front Page award.

Nonetheless, this journalistic coup undoes years of efforts to get   45
an ad schedule from Revlon. Why? Because the Soviet women on our
cover *are not wearing make-up.*

• Four years of research and presentations go into convincing   46
airlines that women now make travel choices and business trips.
United, the first airline to advertise in *Ms.,* is so impressed with the response from our readers that one of its executives appears in a film for
our ad presentations. As usual, good ads get great results.

But we have problems unrelated to such results. For instance: Be-   47
cause American Airlines flight attendants include among their labor
demands the stipulation that they could choose to have their last
names preceded by "Ms." on their name tags—in a long-delayed revolt against the standard. "I am your pilot, Captain Rothgart, and this
is your flight attendant, Cindy Sue"—American officials seem to hold
the magazine responsible. We get no ads.

There is still a different problem at Eastern. A vice president can-   48
cels subscriptions for thousands of copies on Eastern flights. Why? Because he is offended by ads for lesbian poetry journals in the *Ms.*
Classified. A "family airline," as he explains to me coldly on the
phone, has to "draw the line somewhere."

It's obvious that *Ms.* can't exclude lesbians and serve women.   49
We've been trying to make that point ever since our first issue included an article by and about lesbians, and both Suzanne Levine, our
managing editor, and I were lectured by such heavy hitters as Ed Kos-
ner, then editor of *Newsweek* (and now of *New York Magazine*), who insisted that *Ms.* should "position" itself *against* lesbians. But our
advertisers have paid to reach a guaranteed number of readers, and
soliciting new subscriptions to compensate for Eastern would cost
$150,000, plus rebating money in the meantime.

Like almost everything ad-related, this presents an elaborate or-   50
ganizing problem. After days of searching for sympathetic members
of the Eastern board, Frank Thomas, president of the Ford Foundation,
kindly offers to call Roswell Gilpatrick, a director of Eastern. I talk
with Mr. Gilpatrick, who calls Frank Borman, then the president
of Eastern. Frank Borman calls me to say that his airline is not in the
business of censoring magazines: *Ms.* will be returned to Eastern
flights.

• Women's access to insurance and credit is vital, but with the   51
exception of Equitable and a few other ad pioneers, such financial services address men. For almost a decade after the Equal Credit Opportunity Act passes in 1974, we try to convince American Express that
women are a growth market—but nothing works.

Finally, a former professor of Russian named Jerry Welsh be-   52
comes head of marketing. He assumes that women should be cardholders, and persuades his colleagues to feature women in a campaign.
Thanks to this 1980s series, the growth rate for female cardholders surpass that for men.

For this article, I asked Jerry Welsh if he would explain why   53
American Express waited so long. "Sure," he said, "they were afraid of
having a 'pink' card."

• Women of color read *Ms.* in disproportionate numbers. This is a   54
source of pride to *Ms.* staffers, who are also more racially representative
than the editors of other women's magazines. But this reality is obscured
by ads filled with enough white women to make a reader snowblind.

Pat Carbine remembers mostly "astonishment" when she re-   55
quested African American, Hispanic, Asian, and other diverse images.
Marcia Ann Gillespie, a *Ms.* editor who was previously the editor in
chief of *Essence,* witnesses ad bias a second time: Having tried for
Essence to get white advertisers to use black images (Revlon did so
eventually, but L'Oreal, Lauder, Chanel, and other companies never
did), she sees similar problems getting integrated ads for an integrated
magazine. Indeed, the ad world often creates black and Hispanic ads
only for black and Hispanic media. In an exact parallel of the fear that
marketing a product to women will endanger its appeal to men, the response is usually, "But your [white] readers won't identify."

In fact, those we are able to get—for instance, a Max Factor ad   56
made for *Essence* that Linda Wachner gives us after she becomes president—are praised by white readers, too. But there are pathetically few
such images.

• By the end of 1986, production and mailing costs have risen as-   57
tronomically, ad income is flat, and competition for ads is stiffer than
ever. The 60/40 preponderance of edit over ads that we promised to
readers becomes 50/50; children's stories, most poetry, and some fiction
are casualties of less space; in order to get variety into limited pages, the
length (and sometimes the depth) of articles suffers; and, though we do
refuse most of the ads that would look like a parody in our pages, we get
so worn down that some slip through. Still, readers perform miracles.
Though we haven't been able to afford a subscription mailing in two
years, they maintain our guaranteed circulation of 450,000.

Nonetheless, media reports on *Ms.* often insist that our unprof-   58
itability must be due to reader disinterest. The myth that advertisers

simply follow readers is very strong. Not one reporter notes that other comparable magazines our size (say, *Vanity Fair* or *The Atlantic*) have been losing more money in one year than *Ms.* has lost in 16 years. No matter how much never-to-be-recovered cash is poured into starting a magazine or keeping one going, appearances seem to be all that matter. (Which is why we haven't been able to explain our fragile state in public. Nothing causes ad flight like the smell of nonsuccess.)

My healthy response is anger. My not-so-healthy response is   59
constant worry. Also an obsession with finding one more rescue. There is hardly a night when I don't wake up with sweaty palms and pounding heart, scared that we won't be able to pay the printer or the post office; scared most of all that closing our doors will hurt the women's movement.

Out of chutzpah and desperation, I arrange a lunch with Leonard   60
Lauder, president of Estée Lauder. With the exception of Clinique (the brainchild of Carol Philllips), none of Lauder's hundreds of products has been advertised in *Ms.* A year's schedule of ads for just three or four of them could save us. Indeed, as the scion of a family-owned company whose ad practices are followed by the beauty industry, he is one of the few men who could liberate many pages in all women's magazines just by changing his mind about "complementary copy."

Over a lunch that costs more than we can pay for some articles, I ex-   61
plain the need for his leadership. I also lay out the record of *Ms.*: more literary and journalistic prizes won, more new issues introduced into the mainstream, new writers discovered, and impact on society than any other magazine; more articles that became books, stories that became movies, ideas that became television series, and newly advertised products that became profitable; and, most important for him, a place for his ads to reach women who aren't reachable through any other women's magazine. Indeed, if there is one constant characteristic of the ever-changing *Ms.* readership, it is their impact as leaders. Whether it's waiting until later to have first babies, or pioneering PABA as sun protection in cosmetics, *whatever* they are doing today, a third to a half of American women will be doing three to five years from now. It's never failed.

But, he says, *Ms.* readers are not *our* women. They're not inter-   62
ested in things like fragrance and blush-on. If they were, *Ms.* would write articles about them.

On the contrary, I explain, surveys show they are more likely to   63
buy such things than the readers of, say, *Cosmopolitan* or *Vogue.* They're good customers because they're out in the world enough to need several sets of everything: home, work, purse, travel, gym, and so on. They just don't need to read articles about these things. Would he ask a men's magazine to publish monthly columns on how to shave before he advertised Aramis products (his line for men)?

He concedes that beauty features are often concocted more for ad-   64
vertisers than readers. But *Ms.* isn't appropriate for his ads anyway, he explains. Why? Because Estée Lauder is selling "a kept-woman mentality."

I can't quite believe this. Sixty percent of the users of his prod-   65
ucts are salaried, and generally resemble *Ms.* readers. Besides, his
company has the appeal of having been started by a creative and hard-
working woman, his mother, Estée Lauder.

That doesn't matter, he says. He knows his customers, and they   66
would *like* to be kept women. That's why he will never advertise in *Ms.*

In November 1987, by vote of the Ms. Foundation for Education   67
and Communication (*Ms.*'s owner and publisher, the media subsidiary
of the Ms. Foundation for Women), *Ms.* was sold to a company whose
officers, Australian feminists Sandra Yates and Anne Summers, raised
the investment money in their country that *Ms.* couldn't find in its
own. They also started *Sassy* for teenage women.

In their two-year tenure, circulation was raised to 550,000 by in-   68
vestment in circulation mailings, and, to the dismay of some readers,
editorial features on clothes and new products made a more traditional bid for ads. Nonetheless, ad pages fell below previous levels. In
addition, *Sassy*, whose fresh voice and sexual frankness were an unprecedented success with young readers, was targeted by two mothers
from Indiana who began, as one of them put it, "calling every Christian organization I could think of." In response to this controversy,
several crucial advertisers pulled out.

Such links between ads and editorial content was a problem in   69
Australia, too, but to a lesser degree. "Our readers pay two times more
for their magazines," Anne explained, "so advertisers have less power
to threaten a magazine's viability."

"I was shocked," said Sandra Yates with characteristic directness.   70
"In Australia, we think you have freedom of the press—but you don't."

Since Anne and Sandra had not met their budget's projections for   71
ad revenue, their investors forced a sale. In October 1989, *Ms.* and
Sassy were bought by Dale Lang, owner of *Working Mother, Working
Woman,* and one of the few independent publishing companies left
among the conglomerates. In response to a request from the original
Ms. staff—as well as to reader letters urging that *Ms.* continue, plus his
own belief that *Ms.* would benefit his other magazines by blazing a
trail—he agreed to try the ad-free, reader-supported *Ms.* ... and to give
us complete editorial control.

In response to the workplace revolution of the 1970s, traditional   72
women's magazines—that is, "trade books" for women working at
home—were joined by *Savvy, Working Woman,* and other trade books
for women working in offices. But by keeping the fashion/beauty/en-

tertaining articles necessary to get traditional ads and then adding career articles besides, they inadvertently produced the antifeminist stereotype of Super Woman. The male-initiative, dress-for-success woman carrying a briefcase became the media image of a woman worker, even though a blue-collar woman's salary was often higher than her glorified secretarial sister's, and though women at a real briefcase level are statistically rare. Needless to say, these dress-for-success women were also thin, white, and beautiful.

In recent years, advertisers' control over the editorial content of women's magazines has become so institutionalized that it is written into "insertion orders" or dictated to ad salespeople as official policy. The following are recent typical orders to women's magazines: 73

• Dow's Cleaning Products stipulates that ads for its Vivid and Spray 'n Wash products should be adjacent to "children or fashion editorial"; ads for Bathroom Cleaner should be next to "home furnishing/family" features; and so on for other brands. "If a magazine fails for the brands or more," the Dow order warns, "it will be omitted from further consideration."   74

• Bristol-Myers, the parent of Clairol, Windex, Drano, Bufferin, and much more, stipulates that ads be placed next to a "full page of compatible editorial."   75

• S.C. Johnson & Son, makers of Johnson Wax, lawn and laundry products, insect sprays, hair sprays, and so on, orders that its ads *"should not be opposite extremely controversial features or material antithetical to the nature/copy of the advertised product."* (Italics theirs.)   76

• Maidenform, manufacturer of bras and other apparel, leaves a blank for the particular product and states: "The creative concept of the _____ campaign, and the very nature of the product itself appeal to the positive emotions of the reader/consumer. Therefore, it is imperative that all editorial adjacencies reflect that same positive tone. The editorial must not be negative in content or lend itself contrary to the _____ product imagery/message (e.g., *editorial relating to illness, disillusionment, large size fashion, etc.*)." (Italics mine.)   77

• The De Beers diamond company, a big seller of engagement rings, prohibits magazines from placing its ads with "adjacencies to hard news or anti-love/romance themed editorial."   78

• Procter & Gamble, one of this country's most powerful and diversified advertisers, stands out in the memory of Anne Summers and Sandra Yates (no mean feat in this context): Its products were not to be placed in *any* issue that included *any* material on gun control, abortion, the occult, cults, or the disparagement of religion. Caution was also demanded in any issue covering sex or drugs, even for educational purposes.   79

Those are the most obvious chains around women's magazines. There are also rules so clear they needn't be written down: for instance, an overall "look" compatible with beauty and fashion ads.   80

Even "real" nonmodel women photographed for a woman's magazine are usually made up, dressed in credited clothes, and retouched out of all reality. When editors do include articles on less-than-cheerful subjects (for instance, domestic violence), they tend to keep them short and unillustrated. The point is to be "upbeat." Just as women in the street are asked, "Why don't you smile, honey?" women's magazines acquire an institutional smile.

Within the text itself, praise for advertisers' products has become 81 so ritualized that fields like "beauty writing" have been invented. One of its frequent practitioners explained seriously that "It's a difficult art. How many new adjectives can you find? How much greater can you make a lipstick sound? The FDA restricts what companies can say on labels, but we create illusion. And ad agencies are on the phone all the time pushing you to get their product in. A lot of them keep the business based on how many editorial clippings they produce every month. The worst are products" like Lauder's, as the writer confirmed, "with their own name involved. It's all ego."

Often, editorial becomes one giant ad. Last November, for in- 82 stance, *Lear's* featured an elegant woman executive on the cover. On the contents page, we learned she was wearing Guerlain makeup and Samsara, a new fragrance by Guerlain. Inside were full-page ads for Samsara and Guerlain antiwrinkle cream. In the cover profile, we learned that this executive was responsible for launching Samsara and is Guerlain's director of public relations. When the *Columbia Journalism Review* did one of the few articles to include women's magazines in coverage of the influence of ads, editor Frances Lear was quoted as defending her magazine because "this kind of thing is done all the time."

Often, advertisers also plunge odd-shaped ads into the text, no 83 matter what the cost to the readers. At *Woman's Day*, a magazine originally founded by a supermarket chain, editor in chief Ellen Levine said, "The day the copy had to rag around a chicken leg was not a happy one."

Advertisers are also adamant about where in a magazine their 84 ads appear. When Revlon was not placed as the first beauty ad in one Hearst magazine, for instance, Revlon pulled its ads from *all* Hearst magazines. Ruth Whitney, editor in chief of *Glamour*, attributes some of these demands to "ad agencies wanting to prove to a client that they've squeezed the last drop of blood out of a magazine." She also is, she says, "sick and tired of hearing that women's magazines are controlled by cigarette ads." Relatively speaking, she's right. To be as censoring as are many advertisers for women's products, tobacco companies would have to demand articles in praise of smoking and expect glamorous photos of beautiful women smoking their brands.

I don't mean to imply that the editors I quote here share my objec- 85 tions to ads: Most assume that women's magazines have to be the way they are. But it's also true that only former editors can be completely honest. "Most of the pressure came in the form of direct product mentions," explains Sey Chassler, who was editor in chief of *Redbook* from the sixties to the eighties. "We got threats from the big guys, the Revlons, blackmail threats. They wouldn't run ads unless we credited them.

"But it's not fair to single out the beauty advertisers because   86
these pressures came from everybody. Advertisers want to know two things: What are you going to charge me? What else are you going to do for me? It's a holdup. For instance, management felt that fiction took up too much space. They couldn't put any advertising in that. For the last ten years, the number of fiction entries into the National Magazine Awards has declined.

"And pressures are getting worse. More magazines are more   87
bottom-line oriented because they have been taken over by companies with no interest in publishing.

"I also think advertisers do this to women's magazines especially,"   88
he concluded, "because of the general disrespect they have for women."

Even media experts who don't give a damn about women's maga-   89
zines are alarmed by the spread of this ad-edit linkage. In a climate *The Wall Street Journal* describes as an unacknowledged Depression for media, women's products are increasingly able to take their low standards wherever they go. For instance: Newsweeklies publish uncritical stories on fashion and fitness. *The New York Times Magazine* recently ran an article on "firming creams," complete with mentions of advertisers. *Vanity Fair* published a profile of one major advertiser, Ralph Lauren, illustrated by the same photographer who does his ads, and turned the lifestyle of another, Calvin Klein, into a cover story. Even the outrageous *Spy* has toned down since it began to go after fashion ads.

And just to make us really worry, films and books, the last media   90
that go directly to the public without having to attract ads first, are in danger, too. Producers are beginning to depend on payments for displaying products in movies, and books are now being commissioned by companies like Federal Express.

But the truth is that women's products—like women's maga-   91
zines—have never been the subjects of much serious reporting anyway. News and general interest publications, including the "style" or "living" sections of newspapers, write about food and clothing as cooking and fashion, and almost never evaluate such products by brand name. Though chemical additives, pesticides, and animal fats are major health risks in the United States, and clothes, shoddy or not, absorb more consumer dollars than cars, this lack of information is serious. So is ignoring the contents of beauty products that are absorbed into our bodies through our skins, and that have profit margins so big they would make a loan shark blush.

What could women's magazines be like if they were as free as   92
books? as realistic as newspapers? as creative as films? as diverse as
women's lives? We don't know.

But we'll only find out if we take women's magazines seriously.   93
If readers were to act in a concerted way to change traditional practices of *all* women's magazines and the marketing of *all* women's
products, we could do it. After all, they are operating on our consumer
dollars: money that we now control. You and I could:

• write to editors and publishers (with copies to advertisers) that
we're willing to pay *more* for magazines with editorial independence, but
will *not* continue to pay for those that are just editorial extensions of ads;

• write to advertisers (with copies to editors and publishers)
that we want fiction, political reporting, consumer reporting—whatever is, or is not, supported by their ads;

• put as much energy into breaking advertising's control over
content as into changing the images in ads, or protesting ads for harmful products like cigarettes;

• support only those women's magazines and products that
take *us* seriously as readers and consumers.

• Those of us in the magazine world can also use the carrot-and-
stick technique. For instance: Pointing out that, if magazines were a
regulated medium like television, the demands of advertisers would
be against FCC rules. Payola and extortion could be punished. As it is,
there are probably illegalities. A magazine's postal rates are determined by the ratio of ad to edit pages, and the former costs more than
the latter. So much for the stick.

The carrot means appealing to enlightened self-interest. For in-   94
stance: There are many studies showing that the greatest factor in determining an ad's effectiveness is the credibility of its surroundings.
The "higher the rating of editorial believability," concluded a 1987 survey by the *Journal of Advertising Research,* "the higher the rating of the
advertising." Thus, an impenetrable wall between edit and ads would
also be in the best interest of advertisers.

Unfortunately, few agencies or clients hear such arguments. Edi-   95
tors often maintain the false purity of refusing to talk to them at all. Instead, they see ad salespeople who know little about editorial, are
trained in business as usual, and are usually paid by commission. Editors might also band together to take on controversy. That happened
once when all the major women's magazines did articles in the same
month on the Equal Rights Amendment. It could happen again.

It's almost three years away from life between the grindstones of   96
advertising pressures and readers' needs. I'm just beginning to realize
how edges got smoothed down—in spite of all our resistance.

I remember feeling put upon when I changed "Porsche" to "car"   97
in a piece about Nazi imagery in German pornography by Andrea
Dworkin—feeling sure Andrea would understand that Volkswagen,
the distributor of Porsche and one of our few supportive advertisers,
asked only to be far away from Nazi subjects. It's taken me all this
time to realize that Andrea was the one with a right to feel put upon.

Even as I write this, I get a call from a writer for *Elle*, who is   98
doing a whole article on where women part their hair. Why, she wants
to know, do I part mine in the middle?

It's all so familiar. A writer trying to make something of a noth-   99
ing assignment; an editor laboring to think of new ways to attract ads;
readers assuming that other women must want this ridiculous stuff;
more women suffering for lack of information, insight, creativity, and
laughter that could be on these same pages.

I ask you: Can't we do better than this?   100

Examining the Text

1. What do you think of the anecdote at the beginning of the essay, in
which Steinem remarks to a Soviet official that advertising is a way to
limit freedom of the press? Do you think that her essay supports this
assertion? Why or why not?

2. According to Steinem, what is the relationship between advertising
and editorial content in magazines? Does your own reading of magazines support the assertion that advertising affects content?

3. In what ways do women's magazines have a different relationship
to advertising than other magazines? What are some of the significant
problems that *Ms.* encountered in dealing with advertisements and
advertisers?

4. How would you describe the structure of this essay? What effect do
the numerous specific examples Steinem cites in the first and second
parts of the essay have on you as a reader?

For Group Discussion

Steinem asks, "What could women's magazines be like if they were
as free as books? as realistic as newspapers? as creative as films? as diverse as women's lives?" (paragraph 92). How would you answer these
questions? What would be the content of an "ideal" women's magazine?
Would it be different from an "ideal" men's magazine? In what ways? Do
any magazines read by group members approach these "ideals"?

Writing Suggestion

Look at recent issues of several women's magazines and test
Steinem's assertions about the relationship between advertising and

editorial content. Take note of any "complementary copy" in the magazine and any other ways editorial decisions might have been influenced by advertising. In an essay, explore your conclusions about the extent to which advertising affects the content and organization of women's magazines.

ADDITIONAL SUGGESTIONS
FOR WRITING ABOUT ADVERTISING

1. Choose a magazine, television, or radio advertisement that you find particularly interesting, appealing, or puzzling, and write a narrative essay describing your response to the ad.

Begin by recording your initial impressions of the ad. What do you notice first, and why are you drawn to that element of the ad? What emotions or thoughts strike you as you first look at the ad? Then describe your step-by-step progress through the ad. Where does your eye go next? How do your thoughts or emotions change as you notice more of the ad? Finally, record your impressions after you've taken in all of the ad. How does this final impression differ from your first impression?

You might conclude your narrative by commenting on whether, based on your response, the ad achieves its objective of selling the product. In other words, do you think you responded as the designers of the ad intended?

2. Devise your own ad campaign for a product with which you're familiar, including several different ads, each appealing to a different audience.

After deciding on the product, briefly describe each audience group. Choose the form in which you want your advertisements to appear (magazine ads, TV commercials, audio presentations, billboards, or other forms and venues) and then decide on the persuasive methods that you want to use. Do you want to appeal to emotion or intellect or both? What motives will you try to reach? You might refer to Fowles's list of advertising's basic appeals.

Finally, design the ads and briefly explain the reasoning behind each design.

3. Choose recent issues of a women's magazine and a men's magazine, and compare and contrast the ads in each.

How many advertisements are there? What products are being advertised? What techniques are used in the ads and how do these techniques differ significantly between men's and women's magazines? What are the differences in the appeals the ads make? What are the differences in the images of men and women?

From your findings, draw conclusions about how advertisers envision and represent differences in gender. What (if any) stereotypes of men and women do the ads present?

4. Imagine that you are a member of a citizens' group working to improve the quality of advertising. What specific recommendations would you make and what standards would you want to see enforced? Illustrate your ideas with ads you can find that either meet or fall below these standards.

Internet Activities

1. On the Web you'll find sites representing the products and services of almost all major U.S. corporations and of many smaller businesses as well. These corporate Web sites can be seen as extensive advertisements. Though they differ in style and strategy from television and magazine advertisements, they share the goal of informing consumers about a product or service and persuading consumers in their purchasing decisions.

At the *Common Culture* Web site, you'll find links to the sites of companies selling a variety of products. Choose one of those product categories and investigate the links. As you've browse through the companies' Web sites, make a list of the kind of information that's offered there, the organization of the site, the graphics and other interactive elements that are used, the style and tone of the writing, and the mood created at the site. Then write an essay in which you describe the similarities and differences of two or more sites. What strategies do these sites use to promote the company's products and services? Which strategies do you find effective, and why? You might conclude your essay by commenting on the distinctive features of Web sites as advertisements. How are they different from magazine and television ads?

2. You've probably noticed that many Web sites contain advertisements—called "Web banners"—for other sites or for products and services offered by specific companies. These banners usually appear in the top portion of the Web page and invite viewers to click on an icon to get more information. Also on the Web are sponsor links and extra windows that open up to advertise products when one visits a Web site. At the *Common Culture* Web site, you'll find links to examples and additional information about Web advertising. Visit these links and take some time to browse the Web and familiarize yourself with the advertising strategies there. Then, write an essay in which you first describe the characteristics of advertising on the Web, and then compare and contrast Web advertising to television commercials and to print ads. What common features are shared by ads in these different media? How do the differences in media shape the content and style of advertisements?

3

Television

THE BOYS ALWAYS FOUND SUNSET ON
THE PRAIRIE A PARTICULARLY
MOVING EXPERIENCE

Drawing by Glen Baxter; © 1991
The New Yorker Magazine, Inc.

We may laugh at these "boys" who stand in the middle of the barren Southwest desert watching a sunset on TV as the real sun sets behind them. Yet the joke is also on us because—like the cowboys—we might often find ourselves more engaged, more entertained, and even more emotionally touched by what we watch on television than by our own experiences in real life.

Some critics even suggest that people regard what they see on television as more real than what goes on around them and thus virtually narrow their world to what comes to them on "the tube." Paradoxically, television's greatest benefit is its potential to broaden our experience, to bring us to places we could never visit, to people we could never meet, and to a range of ideas otherwise unavailable to many people.

This complex relationship between television and people as individuals and as a society leads thoughtful people to examine closely the way television diverts our attention from what could be our own rich, nonmediated experiences; the way it entertains and informs us through otherwise inaccessible experiences; the way it shapes our perceptions of the world around us.

The readings in the first part of this chapter address some of the important questions raised in regard to this ubiquitous medium. Why do Americans spend so much time watching television? What essential needs and desires does television satisfy? How accurately does television represent reality? How strongly do its distortions of reality affect our ideas and behavior? To what extent does television intervene in our everyday lives, influencing families and communities, domestic space, and leisure time?

The readings in the second part of the chapter expand on these questions and focus on two popular television genres—talk shows and soap operas. The writers use a variety of critical methods to uncover meanings beneath the surface that passive observers (as most of us often are) internalize with little awareness.

As you read these essays, remember the television-entranced cowboys at the opening of the chapter. As you hone your own critical abilities you will go beyond being a passive observer to become an active, critically engaged viewer.

The Cultural Influences of Television

Spudding Out

Barbara Ehrenreich

Do you head straight for the TV when you arrive home after work or school, flicking on the set before you talk to your roommate or feed the cat? If so, you may be exhibiting symptoms of "couch potato" syndrome—a condition cultural critic Barbara Ehrenreich laments in the following essay. Referring to a more active and gregarious America in days past, Ehrenreich observes an onset of a "mass agoraphobia," which she argues has been directly caused by television. This TV-induced phobia—an irrational fear of being away from the tube—has led to a significant loss in human contact and activity, according to Ehrenreich: no longer do people look outside the little box for relaxation or entertainment; instead, Americans have retreated to their living rooms, kitchens, bedrooms, or wherever they lounge comfortably in front of a TV, isolating themselves there before the tube.

Cocooned in chairs, couches, beds, and blankets, and armed with that indispensable accessory of modern life—the remote control keypad—today's Americans are tuned in to the artificial images of TV-land and tuned out from the rest of the world. Moreover, Ehrenreich points to a paradox in our relationship to television: "We love TV because TV brings us a world in which TV does not exist."

As you read *this essay, observe Ehrenreich's tone, which succeeds in being both funny and biting. Notice also how she uses irony and exaggeration to make her critique simultaneously understated and incisive.*

Someone has to speak for them, because they have, to a person, 1
lost the power to speak for themselves. I am referring to that great
mass of Americans who were once known as the "salt of the earth,"
then as "the silent majority," more recently as "the viewing public,"
and now, alas, as "couch potatoes." What drives them—or rather,
leaves them sapped and spineless on their reclining chairs? What are
they seeking—beyond such obvious goals as a tastefully colorized version of *The Maltese Falcon?*

My husband was the first in the family to "spud out," as the ex-   2
pression now goes. Soon everyone wanted one of those zip-up "Couch
Potato Bags," to keep warm in during David Letterman. The youngest

and most thoroughly immobilized member of the family relies on a remote that controls his TV, stereo, and VCR, and can also shut down the neighbor's pacemaker at fifteen yards.

But we never see the neighbors anymore, nor they us. This saddens me, because Americans used to be a great and restless people, fond of the outdoors in all of its manifestations, from Disney World to miniature golf. Some experts say there are virtues in mass agoraphobia, that it strengthens the family and reduces highway deaths. But I would point out that there are still a few things that cannot be done in the den, especially by someone zipped into a body bag. These include racquetball, voting, and meeting strange people in bars.

Most psychologists interpret the couch potato trend as a negative reaction to the outside world. Indeed, the list of reasons to stay safely tucked indoors lengthens yearly. First there was crime, then AIDS, then side-stream smoke. To this list should be added "fear of the infrastructure," for we all know someone who rashly stepped outside only to be buried in a pothole, hurled from a collapsing bridge, or struck by a falling airplane.

But it is not just the outside world that has let us down. Let's face it, despite a decade-long campaign by the "profamily" movement, the family has been a disappointment. The reason lies in an odd circular dynamic: we watch television to escape from our families because television shows us how dull our families really are.

Compare your own family to, for example, the Huxtables, the Keatons, or the peppy young people on *Thirtysomething*. In those families, even the three-year-olds are stand-up comics, and the most insipid remark is hailed with heartening outbursts of canned laughter. When television families aren't gathered around the kitchen table exchanging wisecracks, they are experiencing brief but moving dilemmas, which are handily solved by the youngest child or by some cute extraterrestrial house-guest. Emerging from *Family Ties* or *My Two Dads*, we are forced to acknowledge that our own families are made up of slow-witted, emotionally crippled people who would be lucky to qualify for seats in the studio audience of *Jeopardy!*

But gradually I have come to see that there is something besides fear of the outside and disgust with our families that drives us to spudhood—some positive attraction, some deep cathexis to television itself. For a long time it eluded me. When I watched television, mainly as a way of getting to know my husband and children, I found that my mind wandered to more interesting things, like whether to get up and make ice cubes.

Only after many months of viewing did I begin to understand the force that has transformed the American people into root vegetables. If you watch TV for a very long time, day in, day out, you will begin to notice something eerie and unnatural about the world portrayed therein. I don't mean that it is two-dimensional or lacks a well-developed critique of the capitalist consumer culture or something superficial like that. I mean something so deeply obvious that it's almost scary. When you watch television, you will see people doing many things—chasing fast cars, drinking lite beer, shooting each other at close range, etc. But you will never see people *watching television.* Well, maybe for a second before the phone rings or a brand-new, multiracial adopted child walks into the house. But never *really watching,* hour after hour, the way *real* people do.

Way back in the beginning of the television era, this was not so strange, because real people actually did many of the things people do on TV, even if it was only bickering with their mothers-in-law about which toilet paper to buy. But modern people, i.e., couch potatoes, do nothing that is ever shown on television (because it is either dangerous or would involve getting up from the couch). And what they do do—watch television—is far too boring to be televised for more than a fraction of a second, not even by Andy Warhol, bless his boredom-proof little heart.   9

So why do we keep on watching? The answer, by now, should be perfectly obvious: we love television because television brings us a world in which television does not exist. In fact, deep in their hearts, this is what the spuds crave most: a rich, new, participatory life, in which family members look each other in the eye, in which people walk outside and banter with the neighbors, where there is adventure, possibility, danger, feeling, all in natural color, stereophonic sound, and three dimensions, without commercial interruptions, and starring... us.   10

"You mean some new kind of computerized interactive medium?" the children asked hopefully, pert as the progeny on a Tuesday night sitcom. But before I could expand on this concept—known to our ancestors as "real life"—they were back at the box, which may be, after all, the only place left to find it.   11

Examining the Text

1. Ehrenreich's tone in this essay is basically satirical. Point out several examples of this approach and consider why she adopts this tone. Does she only intend to be amusing or would you say she is making a serious point? If so, what is it?

2. What differences does Ehrenreich note between what we see on television and "real life"? Could these differences be viewed as criticism of television and/or of how we live our lives? Should television reflect the way most people live?

3. "Couch potato" was widely quoted in the media during the middle and late eighties when Ehrenreich wrote this essay, but the term is not as common today. Has the "couch potato" phenomenon been a significant aspect of U.S. culture over the last decade or so? How does the way you answer these questions color your responses to Ehrenreich's essay?

For Group Discussion

Working in a group, choose several currently popular programs that focus on family life and list the characteristics of the families they portray—the relationships among family members, the ways they behave, the problems they face and how they solve them. (For balance, choose at least one situation comedy and one hour-long dramatic series.) How well do these characteristics correspond to those that Ehrenreich notes? As a class, consider how accurately these television families reflect the "average" American family and, in fact, whether there is any such thing as an "average" American family.

Writing Suggestion

Based on your own experiences and your observations of your own family and friends, how would you characterize the television viewing habits of most people? In an essay, analyze the different reasons people have for watching television. In doing so, you may wish to expand upon or counter Ehrenreich's observations.

Television and Cultural Behavior

Conrad P. Kottak

In the following essay Conrad Kottak, a professor of cultural anthropology, chooses an unusual subject for study: the students in his own large Introductory Anthropology course. Treating his classroom as a microcosm that can reveal important information about our society, he extends this comparison even to the point of half jokingly calling his students "natives."

Implicitly arguing with other scholars who might see television as trivial—and against distinctions between "high" and "low" forms of culture—Kottak takes television as his cultural artifact and object of study. The crux of his argument is that years of television watching have fundamentally conditioned the behavior of post-1955 generations of Americans, and that this "teleconditioning" has caused them to adopt behavior styles learned while watching TV. To develop his somewhat unorthodox thesis, Kottak connects his role as a teacher to the role of the television set in modern life. According to Kottak, these behavior patterns manifest themselves in his classroom, where his students react to the "live" instructor—namely, himself—as they would to a TV screen.

For Kottak, television is as powerful as our other societal and cultural institutions—such as family, church, and state—and his attempt to subject it to traditional anthropological study includes the use of academic language and the creation of new terminology such as "teleconditioning."

As you read, consider what you may know of anthropology from your own studies, and notice how Kottak is trying to "modernize" his discipline by treating technology as a contemporary cultural artifact. Consider also the validity of his thesis in your life: Have you been "teleconditioned" into treating a lecturer the same way you would your television set?

Why should a cultural anthropologist, trained to study primitive   1
societies, be interested in television, which is the creation of a complex, industrial society? My interest in television's impact on human social behavior arose mainly through contacts with young Americans. These include my children, their friends, and particularly the college students at the University of Michigan to whom I have been teaching introductory anthropology since 1968.

Most of the freshmen I have taught during the past decade were   2
born after 1955. They belong to the first generation raised after the almost total diffusion of television into the American home. Most of these young Americans have never known a world without TV. The tube has been as much a fixture in their homes as mom or dad. Considering how common divorce has become, the TV set even outlasts the father in many homes. American kids now devote 22–30 hours to television each week. By the end of high school, they will have spent 22,000 hours in front of the set, versus only 11,000 in the classroom (*Ann Arbor News* 1985b). Such prolonged exposure must modify Americans' behavior in several ways.

I have discussed the behavior modification I see in my classroom   3
with university colleagues, and many say they have observed similar changes in students' conduct. The thesis to be defended in this [essay] is somewhat different from those of other studies about television's effects on behavior. Previous researchers have found links between exposure to media content (for example, violence) and individual behavior (hyperactivity, aggression, "acting out"). I also believe that content affects behavior. However, I make a more basic claim: The very habit of watching television has modified the behavior of Americans who have grown up with the tube.

Anyone who has been to a movie house recently has seen exam-   4
ples of TV conditioned behavior—**teleconditioning.** People talk, babies cry, members of the audience file in and out getting snacks and going to the bathroom. Students act similarly in college courses. A decade ago, there was always an isolated student who did these kinds of things. What is new is a behavior pattern, characteristic of a group rather than

an individual. This cultural pattern is becoming more and more pronounced, and I link it directly to televiewing. Stated simply, the pattern is this: *Televiewing causes people to duplicate inappropriately, in other areas of their lives, behavior styles developed while watching television.*

Some examples are in order. Almost nothing bothers professors   5
more than having someone read a newspaper in class. If lecturers take their message and teaching responsibilities seriously, they are understandably perturbed when a student shows more interest in a sports column or "Doonesbury." I don't often get newspapers in class, but one day I noticed a student sitting in the front row reading a paperback novel. Irritated by her audacity, I stopped lecturing and asked "Why are you reading a book in my class?" Her answer: "Oh, I'm not in your class. I just came in here to read my book."

How is this improbable response explained? Why would some-   6
one take the trouble to come into a classroom in order to read? The answer, I think, is this: Because of televiewing, many young Americans have trouble reading unless they have background noise. Research confirms that most Americans do something else while watching television. Often they read. Even I do it. When I get home from work I often turn on the television set, sit down in a comfortable chair, and go through the mail or read the newspaper.

Research on television's impact in other countries confirms that   7
televiewing evolves through certain stages. The first stage when sets are introduced is rapt attention, gazes glued to the screen. Some of us can remember from the late 1940s and 1950s sitting in front of our first TV, dumbly watching even test patterns. Later, as the novelty diminishes, viewers become progressively less attentive. Televiewers in Brazil, whom I began studying systematically in 1983, had already moved past the first stage, but they were still much more attentive than Americans.

A study done in Brazil's largest city, São Paulo, illustrates the con-   8
trast. The study shocked Rede Globo, Brazil's dominant network (and the most watched commercial TV network in the world). It revealed that half the viewers were not paying full attention when commercials were shown. Afraid of losing advertising revenues, Rede Globo attacked the accuracy of the research. American sponsors are so accustomed to inattention and, nowadays, to remote control tune-outs, that it would probably delight them if even half the audience stayed put.

The student who came to my class to read her novel was simply   9
an extreme example of a culture pattern derived from television. Because of her lifelong TV dependency, she had trouble reading without background noise. It didn't matter to her whether the background hum came from a stereo, a TV set, or a live professor. Accustomed to machines that don't talk back, she probably was amazed that I noticed her at all. Perhaps my questioning even prompted her to check her set that night to see if someone real was lurking inside.

Another example of a televiewing effect is students' increasing   10
tendency to enter and leave classrooms at will. Of course, individual
students do occasionally get sick or have a dentist's appointment.
But here again I'm describing a group pattern rather than individual
idiosyncrasies. Only during the past few years have I regularly observed students getting up in mid-lecture, leaving the room for a few
minutes, then returning. Sometimes they bring back a canned soft
drink.

These students intend no disrespect. They are simply transfer-   11
ring a home-grown pattern of snack-and-bathroom break from family
room to classroom. They perceive nothing unusual in acting the same
way in front of a live speaker and fellow students as they do when
they watch television. (A few students manage to remain seated for
only 10–15 minutes. Then they get up and leave the classroom. They
are exhibiting a less flattering pattern. Either they have diarrhea, as
one student told me he did, or they have decided to shut off the "set"
or "change channels.")

Today, almost all Americans talk while watching television.   12
Talking is becoming more common in the classroom, as in the movie
house, and this also illustrates television's effects on our collective behavior. Not only do my students bring food and drink to class, some
lie down on the floor if they arrive too late to get a seat. I have even
seen couples kissing and caressing just a few rows away.

New examples of teleconditioning pop up all the time. In each of   13
the past two semesters that I've taught introductory anthropology, at
least one student has requested that I say publicly "Happy Birthday"
to a friend in the class. These students seem to perceive me as a profes-
sorial analog of Willard Scott, NBC's *Today* show weatherman, who offers birthday greetings (to people 100 and over). Long ago I put into
my syllabus injunctions against reading newspapers and eating
crunchy foods in class. Last semester I felt compelled to announce that
I "don't do birthdays."

All these are examples of effects of televiewing on social behav-   14
ior of young Americans. They are not individual idiosyncrasies (the
subject matter of psychology) but new *culture patterns* that have
emerged since the 1950s. As such they are appropriate objects for anthropological analysis. **Culture,** as defined by anthropologists, consists of knowledge, beliefs, perceptions, attitudes, expectations, values,
and patterns of behavior that people learn by growing up in a given
society. Above all else, culture consists of *shared* learning. In contrast to
education, it extends well beyond what we learn in school, to encompass everything we learn in life. Much of the information that contemporary Americans share comes from their common exposure to the
mass media, particularly television.

TV CONTENT'S CULTURAL IMPACT

TV *content's* impact on American culture enters the story when we   15
consider that contemporary Americans share common information and
experiences because of the programs they have seen. Again, I learn from
my students. The subject matter of introductory anthropology includes
the kinship systems of the United States and other societies. One habit I
acquired about five years ago takes advantage of my students' familiarity with television. My practice is to illustrate changes in American family structure and household organization by contrasting television
programs of the 1950s with more recent examples.

Three decades ago, the usual TV family was a nuclear family   16
consisting of employed father (who often knew best), homemaker
mother, and children. Examples include *Father Knows Best, Ozzie and
Harriet* and *Leave It to Beaver.* These programs, which were appropriate
for the 1950s, are out of sync with the social and economic realities of
the late 1980s. Only 16 million American women worked outside the
home in 1950, compared with three times that number today. By
the mid-1980s, fewer than 10 percent of American households had the
composition that was once considered normal: breadwinner father,
homemaker mother, and two children. Still, today's college students
remain knowledgeable about these 1950s shows through syndicated
reruns. Afternoon television is a pop culture museum that familiarizes
kids with many of the same images, characters, and tales that their
parents saw in recent days of yore.

Virtually all my students have seen reruns of the series *The Brady*   17
Bunch. Its family organization provides an interesting contrast with
earlier programs. It illustrates what anthropologists call "blended family organization." A new (blended) family forms when a widow with
three daughters marries a widower with three sons. Blended families
have been increasing in American society because of more frequent divorce and remarriage. However, a first spouse's death may also lead
to a blended family, as in *The Brady Bunch.* During *The Brady Bunch's*
first run, divorce remained controversial and thus could not give rise
to the Brady household.

The occupation of Mike, the Brady husband-father, a successful   18
architect, illustrates a trend toward upper-middle-class jobs and life-
styles that continues on American television today. TV families tend to
be more professional, more successful, and richer than the average
real-life family. More recent examples include the Huxtables (*The
Cosby Show*) and the Keatons (*Family Ties*). There are also ultra-rich
night-time soap families such as the Carringtons of *Dynasty* and the
Ewings of *Dallas.* Mike and Carol Brady were wealthy enough to employ a housekeeper, Alice. Mirroring American culture when the pro-

gram was made, the career of the wife-mother was part time and subsidiary, if it existed at all. Back then, women like Carol Brady who had
been lucky enough to find a wealthy husband didn't compete with
other women—even professional housekeepers—in the work force.

I use familiar examples like *The Brady Bunch* to teach students   19
how to draw the genealogies and kinship diagrams that anthropologists use routinely in fieldwork and in making cross-cultural comparisons. TV family relationships may be represented with the same
symbols and genealogical charts used for the Bushmen of the Kalahari
Desert of southern Africa, or any other society. In particular, I chart
changes in American family organization, showing how real-life
changes have been reflected in television content, with which students
tend to be familiar. *The Brady Bunch*, for example, illustrates a trend toward showing nontraditional families and households. We also see
this trend in day-time soaps and in prime time, with the marital
breakups, reconciliations, and extended family relationships of *Dallas*,
Dynasty, *Falcon Crest*, and *Knot's Landing*. The trend toward newer
household types is also obvious in *Kate & Allie* and *The Golden Girls*.

Students enjoy learning about anthropological techniques with   20
culturally familiar examples. Each time I begin my kinship lecture, a few
people in the class immediately recognize (from reruns) the nuclear
families of the 1950s. They know the names of all the Cleavers—Ward,
June, Wally, and Beaver. However, when I begin diagramming the
Bradys, my students can't contain themselves. They start shouting out
"Jan," "Bobby," "Greg," "Cindy," "Marsha," "Peter," "Mike," "Carol,"
"Alice." The response mounts. By the time we get to Carol and Alice, almost everyone is taking part in my blackboard kinship chart. Whenever
I give my Brady Bunch lecture, Anthropology 101 resembles a revival
meeting. Hundreds of young natives shout out in unison names made
almost as familiar as their parents' through television reruns.

As the natives take up this chant—learned by growing up in   21
post-1950s America—there is an enthusiasm, a warm glow, that my
course will not recapture until next semester's rerun of my Brady
Bunch lecture. It is as though my students find nirvana, religious ecstasy, through their collective remembrance of the Bradys, in the ritual-
like incantation of their names.

Given my own classroom experiences, I was hardly surprised to   22
read that in a 1986 survey of 1,550 American adults, more people said
they got pleasure from TV than from sex, food, liquor, money, or religion. In that survey, people indicated which of the following "give a
great deal of pleasure and satisfaction." The percentages were as follows:

watching TV	68
friends	61

helping others	59
vacations	58
hobbies	56
reading	55
marriage	45
sexual relationships	42
food	41
money	40
sports	32
religion	32

Furthermore, when people were asked what they liked to do for relaxation, watching TV again topped the list, followed by just relaxing and doing nothing, vacationing, music, reading and going out to eat. Sex and religion were each chosen by a mere one percent.

THE CULTURAL DIMENSION

I often wonder how my more traditional colleagues in anthropol-   23
ogy have managed to avoid becoming interested in television—so striking are the behavioral modifications it has wrought in the natives we see and talk to most frequently: our fellow citizens in modern society. Nationwide and ubiquitous, television cuts across demographic boundaries. It presents to diverse groups a set of common symbols, vocabularies, information, and shared experiences. Televiewing encompasses men and women of different ages, colors, classes, ethnic groups, and levels of educational achievement. Television is seen in cities, suburbs, towns, and country—by farmers, factory workers, and philosophers (although the last may be loath to admit it).

Television is stigmatized as trivial by many people (particularly   24
orthodox intellectuals). However, it is hardly trivial that the average American household has more television sets (2.2 per home) than bathrooms. Given the level of television's penetration of the modern home, we should hardly ignore its effects on socialization and enculturation. The common information that members of a mass society come to share as a result of watching the same thing is indisputably *culture* as anthropologists use the term. This anthropological definition of culture encompasses a much broader spectrum of human life than the definition that focuses on "high culture"—refinement, cultivation, taste, sophistication, education, and appreciation of the fine arts. From the anthropological perspective, not just university graduates, but all people are cultured.

Anthropology's subject matter must include features of modern   25
culture that some regard as too trivial to be worthy of serious study,

such as commercial television. As a cultural product and manifestation, a rock star may be as interesting as a symphony conductor, a comic book as significant as a book-award winner. It is axiomatic in anthropology that the most significant cultural forces are those that affect us every day of our lives. Particularly important are those features influencing children during **enculturation**—the process whereby one grows up in a particular society and absorbs its culture.

Culture is collective, shared, meaningful. It is transmitted by conscious and unconscious learning experiences. People acquire it not through their genes, but as a result of growing up in a particular society. Hundreds of culture-bearers have passed through the Anthropology 101 classroom over the past decade. Many have been unable to recall the full names of their parents' first cousins. Some have forgotten a grandmother's maiden name, and few contemporary students know many Biblical or Shakespearean characters. Most, however, have no trouble identifying names and relationships in mythical families that exist only in televisionland.   26

As the Bible, Shakespeare, and classical mythology did in the past, television influences the names we bestow on our children and answer to all our lives. For example, "Jaime" rose from 70th to 10th most popular girl's name within two years of the debut of *The Bionic Woman*, whose title character was Jaime Sommers. The first name of the program's star, Lindsay Wagner, also became popular. *Charlie's Angels* boosted "Tiffany" and "Sabrina." Younger kids are named "Blake," "Alexis," "Fallon," and "Krystle" (spellings vary) after *Dynasty*'s Carringtons. In other cultures children still receive names of gods (Jesus, Mohammed) and heroes (Ulysses). The comparably honored Olympians of contemporary America lead their glamorous, superhuman lives not on a mountaintop, but in a small square box. We don't even have to go to church to worship them, because we can count on them to come to us in weekly visitations.   27

Psychologists are still debating the precise effects of television on *individual* behavior and psychopathology; TV murders and car chases may indeed influence kids toward aggressive or destructive behavior. However, television's *cultural* effects are indubitable. Examples of the medium's impact on U.S. culture—on the collective behavior and knowledge of contemporary Americans—are everywhere.   28

My conclusions about television can be summarized as follows: New culture patterns related to television's penetration of the American home have emerged since the 1950s. As *technology*, television affects collective behavior, as people duplicate, in many areas of their lives, habits developed while watching TV. Television *content* also influences mass culture because it provides widely shared common knowledge, beliefs, and expectations.   29

I became interested in television because I saw that its effects are   30
comparable to those of humanity's most powerful traditional institutions—family, church, state, and education. Television is creating new
cultural experiences and meanings. It is capable of producing intense,
often irrationally based, feelings of solidarity and *communitas* ("community feeling") shared widely by people who have grown up within
the same cultural tradition. Nothing so important to natives could
long escape the eye of the anthropologist.

Examining the Text

1. Kottak coins the term "teleconditioning" to refer to certain television-
induced patterns of behavior and provides several examples drawn
from movie audiences and students in his classes. What other sorts of
behavior have you observed recently that might be the result of teleconditioning?

2. Given that students in large lectures do exhibit the behavior Kottak
describes—reading newspapers and drifting in and out of class, for example—are there ways to account for this behavior other than teleconditioning? Does Kottak's assertion that such behavior has increased
since the 1960s support his analysis or are there other conditions that
could have contributed to this change?

3. Kottak suggests that television is as powerful an institution in influencing cultures as "family, church, state, and education" (paragraph
30). What examples does he give of this influence? Can you think of
others? Do you think Kottak's assessment is accurate or does he exag-
gerate his case?

For Group Discussion

How closely does Kottak's list of pleasurable activities (22) correspond to your own and those of other college students? Reorder his
list to reflect your own observations, adding and deleting as you wish.
Then compare your group members' lists and try to reach some consensus on an accurate list. Finally, discuss each group's lists as a class.

Writing Suggestion

Kottak discusses the significance of *The Brady Bunch* in his anthropology classes. In an essay, consider other family-based series
from the 1980s and 1990s that are current reruns on TV. What significance do they have both as representations of family structure and as
widely shared points of cultural reference?

Life According to TV

Harry Waters

*The world of television directly influences how people see the "real"
world around them. So says George Gerbner, a noted cultural critic and
communications scholar. Gerbner and his staff spent over fifteen years
studying the televised programs America watches. Their results paint a
damning picture of the TV industry. In the following essay, Harry Waters
summarizes Gerbner's research about how the televised world matches up
to "reality" and to people's perception of reality. To that end, Gerbner
breaks the television-viewing audience into a number of different representative categories—gender, age, race, and lifestyle, just to name a few—and he
observes how people in each category are portrayed in different television
shows.*

*Frequently, Gerbner's results, as detailed by Waters, are surprising.
For example, contrary to most studies of the relationship between TV and
crime, which suggest that television causes people to become more violent,
Gerbner argues that the prevalence of crime on TV creates a "fear of victimization" in the viewer. This fear ultimately leads to a "mean-world syndrome" in which viewers come to see their social surroundings as hostile and
threatening. Waters balances Gerbner's conclusions with comments from network officials who, not surprisingly, often take Gerbner to task.*

As you read *this selection, pay particular attention to the way Waters
maintains his objectivity by attributing most of the opinions and conclusions
to Gerbner and his assistants. Notice, too, how Waters's opinions about Gerbner's research can be detected in phrasing such as "the gospel of Gerbner,"
"tidy explanation," and "comforting."*

Since this is an article originally published in Newsweek, *a magazine
which claims to report the news without bias, you might ask just how* really
objective so-called objective reporting is.

The late Paddy Chayefsky, who created Howard Beale, would   1
have loved George Gerbner. In "Network," Chayefsky marshaled a
scathing, fictional assault on the values and methods of the people
who control the world's most potent communications instrument. In
real life, Gerbner, perhaps the nation's foremost authority on the social
impact of television, is quietly using the disciplines of behavioral research to construct an equally devastating indictment of the medium's
images and messages. More than any spokesman for a pressure group,
Gerbner has become the man that television watches. From his
cramped, book-lined office at the University of Pennsylvania springs a

steady flow of studies that are raising executive blood pressures at the networks' sleek Manhattan command posts.

George Gerbner's work is uniquely important because it transports the scientific examination of television far beyond familiar children-and-violence arguments. Rather than simply studying the link between violence on the tube and crime in the streets, Gerbner is exploring wider and deeper terrain. He has turned his lens on TV's hidden victims—women, the elderly, blacks, blue-collar workers and other groups—to document the ways in which video-entertainment portrayals subliminally condition how we perceive ourselves and how we view those around us. Gerbner's subjects are not merely the impressionable young; they include all the rest of us. And it is his ominous conclusion that heavy watchers of the prime-time mirror are receiving a grossly distorted picture of the real world that they tend to accept more readily than reality itself.

The 63-year-old Gerbner, who is dean of Penn's Annenberg School of Communications, employs a methodology that meshes scholarly observation with mundane legwork. Over the past 15 years, he and a tireless trio of assistants (Larry Gross, Nancy Signorielli and Michael Morgan) videotaped and exhaustively analyzed 1,600 prime-time programs involving more than 15,000 characters. They then drew up multiple-choice questionnaires that offered correct answers about the world at large along with answers that reflected what Gerbner perceived to be the misrepresentations and biases of the world according to TV. Finally, these questions were posed to large samples of citizens from all socioeconomic strata. In every survey, the Annenberg team discovered that heavy viewers of television (those watching more than four hours a day), who account for more than 30 percent of the population, almost invariably chose the TV-influenced answers, while light viewers (less than two hours a day), selected the answers corresponding more closely to actual life. Some of the dimensions of television's reality warp:

SEX

Male prime-time characters outnumber females by 3 to 1 and, with a few star-turn exceptions, women are portrayed as weak, passive satellites to powerful, effective men. TV's male population also plays a vast variety of roles, while females generally get typecast as either lovers or mothers. Less than 20 percent of TV's married women with children work outside the home—as compared with more than 50 percent in real life. The tube's distorted depictions of women, concludes Gerbner, reinforce stereotypical attitudes and increase sexism. In one Annenberg survey, heavy viewers were far more likely than light ones to agree with the proposition: "Women should take care of running their homes and leave running the country to men."

AGE

People over 65, too, are grossly underrepresented on television.   5
Correspondingly, heavy-viewing Annenberg respondents believe that the elderly are a vanishing breed, that they make up a smaller proportion of the population today than they did 20 years ago. In fact, they form the nation's most rapidly expanding age group. Heavy viewers also believe that old people are less healthy today than they were two decades ago, when quite the opposite is true. As with women, the portrayals of old people transmit negative impressions. In general, they are cast as silly, stubborn, sexually inactive and eccentric. "They're often shown as feeble grandparents bearing cookies," says Gerbner. "You never see the power that real old people often have. The best and possibly only time to learn about growing old with decency and grace is in youth. And young people are the most susceptible to TV's messages."

RACE

The problem with the medium's treatment of blacks is more one   6
of image than of visibility. Though a tiny percentage of black characters come across as "unrealistically romanticized," reports Gerbner, the overwhelming majority of them are employed in subservient, supporting roles—such as the white hero's comic sidekick. "When a black child looks at prime time," he says, "most of the people he sees doing interesting and important things are white." That imbalance, he goes on, tends to teach young blacks to accept minority status as naturally inevitable and even deserved. To access the impact of such portrayals on the general audience, the Annenberg survey forms included questions like "Should white people have the right to keep blacks out of their neighborhoods?" and "Should there be laws against marriages between blacks and whites?" The more that viewers watched, the more they answered "yes" to each question.

WORK

Heavy viewers greatly overestimated the proportion of Ameri-   7
cans employed as physicians, lawyers, athletes and entertainers, all of whom inhabit prime-time in hordes. A mere 6 to 10 percent of television

characters hold blue-collar or service jobs vs. about 60 percent in the real work force. Gerbner sees two dangers in TV's skewed division of labor. On the one hand, the tube so overrepresents and glamorizes the elite occupations that it sets up unrealistic expectations among those who must deal with them in actuality. At the same time, TV largely neglects portraying the occupations that most youngsters will have to enter. "You almost never see the farmer, the factory worker or the small businessman," he notes. "Thus not only do lawyers and other professionals find they cannot measure up to the image TV projects of them, but children's occupational aspirations are channeled in unrealistic directions." The Gerbner team feels this emphasis on high-powered jobs poses problems for adolescent girls, who are also presented with views of women as homebodies. The two conflicting views, Gerbner says, add to the frustration over choices they have to make as adults.

HEALTH

Although video characters exist almost entirely on junk food and   8
quaff alcohol 15 times more often than water, they manage to remain slim, healthy and beautiful. Frequent TV watchers, the Annenberg investigators found, eat more, drink more, exercise less and possess an almost mystical faith in the curative powers of medical science. Concludes Gerbner: "Television may well be the single most pervasive source of health information. And its over-idealized images of medical people, coupled with its complacency about unhealthy life-styles, leaves both patients and doctors vulnerable to disappointment, frustration and even litigation."

CRIME

On the small screen, crime rages about 10 times more often than   9
in real life. But while other researchers concentrate on the propensity of TV mayhem to incite aggression, the Annenberg team has studied the hidden side of its imprint: fear of victimization. On television, 55 percent of prime-time characters are involved in violent confrontations once a week; in reality, the figure is less than 1 percent. In all demographic groups in every class of neighborhood, heavy viewers overestimated the statistical chance of violence in their own lives and harbored an exaggerated mistrust of strangers—creating what Gerbner calls "mean-world syndrome." Forty-six percent of heavy viewers who live in cities rated their fear of crime "very serious" as opposed to 26 percent for light viewers. Such paranoia is especially acute among

TV entertainment's most common victims: women, the elderly, non-whites, foreigners and lower-class citizens.

Video violence, proposes Gerbner, is primarily responsible for   10
imparting lessons in social power: it demonstrates who can do what to whom and get away with it. "Television is saying that those at the bottom of the power scale cannot get away with the same things that a white, middle-class American male can," he says. "It potentially conditions people to think of themselves as victims."

At a quick glance, Gerbner's findings seem to contain a cause-   11
and-effect, chicken-or-the-egg question. Does television make heavy viewers view the world the way they do or do heavy viewers come from the poorer, less experienced segment of the populace that regards the world that way to begin with? In other words, does the tube create or simply confirm the unenlightened attitudes of its most loyal audiences? Gerbner, however, was savvy enough to construct a methodology largely immune to such criticism. His samples of heavy viewers cut across all ages, incomes, education levels and ethnic backgrounds—and every category displayed the same tube-induced misconceptions of the world outside.

Needless to say, the networks accept all this as enthusiastically as   12
they would a list of news-coverage complaints from the Ayatollah Khomeini. Even so, their responses tend to be tinged with a singular respect for Gerbner's personal and professional credentials. The man is no ivory-tower recluse. During World War II, the Budapest-born Gerbner parachuted into the mountains of Yugoslavia to join the partisans fighting the Germans. After the war, he hunted down and personally arrested scores of high Nazi officials. Nor is Gerbner some videophobic vigilante. A Ph.D. in communications, he readily acknowledges TV's beneficial effects, noting that it has abolished parochialism, reduced isolation and loneliness and provided the poorest members of society with cheap, plug-in exposure to experiences they otherwise would not have. Funding for his research is supported by such prestigious bodies as the National Institute of Mental Health, the Surgeon General's office, and the American Medical Association, and he is called to testify before congressional committees nearly as often as David Stockman.

MASS ENTERTAINMENT

When challenging Gerbner, network officials focus less on his   13
findings and methods than on what they regard as his own misconceptions of their industry's function. "He's looking at television from the perspective of a social scientist rather than considering what is

mass entertainment," says Alfred Schneider, vice president of standards and practices at ABC. "We strive to balance TV's social effects with what will capture an audience's interests. If you showed strong men being victimized as much as women or the elderly, what would comprise the dramatic conflict? If you did a show truly representative of society's total reality, and nobody watched because it wasn't interesting, what have you achieved?"

CBS senior vice president Gene Mater also believes that Gerbner   14
is implicitly asking for the theoretically impossible. "TV is unique in its problems," says Mater. "Everyone wants a piece of the action. Everyone feels that their racial or ethnic group is underrepresented or should be portrayed as they would like the world to perceive them. No popular entertainment form, including this one, can or should be an accurate reflection of society."

On that point, at least, Gerbner is first to agree; he hardly expects   15
television entertainment to serve as a mirror image of absolute truth. But what fascinates him about this communications medium is its marked difference from all others. In other media, customers carefully choose what they want to hear or read: a movie, a magazine, a best seller. In television, notes Gerbner, viewers rarely tune in for a particular program. Instead, most just habitually turn on the set—and watch by the clock rather than for a specific show. "Television viewing fulfills the criteria of a ritual," he says. "It is the only medium that can bring to people things they otherwise would not select." With such unique power, believes Gerbner, comes unique responsibility: "No other medium reaches into every home or has a comparable, cradle-to-grave influence over what a society learns about itself."

MATCH

In Gerbner's view, virtually all of TV's distortions of reality can   16
be attributed to its obsession with demographics. The viewers that primetime sponsors most want to reach are white, middle-class, female and between 18 and 49—in short, the audience that purchases most of the consumer products advertised on the tube. Accordingly, notes Gerbner, the demographic portrait of TV's fictional characters largely matches that of its prime commercial targets and largely ignores everyone else. "Television," he concludes, "reproduces a world for its own best customers."

Among TV's more candid executives, that theory draws consid-   17
erable support. Yet by pointing a finger at the power of demographics, Gerbner appears to contradict one of his major findings. If female viewers are so dear to the hearts of sponsors, why are female charac-

ters cast in such unflattering light? "In a basically male-oriented power structure," replies Gerbner, "you can't alienate the male viewer. But you can get away with offending women because most women are pretty well brainwashed to accept it." The Annenberg dean has an equally tidy explanation for another curious fact. Since the corporate world provides network television with all of its financial support, one would expect businessmen on TV to be portrayed primarily as good guys. Quite the contrary. As any fan of "Dallas," "Dynasty" or "Falcon Crest" well knows, the image of the company man is usually that of a mendacious, dirty-dealing rapscallion. Why would TV snap at the hand that feeds it? "Credibility is the way to ratings," proposes Gerbner. "This country has a populist tradition of bias against anything big, including big business. So to retain credibility, TV entertainment shows businessman in relatively derogatory ways."

In the medium's Hollywood-based creative community, the [18] gospel of Gerbner finds some passionate adherents. Rarely have TV's best and brightest talents viewed their industry with so much frustration and anger. The most sweeping indictment emanates from David Rintels, a two-time Emmy-winning writer and former president of the Writers Guild of America, West. "Gerbner is absolutely correct and it is the people who run the networks who are to blame," says Rintels. "The networks get bombarded with thoughtful, reality-oriented scripts. They simply won't do them. They slam the door on them. They believe that the only way to get ratings is to feed viewers what conforms to their biases or what has limited resemblance to reality. From 8 to 11 o'clock each night, television is one long lie."

Innovative thinkers such as Norman Lear, whose work has been [19] practically driven off the tube, don't fault the networks so much as the climate in which they operate. Says Lear: "All of this country's institutions have become totally fixated on short-term bottom-line thinking. Everyone grabs for what might succeed today and the hell with tomorrow. Television just catches more of the heat because it's more visible." Perhaps the most perceptive assessment of Gerbner's conclusions is offered by one who has worked both sides of the industry street. Deanne Barkley, a former NBC vice president who now helps run an independent production house, reports that the negative depictions of women on TV have made it "nerve-racking" to function as a woman within TV. "No one takes responsibility for the social impact of their shows," says Barkley. "But then how do you decide where it all begins? Do the networks give viewers what they want? Or are the networks conditioning them to think that way?"

Gerbner himself has no simple answer to that conundrum. Nei- [20] ther a McLuhanesque shaman nor a Naderesque crusader, he hesitates to suggest solutions until pressed. Then out pops a pair of provocative notions. Commercial television will never democratize its treatments of daily life, he believes, until it finds a way to broaden its financial base. Coincidentally, Federal Communications Commission chairman Mark Fowler seems to have arrived at much the same conclusion. In exchange for lifting such government restrictions on TV as the fairness doctrine and the equal-time rule, Fowler would impose a modest levy on station owners called a spectrum-use fee. Funds from the fees would be set aside to finance programs aimed at specialized tastes rather than the mass appetite. Gerbner enthusiastically endorses that proposal: "Let the ratings system dominate most of prime time but not every hour of every day. Let some programs carry advisories that warn: 'This is not for all of you. This is for nonwhites, or for religious people or for the aged and the handicapped. Turn it off unless you'd like to eavesdrop.' That would be a very refreshing thing."

ROLE

In addition, Gerbner would like to see viewers given an active role in steering the overall direction of television instead of being obliged to passively accept whatever the networks offer. In Britain, he points out, political candidates debate the problems of TV as routinely as the issue of crime. In this country, proposes Gerbner, "every political campaign should put television on the public agenda. Candidates talk about schools, they talk about jobs, they talk about social welfare. They're going to have to start discussing this all-pervasive force." 21

There are no outright villains in this docudrama. Even Gerbner recognizes that network potentates don't set out to proselytize a point of view; they are simply businessmen selling a mass-market product. At the same time, their 90 million nightly customers deserve to know the side effects of the ingredients. By the time the typical American child reaches the age of reason, calculates Gerbner, he or she will have absorbed more than 30,000 electronic "stories." These stories, he suggests, have replaced the socializing role of the preindustrial church: they create a "cultural mythology" that establishes the norms of approved behavior and belief. And all Gerbner's research indicates that this new mythological world, with its warped picture of a sizable portion of society, may soon become the one most of us think we live in. 22

Who else is telling us that? Howard Beale and his eloquent alarms have faded into off network reruns. At the very least, it is comforting to know that a real-life Beale is very much with us...and really watching. 23

Examining the Text

1. Waters reports extensive studies by George Gerbner and his associates that show that heavy television viewers have a generally "warped" view of reality, influenced by television's own "reality warp" (paragraph 3). Which viewers do you think would be affected most negatively by these "warped" viewpoints, and why?

2. Gerbner's studies show that "55 percent of prime-time characters are involved in violent confrontations once a week; in reality, the figure is less than 1 percent" (9). While violent crime is known to rank as middle-class America's primary concern, most violent crime occurs in neighborhoods far removed from most middle-class people. How do you explain these discrepancies? Why is "violent confrontation" so common on television? How does the violence you see on television affect you?

3. Waters interviewed a number of different people when he wrote this article for *Newsweek*. Collectively, they offer a variety of explanations for and solutions to the limited images television provides. Look closely at these suggested causes and solutions. Which seem most reasonable to you? In general, is Waters's coverage of the issue balanced? Why or why not?

For Group Discussion

This article was first published more than ten years ago. With your group, look again at Gerbner's categories and discuss what significant recent examples suggest about the way current television programming represents reality. Do today's shows seem more accurate than those of ten years ago? As a class, discuss whether or not most viewers want more "reality" on television.

Writing Suggestion

Starting with Gerbner's six categories, analyze any ways you have come to realize that television distorts your views of reality. In an essay, consider the source of these distortions. How can you perceive reality more accurately, and what do you think the relationship between television images and "real life" could be?

Common Contemporary Themes

Paul Monaco

Paul Monaco believes that we are "awash in wild, but widely believed, claims about the movies, television, and the audiences for them" In fact, he might argue that the previous three articles in this chapter are examples of these "wild claims," of unsound thinking about TV's influence on its viewers.

Monaco, a professor at Montana State University, has written several books on cinema and culture and has produced and directed shows for Montana Public Television. This reading comes from his 1998 book Understanding Society, Culture, and Television, *in which he explains the art of television storytelling and takes issue with the predominant view that TV contributes to various social ills and caters to our desire for depravity. In order to believe this, Monaco argues, we have to assume that TV viewers are "undiscriminating and stupid."*

Monaco's disputes two claims made about television's influence: first, that TV viewing preferences (for instance, the great popularity of the O. J. Simpson trial) indicate that we are a sick society; and second, that TV itself (for instance, the show Beavis and Butthead) *causes our social ills. He provides evidence to the contrary, arguing that our reasons for watching certain programs and the influences of those programs on us are various and idiosyncratic. In short, Monaco argues that the manipulative power of TV has been highly exaggerated.*

Monaco's examples come from TV events in the 1990s: the O. J. Simpson trial and the Murphy Brown–Dan Quayle *episode.* As you read, *think about similar TV events and controversies that are occurring now. What do they indicate about how our society views TV's influence?*

The way most Americans think and talk about TV is remarkable. 1
Federal Communications Commission chairman Newton N. Minow's 1961 description of network television as "a vast wasteland" still is widely quoted. Hardly anyone is aware that at the end of that same year Minow was saying that when viewers on any given night could choose between a drama starring Julie Harris, a special with Yves Montand, or an exposé of a bookie joint, the networks already had led us out of the wasteland.[1] Following that logic, what should we make of television today when a substantial number of viewers can choose from scores of channels?

There is a lot of moaning about what's on TV. Complaints have 2
been steady throughout television's half century of existence. From time to time their character and tone changes but the core idea remains unaltered. We are told that we are watching the wrong programs and too many of them. "Boob tube" and "couch potato" are common terms that nobody questions. Television, however, hardly has an exclusive hold on intellectual shallowness, dishonesty, and exaggeration in our culture.

Owners of $2,500 TV sets routinely call them idiot boxes, with little 3
sense of self contradiction. Several years ago I knew a student who had

---

[1]*Variety*, December 13, 1961.

a bumper sticker on his car that read: "Kill Your Television." On several occasions, however, I overheard him talking with other students about what he had seen the night before on *The David Letterman Show*. People consistently deny that they watch as much television as they actually do. The stigma attached to saying that you like television is strong. Recently, as a panelist on a televised discussion about violence and TV, the moderator asked me if people weren't watching TV "too much." His question implies that there is an answer. I don't believe that there is.

Ellen A. Wartella, the dean of the College of Communications at   4 the University of Texas at Austin, maintains that "the United States is the only English-speaking nation in the world without media education in its public schools."[2] Whether this claim is literally true or not, American schools do spend billions of dollars trying to educate students to distinguish good writing from bad, but almost nothing on their understanding of the media arts. While the nation needs some substantive courses in television analysis and criticism, I would steer clear of the notion that the public schools need an elaborate curriculum or great expenditures of taxpayer dollars to explore television. What is needed, instead, is sound thinking about TV and where it fits into society and culture.

What is really wrong with television? Claims about the me-   5 dium's negative impact upon society are rampant and come from various directions. Take, for example, the matter of how television covers the news. Andrew Tyndall, who tracks the time that television devotes to particular news stories found that from January through September 1995, the major American networks ABC, CBS, and NBC devoted twelve percent of their nightly newscasts to the O. J. Simpson murder trial. This was slightly more time than they devoted to the next two most covered stories *combined:* the war in Bosnia and the deadly bombing of the Murrah Federal Building in Oklahoma City.[3] A similar set of statistics reveals that the opening of the Berlin Wall in 1989 and its immediate aftermath warranted 252 minutes of network newscast coverage over a two-month period. The attack by people associated with Tonya Harding on rival Olympic figure skater Nancy Kerrigan garnered 263 minutes of coverage over a similar sixty days.[4]

In reading these statistics, I suspect that there is a widespread   6 sense that we know what they mean. But what are the demonstrable social consequences of the amount of coverage devoted to specific stories

---

[2]Ellen A. Wartella, "The Context of Television Violence," The Carroll C. Arnold Distinguished Lecture, Needham Heights, MA, Allyn and Bacon, 1997.

[3]Michael Gartner, "O.J. Circus, Blame TV," *USA Today*, October 3, 1995, p. 11A.

[4]Cited in an editorial, *The Bozeman Daily Chronicle*, July 15, 1994, p. 4.

or topics? The O. J. Simpson murder trial coincided with the period in which I did a substantial portion of the research for this [essay] and began writing it. I followed a fair amount of the coverage of that trial, as well as commentary about it, on television. My interest in that trial, however, was in keeping with my own long term interests. I am a fan of Court TV. I saw considerable portions of the trial of William Kennedy Smith on rape charges. I watched some of the Menendez brothers' trial for the murder of their parents. Over the years, I have followed the trials of defendants both obscure and famous. I have even watched traffic court deliberations from various jurisdictions across the United States. I find legal argument and court procedures fascinating. Questions of guilt and innocence are intriguing to me, no matter what the charges against a defendant. Weighing the arguments and the evidence is part of seeing any trial, and awaiting a verdict can be exciting.

Interest in a particular trial may be stimulated by any number of factors, from the celebrity of defendants, such as O. J. Simpson or Joan Collins, to intimations of taboo subjects like incest and sexual abuse, as in the case of Lyle and Erik Menendez. If people wish to hear about the sensational, the macabre and the pathological, there is no clear judgement that we can make about this interest. In and of itself it is neither good nor bad. And it certainly is nothing new. Some critics are appalled by some of today's television talk shows that feature such themes as "mothers who sleep with their daughters' boyfriends." But how does such behavior compare to killing your father and sleeping with your mother? While we venerate *Oedipus Rex* as a cornerstone of Western civilization, we condemn talk show hosts like Jenny Jones, Sally Jesse Raphael, Ricki Lake, and Jerry Springer.   7

We need not apologize for a culture that satisfies a wide range of interests. And we should never fall into the error of believing that widespread fascination with disturbing topics necessarily reveals something fundamentally flawed about our culture. The story of Faust, a man who sold his soul to the devil, inspired various highly regarded literary and dramatic works over several centuries. That we sometimes are fascinated by the darker side of the human spirit is only an acknowledgment that such a side surely exists and not neccesarily an endorsement of it. *The Old Testament*, after all, contains tales of thievery and pillaging, lust and lechery, adultery and incest, rape and murder.   8

We may argue that the O. J. Simpson murder trial, or the William Kennedy Smith rape trial, have no practical connection to the lives of viewers and that their outcomes are of scant historical significance. But such a notion ignores the fact that individuals relate to events for different and complex reasons. If most citizens devoted interest to news and public affairs in direct proportion to their own narrow and immediate interests, most would pay greatest attention to any and all pending revisions in the U.S. tax code. Beyond that, they might focus on issues of broad economic importance, such as the negotiation of an international tariff and trade agreement. And the facination with O. J. Simpson's trial for murder was limited neither to audiences in the United States nor to the least well-educated sectors of the population. Six months after Simpson was acquitted of criminal charges he was the invited guest of the one-hundred-and-seventy-five-year-old Debating Society at Oxford University. From its founding, the American Republic has made court proceedings open to the public and from time to time, dating all the way back to the late eighteenth century, sensational cases have drawn the kind of public attention and media notoriety that turned them into legends.

Tonya Harding and Nancy Kerrigan hardly interested me at all.   9
The competition between these two ladies of the rink never caught my imagination. I couldn't buy this story as an engaging combat between the ice princess from New England and the upstart little roughneck from the pine woods of Oregon. But other people in the potential viewing audience were interested. The TV networks determined this, and hence provided for on going coverage of the physical assault on Kerrigan and its aftermath. In this instance, to what kind of taste were the TV broadcasters appealing? Was the audience full of devotees of the nuances and intricacies of figure skating as sport? Were people tuned in to delight in seeing the long-standing athletic competition between two young ladies turn nasty and ugly? Could viewer interest really have been with Tonya's oafish husband and his band of mean-spirited pranksters who whacked Nancy on the knee?

News is storytelling, and TV news is story-telling with sharp and   10
terse commentary, bountiful pictures, and a compelling sense of immediacy. News is about unusual or significant behavior and events. The unusual and the significant includes the exceptional and the inspiring. It also includes the bizarre and the degrading. What would any of us really make out of an eleven o'clock newscast reporting that during the day 21,318 commercial airline flights had taken off and landed safely in the United States? That we want to know about the one flight that crashed betrays nothing necessarily morbid or insensitive about us. Nor does the interest that humans have in fiction and drama about flawed characters, crimes of passion, criminal escapades, unrequited love, or death and dying mean that our human sensibilities are warped or perverse.

Lots of hype surrounds TV events and shows. But the impulse   11
toward such hype is not television's folly. It is inherent in human beings. Without it we would not strive toward ideas and values that are abstract. With it we have to be continuously assessing and judging what we see and hear. The real issue confronting us with regard to television is how to encourage sharp reasoning and clear thinking

about all that it presents to us. The false issue is blaming television for our social ills, as if changing what is on television would make those problems go away.

In one postmortem on the O. J. Simpson criminal trial David Gel-   12
ernter of Yale University posed a fundamental question about journal-istic judgment, citing a headline from one of the nation's most prestigious newspapers: "'Racism of a Rogue Officer,' *The New York Times* announced in print, 'Casts Suspicions on Police Nationwide.' How much consideration did it give to the headline 'Murder of Mrs. Simpson Casts Suspicion on Black Males Nationwide'?"[5] The impulse to make much out of little and to generalize is not only basic to televi-sion, but also to human thought. We have to constantly sift through in-formation and opinion, deciding what is important and what is not. And, after all, there is little evidence that TV news holds extraordinary sway over viewers. Studies discover that viewers are highly skeptical about believing what they see and hear on television about public af-fairs. TV news not only is *not* hypnotic, it is apparently not even very convincing.[6] Responding to a questionnaire, fully two-thirds of the American viewing public faults news reporting in the United States for being intentionally biased and manipulative.[7]

Even more disconcerting is the common idea that fictions on tele-   13
vision account for poor choices and criminal behavior in society. In 1992, the Vice President of the United States, Dan Quayle, drew global attention when he criticized an episode from the popular TV series *Murphy Brown*. In it the main character, a professional in her forties, decides to give birth to a baby without marrying the child's father. Quayle claimed that this fictional portrayal was providing a negative example for unwed teenage mothers whose situation fuels consider-able social and economic misery in the United States.[8] But what is the evidence that a 15-year-old living in the inner city actually guides her decisions by taking a fictional forty-year-old journalist as her role model? The public is highly inclined to believe that such a 15-year-old

---

[5]David Gelernter, "The Real Story of Orenthal James," *National Review*, October 9, 1995, p. 47.

[6]*USA Today*, May 13, 1996.

[7]Judith Valente, "Do You Believe What Newspeople Tell You?" *Parade Magazine*, March 2, 1997.

[8]See, Richard Zoglin, "Sitcom Politics," *Time*, September 21, 1992, pp. 44–47; Fred Barnes, "Insurrection," *The New Republic*, June 22, 1992, pp. 12, 13; Andrew Rosenthal, "Quayle's Moment," *New York Times Magazine*, July 3, 1992, pp. 10–13. Initially, most commentary criticized Quayle, but for a different opinion, see James Bowman, "Too Much Mr. Nice Guy," *National Review*, June 22, 1992, pp. 21, 22.

is likely to get an undesirable message from the show, namely, that it is just fine to become an unwed mother. Why doesn't the public believe, alternatively, that she might get a *positive* message from the show? That it is desirable to have the freedom and security of a well-educated person who has achieved a responsible and well-paying job is just as much what the character Murphy Brown is about!

Across the political divide from Mr. Quayle, eighteen months   14
later, the Attorney General, Janet Reno, threatened TV-broadcasters with censorship (*legislation* is the polite term) if they did not cut back on the fictional violence reaching America's television screens. Ms. Reno attributed the ultimate evil on the little screen to the asocial antics of two crudely drawn animated characters featured in their own show called *Beavis and Butt-head*.[9] Hence, the American public is left to believe that the nation's highest law enforcement official is convinced that she has discovered a direct connection between the naughty antics of this cartoon duo and violence on America's streets: gang wars, drive-by shootings, pathological serial killing, car-jackings, breaking and entering, murder, mugging, and mayhem!

Rampant this kind of speculation certainly is; well-documented it   15
surely is not. This entire line of thinking is grotesquely convoluted and baffling, and yet it appears to be widely accepted. Talking about the campaigners who consistently attribute negative social effects to television, the British scholar Martin Barker writes: "Their claim is that the materials they judge to be 'harmful' can only influence us by trying to make us the same as them. So horrible things will make us horrible—not horrified. Terrifying things will make us terrifying—not terrified."[10] The single-mindedness of such claims should serve as a first warning to us of their shallowness.

Moreover, counter evidence nearly always is omitted from dis-   16
cussion over the possible influences of the media. As a child in the late 1940s, I was an avid fan of movie cartoons. Like many children, I was

---

[9]See, *U.S. News and World Report*, November 1, 1993, p. 11. Taking up Reno's side, see Gerald Howard, "Divide and Deride: Prevalence of Stupidity in the Mass Media," *The Nation*, December 20, 1993, pp. 772, 773. For more critical views of Reno's position, see Frank McConnell, "Art is Dangerous: Beavis & Butt-head, for Example," *Commonweal*, January 14, 1994, pp. 28–30; Jon Katz, "Beavis and Butt-head," *Rolling Stone*, March 24, 1995, p. 45, amusingly points out that United States Senator Ernest Hollings (Democrat, South Carolina) took up Reno's criticism, repeatedly calling the show "Buff-Coat and Beaver" on the Senate floor. The criticism spread wide. See, for example, Miriam Horn, "Teaching Television Violence," *U.S. News and World Report*, December 27, 1993, p. 91 which recounts CNN-founder and media mogul Ted Turner's testimony to Congress that TV is "the single most significant factor causing violence in America."

[10]Martin Barker, "The Newson Report: A Case Study in 'Common Sense,'" in *Ill Effects: The Media/Violence Debate*, edited by Martin Barker and Julian Petley (London/New York: Routledge, 1997), p. 23.

amused and delighted by the typical antics that presented scenes like beleaguered mice attaching explosives to the rear end of a sassy pussy cat and blasting him into the nether reaches of space. Yet, it never occured to me to copy such behavior in real life. And although I was a devoted fan of Bugs Bunny, I never was tempted to ask my parents to buy me his favorite food—carrots.

From the 1930s to the mid-1960s, the Motion Picture Association   17
of America ("Hollywood") made movies under the "Hays Code" which placed rigid limitations on fictional representations of crime and sex. Kisses on screen were limited to a couple of seconds and never with the mouths open. Scenes of a bedroom, even that of a married couple, showed two beds, lest the sight of one bed for two arouse the prurient interest and erotic passions of the average moviegoer. Criminals might be depicted, but only if their capture and punishment were assured by the movie's end.

From its inception television in America was even more rigidly   18
controlled, given the self-censorship of the networks, the cautious attitudes of advertisers, and governmental regulation by the Federal Communications Commission (FCC). Network executives at CBS, for example, even made sure that the cameras never tilted down to show Elvis Presley's gyrating hips during his TV-premiere on *The Ed Sullivan Show* in 1956. America's children and teenagers were kept safe from even a glimpse of the King's bump-and-grind.

Well into the 1960s, both movies and television in the United States   19
unabashedly portrayed conventional and puritanical values. Nonetheless, the audience nurtured as children on just these media grew into the young adults who gave the nation its sexual revolution and a full-fledged drug culture. In all the talk and writing about media effects, especially about the potential dangers of film and television fare, this history is commonly overlooked. When we are considering why we believe that violence and sex in movies and TV frequently find their way into lived behavior, we need to be asking why wholesome and inoffensive movies and television programming did not prevent the counter-culture changes that occurred in society during the late 1960s?

The other counter evidence that is almost always ignored on the   20
question of media influence and effects comes from other countries. In a rare commentary about what is on television elsewhere, a writer for *Time Magazine* concluded: "Channel surf elsewhere and U.S. television begins to seem as though it were run by so many Roman Catholic schoolgirls.... In Japan...prime-time TV is a mixed menu of soft-core porn, bloodletting drama, and violent animation."[11] Much the same is true, by the way, in many European countries and has been for a num-

---

[11]Ginia Bellafante, "So What's On in Tokyo?" *Time*, February 16, 1996.

ber of years. Yet, the rates for homicide and other violent crime in all these countries vary considerably from the United States, as do the statistics for illegitimate births and school performance as measured by standardized tests. Viewed comparatively, the claims of causal connections between what is on television and what is going on in America's schools, its bedrooms and its streets is nonsensical.

Underlying such nonsense is a widely held belief that fictional   21
movies and television programs represent equivalencies to real life. There is continuing anger about how certain characters are portrayed in films and/or TV programs and public arguments about such portrayals. Some claim that *The Godfather* films as well as other fictional media productions about the Mafia are denigrating to Italian Americans. There are complaints when African Americans are portrayed as street people or muggers. The image of women in the media has drawn extraordinary attention since the end of the 1960s. Indeed, this entire topic of media representation draws a double whammy that fuels all sorts of agendas. Feminists can find in a predictable "buddy" film like *Thelma and Louise* a parable of emancipation in the antics of a pair of women on the run. Conservatives complain that marriage and the family are treated with savage contempt in the movies and on TV. Liberals argue that being unmarried or homosexual assures negative representation in the media. Lawyers do not like their media image. Friends of the unfortunate are offended by scenes in movies or on TV in which the homeless appear menacing or threatening. Friends of the animals condemn scenes set at a rodeo or on a hunting trip. Many African Americans object when Blacks are portrayed as criminal characters, but also complain about representations of high-achieving Black families, as seen on TV's *Cosby Show* or *The Jeffersons,* which they consider to be misleading and unrealistic. Social theorist Paul Ehrlich once proposed that a new federal agency be set up to effectively limit population growth in the United States. Ehrlich wanted the agency to promote what he called "voluntary birth control programs." He also argued that it should have the power to prohibit the broadcast of *all* shows on television "featuring large families."[12]

At base, such thinking and arguing has less to do with these   22
media than with the presumed audience for them, which is believed to be undiscriminating and stupid. This assumption holds that much of the audience will be unduly and negatively influenced by what it sees and hears. But what is the proof for this claim? Audiences for films and TV behave with a great deal of particular discrimination toward productions and their stars. Amid a smorgasbord of media offerings that look like they have much in common with one another, individual

---

[12]Alexander Volkoh, "How Green Is Our Valley?," *Reason,* March, 1995, p. 62.

taste functions as being extraordinarily precise. Some of us like this thriller but not that one; Glenn Close but not Meryl Steep; *Baywatch* but not *Melrose Place*; *The X-Files* but not *Startrek: Voyager*; Jay Leno but not David Letterman. Movie and television culture is unique at specific levels of discrimination and taste. Responses to both these media are extraordinarily precise at this level. Most popular and serious commentary on film and television ignores this. The precision of viewer attitudes is part of the complexity of these media and their appeal.

Contemporary society is awash in wild, but widely believed, claims about the movies, television, and the audiences for them. This, combined with perceptions of the sophisticated electronic technology of movies, video, and TV, contributes to the widespread fear of the manipulative powers of these media. Aside from the rhetoric that maintains their acute manipulative powers over audiences, little evidence supports these fears. Such claims really will not stand up to an examination of them. Moreover, in order to stand up they must be premised on a view that takes humans to be, in great numbers, lacking in rationality and discrimination. Given the insufficient evidence to demonstrate the claimed effects of film and television, as well as the fact that humans are neither as mindless nor as uncritical as they would have to be for such effects to influence them as is claimed, this entire line of thinking is on very shaky ground indeed. 23

Examining the Text

1. In his discussion of TV news programs, Monaco offers an explanation for why so many news stories focus on bizarre, depraved, and disturbing topics. Summarize the points he makes here. Do you find his explanation persuasive? Why or why not?

2. Monaco quotes Martin Barker's summary of how some critics see TV as a negative influence: "horrible things will make us horrible—not horrified. Terrifying things will make us terrifying—not terrified" (paragraph 15). Rewrite this statement in your own words. What's your opinion of the influence of the "horrible" and "terrible" things we see on TV?

3. At several points in the article, Monaco advocates "sharp reasoning" and "clear thinking" about TV's content and cultural impact. Based on his own reasoning in this article, what do you think Monaco means by these phrases? According to Monaco, what are the characteristics of unsound reasoning and erroneous thinking about TV?

For Group Discussion

In his defense of the content of TV news shows, Monaco writes, "If people wish to hear about the sensational, the macabre and the pathological, there is no clear judgment that we can make about this interest. In and of itself it is neither good nor bad." He continues, "And we should never fall into the error of believing that widespread fascincation with disturbing topics necessarily reveals something fundamentally flawed about our culture" (7–8). As a group, discuss your own opinions of why many people seem to be fascinated with bizarre and disturbing stories on news shows. Consider your own habits in viewing the news. What stories interest you most? Why do you suppose this is so?

Writing Suggestion

Monaco believes that there is "little evidence" to support fears that TV has a negative influence on its viewers, and that in order to believe that TV has "acute manipulative powers" we must believe that the viewing audience is "undiscriminating and stupid." Clearly, his views are contrary to the claims made by Kottak and Waters. Choose one of these earlier articles and compare the argument it offers to Monaco's argument. Begin by summarizing the main ideas of each author regarding TV's influence on its viewers. Develop a thesis in which you state the views of each author and present your own opinion on which argument is more persuasive. In the body of your essay, examine each author's points in more detail, and provide evidence from the readings as well as from your own TV-viewing experience to support your position.

1. The Talk Show

Do Ask, Do Tell

Joshua Gamson

Have you ever wondered why people are willing to appear on TV talk shows? They reveal secrets to an audience of strangers and open themselves to embarrassment, ridicule, and perhaps even physical assault. What compels people to take this risk? What rewards are there for appearing on a talk show, other than Andy Warhol's "fifteen minutes of fame" (or ignominy)?

Joshua Gamson, an assistant professor of sociology at Yale University, offers some insight into these issues by focusing on why nonhetersexual guest appear on talk shows. He notes that talk shows are one of very few venues in which people with nonconforming sex and gender identities—gays, lesbians, bisexuals, transsexuals, transvestites—have the opportunity to speak for themselves, to tell their own stories. These guests typically receive support from the host and audience; on most shows it's homophobia, not homosexuality, that is considered deviant.

However, as Gamson points, out, these guests pay a price for their appearance on talk shows. Because talk shows, like all TV shows, are primarily concerned with gaining large viewing audiences and increasing their advertising revenues, they promote their own participants as deviant, bizarre, eccentric, and perhaps even grotesque in order to win ratings. As he puts it, "If you speak, you must be prepared to be use," and being used by a talk show involves, in many cases, playing the role of "freak" and performing in a "parade of pathology."

As you read, recall the talk shows that you've seen on TV. Does Gamson provide a persuasive explanation for why the guests you've seen—heterosexual as well as nonheterosexual—appeared on these shows? Considering the risk and rewards described by Gamson, would you ever want to be a guest on a talk show?

At the end of his 22 years, when Pedro Zamora lost his capacity   1
to speak, all sorts of people stepped into the silence created by the
AIDS-related brain disease that shut him up. MTV began running a
marathon of *The Real World*, its seven-kids-in-an-apartment-with-the-
cameras-running show on which Pedro Zamora starred as Pedro
Zamora, a version of himself: openly gay, Miami Cuban, HIV-positive,
youth activist. MTV offered the marathon as a tribute to Zamora,
which it was, and as a way to raise funds, especially crucial since
Zamora, like so many people with HIV, did not have private insurance. Yet, of course, MTV was also paying tribute to itself, capitalizing
on Pedro's death without quite seeming as monstrous as all that.

President Clinton and Florida governor Lawton Chiles made   2
public statements and publicized phone calls to the hospital room,
praising Zamora as a heroic point of light rather than as a routinely
outspoken critic of their own HIV and AIDS policies. The Clinton administration, in the midst of its clampdown on Cuban immigration,
even granted visas to Zamora's three brothers and a sister in Cuba—a
kindly if cynical act, given the realities of people with AIDS waiting
visas and health care in Guantánamo Bay.

Thus, according to *People* magazine, did Zamora reach a bitter-   3
sweet ending. He was unable to see, hear, or speak, yet with his family
reunited, "his dream had come true." Behind the scenes, one who was
there for Zamora's last weeks told me, the family actually separated
Zamora from his boyfriend—quite out of keeping with the "dreams"
of Pedro's life. When Pedro had his own voice, he had spoken powerfully of how anti-gay ideology and policy, typically framed as "profamily," contributed to teen suicides and the spread of HIV; when he

died, those who spoke for him emphasized individual heroism and the triumph of the heterosexual family.

That others appropriated Zamora on his deathbed hardly tar-   4
nishes his accomplishments. As an MTV star, he had probably reduced suffering among lesbian and gay teenagers more, and affected
their thinking more deeply, than a zillion social service programs. He
spoke publicly to millions in his own words and with the backing of a
reputable media institution, and he did not just tell them to wear condoms, or that AIDS is an equal opportunity destroyer. Nor did he simply fill in the sexual blanks left by prudish government prevention
campaigns. He also told them and showed them: Here is me loving
my boyfriend; here is what a self-possessed gay man looks like hanging out with his roommates; here is what my Cuban family might
have to say about my bringing home a black man; here is me at an
AIDS demonstration, getting medical news, exchanging love vows.

To speak for and about yourself as a gay man or a lesbian on tele-   5
vision, to break silences that are systematically and ubiquitously enforced in public life, is profoundly political. "Don't tell" is more than a
U.S. military policy; it remains U.S. public policy, formally and informally, on sex and gender nonconformitiy. Sex and gender outsiders—
gay men, transsexuals, lesbians, bisexuals—are constantly invited to
lose their voices, or suffer the consequences (job loss, baseball bats) of
using them. Outside of the occasional opening on MTV or sporadic
coverage of a demonstration or a parade, if one is not Melissa
Etheridge or David Geffen, opportunities to speak as a nonheterosexual, or to listen to one, are few and far between. Even if the cameras
soon turn elsewhere, these moments are big breakthroughs, and they
are irresistible, giddy moments for the shut up.

Yet, in a media culture, holding the microphone and the spot-   6
light is a complicated sort of power, not just because people grab them
back from you but because they are never really yours. If you speak,
you must be prepared to be used. The voice that comes out is not quite
yours: It is like listening to yourself on tape (a bit deeper, or more
clipped) or to a version dubbed by your twin. It is you and it is not
you. Zamora's trick, until his voice was taken, was to walk the line between talking and being dubbed. The troubling question, for the silenced and the heard alike, is whether the line is indeed walkable.
Perhaps the best place to turn for answers is the main public space in
which the edict to shut up is reversed: daytime television talk shows.

For lesbians, gay men, bisexuals, drag quens, transsexuals—and   7
combinations thereof—watching daytime television has got to be
spooky. Suddenly, there are renditions of you, chattering away in a system that otherwise ignores or steals your voice at every turn. Sally Jessy
Raphael wants to know what it's like to pass as a different sex, Phil Donahue wants to support you in your battle against gay bashing, Ricki

Lake wants to get you a date, Oprah Winfrey wants you to love without lying. Most of all, they all want you to talk about it publicly, just at a time when everyone else wants you not to. They are interested, if not precisely in "reality," at least not in fictional accounts. For people whose desires and identities go against the norm, this is the only spot in mainstream media culture to speak on their own terms or to hear others speaking for themselves. The fact that talk shows are so much maligned, and for so many good reasons, does not close the case.

The other day, I happened to tune into the *Ricki Lake Show,* the   8 fastest-rising talk show ever. The topic: "I don't want gays around my kids." I caught the last 20 minutes of what amounted to a pro-gay screamfest. Ricki and her audience explicitly attacked a large woman who was denying visitation rights to her gay ex-husband ("I had to explain to a 9-year-old what 'gay' means"; "My child started having nightmares after he visted his father"). And they went at a young couple who believed in keeping children away from gay people on the grounds that the Bible says "homosexuals should die." The gay guests and their supporters had the last word, brought on to argue, to much audience whooping, that loving gays are a positive influence and hateful heterosexuals should stay away from children. The anti-gay guests were denounced on any number of grounds, by host, other guests, and numerous audience members: They are denying children loving influences, they are bigots, they are misinformed, they read the Bible incorrectly, they sound like Mormons, they are resentful that they have put on more weight than their exes. One suburban-looking audience member angrily addressed each "child protector" in turn, along the way coming up with a possible new pageant theme: "And as for you, Miss Homophobia..."

The show was a typical mess, with guests yelling and audiences   9 hooting at the best one-liners about bigotry or body weight, but the virulence with which homophobia was attacked is both typical of these shows and stunning. When Lake cut off a long-sideburned man's argument that "it's a fact that the easiest way to get AIDS is by homosexual sex"("That is not a fact, sir, that is not correct"), I found myself ready to start the chant of "Go, Ricki! Go, Ricki!" that apparently wraps each taping. Even such elementary corrections, and even such a weird form of visibility and support, stands out sharply. Here, the homophobe is the deviant, the freak.

Lake's show is among the new breed of rowdy youth-oriented   10 programs, celebrated as "rock and roll television" by veteran Geraldo Rivera and denigrated as "exploitalk" by cultural critic Neal Gabler. Their sibling shows, the older, tamer "service" programs such as *Oprah* and *Donahue,* support "alternative" sexualities and genders in quieter, but not weaker, ways. Peruse last year's *Donahue:* two teenage lesbian lovers ("Young, courageous people like yourself are blazing the way for other people," says Donahue), a gay construction worker suing his gay boss for harassment ("There's only eight states that protect sexual persuasion," his attorney reports), a bisexual minister, a black lesbian activist, and two members of the African-American theater group Pomo Afro Homos ("We're about trying to build a black gay community," says one), the stars of the gender-crossing *Priscilla, Queen of the Desert* ("I have a lot of friends that are transsexuals," declares an audience member, "and they're the neatest people"), heterosexuals whose best friends are gay, lesbians starting families, gay teens, gay cops, gay men reuniting with their high school sweethearts, a gay talk show. This is a more diverse, self-possessed, and politically outspoken group of nonheterosexuals than I might find, say, at the gay bar around the corner. I can only imagine what this means for people experiencing sexual difference where none is locally visible.

Certainly *Donahue* makes moves to counter its "liberal" reputa-   11
tion, inviting right-wing black preachers and the widely discredited "psychologist" Paul Cameron, who argues that cross-dressing preceded the fall of Rome, that people with AIDS should be quarantined, and that sexuality "is going to get us." But more often than not, Donahue himself is making statements about how "homophobia is global" and "respects no nation," how "we're beating up homosexual people, calling them names, throwing them out of apartments, jobs." The "we" being asserted is an "intolerant" population that needs to get over itself. We are, he says at times, "medieval." In fact, Donahue regularly asserts that "for an advanced, so-called industrialized nation, I think we're the worst."

Oprah Winfrey, the industry leader, is less concerned with the   12
political treatment of difference; she is overwhelmingly oriented toward "honesty" and "openness," especially in interpersonal relationships. As on Lake's show, lesbians and gays are routinely included without incident in more general themes (meeting people through personal ads, fools for love, sons and daughters you never knew), and bigotry is routinely attacked. But Winfrey's distinctive mark is an attack on lies, and thus the closet comes under attack—especially the gay male closet—not just for the damage it does to those in it, but for the betrayals of women it engenders.

On a recent program in which a man revealed his "orientation"   13
after 19 years of marriage, for example, both Winfrey and her audience were concerned not that Steve is gay, but that he was not honest with his wife. As Winfrey put it, "For me, always the issue is how you can be more truthful in your life." One of Steve's two supportive sons echoes Winfrey ("I want people to be able to be who they are"), as does his ex-wife, whose anger is widely supported by the audience ("It makes me feel like my life has been a sham"), and the requisite psychologist ("The main thing underneath all of this is the importance of loving ourselves and being honest and authentic and real in our

lives"). Being truthful, revealing secrets, learning to love oneself: These are the staples of Winfrey-style talk shows. Gay and bisexual guests find a place to speak as gays and bisexuals, and the pathology becomes not sexual "deviance" but the socially imposed closet.

All of this, however, should not be mistaken for dedicated friend-   14
ship. Even when ideological commitments to truth and freedom are at work, the primary commitment of talk shows is, of course, to money. What makes these such inviting spots for nonconforming sex and gen-der identities has mostly to do with the niche talk shows have carved out for ratings. The shows are about talk; the more silence there has been on a subject, the more not-telling, the better a talk topic it is. On talk shows, as media scholar Wayne Munson points out in his book *All Talk* (Temple University Press, 1993), "differences are no longer repressed" but "be-come the talk show's emphasis," as the shows confront "boredom and channel clutter with constant, intensified novelty and 'reality.'" Indeed, according to Munson, Richard Mincer, *Donahue*'s executive producer, encourages prospective guests "to be especially unique or different, to take advantage of rather than repress difference."

While they highlight different sex and gender identities, expres-   15
sions, and practices, the talk shows can be a dangerous place to speak and a difficult place to get heard. With around 20 syndicated talk shows competing for audiences, shows that trade in confrontation and surprise (*Ricki Lake, Jenny Jones, Jerry Springer*) are edging out the milder, topical programs (*Oprah, Donahue*).

As a former *Jane Whitney Show* producer told *TV Guide*, "When   16
you're booking guests, you're thinking, 'How much confrontation can this person provide me?' The more confrontation, the better. You want people just this side of a fistfight."

For members of groups already subject to violence, the visibility of   17
television can prompt more than just a fistfight, as last year's *Jenny Jones* murder underlined. In March, when Scott Amedure appeared on a "se-cret admirer" episode of the *Jenny Jones Show*, the admired Jon Schmitz was apparently expecting a female admirer. Schmitz, not warming to Amedure's fantasy of tying him up in a hammock and spraying whipped cream and champagne on his body, declared himself "100 per-cent heterosexual." Later, back in Michigan, he punctuated this claim by shooting Amedure with a 12-gauge shotgun, telling police that the em-barrassment from the program had "eaten away" at him. Or, as he re-portedly put it in his 911 call, Amedure "fucked me on national TV."

Critics were quick to point out that programming that creates   18
conflict tends to exacerbate it. "The producers made professions of re-gret," Neil Gabler wrote in the *Los Angeles Times* after the Amedure murder, "but one suspects what they really regretted was the killer's indecency of not having pulled out his rifle and committed the crime before their cameras." In the wake of the murder, talk show producers

were likened over and over to drug dealers: Publicist Ken Maley told the *San Franciso Chronicle* that "they've got people strung out on an adrenaline rush," and "they keep raising the dosage"; sociologist Vicki Abt told *People* that "TV allows us to mainline deviance"; Michelangelo Signorile argued in *Out* that some talk show producers "are like crack dealers scouring trailer park America." True enough. Entering the unruly talk show world, one is apt to become, at best, a source of adrenaline rush, and at worst a target of violence.

What most reporting tended to ignore, however, was that most anti-gay violence does not require a talk show "ambush" to trigger it. Like the Oakland County, Michigan, prosecutor who argued that "*Jenny Jones*'s producers' cynical pursuit of ratings and total insensitivity to what could occur here left one person dead and Mr. Schmitz now facing life in prison," many critics focused on the "humiliating" surprise attack on Schmitz with the news that he was desired by another man. As in the image of the "straight" soldier being ogled in the shower, in this logic the revelation of same-sex desire is treated as the danger, and the desired as a victim. The talk show critics thus played to the same "don't tell" logic that makes talk shows such a necessary, if uncomfortable, refuge for some of us.

Although producers' pursuit of ratings is indeed, unsurprisingly, cynical and insensitive, the talk show environment is one of the very few in which the declaration of same-sex desire (and, to a lesser degree, atypical gender identity) is common, heartily defended, and often even incidental. Although they overlook this in their haste to hate trash, the critics of exploitative talk shows help illuminate the odd sort of opportunity these cacophonous settings provide. Same-sex desires become "normal" on these programs not so much because different sorts of lives become clearly visible, but because they get sucked into the spectacular whirlpool of relationship conflicts. They offer a particular kind of visibility and voice. On a recent *Ricki Lake*, it was the voice of an aggressive, screechy gay man who continually reminded viewers, between laughs at his own nasty comments, that he was a regular guy. On other days, it's the take-your-hands-off-my-woman lesbian, or the I'm more-of-a-woman-than-you'll-ever-be transsexual. The vicious voice—shouting that we gay people can be as mean, or petty, or just plain loud, as anybody else—is the first voice talk shows promote. It's one price of entry into mainstream public visibility.

The guests on the talk shows seem to march in what psychologist Jeanne Heaton, co-author of *Tuning in Trouble* (Jossey-Bass, 1995), calls a "parade of pathology." Many talk shows have more than a passing resemblance to freak shows. Neal Gabler, for example, argues that guests are invited to exhibit "their deformities for attention" in a "ritual of debasement" aimed primarily at reassuring the audience of its

19

20

21

superiority. Indeed, the evidence of dehumanization is all over the place, especially when it comes to gender crossing, as in the titles of various recent *Geraldo* programs; the calls of sideshow barkers echo in "Star-Crossed Cross-Dressers: Bizarre Stories of Transvestites and Their Lovers" and "Outrageous Impersonators and Flamboyant Drag Queens" and "When Your Husband Wears the Dress in the Family." As long as talk shows make their bids by being, in Gabler's words, "a psychological freak show," sex and gender outsiders arguably reinforce perceptions of themselves as freaks by entering a discourse in which they may be portrayed as bizarre, outrageous, flamboyant curiosities. (Often, for example, they must relinquish their right to defend themselves to the ubiquitous talk show "experts.")

Talk shows do indeed trade on voyeurism, and it is no secret that   22
those who break with sex and gender norms and fight with each other on camera help the shows win higher ratings. But there is more to the picture: the place where "freaks" talk back. It is a place where Conrad, born and living in a female body, can assert against Sally Jessy Raphael's claims that he "used and betrayed" women in order to have sex with them that women fall in love with him as a man because he considers himself a man; where months later, in a program on "our most outrageous former guests" (all gender crossers), Conrad can reappear, declare himself to have started hormone treatment, and report that the woman he allegedly "used and betrayed" has stood by him. This is a narrow opening, but an opening nonetheless, for the second voice promoted by the talk show: the proud voice of the "freak," even if the freak refuses that term. The fact that talk shows are exploitative spectacles does not negate the fact that they are also opportunities; as Munson points out, they are both spectacle and conversation. They give voice to the systematically silenced, albeit under conditions out of the speaker's control, and in tones that come out tinny, scratched, distant.

These voices, even when they are discounted, sometimes do   23
more than just assert themselves. Whatever their motivations, people sometimes wind up doing more than just pulling up a chair at a noisy, crowded table. Every so often they wind up messing with sexual categories in a way that goes beyond a simple expansion of them. In addition to affirming both homosexuality and heterosexuality as normal and natural, talk show producers often make entertainment by mining the in-between: finding guests who are interesting exactly because they don't fit existing notions of "gay" and "straight" and "man" and "woman," raising the provocative suggestion that the categories are not quite working.

The last time I visited the *Maury Povich Show,* for instance, I   24
found myself distracted by Jason and Tiffanie. Jason, a large 18-year-

old from a small town in Ohio, was in love with Calvin. Calvin was having an affair with Jamie (Jason's twin sister, also the mother of a three-month-old), who was interested in Scott, who had sex with, as I recall, both Calvin and Tiffanie. Tiffanie, who walked on stage holding Jamie's hand, had pretty much had sex with everyone except Jamie. During group sex, Tiffanie explained, she and Jamie did not touch each other. "We're not lesbians," she loudly asserted, against the noisy protestations of some audience members.

The studio audience, in fact, was quick to condemn the kids, who   25 were living together in a one-bedroom apartment with Jamie's baby. Their response was predictably accusatory: You are freaks, some people said; immoral, said others; pathetically bored and in need of a hobby, others asserted. Still other aspects of the "discussion" assumed the validity and normality of homosexuality. Jason, who had recently attempted suicide, was told he needed therapy to help him come to terms with his sexuality, and the other boys were told they too needed to "figure themselves out." Yet much talk also struggled to attach sexual labels to an array of partnerships anarchic enough to throw all labels into disarray. "If you are not lesbians, why were you holding hands?" one woman asked Tiffanie. "If you are not gay," another audience member asked Calvin, "how is it you came to have oral sex with two young men?"

This mix was typically contradictory: condemnation of "immoral   26 sex" but not so much of homosexuality per se, openly gay and bisexual teenagers speaking for themselves while their partners in homosexual activities delare heterosexual identities, a situation in which sexual categories are both assumed and up for grabs. I expect the young guests were mainly in it for the free trip to New York, and the studio audience was mainly in it for the brush with television. Yet the discussion they created, the unsettling of categorical assumptions about genders and desires, if only for a few moments in the midst of judgment and laughter, is found almost nowhere else this side of fiction.

The importance of these conversations, both for those who for   27 safety must shut up about their sexual and gender identities and for those who never think about them, is certainly underestimated. The level of exploitation is certainly not. Like Pedro Zamora, one can keep one's voice for a little while, one finger on the commercial megaphone, until others inevitably step in to claim it for their own purposes. Or one can talk for show, as freak, or expert, or rowdy—limits set by the production strategies within the talk show genre.

Those limits, not the talk shows themselves, are really the point.   28 The story here is not about commercial exploitation, but about just how effective the prohibition on asking and telling is in the United States, how stiff the penalties are, how unsafe this place is for people of atypical sexual and gender identities. You know you're in trouble with Sally Jessy Raphael (strained smile and forced tear behind red glasses) seems like your best bet for being heard, understood, respected, and protected. That for some of us the loopy, hollow light of talk shows seems a safe haven should give us all pause.

———————

Examining the Text

1. Why do you think Gamson begins with the story of Pedro Zamora? Zamora was an actor on MTV's *The Real World*, not on a talk show. What relevance does his story have for talk shows? What does Gamson mean when he writes that "others appropriated Zamora on his deathbed"?

2. How would you describe the structure of Gamson's article? That is, what argument do you think Gamson is making, and how does he structure his points so as to make that argument? Do you think the organization of his article is effective? Why or why not?

3. In his conclusion, Gamson states that the "limits set by the production strategies within the talk show genre.... are really the point." To what limits is he referring? How do those limits constrain self-expression on talk shows?

For Group Discussion

Gamson covers both the positive and negative features of talk shows, stating that "The fact that talk shows are exploitative spectacles does not negate the fact that they are also opportunities..." As a group, make a list summarizing Gamson's points for both perspectives on talk shows—that is, list the ways in which talk shows are "exploitative spectacles" and the ways in which they're "opportunities" for people with nonconforming sex and gender identities. Add any additional points that Gamson hasn't mentioned that would support one side or the other. As a group, discuss which view of talk shows you find more persuasive.

Writing Suggestion

Gamson writes that talk shows can be "a dangerous place to speak and a difficult place to get heard." Test this statement by watching a talk show—taping it, if you can, so that you can view it several times. Pay attention to one of the primary guests on the show. To what extent is the guest allowed to explain his or her views? In what ways does the guest have difficulty in being heard? How do responses from the host, the audience, and other guests on the show interfere with or help this particular guest to tell his or her story? Notice, for example, the number of times the guest is interrupted, challenged, or even ridiculed. Write an essay in which you describe the experience of this guest in telling his or her story and in being heard by the talk show's viewers.

The Talk Show's
Lost Potential

Robin Andersen

Given the raucousness, rowdiness, and downright incivility of many TV talk shows today, it's difficult to imagine that they ever had the potential to help viewers and guests or to contribute to the improvement of social problems. In the early days of talk shows, Phil Donahue invited his guests and studio audience to talk about issues such as consumer rights, feminism, and free speech; the shows were a forum for public debate and a source of accurate information about social issues. In the 1980s and 1990s, Oprah Winfrey shifted the content of talk shows toward more personal topics and the tone of talk shows became more therapeutic, less political. The middle- and late-1990s saw the talk show evolve in a different direction, driven largely by the demand for high ratings. Jerry Springer, Jenny Jones, Sally Jesse Raphael, and others now host very popular talk shows that focus on all manner of deviance and depravity and are characterized by profanity, confrontation, and violence.

In this reading, taken from her 1997 book Consumer Culture and TV Programming, *Robin Andersen analyzes this current generation of TV talk shows. Although they claim to be helpful and informative, Andersen argues that they're pure entertainment—and of the most sensationalist and vulgar sort. The audience isn't there to learn about their own problems or to empathize with the problems of others, but rather to jeer and cheer, like fans at a professional wrestling match. As a result, the guests on talk shows are exploited rather than helped, and the serious issues that talk shows deal with (child abuse, domestic violence, sexualtiy, divorce, and so on) are trivialized and left unsolved.*

As you read, *take note of the way Andersen weaves together broad analytical statements about the talk-show genre with extended examples from specific shows. What general points are her examples intended to prove? How effective do you think these examples are in depicting the current state of TV talk shows?*

What is immediately apparent, even from a cursory glance at   1
talk-show titles, is a selection of topics so bizarre that they verge on the absurd. This is now a routine observation, easily explained by the need to compete in a media environment crowded by one talk show after another. The punchy "teasers" programmed throughout the day have to be provocative and grabby, and the shows themselves, in this age of remote-control technology and intense ratings wars, must hold

the viewer's attention. Any potential that the participatory discourse of inclusion might hold is wiped out by the commercial imperative. The demand for ratings creates an escalating sensationalism that jades the public, made eager for tomorrow's displays only by the most titillating exhibitions. The joke about talk shows these days is that a guest must be more than a nymphomaniac prostitute. She needs to be a nymphomaniac prostitute with HIV-infected children who was abused by her Satan-worshiping stepfather.

But it is not only the demand for ratings that drives producers to   2
find topics so extreme in their sensationalism. Added to the necessity for freak shows that leave the eyes bugged and the jaw slack is the requirement that topics defy rational explanation. This is the logical outcome of a routine cultural practice, influenced by the discourse of consumption, that presents human phenomena disconnected from the larger social and political context. If the topic cannot be held within the pop-psychology discourse of media therapy, it must enter the realm of the utterly fantastic. For instance, by the 1990s a number of talk shows detailed the horrors of Satan worship. Appropriately supernatural, this problem is presented as a manifestation of the forces of evil and its solution requires the intervention of higher powers.

THERAPY AND THE DEVIL

Sometimes the narratives of therapy and the supernatural meet to   3
produce a unified discourse that is more determined than ever to deny social connections. One talk show dealt with the case of a woman who, abused by a family of Satan worshipers, had developed multiple personalities. The show's narrative began by explaining that one of the woman's less dominant personalities had gone to a minister for help. The dominant personality was now suing the minister for performing a forced exorcism. Of course, once the discussion hinged on the issue of exorcism, it entered the realm of predictably hideous spectacle. The minister brought with him a videotaped exorcism that included gruesome visual details of what appeared to be blood spewing from a "possessed" man's mouth. The sticky substance also flowed from his eyes. The grotesque display and the claim of possession by the devil became the focus of the show. In effect, the devil himself was assumed to have occupied the center of a clinical discussion about multiple personalities, with exorcism presented as a therapeutic cure for the disorder. The discussion revolved around unexplainable forces of good and evil.

Real-life clinical cases indicate that the creation of different per-   4
sonalities provides some victims with the distance needed to cope with the pain of abuse. An understanding of this phenomenon as the

effect of extreme childhood abuse might well be helpful to some viewers. It could even further an understanding of the larger public issue of
mental health. But the injection of the supernatural only prevents a
meaningful social discussion. The dimension of Satan worship draws
the discussion away from an understanding of social phenomena and
into the realm of bizarre ratings-boosting curiosity. What does it mean
for a culture to publicly display grotesque depictions of spirit possession as entertainment, and then to assert that such possession is the
cause of child abuse?

OF PERSONAL CULPABILITY
AND PUBLIC RESPONSIBILITY

The July 15, 1992, broadcast of the *Sally Jessy Raphael* program on   5
the subject of "Mothers Who Have Bully Sons" is illustrative of a discourse that exploits the misery of painful problems, backing the participants into a corner of blame, hopelessness, and self-loathing. This
exploitation is accomplished through equal measures of accusations of
individual irresponsibility, social decontextualization, and traditional
gender formulations.

The mothers testify to the brutality of their young thugs, who are   6
of course extreme in their delinquency, having broken bones and
bashed heads with gleeful malevolence. Sobbing, the mothers recount
years of helplessness, detailing the first time he banged his head
against the wall and the first of many humiliating complaints of his
ruthlessness. Then the "understanding " begins.

As the mothers sit crying, bewildered as to "what went wrong,"   7
desperate for reasons, grasping for solutions, a "therapist" planted in
the audience, with hand waving, glibly offers the explanation. It is the
mothers' own fault. In fact, the therapist has written a book on exactly
this topic, and if only the mothers had taught their recalcitrant offspring discipline and respect, this never would have happened. The
obedient audience follows with "If only you had set boundaries," as
they no doubt would have done. Mythic themes, planted in the media
ether, emerge as the social, institutional explanation for delinquency.
In the process, motherhood is devalued by the notion that traditional
families, which once raised wholesome offspring, have been torn apart
by women's selfish desire for liberation.

This explanation hinges on the assumption that mothers are the   8
sole influence on their children's behavior, ignoring a sweeping range
of social influences that affect teenage behavior. In the absence of any
social context for understanding a problem that seems so formidable,
and no doubt strikes fear in the hearts of mothers everywhere, the
mothers of the bullies themselves become the scapegoats.

This "therapeutic" deciphering directs audience sentiments down   9
a discourse not of empathy but of distance—a distance bred by fear
and lack of understanding; a distance that prevents the audience from
having to accept any mutual blame, as members of a shared culture,
for the prevailing social practices of power gained through force and
physical domination; a distance designed to obscure an analytic understanding of the way in which the bullies' aggressive subjectivity
fits within the distorted belligerent power brandished by the "heroes"
of morning television and celebrated in the big-screen action adventures. A week after this show aired, a rock-and-roll radio station in
New York, targeting teenage listeners in the largest market in the
country, held a call-in contest to see who could propose the "most creative way" of breaking Saddam Hussein's fingers.

PRIVATE LIFE IN THE PUBLIC FORUM

Most talk shows are concerned with relationships. Revolving   10
around topics made titillating by taboo, such as "Daddy's Girls," and
"Newlyweds at Each Other's Throat," they engage in marriage counseling and relationship therapy of every persuasion; from psycho-
analysis to the more pedestrian group counseling. Audiences around
the country tune in, trying to "work it out" with their loved ones.

These programs are much more than mass cultural curiosities.   11
They are taken very seriously as helpful forums to which people—
guests, studio audiences, and home viewers—go for help, expression,
and sharing. And on talk shows just about everything is shared. From
murder to incest, crime and punishment, almost no boundaries exist
between what can and cannot be said in public. No revelation, confession, or disclosure is so personal that it cannot be exposed by a talk-
show host. In this atmosphere of total exposure, no secrets are
allowed. For instance, the aforementioned victim of Satan worshiping
described the most intimate details of what her parents did to her and
how it made her feel. On display, no question was inappropriate; so
the audience was not embarrassed to ask her to switch personalities on
command: "Can we see Jenny now?" Men who cross-dress but have
hidden this fact from their families sit in full regalia, entrusting a mass
audience to their innermost passions for a behavior that has isolated
them from their closest relatives. And many people—mothers and
children, brothers and sisters—are reunited for the first time after
years of separation over some deep hurt—on national television.

During one show a husband complains that he's not getting   12
enough sex from his wife; during another, couples learn sexual arousal
through public kissing. The TV talk format represents a profound transformation in this country's formulation of what used to be valued as the

right to privacy. Clearly it appeals to a public whose most intimate needs are not being met by other means. But what types of needs are met on talk shows? How are problems defined and solved through exposure in a public forum? And what are the implications of the shift in positioning between public and private life in this age of TV therapy?

"Don't Tell Me, Tell Her"

Relationship therapy is, of course, about *communicating*. "Don't   13
tell me, tell her," the therapist enjoins. After all, people go on talk shows to talk about their problems. On an *Oprah Winfrey* program entitled, "Newlyweds at Each Other's Throat," three couples bring their marital problems to the small screen. One couple, Stephen and Christy, have a problem that cannot be solved within the realm of private life. Nevertheless, even in this public forum, private solutions are the only ones offered. As Christy puts it "He didn't work for four months, and it's hard. I cannot support the three of us, me and him and our daughter." Throughout the program, both consistently assert that their problems stem entirely from Stephen's inability to find a job. Stephen offers reasons—Christy takes their only car to work and he is forced to stay home with their small child. Nevertheless, his wife has come to resent his unemployed status: "She seems to think there's a standing job for me at Burger King." Christy, meanwhile, believes that her husband has not tried hard enough to get work.

> STEPHEN: I've tooken [sic] jobs picking up garbage out of parking lots   14
> from 11:00 at night until 5:00 or 6:00 in the morning, and I hated it.
> OPRAH: So, the problem, you're saying, is not that you're just waiting on a construction job. You can't find anything.
> STEPHEN: No, I'd take any job that's offered to me, but there's 28,000 construction workers out of work in Palm Beach County, and they're all looking for every job there is that's available.
> OPRAH: Oh OK. Well, coming up, we're going to find out why John thinks Dawn has put his sex life on the skids. We'll be back.

Absolutely incapable of discussing the impact of economic hard-   15
ship on a relationship, the show simply ignores it. To acknowledge it as a fundamental problem would foreclose the possibility of offering a pseudotherapeutic solution. In fact, a therapist, Dr. Gray, is brought on midway through the discussion to tell everyone what their problems are and how to solve them. After all, he has written a book entitled *Men Are from Mars, Women Are from Venus*. Dr. Gray explains, "What they're really—the issue is—what you were talking about,

Oprah, is—the underlying problem in every one of these cases is communication. Nobody's hearing the other person."

But Christy and Stephen are definitely not being heard above the 16
therapeutic din. They continue to ground their discussion on the issue of employment:

> CHRISTY: All I want is— 17
> DR. GRAY: He gets the message that you want to change him, and that hurts a man. That's the most painful thing.
> CHRISTY: I don't want to change him. I just want him to work.

The participants talk at cross-purposes throughout the program 18
because the doctor simply cannot discuss unemployment. He is locked in a therapeutic mode that views the world and its problems solely from an interiorized perspective. Oprah and the doctor translate everything Christy says into a subjective affect devoid of social context. She must "get in touch with her feelings" and "work them out":

> OPRAH: ...What she's really saying is, "I'm scared. I'm scared that what- 19
> ever expectations I had that you were going to be there to take care of me—I am scared that you are not going to be able to fulfill...."
> DR. GRAY: But she's terrified. She's terrified....What she needs is for him to understand and hear that and give her reassurance.

Christy does not seem terrified at all. In fact, she feels confi- 20
dent enough to leave her husband. This is where the therapeutic discourse really goes wrong. An understanding that unemployment is structural leads to the realization that not everyone who looks for work will get it. Viewing her situation from an economic context, Christy might have been more inclined toward patience. Together, she and Stephen might even be able to develop a strategy with which to deal with that situation and thereby alleviate their marital problems. But in the absence of such a discussion, the conventional wisdom that blames the individual is simply presumed. In a culture that continually asserts that anyone who looks for a job will get one, those who do not are considered failures. Those out of work are blamed, just as Christy blames Stephen.

As high-paying skilled jobs are lost and replaced by low-paying 21
service-industry (Burger King) jobs, young couples like Christy and Stephen feel its impact on their personal lives. The injustice of economic disparities and of corporate practices that have taken jobs out of this country by the thousands go unmentioned and therefore unrecognized as significant factors contributing to Christy and Stephen's prob-

lems. In addition, a focus on the general social and economic need for day care might have made this couple's problems seem less individual, and more manageable.

But to include the social and economic context would direct the   22
discussion toward an entire set of contingencies with which the therapeutic discourse is incapable of dealing. That context becomes a Pandora's box, and talk shows strain to keep the lid firmly in place. If they were truly a forum for discussing issues of public concern—for a participatory discourse that would further the goals of democratic practice—they would have to include at least a small range of social, cultural, and economic connections to the human suffering they so effectively exploit. But discussion of such connections would lead to the realization that, in many cases, only economic improvements can ameliorate personal problems. The further discovery might be made that only social participation and citizen involvement in the political process will lead to change. But the amazing talk-show phenomenon prevents literally thousands of people from making those connections, offering self-reflection, instead, as the solution to all our problems. The solution is to work on ourselves rather than on the social problems that render us increasingly miserable as a society.

The therapeutic solution offered to cure Stephen's employment   23
problem is so deficient that the dialogue verges on the absurd.

> DR. GRAY: That's what men want to do, they want to solve the problem.   24
> They want—instead of listening—
> STEPHEN: That's right. I want to solve the problem.
> DR. GRAY: She doesn't want the problem solved. She wants you to understand, empathize. Here. Give her a hug. This lady's starved for a hug. She can't give sex until she gets affection and love and touching and all that stuff. That's what she needs.

John and Dawn are another newlywed couple who are "at each   25
other's throat":

> JOHN: I work six days a week, I'm up at 7:00 every morning to go   26
> to work, OK. Dawn, that's the only thing you have to do, is take care of the baby and clean the house. I go to work and make the money—

TV therapy focuses on private relationships, but as Hillman and   27
Ventura (1992a, 63) point out, "Work may matter just as much as relationship." John's bitter complaint is as much about his work as it is about his wife. Six long days make for an unreasonable schedule, and "in a world where most people do work that is not only unsatisfying

but also, with its pressures, deeply unsettling ... we load all our needs onto a relationship or expect them to be met by our family. And then we wonder why our relationships and family crack under the load" (Hillman and Ventura 1992a, 63). But no one on *Oprah* asks John about his job or his working conditions. Instead, all problems are assumed to hinge on the couple's relationship.

As the discussion continues, John openly belittles the domestic   28
work his wife does. But he does not want her to work outside the home. Rather, he wants more attention from her and clearly would like her life to revolve around his needs: "She takes care of the house, she takes care of the baby, OK, but what about—when is it time to take care of me?" he asks. These demands elicit a negative response from the audience, but Oprah insists, "That is a legitimate—may I say this? Everybody's yelling at him, but that is a legitimate concern."

For Oprah it is a legitimate concern because it is about *feelings*.   29
On talk shows the expression of any feelings is legitimate, even if they are feelings molded by a society in which relationships between men and women are structured in domination. John's devaluation of his wife's domestic work reflects a society in which the sexual division of labor remains dominant. Work in the public sphere is valued and re-warded, whereas domestic labor is "free" and not highly regarded. In addition, John's demand that his wife pay more attention to him exists within a social context that expects women to defer to the needs of their husbands.

But blaming John personally (which is what the predominantly   30
female audience would like to do), without examining the social and economic origins of his attitudes, will do nothing to change his out-look. In her desire to accommodate all feelings (according to the rules of TV therapy), Oprah goes so far as to tell John, "It's not wrong that you think that way, John."

But Dawn certainly thinks it is a problem and has become unin-   31
terested in John as a consequence of his manifest disrespect. And that is the real tragedy of people's lives. Relationships based on inequality are not happy ones. Just as Hope and Michael could never find happi-ness on *thirtysomething* because they had accepted a patriarchal struc-ture that accommodated Michael's needs at the expense of Hope's, these newlyweds play out the unhappy relations of domination. A young woman on the *Oprah* program came close to making such con-nections: "In my opinion, he's not treating her with respect, and peo-ple want to hug and kiss and love when you feel respected." But without a context, her remark fell into a void of no response.

Dr. Gray offers John another nonsolution, similar to the one he   32
had offered Stephen. Simply think of women as different and learn to "deal with it":

And we are different, and so a nice, light way of looking at it is men are   33
from Mars.... It's a whole different world. That's why we're that way.
Women are from Venus. They're just that way. I used to think my wife was
off the wall. Now I know she's from Venus and I—and instead of judging
her, I said, "OK. I need a survival guide for how do you survive on Venus."

What Herbert Marcuse (1966) once referred to as "repressive tol-   34
erance" is offered on the talk show as a solution to problems with relationships that lack equality. Such shows also reassert the biologistic
notion that the sexes are different (a notion that has served to justify
women's second-class status for centuries). And the vast implications
of the social definitions of gender—which include disparities of all
sorts—are reified into mystified categories from outer spece. Admit-
ting that some expectations could be considered unreasonable because
they are based on assumptions of social inequality is beyond the ken
of TV therapy. Thus the soical impact on the formation of human subjectivity is further eclipsed.

To enter into what Marcuse (1966, 301) termed "truly personal
relations," the socially formed character must overcome "modes of
universal alienation." The inequality of socially defined gender positions causes a whole range of conflicts and discontentments in relationships that cannot be alleviated until they are recognized. Only by
acknowledging and understanding the existing social relations of hierarchy will couples be able to overcome the negative impact these relations have on their relationships. If we were to judge talk shows on the
basis of their own rigidly defined individual/psychological terms,
they would fail to satisfy. The reason, as the women's movement
pointed out so long ago, is that the personal is political. That point is
incomprehensible in a discourse where there is no "political." Without
a context, personal feelings and behavior can never be understood.

It is not surprising that by the end of the *Oprah Winfrey* show, the   35
newlyweds are more confused than ever. John, especially, hangs his
head in puzzlement and frustration. In the end, the confusion between
public and private space, and the continual encroachment into private
life, means that nothing gets solved. As with the "new intimacy" of
thirtysomething, talk-show therapy ruptures the connection between
societal conditions and emotional peace of mind. When that link is
broken, paths to well-being become more obscured than ever.

This conspicuous inability to offer solutions that ring with even a   36
modicum of veracity leaves talk shows in the unhappy position of
having to offer their audiences a different set of emotional dynamics
for enjoyment and entertainment. Unfortunately, the programming
strategies used to maintain these audiences in an increasingly competitive environment have taken an unhealthy turn. TV talk therapy's
lack of explanation and understanding has led to strategies that

evoke—not empathy—but ridicule, distance, and moral superiority. *Sally Jessy Raphael's* "I Stole Money to Get Married" show demonstrates talk-show tactics in this age of emotional discontent.

Small-Town Pathology

On *Sally Jessy Raphael* we are introduced to a young couple from   37
a small town in Kentucky, Danny and Jeannie, who recently ended up
in jail on their wedding day. Before the ceremony, they had embarked
on a greedy grab, stealing everything from bridesmaid's dresses to
jewelry, ring cushions, and lingerie. A huge bag filled with what the
audience believes to be the stolen merchandise sits next to Sally. The
girl's cousin, Bobby Ray, is also introduced. These people are talk
show choices, not simply by virtue of their criminality, but because
they have turned on one another. Cousin Bobby is telling a different
story than Danny and Jeannie. They say he stole everything. He says
they did it. They have not spoken to one another since giving the police different stories. They meet again today for the first time.

From the start, Sally asks probing questions, trying to pin some-   38
thing on each of the guests by catching them in an inconsistency. The audience members follow suit, and the program turns into a harsh
inquisition. They ask Jeannie's dress size and shoe size, and the sizes of
the stolen clothes; then they try to find out whether Bobby knew her
sizes. When someone from the audience asks if he had any "idea the
trunk was being filled with merchandise?" Bobby says "No." His im-
plausible denial results in an audible sigh of disbelief from the audience.
From their confused narratives of denial the realization emerges that
none of them is innocent. They are simply trying to blame each other,
causing one audience member to announce, "If any of these people
stood here and told me that Sally's glasses are red, I wouldn't believe it
from any of them." A growing sense of disgust and impatience with the
guests causes Sally to respond with "What do you want from me?" But
she continues on, encouraging everyone to play detective by asking, "If
you were the police, who would you believe and what would you do?"

The audience is provided with dramatization of the theft. From a   39
rack of wedding dresses Jeannie is asked to pick the one most like the
one stolen and to try to fit it under her jacket. Bobby Ray objects, saying, "All these is too long....This was a short dress, come to her knees,
and she knows it."

The audience is led to believe that the items in the bag next to   40
Sally were the actual ones stolen. Sally says, "This is a kind of reenactment of what the police found when they looked in the trunk of
Bobby, the best man's car." She pulls the merchandise out, one item at
a time; playing the scene for maximum impact, she displays each item
and makes comments. With exaggerated artifice she finds the wed-

ding dress: "Now, this—Oh my goodness, this—(*straining to pull it out of the bag*). This is enormously heavy. This is—I'm going to take it this is the wedding dress. But I can hardly—This is very heavy. You know shoplifting is one thing. It has a long train. Whoa...." Then, and a few items later; "Here is the one that somebody said their mother made. No way. This is the ring-bearer thing, right?" Because of the way the items are presented, the audience believes them to be the real ones. Much later, however, during the audience interrogation, one questioner responds with disbelief at Bobby's claim that he did not see Jeannie carrying the wedding dress out of the Bridal Boutique under her coat. The viewer, incredulous, says, "You couldn't see *that* dress?" BOBBY: "The dress wasn't near this big. The dress wasn't even near that size. It wasn't near that size." To this revelation the audience responds with loud grumbles of disapproval for having been misled. SALLY: This is not the—this is the—We didn't take that dress because it's stolen merchandise." This explanation is accepted. No one bothers to ask why a dress so much bigger than the real one was chosen. The next comment comes from someone in the audience: "I think they're all involved in this...." But the show's producers, staff, and Sally are all involved, too. Thieir exaggerations have caused confusion and made the guests look even more mendacious than they really are—and just plain stupid for thinking anyone could believe such nonsense.

As the story unfolds, copious details of different accounts of the 41
theft are argued over. All of the guests refer to police reports they say would verify their claims. Accusations are followed with denials such as "The cops never said no such thing." We find that eight people (all related) were involved in the robbing spree, continuing a drunken episoide that had begun the night before. The argument descends further into a bickering harangue between family members when Jeannie's sister Betty Jo is brought out. The transcript reads as follows:

> BETTY JO (*jailed before her sister's wedding for stealing*): No, I didn't take a 42
>   damn thing.
> SALLY: Nothing?
> BETTY JO: Not a (*expletive deleted*) thing. And if he wants to sit here and
>   tell me I took (*expletive deleted*).
> BOBBY: —damn piece—(*cross-talk*)
> BETTY JO: Yeah, sure, Bobby, sure.
> BOBBY: Why did you sign the papers for it?
> BETTY JO: I didn't sign no (*expletive deleted*) damn papers. Because you
>   (*unintelligible*).

We also find that cousin Bobby is awaiting trial for driving a bus 43
while drunk; one girl is hospitalized with injuries. Bobby counters

with the information that Jeannie's "daddy" robbed a department store, and that Danny and Jeannie have stolen $100,000 worth of merchandise in the past. In addition, someone has tried to burn down the couple's trailer—they blame cousin Bobby for it.

The growing sense of disgust compels Sally to detach herself   44
from these miscreants. To do so she corrects their grammar and mocks their Kentucky drawl. When she asks, "What has this done in the family?" Danny responds that "it's caused peeyur hail."

SALLY: Caused what?   45
DANNY: Peeyur hail.
SALLY: (*sarcastically*) Pure hell.
DANNY: Peeyur hail.

Sally rolls her eyes to create distance between her guests and de-   46
cent people everywhere. They squirm like insects under a microscope. They have been turned into the Other, strange aberrations of the kind created by David Lynch for the cult TV series *Twin Peaks*—itself a view of the unhealthy underbelly of small-town life.

The final insult to the guests comes at the very end as Sally re-   47
turns from the commercial break, saying, "You talk about reality television." She announces having just received a fax from the Ramada Renaissance Hotel (promotional plug), where a hair dryer is missing from the couple's room. All deny having taken it, saying they had their own. The hotel's mini-bar was also "wiped out"—the bill came to $116. As Danny protests, "No, no, no, no, they got that.... That ain't right now," Sally corrects, "That isn't right?"

In a gross violation of privacy, during the next commercial break,   48
the show's staff members rifle through the couple's luggage (or say they have done so) and come up with a hair dryer. (The hair dryer shown has a cord, not like the wall-mounted kind hung in hotel bathrooms.) Sally brandishes the dryer, saying, "There's a hair dryer in the suitcase. Give me the hair dryer. OK (*she says to Jeannie*), you said you used her—." Danny comes to Jeannie's aid, claiming, "That was my fault. I packed the suitcase."

Sally finishes with irritation in her voice: "I don't know what they   49
do in Kentucky, but in New York, this is trouble. I mean, you just can't do this." She continues sternly, "I want the hair dryer back in the hotel...."

As the credits roll, Jeannie and Bobby hang their heads, and we are   50
left with a sinking feeling of disgust, having been exposed to the banality of some senseless malfeasance perpetrated by unhappy miscreants. We have no idea what has gone wrong in their small town and with their lives.

The pathology so blatantly demonstrated on this talk show exists   51
in total contradiction to the mythic political themes developed during

the Democratic convention, which was televised nationally that very same week. In fact, the *Sally Jessy Raphael* program aired the same day that presidential candidate Bill Clinton give his acceptance speech at the convention. Clinton stressed (as dictated by focus groups) his upbringing in the small town of Hope, Arkansas, an upbringing he said had instilled moral character. In short the political myths developed for public consumption at the Democratic convention stand in striking contrast to the representations of small-town pathology developed on *Sally Jessy Raphael*. But this contradiction remains at the level of the repressed; no conscious connection is articulated. Instead, it registers in the deep collective unconscious as the cultural contradiction of marketing culture. The clash of myths is observed, but it remains just below the level of comprehension that would delegitimate the discourse. Indeed, it sits hidden, creating a sense of uneasy awareness that something is desperately wrong—but ever illusive. This awareness, of course, breeds the cynicism so apparent in American culture today.

OF AUTHENTICITY AND ARTIFICE

In the face of Sally's claim to be doing "reality television," it is   52
immediately apparent that everything about her talk show—from the planning stage, to the search for victims, to the development of the gimmicks of the format, to the audience preparation and its group dynamic—is fraudulent. The story of Jeannie, Danny, Bobby Ray, and Betty Jo was formulated and staged. The resulting disgust and hostility on the part of the audience is no accident.

Even though the progam is structured as a detective intrigue,   53
and Sally compels the audience to cross-examine, no real attempt is made to understand what went on. Such an attempt could have been summarized easily at the beginning of the program. All of the guests had already told their stories to the police, and a review of those reports could have been presented. That would have cleared up the majority of contended assertions. But the arguing and lying are ruses— they are the entertainment. The show was deliberately set up to provide toxic fun for an audience invited to play detective, police, and moral arbiter all at the same time.

THE DISCOURSE OF CONFUSION

The shouting, confusing, (expletive deleted) bluster of talk-show   54
"debate" is the formula to which everyone must adhere as a requirement for participation. In *I'm Dysfunctional, You're Dysfunctional*, writer

Wendy Kaminer (1992, 39) explains the preparation she received before appearing on the *Oprah Winfrey* show:

> "Just jump in. Don't wait to be called," one of Oprah's people told us   55
> when she prepped us for the show. "You mean you want us to interrupt
> each other?" I asked; the woman nodded. "You want us to be really
> rude and step on each other's lines?" She nodded again. "You want us
> to act as if we're at a large unruly family dinner on Thanksgiving?" She
> smiled and said, "You got it!"

This format is antithetical to authentic understanding. When the   56
volume is turned up on a cacophony of noise calculated for its dramatic
entertainment value, the "debate" is reduced to grunts and shouts: "I'd
never call what goes on over the turkey a debate," says Kaminer. She
points out, "The trouble with talk shows is that they claim to do so much
more than entertain; they claim to inform and explain. They dominate
the mass marketplace and help make it one that is inimical to ideas"
(1992, 39). This is the most detrimental aspect of the format, whereby the
potential for inclusive discussion of public issues is lost. The wedding
day program was a stereotypical drama featuring a feuding backwoods
clan. It engaged the audience at the level of elitist voyeurism. No one left
more informed; self-righteous superiority is not edification.

The credits at the end of the program that name the professionals   57
who have fixed Sally's hair and designed her clothes are symbolic of
the process by which she has been created. The discourse, too, has
been created. The producers seek people out and provide the hosts
with the notes they have taken. Hosts and the guests alike are thoroughly "prepped." Strategies are developed to frame the discussion itself. Other guests are introduced according to a predetermined
narrative pace and progression. And questions initiated by the host direct the audience to the appropriate topics.

With contrived spontaneity, they talk to one another, these hosts   58
and their allegorical representations of social pathology. These hosts
will often pretend shock or surprise at some revelation after asking a
question they most certainly know the answer to in advance. The same
practice is now apparent on the morning news/talk programs, where,
for example, Regis and Cathy Lee act out a preplanned discussion.
From *Home Show* to Dan Rather's dialogue with a correspondent after
a segment, "reality television" asks itself "Did you know?" and feigns
surprise at the prearranged answer.

The audience members, too, have become actors. They play along,   59
following both the implicit and explicit directions. Indeed, professionals
prep the audience as well as the hosts. Before a *Geraldo* show featuring
"homeless couples," Rivera told studio guests to ask questions about
homeless *relationships* only, not about the causes of homelessness or any

other "general" aspects of the topic. And before the *Phil Donahue Show* gets under way, a coach "revs everybody up a couple of emotional notches," according to one staff member. Applause, used to indicate approval, encourages viewers to ask the toughest questions, or compels guests to reveal the most intimate details of their private life.

THERAPY OR EXPLOITATION?

Such is the sad exploitation for ratings of a daytime parade of   60
human anomalies; but these shows claim to be helping people. By providing information and letting people know "they are not alone," they claim to dispense wisdom about life, along with specific techniques for negotiating adverse situations. Unfortunately, many people, particularly the guests, are not finding help.

Many times, late at night in their hotel rooms, the anxiety of expo-   61
sure overcomes these would-be guests, and, as one staff member put it, "they try to bolt." Talk show producers have devised a strategy to prevent their guests from backing out. Employees of the show are "planted" in hotels to deal with precisely this eventuality. Taking an adjoining room, they are on-site if a guest tries to leave before going on the air. The job of these employees is to "talk them down," and they do so by telling the guests how much they will be helping other people—people with problems just like theirs, who have no one to talk to, nowhere to turn for help. Most of the time this strategy works. But as the *New York Times* (July 18, 1993) reported, an increasing number of people are finding that they feel worse after exposing themselves on national television, and support groups for these people have sprung up.

The devices used to create the smug aloofness with which hosts   62
(Raphael especially) approach their sensational topics offer a convenient way to avoid having to take the blame for setting up these public spectacles. This aloofness denies responsibility for the exploitation of people's pain and distress for ratings. As the topics become more vile and grotesque, everyone involved is compelled to distance themselves from the freakish guests. Despite constant assertions that information is being provided to help others heal, TV therapy is often as much about ridicule as it is about empathy.

In its healthiest manifestation, the talk show *is* about emotional   63
empathy, a hope held out for understanding. But what has bcome apparent is that it functions predominantly as a public confessional. In short, the distinction between confessing and testifying has been effaced. As Kaminer (1992, 30) points out, "The tradition of testifying in court, church, or the marketplace for justice, God, or the public good is a venerable one." Talk shows claim to be engaging in public testimony—for the betterment of all. But when that testimony is gathered

within a social and political void, the once-honorable practice amounts to little more than public humiliation and exposure.

Public testifying for the common good is very different from con-   64
fessing in the pseudotherapeutic context offered on talk shows. As therapy, talk shows are also fraudulent. A genuine therapeutic process involves years of private struggle to attain self-knowledge and come to terms with emotional configurations. It is sometimes argued that talk shows provide a catalyst for healing, by promoting the realization that emotional problems are not unique; but as such shows have devolved into spectacle, any positive gain is canceled out by the formatting strategies employed to contain the discourse within the realm of entertaintment.

That ratings matter more than "healing" the guests is evident   65
from the amount of time the show's producers allot the teletherapists. According to a study done by Vicki Abt, the average amount of time therapists spend on the show is about 2 minutes per guest (cited in Berger 1995, A9). After almost an hour of conflict and cross-talk, these narrative spectacles demand some type of closure. This is when the "tube-shrinks" make their appearance, at the very end of the show. One particularly popular TV therapist, Dr. Gilda Carle (who actually holds a Ph.D in organizational studies) appeared on almost 100 shows in 1994. Dr. Carle is considered one of the best because of her ability to cajole antagonistic guests into hugging just before the credits roll. The quick clichés promoting self-esteem offer dubious therapeutic content, but they do serve to legitimate the TV-talk spectacles.

Therapy as a spectator sport belittles the healing process and serves a different purpose altogether. When the format does not elicit sympathy, it become a destructive public spectacle invoked to confirm, for example, the moral righteousness and superiority of the audience. These formatting strategies produce results that are antithetical to social justice and also to psychic well-being.

Like the ad for Evian that claims to "Refresh Your Inner Self,"   66
talk shows exist within the culture of therapy, forming part of the heart of a heartless world, where a lost public seeks to find a transcendent *self* in a society offering few alternatives. The vast landscape of therapeutic culture promises healing, pleasure, and psychic well-being in a world, it proclaims, that has gone terribly wrong. The therapeutic talk-show discourse of sharing, trust, and disclosure has even taken on spiritual overtones, and is often presented as a way of surpassing the mundane needs of life. But, for the most part, talk shows degrade the emotional and spiritual life of the viewer. In the end, we are left with a profound sense of disgust; viewing other people's pain for our own enjoyment leaves us, at best, feeling empty; at worst, feeling soiled.

On talk shows, the graphic descriptions of abuse turn into   67
grotesque public displays of obscenity—a process that is antithetical to

spiritualism, to say the least. The discourse of blame and the individual culpability of the victim create a morality of condemnation devoid of empathy and magnanimity—and explanations of social cause. Audience engagement at the level of elite voyeurism leaves little but the residue of despair.

THE FAILURE OF THE TALK SHOW

The talk show emerged at a time of increasing ossification of tra-   68
ditional news reporting, public dissatisfaction with the interdependence between the media and the state, and the restriction of a multiplicity of voices so apparent on news and information programming. At first, talk shows held out hope as an alternative space for discursive practice. They seemed to give voice to a public straining to make sense of its own experiences and hoping to take action in its own best interests.

In the final analysis, however, talk shows—like advertising and   69
entertainment programming—address real needs but do not fulfill those needs. Talk shows respond to the need for a public forum on issues of common concern, but, like traditional news formats, they fail to connect personal experience with the larger socioeconomic context. Therefore, they cannot help individuals understand their own lives in relation to the social, political, and economic forces that shape them. The TV therapist has come to replace the expert (or political official) as the voice of wisdom. Talk shows speak with a therapeutic language that examines only a privatized landscape of human experience, further rupturing individual needs from collective solutions. Instead of understanding and knowledge, television talk offers its viewers the voyeuristic pleasure of gazing into the private lives of society's victims. In essence, television's therapeutic discourse prevents the public from understanding social issues and participating in the search for answers to social problems.

Examining the Text

1. According to Andersen, what is the potential that TV talk shows have lost? What good might talk shows have been able to accomplish? Why, according to Andersen, have they failed?

2. At the end of paragraph 12 Andersen asks several broad questions about the format and content of talk shows. Briefly sketch out how her article answers each of these questions.

3. Andersen repeatedly suggests that talk shows exploit human suffering rather than help people understand and alleviate their problems. Choose one of the extended examples discussed by Andersen (Stephen and Christy, John and Dawn, the wedding-day thieves) and summarize the ways in which these guests are exploited. Do you think that they are helped at all by their experience of being on a talk show?

4. Andersen writes that talk shows are "inimical to ideas." What do you think she means by this? What evidence does she provide in her article to support this claim?

Group Discussion

As a group, discuss what changes you think should be made in the content and format of talk shows so that they could indeed achieve their potential as an "alternative space for discursive practice." In other words, decide on several ways in which talk shows could be improved so that they would actually provide some benefit for guests and viewers. What topics would be discussed? What role would the host play? What kinds of "experts" would be invited to appear? What role would the studio audience play? Finally, having sketched out your ideal TV talk show, do you think that people would actually watch it? Why or why not?

Writing Suggestion

Andersen's major criticism of talk shows is that they ignore the social, cultural, political, and economic causes of the guests' problems and therefore cannot offer adequate solutions to those problems. Test her hypothesis by watching a talk show and analyzing the problem or conflict being discussed by the guests. Write an essay in which you first describe what the problem is and then analyze whether social, cultural, political, and economic fators contribute to or cause this problem. Could the problem be solved on a purely personal level, or do broader social changes need to be made in order for the guests to be helped? As a model for your essay, look at the three extended examples discussed by Andersen in her article.

2. The Soap Opera

The following two essays are more academic in presentation than the previous two. The writers, for example, cite a number of previously published critical works to substantiate their own views. However, both can be easily read by an educated popular audience because neither writer relies heavily on technical concepts and language.

Soaps Day and Night

Ronald Berman

*"And as sands through the hourglass, so are the days of our lives."
Even the most ardent critic of soap operas will likely recognize this tag line
from one of daytime television's most popular series, and whether we hate or
love them, we have to acknowledge the widespread popularity of the soaps and
the hold they exert over the hearts and minds of millions of Americans.*

In this chapter from his book How Television Sees Its Audience, *Ronald Berman argues that modern-day soap operas are a form of the serial
fiction of an earlier time, available and accessible to the masses. Still there are
differences, and Berman points out many of the characteristics that make the
soap opera a unique genre. For example, despite its emphasis upon sex and the
physical aspects of relationships, at the center of the soap opera is the family
unit; it is the family that holds the episodes together and provides a cohesive
structure. Further, the plots tend to be nonlinear and the dialogue tends toward stream-of-consciousness narration, used less to move the plot forward or
direct the action than simply to express states of mind.*

*Berman contrasts nighttime and daytime soaps and finds marked class
differences between the two. Nighttime characters tend to be more glamorous
and have more money, so there is more fantasy involved, whereas daytime
characters cut across a wider socioeconomic stratum and are therefore more
"realistic." Both types of soap, however, enact a kind of "middle-class fantasy," where wealth is "the good," and it is this preoccupation with money
and the self, Berman suggests, that places the genre within its contemporary
cultural and social context.*

*As **you read** this piece, think about Berman's analysis of the role of wealth
in terms of our possibilities for expression and action in a material world. How
can money (and preoccupation with financial conditions) either free or limit our
consciousness? Notice, too, that Berman draws comparisons between soap characters and the characters of Shakespeare. Shakespeare was a producer of the popular culture in his day, but are his works and soap operas of equal value?*

STORIES AND SELVES

Serial fiction isn't new; it began when publication caught up with   1
demand. In the early part of the nineteenth century, books were expensive and writers like Dickens and Thackeray could not reach all
their potential customers. Literacy had in effect become a commodity.

For the Victorians the problem was solved by printing novels in monthly or even weekly installments. For a shilling the customer could get the latest chapter of *Pickwick Papers*. He or she could join a sympathetic group of equals gathered around a London newsstand (or, for that matter, a newsstand in Bombay), anxious to know the fate of Little Nell. Serial publication, like soap opera on television, brought together fiction and a mass public.

Emotions once reserved for high tragedy were drawn out of every-   2
day life. Here is an excerpt from a letter to Dickens about the death of Paul Dombey in *Dombey and Son:* "Oh my dear dear Dickens! . . . I have so cried and sobbed over it last night, and again this morning: and felt my heart purified by those tears." Judging from other responses, this is, I think, pretty much representative. One's deepest feelings were affected by stories about one's own time, place, and social condition. Horror and pity, once the subjects of Shakespeare or Sophocles, became feelings attached to life and death in the middle class.

Now the novel has been supplanted, and the work it used to do,   3
telling us about daily life, has been taken on by other forms. They don't do it as well, but that matters little to their audience, who demand from our own kind of serial fiction a limited number of effects. The soap opera audience, although much less literate than the audience for the novel, wants also to know about self and social class, about money, about rising and falling in the world, and about love.

I suppose you could say that the soap opera has risen a notch or   4
two in social class since the novel established caste and class as interests of fiction. The romance once associated with love is now attached to money. Although the broad range of daytime soaps concern themselves with jobs and careers, the nighttime programs are about big money. Like a historical novel, the soap of the eighties is about the various generations of a family. During the day this family tends to be organized around business or professions. At night, in a more fantastic world, it is gathered around oil wells or ranches—the struggle is not for survival but for control. Like so many little King Lears, the fathers of nighttime soaps are surrounded by the ungrateful young. This may be either a convenient literary strategy or a sign of the times. At any rate, the family of either day or nighttime soap opera is split around opposed interests. Parents and children disapprove of each other's business tactics or consultants or, now and then, lovers. But the essential fact in the structure of any soap is the family caught up in various ways with some kind of enterprise.

During the day we see more of communities than simply of Col-   5
bys or Carringtons. There will be a greater variety of character, more minorities, more of a sense of necessity in choosing careers, mates, or

opportunities. Daytime soaps are on a much smaller economic scale, and will show us dramas about the fate of housemaids or police officers. Social class really means something on daytime soaps—it is not just a fantasy of wealth but something you can climb into or fall out of.

On either kind of soap love is probably less interesting than its after-effects. People are unquestionably drawn to each other, and acts of passion naturally result, but they are characterized by social self-consciousness. Men and women on soaps, before and after bed, ask themselves and each other if this has been "right" for them; if it suggests a break in their social lives; if it betrays their wives or husbands; what effect it has on their friends, acquaintances, former lovers, or spouses; and how it will affect business. 6

This is all natural to domestic fiction. The real issues always have been the social effects of personal actions. And of course in an age such as our own, when both men and women work, one's real interest is reserved for the long haul, not for happy interludes. So that soaps, which may get steamy now and then, and which feature altogether wonderful characters like Susan Lucci or Joan Collins, nevertheless concentrate far more on lives, money, and careers than they do on love. A great American critic, Lionel Trilling, once wrote that we learned from the novel "most of what we know about modern society, about class and its strange rituals, about power and influence and about money." With very little transposition the same could now be said about soaps. They don't teach as well, but they do show us what we know—and they show us ourselves. 7

How does a soap proceed? Not like a movie, which has a beginning, a middle, and an end. Nor like a novel, which defines and develops characters. A soap is new every time we see it, even from Monday to Tuesday. This tends to be confusing to those of us educated under the old dispensation. If you cannot instantly disengage your expectations, to say nothing of your memory, you will not be able to watch a soap comfortably. It is a chronicle, not a history. 8

In soap opera it is perfectly possible to mislay a character. You can be born into or die out of the show—and there are probably more deaths on soaps due to accountants than to mortality. The obverse can also be true: It is easy to be resurrected. If one of the cast should happen to die in a car crash, it will be no surprise months later to find him flourishing although amnesiac. One of the reasons for this is that the crash is rarely portrayed in detail on film—it is simply said to have happened. 9

This has real implications for the rest of the soap story. Like the car crash that may or may not have happened as reported, the soap is built around ambiguities. One hardly knows who is alive or dead, who is an imposter or the real thing. Soaps are full of long-lost brothers who are as genuine as the script allows them to be. The key to the 10 soap is not the action, but the script. Again, this is something hard to grasp for those brought up on different kinds of fiction. Reality is not what the plot suggests—nor even what the camera observes. Reality is what the script says it is.

Over the short term this doesn't matter much. Over the long term, however, the soap is basically incomprehensible. If a show has had a run of a few years its plot will look like a particularly ingeniously confused Turkish carpet. Its action spreads out laterally instead of developing in a progressive line.   11

DRAMA OR MONOLOGUE?

The soap *looks* like a drama, and it involves adversarial figures and answering dialogue, but it does not really depend on interaction. The one great essential about soaps is that they are literally all talk. There really is very little action in proportion to production time.   12

In any drama the dialogue has some special meaning. It is shot through with particular themes and ideas, articulated through significant images. It corresponds to, is tailored for, individual characters. In a drama, everyone has his or her own vocabulary. Very little of this is true for soaps. In fact, it can be said with little exaggeration that on a soap the dialogue doesn't have dramatic meaning. It may not have *any* meaning. That is because soap dialogue is not meant to further the action. It is a series of *statements* or expressions that show us not what people are thinking but what is on their minds, which is different. The soap script is designed to allow characters to empty themselves out, to cleanse themselves emotionally. Think not of the drama or the novel when looking at soap opera, but of the diary or journal.   13

Soap dialogue allows one to listen to oneself. It is almost purely expressive and subjective. Of course its subject will always be the self measuring its own claims to happiness, or stating its own consciousness, or simply letting off steam.   14

Soap dialogue has an odd resemblance to the talk of a patient to an analyst. The most common moment in soap conversation involves two people, one with personal emotional anguish that must be stated, and the other with no business but to witness that. Unhappiness does not really require a necessary cause—the characters of soapland are unhappy from the beginning. They have been or are insufficiently loved; perhaps they have been wounded in their self-conception. Or they have been emotionally traumatized in the past. They seem to be constructs of some common psychological needs now popular. We all evidently need far more emotional gratification than we get. Even if we *succeed* in life we may be deeply deprived. Our own self-worth is   15 rarely visible to others. Born with this attitude, soap opera people do not really need what have been called the "blocking characters" of drama or the novel. Regardless of the opposition of villains, life on soaps would be psychologically unhappy. If Dickens had written a soap instead of a novel, David Copperfield would not have needed Uriah Heep to complicate his life. He would have needed only to let us know that he was unhappy with himself, or uncertain about his career or sexual choices. Soaps have many villains, but most people make their own troubles for themselves.

What is the first rule of soap opera? No one should suffer in si-   16
lence. Not to express all of one's anxiety would be an unthinkable deviation. There may be secrets suppressed in order to advance the plot,
but no one ever hides the sources of his or her own discontent. They
are all talked out. This is pretty much the opposite of real life, which
may constitute one of the principal attractions of the soap opera. Few
of us ever get to let the world know exactly how we feel. Clearly, the
audience of soap opera is smitten not so much with melodrama as
with psychodrama.

Since a soap is literally all talk, it becomes necessary to institu-   17
tionalize the role of listener or confidante. The confidante, long a part
of sentimental drama, becomes the most obvious fixture of soaps and
their stories. Every character has a friend who listens to his or her
story. A social illusion is necessarily created that no one is solitary. In
the world of soaps, not only do we express our deepest feelings, but
the social world listens and responds to them. We are *visible* in the
world of soap opera, far more visible than in reality. And the most visible thing about us is our psychology. The main characters (and many
of the minor ones) reveal themselves in bursts of emotional rhetoric: in
apology or declaration or demand or revelation of some kind. Common to most kinds of dialogue (or, frequently, monologue shared by
two people) is the theme of subjectivity. The soaps are the product of
an era fascinated by the self-evident topics of magazines like *People* or
Self, which is to say that they cash in on the democratic tendency to reduce all things to a certain size. On soaps, what matters is not the state
of the world but how you feel about it.

There is one large problem that soaps have not been able to solve: 18
Their language is dreary, imprecise, not really capable of expressing
much meaning. This really hurts because self-awareness, self-pity, and
self-consciousness are, after all, interesting things. But, as the following
collection of samples, from a single episode of *General Hospital* indicates,
the characters don't often get the tools they need from the writers:

And that means trouble.
I'd better get to her before...

I've got an idea.
I'll get to the bottom of it.
I'm going to lose him.
I know how you feel.
We must look to the future.
All our troubles are over.

These clichés can't really express the emotional depth of suffer-   19
ing. Pitched to the general illiteracy of the audience, the soap tries to
find a language that everyone will understand. It is not surprising that
soap language, which needs help so badly, gets it from spectacle and
music. Deep emotion is suggested not by adequate statement but by
the universal heavy sigh repeated every few minutes every day, from
The Young and the Restless through *One Life to Live*. Everyone on soap
opera has that sigh, followed by a little wince. And there is music all
the time. Music serves the same purpose for the soap that the laugh
track serves for comedy. It is heavy, portentous, and sentimental. And
it is there all the time, covering stretches between dialogue, instructing
us how to feel, trying to do what language has already failed to do.

The soap is full of nonverbal clues to character and feeling. To   20
sigh is to have feelings. To wear a hat or especially a turban is (for
women) the infallible sign of great wealth. To respond to animals or
infants is to indicate moral value. To listen earnestly is to suggest
moral purpose.

Even when tempered, as it is now, by fantasy, the soap is about   21
husbands and wives. Its central institution is the family. One of the
basic soap plots is about the formation of a family, from the first attraction between two individuals to the social resonance caused by
their eventual connection.

In the good old days of radio, where soaps originated, family   22
problems tended to be simple and solutions tended to be moral. Domestic uncertainty and unhappiness were the great subjects, and they
were looked at from a woman's point of view. Today we are much
more likely to hear about issues, many of them involving social
change. Soap characters are involved in running corporations and
vineyards and oil wells. They brush up against politics (although most
of the ideas are carefully washed out). They are threatened by technology; for example, on one of the nighttime soaps, the ongoing pollution
of inherited property. We hear now in the soaps about abortion and
computers, about working women and market trends.

Clearly the biggest issue of social change is the liberation of   23
women. Since the soap is designed for a female audience, the issue is a
natural. The news of the day tells us that more women are now in the
work force—and the soap responds by mixing career women in

among housewives. Statistics indicate that many of these women are now executives—and the soap shows us women in skyscraper offices running financial empires. The news reveals the new sexual morality—and the soap is now about women attracted to (or suffering from) sexual freedom. The old standard problem of the soap opera, getting married, has been joined by the new one of extracting a "commitment" and maintaining a "relationship."

But for every social action there is bound to be a reaction. Not everyone in the audience is liberated. So the soaps keep men on in positions of authority—as physicians and lawyers and heads of households. Mothers continue to be best sources of love, sympathy, and advice. And, according to one survey, the soap is in some ways antifeminist: 24

> Conservative, nurturing women tended to be good characters, while evil women were career-oriented and nontraditional in their behavior. *All My Children*'s Erica Kane Martin, who informed her mother that she was a feminist (November 1, 1982, episode, and others), is the classic example of a selfish, ambitious, "bad" woman. This example suggests that soaps equate "good" with traditional, sex-typed behavior; that is, a "good" woman is not career-oriented and ambitious.

The information is interesting, but I'm not sure about the interpretation. The passage cited above seems to confuse character with occupation. Erica (or Alexis on *Dynasty*) would be what they are whether they had careers or were locked in a closet. And "badness" is relative—the audience is I think quite pleased to see Joan Collins sexually and financially triumphant. In fiction, *good* and *bad* are tricky terms—remember that Shylock and Iago take all the curtain calls. 25

CHARACTER AND SOCIAL VALUES

The soap opera is never funny about anything. It would be as out of place to be witty on this kind of show as in a campaign for state assemblyman. It might even be said that the soap has less of a sense of humor than almost any other fictional genre. In a way this is understandable: Some of the roles are already like cartoons and might lose their credibility if they were questioned. A sense of humor questions everything. But why are soaps so relentlessly *serious?* Serious especially about character and social values? There are comic characters even in *Hamlet* and *King Lear*. Is it the case that middle-class values or aspirations are too important for laughter? Or that the soap avoids any modality that might allow the viewer to look at the show in more than one designated way? 26

In soap opera, no social institution is ever satirized. The hospital   27
and the ranch and the corporation all seem to be good by definition.
The life they encourage, if lived rightly, seems to be just fine. This has
several consequences for character. No one is ever allowed to be ambivalent about "basic" values. Characters may from time to time not
know what they want, or make the wrong choice of bed, board, or career, but their philosophy is never in doubt. To see a soap requires
more than one kind of suspension of disbelief. We have to accept that
all its troubles occur in a social universe that really hasn't been responsible for causing them.

One of the big values on soap opera is money. The "bad" charac-   28
ters are corrupt in pursuit of it, but the money itself is okay. In fact, the
"good" characters seem innocent enough in its pursuit. On certain soap
operas what money does is fiercely admired by the cast and, one imagines, by the audience. Money and what it can buy are always on display
and we are invited to pant over its power and uses. The set and costumes
have come to matter increasingly, and soaps have become visual displays for *haute couture*. Current nighttime soaps are very nearly pornographic about wealth. One doesn't know what matters most to the
producers, Joan Collins's body or her wardrobe—probably the
wardrobe. Her clothes are calculated to be the last word not in style or
beauty but in the appearance of expense. As in the commercials she now
does for *Time* and other magazines, they are "statements" about acquisition. Although Joan Collins is often viewed as a middle-aged sex goddess, she may be much more like Imelda Marcos than *Venus Geriatrix*.

In the mid-1980s, the soaps seem to have moved away from   29
middle-class actuality and toward middle-class fantasy. They are now
about conspicuous consumption. In some ways the soaps are fictional
versions of *Lifestyles of the Rich and Famous*. But there is a real difference between interest in wealth and the depiction of wealth as a value
in itself. Possibly the writers of *Dallas* and *Dynasty* are saying with a
straight face what F. Scott Fitzgerald once wrote satirically: "The richer
a fella is, the better I like him."

In more traditional fiction wealth is an object of suspicion, and its   30
acquisition is part of a tension between ambition and surrender to its
values. Especially in the last two centuries, the centuries both of the
modern novel and the modern experience of "rising" into the "upper"
middle class, getting money has been a major theme of both life and art.
And serious literature has used the theme well. If one looks over Fitzgerald and Hemingway—or Balzac and Dickens—it's fairly plain that
wealth has a Faustian effect on character. It frees us from the ordinary
human fate. We are no longer compelled by necessity. Which means that
we are free to act out what we really are. Wealth allows character to reveal itself, finally, because there is no need any longer to subscribe to the

hypocrisies of manners and morals. The rich, like Tom Buchanan in *The Great Gatsby*, are free to be themselves. Or, like the inimitable Joan Collins, to show the world actual human desires unmediated by conscience or other social inhibitions. In great literature—and now and then on soaps—wealth really does free character and express nature. It certainly disposes of the merely social obstacles to self-expression.

For the most part, however, soaps do not rise to the occasion. To   31
be rich, like the Colbys or the Carringtons, means to be very much like the audience. To have money is to be lucky rather than different. The character of Blake Carrington is passive to the extent of being dimwitted. Wealth has done nothing for him psychologically except allow him to pay his bills.

I've suggested that there is a kind of pornography of wealth on   32
soap opera—the audience is invited to lust after houses and jewels and stock-market options. The women of soap are not undressed, as moralists might fear, but overdressed. Again, there are some interesting differences between the fiction of high culture and this offshoot mass culture. In Fitzgerald's short story "The Diamond as Big as the Ritz," there are some great lines describing the reaction of the middle class to the real thing, big money. The hero of the story, John T. Ungar, from the small and super respectable town of Hades on the Mississippi, has just gotten into a preposterous automobile owned by the Washington family. It is lavish beyond belief: The upholstery is made of tapestry and embroidery, covered with woven gold and even with the supererogatory "ends of ostrich feathers." It is This Year's Model in spades. But the appropriate reaction to the display of buying power is very far from laughter:

> If the car was any indication of what John would see, he was prepared
> to be astonished indeed. The simple piety prevalent in Hades has the
> earnest worship of and respect for riches as the first article of its creed—
> had John felt otherwise than radiantly humble before them, his parents
> would have turned away in horror at his blasphemy.

And so, one imagines, would the producer turn away in horror if it had occurred to him or her that the world of wealth on soaps was not a proper world at all. Or that characters could become caricatures if they were defined entirely by having money and acting out our dreams of consumption.

DUALITIES

There are some characters on soaps, brilliantly acted, who escape   33
the general fate. They are not reductive because money is for them a means to power—so is sex. Everything refers itself to a motive, and

not merely the generalized desire for "happiness." J.R. Ewing of *Dallas*, Alexis of *Dynasty*, and Erica of *All My Children* are motivated by genuine self-interest and because of this are morally isolated from other characters on their shows. Those others, who serve as foils for Alexis and Erica and J.R., are radically innocent. They are convinced of two things in general: One is that the happiness of others is implied by their own, and the second is that the pursuit (and even capture) of happiness is a natural right. The burden of the many monologues and dialogues of soap opera is that there must be a solution to human problems. Since nothing is wrong with the world as it is, and since the pursuit of wealth, power, love and, "happiness" is normative, the failure to get what you want is only a failure of means.

This philosophy underlies soap-opera motivation and discourse. 34 The typical argument unfolded in a moment of truth on screen will be that if something had been done in the past, if some opportunity had been taken or some temptation resisted, then things in the present would have been uncritically good. If only the right advice had been listened to, or the rules observed more closely. This view, pretty much by definition, is the opposite of tragic—and there will be some who call it the opposite of realistic. Nothing in the nature of things except for decisions accounts for happiness or unhappiness. No "star-crossed" lovers for the soaps.

In his recent book *The Culture of Narcissism*, Christopher Lasch 35 has described a change in cultural definition: "The pursuit of self-interest, formerly identified with the rational pursuit of gain and the accumulation of wealth, has become a search for pleasure and psychic survival." The observation seems especially accurate for soap opera, which is in its own way a mirror of the times, except that on soaps, characters are liable to practice both kinds of self-interest at once. It is altogether fascinating to see how J.R., Erica, and Alexis link the two kinds of pleasure, money and sex. Most of their encounters in the bedroom lead to changes in stock options. And there is a kind of cross-fertilization, as attitudes conventional for business are transposed in love. It is no wonder that, at a time when the mass media's other forms ceaselessly exhort us to see ourselves as upwardly mobile consumers of every kind of property or pleasure, that these characters should have become cultural heroes. Joan Collins finds her natural metier, the advertisement; Larry Hagman comes to symbolize American manners and mores on the television sets of Namibia, Chad, and Tongo; and Susan Lucci is a conglomerate of her own:

> Television's greatest villainess isn't really Alexis (Joan Collins) on "Dynasty." The real vixen in TV is Erica Kane (Susan Lucci) on the popular ABC soap opera "All My Children." The network has been literally holding its corporate breath waiting to see what Lucci might do once her

contract ended.... She was entertaining offers from all the networks and lots of other organizations too.

What do these great consumers of love and money bring to their   36
shows? Unlike their foils, they are self-aware. They are capable of
being jealous without cause, of bringing down destruction for a whim,
like the ancient gods. Like Alexis, they do what they want. Like Erica,
they do what is easiest. But whatever they do is conceived as an extension of ordinary human possibility: They take the logic of the situation
past the point that most of us dare to.

Their victims believe that happiness for one person means happi-   37
ness for someone else as well. But Erica and company have given a
certain amount of thought to the subject, and have concluded that
their own happiness does not depend on that of anyone else. Nor need
it make anyone else happy. They are perfectly subjective, images of
psychological change in our national self-conception. The majority of
innocent, striving characters of soap opera seem not to realize that
there are those to whom the happiness of others is offensive.

This heightened sense of character, and of its intensely subjective   38
values, makes it difficult to agree that the soap opera is confined to
domestic themes. One recent summary of studies on the subject
concludes that the soap is "a world dominated by interpersonal relationships, where characters discuss romantic, marital, and family
problems, and where health and work are major concerns within these
contexts." Within limits this is true enough. But the soap does other
kinds of work as well. In trying to keep up with the present it alters
the old form. Right now, in the middle of the eighties, the major characters of the soaps are not very domestic. They display all the signs
that we have come to associate with the personal liberation that marks
this decade. They are alone, very much self-concerned, and interested
in the various kinds of power, both material and emotional. They are
not romantic—even though deep sexuality is hinted at, it turns out
that sexual relationships are rarely ends in themselves. The major
characters—those most enthusiastically accepted by the American
(and even the world) audience—may live in family circumstances, but
they go through sequential marriages and "relationships." If art imi-
tates life, then these kinds of characters show the decade to itself.

My own guess, then, is that two kinds of social change are the   39
underlying subjects of soap opera. One is fairly visible: These programs now translate news events into fiction. They show us the use
and abuse of controlled substances. They have the latest attitudes toward alcoholism or sexual deviation. They are definitively about the
new status of women—and, consequently, of men. They suggest the
high incidence of crime in actual life and of terrorism. They contain
characters far from the small town that was the origin of the genre,

characters who step in from the vagueness of outer geography to the *mise-en-scène* of Texas or Colorado. The "interpersonal relationships" of soap opera now are incredibly complicated because of the current history they are meant to represent. In this respect, then, the soap is almost literally a form of "news of the day."

But it is in a second respect that the soap displays social change 40
more tellingly. It has two sets of characters, the simple and the complex, who tell us not about the news but about ourselves. The simple—who are often victims of the complex—represent in their innocent way all the hopes and desires of their audience. And their attitude is certainly representative: Without any sense of hubris at all they demand from life every natural right that has been drafted since 1789. They want happiness—and in order to get it they construe the social, political, and psychological world as if it existed only to respond to human desires. These characters worry us even when they are blameless. Always talking of themselves, always invoking happy moments of their past, always demanding that the world listen to them, they seem to have sprung up from the shelves of self-help and self-fulfillment. The complex characters are, paradoxically, more comfortable to understand. They hover on the edge of drama because they demand real "interaction." And in their powerful self-awareness and emotional selfishness they too help delineate the portrait of an age. Both kinds of characters unite to show some new social values, and we draw from their depiction an uneasy recognition of individualism concerned not with political freedom but with emotional indulgence. Are the soaps an art form? Not to me. Are they meaningful? Very much so. Better than most other forms of fiction in our time, they show us the passionate concern with the self that has been made possible by a new kind of cultural economy.

Examining the Text

1. How would you describe Berman's attitude toward soap operas? What does he see as the similarities and differences between serial fiction of the nineteenth century and the soap operas of today? Why does he make this comparison?

2. Soaps, says Berman, are "literally all talk" (paragraph 12), but the language consists of "clichés...pitched to the general illiteracy of the audience" (19). Analyze Berman's criticism of the dialogue in soap operas (12–19). From your experiences watching soap operas, do you find his criticisms valid?

3. According to Berman, "nothing in the nature of things except for decisions accounts for happiness or unhappiness" in soap operas (34). What does he mean by this statement, and what are its broader social and economic implications? Do you agree that, in general, soap opera characters are "happy" or "unhappy" based exclusively on the decisions they've made in the past?

For Group Discussion

Writing about prime-time soap operas popular during the early 1980s, such as *Dallas* and *Dynasty*, Berman suggests that "a kind of pornography of wealth" was fundamental to their appeal (32). As a group, discuss two or three more recent prime-time soap operas, such as *Melrose Place* and *Beverly Hills 90210*; if possible, you might also consider a prime-time soap opera from an earlier decade, such as *Family* or *Peyton Place*. In what ways do these other shows reflect the values Berman describes? In what ways do they rely on different values for their appeal? As a class, consider the extent to which the appeal of prime-time soap operas reflects the mood of the country.

Writing Suggestion

In an essay, evaluate Berman's statement that "the soap opera is never funny about anything" (26). According to his interpretation, why are soap operas so serious in regard to character and social values? Can you use his point to distinguish "soap operas" from other serial-like programs that are often funny, such as *LA Law* and *Northern Exposure?*

Soap Opera, Melodrama, and Women's Anger

Tania Modleski

The following selection, excerpted from Tania Modleski's Loving with a Vengeance: Mass-Produced Fantasies for Women, *is more scholarly than previous essays in this chapter. Modleski weaves together elements of psychoanalytic theory, film criticism, and statistical research. Her strategy is to use the texts of "high" critical theory to raise the status of popular art and then to argue that the soap opera itself is "in the vanguard" of popular aesthetic forms.*

Frequently dismissed by critics as the worst of television—and possibly the "nadir of art forms"—the soap opera is instead, Modleski argues, a central and primary female narrative form. Given the data (she notes that of approximately 20 million daily viewers, 90 percent are women), Modleski sets out to account for the widespread appeal of the soaps, which initially she pinpoints to be the pleasure women find in the narrative. Modleski draws constant parallels between the narrative structure of the soap opera and the structure of a woman's life in late twentieth-century America. For example, she compares the suspended conclusion, the delay of gratification, to what she sees as the essential condition of a woman's life: waiting. Further, in linking morality and goodness with the category of motherhood, the soaps "affirm the primacy of the family." Yet despite the benevolence of the heroines, true power resides in the villainesses. Viewers, Modleski suggests, can thus identify with both, simultaneously playing out their fantasies of domesticity and of power.

As you read, notice how Modleski reads the soap opera as a "text" and how she analyzes it in terms of its "codes" and structure. Despite her insistent focus upon popular art forms, Modleski's work is formulated with an academic audience in mind; she cites other scholars to lend credibility to her own points. You might think of each of her sources as threads she weaves together to support her own argument, a strategy you may want to use in your own academic writing.

———

Approximately twelve soap operas are shown daily, each half an   1
hour to an hour and a half long. The first of them goes on the air at about 10:00 A.M., and they run almost continuously until about 3:30 P.M. (of course, the times vary according to local programming schedule). In 1975 the *New York Times Magazine* reported that 20 million people watch soap operas daily, the average program attracting 6.7 million viewers, almost 90 percent of them female. Further:

> The households break down economically and educationally in proportions similar to the population as a whole—51.3 percent with household incomes under $10,000, for instance, and 23.9 percent with incomes over $15,000. About 24.8 percent of household heads have only an elementary school education, while 56.2 percent have a high school education or better.... The programs gross more than $300 million a year from the makers of soaps, deodorants, cake mixes and other household products, providing a disproportionate share of network profits though nighttime budgets are much larger.[1]

With the exception of "Ryan's Hope," which takes place in a big   2
city, the soap operas are set in small towns and involve two or three families intimately connected with one another. Families are often composed of several generations, and the proliferation of generations is accelerated by the propensity of soap opera characters to mature at an incredibly rapid rate; thus, the matriarch on "Days of Our Lives," who looks to be about 65, has managed over the years to become a great-great-grandmother. Sometimes on a soap opera one of the families will

———

[1]Anthony Astrachan, quoted in Dan Wakefield, *All Her Children*, p. 149.

be fairly well-to-do, and another somewhat lower on the social scale though still, as a rule, identifiably middle-class. In any case, since there is so much intermingling and intermarrying, class distinctions quickly become hopelessly blurred. Children figure largely in many of the plots, but they don't appear on the screen all that often; nor do the very old. Blacks and other minorities are almost completely excluded.

Women as well as men frequently work outside the home, usu-   3 ally in professions such as law and medicine, and women are generally on a professional par with men. But most of everyone's time is spent experiencing and discussing personal and domestic crises. Kathryn Weibel lists "some of the most frequent themes":

> the evil woman
> the great sacrifice
> the winning back of an estranged lover/spouse
> marrying her for her money, respectability, etc.
> the unwed mother
> deceptions about the paternity of children
> career vs. housewife
> the alcoholic woman (and occasionally man).[2]

Controversial social problems are introduced from time to time: 4 rape was recently an issue on several soap operas and was, for the most part, handled in a sensitive manner. In spite of the fact that soap operas contain more references to social problems than do most other forms of mass entertainment, critics tend to fault them heavily for their lack of social realism.

If television is considered by some to be a vast wasteland, soap   5 operas are thought to be the least nourishing spot in the desert. The surest way to damn a film, a television program, or even a situation in real life is to invoke an analogy to soap operas. In the same way that men are often concerned to show that what they are, above all, is not women, not "feminine," so television programs and movies will, surprisingly often, tell us that they are not soap operas. On a recent "Phil Donahue Show," a group of handicapped Vietnam War Veterans were bitterly relating their experiences; at one point Donahue interrupted the conversation to assure his audience (comprised almost entirely of women) that he was not giving them soap opera, but he thought it important to "personalize" the war experience. An afternoon "Money Movie," *Middle of the Night,* an interminable Paddy Chayevsky affair starring Frederick March, dealt with one man's life-crisis as, on the

---

[2]Weibel, p. 56.

brink of old age, he falls in love with a very young Kim Novak and struggles against the petty and destructive jealousy of his sister and daughter. "This is *not* a soap opera," he reprimands the sister at one point. Since to me it had all the ingredients of one, I could only conclude that men's soap operas are not to be thought of as soap operas only because they are *for men* (or about men).

It is refreshing, therefore, to read Horace Newcomb's book, *T.V.:*   6
The Most Popular Art, in which he suggests that far from being the nadir of art forms, as most people take them to be, soap operas represent in some ways the furthest advance of T.V. art. In other words, for all their stereotypical qualities, they combine to the highest degree two of the most important elements of the television aesthetic: "intimacy" and "continuity." Television, says Newcomb, is uniquely suited to deal with character and interpersonal relations rather than with action and selling. Soap operas, of course, play exclusively on the intimate properties of the medium. Newcomb also points out that because of the serial nature of the programs, television can offer us depictions of people in situations which grow and change over time, allowing for a greater "audience involvement, a sense of becoming a part of the lives and actions of the characters they see."[3] Thus far it is mainly soap opera which has taken advantage of these possibilities for continuity, nighttime programs, by and large, tending to "forget" from week to week all of the conflicts and lessons which have gone before.

Newcomb's book is important in that, by refusing to indulge in   7
an antifeminine bias against soap operas, it reveals a new way of seeing these programs which allows them to be placed in the vanguard of T.V. aesthetics (dubious as this distinction may seem to many people). My approach is different from, though in no sense opposed to Newcomb's. I propose not to ignore what is "feminine" about soap operas but to focus on it, to show how they provide a unique narrative pleasure which, while it has become thoroughly adapted to the rhythms of women's lives in the home, provides an alternative to the dominant "pleasures of the text" analyzed by Roland Barthes and others. Soap operas may be in the vanguard not just of T.V. art but of all popular narrative art.

Whereas the meaning of Harlequin Romances depends almost   8
entirely on the sense of an ending, soap operas are important to their viewers in part because they never end. Whereas Harlequins encourage our identification with one character, soap operas invite identification with numerous personalities. And whereas Harlequins are

---

[3]Horace Newcomb, *T.V.: The Most Popular Art,* p. 253.

structured around two basic enigmas, in soap operas, the enigmas proliferate: "Will Bill find out that his wife's sister's baby is really his by artificial insemination? Will his wife submit to her sister's blackmail attempts, or will she finally let Bill know the truth? If he discovers the truth, will this lead to another nervous breakdown, causing him to go back to Spring General where his ex-wife and his illegitimate daughter are both doctors and sworn enemies?" Tune in tomorrow, not in order to find out the answers, but to see what further complications will defer the resolutions and introduce new questions. Thus the narrative, by placing ever more complex obstacles between desire and fulfillment, makes anticipation of an end an end in itself. Soap operas invest exquisite pleasure in the central condition of a woman's life: waiting—whether for her phone to ring, for the baby to take its nap, or for the family to be reunited shortly after the day's final soap opera has left *its* family still struggling against dissolution.

According to Roland Barthes, the hermeneutic code,[4] which propounds the enigmas, functions by making "expectation...the basic condition for truth: truth, these narratives tell us, is what is *at the end* of expectation. This design implies a return to order, for expectation is a disorder."[5] But, of course, soap operas do not end. Consequently, truth for women is seen to lie not "at the end of expectation," but *in* expectation, not in the "return to order," but in (familial) disorder.

Many critics have considered endings to be crucial to narratives. Frank Kermode speculates that fictive ends are probably "figures" for death.[6] In his essay on "The Storyteller," Walter Benjamin comes to a similar conclusion:

> The novel is significant...not because it presents someone else's fate to us, perhaps didactically, but because this stranger's fate by virtue of the flame which consumes it yields us the warmth which we never draw from our own fate. What draws the reader to the novel is the hope of warming his shivering life with a death he reads about.[7]

---

[4]**Hermeneutic code:** In Roland Barthes's theory of fiction, everything in a story is understood in terms of one or more of five codes. One of these, the hermeneutic code, organizes the reader's desire to find out the truth about the characters and events in any story. This code is very active in detective stories, of course, but it is present in every kind of narrative. Modleski's point, in the present case, is that soap operas are different from most kinds of narrative, in that they will never reach that conclusion in which everything is revealed. If there is truth in them, it cannot be the kind of truth we learn only at the end of the tale. [Eds.]

[5]Barthes, *S/Z*, p. 76.

[6]Frank Kermode, *The Sense of an Ending*, p. 7.

[7]Walter Benjamin, "The Storyteller," in his *Illuminations*, p. 101.

But soap operas offer the promise of immortality and eternal re- 11
turn—same time tomorrow. Although at first glance, soap opera
seems in this respect to be diametrically opposed to the female domestic novels of the nineteenth century, which were preoccupied with
death, especially the deaths of infants and small children, a second
look tells us that the fantasy of immortality embodied in modern
melodrama is not so very different from the fantasies expressed in the
older works. In the latter, it is not the case that, in Benjamin's words,
"the 'meaning' of a character's life is revealed only in his death";[8]
rather, for women writers and readers, forced to endure repeatedly the
premature loss of their children, it was the meaning of the character's
death that had to be ascertained, and this meaning was revealed only
in the afterlife, only in projections of eternity.

"[T]racts of time unpunctuated by meaning derived from the 12
end are not to be borne," says Frank Kermode, confidently.[9] But
perhaps, for women (no doubt for men too) certain kinds of endings
are attended by a sense of meaninglessness even less capable of
being borne than limitless expanses of time which at least hold open
the possibility that something may sometime happen to confer sense
upon the present. The loss of a child was, for nineteenth century
women, an example of such an unbearable ending: it was, as Helen Papashvily has called it, "a double tragedy—the loss of a precious individual and the negation of her creativity,"[10] and it threatened, perhaps
more than any other experience, to give the lie to the belief in a benevolent God and the ultimate rightness of the world order. And so, it
was necessary to believe that the child would join a heavenly family
for all eternity.

For twentieth-century woman, the loss of her family, not through 13
death, but through abandonment (children growing up and leaving
home) is perhaps another "ending" which is feared because it leaves
women lonely and isolated and without significant purpose in life. The
fear, as Barbara Easton persuasively argues, is not without foundation:

> With the geographical mobility and breakdown of communities of the
> twentieth century, women's support networks outside the family have
> weakened, and they are likely to turn to their husbands for intimacy that
> earlier generations would have found elsewhere.[11]

---

[8]Benjamin, "The Storyteller," pp. 100–101.

[9]Kermode, p. 162.

[10]Papashvily, p. 194.

[11]Barbara Easton, "Feminism and the Contemporary Family," p. 30.

The family is, for many women, their only support, and soap op-   14
eras offer the assurance of its immortality.[12] They present the viewer
with a picture of a family which, though it is always in the process of
breaking down, stays together no matter how intolerable its situation
may get. Or, perhaps more accurately, the family remains close precisely because it is perpetually in a chaotic state. The unhappiness generated by the family can only be solved in the family. Misery becomes
riot, as in many nineteenth-century women's novels, the consequence
and sign of the family's breakdown, but the very means of its functioning and perpetuation. As long as the children are unhappy, as long
as things *don't* come to a satisfying conclusion, the mother will be
needed as confidante and adviser, and her function will never end.

One critic of soap opera remarks, "If...as Aristotle so reasonably   15
claimed, drama is the imitation of a human action that has a beginning,
a middle, and an end, soap opera belongs to a separate genus that is entirely composed of an indefinitely expandable middle."[13] It is not only
that successful soap operas do not end, it is also that they cannot end. In
The Complete Soap Opera Book, an interesting and lively work on the subject, the authors show how a radio serial forced off the air by television
tried to wrap up its story.[14] It was an impossible task. Most of the story-
line had to be discarded and only one element could be followed
through to its end—an important example of a situation in which what
Barthes calls the "discourse's instinct for preservation" has virtually triumphed over authorial control.[15] Furthermore, it is not simply that the
story's completion would have taken too long for the amount of time allotted by the producers. More importantly, I believe it would have been
impossible to resolve the contradiction between the imperatives of
melodrama—the good must be rewarded and the wicked punished—
and the latent message of soap operas—everyone cannot be happy at the
same time, no matter how deserving they are. The claims of any two
people, especially in love matters, are often mutually exclusive.

John Cawelti defines melodrama as having

at its center the moral fantasy of showing forth the essential 'rightness'   16
of the world order....Because of this, melodramas are usually rather

---

[12]Not only can women count on a never ending story line; they can also, to a great extent, rely upon the fact that their favorite characters will never desert them. To take a
rather extreme example: when, on one soap opera, the writers killed off a popular female character and viewers were unhappy, the actress was brought back to portray the
character's twin sister. See Madeleine Edmondson and David Rounds, *From Mary Noble
to Mary Hartman: The Complete Soap Opera Book,* p. 208.

[13]Dennis Porter, "Soap Time: Thoughts on a Commodity Art Form," p. 783.

[14]Edmondson and Rounds, *The Complete Soap Opera Book,* pp. 104–110.

[15]Barthes, *S/Z*, p. 135.

complicated in plot and character; instead of identifying with a single protagonist through his line of action, the melodrama typically makes us intersect imaginatively with many lives. Subplots multiply, and the point of view continually shifts in order to involve us in a complex of destinies. Through this complex of characters and plots we see not so much the working of individual fates but the underlying moral process of the world.[16]

It is scarcely an accident that this essentially nineteenth-century   17
form continues to appeal strongly to women, whereas the classic (male) narrative film is, as Laura Mulvey points out, structured "around a main controlling figure with whom the spectator can identify."[17] Soap operas continually insist on the insignificance of the individual life. A viewer might at one moment be asked to identify with a woman finally reunited with her love, only to have that identification broken in a moment of intensity and attention focused on the sufferings of the woman's rival.

If, as Mulvey claims, the identification of the spectator with "a   18
main male protagonist" results in the spectator's becoming "the representative of power,"[18] the multiple identification which occurs in soap opera results in the spectator's being divested of power. For the spectator is never permitted to identify with a character completing an entire action. Instead of giving us one "powerful ideal ego...who can make things happen and control events better than the subject/spectator can,"[19] soap operas present us with numerous limited egos, each in conflict with the others, and continually thwarted in its attempts to control events because of inadequate knowledge of other peoples' plans, motivations, and schemes. Sometimes, indeed, the spectator, frustrated by the sense of powerlessness induced by soap operas, will, like an interfering mother, try to control events directly:

> Thousands and thousands of letters [from soap fans to actors] give advice, warn the heroine of impending doom, caution the innocent to beware of the nasties ("Can't you see that your brother-in-law is up to no good?"), inform one character of another's doings, or reprimand a character for unseemly behavior.[20]

Presumably, this intervention is ineffectual, and feminine power-   19
lessness is reinforced on yet another level.

---

[16]John G. Cawelti, *Adventure, Mystery and Romance,* pp. 45–46.

[17]Laura Mulvey, "Visual Pleasure and Narrative Cinema," p. 420.

[18]Mulvey, p. 420.

[19]Mulvey, p. 420.

[20]Edmondson and Rounds, p. 193.

The subject/spectator of soap operas, it could be said, is consti- 20
tuted as a sort of ideal mother: a person who possesses greater wisdom
than all her children, whose sympathy is large enough to encompass the
conflicting claims of her family (she identifies with them all), and who
has no demands or claims of her own (she identifies with no one character exclusively). The connection between melodrama and mothers is an
old one. Harriet Beecher Stowe, of course, made it explicit in *Uncle Tom's
Cabin,* believing that if her book could bring its female readers to see the
world as one extended family, the world would be vastly improved. But
in Stowe's novel, the frequent shifting of perspective identifies the
reader with a variety of characters in order ultimately to ally her with
the mother/author and with God who, in their higher wisdom and understanding, can make all the hurts of the world go away, thus insuring
the "essential 'rightness' of the world order." Soap opera, however, denies the "mother" this extremely flattering illusion of her power. On the
one hand, it plays upon the spectator's expectation of the melodramatic
form, continually stimulating (by means of the hermeneutic code) the
desire for a just conclusion to the story, and, on the other hand, it constantly presents the desire as unrealizable, by showing that conclusions
only lead to further tension and suffering. Thus soap operas convince
women that their highest goal is to see their families united and happy,
while consoling them for their inability to realize this ideal and bring
about familial harmony.

This is reinforced by the character of the good mother on soap op- 21
eras. In contrast to the manipulating mother who tries to interfere with
her children's lives, the good mother must sit helplessly by as her children's lives disintegrate; her advice, which she gives only when asked,
is temporarily soothing, but usually ineffectual. Her primary function is
to be sympathetic, to tolerate the foibles and errors of others. Maeve
Ryan, the mother on "Ryan's Hope," is a perfect example. "Ryan's
Hope," a soap opera centered around an Irish-Catholic bar owning family which, unlike the majority of soap families, lives in a large city, was
originally intended to be more "realistic," more socially oriented than
the majority of soap operas.[21] Nevertheless, the function of the mother is
unchanged: she is there to console her children and try to understand
them as they have illegitimate babies, separate from their spouses
(miraculously obtaining annulments instead of divorces), and dispense
birth control information in the poor neighborhoods.

It is important to recognize that soap operas serve to affirm the 22
primacy of the family not by presenting an ideal family, but by portraying a family in constant turmoil and appealing to the spectator to

---

[21]See Paul Mayer, "Creating 'Ryan's Hope.'"

be understanding and tolerant of the many evils which go on within that family. The spectator/mother, identifying with each character in turn, is made to see "the larger picture" and extend her sympathy to both the sinner and the victim. She is thus in a position to forgive all. As a rule, only those issues which can be tolerated and ultimately pardoned are introduced on soap operas. The list includes careers for women, abortions, premarital and extramarital sex, alcoholism, divorce, mental and even physical cruelty. An issue like homosexuality, which could explode the family structure rather than temporarily disrupt it, is simply ignored. Soap operas, contrary to many people's conception of them, are not conservative but liberal, and the mother is the liberal par excellence. By constantly presenting her with the many-sidedness of any question, by never reaching a permanent conclusion, soap operas undermine her capacity to form unambiguous judgments.

In this respect, soap opera melodrama can be said to create in the spectator a divisiveness of feeling totally different from the "monopathic" feeling Robert Heilman sees as constituting the appeal of traditional melodrama. There, he writes, "one enjoys the wholeness of a practical competence that leads to swift and sure action; one is untroubled by psychic fumbling, by indecisiveness, by awareness of alternate courses, by weak muscles or strong counter imperatives."[22] But in soap operas, we are constantly troubled by "psychic fumbling" and by "strong counter-imperatives." To take one example, Trish, on "Days of Our Lives," takes her small son and runs away from her husband David in order to advance her singing career. When she gets an opportunity to go to London to star in a show, she leaves the child with her mother. When the show folds, she becomes desperate to get back home to see her child, but since she has no money, she has to prostitute herself. Finally she is able to return, and after experiencing a series of difficulties, she locates her son, who is now staying with his father. Once she is in town, a number of people, angry at the suffering she has caused David, are hostile and cruel towards her. Thus far, the story seems to bear out the contention of the critics who claim that soap opera characters who leave the protection of the family are unequivocally punished. But the matter is not so simple. For the unforgiving people are shown to have limited perspectives. The larger view is summed up by Margo, a woman who has a mysterious and perhaps fatal disease and who, moreover, has every reason to be jealous of Trish since Trish was the first love of Margo's husband. Margo claims that no one can ever fully know what private motives drove Trish to abandon her family; besides, she says, life is too short to bear grudges and inflict pain. The spectator, who sees the ex-

23

---

[22]Robert B. Heilman, *Tragedy and Melodrama*, p. 85.

tremity of Trish's sorrow, assents. And at the same time, the spectator is made to forgive and understand the unforgiving characters, for she is intimately drawn into their anguish and suffering as well.

These remarks must be qualified. If soap operas keep us caring   24
about everyone, if they refuse to allow us to condemn most characters and actions until all the evidence is in (and, of course, it never is), there is one character whom we are allowed to hate unreservedly: the villainess, the negative image of the spectator's ideal self.[23] Although much of the suffering on soap opera is presented as unavoidable, the surplus suffering is often the fault of the villainess who tries to "make things happen and control events better than the subject/spectator can." The villainess might very possibly be a mother trying to manipulate her children's lives or ruin their marriages. Or perhaps she is a woman avenging herself on her husband's family because it has never fully accepted her.

This character cannot be dismissed as easily as many critics seem   25
to think.[24] The extreme delight viewers apparently take in despising the villainess testifies to the enormous amount of energy involved in the spectator's repression and to her (albeit unconscious) resentment at being constituted as an egoless receptacle for the suffering of others.[25] The villainess embodies the "split-off fury" which in the words of Dorothy Dinnerstein, is "the underside of the 'truly feminine' woman's monstrously overdeveloped talent for unreciprocated empathy."[26] This aspect of melodrama can be traced back to the middle of the nineteenth century when *Lady Audley's Secret*, a drama based on Mary Elizabeth Braddon's novel about a governess turned bigamist and murderess, became one of the most popular stage melodramas of all time.[27] In her discussion of the novel, Elaine Showalter shows how the author, while paying lipservice to conventional notions about the feminine role, managed to appeal to "thwarted female energy":

---

[23]There are still villains on soap operas, but their numbers have declined considerably since radio days—to the point where they are no longer indispensable to the formula. "The Young and the Restless," for example, does without them.

[24]According to Weibel, we quite simply "deplore" the victimizers and totally identify with the victim (p. 62).

[25]"A soap opera without a bitch is a soap opera that doesn't get watched. The more hateful the bitch the better. Erica of 'All My Children' is a classic. If you want to hear some hairy rap, just listen to a bunch of women discussing Erica.

'Girl, that Erica needs her tail whipped.'

'I wish she'd try to steal my man and plant some marijuana in my purse. I'd be mopping up the street with her new hairdo.'" Bebe Moore Campbell, "Hooked on Soaps," p. 103.

[26]Dorothy Dinnerstein, *The Mermaid and The Minotaur*, p. 236.

[27]"The author, Mary Elizabeth Braddon, belonged to that class of writers called by Charles Reade 'obstacles to domestic industry.'" Frank Rahill, *The World of Melodrama*, p. 204.

The brilliance of *Lady Audley's Secret* is that Braddon makes her would-be murderess the fragile blond angel of domestic realism. . . . The dangerous woman is not the rebel or the bluestocking, but the "pretty little girl" whose indoctrination in the female role has taught her secrecy and deceitfulness, almost as secondary sex characteristics.[28]

Thus the villainess is able to transform traditional feminine   26
weaknesses into the sources of her strength.

Similarly, on soap operas, the villainess seizes those aspects of a   27
woman's life which normally render her most helpless and tries to turn them into weapons for manipulating other characters. She is, for instance, especially good at manipulating pregnancy, unlike most women, who, as Mary Ellmann wittily points out, tend to feel manipulated by it:

At the same time, women cannot help observing that conception (their highest virtue, by all reports) simply happens or doesn't. It lacks the style of enterprise. It can be prevented by foresight and device (though success here, as abortion rates show, is exaggerated), but it is accomplished by luck (good or bad). Purpose often seems if anything, a deterrent. A devious business benefiting by indirection, by pretending not to care, as though the self must trick the body. In the regrettable conception, the body instead tricks the self—much as it does in illness or death.[29]

In contrast to the numerous women on soap operas who are ei-   28
ther trying unsuccessfully to become pregnant or who have become pregnant as a consequence of a single unguarded moment in their lives, the villainess manages, for a time at least, to make pregnancy work for her. She gives it the "style of enterprise." If she decides she wants to marry a man, she will take advantage of him one night when he is feeling especially vulnerable and seduce him. And if she doesn't achieve the hoped-for pregnancy, undaunted, she simply lies to her lover about being pregnant. The villainess thus reverses male/female roles: anxiety about conception is transferred to the male. He is the one who had better watch his step and curb his promiscuous desires or he will find himself burdened with an unwanted child.

Some episodes on "The Young and the Restless" perfectly illus-   29
trate the point. Lori's sister Leslie engages in a one-night sexual encounter with Lori's husband, Lance. Of course, she becomes pregnant as a result. Meanwhile Lori and Lance have been having marital diffi-

---

[28]Elaine Showalter, *A Literature of Their Own*, p. 204.

[29]Mary Ellmann, *Thinking About Women*, p. 181. Molly Haskell makes a similar point in her discussion of "The Woman's Film," in *From Reverence to Rape*, pp. 172–73.

culties, and Lori tries to conceive a child, hoping this will bring her closer to her husband. When she finds out about her sister and Lance, she becomes frantic about her inability to conceive, realizing that if Lance ever finds out he is the father of Leslie's child, he will be drawn to Leslie and reject her. Vanessa, Lance's mother and a classic villainess, uses her knowledge of the situation to play on Lori's insecurities and drive a wedge between her and Lance. At the same time, Lori's father has been seduced by Jill Foster, another villainess, who immediately becomes pregnant, thus forcing him to marry her.

Furthermore, the villainess, far from allowing her children to rule　　30 her life, often uses them in order to further her own selfish ambitions. One of her typical ploys is to threaten the father or the woman possessing custody of the child with the deprivation of that child. She is the opposite of the woman at home, who at first is forced to have her children constantly with her, and later is forced to let them go—for a time on a daily recurring basis and then permanently. The villainess enacts for the spectator a kind of reverse *fort-da* game, in which the mother is the one who attempts to send the child away and bring it back at will, striving to overcome feminine passivity in the process of the child's appearance and loss.[30] Into the bargain, she also tries to manipulate the man's disappearance and return by keeping the fate of his child always hanging in the balance. And again, male and female roles tend to get reversed: the male suffers the typically feminine anxiety over the threatened absence of his children. On "Ryan's Hope," for example, Delia continually uses her son to control her husband and his family. At one point she clashes with another villainess, Raye Woodward, over the child and the child's father, Frank Ryan, from whom Delia is divorced. Raye realizes that the best way to get Frank interested in her is by taking a maternal interest in his child. When Delia uncovers Raye's scheme, she becomes determined to foil it by regaining custody of the boy. On "The Young and the Restless," to take another example, Derek is on his way out of the house to try to intercept Jill Foster on her way to the altar and persuade her to marry him instead of Stuart Brooks. Derek's ex-wife Suzanne thwarts the at-

---

[30]The game, observed by Freud, in which the child plays "disappearance and return" with a wooden reel tied to a string. "What he did was to hold the reel by the string and very skillfully throw it over the edge of his curtained cot, so that it disappeared into it, at the same time uttering his expressive 'O-O-O-O'. [Freud speculates that this represents the German word *'fort'* or *'gone.'*] He then pulled the reel out of the cot again by the string and hailed its reappearance with a joyful *'da'* ['there']." According to Freud, "Throwing away the object so that it was 'gone' might satisfy an impulse of the child's, which was suppressed in his actual life, to revenge himself on his mother for going away from him. In that case it would have a defiant meaning: 'All right then, go away! I don't need you. I'm sending you away myself.'" Sigmund Freud, *Beyond the Pleasure Principle*, pp. 10–11.

tempt by choosing that moment to inform him that their son is in a mental hospital.

The villainess thus continually works to make the most out of 31
events which render other characters totally helpless. Literal paralysis turns out, for one villainess, to be an active blessing, since it prevents her husband from carrying out his plans to leave her; when she gets back the use of her legs, therefore, she doesn't tell anyone. And even death doesn't stop another villainess from wreaking havoc; she returns to haunt her husband and convince him to try to kill his new wife.

The popularity of the villainess would seem to be explained in 32
part by the theory of repetition compulsion, which Freud saw as resulting from the individual's attempt to become an active manipulator of her/his own powerlessness.[31] The spectator, it might be thought, continually tunes into soap operas to watch the villainess as she tries to gain control over her feminine passivity, thereby acting out the spectator's fantasies of power. Of course, most formula stories (like the Western) appeal to the spectator/reader's compulsion to repeat: the spectator constantly returns to the same story in order to identify with the main character and achieve, temporarily, the illusion of mastery denied him or her in real life. But soap operas refuse the spectator even this temporary illusion of mastery. The villainess's painstaking attempts to turn her powerlessness to her own advantage are always thwarted just when victory seems most assured, and she must begin her machinations all over again. Moreover, the spectator does not comfortably identify with the villainess. Since the spectator despises the villainess as the negative image of her ideal self, she not only watches the villainess act out her own hidden wishes, but simultaneously sides with the forces conspiring against fulfillment of those wishes. As a result of this "internal contestation,"[32] the spectator comes to enjoy repetition for its own sake and takes her adequate pleasure in the building up and tearing down of the plot. In this way, perhaps, soap operas help reconcile her to the meaningless, repetitive nature of much of her life and work within the home.

Soap operas, then, while constituting the spectator as a "good 33
mother," provide in the person of the villainess an outlet for feminine anger: in particular, as we have seen, the spectator has the satisfaction

---

[31]Speaking of the child's *fort-da* game, Freud notes, "At the outset he was in a passive situation—he was overpowered by experience; but by repeating it, unpleasurable though it was, as a game, he took on an active part. These efforts might be put down to an instinct for mastery that was acting independently of whether the memory was in itself pleasurable or not." In *Beyond the Pleasure Principle*, p. 10.

[32]Jean-Paul Sartre's phrase for the tension surrealism's created object sets up in the spectator is remarkably appropriate here. See *What Is Literature?*, p. 133n.

of seeing men suffer the same anxieties and guilt that women usually experience and seeing them receive similar kinds of punishment for their transgressions. But that anger is neutralized at every moment in that it is the special object of the spectator's hatred. The spectator, encouraged to sympathize with almost everyone, can vent her frustration on the one character who refuses to accept her own powerlessness and who is unashamedly self-seeking. Woman's anger is directed at woman's anger, and an eternal cycle is created.

And yet, if the villainess never succeeds, if, in accordance with 34 the spectator's conflicting desires, she is doomed to eternal repetition, then she obviously never permanently fails either. When, as occasionally happens, a villainess reforms, a new one immediately supplants her. Generally, however, a popular villainess will remain true to her character for most or all of the soap opera's duration. And if the villainess constantly suffers because she is always foiled, we should remember that she suffers no more than the good characters, who don't even try to interfere with their fates. Again, this may be contrasted to the usual imperatives of melodrama, which demand an ending to justify the suffering of the good and punish the wicked. While soap operas thrive they present a continual reminder that women's anger is alive, if not exactly well.

WORKS CITED

Barthes, Roland. *S/Z*. Translated by Richard Miller. New York: Hill and Wang, 1974.

Benjamin, Walter. *Illuminations*. Translated by Harry Zohn. Edited by Hannah Arendt. New York: Schocken Books, 1969.

Campbell, Bebe Moore. "Hooked on Soaps." *Essence*, November 1978, pp. 100–103.

Cawelti, John G. *Adventure, Mystery, and Romance*. Chicago: University of Chicago Press, 1976.

Dinnerstein, Dorothy. *The Mermaid and the Minotaur: Sexual Arrangements and Human Malaise*. New York: Harper & Row, 1976.

Easton, Barbara. "Feminism and the Contemporary Family." *Socialist Review* 8, no. 3 (1978), pp. 11–36.

Edmondson, Madeleine, and Rounds, David. *From Mary Noble to Mary Hartman: The Complete Soap Opera Book*. New York: Stein and Day, 1976.

Ellmann, Mary. *Thinking about Women*. New York: Harvest Books, 1968.

Freud, Sigmund. *Beyond the Pleasure Principle*. Translated by James Strachey. New York: W. W. Norton, 1961.

Haskell, Molly. *From Reverence to Rape: The Treatment of Women in the Movies.* New York: Penguin, 1974.

Heilman, Robert B. *Tragedy and Melodrama: Versions of Experience.* Seattle: University of Washington Press, 1968.

Kermode, Frank. *The Sense of an Ending: Studies in the Theory of Fiction.* New York: Oxford University Press, 1967.

Mayer, Paul. "Creating 'Ryan's Hope.'" In *T.V. Book.* Edited by Judy Fireman. New York: Workman Publishing Co., 1977.

Mulvey, Laura. "Visual Pleasure and Narrative Cinema." In *Women and the Cinema.* Edited by Karyn Kay and Gerald Peary. New York: E. P. Dutton, 1977.

Newcomb, Horace. *TV: The Most Popular Art.* New York: Anchor Books, 1974.

Papashvily, Helen Waite. *All the Happy Endings: A Study of the Domestic Novel in America, the Women Who Wrote It, the Women Who Read It, in the Nineteenth Century.* New York: Harper & Brothers, 1956.

Porter, Dennis. "Soap Time: Thoughts on a Commodity Art Form." *College English* 38 (1977): 782–88.

Rahill, Frank. *The World of Melodrama.* University Park: Pennsylvania State University Press, 1967.

Sartre, Jean-Paul. *What Is Literature?* Translated by Bernard Frechtman. New York: Washington Square Press, 1966.

Showalter, Elaine. *A Literature of Their Own.* Princeton: Princeton University Press, 1977.

Wakefield, Dan. *All Her Children.* Garden City, N.Y.: Doubleday & Co., 1976.

Weibel, Kathryn. *Mirror, Mirror: Images of Women Reflected in Popular Culture.* Garden City, N.Y.: Anchor Books, 1977.

Examining the Text

1. Modleski's attitude toward soap operas seems much more positive than Berman's. Point to some instances of her praise. How does her focus on "intimacy" and "continuity" (paragraph 6) and on the "feminine" (7) in soap operas color her attitude?

2. In soap operas, Modleski says, "the enigmas proliferate,...the narrative, by placing ever more complex obstacles between desire and fulfillment, makes anticipation of an end an end in itself" (8). What does she mean? How does the fact that soap operas "cannot end" (15) contribute to her comparison of this genre and traditional melodrama? Do Modleski's observations correspond to your own experience of soap operas?

3. Modleski focuses on the image of women in soap operas and their relationship to the spectator (the "ideal" but "ineffectual" spectator/ mother, able "to forgive both the sinner and the victim," and "the villainess, the negative image of the spectator's ideal self"). How does she relate these opposing images to feminine powerlessness? How do they contribute to the dynamics and appeal of soap operas?

For Group Discussion

Modleski argues that soap operas "are not conservative but liberal" (22). As a group, determine what she means by "liberal" in this context and how you think soap operas do or do not fit this definition. As a class, evaluate Modleski's analysis of soap operas. Do you agree or disagree with her basic assertions?

Writing Suggestion

Modleski notes that in 1982, when she was writing about daytime soap operas, approximately twelve were on the air. Almost as many are broadcast today, mostly the same ones. In an essay consider the extent to which Modleski's observations hold true today and the extent to which there may be changes. Are soap operas still marked by "intimacy" and "continuity"? Are the plot dynamics similar and the basic roles of "good mother" and "villainess" still prominent? Have there been changes in the representation of minorities (2) and the presentation of controversial issues, such as abortion and homosexuality (22)? What can you conclude about soap operas' essential appeal and the extent to which they adapt to changing audiences?

ADDITIONAL SUGGESTIONS FOR WRITING ABOUT TELEVISION

1. This chapter includes essays about two genres of television: talk shows and soap operas. Choose another genre (such as game shows, dating-game shows, tabloid news shows, situation comedies, detective shows, cartoons, or live police dramas) and analyze the underlying presuppositions of this genre. What specific beliefs, actions, and relationships do these shows encourage? How and why do these shows appeal to the audience? If everything that you knew were based on your exposure to this genre of show, what kind of world would you expect to encounter, how would you expect people to behave toward each other, and what sort of values would you expect them to have? To support your analysis of the genre, use examples from specific shows, but keep in mind that your essay should address the genre or category of shows in general.

2. According to sociologists and psychologists, human beings are driven by certain basic needs and desires. All of the essays in this chapter attempt to account for the powerful appeal of television in our culture, and several suggest that we rely on television to fulfill needs that aren't met elsewhere. Consider some of the following basic needs and desires that television might satisfy for you or for the broader viewing public:

> to be amused
> to gain information about the world
> to have shared experiences
> to find models to imitate
> to see authority figures exalted or deflated
> to experience, in a controlled and guilt-free situation, extreme emotions
> to see order imposed on the world
> to reinforce our belief in justice
> to experience thrilling or frightening situations
> to believe in romantic love
> to believe in magic, the marvelous and the miraculous
> to avoid the harsh realities of life
> to see others make mistakes

Referring to items on this list, or formulating your own list of needs and desires, compose an essay in which you argue that television succeeds or fails in meeting our basic needs and desires. Use specific television programs that you're familiar with as concrete evidence for your assertions.

3. Modleski and Berman disagree on whether soap operas should be considered "art." Relying on the essays in this chapter along with outside reading, devise your own definition of "art" and apply this to three or four specific shows that you know relatively well. To what degree do these meet your criteria of "art"?

Internet Activities
1. Game shows have long been a popular television genre, and their popularity of late seems to be on the rise. One reason may be that they allow for a degree of audience interactivity that scripted shows like dramas and comedies lack; after all, viewers can become participants on game shows and gain instant celebrity if they do well. Game shows also seem to appeal to our greed (or our desire to get rich quickly and without too much work) as well as to our competitive nature. In preparation for writing an essay on game shows, recall some of the ones that you've seen on TV, and check the *Common Culture* Web site for links to sites related to game shows. Then, write an essay in which you analyze the reasons why this television genre is appealing to

viewers. As part of your essay, you might decide to compare and contrast game shows to one of the other television genres discussed in this chaper.

2. Although it's difficult to predict developments having to do with the Internet, a possibility discussed by experts is that television and the World Wide Web will, in some way, merge. Perhaps your TV screen will become your computer monitor, or you'll be able to order movies and view television shows through your computer and Internet connection. Already we see some early connections between the two media, for instance in the live Web casts that some TV shows are doing, or in exclusive Web casts (that is, programs or videos that are shown only on the Web and not on TV). In addition, most news and sports shows have companion Web sites that offer viewers additional information, pictures, interviews, etc. Consider some of these developments, discussed in further detail at the links provided at the *Common Culture* Web site. Then, write an essay in which you discuss the ways in which the Web competes with or complements television. Do the two media provide the same kind of information and entertainment, or do they offer fundamentally different viewing experiences?

4

Popular Music

A naked man, arms outstretched suggestive of Christ on the cross or an Olympian swimmer about to take the plunge, stands atop a cassette deck. Electric pulses from the tape player reach his brain through headphones as he gazes heavenward as if in a trance. The phrase "Be the music" scrolls about his midsection, concealing—perhaps replacing—his maleness, as the music fills his every cell. Such is the power music has over us, this TDK as suggests, that it can take us over completely—mentally, physically, emotionally.

By virtue of its sheer volume, rhythm, and encompassing presentation, music has the capacity to take us to "completely different" psychic spaces. It can lift us from our ordinary sense of reality and profoundly affect our moods, emotions, energy level, and even our level of sexual arousal. Furthermore, the lyrics, when combined with these powerful aural appeals, become all the more potent and suggestive, influencing our feelings of isolation or belonging, our relation to parents and friends, our attitudes toward authority figures, our notions about romance, and our views about gender and race.

The articles in this chapter discuss the ways in which people are "constructed" by what they hear—that is, how their beliefs, values, attitudes, and morals are shaped by the music they listen to. Allan Bloom, in "Music," sees this phenomenon as potentially dangerous, since it encourages people—especially young people—to transgress the boundaries imposed by civilized society. However, other critics contend that popular music plays a very positive role in contemporary society, since it allows people to voice feelings and ideas that would otherwise not be widely heard. This is especially the case with rap and hip-hop music, as several writers in the second section of this chapter observe. Originally created by and intended for young, African-American inner-city audiences, this music has gained more widespread acceptance, to the point that it appears regularly on MTV and has been adopted by major recording labels, thus giving previously disenfranchised urban youth a more pervasive presence in the popular culture.

As you read these essays, perhaps hooked up to your Walkman and blasting the latest Jamiroquai, Phish, Sarah McLachlan, Chemical Brothers, or Tupac posthumous release, you might consider the implications of music in your life: the reasons why you listen to certain kinds of music, the messages embodied in their lyrics and rhythm, and the pleasures and possible dangers inherent in letting popular music move you to a "completely different" frame of mind.

Rock and Rap:
Musical Controversies

Music

Allan Bloom

Throughout its forty-odd year history, rock music has been criticized variously as wicked, immoral, and depraved. But in the late 1980s rock and its proponents found themselves the object of a new criticism.

In his controversial and widely read study of American culture, The Closing of the American Mind *(1987), Allan Bloom contends that rock music is worthless "junk food for the soul" and focuses on rock's antithetical relationship to "high" learning, civilization, and the classical tradition. Bloom, for many years a professor at the University of Chicago, argues that rock music debilitates listeners' capacity to reason, and he charges that its effects on the imagination of today's youth are crippling and druglike. Bloom believes that music, in its ideal form, should cultivate a sense of harmony and unity that uplifts the human subject to a higher good, and he laments the fact that crucial moral and spiritual values have been lost as rock has supplemented other, classically oriented forms of music in the second half of the twentieth century. More than anything, perhaps, Bloom is concerned with the passionate drives that rock music taps and releases in listeners. For Bloom, rock turns life into a "masturbational fantasy," and as such poses a threat to the psychological and sociological balance of human rationality. In its "barbaric appeal to sexual desire," rock plugs into an unconscious and untamed passion, one which leads humanity away from the order of civilization: Bloom argues that this escape into an irrational and primitive fantasy world has contributed to the deterioration of the great Western cultural tradition.*

As you read, note how Bloom calls on a long tradition of "high" culture and his own experience as a teacher to bolster his authority. Where do you find his argument most persuasive? Least convincing?

Though students do not have books, they most emphatically do have music. Nothing is more singular about this generation than its addiction to music. This is the age of music and the states of soul that accompany it. To find a rival to this enthusiasm, one would have to go back at least a century to Germany and the passion for Wagner's operas. They had the religious sense that Wagner was creating the meaning of life and that they were not merely listening to his works but experiencing that meaning. Today, a very large proportion of young people between the ages of ten and twenty live for music. It is their passion; nothing else excites them as it does; they cannot take seriously anything alien to music. When they are in school and with their families, they are longing to plug themselves back into their music. Nothing surrounding them—school, family, church—has anything to do with their musical world. At best that ordinary life is neutral, but mostly it is an impediment, drained of vital content, even a thing to be rebelled against. Of course, the enthusiasm for Wagner was limited to a small class, could be indulged only rarely and only in a few places, and had to wait on the composer's slow output. The music of the new votaries, on the other hand, knows neither class nor nation. It is available twenty-four hours a day, everywhere. There is the stereo in the home, in the car; there are concerts; there are music videos, with special channels exclusively devoted to them, on the air nonstop; there are the Walkmans so that no place—not public transportation, not the library—prevents students from communing with the Muse, even while studying. And, above all, the musical soil has become tropically rich. No need to wait for unpredictable genius. Now there are many geniuses, producing all the time, two new ones rising to take the place of every fallen hero. There is no dearth of the new and the startling.

The power of music in the soul—described to Jessica marvelously by Lorenzo in the *Merchant of Venice*—has been recovered after a long period of desuetude. And it is rock music alone that has effected this restoration. Classical music is dead among the young. This assertion will, I know, be hotly disputed by many who, unwilling to admit tidal changes, can point to the proliferation on campuses of classes in classical music appreciation and practice, as well as performance groups of all kinds. Their presence is undeniable, but they involve not more than 5 to 10 percent of the students. Classical music is now a special taste, like Greek language or pre-Colombian archaeology, not a common culture of reciprocal communication and psychological shorthand. Thirty years ago, most middle-class families made some of the old European music a part of the home, partly because they liked it, partly because they thought it was good for the kids. University students usually had some early emotive association with Beethoven, Chopin, and Brahms, which was a permanent part of their makeup and to which they were likely to respond throughout their lives. This was probably the only regularly recognizable class distinction between educated and uneducated in America. Many, or even most, of the young people of that generation also swung with Benny Goodman, but with an element of self-consciousness—to be hip, to prove they weren't snobs, to show solidarity with the democratic ideal of a pop culture out of which would grow a new high culture. So there remained a class distinction between high and low, although private taste was beginning to create doubts about whether one really liked the high very much. But all that has changed. Rock music is as unquestioned and unproblematic as the air the students breathe, and very few have any acquaintance at all with classical music. This is a constant surprise to me. And one of the strange aspects of my relations with good students I come to know well is that I frequently introduce them to Mozart. This is a pleasure to me, inasmuch as it is always pleasant to give people gifts that please them. It is interesting to see whether and in what ways their studies are complemented by such music. But this is something utterly new to me as a teacher; formerly my students usually knew much more classical music than I did.

Music was not all that important for the generation of students 3 preceding the current one. The romanticism that had dominated serious music since Beethoven appealed to refinements—perhaps over-refinements—of sentiments that are hardly to be found in the contemporary world. The lives people lead or wish to lead and their prevailing passions are of a different sort than those of the highly educated German and French bourgeoisie, who were avidly reading Rousseau and Baudelaire, Goethe and Heine, for their spiritual satisfaction. The music that had been designed to produce, as well as to please, such exquisite sensibilities had a very tenuous relation to American lives of any kind. So romantic musical culture in America had had for a long time the character of a veneer, as easily susceptible to ridicule as were Margaret Dumont's displays of coquettish chasteness, so aptly exploited by Groucho Marx in *A Night at the Opera*. I noticed this when I first started teaching and lived in a house for gifted students. The "good" ones studied their physics and then listened to classical music. The students who did not fit so easily into the groove, some of them just vulgar and restive under the cultural tyranny, but some of them also serious, were looking for things that really responded to their needs. Almost always they responded to the beat of the newly emerging rock music. They were a bit ashamed of their taste, for it was not respectable. But I instinctively sided with the second group, with real, if coarse, feelings as opposed to artificial and dead ones. Then their musical sans-culotteism won the revolution and reigns unabashed today. No classical music has been produced that can speak of this generation.

Symptomatic of this change is how seriously students now take 4 the famous passages on musical education in Plato's *Republic*. In the past, students, good liberals that they always are, were indignant at the censorship of poetry, as a threat to free inquiry. But they were really thinking of science and politics. They hardly paid attention to the discussion of music itself and, to the extent that they even thought about it, were really puzzled by Plato's devoting time to rhythm and melody in a serious treatise on political philosophy. Their experience of music was as an entertainment, a matter of indifference to political and moral life. Students today, on the contrary, know exactly why Plato takes music so seriously. They know it affects life very profoundly and are indignant because Plato seems to want to rob them of their most intimate pleasure. They are drawn into argument with Plato about the experience of music, and the dispute centers on how to evaluate it and deal with it. This encounter not only helps to illuminate the phenomenon of contemporary music, but also provides a model of how contemporary students can profitably engage with a classic text. The very fact of their fury shows how much Plato threatens what is dear and intimate to them. They are little able to defend their experience, which has seemed unquestionable until questioned, and it is most resistant to cool analysis. Yet if a student can—and this is most difficult and unusual—draw back, get a critical distance on what he clings to, come to doubt the ultimate value of what he loves, he has taken the first and most difficult step toward the philosophic conversion. Indignation is the soul's defense against the wound of doubt about its own; it reorders the cosmos to support the justice of its cause. It justifies putting Socrates to death. Recognizing indignation for what it is constitutes knowledge of the soul, and is thus an experience more philosophic than the study of mathematics. It is Plato's teaching that music, by its nature, encompasses all that is today most resistant to philosophy. So it may well be that through the thicket of our greatest corruption runs the path to awareness of the oldest truths.

Plato's teaching about music is, put simply, that rhythm and   5 melody, accompanied by dance, are the barbarous expression of the soul. Barbarous, not animal. Music is the medium of the *human* soul in its most ecstatic condition of wonder and terror. Nietzsche, who in large measure agrees with Plato's analysis, says in *The Birth of Tragedy* (not to be forgotten is the rest of the title, *Out of the Spirit of Music*) that a mixture of cruelty and coarse sensuality characterized this state, which of course was religious, in the service of gods. Music is the soul's primitive and primary speech and it is *alogon*, without articulate speech or reason. It is not only not reasonable, it is hostile to reason. Even when articulate speech is added, it is utterly subordinate to and determined by the music and the passions it expresses.

Civilization or, to say the same thing, education is the taming or   6 domestication of the soul's raw passions—not suppressing or excising them, which would deprive the soul of its energy—but forming and informing them as art. The goal of harmonizing the enthusiastic part of the soul with what develops later, the rational part, is perhaps impossible to attain. But without it, man can never be whole. Music, or poetry, which is what music becomes as reason emerges, always involves a delicate balance between passion and reason, and, even in its highest and most developed forms—religious, warlike, and erotic— that balance is always tipped, if ever so slightly, toward the passionate. Music, as everyone experiences, provides an unquestionable justification and a fulfilling pleasure for the activities it accompanies: the soldier who hears the marching band is enthralled and reassured; the religious man is exalted in his prayer by the sound of the organ in the church; and the lover is carried away and his conscience stilled by the romantic guitar. Armed with music, man can damn rational doubt. Out of the music emerge the gods that suit it, and they educate men by their example and their commandments.

Plato's Socrates disciplines the ecstasies and thereby provides little consolation or hope to men. According to the Socratic formula, the lyrics—speech and, hence, reason—must determine the music—harmony and rhythm. Pure music can never endure this constraint. Students are not in a position to know the pleasures of reason; they can only see it as a disciplinary and repressive parent. But they do see, in the case of Plato, that that parent has figured out what they are up to. Plato teaches that, in order to take the spiritual temperature of an individual or a society, one must "mark the music." To Plato and Nietzsche, the history of music is a series of attempts to give form and beauty to the, dark, chaotic, premonitory forces in the soul—to make them serve a higher purpose, an ideal, to give man's duties a fullness. Bach's religious intentions and Beethoven's revolutionary and humane ones are clear enough examples. Such cultivation of the soul uses the passions and satisfies them while sublimating them and giving them an artistic unity. A man whose noblest activities are accompanied by a music that expresses them while providing a pleasure extending from the lowest bodily to the highest spiritual, is whole, and there is no tension in him between the pleasant and the good. By contrast a man whose business life is prosaic and unmusical and whose leisure is made up of coarse, intense entertainments, is divided, and each side of his existence is undermined by the other. 7

Hence, for those who are interested in psychological health, music is at the center of education, both for giving the passions their due and for preparing the soul for the unhampered use of reason. The centrality of such education was recognized by all the ancient educators. It is hardly noticed today that in Aristotle's *Politics* the most important passages about the best regime concern musical education, or that the *Poetics* is an appendix to the *Politics*. Classical philosophy did not censor the singers. It persuaded them. And it gave them a goal, one that was understood by them, until only yesterday. But those who do not notice the 8 role of music in Aristotle and despise it in Plato went to school with Hobbes, Locke, and Smith, where such considerations have become unnecessary. The triumphant Enlightenment rationalism thought that it had discovered other ways to deal with the irrational part of the soul, and that reason needed less support from it. Only in those great critics of Enlightenment and rationalism, Rousseau and Nietzsche, does music return, and they were the most musical of philosophers. Both thought that the passions—and along with them their ministerial arts—had become thin under the rule of reason and that, therefore, man *himself* and what he sees in the world have become correspondingly thin. They wanted to cultivate the enthusiastic states of the soul and to reexperience the Corybantic possession deemed a pathology by Plato. Nietzsche, particularly, sought to tap again the irrational sources of vitality, to replenish our dried-up stream from barbaric sources, and thus encouraged the Dionysian and the music derivative from it.

This is the significance of rock music. I do not suggest that it has   9
any high intellectual sources. But it has risen to its current heights in the education of the young on the ashes of classical music, and in an atmosphere in which there is no intellectual resistance to attempts to tap the rawest passions. Modern-day rationalists, such as economists, are indifferent to it and what it represents. The irrationalists are all for it. There is no need to fear that "the blond beasts" are going to come forth from the bland souls of our adolescents. But rock music has one appeal only, a barbaric appeal, to sexual desire—not love, not *eros*, but sexual desire undeveloped and untutored. It acknowledges the first emanations of children's emerging sensuality and addresses them seriously, eliciting them and legitimating them, not as little sprouts that must be carefully tended in order to grow into gorgeous flowers, but as the real thing. Rock gives children, on a silver platter, with all the public authority of the entertainment industry, everything their parents always used to tell them they had to wait for until they grew up and would understand later.

Young people know that rock has the beat of sexual intercourse.   10
That is why Ravel's *Bolero* is the one piece of classical music that is commonly known and liked by them. In alliance with some real art and a lot of pseudo-art, an enormous industry cultivates the taste for the orgiastic state of feeling connected with sex, providing a constant flood of fresh material for voracious appetites. Never was there an art form directed so exclusively to children.

Ministering to and according with the arousing and cathartic   11
music, the lyrics celebrate puppy love as well as polymorphous attractions, and fortify them against traditional ridicule and shame. The words implicitly and explicitly describe bodily acts that satisfy sexual desire and treat them as its only natural and routine culmination for

children who do not yet have the slightest imagination of love, marriage, or family. This has a much more powerful effect than does pornography on youngsters, who have no need to watch others do grossly what they can so easily do themselves. Voyeurism is for old perverts; active sexual relations are for the young. All they need is encouragement.

The inevitable corollary of such sexual interest is rebellion against   12
the parental authority that represses it. Selfishness thus becomes indignation and then transforms itself into morality. The sexual revolution must overthrow all the forces of domination, the enemies of nature and happiness. From love comes hate, masquerading as social reform. A worldview is balanced on the sexual fulcrum. What were once unconscious or half-conscious childish resentments become the new Scripture. And then comes the longing for the classless, prejudice-free, conflictless, universal society that necessarily results from liberated consciousness—"We Are the World," a pubescent version of *Alle Menschen werden Brüder*, the fulfillment of which has been inhibited by the political equivalents of Mom and Dad. These are the three great lyrical themes: sex, hate, and a smarmy, hypocritical version of brotherly love. Such polluted sources issue in a muddy stream where only monsters can swim. A glance at the videos that project images on the wall of Plato's cave since MTV took it over suffices to prove this. Hitler's image recurs frequently enough in exciting contexts to give one pause. Nothing noble, sublime, profound, delicate, tasteful, or even decent can find a place in such tableaux. There is room only for the intense, changing, crude, and immediate, which Tocqueville warned us would be the character of democratic art, combined with a pervasiveness, importance, and content beyond Tocqueville's wildest imagination.

Picture a thirteen-year-old boy sitting in the living room of his   13
family home doing his math assignment while wearing his Walkman headphones or watching MTV. He enjoys the liberties hard won over centuries by the alliance of philosophic genius and political heroism, consecrated by the blood of martyrs; he is provided with comfort and leisure by the most productive economy ever known to mankind; science has penetrated the secrets of nature in order to provide him with the marvelous, lifelike electronic sound and image reproduction he is enjoying. And in what does progress culminate? A pubescent child whose body throbs with orgasmic rhythms; whose feelings are made articulate in hymns to the joys of onanism or the killing of parents; whose ambition is to win fame and wealth in imitating the drag-queen who makes the music. In short, life is made into a nonstop, commercially prepackaged masturbational fantasy.

This description may seem exaggerated, but only because some   14
would prefer to regard it as such. The continuing exposure to rock music

is a reality, not one confined to a particular class or type of child. One need only ask first-year university students what music they listen to, how much of it, and what it means to them, in order to discover that the phenomenon is universal in America, that it begins in adolescence or a bit before and continues through the college years. It is *the* youth culture and, as I have so often insisted, there is now no other countervailing nourishment for the spirit. Some of this culture's power comes from the fact that it is so loud. It makes conversation impossible, so that much of friendship must be without the shared speech that Aristotle asserts is the essence of friendship and the only true common ground. With rock, illusions of shared feelings, bodily contact and grunted formulas, which are supposed to contain so much meaning beyond speech, are the basis of association. None of this contradicts going about the business of life, attending classes, and doing the assignments for them. But the meaningful inner life is with the music.

This phenomenon is both astounding and indigestible, and is   15
hardly noticed, routine and habitual. But it is of historic proportions that a society's best young and their best energies should be so occupied. People of future civilizations will wonder at this and find it as incomprehensible as we do the caste system, witch-burning, harems, cannibalism, and gladiatorial combats. It may well be that a society's greatest madness seems normal to itself. The child described has parents who have sacrificed to provide him with a good life and who have a great stake in his future happiness. They cannot believe that the musical vocation will contribute very much to that happiness. But there is nothing they can do about it. The family spiritual void has left the field open to rock music, and they cannot possibly forbid their children to listen to it. It is everywhere; all children listen to it; forbidding it would simply cause them to lose their children's affection and obedience. When they turn on the television, they will see President Reagan warmly grasping the daintily proffered gloved hand of Michael Jackson and praising him enthusiastically. Better to set the faculty of denial in motion—avoid noticing what the words say, assume the kid will get over it. If he has early sex, that won't get in the way of his having stable relationships later. His drug use will certainly stop at pot. School is providing real values. And popular historicism provides the final salvation; there are new lifestyles for new situations, and the older generation is there not to impose its values but to help the younger one to find its own. TV, which compared to music plays a comparatively small role in the formation of young people's character and taste, is a consensus monster—the Right monitors its content for sex, the Left for violence, and many other interested sects for many other things. But the music has hardly been touched, and what efforts have been made are both ineffectual and misguided about the nature and extent of the problem.

The result is nothing less than parents' loss of control over their   16
children's moral education at a time when no one else is seriously concerned with it. This has been achieved by an alliance between the
strange young males who have the gift of divining the mob's emergent
wishes—our versions of Thrasymachus, Socrates' rhetorical adver-
sary—and the record-company executives, the new robber barons, who
mine gold out of rock. They discovered a few years back that children
are one of the few groups in the country with considerable disposable
income, in the form of allowances. Their parents spend all they have
providing for the kids. Appealing to them over their parents' heads, creating a world of delight for them, constitutes one of the richest markets
in the postwar world. The rock business is perfect capitalism, supplying
to demand and helping to create it. It has all the moral dignity of drug
trafficking, but it was so totally new and unexpected that nobody
thought to control it, and now it is too late. Progress may be made
against cigarette smoking because our absence of standards or our rela-
tivism does not extend to matters of bodily health. In all other things the
market determines the value. (Yoko Ono is among America's small
group of billionaires, along with oil and computer magnates, her late
husband having produced and sold a commodity of worth comparable
to theirs.) Rock is a very big business, bigger than the movies, bigger
than professional sports, bigger than television, and this accounts for
much of the respectability of the music business. It is difficult to adjust
our vision to the changes in the economy and to see what is really important. McDonald's now has more employees than U.S. Steel, and likewise the purveyors of junk food for the soul have supplanted what still
seems to be more basic callings.

This change has been happening for some time. In the late fifties,   17
DeGaulle gave Brigitte Bardot one of France's highest honors. I could
not understand this, but it turned out that she, along with Peugeot,
was France's biggest export item. As Western nations became more
prosperous, leisure, which had been put off for several centuries in
favor of the pursuit of property, the means to leisure, finally began to
be of primary concern. But, in the meantime, any notion of the serious
life of leisure, as well as men's taste and capacity to live it, had disappeared. Leisure became entertainment. The end for which they had la-
bored for so long has turned out to be amusement, a justified
conclusion if the means justify the ends. The music business is peculiar
only in that it caters almost exclusively to children, treating legally and
naturally imperfect human beings as though they were ready to enjoy
the final or complete satisfaction. It perhaps thus reveals the nature of
all our entertainment and our loss of a clear view of what adulthood or
maturity is, and our incapacity to conceive ends. The emptiness of *values* results in the acceptance of the natural *facts* as the ends. In this case

infantile sexuality is the end, and I suspect that, in absence of other ends, many adults have to agree that it is.

It is interesting to note that the Left, which prides itself on its crit-   18
ical approach to "late capitalism" and is unrelenting and unsparing in its analysis of our other cultural phenomena, has in general given rock music a free ride. Abstracting from the capitalist element in which it flourishes, they regard it as a people's art, coming from beneath the bourgeoisie's layers of cultural repression. Its antinomianism and its longing for a world without constraint might seem to be the clarion of the proletarian revolution, and Marxists certainly do see that rock music dissolves the beliefs and morals necessary for liberal society and would approve of it for that alone. But the harmony between the young intellectual Left and rock is probably profounder than that. Herbert Marcuse appealed to university students in the sixties with a combination of Marx and Freud. In *Eros and Civilization* and *One Dimensional Man* he promised that the overcoming of capitalism and its false consciousness will result in a society where the greatest satisfactions are sexual, of a sort that the bourgeois moralist Freud called polymorphous and infantile. Rock music touches the same chord in the young. Free sexual expression, anarchism, mining of the irrational unconscious and giving it free rein are what they have in common. The high intellectual life...and the low rock world are partners in the same entertainment enterprise. They must both be interpreted as parts of the cultural fabric of late capitalism. Their success comes from the bourgeois's need to feel that he is not bourgeois, to have undangerous experiments with the unlimited. He is willing to pay dearly for them. The Left is better interpreted by Nietzsche than by Marx. The critical theory of late capitalism is at once late capitalism's subtlest and crudest expression. Antibourgeois ire is the opiate of the Last Man.

This strong stimulant, which Nietzsche called Nihiline, was for a   19
very long time, almost fifteen years, epitomized in a single figure, Mick Jagger. A shrewd, middle-class boy, he played the possessed lower-class demon and teen-aged satyr up until he was forty, with one eye on the mobs of children of both sexes whom he stimulated to a sensual frenzy and the other eye winking at the unerotic, commercially motivated adults who handled the money. In his act he was male and female, heterosexual and homosexual; unencumbered by modesty, he could enter everyone's dreams, promising to do everything with everyone; and, above all, he legitimated drugs, which were the real thrill that parents and policemen conspired to deny his youthful audience. He was beyond the law, moral and political, and thumbed his nose at it. Along with all this, there were nasty little appeals to the suppressed inclinations toward sexism, racism, and violence, indulgence in which is not now publicly respectable. Never-

theless, he managed not to appear to contradict the rock ideal of a universal classless society founded on love, with the distinction between brotherly and bodily blurred. He was the hero and the model for countless young persons in universities, as well as elsewhere. I discovered that students who boasted of having no heroes secretly had a passion to be like Mick Jagger, to live his life, have his fame. They were ashamed to admit this in a university, although I am not certain that the reason has anything to do with a higher standard of taste. It is probably that they are not supposed to have heroes. Rock music itself and talking about it with infinite seriousness are perfectly respectable. It has proved to be the ultimate leveler of intellectual snobbism. But it is not respectable to think of it as providing weak and ordinary persons with a fashionable behavior, the imitation of which will make others esteem them and boost their own self-esteem. Unaware and unwillingly, however, Mick Jagger played the role in their lives that Napoleon played in the lives of ordinary young Frenchmen throughout the nineteenth century. Everyone else was so boring and unable to charm youthful passions. Jagger caught on.

In the last couple of years, Jagger has begun to fade. Whether Michael Jackson, Prince, or Boy George can take his place is uncertain. They are even weirder than he is, and one wonders what new strata of taste they have discovered. Although each differs from the others, the essential character of musical entertainment is not changing. There is only a constant search for variations on the theme. And this gutter phenomenon is apparently the fulfillment of the promise made by so much psychology and literature that our weak and exhausted Western civilization would find refreshment in the true source, the unconscious, which appeared to the late romantic imagination to be identical to Africa, the dark and unexplored continent. Now all has been explored; light has been cast everywhere; the unconscious has been made conscious, the repressed expressed. And what have we found? Not creative devils, but show business glitz. Mick Jagger tarting it up on the stage is all we brought back from the voyage to the underworld. 20

My concern here is not with the moral effects of this music— whether it leads to sex, violence, or drugs. The issue here is its effect on education, and I believe it ruins the imagination of young people and makes it very difficult for them to have a passionate relationship to the art and thought that are the substance of liberal education. The first sensuous experiences are decisive in determining the taste for the whole of life, and they are the link between the animal and spiritual in us. The period of nascent sensuality has always been used for sublimation, in the sense of making sublime, for attaching youthful inclinations and longings to music, pictures, and stories that provide the transition to the fulfillment of the human duties and the enjoyment of the human pleasures. 21

Lessing, speaking of Greek sculpture, said "beautiful men made beautiful statues, and the city had beautiful statues in part to thank for beautiful citizens." This formula encapsulates the fundamental principle of the esthetic education of man. Young men and women were attracted by the beauty of heroes whose very bodies expressed their nobility. The deeper understanding of the meaning of nobility comes later, but is prepared for by the sensuous experience and is actually contained in it. What the senses long for as well as what reason later sees as good are thereby not at tension with one another. Education is not sermonizing to children against their instincts and pleasures, but providing a natural continuity between what they feel and what they can and should be. But this is a lost art. Now we have come to exactly the opposite point. Rock music encourages passions and provides models that have no relation to any life the young people who go to universities can possibly lead, or to the kinds of admiration encouraged by liberal studies. Without the cooperation of the sentiments, anything other than technical education is a dead letter.

Rock music provides premature ecstasy and, in this respect, is   22 like the drugs with which it is allied. It artificially induces the exaltation naturally attached to the completion of the greatest endeavors—victory in a just war, consummated love, artistic creation, religious devotion, and discovery of the truth. Without effort, without talent, without virtue, without exercise of the faculties, anyone and everyone is accorded the equal right to the enjoyment of their fruits. In my experience, students who have had a serious fling with drugs—and gotten over it—find it difficult to have enthusiasms or great expectations. It is as though the color has been drained out of their lives and they see everything in black and white. The pleasure they experienced in the beginning was so intense that they no longer look for it at the end, or as the end. They may function perfectly well, but dryly, routinely. Their energy has been sapped, and they do not expect their life's activity to produce anything but a living, whereas liberal education is supposed to encourage the belief that the good life is the pleasant life and that the best life is the most pleasant life. I suspect that the rock addiction, particularly in the absence of strong counterattractions, has an effect similar to that of drugs. The students will get over this music, or at least the exclusive passion for it. But they will do so in the same way Freud says that men accept the reality principle—as something harsh, grim, and essentially unattractive, a mere necessity. These students will assiduously study economics or the professions and the Michael Jackson costume will slip off to reveal a Brooks Brothers suit beneath. They will want to get ahead and live comfortably. But this life is as empty and false as the one they left behind. The choice is not between quick fixes and dull calculation. This is what liberal education is meant to show them. But as long as they have the Walkman on, they cannot hear what the great tradition has to say. And, after its prolonged use, when they take it off, they find they are deaf.

Examining the Text

1. Why did Bloom "instinctively" side with rock-listening students when he was young (paragraph 3)? What drew him to this group of listeners, or to the music itself? What would he say led him to change his opinion? Do you think anything else might have contributed to this change?

2. What does Bloom mean by the statement, "Indignation is the soul's defense against the wound of doubt about its own; it reorders the cosmos to support the justice of its cause" (4)? Does anything in Bloom's argument make you "indignant"? Why does Bloom want students to recognize such indignations "for what it is"?

3. Explain the statement "Antibourgeois ire is the opiate of the Last Man" (18), in light of Bloom's discussion of the relationship among capitalism, the Left, Marxism, and rock music. Do you agree that rock music today embodies this superficial antibourgeois ire?

For Group Discussion

What, according to Bloom, is the singular appeal of rock music to young people? As a group, use Jib Fowles' catalog (p. 63) of advertising's psychological appeals—sex, affiliation, nurturing, and so forth—to list and explore possible additional appeals that rock music may have to its listeners.

Writing Suggestion

Consider Bloom's assertion that when students are "in school and with their families, they are longing to plug themselves back into their music." In an essay, explain the broad social point Bloom is making about the role of popular music in young people's lives, and then go on to discuss the role of popular music in your own life, citing examples from your experience and that of your friends and peers.

Rock and Sexuality

Simon Frith

The expression of explicit sexuality has become increasingly prevalent in rock lyrics and musical performances, a phenomenon described by many critics as radical—even subversive. However, while many believe that rock

music and musicians are becoming more and more liberated, other critics
argue that contemporary popular music may in fact be expressing conserva-
tive ideologies in a new, different—and frequently disguised—form.

In the following historical analysis of the relationship between rock and
sexuality, Simon Frith carefully distinguishes between sexual practice and
sexual ideology as he argues that rock music often contributes to ordering
and normalizing certain codes of gender and sexual behavior. For example, he
argues that gender hierarchies and a "sexual double standard" are absolutely
bound up with the sexual ideology of rock 'n' roll in the 1950s and 1960s. It
wasn't until the advent of the punk and disco movements, Frith argues, that
women finally found an aesthetic and erotic niche of their own within the nar-
row sexual confines of rock music. An interesting sidebar to Frith's argument
is his discussion of the "gay aesthetic" of the disco movement: dedicated to
eroticism and intensity, disco dancing created a new arena for physical plea-
sure, even ecstasy.

A well-known rock journalist and university professor in England,
Frith has written for The Village Voice, Creem, *and* In These Times. *His*
books include Art into Pop, Music for Pleasure, Facing the Music, *and*
Sound Effects: Youth, Leisure, and the Politics of Rock 'n' Roll, *from*
which the following selection is taken. **As you read,** *notice that he incorpo-*
rates ideology, economics, and social behavior into the analysis. Look for ex-
amples of each means of study.

The girl culture…is teenage culture, essentially working-class,   1
but such leisure constraints also apply to student culture, even if the
sexual differentiation of economic opportunity is less blatant for
middle-class youth. Indeed it was on college campuses in the 1920s
that many of the conventions of postwar teenage sexual behavior were
first established: it was college girls who first decided which sex acts a
respectable girl could enjoy, which were illicit; it was college boys who
first organized sex as a collective male activity, turned seductions into
"scores"; it was at college that petting (an extraordinary American sexual institution) was first turned into a routine. College youth culture
was interpreted at the time as "liberating," particularly for the girls,
but they weren't liberated from the double standard.

If girls' leisure is limited by its use as the setting for courtship,   2
courtship itself has to be understood in the context of a particular sort
of ideology of marriage, an ideology that does give girls a freedom—
the freedom to choose partners. Historians have argued that boys had
a youth, a time of transition from childhood to adulthood as they
moved from home to work, long before girls. Adolescence as a social
status is predicated on a degree of independence, and as long as girls
were protected through puberty, confined to one household until they

were given away in marriage to another, they had no youth. Girls could only become teenagers when free marital choice became the norm, when marriage was expected to be preceded by love. Only then did a transitional period become necessary for women too, a period when they could play the marriage field for themselves. This ideology only began to be a general norm at the beginning of this century, as ragtime and the dance craze began. Rudi Blesh and Harriet Janis quote the *Sedalia Times* from 1900:

> When the girls walk out evenings with the sole purpose of picking up a young man and continuing the walk, it is time to have a curfew law that will include children over sixteen. The restlessness that comes upon girls upon summer evenings results in lasting trouble unless it is speedily controlled. The right kind of man does not look for a wife on the streets, and the right kind of girl waits till the man comes to her home for her.[1]

Lawrence Stone, in his history *The Family, Sex and Marriage in England*, argues that the ideology of sentimental love and "well-tried personal affection" as the basis of marriage spread from the aristocracy to the bourgeoisie in Europe in the latter part of the eighteenth century (the move was marked by the rise of the romantic novel) and moved gradually down the social scale during the nineteenth century. But this was neither a natural nor an uncomplicated change of ideas. Youthful courtship carried dangers—the threat of sexual disorder, a challenge to parental authority. 3

These dangers seemed to be multiplied by the emergence of working-class adolescents. From early in the nineteenth century, the feature of the industrial revolution that most concerned middle-class moralists was its apparent effect on the working-class family, as girls worked in the new factories alongside boys, achieving with them an "unnatural" independence from their parents. The bourgeoisie themselves were slowly adopting the ideology of romantic love as a way of regulating adolescent sexuality and guaranteeing their children's orderly transition to adult respectability. Romantic love was idealized in bourgeois fiction, in love songs, stories, and poetry, and routinized in the suburbs, in middle-class clubs and sports and dances where girls could meet boys who would be guaranteed to be suitable partners for love and marriage. Peer groups began to take over from parents as the arbiters of correct sexual behavior. 4

By the end of the nineteenth century middle-class reformers were beginning to apply the romantic approach to the problem of working-class adolescence too—in England and France, for example, 5

---

[1]Rudi Blesh and Harriet Janis, *They All Played Ragtime* (New York, 1950), p. 33.

romance was promoted as a replacement for community control of working-class sexuality, and young workers were encouraged to join their own "rational" peer-group leisure associations—youth clubs, cycle clubs, sports clubs, and so forth. In the USA the most important institution for the control of adolescent sexuality was, at least after 1918, the high school. Paula Fass suggests that the 1920s, in particular, were crucial for the development of American youth culture, because it was then that the ideology of sentimental love was fused with a new kind of advocacy of sexual pleasure. It was, in her words, the "dual process of the sexualization of love and the glorification of sex that helped to anchor the twentieth-century American marriage pattern, the horse-and-carriage ideal."

The "sexualization of love" was made possible by the spread of   6
relatively efficient contraception. Delayed small families encouraged compassionate marriages; sex itself, freed from conception, was reinterpreted as a form of emotional expression, a source of mutual pleasure—from the 1920s, middle-class marriage manuals recognized female sexuality. But the other side of this process was the domestication of sex. If sexual expression, for its own sake, became one of the pleasures and purposes of marriage, so marriage itself was defined as the necessary setting for the most pleasurable sex—necessary now not in terms of traditional morality but in terms of romance: love had become the reason for sex, and true love involved a commitment to marriage. First an engagement, later going steady, became the moment in youth culture when it was morally permissible to go all the way; and from the 1920s, middle-class girls, as prospective wives, could express their "sexual personalities" publicly, could use sexual devices, like makeup, that had previously been confined to prostitutes, to "loose women."

What made this ideology initially shocking was that it legiti-   7
mated youthful sexual activity as an aspect of efficient mate selection; parents lost control not only over their children's marriage choices but also over their sexual behavior. Their place was taken, once more, by peer groups, which elaborated new rules of sexuality according to which some premarital pleasure was permissible, for girls and boys alike, but not such pleasure as would disrupt the romantic transition to marriage. Paula Fass quotes a female student from Ohio State University writing in 1922 in defense of her physical enjoyment of "smoking, dancing like voodoo devotees, dressing décolleté, petting and drinking." Her point was that although

> our tastes may appear riotous and unrestrained, the aspect of the situation is not alarming. The college girl—particularly the girl in the coeducational institution—is a plucky, coolheaded individual who thinks naturally. She doesn't lose her head—she knows her game and can play

it dexterously. She is armed with sexual knowledge.... She is secure in the most critical situations—she knows the limits, and because of her safety in such knowledge she is able to run almost the complete gamut of experience.[2]

By the 1950s, knowledge of "the limits" was an aspect of teenage   8
culture generally, but if the task of teenage peer groups was to control teenage sexuality, the issue was, really, girls' sexual behavior. It was female morality that was defined as chastity, female "trouble" that meant pregnancy. Adults worried about boys in terms of violence, the threat to order; they only worried about girls in terms of sex, the threat to the family. And they worried about all girls in these terms, their fears weren't confined to "delinquents."

Nineteen-fifties rock 'n' roll is usually described as a particularly   9
sexual form of expression, a source of physical "liberation," but teenage culture was already sexualized by the time it appeared. The question we really have to examine concerns the use of music not in the general expression of sexuality but in its ordering. Sexuality is not a single phenomenon that is either expressed or repressed; the term refers, rather, to a range of pleasures and experiences, a range of ways in which people make sense of themselves as sexed subjects. Sexual discourses determine prohibitions as well as possibilities, what can't be expressed as well as what can. But the most important function of 1950s teenage culture wasn't to "repress" sexuality but to articulate it in a setting of love and marriage such that male and female sexuality were organized in quite different ways. And rock 'n' roll didn't change that sexual order. Elvis Presley's sexuality, for example, meant different things to his male and female fans. There was an obvious tension between his male appropriation as cock-rocker and his female appropriation as a teeny-bop idol. Rock 'n' roll was, say its historians significantly, "emasculated," but its "decline" (from crude, wild dance music to crafted romantic ballads and spruce idols) marked not a defused rebellion but a shift of sexual discourse as the music moved from the street to the bedroom. In neither place did it challenge the conventions of peer-group sex.

The youth culture that developed in the 1960s was, in sexual terms,   10
more rebellious: the family was part of the system under attack. Domestic ideology was subverted, sexuality separated from marriage, romantic love intercut with fleeting hedonism. In Tom Hayden's words, there was "a generation of young whites with a new, less repressed attitude toward sex and pleasure, and music has been the means of their liberation."

---

[2]Paula S. Fass, *The Damned and the Beautiful: American Youth in the 1920s* (New York: Oxford University Press, 1977), p. 307.

Rock was experienced as a new sort of sexual articulation by   11
women as well as men. The music was, in Sheila Rowbotham's words,
"like a great release after all those super-consolation ballads." Rock,
writes Karen Durbin, "provided me and a lot of women with a channel
for saying 'want,' and for asserting our sexuality without apologies and
without having to pretty up every passion with the traditionally 'feminine' desire for true love and marriage, and that was a useful step towards liberation." At a time when girls were still being encouraged from
all directions to interpret their sexuality in terms of romance, to give pri-
ority to notions of love and commitment, rock performers like the
Rolling Stones were exhilarating because of their antiromanticism, their
concern for "the dark side of passion," their interest in sex as power and
feeling. But the problem quickly became a different one: not whether
rock stars were sexist, but whether women could enter their discourse,
appropriate their music, without having to become "one of the boys."

ROCK AND SEXUAL LIBERATION

Male sexuality is no more "naturally" aggressive, assertive, and   12
urgent than female sexuality is "naturally" passive, meek, and sensitive.
But the issue is not the nature of sex and its representations, and they
work not by describing feelings, but by constructing them. The sexual
content of rock can't be read off its texts unambiguously—lyrics are the
sign of a voice, instrumental sounds don't have fixed connotations. The
sexuality of music is usually referred to in terms of its rhythm—it is
the beat that commands a directly physical response—but rock sexuality has other components too. The rock experience is a social experience,
involves relationships among the listeners, refers to people's appreciation of other genres, other sound associations; and in sexual terms our
musical response is, perhaps above all, to the grain of a voice, the
"touch" someone has on an instrument, the sense of personality at play.
The "pleasure of the text" is the pleasure of music production itself, and
one reason for the dissolution of rock's liberating promises to the male
routines of the 1970s was simply the inevitable translation of an open
text into a closed formula: cock-rock, by definition, rules out the possibilities of surprise and delight. But the question remains: Why this formula? Nineteen-sixties rock was expressly opposed to the love and
marriage ideology of traditional teenage culture; how then did it come
to articulate an even more rigid sexual double standard?

The concept of youth developed in the 1960s by rock (among   13
other media) involved the assumption that good sex meant spontaneity, free expression, an "honesty" that could only be judged in terms of
immediate feelings. Sex was thus best experienced *outside* the restrictive sphere of marriage, with its distracting deceits of love and long-

term commitment. This was, in principle, an ideology of sexual equality—men and women alike were entitled to set their own limits on their sexual experiences.

Such permissiveness reflected a number of shifts in the material   14
situation of middle-class youth: an increasing number of them were at college for an increasing length of time (by the end of the 1960s more than a quarter of *all* twenty-one to twenty-four-year-olds in the USA were in school), and they were enjoying new levels of affluence (a reflection of rising parental income), mobility, and independence. It was, therefore, increasingly possible to enjoy sex without any reference to marriage; and the pill, in particular, enabled women to manage their sex lives without reference to family, community, or peer group. Sex became just another form of leisure, and the ideology of leisure itself began to change. Free time was used increasingly impulsively, irrationally, unproductively, with reference to immediate gratification rather than to usefulness or respectability or sense of consequence. The expansion of sexual opportunity, in other words, occurred in the context of a new leisure stress on hedonism, and the result was that sex became an experience to be consumed, used up in the moment, like any other leisure good. Sex was now defined without reference to domestic ideology or romantic love, but it was still gender-bound: men were, by and large, the sexual consumers; women were, by and large, the sexual commodities, their charms laid out for customer approval in a never-ending supply of magazines and films and "spreads."

Rock sexuality developed in this permissive context, but defined   15
itself (initially, at least) against such "plastic" consumer sex. Rock sex was bohemian sex—earthy, real, "free." The woman's place, though, remained subordinate.

Bohemian freedom, particularly in its young rebel version, is de-   16
fined primarily against the family. It is from their families that the young must escape, it is through their family quarrels that they first recognize themselves as rebels, and it is their refusal to settle down to a respectable domestic life that makes their rebellion permanent. Youthful bohemia begins, then, as a revolt against women, who are identified with the home as mothers, sisters, potential domesticators. The young rebel has to be a loner, to move on, and female sexuality becomes, in itself, something repressive, confining, enveloping. In the Hollywood version of the young rebel's story (a story repeated in numerous films over the last thirty years, although James Dean remains the model for rock 'n' roll's rebellious style), the message is plain enough: the boy must get out, the girl tries to hold him back. The original middle-class youth rebels in America, the bohemians drawn to big-city life and leisure at the turn of the century, were fascinated precisely by those proletarian institutions—gambling, drinking, sports like pool—which were, in Ned Polsky's words, aspects of a "bachelor subculture": they were institutions

for men without women, and the only intimate relationships bohemians can have are with each other, as friends.

Even rebels need sexual and domestic female services, though (one 1960s result was the symbolic hippie woman, the fleet-footed earth mother), and, traditionally, the ideal bohemian woman is the "innocent" prostitute—antidomestic and a symbol of sex as transitory pleasure. The prostitute can be treated (as rock stars treat groupies) with a mixture of condescension and contempt, as someone without an autonomous sexuality. Sex as self-expression remains the prerogative of the man; the woman is the object of *his* needs and fantasies, admired, in a way, for her lack of romantic hypocrisy but despised for her anonymity.   17

Sexual relationships involve a number of necessary oppositions. These oppositions don't have to be divided between sexual partners, aren't gender defined, but mean constant negotiation, exploration, struggle, and experiment. These negotiations are the source of sexual pleasure as well as pain, and the issues at stake—independence/dependence, risk/security, activity/passivity, movement/stability, incident/routine, creation/consumption—inform the best rock music, which deals with the sexual *frisson* of relationships, the fact that all interesting affairs are alive. But, in general (and whatever the concerns of individual musicians like Neil Young or Van Morrison or Joni Mitchell), rock performers lay claim to sexual values—movement, independence, creativity, action, risk—in such a way that female sexuality is defined (just as in working-class street culture) by the opposite values—stability, dependence, inaction, security. Women are excluded from this "rebellion" by definition; rock's antidomestic ideology doesn't move women out of the home, but leaves them in it, as inadequates.   18

The issue here is sexual ideology, not sexual practice. The actual behavior of men and women is far more complicated than the ideology implies.... But there is one more practical point to be made. Nineteen-sixties youth culture opposed impulse to calculation, irrationality to rationality, the present to the future; but these values posed quite different problems for boys than for girls. Girls have to keep control. They can't get drunk or drugged with the same abandon as boys because to lose control is to face consequences—pregnancy most obviously ("I got drunk at a party..."), a bad reputation more generally ("She'll do *anything*..."). As long as female attraction is defined by the male gaze, girls are under constant pressure too to keep control of their appearance; they can't afford to let their performance go. A drunken, "raddled" woman remains a potent image of ugliness; a haggard Keith Richards retains a far more *glamorous* appeal than a haggard Janis Joplin or Grace Slick. The irrational elements of the counterculture—in other words, the sex and drugs and rock 'n 'roll—could not be appropriated by girls as they were by boys without affecting their self-definitions, their relationships, their lives.   19

By the 1970s women were giving their own answers to the coun-   20
tercultural questions about sex and domesticity and love—the terms of
male domination were challenged. One effect of the feminist rewriting
of the sexual rule book has been a male movement to more irrational
forms of sexual power—rape, violent fantasy, a neurotic inability to
sustain any sexual relationship. As one male property right (as husband) is denied, another (as purchaser) is asserted; sex, and therefore
women, have been commoditized. "I think," writes Lester Bangs about
Debbie Harry at the end of the decade, "that if most guys in America
could somehow get their fave-rave poster girl in bed and have total license to do whatever they wanted with this legendary body for one afternoon, at least 75 percent of the guys in the country would elect to
beat her up." It is in this context that we have to analyze the musical
forms of 1970s sexuality—punk and disco.

PUNK SEX AND DISCO PLEASURE

Punks rejected both romantic and permissive conventions, and   21
refused, in particular, to allow sexuality to be constructed as a commodity. They flaunted sex-shop goods in public, exposing the mass
production of porno fantasy, dissolving its dehumanizing effects
through shock—"Oh bondage! Up yours!" (not that this stopped the
media from running numerous pictures of "punkettes" in corsets and
fishnet tights). Punks denied that their sexuality had any significance
at all—"My love lies limp," boasted Mark Perry of Alternative TV;
"What is sex anyway?" asked Johnny Rotten. "Just thirty seconds of
squelching noises."

Punk was the first form of youth music not to rest on love songs   22
(romance remained the staple of rock lyrics throughout the countercultural 1960s), and one consequence of this was that new female
voices were heard on record, stage, and radio—shrill, assertive, im-
pure, individual voices, singer as subject not object. Punk's female musicians had a strident insistence that was far removed from the appeal
of most postwar glamour girls (the only sexual surprise of a self-
conscious siren like Debbie Harry, for example, was that she became a
teeny-bop idol for a generation of young girls).

Punk interrupted the long-standing rock equation of sex and   23
pleasure, though the implications of this interruption still remain un-
clear. British punk subculture itself hardly differed, in sexual terms,
from any other working-class street movement—the boys led, the girls
(fewer of them) hung on; and in the end it was probably punk's sexual
effect on performers rather than on audiences that mattered—women
were brought into a musical community from which they'd previously
been excluded, and they brought with them new questions about

sound and convention and image, about the sexuality of performance and the performance of sexuality. Whether these questions get answered we have yet to see, but at least punks opened the possibility that rock could be *against* sexism.

Disco, which between 1974 and 1978 became the dominant sound   24 of mass music across the world, had different origins and different effects. The success of *Saturday Night Fever* simply confirmed the resonance of a genre that was already an $8-billion-per-year industry in the USA, already accounted for half the albums and singles in *Billboard*'s hot hundreds. Disco had changed the sound of radio, the organization of record companies, the status of club deejays, the meaning of a good night out, and all this has to be understood in the context of the 1970s sexual mores. Disco was not a response (like punk) to rock itself, but challenged it indirectly, by the questions it asked about music and *dance*.

The dance floor is the most public setting for music as sexual ex-   25 pression and has been an important arena for youth culture since the dance crazes of the beginning of the century when Afro-American rhythms began to structure white middle-class leisure, to set new norms for physical display, contact, and movement. Dance has been, ever since, central to the meaning of popular music. Girls, in particular, have always flocked to dance halls, concerned not just about finding a husband, but also about pursuing their own pleasure. They may be attracting the lurking boys through their clothes, makeup, and appearance, but on the dance floor their energy and agility is their own affair. The most dedicated dancers in Britain, for example, the Northern soul fans, are completely self-absorbed, and even in *Saturday Night Fever* (in which dancing power was diluted by pop interests) John Travolta transcended Hollywood's clumsy choreography with the sheer quality of his commitment—from the opening shots of his strut through the streets, his gaze on himself never falters; the essence of dance floor sex is physical control, and, whatever happens, John Travolta is never going to let himself go.

Dancing as a way of life, an obsession, has a long American his-   26 tory. Shorty Snowden, the John Travolta of the Savoy Ballroom in the 1920s, suffered from "Sunday Night Fever": "We started getting ready for Sunday on Saturday. The ideal was to get our one sharp suit to the tailor to be pressed on Saturday afternoon. Then we'd meet at the poolroom and brag about what we were going to do on the dance floor the next night...."[3]

The 1920s dance cult spread quickly to "hep" white teenagers   27 who tried to dress, dance, move like these sharp black "dudes," and

---

[3]Marshall and Jean Stearns, p. 322

the Depression stimulated dancing among the nonhep too. Thousands of small, cheap bars with dance floors, used pianos, record players, radios, and jukeboxes to fill the weekends with noise. Such working-class dance halls were crucial to the culture of courtship, but dancing meant something else even more important: it was an escape, a suspension of real time, a way in which even the unemployed could enjoy their bodies, their physical skills, the sense of human power their lives otherwise denied. Such power does not need to be rooted in sexual competition (though it often enough is); parties, Friday and Saturday night bursts of physical pleasure, sex or no sex, have always been the most intense setting for working-class musics, from ragtime to punk.

A party matters most, of course, to those people who most need   28
to party, and, whatever else happened to mass music in the 1950s and 1960s, there were many people (black working-class Americans, British working-class teenagers, using much the same music) who never stopped dancing—1970s disco itself emerged musically from black clubs, depended commercially on its continuing white youth appeal. But, sexually, disco was most important as a gay aesthetic, and what was surprising, socially, was the appropriation of this aesthetic by the mass middle class.

Disco is dance music in the abstract, its content determined by its   29
form. Middle-class dance music in the past, even in the 1930s, was a form determined by its content—there were still influential dance hall instructors, sheet music salesmen, and band leaders who laid down rules of partnership, decorum, uplift, and grace. There are no such rules in disco, but, on the other hand, individual expression means nothing when there is nothing individual to express. Disco is not, despite its critics, anything like Muzak. Muzak's effect is subliminal; its purpose is to encourage its hearers to do anything but listen to it. Disco's effect is material; its purpose is to encourage its hearers to do nothing but listen to it.

What do they hear? An erotic appeal, most obviously—what   30
Richard Dyer calls "whole body eroticism." All dancing means a commitment to physical sensation, but disco expanded the possibilities of sensation. Disco pleasure is not closed off, bound by the song structures, musical beginnings and ends, but is expressed, rather, through an open-ended series of repetitions, a shifting *intensity* of involvement. And disco, as Dyer suggests, shares rock's rhythmic pulse, while avoiding rock's phallocentrism: disco is committed to the 4:4 beat in all its implications. Disco dancing is sinuous, it avoids the jerk and grind and thrust of rock; disco dancers hustle and slide, they use all their bodies' erotic possibilities.

Dancing has always been a physical pleasure sufficiently intense   31
to block out, for the moment, all other concerns, but disco pushed such enjoyment to new extremes: the disco experience is an overwhelming

experience of *now-ness*, an experience intensified still further by drugs like amyl nitrite, an experience in which the dancer is, simultaneously, completely self-centered and quite selfless, completely sexualized and, in gender terms, quite sexless. On the disco floor there is no overt competition for partners, no isolation; and disco (unlike bohemia) signifies nothing, makes no expressive claims—if bohemia suggests a different way of life, disco simply offers a different experience of it.

The disco version of eroticism and ecstasy is not, in itself, homo-   32
sexual, but the aesthetic uses of these experiences did reflect gay consciousness. They were imbued, for example, with gay romanticism: disco sensations were associated with the fleeting emotional contacts, the passing relationships of a culture in which everything in a love affair can happen in a night. Disco eroticism became, too, the sign of a sexuality that was always being constructed. It was the process of construction, the very artificiality of the disco experience, that made it erotic. Disco was a version of camp: the best disco records were those made with a sense of irony, an aggressive self-consciousness, a concern for appearances. There was an obvious link between the vocal styles of disco and 1930s torch songs: Billie Holiday and Donna Summer alike stylized feelings, distanced pain, opened up the texts of sexuality (and for this reason, disco, despised by punk-rockers on principle, had an immense appeal to the postpunk avant-garde).

Mainstream disco, the Saturday night fever of the teenage work-   33
ing class, continued to operate according to the traditional street party line; teenagers danced in different ways, to different sounds than gays. But it was the gay disco aesthetic that middle-class dancers began to appropriate from 1974 on. If 1960s "permissive" sexual ideology had reflected new leisure and sexual opportunities, then 1970s disco culture reflected their emotional consequences. Disco was music for singles bars, sexual mobility, heterosexual cruising, weekend flings, and transitory fantasies. Gay culture reflected, in its own way, the problems and possibilities of sex without domesticity, love without the conventional distinctions of male and female. These problems and possibilities had become important now for heterosexuals too.

Disco was about eroticism and ecstasy as material goods, pro-   34
duced not by spiritual or emotional work, God or love, but by technology, chemistry, wealth. The disco experience (the music and the mood, the poppers and the lights) revealed the artificiality and transience of sexual feelings—they were produced to be consumed; and disco pleasure, as it moved into the commercial mainstream, became the pleasure of consumption itself. This was obvious enough in the chic appeal of Studio 54, but was just as important for the strut of the factory girls, equally chic, up the steps of Tiffany's in provincial Britain. Disco made no claims to folk status; there was no creative disco community. The music was, rather, the new international symbol of American con-

sumer society. Chic discos sprang up around the world, each offering the secret of eternal American youth; the pleasures of consumption and the pleasures of sex became, in such settings, the same thing.

The problem with escapism is not the escape itself, but what's still there when it's over—the rain still falls when Monday morning dawns. Once something's been consumed it's gone; new goods are necessary, new experiences, new highs, new sex. As many observers commented, by the end of the 1970s disco had become a drug, but it was leisure itself that had a new desperation. In Andrew Holleran's disco novel, *Dancer from the Dance*, the most dedicated disco-goers are the most eager to escape:

35

> They seldom looked happy. They passed one another without a word in the elevator, like silent shades in hell, hell-bent on their next look from a handsome stranger. Their next rush from a popper. The next song that turned their bones to jelly and left them all on the dance floor with heads back, eyes nearly closed, in the ecstasy of saints receiving the stigmata. They pursued these things with such devotion that they acquired, after a few seasons, a haggard look, a look of deadly seriousness. Some wiped everything they could off their faces and reduced themselves to blanks. Yet even these, when you entered the hallway where they stood waiting to go in, would turn toward you all at once in that one unpremeditated moment (as when we see ourselves in a mirror we didn't know was there), the same look on their faces: Take me away from this.[4]

Examining the Text

1. In what ways, by Frith's account, did rock music in the 1960s provide women a "useful step toward liberation" (paragraph 11)? What problems grew out of this "useful step"? Do you agree with Frith that there is no "natural" male or female sexuality?

2. Frith says that "rock's antidomestic ideology doesn't move women out of the home, but leaves them in it, as inadequates" (18). How, according to Frith, does rock music exclude women from rebellion against such qualities as dependence and passivity? What are your responses to these observations?

3. How does disco music reflect gay consciousness, according to Frith (28–22)? What caused the "demise" of disco, at the end of the 1970s, and what do you think accounts for its fairly consistent rebursts of popularity in the years since?

---

[4]Andrew Holleran, *Dancer from the Dance* (New York: Morrow, 1978), pp. 38–39.

For Group Discussion

Frith states, "Nineteen-sixties rock was expressly opposed to the love and marriage ideology of traditional teenage culture" (12), but he also suggests that rock "articulated" a more rigid sexual double standard. In a group discussion, explain and comment on this apparent paradox, based upon Frith's discussion of the evolution of contemporary youth culture. List some specific ways in which rock and rap in the 1990s differ from (or are similar to) this earlier music in its messages about sexuality.

Writing Suggestion

Toward the end of this piece, Frith comments that, with punk rock, "women were brought into a musical community from which they'd previously been excluded, and they brought with them new questions about sound and convention and image, about the sexuality of performance and the performance of sexuality. Whether these questions get answered we have yet to see..." (23). In an essay explain and respond to this comment: how has popular music in recent years contributed to reducing or perpetuating sexism among young people? Use specific examples from rock and rap songs to substantiate your assertions.

The Rap on Rap

David Samuels

In 1989, with the success of Public Enemy's "Fight the Power," the birth of "Yo! MTV Raps," and the controversial first album of N.W.A., rap music began a meteoric rise to national attention. After computerized reporting of record sales went into effect in 1991, the widespread popularity of rap became even clearer; surprised industry observers discovered rap's largest audience to be white, suburban males.

In this article written for The New Republic, *a monthly magazine with a moderate to conservative editorial slant, David Samuels argues that these white consumers have come to largely dictate rap's form and content. Rap's appeal to white male teenagers, Samuels believes, lies in its representation of a "foreign, sexually charged, and criminal underworld. " Rap music offers middle-class white listeners their exotic "other" in a prepackaged, easily consumable form, providing the vicarious thrills of transgression (drugs, guns, and sex) without the risk. Moreover, Samuels maintains, in order to appeal to these white fans, rap musicians and producers have created an increasingly violent and antisocial image of black males, an image that has important—and in many ways negative—repercussions.*

As you read this selection, think about whether you agree with Samuels's basic premise that the images presented in much of rap music are dictated more by the demands of white consumers than by black culture. You might also be reflecting on whether it is possible for any musical form to achieve widespread popularity without falling under the influence of bourgeois white America.

This summer Soundscan, a computerized scanning system, changed *Billboard* magazine's method of counting record sales in the United States. Replacing a haphazard system that relied on big-city record stores, Soundscan measured the number of records sold nationally by scanning the bar codes at chain store cash registers. Within weeks the number of computed record sales leapt, as demographics shifted from minority-focused urban centers to white, suburban, middle-class malls. So it was that America awoke on June 22, 1991, to find that its favorite record was not *Out of Time*, by aging college-boy rockers R.E.M., but *Niggaz4life*, a musical celebration of gang rape and other violence by N.W.A., or Niggers With Attitude, a rap group from the Los Angeles ghetto of Compton whose records had never before risen above No. 27 on the *Billboard* charts.

From *Niggaz4life* to *Boyz N the Hood*, young black men committing acts of violence were available this summer in a wide variety of entertainment formats. Of these none is more popular than rap. And none has received quite the level of critical attention and concern. Writers on the left have long viewed rap as the heartbeat of urban America, its authors, in Arthur Kempton's words, "the pre-eminent young dramaturgists in the clamorous theater of the street." On the right, this assumption has been shared, but greeted with predictable disdain.

Neither side of the debate has been prepared, however, to confront what the entertainment industry's receipts from this summer prove beyond doubt: although rap is still proportionally more popular among blacks, its primary audience is white and lives in the suburbs. And the history of rap's degeneration from insurgent black street music to mainstream pop points to another dispiriting conclusion: the more rappers were packaged as violent black criminals, the bigger their white audiences became.

If the racial makeup of rap's audience has been largely misunderstood, so have the origins of its authors. Since the early 1980s a tightly knit group of mostly young, middle-class, black New Yorkers, in close concert with white record producers, executives, and publicists, has been making rap music for an audience that industry executives concede is primarily composed of white suburban males. Building upon a form pioneered by lower-class black artists in New York between 1975 and 1983, despite an effective boycott of the music by both black and white radio that continues to this day, they created the most influential pop music of the 1980s. Rap's appeal to whites rested in its invocation of an age-old image of blackness: a foreign, sexually charged, and criminal underworld against which the norms of white society are defined, and, by extension, through which they may be defied. It was the truth of this latter proposition that rap would test in its journey into the mainstream.

"Hip-hop," the music behind the lyrics, which are "rapped," is a   5
form of sonic bricolage with roots in "toasting," a style of making music by speaking over records. (For simplicity, I'll use the term "rap" interchangeably with "hip-hop" throughout this article.) Toasting first took hold in Jamaica in the mid-1960s, a response, legend has it, to the limited availability of expensive Western instruments and the concurrent proliferation of cheap R&B instrumental singles on Memphis-based labels such as Stax-Volt. Cool DJ Herc, a Jamaican who settled in the South Bronx, is widely credited with having brought toasting to New York City. Rap spread quickly through New York's poor black neighborhoods in the mid- and late 1970s. Jams were held in local playgrounds, parks, and community centers, in the South and North Bronx, Brooklyn, and Harlem.

Although much is made of rap as a kind of urban streetgeist, early   6
rap had a more basic function: dance music. Bill Stephney, considered by many to be the smartest man in the rap business, recalls the first time he heard hip-hop: "The point wasn't rapping, it was rhythm, DJs cutting records left and right, taking the big drum break from Led Zeppelin's 'When the Levee Breaks,' mixing it together with 'Ring My Bell,' then with a Bob James Mardi Gras jazz record and some James Brown. You'd have 2,000 kids in any community center in New York, moving back and forth, back and forth, like some kind of tribal war dance, you might say. It was the rapper's role to match this intensity rhythmically. No one knew what he was saying. He was just rocking the mike."

Rap quickly spread from New York to Philadelphia, Chicago,   7
Boston, and other cities with substantial black populations. Its popularity was sustained by the ease with which it could be made. The music on early rap records sounded like the black music of the day: funk or, more often, disco. Performers were unsophisticated about image and presentation, tending toward gold lamé jumpsuits and Jeri-curls, a second-rate appropriation of the stylings of funk musicians like George Clinton and Bootsy Collins.

The first rap record to make it big was "Rapper's Delight," re-   8
leased in 1979 by the Sugar Hill Gang, an ad hoc all-star team drawn

from three New York groups on Sylvia and Joey Robinson's Sugar Hill label. Thanks to Sylvia Robinson's soul music and background, the first thirty seconds of "Rapper's Delight" were indistinguishable from the disco records of the day: light guitars, high-hat drumming, and hand-claps over a deep funk bass line. What followed will be immediately familiar to anyone who was young in New York City that summer:

> I said, hip-hop, de-hibby, de-hibby-dibby,
> Hip-hip-hop you don't stop.
> Rock it out, Baby Bubba to the boogie de-bang-bang,
> Boogie to the boogie to be.
> Now what you hear is not a test,
> I'm rapping to the beat...
> I said, "By the way, baby, what's your name?"
> She said, "I go by the name Lois Lane
> And you can be my boyfriend, you surely can
> Just let me quit my boyfriend, he's called Superman."
> I said, "he's a fairy, I do suppose
> Flying through the air in pantyhose...
> You need a man who's got finesse
> And his whole name across his chest"...

Like disco music and jumpsuits, the social commentaries of early   9
rappers like Grandmaster Flash and Mellie Mel were for the most part transparent attempts to sell records to whites by any means necessary. Songs like "White Lines" (with its anti-drug theme) and "The Message" (about ghetto life) had the desired effect, drawing fulsome praise from white rock critics, raised on the protest ballads of Bob Dylan and Phil Ochs. The reaction on the street was somewhat less favorable. "The Message" is a case in point. "People hated that record," recalls Russell Simmons, president of Def Jam Records. "I remember the Junebug, a famous DJS of the time, was playing it up at the Fever, and Ronnie DJ put a pistol to his head and said, 'Take that record off and break it or I'll blow your fucking head off.' The whole club stopped until he broke that record and put it in the garbage."

It was not until 1984 that rap broke through to a mass white au-   10
dience. The first group to do so was Run-DMC, with the release of its debut album, *Run-DMC*, and with *King of Rock* one year later. These albums blazed the trail that rap would travel into the musical mainstream. Bill Adler, a former rock critic and rap's best-known publicist, explains: "They were the first group that came on stage as if they had just come off the street corner. But unlike the first generation of rappers, they were solidly middle class. Both of Run's parents were college-educated. DMC was a good Catholic schoolkid, a mama's boy. Neither of them was deprived and neither of them ever ran with a

gang, but on stage they became the biggest, baddest, streetest guys in the world." When Run-DMC covered the Aerosmith classic "Walk This Way," the resulting video made it onto MTV, and the record went gold.

Rap's new mass audience was in large part the brainchild of Rick   11
Rubin, a Jewish punk rocker from suburban Long Island who produced the music behind many of rap's biggest acts. Like many New Yorkers his age, Rick grew up listening to Mr. Magic's Rap Attack, a rap radio show on WHBI. In 1983, at the age of 19, Rubin founded Def Jam Records in his NYU dorm room. (Simmons bought part of Def Jam in 1984 and took full control of the company in 1989.) Rubin's next group, the Beastie Boys, was a white punk rock band whose transformation into a rap group pointed rap's way into the future. The Beasties' first album, *Licensed to Kill*, backed by airplay of its authentic frat-party single "You've Got to Fight for Your Right to Party," became the first rap record to sell a million copies.

The appearance of white groups in a black musical form has his-   12
torically prefigured the mainstreaming of the form, the growth of the white audience, and the resulting dominance of white performers. With rap, however, this process took an unexpected turn: white demand indeed began to determine the direction of the genre, but what it wanted was music more defiantly black. The result was Public Enemy, produced and marketed by Rubin, the next group significantly to broaden rap's appeal to young whites.

Public Enemy's now familiar mélange of polemic and dance   13
music was formed not on inner-city streets but in the suburban Long Island towns in which the group's members grew up. The children of successful black middle-class professionals, they gave voice to the feeling that, despite progress toward equality, blacks still did not quite belong in white America. They complained of unequal treatment by the police, of never quite overcoming the color of their skin: "We were suburban college kids doing what we were supposed to do, but we were always made to feel like something else," explains Stephney, the group's executive producer.

Public Enemy's abrasive and highly politicized style made it a   14
fast favorite of the white avant-garde, much like the English punk rock band The Clash ten years before. Public Enemy's music, produced by the Shocklee brothers Hank and Keith, was faster, harder, and more abrasive than the rap of the day, music that moved behind the vocals like a full-scale band. But the root of Public Enemy's success was a highly charged theater of race in which white listeners became guilty eavesdroppers on the putative private conversation of the inner city. Chuck D denounced his enemies (the media, some radio stations), proclaimed himself "Public Enemy #1," and praised Louis Farrakhan in stentorian tones, flanked onstage by black-clad security guards from

the Nation of Islam, the SIWS, led by Chuck's political mentor, Professor Griff. Flavor Flav, Chuck's homeboy sidekick, parodied street style: oversize sunglasses, baseball cap cocked to one side, a clock the size of a silver plate draped around his neck, going off on wild verbal riffs that often meant nothing at all.

The closer rap moved to the white mainstream, the more it became like rock 'n' roll, a celebration of posturing over rhythm. The back catalogs of artists like James Brown and George Clinton were relentlessly plundered for catchy hooks, then overlaid with dance beats and social commentary. Public Enemy's single "Fight the Power" was the biggest college hit of 1989:   15

> Elvis was a hero to most
> But he never meant shit to me, you see
> Straight-up racist that sucker was simple and plain
> Motherfuck him and John Wayne
> 'Cause I'm black and I'm proud
> I'm ready and hyped, plus I'm amped
> Most of my heroes don't appear on no stamps
> Sample a look back, you look and find
> Nothing but rednecks for 400 years if you check.

After the release of "Fight the Power," Professor Griff made a series of anti-Semitic remarks in an interview with *The Washington Times*. Griff was subsequently asked to leave the group, for what Chuck D termed errors in judgment. Although these errors were lambasted in editorials across the country, they do not seem to have affected Public Enemy's credibility with its young white fans.

Public Enemy's theatrical black nationalism and sophisticated noise ushered in what is fast coming to be seen as rap's golden age, a heady mix of art, music, and politics. Between 1988 and 1989 a host of innovative acts broke into the mainstream. KRS-One, now a regular on the Ivy League lecture circuit, grew up poor, living on the streets of the South Bronx until he met a New York City social worker, Scott La Rock, later murdered in a drive-by shooting. Together they formed BDP, Boogie Down Productions, recording for the jive label on RCA. Although songs like "My Philosophy" and "Love's Gonna Get 'Cha (Material Love)" were clever and self-critical, BDP's roots remained firmly planted in the guns-and-posturing of the mainstream rap ghetto.   16

The ease with which rap can create such aural cartoons, says Hank Shocklee, lies at the very heart of its appeal as entertainment: "Whites have always liked black music," he explains. "That part is hardly new. The difference with rap was that the imagery of black artists, for the first time, reached the level of black music. The sheer   17

number of words in a rap song allows for the creation of full characters impossible in R&B. Rappers become like superheroes. Captain
America or the Fantastic Four."

By 1988 the conscious manipulation of racial stereotypes had be-   18
come rap's leading edge, a trend best exemplified by the rise to stardom
of Schoolly D, a Philadelphia rapper on the Jive label who sold more
than half a million records with little mainstream notice. It was not that
the media had never heard of Schoolly D: white critics and fans, for the
first time, were simply at a loss for words. His voice, fierce and deeply
textured, could alone frighten listeners. He used it as a rhythmic device
that made no concessions to pop-song form, talking evenly about smoking crack and using women for sex, proclaiming his blackness, accusing
other rappers of not being black enough. What Schoolly D meant by
blackness was abundantly clear. Schoolly D was a misogynist and a
thug. If listening to Public Enemy was like eavesdropping on a conversation, Schoolly D was like getting mugged. This, aficionados agreed,
was what they had been waiting for: a rapper from whom you would
flee in abject terror if you saw him walking toward you late at night.

It remained for N.W.A., a more conventional group of rappers   19
from Los Angeles, to adapt Schoolly D's stylistic advance for the mass
white market with its first album-length release, *Straight Out of Compton*, in 1989. The much-quoted rap from that album, "Fuck the Police,"
was the target of an FBI warning to police departments across the country, and a constant presence at certain college parties, white and black:

> "Fuck the Police" coming straight out the underground
> A young nigger got it bad 'cause I'm brown
> And not the other color. Some police think
> They have the authority to kill the minority...
> A young nigger on the warpath
> And when I'm finished, it's gonna be a bloodbath
> Of cops, dying in L.A.
> Yo, Dre I've got something to say: Fuck the Police.

Other songs spoke of trading oral sex for crack and shooting   20
strangers for fun. After the release of *Straight Out of Compton*, N.W.A.'s
lead rapper and chief lyricist, Ice Cube, left the group. Billing himself
as "the nigger you love to hate," Ice Cube released a solo album,
Amerikkka's Most Wanted, which gleefully pushed the limits of rap's
ability to give offense. One verse ran:

> I'm thinking to myself, "why did I bang her?"
> Now I'm in the closet, looking for the hanger.

But what made *Amerikkka's Most Wanted* so shocking to so many   21
record buyers was the title track's violation of rap's most iron-clad
taboo—black on white violence:

> Word, yo, but who the fuck is heard:
> It's time you take a trip to the suburbs.
> Let 'em see a nigger invasion
> Point blank, on a Caucasian.
> Cock the hammer and crack a smile:
> "Take me to your house, pal..."

Ice Cube took his act to the big screen this summer in *Boyz N the*   22
Hood, drawing rave reviews for his portrayal of a young black drug
dealer whose life of crime leads him to an untimely end. The crime-
doesn't-pay message, an inheritance from the grade-B gangster film is
the stock-in-trade of another L.A. rapper-turned-actor. Ice-T of *New Jack*
City fame, a favorite of socially conscious rock critics. Taking unhappy
endings onto glorifications of drug dealing and gang warfare, Ice-T offers all the thrills of the form while alleviating any guilt listeners may
have felt about consuming drive-by shootings along with their popcorn.

It was in this spirit that "Yo! MTV Raps" debuted in 1989 as the first   23
national broadcast forum for rap music. The videos were often poorly
produced, but the music and visual presence of stars like KRS-One, LL
Cool J, and Chuck D proved enormously compelling, rocketing "Yo!" to
the top of the MTV ratings. On weekends bands were interviewed and
videos introduced by Fab Five Freddie; hip young white professionals
watched his shows to keep up with urban black slang and fashion.
Younger viewers rushed home from school on weekdays to catch ex-
Beastie Boys DJ Dr. Dre, a sweatsuit-clad mountain of a man, well over
300 pounds, and Ed Lover, who evolved a unique brand of homeboy
Laurel and Hardy mixed with occasional social comment.

With "Yo! MTV Raps," rap became for the first time the music of   24
choice in the white suburbs of middle America. From the beginning,
says Doug Herzog, MTV's vice president for programming, the show's
audience was primarily white, male, suburban, and between the ages
of 16 and 24, a demographic profile that "Yo!"'s success helped set in
stone. For its daytime audience, MTV spawned an ethnic rainbow of
well-scrubbed pop rappers from MC Hammer to Vanilla Ice to Ger-
ardo, a Hispanic actor turned rap star. For "Yo" itself, rap became
more overtly politicized as it expanded its audience. Sound bites from
the speeches of Malcolm X and Martin Luther King became de rigueur
introductions to formulaic assaults on white America mixed with
hymns to gang violence and crude sexual caricature.

Holding such polyglot records together is what *Village Voice* critic   25
Nelson George has labeled "ghettocentrism," a style-driven cult of

blackness defined by crude stereotypes. P.R. releases, like a recent one for Los Angeles rapper DJ Quik, take special care to mention artists' police records, often enhanced to provide extra street credibility. When Def Jam star Slick Rick was arrested for attempted homicide, Def Jam incorporated the arrest into its publicity campaign for Rick's new album, bartering exclusive rights to the story to *Vanity Fair* in exchange for the promise of a lengthy profile. Muslim groups such as Brand Nubian proclaim their hatred for white devils, especially those who plot to poison black babies. That Brand Nubian believes the things said on its records is unlikely: the group seems to get along quite well with its white Jewish publicist, Beth Jacobson of Electra Records. Anti-white, and, in this case, anti-Semitic, rhymes are a shorthand way of defining one's opposition to the mainstream. Racism is reduced to fashion, by the rappers who use it and by the white audiences to whom such images appeal. What's significant here are not so much the intentions of artist and audience as a dynamic in which anti-Semitic slurs and black criminality correspond to "authenticity," and "authenticity" sells records.

The selling of this kind of authenticity to a young white audience   26
is the stock-in-trade of *The Source*, a full-color monthly magazine devoted exclusively to rap music, founded by Jon Shecter while still an undergraduate at Harvard. Shecter is what is known in the rap business as a Young Black Teenager. He wears a Brooklyn Dodgers baseball cap, like Spike Lee, and a Source T-shirt. As editor of *The Source*, Shecter has become a necessary quote for stories about rap in *Time* and other national magazines.

An upper-middle-class white, Shecter has come in for his share   27
of criticism, the most recent of which appeared as a diatribe by the sometime critic and tinpot racist Harry Allen in a black community newspaper, *The City Sun*, which pointed out that Shecter is Jewish. "There's no place for me to say anything," Shecter responds. "Given what I'm doing, my viewpoint has to be that whatever comes of the black community, the hip-hop community which is the black community, is the right thing. I know my place. The only way in which criticism can be raised is on a personal level, because the way that things are set up, with the white-controlled media, prevents sincere back-and-forth discussion from taking place." The latest venture in hip-hop marketing, a magazine planned by Time Warner, will also be edited by a young white, Jonathan van Meter, a former Condé Nast editor.

In part because of young whites like Shecter and van Meter, rap's   28
influence on the street continues to decline. "You put out a record by Big Daddy Kane," Rubin says, "and then put out the same record by a pop performer like Janet Jackson. Not only will the Janet Jackson record sell ten times more copies, it will also be the cool record to play

in clubs." Stephney agrees: "Kids in my neighborhood pump dance hall reggae on their systems all night long, because that's where the rhythm is....People complain about how white kids stole black culture. The truth of the matter is that no one can steal a culture." Whatever its continuing significance in the realm of racial politics, rap's hour as innovative popular music has come and gone. Rap forfeited whatever claim it may have had to particularity by acquiring a mainstream white audience whose tastes increasingly determined the nature of the form. What whites wanted was not music, but black music, which as a result stopped really being either.

White fascination with rap sprang from a particular kind of cultural tourism pioneered by the Jazz Age novelist Carl Van Vechten. Van Vechten's 1926 best seller *Nigger Heaven* imagined a masculine, criminal, yet friendly black ghetto world that functioned, for Van Vechten and for his readers, as a refuge from white middle-class boredom. In *Really the Blues*, the white jazzman Mezz Mezzrow went one step further, claiming that his own life among black people in Harlem had physically transformed him into a member of the Negro race, whose unique sensibility he had now come to share. By inverting the moral values attached to contemporary racial stereotypes, Van Vechten and Mezzrow at once appealed to and sought to undermine the prevailing racial order. Both men, it should be stressed, conducted their tours in person.

The moral inversion of racist stereotypes as entertainment has lost whatever transformative power it may arguably have had fifty years ago. MC Serch of 3rd Bass, a white rap traditionalist, with short-cropped hair and thick-rimmed Buddy Holly glasses, formed his style in the uptown hip-hop clubs like the L.Q. in the early 1980s. "Ten or eleven years ago," he remarks, "when I was wearing my permanent-press Lee's with a beige campus shirt and matching Adidas sneakers, kids I went to school with were calling me a 'wigger,' 'black wanna-be,' all kinds of racist names. Now those same kids are driving Jeeps with MCM leather interiors and pumping Public Enemy."

The ways in which rap has been consumed and popularized speak not of cross-cultural understanding, musical or otherwise, but of a voyeurism and tolerance of racism in which black and white are both complicit. "Both the rappers and their white fans affect and commodify their own visions of street culture," argues Henry Louis Gates, Jr., of Harvard University, "like buying Navajo blankets at a reservation roadstop. A lot of what you see in rap is the guilt of the black middle class about its economic success, its inability to put forth a culture of its own. Instead they do the worst possible thing, falling back on fantasies of street life. In turn, white college students with impeccable gender credentials buy nasty sex lyrics under the cover of getting at some kind of authentic black experience."

Gates goes on to make the more worrying point: "What is poten-   32
tially very dangerous about this is the feeling that by buying records they have made some kind of valid social commitment." Where the assimilation of black street culture by whites once required a degree of human contact between the races, the street is now available at the flick of a cable channel—to black and white middle class alike. "People want to consume and they want to consume easy," Hank Shocklee says. "If you're a suburban white kid and you want to find out what life is like for a black city teenager, you buy a record by N.W.A. It's like going to an amusement park and getting on a roller coaster ride— records are safe, they're controlled fear, and you always have the choice of turning it off. That's why nobody ever takes a train up to 125th Street and gets out and starts walking around. Because then you're not in control anymore: it's a whole other ball game." This kind of consumption—of racist stereotypes, of brutality toward women, or even of uplifting tributes to Dr. Martin Luther King—is of a particularly corrupting kind. The values it instills find their ultimate expression in the ease with which we watch young black men killing each other: in movies, on records, and on the streets of cities and towns across the country.

Examining the Text

1. According to Samuels, why did "white suburban males" begin listening to rap in such large numbers during the 1980s? What black stereotypes does rap perpetuate? Does Samuels's causal analysis correspond to your experience?

2. How, by Samuels's account, did Run-DMC contribute to moving rap into the "musical mainstream" of young American society? How persuasive do you find Samuels's reasoning here?

3. What does *Village Voice* critic Nelson George mean by his term "ghettocentrism" (paragraph 25)? How might this phenomenon encourage the tolerance of racism, as Samuels suggests it does? What forces in our culture do you see as bearing the greatest responsibility for the "crude stereotype" promulgated in much rap music?

For Group Discussion

In this selection, Samuels describes a historical phenomenon: "The appearance of white groups in a black musical form has historically prefigured the mainstreaming of the form, the growth of the white audience, and the resulting dominance of white performers" (12). As a group activity, paraphrase this statement to derive its central meaning, and then discuss the validity of Samuels's views on "mainstreaming," listing several examples that prove or disprove his central point.

Writing Suggestion

Samuels sees rap as a musical form on the decline: "Whatever its continuing significance in the realm of racial politics, rap's hour as innovative popular music has come and gone" (28). In an essay, explain what Samuels means by this statement, state whether or not you agree with him, and cite examples of rap music that either support or disprove his claim.

Hip-Hop Nation: There's More To Rap Than Just Rhythms and Rhymes

Melissa August, Leslie Everton Brice, Laird Harrison, Todd Murphy, and David E. Thigpen

In this article, co-written by a group of young experts in rap and hip-hop music, the authors argue that rap has become a predominant force in the United States popular culture and has found its way into a wide variety of other artistic forms, such as literature and film. According to this article, 81 million rap CDs were sold last year, outpacing every other musical category, popular or otherwise; furthermore, in that same period, sales of rap and hip-hop recordings jumped over 31 percent.

The authors provide an encapsulated view of hip-hop's social and historical roots, noting that this pop-music force derived originally from the Bronx, New York, with inspiration from some reggae-related musical activities in Kingston, Jamaica. They supplement that historical overview with a timeline at the end of the article, chronicling notable points in rap's development. Finally, the authors explore the popularity of this musical form with white audiences and discuss the responses of the African-American community to this mainstream "appropriation" of an originally black art form.

As you read *this article, note the ways in which this writing differs from the kinds of linear, logically sequenced prose you are accustomed to reading in academic essays and textbooks. For example, pay attention to the way that the authors attempt to suggest some of hip-hop's flavor, by interspersing* *"sampled" rap-related excerpts and discussions throughout, and by including a collage of quotations to conclude this piece.*

———————

Music mixes with memory. As we think back over the 20th cen-   1
tury, every decade has a melody, a rhythm, a sound track. The years and
the sounds bleed together as we scan through them in our recollections,
a car radio searching for a clear station. The century starts off blue:
Robert Johnson selling his soul to the devil at the crossroads. Then the
jazz age: Louis Armstrong, Duke Ellington and, later on, Benny Goodman and "Strange fruit hanging from the poplar trees." Midcentury,
things start to rock with Chuck Berry, "Wop-bop-a-loo-bop a-lop bam
boom!" the Beatles, Aretha Franklin, "a hard rain's a-going to fall," Bob
Marley, Stevie Wonder. It might be better to forget the '80s—the posturing heavy-metal bands, Debbie Gibson, "Let's get physical—physical,"
the guy with the haircut in Flock of Seagulls. Perhaps the remembered
sounds of R.E.M., U2 and Prince can drown them all out.

And how will we remember the last days of the '90s? Most likely,   2
to the rough-hewn beat of rap. Just as F. Scott Fitzgerald lived in the
jazz age, just as Dylan and Jimi Hendrix were among the rulers of the
age of rock, it could be argued that we are living in the age of hip-hop.
"Rock is old," says Russell Simmons, head of the hip-hop label Def
Jam, which took in nearly $200 million in 1998. "It's old people's shit.
The creative people who are great, who are talking about youth culture in a way that makes sense, happen to be rappers."

Consider the numbers. In 1998, for the first time ever, rap outsold   3
what previously had been America's top-selling format, country
music. Rap sold more than 81 million CDs, tapes and albums last year,
compared with 72 million for country. Rap sales increased a stunning
31% from 1997 to 1998, in contrast to 2% gains for country, 6% for rock
and 9% for the music industry overall. Boasts rapper Jay-Z, whose current album, *Vol. 2 . . . Hard Knock Life* (Def Jam), has sold more than 3
million copies: "Hip-hop is the rebellious voice of the youth. It's what
people want to hear."

Even if you're not into rap, hip-hop is all around you. It pulses   4
from the films you watch (Seen a Will Smith movie lately?), the books
you read (even Tom Wolfe peels off a few raps in his best-selling new
novel), the fashion you wear (Tommy Hilfiger, FUBU). Some definitions
are in order: rap is a form of rhythmic speaking in rhyme; hip-hop refers
to the backing music for rap, which is often composed of a collage of excerpts, or "samples," from other songs; hip-hop also refers to the culture
of rap. The two terms are nearly, but not completely, interchangeable.

Rap music was once called a fad, but it's now celebrating a 20th   5
anniversary of sorts. The first hip-hop hit, "Rapper's Delight" by the

Sugar Hill Gang, came out in 1979. Hip-hop got its start in black America, but now more than 70% of hip-hop albums are purchased by whites. In fact, a whole generation of kids—black, white, Latino, Asian—has grown up immersed in hip-hop. "I'm hip-hop every day," declares 28-year old Marlon Irving, a black record-store employee in Portland, Ore. "I don't put on my hip-hop." Says Sean Fleming, a white 15-year-old from Canton, Ga.: "It's a totally different perspective, and I like that about it." Adds Katie Szopa, 22, a white page at NBC in New York City: "You do develop a sense of self through it. You listen and you say, 'Yeah, that's right.'"

Hip-hop represents a realignment of America's cultural aesthet-   6
ics. Rap songs deliver the message, again and again, to keep it real. The poet Rainer Maria Rilke wrote that "a work of art is good if it has sprung from necessity." Rap is the music of necessity, of finding poetry in the colloquial, beauty in anger, and lyricism even in violence. Hip-hop, much as the blues and jazz did in past eras, has compelled young people of all races to search for excitement, artistic fulfillment and even a sense of identity by exploring the black underclass. "And I know because of [rapper] KRS-1," the white ska-rap singer Bradley Nowell of Sublime once sang in tribute to rap. Hip-hop has forced advertisers, filmmakers and writers to adopt "street" signifiers like cornrows and terms like player hater. Invisibility has been a long-standing metaphor for the status of blacks in America. "Don't see us / but we see you," hip-hop band the Roots raps on a new song. Hip-hop has given invisibility a voice.

But what does that voice have to say?   7

Now tell me your philosophy / On exactly what an artist should be.
                                          —Lauryn Hill, Superstar

It's a Friday night, early December 1998, and you're backstage at   8
Saturday Night Live. You're hanging out in the dressing room with Lauryn Hill, who is sitting on the couch, flipping through a script. The 23-year-old rapper-singer-actress is the musical guest on this week's show. It's her coming-out party, the first live TV performance she's done since releasing her critically acclaimed and best-selling album *The Miseducation of Lauryn Hill*. She might also do a little acting on the show—*SNL* staff members have asked her to appear in a skit. But as Hill reads, her small rose-blossom lips wilt into a frown. She hands you the script. It's titled Pimp Chat—it's a sketch about a street hustler with a talk show. Hill's role: a 'ho. Or, if she's uncomfortable with that, she can play a female pimp. Hmmm. Now, being in an *SNL* sketch is a big opportunity—but this one might chip away at her image as a socially conscious artist. What's it going to be?

It's all about the Benjamins, baby.
            —Sean ("Puffy") Combs, It's All About the Benjamins

You are in a recording studio in midtown Manhattan, hanging   9
out with hip-hop superproducer Sean ("Puffy") Combs. It's 1997, and
Puffy is keeping a low profile, working on his new album, his first as a
solo performer. This album will be his coming-out party. He's eager to
play a few tracks for you. People have him all wrong, he says. He majored in business management at Howard. He's not just about gangsta
rap. Sounds from his new album fill the room. One song is based on a
bit from the score to *Rocky*. Another, a sweeping, elegiac number, uses
a portion of "Do You Know Where You're Going To?" That's what he's
about, Combs says. Classic pop. "I'm living my life right," he says. "So
when it comes time for me to be judged, I can be judged by God."

You're mad because my style you're admiring / Don't be mad—UPS is
hiring.
            —The Notorious B.I.G., Flava in Your Ear (Remix)

Hip-hop is perhaps the only art form that celebrates capitalism   10
openly. To be sure, filmmakers pore over weekend grosses, but it
would be surprising for a character in a Spielberg film to suddenly
turn toward the camera and shout, "This picture's grossed $100 mil-
lion, y'all! Shout out to DreamWorks!" Raps' unabashed materialism
distinguishes it sharply from some of the dominant musical genres of
the past century. For example, nobody expects bluesmen to be money-
makers—that's why they're singing the blues. It's not called the
greens, after all. As for alternative rockers, they have the same relationship toward success that one imagines Ally McBeal has toward
food: even a small slice of pie leaves waves of guilt. Rappers make
money without remorse. "These guys are so real, they brag about
money," says Def Jam's Simmons. "They don't regret getting a Coca-
Cola deal. They brag about a Coca-Cola deal."

Major labels, a bit confused by the rhythms of the time, have re-   11
lied on smaller, closer-to-the-street labels to help them find fresh rap
talent. Lauryn Hill is signed to Ruffhouse, which has a distribution
deal with the larger Columbia. Similar arrangements have made tens
of millions of dollars for the heads of these smaller labels, such as
Combs (Bad Boy), Master P (No Limit), Jermaine Dupri (So So Def),
and Ronald and Bryan Williams (co-CEOs of Cash Money, home to
rising rapper Juvenile).

"I'm not a role model," rapper-mogul-aspiring-NBA-player Mas-   12
ter P says. "But I see myself as a resource for kids. They can say, 'Master
P has been through a lot, but he changed his life, and look at him. I can
do the same thing.' I think anyone who's a success is an inspiration."

Master P introduced something new to contemporary pop: shame-   13
less, relentless and canny cross-promotion. Each of the releases on his
New Orleans-based No Limit label contains promotional materials for
his other releases. His established artists (like Snoop Dogg) make guest
appearances on CDs released by his newer acts, helping to launch their
debuts. And his performers are given to shouting out catchphrases like
"No Limit soldiers!" in the middle of their songs—good advertising for
the label when the song is being played on the radio.

Madison Avenue has taken notice of rap's entrepreneurial spirit.   14
Tommy Hilfiger has positioned his apparel company as the clothier of
the hip-hop set, and he now does a billion dollars a year in oversize
shirts, loose jeans and so on. "There are no boundaries," says Hilfiger.
"Hip-hop has created a style that is embraced by an array of people
from all backgrounds and races." However, fans are wary of profiteers
looking to sell them back their own culture. Says Michael Sewell, 23, a
white congressional staff member and rap fan: "I've heard rap used in
advertising, and I think it's kind of hokey—kind of a goofy version of
the way old white men perceive rap."

But the ads are becoming stealthier and streetier. Five years ago,   15
Sprite recast its ads to rely heavily on hip-hop themes. Its newest series
features several up-and-coming rap stars (Common, Fat Joe, Goodie
Mob) in fast-moving animated clips that are intelligible only to viewers
raised on Bone-Thugs-N-Harmony and Playstation. According to Sprite
brand manager Pina Sciarra, the rap campaign has quadrupled the
number of people who say that Sprite is their favorite soda.

Hollywood too is feeling the rap beat. After Lauryn Hill passed   16
on a role in *The Cider-House Rules* (an adaptation of the John Irving
book), filmmakers cast hip-hop soul singer Erykah Badu. Ice Cube,
who has appeared in such movies as *Boyz N the Hood* and *Fridays*, will
soon star with George Clooney in the Gulf War thriller *Three Kings.*
Queen Latifah, featured in the recent film *Living Out Loud,* is now set
to be the host of a TV talk show. And the former Fresh Prince, Will
Smith, has become one of the most in-demand actors around. Ice
Cube—who performed a song with Public Enemy titled "Burn Hollywood Burn" in 1990—says Tinseltown wants rapper actors because
"we add a sense of realism where sometimes a trained actor can't deliver that reality the way it needs to be done."

Warren Beatty, who directed and starred in *Bulworth,* a comedy   17
about a Senator who becomes possessed by the spirit of hip-hop, became interested in the subject because "it seemed to have a similar
protest energy to the Russian poets of the 1960s. The Russian poets
reigned in Moscow almost like rock itself reigned in the U.S. Ultimately it seemed to me that hip-hop is where the voice of protest is
going in the inner city and possibly far beyond because the culture has
become so dominated by entertainment."

Even Tom Wolfe, who documented the counterculture in the '60s   18
and greed in the '80s, found himself buying a stack of hip-hop records
in order to understand Atlanta in the '90s for his best-selling book *A
Man in Full*. In several sections of his novel, Wolfe offers his own sly
parodies of today's rap styles: "How'm I spose a love her / Catch her
mackin' with the brothers," Wolfe writes in a passage. "Ram yo'
booty! Ram yo' booty!" Most of the characters in *A Man in Full* are a bit
frightened by rap's passion. It's Wolfe's view that "hip-hop music
quite intentionally excludes people who are not in that world." That
world, however, is growing.

> *Poetic language emerges out of the ruins of prose.*
> —Jean-Paul Sartre, *Art and Action*

The hip-hop world began in the Bronx in 1971. Cindy Campbell   19
needed a little back-to-school money, so she asked her brother Clive to
throw a party. Back in Kingston, Jamaica, his hometown, Clive used to
watch dancehall revelers. He loved reggae, Bob Marley and Don
Drummond and the Skatalites. He loved the big sound systems the
deejays had, the way they'd "toast" in a singsong voice before each
song. When he moved to the U.S. at age 13, he used to tear the speakers out of abandoned cars and hook them onto a stereo in his room.

The after-school party, held in a rec room of a Bronx high-rise,   20
was a success: Clive and Cindy charged 25 [cents] for girls and
50 [cents] for boys, and it went till 4 A.M. Pretty soon Clive was getting
requests to do more parties, and in 1973 he gave his first block party.
He was Kool Herc now—that was the graffito tag he used to write on
subway cars—and he got respect. At 18 he was the first break-beat
deejay, reciting rhymes over the "break," or instrumental, part of the
records he was spinning. He had two turntables going and two copies
of each record, so he could play the break over and over, on one
turntable and then the next. Americans didn't get reggae, he thought,
so he tried to capture that feel with U.S. funk songs—James Brown
and Mandrill. He had dancers who did their thing in the break—break
dancers, or, as he called them, b-boys. As they danced, Herc rapped,
"Rocking and jamming / That's all we play / When push comes to
shove / The Herculoids won't budge / So rock on, my brother..."

Joseph Saddler loved music too. He thought Kool Herc was a   21
god—but he thought he could do better. Saddler figured most songs
had only about 10 seconds that were good, that really got the party
going, so he wanted to stretch those 10 seconds out, create long nights
of mixing and dancing. Holed up in his Bronx bedroom, he figured out
a way to listen to one turntable on headphones while the other
turntable was revving up the crowd. That way a deejay could keep

two records spinning seamlessly, over and over again. Herc was doing it by feel. Saddler wanted the show to be perfect.

So he became Grandmaster Flash. He played his turntables as if he 22 were Jimi Hendrix, cuing records with his elbow, his feet, behind his back. He invented "scratching"—spinning a record back and forth to create a scratchy sound. He tried rapping, but he couldn't do it, so he gathered a crew around him—the Furious Five, rap's first supergroup.

Things happened fast. This is the remix. There were start-up la- 23 bels like Sugar Hill and Tommy Boy. Then in 1979 came Rapper's Delight—the first rap song most people remember. Grandmaster Flash warned, "Don't touch me 'cause I'm close to the edge." Then there was Run-D.M.C. rocking the house, and the Beastie Boys hollering, "You gotta fight for your right—to party!" and Public Enemy saying, "Don't believe the hype," and Hammer's harem-style balloon pants. Then gangsta rap: N.W.A. rapping "Fuck tha police"; Snoop drawling "187 on an undercover cop"; and Tupac crying, "Even as a crack fiend, mama / You always was a black queen, mama." Then Mary J. Blige singing hip-hop soul; Guru and Digable Planets mixing rap with bebop; the Fugees "Killing me softly with his song"; Puffy mourning Biggie on CD and MTV.

We in the '90s And finally it's looking good / Hip-hop took it to billions I knew we would.
                                                              —Nas, We Will Survive

All major modern musical forms with roots in the black commu- 24 nity—jazz, rock, even gospel—faced criticism early on. Langston Hughes, in 1926, defended the blues and jazz from cultural critics. Hardcore rap has triumphed commercially, in part, because rap's aesthetic of sampling connects it closely to what is musically palatable. Some of the songs hard-core rappers sample are surprisingly mainstream. DMX raps about such subjects as having sex with bloody corpses. But one of his songs, "I Can Feel It," is based on Phil Collins' easy-listening staple "In the Air Tonight." Jay-Z's hit song "Hard-Knock Life" draws from the musical *Annie*. Tupac's "Changes" uses Bruce Hornsby. Silkk the Shocker samples the not-so-shocking Lionel Richie.

The underlying message is this: the violence and misogyny and 25 lustful materialism that characterizes some rap songs are as deeply American as the hokey music that rappers appropriate. The fact is, this country was in love with outlaws and crime and violence long before hip-hop—think of Jesse James, and Bonnie and Clyde—and then think of the movie *Bonnie and Clyde*, as well as *Scarface* and the *Godfather* saga. In the movie *You've Got Mail*, Tom Hanks even refers to the *Godfather* triology as the perfect guide to life, the I-Ching for guys.

Rappers seem to agree. Snoop Dogg's sophomore album was titled *The Doggfather*. Silkk the Shocker's new album is called *Made Man*. On his song "Boomerang," Big Pun echoes James Cagney in *White Heat*, yelling, "Top of the world, Ma! Top of the world!"

Corporate America's infatuation with rap has increased as the 26 genre's political content has withered. Ice Cube's early songs attacked white racism; Ice-T sang about a Cop Killer; Public Enemy challenged listeners to "fight the power." But many newer acts such as DMX and Master P are focused almost entirely on pathologies within the black community. They rap about shooting other blacks but almost never about challenging governmental authority or encouraging social activism. "The stuff today is not revolutionary," says Bob Law, vice president of programming at WWRL, a black talk-radio station in New York City. "It's just, 'Give me a piece of the action.'"

Hip-hop is getting a new push toward activism from an unlikely 27 source—the Beastie Boys. The white rap trio began as a Dionysian semiparody of hip-hop, rapping about parties, girls and beer. Today they are the founders and headliners of the Tibetan Freedom Concert, an annual concert that raises money for and awareness about human-rights issues in Tibet. Last week Beastie Boys, along with the hip-hop-charged hard-rock band Rage Against the Machine and the progressive rap duo Black Star, staged a controversial concert in New Jersey to raise money for the legal fees of Mumia Abu-Jamal, a black inmate on death row for killing a police officer. Says Beastie Boy Adam Yauch: "There's a tremendous amount of evidence that he didn't do it and he was a scapegoat."

Yauch says rap's verbal texture makes it an ideal vessel to commu- 28 nicate ideas, whether satirical, personal or political. That isn't always a good thing. "We've put out songs with lyrics in them that we thought people would think were funny, but they ended up having a lot of really negative effects on people. [Performers] need to be aware that when you're creating music it has a tremendous influence on society."

Sitting in the conference room on the 24th floor of the Time & 29 Life Building, Kool Herc thinks back to the start of rap with a mixture of fondness and sadness. He'd like to see rappers "recognize their power, in terms of politics and economics." Hip-hop has not made him powerful or rich. "I never looked at it like that," he says. "I was just having fun. It was like a hobby to me." But he would appreciate more recognition. When he calls local radio stations, looking for an extra ticket or two for a hip-hop show, he's often told there are none available—even for the father of the form. Still, he's planning a comeback. He's holding a talent contest later this year, and also hopes to record his first full album. Says Herc: "Respect is due."

Friday night at Life, a dance club in lower Manhattan. Grand- 30 master Flash pulls the 11 P.M. to 2 A.M. shift, and he's doing his thing.

The Furious Five have long since broken up. Flash had drug problems, money problems and a court battle with his old record company, Sugar Hill, but he says today he has no ill will. He's the musical director on HBO's popular *Chris Rock Show*. And he's helping to develop a movie script about his life. "I was bitter a while back because I got into this for the love," says Flash. "I gave these people the biggest rap group of all time. But as long as there's a God, as long as I'm physically able to do what I do—what I did—I can do it again."

The dance floor is getting crowded. Flash puts on a record. Does   31
a little scratching. He plays the instrumental intro again and again and then lets it play through. "Ain't no stopping us now ..."

At first I did not know what I wanted. But in the end I understood the language. I understood it, I understood it, I understood it all wrong perhaps. That is not what matters ... Does this mean that I am freer than I was?
—Samuel Beckett, *Malloy*

In Mill Valley, Calif., in a one-bedroom apartment above a coin-   32
operated laundry, Andre Mehr, a white 17-year-old with a crew cut, and Emiliano Obiedo, a ponytailed 16-year-old who is half white and half Hispanic, are huddled over a PC. A beat spirals up. Obiedo offers some advice, and Mehr clatters away at the keyboard. They are making music. Once they settle on a beat, Obiedo will take a diskette bearing a rhythm track home and lay down some rhymes. Soon they hope to have enough for a CD. Boasts Obiedo: "I'm going to change rap."

Across the country, similar scenes are playing out as kids outside   33
the black community make their own hip-hop or just listen in. Some say they don't pay much attention to the lyrics, they just like the beat. "I can't relate to the guns and killings," says Mehr. Others are touched more deeply. Says 15-year-old Sean Fleming: "I can relate more and get a better understanding of what urban blacks have to go through."

Todd Boyd, a professor of critical studies at the University of   34
Southern California, says rap can bring races together: "It's a little more difficult to go out and talk about hate when your music collection is full of black artists. That is not to say that buying an OutKast record is the same as dealing with real people, but it is reason to hope." Ice Cube is a bit more cynical: "It's kinda like being at the zoo. You can look into that world, but you don't have to touch it. It's safe."

Nonblack performers are increasingly drawing from rap. Beck   35
expertly combined folk and hip-hop. Hanson's hit "MMMBop" included deejay scratching. Portishead refashioned hip-hop into ethereal trip-hop. Singer Beth Orton, whose enchantingly moody album *Central Reservation* is due out in March, blends folksy guitars with samples and beats. Doug Century, author of *Street Kingdom: Five Years Inside the Franklin Avenue Posse,* studied hip-hop culture as he documented the

lives of gang members; he predicts white acts will eventually domi-
nate rap, just as white rockers pushed out rock's black forerunners.
"It's possible that in 15 years all hip-hop will be white," Century says.
"[Then] black youth culture will transform itself again."

Already the white b-boy has become an iconic figure—ridiculed   36
in movies like *Can't Hardly Wait* and the forthcoming *Go*, and in songs
like Offspring's "Pretty Fly (for a White Guy)." In "Pretty Fly" the
punk band Offspring mocks whites who adopt hip-hop styles, singing,
"He may not have a clue / And he may not have style / But everything he lacks / Well he makes up in denial." Irish-American rap-
rocker Everlast, whose new CD, *Whitey Ford Sings the Blues,* has
proved to be a commercial hit, says the song makes him laugh: "They
ain't talking about me, 'cause I'll beat the s____ out of every one of
those guys." In fact, Everlast feels confident enough about his standing in the rap world to take a verbal swipe at Puffy Combs: "I don't
think Puffy really cares about what he's doing. He's a brilliant businessman, but he's no different from the Backstreet Boys or the Spice
Girls because he's just creating a product."

Wu-Tang Clan producer-rapper RZA is also concerned about   37
maintaining standards. He believes many performers are embracing
the genre's style—rapping—but missing its essence, the culture of hip-
hop. "I don't think the creativity has been big. I think the sales have
been big, and the exposure has been big," says RZA. "Will Smith is
rap. That's not hip-hop. It's been a big year for rap. It's been a poor
year for hip-hop."

Underground rap is available for those industrious enough to seek   38
it out. At New York City's Fat Beats record store, you can pick up vinyl
editions of independently released songs by such promising new acts as
the Philadelphia-based Maylay Sparks (call 215-492-4257 for more
information) and the all-female antimisogyny hip-hop collective
Anomolies (917-876-0726). Maylay Sparks' spirited "I Mani" and the New
York City-based Anomolies' raucous tune "Black-listed" (a collaboration
with the group Arsonists) are two of the best songs to come out this year.

Other groups, signed to major labels, are trying to perpetuate   39
rap's original spirit of creativity. The rapper Nas' forthcoming album *I
Am...the Autobiography* promises to be tough, smart and personal.
And the Atlanta-based duo OutKast's current album, *Aquemini,*
weaves chants, neo-soul and hip-hop into an enthralling mix. Says
OutKast's Big Boi: "We're not scared to experiment."

One of the most ambitious new CDs is the Roots' *Things Fall Apart*   40
(named after the book by the Nigerian Nobel laureate Chinua Achebe).
The CD features live instrumentation, lyrics suitable for a poetry slam
and a cameo from Erykah Badu. Roots drummer Ahmir hopes, in the future, the more creative wing of performers in hip-hop will form a sup-

port network. "There are some people in hip-hop that care about leaving a mark," he says. "There are some of us that look at *Innervisions* as a benchmark, or *Blood on the Tracks* or *Blue* or *Purple Rain*. Leaving a mark is more important than getting a dollar. I think Lauryn's album is one of the first gunshots of hip-hop art the world is going to get."

> *You could get the money / You could get the power But keep your eyes on the final hour.*
> —Lauryn Hill, Final Hour

It's Puffy's 29th birthday party, and the celebration is being held on Wall Street. Inside the party, women in thongs dance in glass cages. Above the door a huge purple spotlight projects some of Puffy's corporate logos: Bad Boy (his record company) and Sean John (his new clothing label). But where's Puffy?   41

The music stops. The crowd parts. Muhammad Ali arrives. He's only the appetizer. The score to Rocky booms over the speakers. Only then does Puffy enter, in a light-colored three-piece suit. Forget being street. He's Wall Street, he's Madison Avenue, he's le Champs Elysees. Donald Trump is at his side. It's Puffy's moment. His album *No Way Out* played on some familiar gangsta themes, but it's a smash hit. Puffy is a household name, a brand name. In fact his name comes up again and again, in gossip columns and other people's rap songs. He has transformed himself into a human sample. He is swallowed by the crowd.   42

You are at the Emporio Armani store on Fifth Avenue in downtown Manhattan. There's a benefit here tonight for the Refugee Project, a nonprofit organization Lauryn Hill founded to encourage social activism among urban youth. Hill is here, and the cameras are flashing. Her musical performance on *Saturday Night Live* has boosted her album back to the upper reaches of the charts. In a few days she will receive 10 Grammy nominations, the most ever by a female artist.   43

She never did do that *SNL* skit about the hooker. She says she feels too connected to hip-hop to do a movie or TV role that might compromise the message in her music. She addresses the crowd. "I'm just a vehicle through which this thing moves," she says. "It's not about me at all." You think back to some of the rappers you've talked to—Jay-Z, Nas, the Roots, Grandmaster Flash. A record cues up in your mind: "Ain't no stopping us now..."   44

20 YEARS OF HIP-HOP

1979 THE SUGAR HILL GANG. Six years after Kool Herc introduced rap to partyers in the Bronx, the Sugar Hill Gang serves it up to a national audience in the form of the classic catchy song Rapper's Delight.

1984 RUSSELL SIMMONS. He co-founds Def Jam Recordings and goes on to become one of the richest, most influential forces in pop music.

1984 RUN-D.M.C. Hailing from Hollis, Queens, the supergroup rocks the house and introduces some rap signifiers—gold chains and untied sneakers.

1986 BEASTIE BOYS. The white rap trio's mix of hard rock and hip-hop make License to Ill a favorite at frat parties everywhere and the first rap album to hit the top of the charts.

1988 THE SOURCE. Harvard undergrads Jon Shecter and David Mays publish the first issue of their hip-hop mag out of their dorm room. Although it no longer has the field to itself and isn't even the largest publication covering the rap scene today, the Source remains a widely read source on hip-hop.

1989 N.W.A. The California act's Straight Outta Compton sparks gangsta rap and foreshadows the Los Angeles uprising of '92.

1989 2 LIVE CREW. (Remember "Me so horny?") This proudly foulmouthed group is pushed into the national spotlight in a Florida battle over freedom of speech.

1990 VANILLA ICE. Admit it. You like Ice, Ice Baby. And so do the 7 million others who buy this one-hit wonder's To the Extreme.

1990 WILL SMITH. The sitcom The Fresh Prince of Bel-Air debuts on NBC, bringing suburban-flavored rap to the small screen. A new acting star is born.

1991 NEW JACK CITY. The crime thriller co-starring Ice-T is a surprise box-office hit and helps usher in a new genre of urban films, such as Boyz N the Hood and Menace II Society.

1992 SISTER SOULJAH. Her music and its message become a campaign issue when presidential candidate Bill Clinton attacks her militant views on race.

1993 SNOOP DOGGY DOGG. The pop-gangsta rapper releases Doggystyle, and it immediately rockets to the No. 1 spot on the charts.

1996 THE FUGEES. The trio's album The Score features head-bobbing beats, reggae and smart lyrics. It becomes a worldwide smash.

1996 TUPAC SHAKUR. The year after he releases his best album, Me Against the World, the rapper dies in a drive-by killing.

1997 BIGGIE SMALLS. The Notorious B.I.G. is shot. His album Life After Death is a hit.

1997 PUFF DADDY. His galvanizing rendition of I'll Be Missing You at the MTV Music Awards awakens millions of pop fans and ushers in a new era of positivism in hip-hop.

1998 BULWORTH. Warren Beatty's comedy uses the language of rap to critique politics.

1999 LAURYN HILL. She grabs 10 Grammy nods, begins first solo tour and eyes a film career.

QUOTES

Ya rock and ya don't stop and this is the sounds of DJ Kool Herc and the Sound System.   —DJ Kool Herc

So don't push me 'cause I'm close to the edge. I'm tryin' not to lose my head.   —Grandmaster Flash

You gotta fight for your right to party.   —Beastie Boys

Who you callin' a Bitch?   —Queen Latifah

Ain't nothin' but a G thang, baaaaabay!   —Dr. Dre

You might win some but you just lost one.   —Lauryn Hill

Let's talk about sex, baby. Let's talk about you and me.   —Salt-N-Pepa

Fuck tha police. Comin' straight from the underground.   —N.W.A.

Been spending most our lives, living in a gangsta's paradise.   —Coolio

Me against the world. It's just me against the world.   —Tupac Shakur

U can't touch this.   —Hammer

I made the change from a common thief, to up close and personal with Robin Leach.   —Notorious B.I.G.

Gettin' jiggy wit it.   —Will Smith

I got the hook up, holla if you hear me.   —Master P

Examining the Text

1. What concrete examples do the authors of this article cite to support their article's thesis: that hip-hop is today's pervasive pop-music form? Based on your own experience, what additional examples can you cite? Are there any other pop-music forms that have similar influence, in your experience?

2. In what ways, according to this article, has hip-hop music and culture infiltrated and dramatically changed institutions of the American financial mainstream, such as advertising, fashion, literary publishing, and the Hollywood film industry?

3. Outline the historical roots of hip-hop, as laid out in this article. What social and/or personal concerns does this music reflect? What, according to this article, is the thematic function of "the violence and misogyny and lustful materialism that characterize some rap songs"?

4. What is the function of the quoted passages throughout this article? What key points do they help deliver? How does this article's inclusion of quoted passages resemble certain features of hip-hop music?

5. What is the influence of hip-hop on the "nonblack" American youth culture, according to this article? How do some African-American critics feel about hip-hop's move into the white mainstream?

For Group Discussion

Discuss the viewpoint expressed by the authors that "Hip-hop is perhaps the only art form that celebrates capitalism openly." From your own experience, cite musical examples that support this assertion, and/or examples that disprove it. If you find examples of non-commercial, or anticommercial hip-hop, what does this say about hip-hop as a genre? Is there one hip-hop music, or a number of sub-genres of this art form, each with its own style and point of view?

Writing Suggestion

In an essay, consider honestly the notion expressed by Russell Simmons, head of the hip-hop label Def Jam, that rock & roll is old people's music. In particular, discuss the two premises inherent in this assertion: (1) that rock is a dead or dying art form, in which young people (such as yourself) have little interest; and (2) that "old people's music"—for example, jazz, blues, rock, and even classical music—are not "what people want to hear," as Simmons suggests.

All the Rage

Michael Crowley

Picture a large arena packed with several thousand chain-smoking, tattooed, body-pierced twenty-somethings, all slamming their bodies into each other in a music-driven frenzy. These are the persons to whom members of the pop/politico/hip-hop band Rage Against the Machine are singing...but their message is not getting through, according to Michael Crowley in this article. Crowley commends the band's members for writing lyrics that encourage listeners to become involved in the sociopolitical issues of today. However, although the band's messages consciously encourage teens and twenty-something Americans to become more politically aware and active, Crowley believes the band's songs receive a typical pop-musical media play that strips the music of much of its social relevance.

As you read, *think about the information-giving potential that a channel such as* MTV *has, compared with that of a television news channel. Although you probably watch* MTV *for entertainment, does it also impart information—political, social, or otherwise? If so, what are some of the messages it delivers? Also consider the motivating effect of song lyrics: are you moved to political action (or any other kind of action) by certain lyrics, while you listen to a compact disc, watch a video...or mosh at a concert? Finally, think about how your younger or older siblings, mom or dad, would react to the messages being portrayed in the music you enjoy. How is each person likely to be affected by the lyrics, tone, and style of the songs?*

Nothing planted the concept of Generation X so firmly in the   1
zeitgeist as the explosion of grunge music in the early 1990s. Like the youth culture it supposedly represented, the music of bands like Nirvana was an apolitical melange of glum alienation and apathetic cynicism. Since then grunge has been backlashed to death, and young Seattle—Michael Kinsley or no—is becoming better known for heroin than trendsetting. But this election year a new attention to youth politics as panache has burbled into the marketing of both performers and media outlets, and it is frequently both calculated and facile.

A prime example is Rage Against the Machine, a leftist foursome   2
who belt out a whipcrack fusion of punk and rap. What makes them notable is that, in the era of MTV hegemony, no band so doggedly political has hit the mainstream jackpot as this self-styled revolutionary cadre has: Rage's second album, *Evil Empire,* entered the Billboard charts last month at number one, filling a slot routinely held by vacuous Nirvana xeroxes and Snoop Doggy Dogg-ites.

Rage cribs conspicuously from a parade of leftists, socialists and   3
rebels and shouts down enemies from nafta to the IMF to the ivory tower: "The present curriculums/ I put my fist in 'em/ Eurocentric every last one of 'em," yelps dreadlocked lead singer Zack De La Rocha. Rage even got kicked off "Saturday Night Live" for planning a denunciation of guest-host Steve Forbes.

This fever-pitched crusading has caught on. MTV News cheered   4
the band's "intense political sensibility which extends way beyond issue-oriented lyrics" to pamphleting at concerts and flogging books by lefty thinkers from Chomsky to Marx. A typical "Rage page" on the Web exhorts: "wake up people!!! do something, even if it sucks, register to vote by clicking here."

As always with the marketing of rebellion, there are some unfor-   5
tunate contradictions. "GE is gonna flex and try and annex the truth,"
De La Rocha sings. "NBC is gonna flex and cast their image in you/
Disney bought the fantasies and piles of eyes/ And ABC's new thrill
rides of trials and lies." Rage's revolution, however, is brought to us
by Sony and televised ad nauseam by MTV. Guitarist Tom Morello did
not emerge from the misty hills of Nicaragua but from Harvard University and, later, the office of Senator Alan Cranston, where he
worked as a scheduler.

But at least Rage's screeds, while coopted by the band's sup-   6
posed enemies, have a bottom-up credibility. More and more, the politics of rebellion comes top down, through youth-targeted advertising.
Channel One, the commercial news network for schoolkids, has
launched a bafflingly vacant ad campaign that purports to display
"the impact" the network has on "the way teenagers view their
world." The full-page ads show the floating heads of teenagers deep in
thought, as nuggets of breathtakingly shallow political pith hover
above them. "I'd like to vote for Clinton," muses dark-eyed An-
toneilia, 17, "but as far as I can tell he hasn't really done anything. I
guess that leaves Dole."

Ramon, also 17, wears thinker's glasses, as well as an earring,   7
goatee and braids. What's Channel One got him thinking about?
"Dole? You can't vote for Dole. The guy's totally stale." In another ad,
one teen simply ponders the word "Recognize." The campaign plays
up the look of political engagement with nary a nod to its substance.
This isn't politics, it's posing.

Examining the Text

1. Crowley refers to "the concept of Generation X" in his first paragraph. To what specific social group is he referring with the term Generation X? Where and when did this term first come into popular
awareness? What are the stereotypes usually associated with this term?
How do you and your friends fit or contradict these stereotypes?

2. Early in the article, Crowley seems to be objectively reporting information about youth politics as embodied in Rage Against the Machine's lyrics, rather than taking a personal stance on the issue. At
what point in the article does his opinion filter in? What is his opinion
about the Rage Against the Machine phenomenon, and why does
Crowley choose to let his own biases come in when he does?

3. How does the author of this article characterize the political awareness of young Americans? What does he mean by the statement, "This

isn't politics, it's posing" (paragraph 7)? How does this statement relate specifically to his discussion of Rage Against the Machine's music and social stance?

For Group Discussion

Discuss Crowley's assessment of 1990s music—and, by extension, youth culture in general—as an "apolitical melange of glum alienation and apathetic criticism" (1). What does he mean by "glum alienation?" Are you and your generation more guilty of this characteristic than previous generations? If so, what specific factors might account for the apathy and alienation of Generation X? If you don't believe your generation is as apolitical and glum as some social critics say it is, how did your generation get its undeserved bad reputation? Cite specific examples that dispute the negative stereotype of contemporary youth culture.

Writing Suggestion

Crowley says of the presidential election of 1996, "... this election year a new attention to youth politics as panache has burbled into the marketing of both performers and media outlets, and it is frequently both calculated and facile" (1). By this statement he seems to be implying that corporate executives in the entertainment industry are coopting young people's political awareness to sell products. Ironically, as it turned out, voting participation by young people was at an all-time low in the past election. Write an essay in which you discuss the political awareness and commitment of your generation. What specific factors might account for the low turnout at the polls by young voters? Use your own experiences—and perhaps the reported experiences of your friends—as concrete support for your assertions. Toward the end of your essay, you might move your thesis in the direction of the rhetorical mode known as the formal recommendation essay, by making some specific suggestions for increasing political participation on the part of young people.

Popular Music's Influence on Lifestyle

Popular Music: Emotional Use and Management

Alan Wells

If you've ever used a particular song or album to alter your state of mind—to relax, to stimulate feelings of nostalgia, or to "pump up" for a party, then you're a typical pop music listener, according to Alan Wells. In this 1987 qualitative study of youth's relationship to popular music, Wells suggests that young people use music to manipulate their moods and behaviors, finding "deep emotional meaning" in the rhythm, melody, and lyrics of popular responses.

In surveying his respondents' favorite music for listening and dancing, Wells found slight but significant gender differences in young people's uses of and responses to pop music. For example, female respondents listed "happiness" and "love" as predominant themes and emotions elicited by popular music, while "excitement" above those two was on the top of the list for males. Although "proving" that men and women respond differently to similar musical stimuli, Wells still believes both genders use music as a form of "self-administered psychotherapy" to create and control their emotional responses.

As you read this essay, observe how heavily Wells, a sociologist by profession, relies on percentile norms and other numerical values as his data, a research strategy which writers in the social and "hard" sciences use to lend validity to their conclusions. However, you may also test his conclusions against your own musical experience. How closely do you conform to the conclusions which Wells draws in this article? Do you rely on your favorite music in ways that Wells's survey suggests?

The study of popular music is a relatively new field in communication (Chaffee, 1985). Recent book length treatments of the topic (Frith, 1981; Lull, 1987), the continuation of the scholarly journal *Popular Music and Society*, and articles published in other journals, are adding to existing knowledge. (Curtis 1987:2) has noted that technology and the audience are the least studied aspects of popular music. Similarly, Lewis (1981, 1983) urges the desirability of the "uses and gratifications" approach to fill gaps in our knowledge of popular music. The study reported here is in this tradition, and also employs ideas from the sociology of emotions that has recently emerged from symbolic interaction theory.

A survey of college students was conducted to gauge their consumption and use of popular music. The focus was on dance and emotions, and gender is the single independent variable. They were asked to select their favorite type of music, and indicate their dance activity and favorite dance music. Subjects were then asked to list their three favorite songs and identify emotions that they associated with them. Finally, they were asked what effect they thought music had on them and whether they ever use music to change their mood.   2

Three previous studies have a bearing on the research reported here. Gantz *et al* (1978) studied the gratification of popular music claimed by a sample of secondary and college students. The listeners, they found, used music primarily to relieve boredom, ease tensions, manipulate their moods, and fight loneliness. The researchers, however, did not examine emotional uses or identify music preferences.   3

Rosenbaum and Prinsky (1987) asked a junior and senior high school sample to choose their favorite three songs and select one of seven reasons for liking them. Except for dance, differences between the genders were small. In order of preference, the reasons the songs were chosen were (1987:85): "It helps me to relax and stop thinking about things" (30% Male, 34% Female); "Helps get me into the right mood" (25% Male, 29% Female); "It's good to dance to" (16% Male, 35% Female); "Words express how I feel" (17% Male, 24% Female); "It creates a good atmosphere when I'm with others" (16% Male, 13% Female); "It helps pass the time" (13% Male, 10% Female); and "I want to listen to the words" (11% Male, 7% Female). Dance or emotional impact are highly represented.   4

In a survey of college students similar to that employed here, Melton and Galician consciously employ a uses and gratification model. They found that "Respondents felt that both radio and music videos provided need satisfaction in passing time, relieving tension, relaxation, mood shifting, and forgetting about problems" (1987:41).   5

SAMPLE

Self-administered questionnaires were completed by two groups of college students, 105 from a sociology class at a medium-size rural campus in New England, and 119 in a communication class at a large East Coast University. Both colleges are state supported and serve a broad range of social classes. Although the sample cannot be claimed to be representative of college youth, high agreement exists between   6 the two groups, and with a Midwestern sample of 141 (predominantly middle class) students in a similar study (Wells, 1985). The results may be suggestive for a larger universe.

The mean age of the subject was 19.6 years. Approximately 32 percent were 18 years old or less; 30% were 19 or 20; 22% were 21 or 22; and 7% were 23 years or older. There were 115 males and 119 females, of whom 19 identified themselves as minorities (Black 16, Hispanic 3, all in East Coast group). Because of the similarities between the two groups the findings report for the entire sample. Any large discrepancies are noted in the discussion.

FINDINGS: MUSIC CHOICE, DANCE, EMOTIONS AND MEANINGS

(1) Favorite music. Respondents were asked to indicate their favorite type of music from the following list: Classical, Easy listening, Heavy metal, jazz, R & B/Soul, Country, Pop, Rock, and Other (which they were encouraged to specify. (Only one respondent questioned these terms, asking "What the hell is pop!")

Table I shows the respondents' favorite type of music. Rock and pop are clearly the dominant forms of music. The popularity of R & B/ Soul can be attributed largely to Black respondents: 9 of the 16 made it their top choice. Country music had less than a one percent following, and classical and jazz had minuscule followings. The musics that are grouped under the heading "new wave" were the only significant addition to the list provided. The response to heavy metal is perhaps the least expected. The music is usually thought to appeal to young males, while women prefer softer, romantic rock (Frith, 1981; Weinstein,

Table I: Favorite Popular Music, by Gender (Percent Choosing Music Type)

	Males (n = 115)	Females (n = 119)	Total (n = 234)
Rock	53	40	47
Pop	14	29	22
R & B/Soul	7	11	9
New wave[1]	7	8	7
Heavy metal	3	3	3
Easy listening	1	3	2
Jazz	1	1	1
Classical	0	2	1
Reggae	2	1	1
Multiple/All	5	1	3
Other/NR	6	1	3

[1]Includes progressive, punk, hardcore, underground, and new music.

1983). While the latter may be true (women's higher preference for pop), male respondents had a low approval of heavy metal, the same as that for females. Perhaps the male respondents are already beyond the "metal" age.

The variety available in popular music is indicated by the respondents' choices of popular songs. Most were able to identify three favorites, and selected from an approximately 20-year pool of popular songs. Many were first heard by the respondents in their early teens. While current hits are represented, the bulk of the choices indicate a broad variety of musical preference. Nor can music be seen as a purely youth phenomenon, since respondents are now selecting music from their parents' generation. While younger listeners may only know current hits (Stipp, 1985), tastes of college-age people are much more varied.

In all, 277 artists or groups were mentioned as favorites (out of a total of 702 possible choices), which indicates a wide variety of popular music. The top choice, the contemporary Irish group U2, received 26 mentions. The next eight most popular choices have been performing for more than a decade: Pink Floyd (18), Bruce Springsteen (17), Led Zeppelin (11), Genesis and Bob Marley (12), Billy Joel (11), Elton John, and the Beatles (10). Contemporary "star" George Michael completes the top ten artists with 9 mentions. There were twenty-two other artists receiving four or more mentions. Only two were women—Whitney Houston and Madonna. Only a few were relatively new groups (The Cure, R.E.M. Prince, The Smiths (Morrissey), the remainder veterans of pop music (Eagles, Rolling Stones, Journey, Peter Gabriel, the Police, Boston, Van Halen, Stevie Wonder, Lynyrd Skynyrd, Phil Collins, Sting, the Who, Queen, Steve Winwood, Elvis Presley, and Vivaldi).

The favorite song artists were identified by gender and the choices of male and female respondents are shown in Table II. As expected, females were more likely than men to choose female artists or mixed gender groups. But like male respondents, women still usually choose songs by male artists. During the Madonna, Cyndi Lauper, Tina Turner peak (Wells 1985), 30% of a similar sample of women chose female or mixed groups.

Table II: Gender and Favorite Songs, Artists by Respondent's Gender

Gender of Artists	Female	Male	Total
Male	91 (83%)	99 (93%)	190
Female	16 (15%)	7 (7%)	23
Males and females	3 (3%)	1 (1%)	4
	110 (100%)	107 (100%)	217

17 choices could not be identified by artists' gender and are omitted.

Table III: Dance Frequency by Gender

Frequency	Females (%)	Males (%)
Everyday	15 (13)	13 (11)
Twice or more/week	39 (33)	17 (15)
Once per week	32 (27)	15 (13)
Once per month	17 (14)	36 (31)
Seldom/never	11 (9)	29 (25)
No response	5 (4)	5 (1)
Total	119 (100)	115 (99)

(2) Music for Dancing. The survey provides information on 13 how often respondents dance, and what type of music they dance to. Table III shows dance frequency by gender. Women clearly dance more often than men, in part, perhaps, because it is socially acceptable for women to dance together. Both males and females in the New England sample danced more than the East Coast respondents (except in the "everyday" category, inflated for the East by 6 of 11 Black females). Seventy-three percent of the women dance at least once per week, compared to 39 percent of the men.

If popular music is primarily for dancing, the choice of dance 14 music should be similar to the favorite music shown in Table I. Since women apparently dance the most, it should be especially true for them. Table IV shows to what degree this holds. While it is true that Rock, Pop and R & B/Soul are the most popular types of music, pop is used more for dancing, rock for listening. While new wave is about equally valued, the other types of music (all "write-ins") are chosen

Table IV: Favorite Dance Music by Gender (Percent Choosing Music Type)

	Males (n = 115)	Females (n = 119)	Total (n = 234)
Pop /Top 40	22	33	28
Rock	18	13	16
R & B/Soul	12	11	12
Dance/Club	9	7	8
New wave	7	9	8
Disco funk	5	7	6
Reggae	1	1	2
Other	6	9	8
No response	18	7	12
	98*	98*	99*

*Less than 100 due to rounding and omitting Jazz, Country, Easy Listening, and Heavy Metal which each had less than 1% response.

specifically for dancing. Thus dance/club and disco/funk are represented in Table IV, but not Table I. The relatively high no response category represents primarily non-dancers. Clearly dancing is one use of popular music, but it is not the most important use for the most popular (overall) type of music, rock. Dance, however, does popularize types of music that capitalize on dancability over other qualities.

(3) Music and Emotions.   Christenson and Lindlof have summarized what is known from the scarce studies of the effects of music on children. It may "…have a significant *emotional* or *affective* impact… there is evidence that two of the prime determinants of children's musical preferences are the mood and sentiment of the music…Most rock music is by its very nature an excitatory stimulus and can arouse the listener" (1983:36). The same effects can be expected in young adults. 15

Hochschild (1981) has analyzed some of the complexities of a single emotion, love, and the differing ways that males and females deal with it. Hochschild (1983) has also persuasively argued that the genders manage their emotions in different ways. We can therefore hypothesize gender differences in the emotional use of music. 16

Love, in its many varieties, is widely acknowledged to be the most common component of western popular music, a claim supported by the findings reported below. Denisoff and Bridges (1983) have cited the numerous studies on the love component of American popular music and the differing uses of music by males and females. Similarly, Frith (1981) discusses at length the meaning of pop music to British teenagers. He describes the features of female youth culture (1981:225–234) which produces the "dream lover" phenomenon while males gravitate to "macho" music. While he notes that rock has been a force in liberating sexuality (1981:235–248) there is neither sexual equality among performing artists nor a unisex homogenization of musical tastes. Of course, the expression of a range of emotions in popular music is complex. The music itself may imply emotions and the artist's interpretation of lyrics can convey other than their surface meaning. A recent song by John Waite, for example, used the repeated line "I ain't missing you." Rather than a simple declaration of fact, the artist's intonation implied alternatively anger, hate, sadness and remorse. The analysis here suspends such considerations and deals only with emotional content of a song perceived by the listener-respondent. 17

Respondents were presented the list of emotions and asked to identify those (if any) which they thought were expressed in their chosen songs. The emotions were chosen from the most frequently cited terms in the Dictionary of Emotional Meaning (Davitz, 1969:11). They were: 18

| Fear | Anger | Hate | Relief |
| Hope | Confidence | Passion | Shame |

Love	Delight	Pity	Grief
Surprise	Happiness	Pride	Excitement

Respondents were also encouraged to add the emotions not on the list. The results are shown in Table V.

Very few respondents had any difficulty in their selection. None claimed that songs do not express emotions. As Table V shows, women selected slightly less emotions on average than males. Contrary to the pernicious "non-emotional" stereotype of males, they do in fact exhibit strong emotional use of music. Overall, there is a striking congruence of the frequency of male and female selections of emotions.   19

As would be expected, love is high on the list. It is often claimed to be the overwhelming theme of popular music. Happiness, however, is a more frequent choice for both males and females, and the males' top choice was excitement. While popular music exposes the listener to a broad range of emotional feelings, the top seven in Table V appear to be the most common. The same emotions were also the most chosen in Wells (1985).   20

Gender differences do not appear to be great. Women chose songs that express hope, happiness, passion and grief slightly more than men. Men are a little more swayed by excitement, delight, anger and hate.   21

Table V: Emotions Identified in Favorite Songs, by Gender

	Female (n = 119)		Males (n = 115)		Total (n = 234)
Emotion	No. of Mentions	Per Respondent	No. of Mentions	Per Respondent	No. of Mentions
Happiness	131	1.10	88	.77	219
Excitement	86	.72	121	1.05	207
Love	109	.92	71	.61	183
Hope	79	.66	55	.48	134
Confidence	59	.50	73	.63	132
Delight	49	.11	81	.70	130
Passion	66	.55	18	.42	114
Pride	19	.16	36	.31	55
Grief	33	.28	17	.15	50
Anger	7	.06	35	.30	42
Relief	13	.11	24	.21	37
Fear	12	.10	19	.17	31
Pity	11	.09	12	.10	23
Hate	1	.01	9	.08	10
Surprise	5	.01	5	.01	10
Shame	2	.02	4	.03	6
Total	701	5.89	733	6.36	1134

The tendency for women to be a little more positive than men   22
was indicated by comments explaining their choices in Wells (1985):
"It's a love song; it talks about the importance and feeling of a relationship." "I like soft music usually, words about love or lost love," or "I
want to know what love is." All is not optimism, however. "The songs
are all about hope and love but there is also anger at times." Another
writes "loneliness, despair—small doses of unhappiness are good for a
person."

Men are perhaps less tranquil. A few are pessimistic, alienated   23
and angry. One male describing a song that expresses fear, anger and
grief says that "...irregardless of what happens, what you do, who
you are—is of no consequence, it's all bigger than us and we have no
control over it." Another selects a song that expresses fear, trouble,
anger and recounts "...how the U.S. is facing bad times with unemployment, murders, and misguided youth." No songs of this genre
were chosen by women.

(4) Effects of Music. Qualitative comments indicate that   24
there may be differences between male and female uses of music
as Frith (1981) has suggested. In an earlier study (Wells, 1985) a
minority of the men liked "head-banger," so called "heavy metal"
music, which they claimed energizes them, sometimes within a
sexual context: "The songs can get you up and make you wild with
your girlfriends." Others commented that it gets them in the mood
"to party": "It's a kick-ass song when you're stoned." Women were
more likely to comment that their favorite music relaxes them: "It
makes me feel as if the world is just so beautiful and there are no
troubles to worry about." Another claimed her favorite choices
were "good to put you in a relaxed state." Overall, then, men may
use music to "wind up," women to "wind down."

Many of the comments on effects indicate the intensity that music   25
inspires. Only two people said music had no effect on them, and most

Table VI: Music Effects. Responses to the
question: "What effect does listening to music have
on you?" Percentage of responses falling in category.

	Male	Female
Mellows out, relaxes	18	14
Excites or relaxes	13	21
Makes me happy	4	8
Memories	3	7
Uplifts	4	2

express an emotional, personal impact that is probably far more important to them than, for example, watching a TV soap opera or reading a textbook. A female claims "music to me is the difference between merely existing and living." Males add "music has more effect on me than anything else," "sometimes I feel as if I'm addicted to music," and "music is the essence of life, as important as food. It helps free my mind." A male musician attests "It's the ultimate thing in my life" and another male claims "I often lose myself in the music. I have been known to listen for as much as 6 hours at a time, never leaving my room."

Both males and females commonly associate songs with current   26
or past loves. Respondents in the Midwest (Wells, 1985) claim "Me and my girlfriend's song" (male); and (female) "I like the...songs because they remind me of my boyfriend and our love." Songs can also evoke other memories, sometimes tragic ones: "It has sentimental value because it was a favorite song of a good friend who died in a car accident" (female respondent). Similar comments were made in this study. A male says "music is like a time machine and when I want to return to certain past experiences I listen to the music that was present at that time." A female adds "It makes me feel love and brings back memories of the past that I cherish." The results, however, are not always positive. A male notes, "when I hear certain songs, it makes me think about girls I used to go out with and gets me a little depressed." Music, then, appears to be a major link of biography and nostalgia.

(5) Emotional Management. The respondents were asked if   27
they ever use music to change their mood. Their answers often showed an unanticipated passion. A female replies "Yes, most definitely. All I need to do is to put on the radio and after a long day of being cranky and irritable it completely changes my mood." Another says "Yes! Whenever I'm angry or upset I use music to calm me, sometimes I use it to pep me up." A third is even more emphatic: "Yes!! I find that music is a large contributor to my emotional standing." A similarly enthusiastic male adds "Yes!! If I am bored or down I listen to my favorite music and it usually picks me up."

Table VII shows the grouping of responses to the open ended   28
question on mood management. A high percentage of both females and males claim to use music in this way. A minority of each gender say that they use music to enhance an existing mood. One replies "Yes. To accent the mood, like getting ready for a party." Another says "I usually use it to enhance a mood—Dance music when I'm happy, the Carpenters when I'm suicidal." A higher proportion of men than women replied that they do not use music in this way.

Many of the "yes" responses fell into the broad categories shown   29
in the table. The most common for both genders was combating de-

Table VII: Emotional Management by Gender. Responses to the question:
"Do you ever use music to change your mood?"

	Percent of Females (n = 118)	Percent of Males (n = 107)
Yes	85	71
Lift spirits	(44)	(30)
Pick up and calm down	(16)	(13)
Mellow out, relax	(10)	(10)
Get pumped up	(1)	(11)
Multiple uses	(7)	(3)
Enhance mood	7	10
Both (change and enhance)	3	3
No	6	13

pression or being upset. Music, they claimed, could lift their spirits. Thus a male says "If I am depressed I will play some of my favorite music to cheer me up." Others claim that music helps them calm down, to "mellow out," or relax. For example a female says "If I'm ever mad at someone I use music to relax, calm down." A few respondents claimed both uses, to pick themselves up or calm themselves: "When I'm depressed, angry or bored, music can either calm me down or cheer me up" (female). "I can listen to an AC/DC album and get really rowdy yet if I listen to a soft Elton John song I turn melancholy" (male). A few respondents, more females than males, report multiple changes in moods.

The most noticeable gender difference was in reporting that music could enervate the listener. Males said they use music to "pump themselves up" for parties or sports competition. One says that "... before every [hockey] game I listen to some Rock psych songs to get myself pumped up." Others claim "music ... psyches me up when I play sports," and "before I go to parties I listen to some Elvis Costello to get me pumped up." Parties are perhaps the equivalent to sports events for males, and both demand vigorous physical performance.

All "yes" responses could not be subsumed in the subcategories listed in Table VII. Individual replies point to the diversity of mood management uses. For one male music counters alcohol abuse: "If I'm hung over, I listen to mellow Zeppelin or Hendrix blues to get me going again." Another reports "It makes me feel as though I'm not experiencing something alone—I know someone else went through it before." A female adds "listening to music is a very inner and personal thing to me. It makes me more confident and more caring about myself and others."

CONCLUSIONS

While the subjects in the study were not a representative sample   32
of college students or young American adults, the similarities between
the East Coast and New England groups may indicate that the findings may at least be suggestive for these populations. Music, clearly, is
important in the lives of many young adults. The most popular music
genres are pop and rock, but there is a broad diversity of favorite
choices within them. Favorite music is not predominantly current hits,
but chosen from a two decades or more catalogue of music. Dance is
one popular use of music, but subjects discriminate between dancability and deeper musical values.

Gender differences in the use of music are present, but as Melton   33
and Galician (1987) found, often less significant than expected.
Women dance more than men, prefer softer music, and derive somewhat different gratifications. But music also represents something that
is shared and has meaning across genders. Males and females not only
dance and listen to music together, they may also judge one another
on the basis of musical preference.

Music has deep emotional meaning, both in its sound and lyrics.   34
It can also have meaning by its association with personal experiences.
Both genders report that they use music to change their moods and
manipulate emotions. It is not just noise or entertainment, but a self-
administered psychotherapy that works.

SUGGESTIONS FOR FURTHER READING

Chaffee, Steven. 1985. "Popular music and communication research:
     an editorial epilogue," *Communication Research*, 12:413–424.
Christenson, Peter G. and Lindlof, Thomas R. 1983 "The Role of Audio
     Media in the Lives of Children," *Popular Music and Society*, ix:3,
     pp. 25–40.
Curtis, Jim. 1987. *Rock Eras: Interpretations of Music and Society,
     1954–1984.* Bowling Green, Ohio: Bowling Green State Univer-
     sity Press.
Davitz, Joel R. 1969. *The Language of Emotion.* New York: Academic Press.
Frith, Simon. 1981. *Sound Effects: Youth, Leisure and the Politics of Rock
     'n' Roll.* New York: Pantheon.
Gantz, Walter, Gattenberg, Howard M., Pearson, Martin I., & Schiller,
     Seth O. 1978. "Gratifications and Expectations Associated with Pop
     Music Among Adolescents," *Popular Music and Society*, 6:81–89.
Hochschild, Arlie Russell. 1981. "Attending to Codifying and Manag-
     ing Feelings: Sex Differences in Love." In Laurel Walum-

Richardson & Verta Taylor (eds.) *Sex and Gender.* New York: Heath. 1983 *The Managed Heart.* Berkeley and Los Angeles: University of California Press.

Lewis, George I. 1983. "The meaning's in the music and the music's in me: popular music as symbolic communication," *Theory, Culture and Society* I (3):133–141.

———. 1981. "Towards a Uses and Gratification Approach: An Examination of Commitment and Involvement in Popular Music," *Popular Music and Society,* 8 (1):10–18.

Lull, James (ed.). 1987. *Popular Music and Communication,* Beverly Hills, CA: Sage.

Melton, Gary W. and Mary-Lou Galician. 1987. "A Sociological Approach to the Pop Music Phenomenon: Radio and Music Video Utilization for Expectation, Motivation and Satisfaction," *Popular Music and Society,* Vol. 11, No. 3 (Fall), pp. 35–46.

Stipp, Horst. 1985. "Children's Knowledge of and Taste in Popular Music," *Popular Music and Society,* 10:2, pp. 1–17.

Weinstein, Deena. 1983. "Rock: Youth and Its Music," *Popular Music and Society,* ix:3, pp. 2–16.

Wells, Alan. 1985. "Gender, Emotions and Popular Music." Paper presented at the Midwest Sociological Society Annual Meeting, St. Louis.

Examining the Text

1. What does Wells mean by the term "uses and gratifications" as it applies to the study of popular music? What are your own "uses and gratifications" in regard to popular music? In what other fields of study might such a focus be useful?

2. The author contends, "Nor can music be seen as a purely youth phenomenon, since respondents are now selecting music from their parents' generation" (paragraph 10). What point is he making about the musical tastes of the current generation? In your experience, are his observations apt?

3. As a class, complete Wells's survey, totaling up responses and break them down by gender. Do your class results support Wells's? How do you account for similarities or differences?

For Group Discussion

In assessing his sample research population, Wells found that "approximately 32 percent were 18 years or less; 30% were 19 or 20;

22% were 21 or 22; and 7% were 23 years or older. There were 115 males and 119 females, of whom 19 identified themselves as minorities (Black 16, Hispanic 3, all in East coast group)" (7). Consider your class as a sample research population. How might the ethnic/gender makeup of your class make your results different from Wells's?

Writing Suggestion

Wells conducted this study in 1987. Write an essay in which you examine the changes that have taken place in popular music since then. How would you suggest the results of Wells's study would be modified by current trends in music? Be as specific as you can in considering contemporary movements in popular music.

Punks in LA: It's Kiss or Kill

Jon Lewis

In the mid-1970s, an unprecedented and provocative subculture emerged on the American scene: the punk movement. At that time, bewildered mainstream pop music critics and social observers derided punk music as atonal, arrhythmic noise, and its adherents as mindlessly disruptive—which, in truth, they often were. But that was the point (if so antiintellectual a movement can be said to have had a point).

Based on his studies of punks in Los Angeles, Jon Lewis, a professor of film and video at Oregon State University, gives us a historical retrospective and sociological analysis of the entire movement, as well as its relationship to rock 'n' roll and other youth subcultures. Marked by a continual threat of violence, riots, and antisocial behavior, the "self-effacing, self-mutilating, self-abusive" punk crowd was at home in clubs in L.A.'s worst neighborhoods. As a "celebration of resignation," the punk movement attracted and produced a subculture of disenfranchised youth drawn to self-destruction as a means of expressing their sense of alienation and desperation. Lewis argues that "disdain public propriety" was the lifeblood of the punks, accounting for their embrace of drugs, alcohol, violent slamdancing, graffiti, and nipple-piercing— all emblematic of their tendencies toward excess, illegality, and crude obscenity.

*Writing not as an outraged, moralizing citizen, but rather as an objective (even sympathetic) cultural theorist, Lewis argues that the punk movement was but one scene in the ongoing drama of pop culture. Following his interest in cultural and revolutionary disruption, Lewis recreates the spectacles of punk music, videos, movies, and art, giving us the chance to live those chaotic and dangerous times vicariously. **As you read** about the brief existence of the movement—and its eventual assimilation into the mainstream of* *music and fashion culture, consider whether any youth subculture can be truly subversive.*

———————————

Punk surfaced in Los Angeles in the late seventies as a curious   1
blend of anarchy and anomie—as one last desperate attempt for white, urban, lower middle class youths to dramatically express their distaste for a society that had long since expressed its disinterest in them. What follows is a selective description of the movement; an analysis of its ideology and its symbiotic relationship to mainstream rock and roll and an attempt to contextualize punk as a unique moment in the history of American youth culture.

The LA punk movement began around 1977 and ended in the   2
first few years of the 1980s. For the duration of its brief hold on the disenfranchised youth of urban LA, punk unapologetically paraded a variety of misanthropic and misogynist tendencies: Nazism, fascism, racism and self-hate. No youth movement before or since has hinged so tenuously on bizarre and frightening ceremonies of attraction and repulsion and public displays of absolute anti-social behavior. No youth movement before or since has laid so bare the desperation residing at the heart of the now failed urban American dream.

Like the New York or London based punk movements, the LA   3
variation gained definition as an urban performance art form. The chaos and penchant for public obscenity which were punk's stock in trade found a milieu in the Masque, Madame Wong's and the Hong Kong Cafe—punk clubs in the heart of LA's very worst neighborhoods. Imminent danger characterized every venture to a punk club and the media attention to the savagery and very real violence integral to every punk performance and experience made it virtually impossible for anyone to "be there" completely by mistake.

From the start punk's droll, black comic and only marginally ironic   4
celebration of urban squalor and senseless violence generated a kind of outsider mystique. Punk performances—here a very broad term indeed—generally manifested itself in ritual terms; shared act, or activities displaying a ceremonial and privileged significance. Punk attire and behavior was opposed to convention; which was consistent with the movement's tendency towards celebrating its members' alienation from the mainstream of bourgeois city life. As a rejection of the late seventies/early eighties gearing up of the yuppie lifestyle, the LA punk movement paraded a glib and steadfast embrace of the frustrations inherent to their outsider status, maintaining an essential insider subculture—one which was simply too extreme to court the likes of the urban bourgeoisie as anything more than dumbfounded spectators.

As with so many urban subcultures, punk generated its own pecu-   5
liar performance art scene, headed up by the redoubtable Sergio Premoli. In his most famous performance to date, Premoli, stationed in
front of Gucci's status-packed Italian boutique on Beverly Hills' famed
Rodeo Drive, hefted a 120-pound wooden American flag up on his back.
"To carry something this heavy, it takes a lot of faith to do it," Premoli
told spectators, "That's why Christ was so special." Viewing Premoli
bearing his cross down the ritziest commercial LA street, the proprietor
of ("the intelligent and tasteful mens' store") Madonna Man suggested
that Premoli (clad topless, with loose fitting sweatpants over his bottom
half) should have worn something more elegant, like a black raincoat by
Benedetto (the Blessed One) of New York. Premoli, citing the gravity of
his task was hardly thinking of fashion, even on so auspicious an avenue. When asked how he felt once he secured the flag on his shoulders,
Premoli replied, "Eeets a fucking heavy."[1]

Premoli's art is provocation and it is meant to be offensive. By   6
mixing his metaphors to God and country, Premoli complicates matters with his choice of locale (commercial America; the one street on
earth most completely associated with conspicuous consumption).
That there is an element of social commentary here is not all that unusual for punk. And that the commentary is obscene (in the Henry
Miller sense of the word: as not pornographic or titillating, but ugly
and revelatory) and to a great extent confusing and confused, is quite
consistent with the peculiar artistic oeuvre of the LA punk scene.

The punk predilection for obscenity is similarly exposed in the   7
LA punk literature: godfathered by the now legendary Charles
Bukowski, featured in the unique punk fanzines like *Wet, Slash, Conta-
gion, No Mag* and *The Lowest Common Denominator* and publically exhibited on bathroom walls and decaying building edifices in the often
misanthropic/misogynist, existential or absurdist punk graffiti.

Bukowski, like his more famous counterpart William Burroughs   8
in New York, has been credited as the movement's literary avatar, its
truly gifted muse. But like Burroughs, whose reputation and income
soared due to an identification with the movement, Bukowski's relationship to the punks themselves is peripheral at most. His readership
is comprised primarily of those who viewed punk with fascination
(but at arms' length). Bukowski's alcohol-soaked prose and anti-
heroic, macho, bar-brawling heroes coincide and resonate with punk
anti-social behavior and lifestyle, but aside from his alleged influence
on the punk band X, Bukowski and the punks literally live at opposite
ends of town; he in Venice by the sea, the punks far east of La Brea in
the heat and smog of downtown.

---

[1]"Eeets a Fuckin' Heavy: Christ Comes to Rodeo Drive," *Wet*, May/June 1981, p. 55.

For those on the inside, graffiti was the "pure punk" form, as it is   9
public, obscene, often misspelled and ungrammatical, generally reductive and emblematic (rather than symbolic or allusive) and illegal. A familiar mix of crude drawing and aphoristic outrage, punk graffiti effaced
already crumbling property, calling attention to (but never asking anyone to change) the dreadful landscape of decaying urban America.

The graffiti look and literary style is clearly evident in the unique   10
and irreverent punk fanzines. These fan magazines, staffed, funded
and distributed from within the punk subculture, provided information on the punk bands and featured pseudo-gonzo New Journalism
(apeing Hunter Thompson and Terry Southern) replete with anti-
social and often paradoxical and paranoid nihilist rants (for example
Richard Meltzer's bizarre punk treatise on communism, "Go for the
hammer/go for the sickle/you'll be glad you did.... Hitler was just a
fairy who dug blue-eyed South Bay surfer boys").[2]

The fanzines all featured a graffiti layout style, literalizing the ef-   11
fect of cutting and pasting. Unlike *Rolling Stone* and the other popular
music magazines, the punk fanzines de-emphasized the stardom of
the bands. While *Rolling Stone* et al institutionalized the glamour of the
industry, the fanzines wallowed in the glamourlessness of punk.

The punk sense of humor exhibited in the fanzines was charac-   12
teristically irreverent. For example, when Ronald Reagan's Commission on the Eighties found that for the first time in U.S. history more
than one-half of the American population lived west of the Mississippi, *Wet* responded to the rising political influence of the conservative southwest with a black-comical mock advertisement for a solar
powered electric chair, touting "Organic Executions for the Sunbelt."
The ad credits the chair to New York designer James Hong and guar-
antees that the device "provides effectiveness even on a partly cloudy
day." The chair, as advertised, is "slow rotisserie effective," with "capabilities for torture most of us haven't dreamed about since the days
of the Protestant Reformation." And with a typical bit of (not really
tongue in cheek) punk social theory, the ad concludes: "Just the thing
to stamp out those food stamp cheating single mothers."[3]

Two films, both by UCLA film school graduates who were in LA   13
in the late seventies, articulate (for audiences outside LA) the essence
of the LA punks: Penelope Spheeris' *The Decline of Western Civilization*
and Alex Cox's cult-hit *Repo Man*, a film that juxtaposes the punk hallmark anti-commercialism to the crude narratives and visual styles of
truly bad B-films.

---

[2]David E. James, "Poetry/Punk/Performance: Some Recent Writing in LA," the *Minnesota Review*, Fall 1984, p. 135.

[3]"Creative Methodologies," *Wet*, May/June 1981, p. 61.

The attraction of punk culture to graduate students, to upper   14
middle class, white, well educated men and women (despite the fact
that they were often the target of punk tirades), was a curious phenomenon in late seventies' LA. For those in search of a youth movement in post-Vietnam America, punk positioned itself in diametric
opposition to the optimistic and idealistic flower children of the previous decade. In fact, the punks often railed against the hippies. One
punk (sporting a swastika medallion on his chest) wryly quips (in an
interview with Penelope Spheeris in *The Decline of Western Civilization*):
"Like I'm not going to go out and kill some Jew. C'mon—Maybe a hippie." Such blank, emotionless threats of violence abound in Spheeris'
film. One punk argues that fighting is the only thing that makes him
feel good. Claude Bessy, AKA Kickboy Face, *Slash* editor and lead
singer of the punk band Catholic Discipline puts it all in the peculiar
punk perspective: "We're not grooving on the same vibes anymore.
We're grooving on different vibes...ugly vibes."

Eugene, a skinhead who opens *The Decline of Western Civilization*   15
with a treatise on how punk has "no stars—no bullshit," expresses his
rationale for rebellion via vague references to buses and poseurs. For
him, as for so many other punks, the city is both subject and object, at
once sacred and profane, a kind of indecipherable, repugnant yet seductive fact of life.

The most obvious performative outlet for this familiar urban   16
frustration was the phenomenon of pogo. A dance, done to music exe-
cuted at 250 beats a minute (disco for example is performed at half that
speed), pogo (and its offspring, the even less structured slam dance)
was pure and simple the performance of violence. Whereas mainstream rock and roll sugarcoats an essential misanthropy and misogyny as teenage romance and rebellion, the punks accepted the
"teenage wasteland" for what it is. Punk was the celebration of resignation. It was anomie as artistic impulse. And in a cult of aggressive
egalitarianism (everyone is worthless/everyone is the same) everyone
involved in the punk performance was part of the performance.

To Spheeris' credit (and coincident with her decision to docu-   17
ment rather than comment on the LA punk scene), the concert material
in *The Decline of Western Civilization* is almost exclusively shot from the
point of view of the audience. There the camera is obscured, jostled,
harassed, threatened, knocked over, kicked and cursed and abused by
the maniacal pogo dancing punks. "Actually there is no difference between dancing and fighting," a bouncer muses as he grabs a security
guard by the throat. Shaking his co-worker like a rag doll he adds,
"This, for example, is dancing."

Alex Cox's cult-fiction film *Repo Man* purposefully attends to the   18
significance of the city to LA punk culture. The film's focus on the
unglamorous East LA city-scape as opposed to the fun, sun and surf

allure of Santa Monica, Malibu or Venice (where the majority of mainstream TV and cinema are shot) depicts the city as just one large bad
neighborhood.

From the opening credit sequence to the closing scene hovering   19
above the night-lit city in a radioactive automobile, *Repo Man* leaps
and lunges from one thing to the next, never effacing (in fact celebrating) the anti-aesthetics of the low budget B movie. Much of the film is
comical and ridiculous, banking on postmortem pastiche, kitsch and
camp. The film features aliens, a radioactive car and an obscure plot
involving repo men battling g-men. The film's truth-teller, Miller, who
waxes philosophical while burning garbage under the striking LA
smog sunset, talks of the cosmic relevance of "plates of shrimp" and
argues that (in of all places LA) "the more you drive the less intelligent
you are." His revelations are characteristically off-center which explains why he has such authority in the film.

Repo Man rather blankly wades through hackneyed dialogue   20
reminiscent of the strained seriousness of 50's B movie teenage melodramas, as evident in the following scene: Duke (dying from a gun-
shot wound suffered while robbing a 7-11): "I know a life of crime has
led me to this sorry fate. And yet I blame society—Society made me
what I am." Otto (the punk cum repo man hero of the film played by
Emilio Estevez): "That's bullshit. You're a white suburban punk just
like me." Duke: "But it still hurts," (and he dies).

The helter skelter pace of the film not only punctuates the searing   21
punk music score, but allows filmic material to simply appear and disappear without much coherence or apparent authorial organization, as
if any pretense to order would betray the punk sensibility of the film.
But despite its B-movie clichés and scatterbrained narrative, *Repo Man*
successfully posits a realistic and depressing view of the city and its
youth. When Kevin, Otto's straight friend, mindlessly stacks and prices
cans of generic cling peaches in a small city supermarket he sings the
7-Up jingle ("Feeling' 7-Up/I'm feelin' 7-Up"). Later on in the film,
Kevin peruses the want ads, "There's room to move as a fry cook," he
says, "in two years I'll be assistant manager. It's key." That Otto rejects
such acquiescence helps to define his separation and heroism.

There is a progressive argument to be made about *Repo Man*—a   22
critical position seldom staked with regard to punk art and lifestyle.
Fred Pfeil argues that *Repo Man* "reproduces the relation between the
bone-numbing vacuity and circularity of daily life…" noting that the
film's "sudden jolts of idiotic violence"[4] offer a profound if parodic
(Pfeil would argue postmodern) critique of "the nowhere city." Pfeil

---

[4]Fred Pfeil, "Makin' Flippy Floppy: Postmodernism and the Baby Boom PMC," in *The Year Left* (London: Verso Press, 1986), p. 285.

then comments on "the simultaneous desire and dread of some ultimate, externally imposed moment of truth" in *Repo Man*; a moment
that "once and for all would put an end to the endless, senseless repetitions of which our lives seem to be made."[5]

Repo Man, though deliberately narratologically incoherent, does   23
evince a coherent tract on the effect of the city on its disenfranchised
youth. And though the film has been championed by its primarily
postpunk, white urban and suburban youth audience—and I suppose
in effect misunderstood by them as a camp teen film comedy, a *Beach
Party* with 80's nudity, bad language and technology—*Repo Man*
should not be disparaged because of its popularity. It is just unfortunate that punk, as with all other youth movements, has been annexed
into mainstream popular culture, and, as is so often the case, it has re-
surfaced as far less threatening and far less politically important to
those too young or too rich or too suburban to really understand what
the movement meant less than a decade past.

Certainly mainstream rock and roll has had a significant effect on   24
the American teenage population. And apropos to Tipper Gore, the
music and the multi-billion dollar consumer culture that accompanies
it stupidly celebrates sex and drugs and anti-social behavior.

Punk on the other hand offered no escapist merchandising   25
scheme. The self-effacing, self-mutilating, self-abusive tendencies of
punk—shared by its performers and fans to the point of establishing the
movement's most significant bond—were dramatically "performed" in
ceremonies of complete sexual and physical surrender. Punk slam and
pogo dancing guaranteed physical injury. The indiscriminate abuse of
drugs and alcohol common among the punks involved none of the
glamour and pretense to being cool commonly associated with mainstream rock and roll. Rather, substance abuse among the punks was pur-
poseful. It was a ritual of self-destruction; subsuming the self, not to the
commodity (as in conventional rock and roll), but to a senseless, stupid
culture revealed in a decaying urban environment where glamour, romance and petty teenage angst are comical and unacceptable.

A sense of desperation is captured in the music. And despite the   26
speed and volume of the songs, the lyrics are audible and (because
they are simplistic and repeated several times) comprehensible. In the
baiting, the heckling, the fistfights between band members and the
crowd, a kind of bizarre kinship is maintained. Club owner Brenden
Mullen called punk the folk music of the 1980's; and in the purest

---

[5]Pfeil, p. 286.

sense of the term "folk," he is right. For the appropriately initiated, the ritual nature of punk was far more significant than it has ever been or ever will be for mainstream rock and roll.

The cultural importance of popular music since the advent of rock   27
and roll some thirty years ago is the subject of a rather divergent debate. Some culture critics, here most notably the proponents of the Frankfurt School, cite the almost immediate commodification of rock and roll by "the culture industry." Just as "youth culture" surfaced as a critical term, the same 9–14 and 15–24 year olds became the principal media and consumer target groups. Other critics, many of them rock and roll historians like Robert Christgau, Greil Marcus and Dick Hebdige maintain arguments regarding rock and roll's unifying, even emancipatory function. Bernard Gendron summarizes this idealistic approach as follows: "...rock and roll's appearance at a particular juncture of class, generational and cultural struggle has given it a preeminent role among mass cultural artifacts as an instrument of opposition and liberation."[6]

In "On Popular Music" (first published in 1941) Theodor Adorno   28
juxtaposes mass market, assembly line commodity production with the "Tin Pan Alley culture industry" that "standardizes" popular music. By connecting popular music to factory production Adorno vents his rage against a popular culture industry that stupefies its audience. In punk, Adorno's fears regarding the repetitive and reductive tendencies of popular music are dramatically played out, but to a significantly different ideological effect.

Punk music is fast, loud and for the most part simplistic. The   29
songs seldom last more than a scant two minutes and are often indistinguishable from one another. LA punk bands like Black Flag and the Circle Jerks actually highlight the indistinguishability of their songs, allowing one number to run into (or over) another. This standardization, so abhorred by Adorno and so much a part of his critique of the culture industry, is in punk music part of a unifying ceremonial performance. For punk, musical and lyrical repetition bears a dramatic political and collective ritual import.

Punk music is simple enough and standard enough to consis-   30
tently incite violence and riot. In the purest sense punk, however politically confused on the surface, realizes the ever so elusive emancipatory popular culture so optimistically envisioned by Walter Benjamin and so skeptically lamented by Adorno, fellow Frankfurt School theorists Max Horkheimer and Herbert Marcuse, C. Wright

---

[6]Bernard Gendron, "Theodor Adorno Meets the Cadillacs," in *Studies in Entertainment*, ed. by Tania Modleski (Bloomington and Indianapolis: University of Indiana Press, 1986), p. 19.

Mills and Robert Warshow, who argues the following in his landmark study, *The Immediate Experience*:..."the chief function of mass culture is to relieve one of the necessity of experiencing one's life directly."[7]

However we view the function and significance of popular culture in America today, the issue of the specific ideological agenda of punk remains a difficult issue. The songs performed by X, Black Flag, the Circle Jerks, the Germs, Catholic Discipline and Fear often feature overtly political lyrics, but given the setting and performance the precise point is often obscure or paradoxical. Black Flag, for example, a band fronted by an Hispanic lead singer who lives in a gutted church, perform "White Minority," a fascist, racist rant made altogether paradoxical by the lead singer's ethnicity. Another of their songs, "Depression," heralds a conventional rock and roll sentiment, teenage angst, but with a clearly more angry and desperate subtext: "Got no friends/No girls want to touch me/I don't need your fucking sympathy."

X, the one LA punk band to achieve commercial success (by necessarily abandoning the movement) match high speed rhythms essential for pogo and slam dancing with ironic, black comic lyrics. Their best known song "Nausea," about vomiting blood after drinking too much is a classic rock and roll bar song with a shifted focus (to the morning after) and "Johnny Hit and Run Pauline," which uncritically tells of a violent rape fantasy, takes the mainstream rock and roll penchant for misogyny and sexual violence to graphic extremes. X, who were discovered by former Doors' member Ray Manzarek, also display a more self-conscious and ironic side with songs about Jacqueline Susann, "sex and dying in high society," and landlord tenant relations (in the classic, "We're Desperate," lyrics as follows: We're desperate/Get used to it/ We're desperate/It's kiss or kill.)

Exene, the lead singer of X who met fellow X member John Doe at a poetry workshop in Venice, argues that "the only performance that 'makes it' is the one that achieves total madness." Curiously, Exene's remark is a direct quote from the British New Wave film *Performance*, written and directed by Nick Roeg in 1970. In *Performance*, Rolling Stones' lead singer Mick Jagger plays a down and out rock and roll performer who finally decides that suicide is (on so many levels) the ultimate public act.

The LA punk bands all seem to share Exene's fixation with madness. In the late seventies the most interesting bands made their reputation by getting barred from one club or another for inciting riots. Black Flag, for example, introduce one of their numbers in *The Decline of Western Civilization* with the following: "This song is for the *L.A.P.D.* We got

---

[7]Robert Warshow, *The Immediate Experience* (New York: Athenium, 1970), p. 38.

arrested the other night . . . for playing punk rock music . . . they called it a public nuisance. This song is for them and it's called 'Revenge.'"

Since musicianship and professionalism are the trappings of   35
commercial rock and roll, many of the LA punk bands made a spectacle out of their own lack of musical talent. (In this too there are the seeds of a true egalitarian, proletarian art, supported by standardization and simplicity.) Here the Germs provide a most telling example. Germs' performances were never organized around songs but "gained meaning" from the bizarre ramblings and completely drug-altered behavior of their lead singer Darby Crash. As it may not have been evident at the time, Crash's on stage performance was a thinly veiled public suicide ritual. What had its perversely funny moments (Crash's habit for forgetting to sing into the microphone, for example) also had its darker side. Every Germs performance ended with Crash hurling himself limp-limbed into the audience. When he'd emerge he'd be effaced with magic marker drawings all over his face and chest, or worse, cut by a knife or piece of glass in the melee on the floor. When Crash died of a drug overdose at the height of his "fame," he became the movement's unlikely martyr, its rebel, its James Dean.

Though terms like "star" and "fame" were anathema to the   36
punks, Crash was the movement's best known figure—a kind of scene-maker who precisely because of his lack of true star qualities (charisma, attractiveness, wit, etc.) became a punk legend. His death, a familiar fate to so many punks who similarly abused drugs, seemed appropriate, like Dean's death (which so symbolized living fast and dying young to his teenage fans).

The Circle Jerks, whose "hits" include "Red Tape," "Beverly   37
Hills" (beginning with the lyrics: "Beverly Hills/Century City/everything/looks so pretty/all the people/look the same/don't they know they're fucking lame"), "I just Want Some Skank" and "Back Against the Wall" (featuring the chorus: "You can curse/spit/throw bottles . . . but it all ends with a swift kick in the ass") efface musicality and professional performance by standardizing their songs to lengths under sixty seconds. Every Circle Jerks' song reveals an identical chord pattern. One song simply begins as another ends. There are no refrains, no codas, no hooks and no payoff endings.

Catholic Discipline, a band founded by a charismatic, misplaced   38
Paris aesthete Claude Bessy, takes its name from graffiti found on the men's room wall in the Masque. Bessy's performance features a caustic harangue at the audience, which is typical of punk. "I just want (the audience) to hate me," Bessy says, "It makes me feel good." Bessy, like performance artist Sergio Premoli, fashions himself an artiste and his songs bear out an irreverent penchant for the mixed metaphor. Catholic Discipline's best known compositions are "Barbie Doll Love," chronicling Bessy's habit of fondling the famous doll in his pocket and

"Underground Babylon," featuring references to the Bible, DW Griffith's *Intolerance* and Kenneth Anger's *Hollywood Babylon*.

Of all the bands, Fear was the most provocative and charismatic.   39
Once featured on "Saturday Night Live," their performance was so savage and anarchic and their pogo dancing entourage so out of control that NBC executives forced the show's producer, Lorne Michaels, to cut to commercial long before the set was complete. Their front man, Lee Ving (now something of a film star after his role as a sleazy club owner in *Flashdance*), like Bessy, purposefully provoked the audience between numbers. His remarks were characteristically obscene and bitter and his disdain for public propriety was the kind of punk performance that "made it"—that achieved the madness of public outrage and riot.

In response to a heckler in *The Decline of Western Civilization*, Ving   40
shouts: "Next time don't bite so hard when I come." Preceding their final number in the film, Ving attacks the record industry: "If there are any A and R people out there, go die!" Ving is unapologetic and he is not ironic or parodic. When he mocks homosexuals ("We're from Frisco," he says hanging his wrist limply, "We think you're a bunch of queers..."), there is no liberal critical distance. When he says "You know why chicks have their holes so close together?...so you can carry them around like sixpacks," his disdain for public propriety is the point of his performance; it is the only real rationale for performance.

Fear's live set includes: "Beef Bologna" (revealing Ving's girl-   41
friend's taste with regard to cuts of meat), "Let's Have a War/So You Can Go Die" (Fear's answer to the population explosion), "I Don't Care About You/Fuck You," and the punk anthem "I Love Livin' in the City" (lyrics as follows: "My house smells just like a zoo/It's chock full of shit and puke/cockroaches on my walls/crabs are crawlin' on my balls/oh I'm so clean cut/ I just want to fuck some slut/ I love livin' in the city...suburban scumbags/they don't care/they just get fat/and dye their hair/I love livin' in the city.") Their performance in *The Decline of Western Civilization* closes with a satire of the national anthem: "O'er the land of the free/and the homos and Jews."

As a cultural artifact—as a cultural phenomenon—the LA punks   42
dramatically raise certain central questions regarding the relative autonomy of youth culture and the liberating potential of popular culture in general and rock and roll in specific. Bernard Gendron, deferring to the Birmingham School of Culture Theory, paraphrases Dick Hebdige when he writes: "One cannot understand the meaning of a rock and roll record without situating it within the youth cultures which typically consume it. In effect...the punks rewrite the recorded text...by recontextualizing it within their practices and rituals."[8]

---

[8]Gendron, p. 34.

Citing such a point of view in conjunction with Roland Barthes'   43
concept of a "readerly text," Gendron posits the following (familiar)
ideological conclusion: "If either the artist or the consuming public is
the primary creator of—meaning, then rock and roll does have the lib-
eratory power so often claimed for it."[9]

David E. James characterizes punk "as the final modernist capit-   44
ulation to decadence, irrationality and despair," and posits his argument, finally, in ideological (mass cultural), terms: "(Punk is) a
recalcitrant stance against the bland conformity of mass society."
James goes on to cite punk as "avant garde and populist,"[10] though
here his "progressive ideological" approach and desire to affix a
method to the madness that so dominated downtown LA in the late
seventies gets the better of him. Certainly punk has many of the qualities of an avant garde practice akin to the Dadaists and Surrealists,
though it is stretching things to view the LA of the late seventies as a
rebirth of the Paris of the 1920's. More obvious and telling are the unsettling parallels to Berlin circa 1925–1933.

By 1981 punk had all but vanished from the LA club scene. X ap-   45
peared on "American Bandstand" with Dick Clark and accepted a
major label record contract. The clubs that had made their reputations
on the riots incited by Fear, Black Flag and the other punk bands
began showcasing "safer" acts.

Punk's brief hold on a very unhappy segment of the urban LA   46
population testifies to a mass cultural conclusion made by Dana Polan
in "'Brief Encounters': Mass Culture and the Evacuation of Sense":
"…the new mass culture may operate by offering no models whatsoever, preferring instead a situation in which there are no stable values,
in which there are no effective roles that one can follow from beginning to end."[11] In such a scenario, all popular culture becomes part of
an intertextual spectacle in which punk was (at the very least) a very
significant and disturbing scene.

Examining the Text

1. According to Lewis, why did Sergio Premoli hoist a 120-pound
American flag on his back in the poshest shopping area of Beverly

---

[9]Gendron, p. 34.

[10]James, p. 131.

[11]Dana Polan, "Brief Encounters': Mass Culture and the Evacuation of Sense," in *Studies in Entertainment*, p. 182.

Hills (paragraph 5)? How might this artistic gesture be emblematic of the punk "aesthetic"?

2. What was the "literary style" of punk graffiti? By the author's account, how did punk graffiti influence other forms of popular writing, such as magazines? Do you continue to see this influence anywhere?

3. What was Teodor Adorno's primary objection to popular music (28)? How did punk rock support or refute Adorno's ideas about pop music?

For Group Discussion

As a group, make a list of ways in which punk music's influence might be evident in today's popular concerts, dances, and recorded music. Are punk's "contributions" to contemporary pop culture dead, or might they live on in some modified and updated form?

Writing Suggestion

The author contends that the LA punk movement reflected the "desperation residing at the heart of the now failed urban American dream" (2). In an essay, first explain how the "American dream" might be perceived as having "failed," citing economic and cultural examples as support for your thesis. Then discuss the ways in which popular music, including the punk movement, might reflect this failure, drawing upon your knowledge of various pop-music forms to support and develop your points.

Crossing Pop Lines:
Attention to Latinos Is Overdue,
But Sometimes Off-Target

Alisa Valdes-Rodriguez

According to a recent article in Time *magazine, "Ricky Martin is what's going on. The hip-shaking Latin pop star has the No. 1 song in America, 'Livin' la Vida Loca.' His self-titled new CD is setting sales records at stores across the U.S. And Martin is at the center of something bigger than himself." In this article, the author examines the media's portrayal of Puerto Rican pop star Martin—and other contemporary Latino pop stars in the country, such as vocalist Marc Anthony and actress-turned-pop-diva Jennifer Lopez—by using superheated adjectives such as "spicy" and "hip-shaking" to focus on their sexuality rather than their music. She concludes that the media's portrayal of these artists is not so "hot": that is, the media tend to put forth stereotypically one-dimensional depictions of the individuals in question, often at the expense of accurately portraying their music, individualized personalities, and ethnic heritage.*

Furthermore, says Valdes-Rodriguez, the media have a tendency to lump all Americans of Spanish-speaking descent into one heterogeneous category, or to identify certain artists as belonging to the wrong ethnic group. In short, reporters, critics and others ignore the complex backgrounds, allegiances, and social forces at play when they employ the umbrella term "Hispanics." While the author does not find this situation utterly hopeless, she does not suggest that remedying this situation would involve a dramatically heightened historical consciousness and a correspondingly increased complexity of thought ... qualities which, in her view, media purveyors seem not to be interested in developing. As you read, then, consider the preconceptions you bring to media portrayals of certain ethnic artists: do you accept the kinds of potrayals Valdes-Rodriguez describes as harmless, or do you agree with her indignation?

First, the well-known facts: Puerto Rican pop star Ricky Martin is   1
enjoying phenomenal success with his first English-language album, and more Latino pop artists, such as Enrique Iglesias, are vying to do the same. This has led the U.S. media—including a *Time* magazine cover story—to trumpet a new "Latin crossover phenomenon."

Now, the lesser-known facts.   2

One: Many of the so-called crossover artists are American by birth,   3
including Martin. But the pervasive impression in the media and in the culture at large is that these artists are exotic foreigners. Example? *USA Today* calling Martin's sounds "south-of-the-border," even though residents of his native Puerto Rico have been United States citizens since 1917, and the island's signature musical genre, salsa, was invented in the 1960s in a city south of the Connecticut border: New York.

Two: Even though in the pop music business "crossover" gener-   4
ally means switching genres, Martin's music—pop by any standards—has not changed, only the language he sings in. He is not, as some publications have posited, a salsa singer.

For Martin and others, the only real "crossover" is their lan-   5
guage; it's an unusual category, and one that French-speaking Canadian Celine Dion managed to avoid. Latinos, even those U.S.-born like Martin, are not afforded the same leeway.

Shakira, for example, is a Colombian rock singer whose style has   6
been compared to Alanis Morissette; her "crossover" album will consist of translations of rock songs she has recorded in Spanish. Enrique Iglesias sings syrupy ballads in the tradition of Air Supply; it's a formula that will likely work as well for him in English. And Martin's music,

while injected occasionally with percussive instruments, is no more or less "Latin" than that of, say, Puff Daddy, who also uses Spanish phrases.

All of this has led East Harlem's Marc Anthony, who records salsa   7
in Spanish and R & B dance music in English, to declare "crossover" irrelevant, venturing to say the term has only been applied to these artists because they are Latinos on the mainstream charts, not because they perform Latin music on the mainstream charts.

While no one denies that focusing the mainstream media spot-   8
light on Latino musicians and singers is overdue, the recent storm of coverage has exposed an abysmal ignorance about the complexity, diversity and reality of Latinos and Latin music.

Lost in the frenzy to cover "crossover" artists have been two sim-   9
ple facts: Latino artists do not necessarily perform in Latin music genres; and Latin music is not always performed by Latinos.

In the case of Jennifer Lopez, who is often lumped into this   10
nascent category, the only "crossover" is in the minds of a media establishment oblivious to the fact that she is a Bronx native who has recorded her debut album of commercial pop songs in her "native tongue": English. Yes, Lopez has two Spanish-language pop songs on the album, but artists from Madonna to Bon Jovi have been recording in Spanish for release in Latin America for years, and yet no one has called them crossover artists.

Beyond the assumptions about Latino Americans seeming some-   11
how foreign, there is another, more unsettling bit of stereotyping being done in the media about the new "crossover" stars.

Clichéd adjectives are used over and over in the mainstream press   12
in general but take on a different connotation when used to describe artists such as Martin, Lopez, Anthony and others. Words such as "hot," "spicy" and "passionate" are taken, one assumes, from the flavors of Mexican cuisine and outdated stereotypes of the "Latin lover."

Particularly upsetting is the media propensity to comment on   13
certain body parts when writing about Latino artists, namely hips and rear ends. *Entertainment Weekly* labeled Martin "hot hips." And the vast majority of stories on Lopez refer to her hind side. This is no mere coincidence; several academics have shown direct links between the view European settlers took of the American land and indigenous peoples, both of which were seen as wild, sexual and, in their view, in need of taming.

Speaking of hot: According to *Billboard* magazine, Ricky Martin   14
is a "hot tamale." This phrase appears several times, and is ridiculous because Martin hails from Puerto Rico, where the local cuisine includes neither chili peppers nor tamales, both of which come from Mexico. The recent *TV Guide* cover story on Martin made it only three paragraphs before calling the singer "spicy," and a few paragraphs later made reference to his wiggling hips.

According to the *New York Daily News,* Martin is "red hot," while   14
the *Atlanta Constitution* calls him "hot stuff." The *Seattle Times* says Martin is "incendiary" (gives them credit for consulting a thesaurus, at
least). The list goes on and on. Even the *New York Times* has not been immune to the stereotyping; the headline of its recent concert review of
Chayanne—a singer who appeared in the film "Dance With Me" alongside Vanessa Willilams and who has plans to release an English-only
album soon—read: Amor (Those Hips!) Pasion: (Those Lips!).

When it comes to Lopez, the coverage is even more troubling,   15
tainted with sexism and sexual innuendo in addition to ignorance.
Lopez was called "salsa-hot" by the *Hartford Courant.* Like Martin,
Lopez is Puerto Rican; once more, on that island, salsa is to be danced,
not eaten. The *New York Daily News* calls Lopez a "hot tamale." Even in
Canada the stereotypes, and mistakes, persist: The *Ottawa Citizen*
called Lopez "a hot-blooded Cuban."

Marc Anthony is so disgusted with the "heated" coverage he and   16
others are getting in the mainstream press—he has been called "red-
hot" by the *Boston Herald* and "white-hot" by the *New York Daily
News*—that he has started refusing to do some interviews. He jokingly
told his publicist that he will "jump off a bridge" if he is called "hot"
or "spicy" by one more publication.

TOO COMPLEX TO BE LUMPED AS "LATIN MUSIC"

To understand why this type of writing is so offensive, one must   17
be familiar with the complex reality of Latinos and the dozens of musical genres that have been lumped into the amorphous "Latin music"
category.

Most of the 30 million Latinos in the U.S. speak English as their
primary language. Beyond that, they are as racially and economically
diverse as the entire U.S. population. While many people continue to
believe that all Latinos are "brown," this is simply not true.

In fact, the history of the U.S. is parallel to that of Latin America: 18
The Native American inhabitants were "conquered" by Europeans;
many Native Americans were killed in the process, and Africans were
"imported" to replace them as slaves. Documents from slave ships
show that fully 95% of the Africans brought to the Americas as slaves
went to Latin America, according to historians.

Brazil is home to the largest African American population on   19
Earth, and five of every six Dominicans is of African descent. My father's birth was dedicated to the Yoruba god Obatala, as were those of
most other white kids in his neighborhood in Cuba; he has often said
that to be a Caribbean Latino is to be African, regardless of color.

At this moment, there are plenty of black Latinos succeeding in   20
mainstream American pop music, but few, if any, ever get mentioned

in the Latin crossover write-ups. In some instances, this is due to the artist's decision not to make his or her background known. But in other cases, as in the exclusion of R&B crooner Maxwell, who is half Puerto Rican, it's due mostly to reluctance on the part of both the English and Spanish media to include blacks in the discussion at all.

Pop singer Usher is half Panamanian. Other Puerto Ricans include TLC rapper Lisa "Left Eye" Lopes, "Ghetto Superstar" singer Mya—who has recorded in Spanish—and rappers Fat Joe and Big Pun. And Mariah Carey, who describes her father as a black Venezuelan and who routinely includes Spanish singles on her albums for import to Latin America, is also absent from the crossover discussion.   21

With one notable exception in the *New York Times* last month, merengue singer Elvis Crespo has been left out of the crossover equation too, even though he is probably the only Latin artist who currently qualifies in the traditional sense of the term. Crespo currently has two Spanish-language albums on the Billboard 200 mainstream chart.   22

Some music executives, including Sony Music Chairman and CEO Thomas D. Mottola, have said outright that they are excited about Martin and other crossover candidates because these artists fill the role of the white male pop star that has been vacant since the glory days of George Michael.   23

While a white Latino is just as Latino as a brown or black one, it unfortunately seems that in the world of American pop culture, Latinos are still only palatable as long as they appeal to a mainstream, Caucasian standard of beauty. Jennifer Lopez seems to have figured this one out: Her naturally wavy, dark brown hair has been lightened and straightened, and her once-fuller body has been whittled down by a fitness guru to something virtually indistinguishable from the lean, muscular Madonna.   24

All of this brings us to the ungainly truth no one seems to want to embrace in this country: Simply, there is no such thing as a singular "Latino," and efforts, no matter how well-intentioned, to classify 30 million racially, economically and educationally diverse individuals as one unit is ignorant—and irresponsible.   25

The term "Hispanic" was invented by the U.S. Census Bureau in the 1970s in order to classify a group of Americans ostensibly linked through a common language—Spanish. Hispanics, or Latinos, don't exist in Latin America where people identify themselves by nationality, class and race—just like here. "Latinos" have been invented in the U.S. for the convenience of politics and marketing, overlooking considerable cultural differences and complexity that can make your head spin.   26

Think about this: Much of what we call "Mexican food" today is really Native American food; the unifying "Latino" language, Spanish,   27 is a European import, just like English; the backbone of salsa music, the clave rhythm, comes from West Africa, as does merengue's two-headed tambora drum; Mexican norteno and banda music is rooted in Germany and Poland...but Cajuns in Louisiana who play essentially the same stuff in French are not Latinos. Got that?

Complexity! It is anathema to good capitalist marketing plans, which promise big bucks to whomever can lasso the elusive buyers of the world. And yet history is complex—all of ours—and journalists owe it to everyone to accurately chronicle the history of our world and one of its most powerful cultural forces: music.   28

We leave you with a sadly typical example of the comedy and tragedy of simplification of Latinos and Latin music. It happened, of all places, at a recent Los Angeles Dodgers game. As each Dodger goes to bat, the scoreboard lists personal facts, including the player's favorite band. A snippet from said band is then played over the loudspeakers. Two Dominican players both listed the New Jersey-based merengue group Oro Solido as their favorite. Yet when one came up to the plate, the folks in charge of the public address system chose instead to play...Ricky Martin!   29

To many a Dominican, the exchange of Martin for Oro Solido could be seen as a slap in the face; first, merengue is the official national dance of the Dominican Republic. Secondly, there is a long history of tension between Puerto Ricans and Dominicans over class and citizenship issues. In this context, replacing Oro Solido with Martin was not only ignorant, but possibly even insulting. But to know this means to study history. It means entertaining complex thought. And that, in a trend-driven pop culture obsessed with simple marketing categories and the almighty dollar, is apparently too much work.   30

Examining the Text

1. Explain the parallel Valdes-Rodriguez draws between the media's commenting on the "hips and rear ends" (paragraph 13) of certain Latino musicians and "the view European settlers took of the American land and indigenous peoples."

2. Why has East Harlem salsa and R & B musician Marc Anthony threatened to jump off a bridge if he is called "hot" or "spicy" in one more publication? What does he—and the author of this article—find particularly offensive in that portrayal?

3. What is the problem with lumping all Latinos together into one ethnic group or all Latin music into one genre, according to Valdes-Rodriguez?

4. What positive steps—as implied in the conclusion of this article—might one take to counteract the negative effects of ethnic stereotyping?

For Group Discussion

What are Valdes-Rodriguez's objections to the media's portrayal of Ricky Martin's hips and Jennifer Lopez's hind quarters, as presented in this article? In class discussion, explore the ways in which the media might focus on the nonartistic aspects (e.g., physical attributes) of other popular musicians, Latino and otherwise.

Writing Suggestion

In an essay, respond to the author's thematic position: that the media stereotype Latin artists and often portray their music and their cultural backgrounds inaccurately. Do you find more instances of this phenomenon occurring with certain "minority" groups, or do the media focus on the physical attributes of all musicians, regardless of ethnicity, in your opinion? Whatever position you end up taking with regard to this question, be sure to support your assertions with evidence based on your own experience with media artifacts, including television (such as MTV), magazines, newspapers, radio, and so forth.

Dreaming America

Danyel Smith

The following essay by Danyel Smith focuses on popular music as the embodiment of the urban experience in contemporary America. Smith creates a fictional character, "Ms. Hip Hop," a street-wise, fast-moving, musically attuned young woman who is more at home among the run-down buildings, the exhaust fumes and cutthroat characters of New York City than in the "big country town" of California. For Smith, Ms. Hip Hop—and by association, contemporary urban music—represents all that is compelling about the city. Using this character, Smith is able to contrast various aspects of modern life—the differences between city and country life, between Eastern and Western cities, between various ethnic groups, between cities past and present.

This piece first appeared in Spin *magazine, a nonacademic journal devoted to current trends in popular music. For that reason, Smith's article doesn't develop in the way that academic essays do. You will notice that it lacks a focused and coherent thesis statement; it doesn't proceed logically with each abstract point developed with evidence and examples, followed by the next, nor does it conclude with a neat thematic summation. Nevertheless, the article certainly does have a thesis, and it uses rich language to get that point across. As you read this piece, attempt to discover the creative ways in which Smith uses*

descriptions of Ms. Hip Hop to suggest meanings about the inner-city experi-
ence of New York City specifically and modern-day America generally.

The music is my life.

Is New York, New York, really the birthplace of hip hop? Is this   1
ultimate city—the preferred setting for most modern-day film fables—
the place where the seed took hold? Where the rhymes first flowed
and a culture took form? This compressed, dirty place, this mainstream cultural stronghold, is the steamy-hot/snowy region where a
generation found an identity, where all the shit went down?

It's where DJ Scott LaRock died and Slick Rick went to prison.   2
Where Run found Christ and Griff got dismissed. Where sneakers became the rule and not the exception: where Latifah grew Treach, and
where the Guru *squoze* hip hop out of Bird's horn.

And here she is, Ms. Hip Hop, generic girl-fan. In that place. The   3
city. Looking around for the elusive ticket, the line, the string that tied
it all together and turned the music into a thing, a movement—music.

She is a native Californian in New York for the third time. She   4
never stays long. She always flies back West, over the mountains and the
lakes, relieved when she sees Lake Tahoe, ecstatic when she spots the
Golden Gate Bridge, its yawning red span as welcoming as a familiar
mouth upturned in a smile. Then she knows she is in California, a sub-
division of the U.S.A. as long and thin as she would like to be—a huge
state broken up into sprawling counties, the seductively warm state she
calls her home. California has its glories, and it holds on tight to its trophies—the Eagles, Sly and the Family Stone, Jefferson Airplane, Tower
of Power. But as grand and forthright as Cali hip hop is circa 1993—the
Coup, Snoop Dogg, Souls of Mischief—in the East lay the lungs and
heart of hip hop and so the West holds court in its long shadow.

Tommy Boy president Monica Lynch asked, "Has New York   5
fallen the fuck off?" a long time ago, like maybe it would jar East Coast
B-boys and -girls into action. But to no avail. The cast pumps hip hop
blood, but out West are the sinewy appendages, out West is where
folks are walking and talking it.

New York beckons, though, like an old buddy with gossip, like a   6
preacher who just might know the Truth. The buildings are older, the
street fumes stronger, every other car is a taxi. The periodicals seem
vital, seem to have more than a tenuous connection to the city. The trains
hiss and moan and chug. The place is cutthroat, envious, and mean.
Pleasantries are hoarded like money and doled out without enthusiasm.
California is one big country town compared with Manhattan and the
surrounding boroughs. California piles on big-city makeup in L.A. and

Oakland, San Diego and San Francisco—but really, the place is spread out like a big cabbage farm, like the far-flung desert it is.

But cabbage farm or no, in urban southern California, even a 7 mostly middle-class Catholic schoolgirl like Ms. Hip Hop knows which neighborhood is blue and which is red. She knows when to hit the asphalt in the parking lot of Shakey's or Astro Burger because boys are shooting bullets in the air or at certain cars because their varsity hoop squad lost. Or because they won.

She remembers when "urban" didn't have a negative connota- 8 tion, when urban meant of or having to do with a city or a metropolis. She remembers when "city" didn't mean dank and dark and poor. She vaguely recalls when black people weren't automatically associated with cities and urbanity. She's read about it, about when African-Americans lived mostly on farms and in the "country" and in the South. Arrested Development's Speech reminisces about that era in "Tennessee." Making myth of the post-sharecropping era and country life, he talks convincingly, painfully about climbing the trees his fore-fathers hung from. It sounds so cleansing and sad and fine. Just as American black people are automatically associated with cities and all of their ills, Speech wants the old life, the old values, the old ways—back to the earth. To being "natural." As if that state—"naturalness"—is an option at this point in Western civilization.

The Catholic schoolgirl, the smart hip hop girl—she is ever anx- 9 ious for peace for her people and her own state of mind. She wildly reaches for this "oldness," this better way of being. But even as a mindset, while she stands on the streets of New York or West Los An-geles or Fresno or Kettleman or Napa, California—it doesn't work. Im-ages of wooden porches and backyard cornstalks, or roosters pecking and kente cloth flowing, the brightly painted pictures in her desperate imagination fade like a mirage in an old cartoon: quickly and com-pletely in its place are frowns and guns, televisions and straightened hair, housing projects and stucco single-family homes. Fast cars and loud music. Hip hop MC Breed and Too Short. Onyx and Ice Cube.

Still she looks for hip hop's heart in New York City, believing she 10 can find it, thinking naively that if she sees it, she could define it and the definition would make a difference in all that she sees, in all that her mind conjures and remembers. So she presses on.

Examining the Text

1. Smith describes New York City as the place "where sneakers be-came the rule and not the exception; where Latifah grew Treach, and where the Guru *squoze* hip hop out of Bird's horn" (paragraph 2). Explain the references to sneakers, Latifah, the word *squoze*, and Bird.

2. When Smith says "out West are the sinewy appendages, out West is where folks are walking and talking it" (5), what does she mean by "it"? What does this statement suggest about the shift in geographic influence in the current hip-hop world?

3. What is the significance of the statement "even a mostly middle-class Catholic schoolgirl like Ms. Hip Hop knows which neighborhood is blue and which is red" (7)? What is the point of this image of the "Catholic schoolgirl" in the rest of the essay?

For Group Discussion

As a group, describe Ms. Hip Hop as she is portrayed by Smith, listing as many descriptive words and phrases as you can. Having described this character at some length, discuss as a class the function this character serves for Smith as she develops her ideas about hip-hop.

Writing Suggestion

Smith says that California is "spread out like a big cabbage farm, like the far-flung desert it is" (6), a fact which is reflected in the music that comes out of that area. Write an essay that describes a geographical area, ideally one with which you are quite familiar, focusing on locally popular music as a central feature in your description.

ADDITIONAL SUGGESTIONS
FOR WRITING ABOUT POPULAR MUSIC

1. Americans receive a great deal of information about important issues—for example, presidential elections, gender-role attitudes, the legalization of drugs—from popular music and the media that purvey it. Write an essay in which you examine the representation of one important social issue or problem through music. For instance, you might focus on how AIDS is represented in recent song lyrics, on AM and FM radio stations, and in videos and advertisements on channels such as MTV and VH1.

2. Write a essay modeled after "All the Rage" by Michael Crowley, in which you first construct a detailed description of a band whose music you know very well, and then analyze the themes embodied in that band's songs. Discuss the effects the band's music has on its listeners and some possible reasons for the band's popularity or lack thereof with mainstream listeners.

3. Imagine that you've recently arrived in the United States; you turn on the television and find yourself watching an hour of programming on MTV. Based on this one hour of viewing, write a description of the interests, attitudes, lifestyles, and customs of young Americans. Try to include information that you gather from everything you've seen during that hour—the videos, game shows, advertisements, promos for upcoming shows, and so on—and make sure that you render your descriptions in vivid detail, so that somebody from another country might visualize all the elements you describe.

4. Write an essay in which you discuss the relative advantages and disadvantages of the three primary sources of popular music: television, radio, and record albums or compact discs. Which one of the three do you think most effectively conveys the messages intended by contemporary recording artists, and why? Which source do you think trivializes the music, turning it into a popular product without redeeming social relevance? What are the advantages and disadvantages of each pop-music source?

Internet Activities

1. Visit the Web sites of some diverse musicians (possible options are available on the *Common Culture* Web site). Write an essay describing these sites. What features do these Web sites offer? What differences/similarities can you note in the presentations of the different musical genres? How would you account for these differences/similarities? For instance, is there anything offered on a Web site devoted to a rock group that isn't available on a jazz Web site? Are the Web site's features indicative of the genre in any way; that is, do the form/appearance/layout of the site mirror the musical genre it presents?

2. With the advent of various forms of media on the Web, such as radio broadcasts and videos, music has a new forum to reach an immediate, worldwide audience. Explore some sites that offer music from across the country and the world (options are available at the *Common Culture* Web site). Once you have sampled a diverse selection of music, write an essay categorizing and/or describing your findings. How is the availability of music on the Web changing how listeners access music and what they listen to? What type of music is available? Are any musical types represented more heavily than others? Are any music genres woefully lacking, in your opinion? How would you account for this representation (or lack thereof)?

5

Cyberculture

"I don't understand #11...
*Thou shalt not be obscene
on the Internet."*

Computer culture—in the form of electronic mail, word processing, the World Wide Web, "cyberpunk," arcade-style games, chat
rooms, hypertext, digital multimedia, and on and on—is no longer
merely an emerging phenomenon; it has become driving force in contemporary America and the world. In fact, computers have become so
much a part of our lives that the social conventions surrounding computers have taken on the importance of Biblical commandments, as
suggested by the above cartoon.

Furthermore, the bewildered attitude of the cartoon "Moses" indicates that computer technology, and the culture surrounding it,
evolves with such rapidity that many (or perhaps most) people find
themselves confused, awash in a white-noise sea of nagging questions:
what is the meaning of those weird terms—gigabytes and baud rates
and MOOs and flaming—that tech-nerds use; is nonlinear writing, as

modeled by the World Wide Web and other hypertext-formatted documents, really going to replace traditional expository writing, with its linear, logical, structure; will the average individual need to be fully computer literate to survive and even prosper in the economy of the next millennium; how will the computer redefine people's notions of work, leisure time, and social interaction; how will the aesthetic worlds of music and visual art be influenced by the continuing use of computer technology; and will "virtual reality"—the real-time, interactive, computerized simulation of sensory experiences—become a practical reality in succeeding decades? This chapter, by exploring some specialized topics within the broad area of computer culture, and by providing a "casebook" on computer-aided "virtual communities," will suggest answers to many of those questions.

The first half of this chapter deals with some relatively controversial issues relating to computer culture. Jessica Heland, in "Digital Soup," explores the emerging technology of interactive media, attempting to discover whether computerized narrative will emerge as a viable alternative to traditional storytelling methods. Gary Chapman's "Flamers: Cranks, Fetishists and Monomaniacs" studies and posits some social theories about those individuals who use the e-mail and computerized chat groups as a means of expressing rage or indulging erotic obsession. Joshua Quittner, in his "Free Speech for the Net: A Panel of Federal Judges Overturns the Communications Decency Act," discusses the social implications of pornography on the Internet, specifically with regard to questions of regulation and censorship. Finally, the last article in the first half of the chapter, McKenzie Wark's "Cyberpunk—Subculture or Mainstream?" examines a new form of literature and the accompanying subcultural movement, known as "cyberpunk."

The second half of this chapter explores the phenomenon of "virtual communities"—the chat rooms, "multi user dungeons," mailing lists, and other virtual gathering places that constitute a large portion of the Internet. With nothing more than a computer and a modem, people can congregate electronically with others who share an interest in every topic imaginable, from skateboards to romance novels to rubber undergarments. In virtual communities people meet to converse, to give and get advice, to find romance, to share their joy or vent their rage, to play games: the same activities that people undertake in real-world communities, but without the constraints of geography or time. The authors of two essays in this section—John Perry Barlow and Sherry Turkle—offer opinions as to whether the trend toward computer-aided community is a healthy one. Some suggest that it's a dehumanizing influence, drawing time and attention away from real human contact, while other contend that computer-based interaction makes up for the lack of community spirit in contemporary America by providing opportunities for meaningful human contact. The other two essays in this section focus on problems that specific groups of people face in gaining access to the Internet and feeling welcome there. Colin Beckles describes the barriers that constrain African Americans from fuller participation on the Internet, while L. Jean Camp and Anita Borg describe an Internet community called Systers that is exclusively for women. These two articles make it clear that we need to consider the demographics of virtual communities: who's invited to join, who's excluded, and why.

Given that computers and virtual relationships will certainly become more prevalent and influential in the years ahead, you might take the readings in this chapter as an invitation and opportunity to reflect on your attitudes about and level of involvement in computer culture. In what ways have computers influenced your life already, and how do you imagine they will affect you personally and professionally in the next century?

Life on the Internet

Digital Soup

Jessica Heland

When you first read the novel Catcher In the Rye, *how easy was it for you to relate to Salinger's protagonist, Holden Caulfield? Did you feel you understood his motivations and ambivalent impulses? Would the novel have been more comprehensible had someone altered it so that you could observe the events of the story and its complex protagonist from a number of different perspectives...or so that you could even participate in the story? In this essay, Jessica Heland describes the concept of "interactive media" as an alternative to traditional storytelling technique and practice.*

Various forms of interactive media—from choose-your-own-plot computerized mystery games to hypertextual fiction that encourages the reader to follow any number of narrative threads—have become a viable late twentieth-century outlet for literary distribution and consumption. By displaying literary works on a computer screen, the reader has the option of passing on her or his own perspective of the text by altering its narrative structure. It is the challenge of the media designers, says Heland, "to mediate this interaction," to design interactive, computer-aided stories that deliver satisfaction equal to the traditional narrative in novels, plays, and films.

Heland compares and contrasts the conventions of classical storytelling with the advantages of interactive media for both the participants and the designers. While different perspectives may help to spice up the text or convey a better understanding of the original, there exists some concern over corrupting the original text in the case of original works that are adapted to a more interactive, computer-based access. Furthermore, the advent of "hypertext," written language that contains "hot" word-links (the World Wide Web being the most prevalent forum for this kind of hypertextual writing), makes storytellers consider audience participation in the literary process: where reading used to be a relatively passive activity, hypertextual writing makes the reader a much more active participant in the story.

As you read, consider your own novel-reading and movie-viewing habits. Do you find it relaxing and satisfying to be passively "manipulated" by a writer's or filmmaker's carefully plotted story, or would you prefer a more participatory narrative experience, as hypertextual writing promises to deliver?

Over dinner recently, my mother recounted a passage from *The* 1
Alexandria Quartet. She had read the book twice, though not recently;
still her face lit up as she cited certain key moments—the names of
characters, descriptions of settings, memorable fragments of her own
reading of this text. Her detailed recollections were delivered with enthusiasm and delight, a testament to the evocative durability of
Lawrence Durrell's epic tale.

It occurred to me that I had never heard anyone describe an ex- 2
perience with interactive media in quite the same way. What is it that
makes a story memorable? This book clearly meant something to my
mother. And even had Durrell not structured the four volumes of the
Quartet to be read in any order—an early, and by contemporary standards, crude, experiment in interactivity—I suspect she would have
derived the same pleasure from the novels. Her references were personal, idiosyncratic; her interpretations specific to her own life experience. By rereading the story years later, she had further enriched her
enjoyment of its narrative, characters, and unusual dimensions.

One of the great promises of fiction is its ability to do precisely 3
this: to transport us to a different time and place, an alternative
"space" in which we make silent observations, casting ourselves inside
a story's domain. We often experience a trip to the movies in a similar
way. Captive in a darkened room, we find the immense scale of the
screen exorcises any dueling reality, leaving our focus streamlined and
our attention riveted.

Does this kind of mesmerizing interaction demand immense 4
scale and total darkness in order to succeed? Or can interactive technologies—and their designers—hope to achieve a similar goal?

Up until very recently, "interactivity" with the screen has been 5
primarily a consequence of seeing and responding to a moment observed. For over a century, it has remained the role of the writer, director, and cinematographer (and, on occasion, designer) to render time
through plot and character, sound, motion, and image. As technology
grew to support greater complexity in filmmaking, so, too, did the experience of responding to the screen expand to elicit in us a variety of
reactions: pain, laughter, fear, terror, anticipation, excitement. The
public's continued love affair with the movies is a reminder of the enduring power of the screen as an engaging, seductive, even hypnotic
medium.

As we struggle to reconcile our conflicting reactions to informa- 6
tion overload, the dramatic and dynamic model of filmic storytelling
offers a more compelling way to think about the power of visual narrative. From scene to sequence, montage to mise-en-scene, visual stag-
ing on the screen has a long and distinguished history. Why has this

rich legacy been virtually ignored in the design and development of interactive, screen-based media?

The growth of the consumer electronics market over the last   7
decade has introduced opportunities for designers ranging from on-air graphics to video games to a host of digitally engineered products and information services. All require a skill known as interface, or more appropriately, interaction design. Led (and quite often restricted) by current technology, electronic media have generated their own visual vocabulary largely as a reductive pictorial syntax, an ironic casualty of late-20th-century Modernism taken to an infographic extreme. Efforts to make complex information accessible have resulted in a global language of sterile, stilted iconography. We are overrun by miniature hieroglyphs featuring cartoon-like facsimiles of task-driven processes: file folders and trashcans and, most recently (and to my mind, lamentably), emoticons. In earlier columns, I have discussed what critic Andrew Olds dubs an "ideogrammatic mode of organization," expressing my own dissatisfaction with the desktop legacy: the icon-driven graphical language that is, to date, the dubious esthetic hallmark of the so-called computer age.

Today, these intransigent emblems of consumer technology offer   8
little leeway for expressing the greater complexities introduced by dynamic, time-based media. Better to look at the narrative models suggested by screens other than the computer: most notably, the silver one.

For the better part of this century, the designer's contribution to   9
film has resided largely in the creation of title sequences. Like the shaping of information on a package or book jacket, titles are critical to our immediate perception of the underlying content. They bespeak, in a sense, the film's corporate identity. Uniting form and content, they are uniquely, critically connected to our immediate responses, responses that are reflected in box office receipts and Oscar nominations and, ultimately, the economic livelihood of the movie industry as a whole.

Yet even given some of the more inspired examples—Saul Bass'   10
Man with the Golden Arm, R. Greenberg's *Superman*—titles dwell at the physical peripheries of films themselves. Ultimately, their role lies somewhere between promotion and propaganda. Their principal duty is to introduce functional information rooted in contractual imperatives: Billing and credits are serious business, particularly if you're the star and you have an agreement stipulating that your name precede the title of the film itself. From this perspective, the design challenge becomes a strategic mediation between storytelling and story selling.

This is not to minimize the impact titles can and should have on   11
a film's identity and on the introduction of film narrative. Like any other design process, the design of titles requires the ability to understand and translate content into a dynamic form that is at once suitable

and surprising. There is a choreographic component to all of this that demands attention to the relationship between visual and aural stimuli, matching representative sequences to cuts from the film's soundtrack, for instance.

The design of titles, however, is a highly controlled process. 12 More and more, as we enter a world where viewers, not designers, control the dissemination of information, we must remodel the kind of thinking that once drove such one-way design decisions. With interaction comes choice, followed invariably by chaos unless "good design" intervenes in the form of navigational support.

Actually, that's not true. 13

Interaction design is not only information design: It demands 14 more comprehensive thinking involving cognitive, spatial, and ergonomic considerations. As content of ever-growing complexity finds its way into the electronic sphere, design challenges for shaping that content will demand more than mere attention to directional clarity. Like the cinematic model cited earlier, successful visual communication will depend on our understanding of narrative, audience, and drama.

The classic Aristotelian definition of narrative—a story that has a 15 beginning, a middle, and an end—is freshly challenged with each new wave of critical theory and more and more admits the reader's role as collaborator in the narrative process, co-inventing text in the very process of consuming it. A contemporary perspective on storytelling that may be relevant to the practice of interaction design is described by design critic Hamett Nurosim, who posits "the presentation of an event or a sequence of events that are connected by subject matter and related by time and space." His own bifurcated analysis suggests a deconstruction of narrative that distinguishes between "storyteller" and "story." The early-20th-century novelist D. H. Lawrence held a more conservative view that raises potentially relevant questions about the roles of author and audience. "Trust the tale," wrote Lawrence, "not the teller."

Lawrence's loyalty to the narrative, though commendable, may 16 soon become obsolete. What happens when the story, by virtue of its distribution in a digital environment, becomes infinitely changeable? In time-based media, we no longer have control over hierarchical relationships. Stories don't necessarily have a beginning, middle, and end. Communication is no longer rhetorical. How do we design for such perpetual and unpredictable interruption?

If each viewer becomes a de facto storyteller, can we still main- 17 tain the integrity of authorship, the focus of plot, the particular cadences of a writer's voice and point-of view? As interactive technologies grow more sophisticated and complex, we are witnessing the emergence of a kind of shared authorship in which the linear parameters of classic narrative structure may no longer apply.

If, as designers, we are asked to consider the permutations of a   18
story, our role typically involves making the abstract visually concrete.
We think in terms of point and counterpoint, word and image, pacing
and sequencing, cropping and juxtaposing. With dynamic media,
however, we must devise new methods for understanding stories in
multiple layers.

One of these layers, of course, is visual. Another is textural. An-   19
other is informational. Still another is dramatic. There is time and motion and sound to be considered, and finally, there is "hypertext"—the
ability to link ideas and images—which redefines the message transmitted, by virtue of its connection to the message received.

The interpretive flexibility inherent in such new media suggests   20
that point-of-view is itself a powerful narrative tool. Consider Akira
Kurosawa's classic 1951 film, *Rashomon*. Here, the spine of the story consists of a single crime represented through the "viewpoints" of various
characters. Within this tapestry of perspectives, our attention is riveted
by the telling of each individual tale: multiple points of entry with a singular plot line. Each character in the film is an eyewitness: So, too, are we.

The concept of the eyewitness is central to thinking about the   21
new visual narrative. It places the emphasis on the viewer, the end
user. It values the power of individual observation over the one-
sidedness of oration, and, in so doing, makes the experience of viewing that much more memorable. The audience, central to this
interaction, is the protagonist.

The designer's challenge, then, is to mediate this interaction.   22
Film director Sergei Eisenstein, who was trained as an engineer and
architect, described his responsibility as a visual storyteller as a "con-
trapuntal (method) combining visual and aural images." His ultimate
goal was to reduce this complexity to a "common denominator" on behalf of what he considered to be a singular audience. Though perhaps
no longer applicable in today's climate of media convergence, Eisenstein's goal of representing the intricacies of human experience
through a carefully articulated armature of audiovisual phenomena
remains a timeless model for study.

With today's interactive products comes a revised definition of au-   23
dience: No longer passive, theirs is a new kind of authority, offering enhanced choice as well as enhanced participation. This emphasis on
participation remains the most compelling aspect of interactive technologies, yet jeopardizes our classic understanding of narrative form.
The structural disturbances introduced by true interpersonal interaction
force us to rethink the rules and conventions of classic storytelling. Will
such audience participation breed chaos, or even contempt?

Such random, wanton "choice" may not, in the end, be a neces-   24
sary incentive to viewer interest. The screen is and has always been an

inmersive medium. In the movies, our participation may be physically passive, but visually and, psychologically, we have always been riveted because of the medium's evocative capacity to draw us in. This remains one of the most enduring legacies of film, and one today's interactive "screen" designers would do well to consider.

Examining the Text

1. What does Heland mean when she describes traditional narrative's ability "to transport us to a different time and place, an alternative 'space'"? (paragraph 3). How does this statement relate to the author's thesis about the new, interactive narrative structures? Does hypertextual writing, according to the author, have the same power to transport the reader?

2. What point does Heland hope to convey to the reader when she says(5): "As technology grew to support greater complexity in filmmaking so, too, did the experience of responding to the screen expand to elicit in us a variety of reactions: pain, laughter, fear, terror, anticipation, excitement? If pain, laughter, fear, terror, and so on, are feelings elicited by advancements in filmmaking, what do you suppose will be the reactions to similar advancements in other multimedia outlets? In the long run, does interactive media technology represent a positive or negative advancement, according to Heland?

3. Heland says of the position of the interactive media audience, "No longer passive, theirs is a new kind of authority, offering enhanced choice as well as enhanced participation"(23). She then goes on to say that such reader participation "jeopardizes our classic understanding of narrative form"(23). What is the problem with interactive media, according to the author? Is there a possibility that traditional narrative structures will become extinct, or will people always be drawn to the classic Aristotelian plot, that is, "a story that has a beginning, a middle, and an end"(14)?

For Group Discussion

When comparing the classic Aristotelian definition of storytelling to the newer, interactive narrative structure, Heland emphasizes "the reader's role as collaborator in the narrative process, co-inventing text in the very process of consuming it." How does the role of the reader of interactive media differ from the role of the reader of classic narrative? Consider Heland's first paragraph of the article: how does the idea of an interactive reader relate to the way her mother responded to the novel series she loved so much, Durrell's *Alexandria*

Quartet? Describe as concretely as possible your own responses to your favorite movie or Stephen King novel: how do those pop culture artifacts make you feel? Do you believe it would be possible for interactive stories to elicit the same responses—or other, equally gratifying responses—in you?

Writing Suggestion

In an essay, answer Heland's question "What happens when the story, by virtue of its distribution in a digital environment, becomes infinitely changeable?" In other words, in what specific ways do you believe interactive media will change storytelling? You might begin your paper by explaining why the Aristotelian plot model, as described by Heland, has remained successful all these years: what basic human needs does it satisfy? Then, after developing several paragraphs that catalog the narrative changes you believe interactive media will bring about in subsequent decades, you might go on to construct an argument for or against interactive media. Based on your own experience as reader and viewer, do you welcome the advent of interactive technology? Why or why not?

Flamers: Cranks, Fetishists and Monomaniacs

Gary Chapman

When it comes to the Internet, there seems to exist a broad range of participants in this relatively new form of communication. Some people abhor technological "advances," such as e-mail or online chat groups, and either avoid them altogether or engage in them grudgingly, because it's what everybody else is doing. Other people enjoy sharing electronic discussion with friends or individuals who have mutual interests: surfing, collecting Barbie dolls, guitar-playing, organic gardening, whatever. At the far end of the spectrum, however, there are increasing numbers of individuals who have developed a psychological dependence on various forms of computer-aided communication. Many of these people, according to Chapman, have begun to use the Internet as a forum for venting their frustrations or sexual obsessions—with the result that many former participants are gradually losing interest in participating in Internet-based forms of communication.

Phenomena such as "flame wars"—the ranting diatribes of hate-filled individuals—along with growing numbers of adolescents posing as sexually experienced adults, middle-aged men representing themselves as young girls, bigots, homophobes, women-haters, and militia fanatics have all added to the depreciation of a potentially civilizing, democratic communication system.

Chapman laments this trend in Internet culture, because he views the Net as a potential factor in harmonizing diverse cultures. He hopes that more rational minds will prevail with respect to computer-based communication; in his words, "If we can treat each other with respect over e-mail, we may go a long way toward solving some of the basic dilemmas of democracy."

As you read, *think about whether or not Chapman's hope for social courtesy and democratic salvation is possible today. How can the Internet help bring people together? Conversely, how can it serve as a means of driving wider wedges between individuals and subcultural groups? Finally, consider your own position on Net-based communication: what are your personal feelings about facilities such as e-mail and chat groups, both as conveniences and as agents for social harmony or disruption?*

A joke floating around the Internet: Q: How many Internet contributors does it take to change a light bulb? A: What are you trying to say, you worthless, scumbag jerk? Computer networks are increasingly hyped as a new medium of virtuous democratic and social discourse, the cyber version of the Acropolis. A *Time* magazine reviewer recently called the Internet "the ultimate salon" of conversation, and *The Utne Reader* is promoting "electronic salons" to soothe the anomie and coarseness of contemporary life. Author Howard Rheingold has celebrated the "virtual community" as a source of solace and fraternity, and columnist David Broder has written paeans to the new spirit of civic participation allegedly found on computer networks.   1

Electronic conversations—if that's what they are to be called—on the Internet and various other computer networks such as America Online, Prodigy and CompuServe, are certainly a new and interesting feature of American social life and manners. The terabytes of gab on these systems, engaging millions of people, are perhaps the first display of the direct voice of the American people in an ongoing, semi-organized, public forum. People are talking about everything under the sun—politics, pet care, even deliberate gibberish. Consequently, politicians, pollsters, reporters, marketers and social analysts are keenly interested in what our fellow citizens are thinking and saying on-line. Electronic conversations, to our benefit, allow people to circumvent the managed public dialogue that politicians and P.R.-types try to shape to serve their own ends.   2

But the evidence of public virtue in cyberspace is so far more discouraging and alarming than noble and salutary. Electronic salons already contain broken furniture and have mud on their walls. The notorious phenomenon of "flaming"—issuing a nasty and often profane diatribe—is now a familiar sociological curiosity. UseNet news groups—open, topical conversations accessible over the Internet and   3 other systems—have become vast libraries of pyrotechnic insults. Mark Dery, editor of a new book, *Flame Wars,* offers a few choice examples: "You syphilitic bovine harpy." "You heaving purulent mammoth." "You twitching gelatinous yolk of rancid smegma." You get the idea. Many retorts are merely terse, obscene snarls, but Internet users have also developed a competition in rococo, smart-alecky taunts, such as this one: "Your reply was most impressive. You seem to have the ability to respond to e-mail with either profanity, inanity or pointless threats of physical violence. Why don't you try those pills the doctor gave you, and take a nice long rest. It may do you no good, but I am sure the remainder of the viewers would be pleased by the absence of your moronic and asinine diatribes." It's hard to imagine such exchanges at a PTA meeting or a cocktail party. Electronic communication is providing a disturbing glimpse of what may be smoldering, heretofore unsaid, in the minds of many Americans.

More generally, electronic conversations appear to be prone misinterpretation, sudden and rapidly escalating hostility between participants, and a weird kind of implosion when the conversants express their anger with sulking silence. This may be because, unlike in face-to-face conversation, there are no visual cues, what linguist Peter Farb calls "paralanguage." It may also be because people who are completely removed from one another physically can assault each other verbally without fear of bodily harm, a suggestion that our evolutionary heritage is still at work in restraining our behavior in everyday encounters. 4

Electronic anonymity also encourages fantasy life, often tilting toward the dark side. Dedicated network denizens frequently inhabit alter egos attached to their computer names. Some computer users have identities in cyberspace that correspond to exotic names, such as Phreak or Acid, two well-known hacker monikers, rather than to their prosaically named real-world personae. While a middle-class, suburban white man may tend not to adopt a nom d'ordinateur, millions of electronic Walter Mittys nationwide do take on a more aggressive personality behind a computer and a modem—ferociously pouring out their otherwise sublimated middle-class angst. 5

A cyberspace alter ego often goes beyond a new name and a release of inhibition. Network users lie, sometimes spectacularly. Pavel Curtis, a Xerox researcher who runs a fascinating Multi-User Dimension (or MUD)—a kind of a "virtual world" within the Internet with its own simulated geography, characters and interactions—reports that a significant portion of people logging into his system switch genders for the identities they assume. Most common are young men who portray themselves as women; indeed, it's become a rule of thumb that any sexually aggressive female on this mud is really a man. Peter Lewis, *The New York Times*'s cyberspace reporter, tells a story about a man who conducted a protracted and intimate electronic romance 6 over the Internet with a pen pal, who said she was a 26-year-old graduate student. When he met her in person, he learned that she was in fact a 13-year-old girl.

As the French discovered in their national Minitel system, sex 7
often dominates electronic encounters. The majority of messages on Minitel have been advertisements for sex or sex talk, and, national character notwithstanding, Americans are no slackers in this regard. Computer communication seems to bring out the id screaming for attention. In February, a University of Michigan student, Jake Baker, was arrested for posting to the university's computer network a graphic fantasy of the rape, torture and murder of a fellow student; though such stories are common on a few news groups, Baker actually named his victim, which police interpreted as a threat. A reporter for *Computer Life* magazine posed on the Internet as a 15-year-old cheerleader and got more than thirty e-mail messages of a sexual nature, including requests for her panties and her telephone number. Harassment of women is so common that women often pretend to be men to avoid sexually suggestive e-mail.

Bigotry and misogyny are prevalent as well. As Amy Harmon 8
noted recently in *The Los Angeles Times,* bigots are showing up on computer networks with increasing frequency because they can't get a hearing anywhere else. Networks are a cheap means for white supremacists and neo-Nazis to get their hate messages to thousands of people at once. The Simon Wiesenthal Center has protested to Prodigy about frequent anti-Semitic rants on that system. Prodigy officials are caught, to their embarrassment, in a tug-of-war between freedom of speech and the basic civilities that many users expect.

Finally, the general quality of the rhetoric on the Internet is dis- 9
couraging in itself. Even without all the cranks, poseurs, charlatans, fetishists, single-issue monomaniacs, sex-starved lonely hearts, mischievous teenagers, sexists, racists and right-wing haranguers many participants in unstructured Internet conversations have little of interest to say but a lot of room in which to say it. Goofy opinions and comical disregard for facts are rampant. Spelling is haphazard and even simple typos sometimes produce absurd flaming firefights. Nearly every reasonable discussion is sooner or later discovered by someone with a hobby horse or an abrasive personality or both, and there are few reliable ways to shunt such people elsewhere. It's pretty clear, too, that quite a few messages come from people who must be drunk; there are as yet no sobriety checkpoints on the "information superhighway." The new electronic Acropolis seems to foster rhetoric stylistically closer to Beavis and Butt-head than to Pericles.

Fifteen years ago, the forerunner of the Internet, the Arpanet, 10
was used almost exclusively by top computer scientists and other elite engineers and scientists, who tend to be a refined bunch, partial to

classical music and good books. Many are now appalled by what networking has become. Some have dropped off the net altogether.

This suggests that the Internet may be on a path similar to that followed by television and other communications media: the introduction of the masses so alienates well-educated, cosmopolitan people that they abandon the medium or resort to a specialized class of cultural material that advertises its disdain for mass tastes. There are already signs that this is happening on the Internet: while veterans of the net have tended to narrow their presence to a select group of exclusive and low-profile mailing lists, more recent users are complaining loudly about the influx of hundreds of thousands of newcomers via America Online, "newbies" who are stumbling around the net asking greenhorn questions and committing faux pas of "netiquette." Many people with pressing schedules are starting to regard the cacophonous noise as a waste of time. Their exits raise the proportion of nuts, creeps and boors. Thus an inevitable backlash against the lofty hype surrounding the Internet is building, such as in Cliff Stoll's new book, *Silicon Snake Oil: Second Thoughts on the Information Highway*.   11

This all sounds like an anti-democratic trend, in contrast to the democratization that computer networks are supposed to both exemplify and support. Is cyberspace already sorting itself into two camps, a jaded, invisible elite and a teeming mass of wrassling rubes? This image wouldn't be unusual in the history of American popular culture. It seems clear that cultural polarization and low behavior in cyberspace reflect trends in American society as a whole, but the peculiar features of computer communication are amplifying the decline of our national mores and manners, and, at the same time, giving us an unprecedented bird's-eye view of what we've become.   12

Of course, we can always hope that computer networks are undergoing a metamorphosis from childhood to adolescence these days, with an anticipated maturation into adulthood sometime in the future. We'll have to develop manners in cyberspace just as we have in our everyday, real-world encounters, and that could entail a long process of evolution and refinement. If we don't develop virtual manners, cyberspace will continue to resemble a mud wrestling event. But if we can treat each other with respect over e-mail, we may go a long way toward solving some of the basic dilemmas of democracy.   13

Examining the Text

1. In Chapman's first paragraph he includes a comment by author Howard Rheingold, who has "celebrated the virtual community as a source of solace and fraternity." Explain what Rheingold means by making such a pronouncement. If people rely on the Internet as a surrogate family, how might this affect the sociology of familial relationships in the next century?

2. Chapman says that the Internet is "perhaps the first display of the direct voice of the American people in an ongoing, semi-organized, public forum"(2). Do you agree with this statement, or do you believe there have been other, equally valid, public forums in the past? Do you see any irony, intentional or otherwise, for praising the "directness" of the Internet?

3. What does Chapman's term, "cyberspace alter ego"(6) mean? How does computer-based communication encourage people to adopt personae, that is, masks, to conceal their true identities? Is this tendency in certain Internet habitués a positive or negative thing, according to Chapman? What are your own feelings about people using alter egos during Net encounters?

For Group Discussion

Spend a few minutes of class time freewriting about your own feelings and thoughts about the Internet. Are you an enthusiastic participant in this new form of communication, or are you suspicious of its potential to dehumanize, divide, and make people less civilized? Having completed the freewrite, discuss the pros and cons of Net-based communication as a class, attempting to list specific details in support of both positions. Finally, make some concrete suggestions for making the Net a more congenial place for all people to visit, whatever their unique personal agendas might be.

Writing Suggestion

Chapman asks the provocative question, "Is cyberspace already sorting itself into two camps, a jaded, invisible elite and a teeming mass of wrassling rubes?" and then adds, "This image wouldn't be unusual in the history of American popular culture." Answer Chapman's question, using his article, outside sources and your own experiences with the Internet. Having completed that initial task, next consider the comment that America has, in the past, divided itself into an educated, elite class and a relatively ignorant underclass. Cite a specific historical event, or several events, that might exemplify or disprove Chapman's division of American culture into these two camps.

Free Speech for the Net:
A Panel of Federal Judges Overturns
the Communications Decency Act

Joshua Quittner

What's the first thing that springs to mind when you hear or read the word "censorship": the banning of certain books from high school libraries; rap lyrics condemned by certain socially concerned groups; outraged citizens protesting the portrayal of Jesus in the film The Last Temptation of Christ? *Nowadays, with the Internet-driven "information revolution" at hand, there is more opportunity for free expression than ever before...which means, ironically, that there is a correspondingly higher likelihood of censorship.*

As Joshua Quittner asserts, the world of the Internet is the newest target for the entrepreneurs of censorship. Members of the Christian Coalition and similar "family-values" groups argued in support of the Communications Decency Act (CDA), signed into law by President Clinton in 1996. The act was conceived and passed in order to ban online pornography, yet the "legislation was so vague and broad" that it virtually fell apart under scrutiny by the United States Supreme Court. In this article, Quittner considers the motivating factors behind both the passage of the CDA and its eventual overturning, concluding with this statement: "Any content-based regulation of the Internet, no matter how benign the purpose, could burn the global village to roast the pig." In other words, the act of protecting our citizens from cyberporn might seriously endanger our Constitutional right to free speech and thereby undermine one of the foundations of American democracy.

As you read, *consider the reasons, both overt and covert, for the enactment and subsequent reversal of the Communications Decency Act, and consider your own position with regard to this issue. Furthermore, think about how other types of "pornographic" content—whether in books or music, or films—might be different from the risqué material encountered through cyberspace media. Is the Internet-based pornography market accessed more easily and therefore in need of more serious regulation?*

It's been a suspenseful spring in cyberspace. Everyone has felt it,   1
from the folks who gather for online chats at Bianca's Smut Shack to the
Netizens who post daily dispatches to the "fight censorship" E-mail list.
The whole information revolution was jeopardized, the cybernauts believed, by a primly named federal statute called the Communications

Decency Act. Signed into law by President Clinton on Feb. 8, after being passed by an admittedly Net-illiterate Congress, the CDA was supposed to squelch online pornography and make the Net safe for children by banning "indecent" content. But the legislation was so vague and broad that uploading *Ulysses* to the World Wide Web could have been construed as a felony offense punishable by a $250,000 fine and two years in jail. If that's the kind of treatment James Joyce would get, what hope would there be for poor Bianca and her Smut Shack?

Relief came last week in a landmark ruling that firmly extends the umbrella of the First Amendment over cyberspace. A panel of three federal judges, specially convened in Philadelphia to review the new law, pronounced the government's attempt to regulate online content more closely than print or broadcast media "unconstitutional on its face" and "profoundly repugnant." The Justice Department was enjoined from not only enforcing the act but even investigating alleged malfeasance, at least for now.

The court went further than the most ardent civil libertarians had dreamed. In a striking 175-page memorandum that was published online within minutes of being handed down, the judges declared the Internet a medium of historic importance, a profoundly democratic channel for communication that should be nurtured, not stifled. Because the Net is still in its infancy, the judges said, it deserved at least as much constitutional safekeeping as books and newspapers, if not more. "As the most participatory form of mass speech yet developed," wrote Judge Stewart Dalzell in an eloquently crafted opinion, "the Internet deserves the highest protection from governmental intrusion."

The unanimous ruling was hailed by civil libertarians as a signal moment in the struggle for free speech. "This is as historic a case as we've had in our history of First Amendment fights," said Ira Glasser, executive director of the American Civil Liberties Union, which led the court challenge on behalf of some 50 plaintiffs ranging from the American Library Association to Microsoft. Marc Rotenberg of the Electronic Privacy Information Center called the decision "the Times *v.* Sullivan of cyberspace," a reference to the 1964 Supreme Court decision that granted broad protection to journalists.

The legal battle is not over yet. The Department of Justice has 20 days to decide whether to ask the Supreme Court to review the case. While a Justice Department spokesman was noncommittal last week lawyers for the government said from the outset that they would appeal an adverse decision to the highest court. Which is where proponents of the CDA say the case belongs. "We wrote this law based on previous Supreme Court decisions that have a lot of merit, so it will be looked on very carefully," says Senator J. James Exon, who introduced the original bill and believes, despite last week's rebuke, that it will be sustained.

The proponents of the CDA are fueled by outrage that hard-core 6
pornography can be found on a computer network to which children
have access. "We're talking about material going into the hands of
young people whose lives can be permanently altered," says Mike
Russell, spokesman for the Christian Coalition, which campaigned
hard to get Congress to do something about it.

But the Philadelphia jurists (two Bush appointees, one Carter) 7
found no indication that children were at particular risk to exposure to
smut online—*Time*'s controversial "cyberporn" cover story last summer notwithstanding. In a kind of Socratic online safari, the judges
spent weeks learning their way around the Net. Guided by experts
who brought computers and an Internet connection into the court-
room, they searched for online porn and tested software that allows
parents to screen out offensive material. They finally concluded that
whatever danger was posed for kids by the presence of "indecent" offerings online was best addressed by parents or teachers. Obscenity
and child pornography, the judges noted, are already illegal under
current statutes.

"There is no evidence that sexually oriented material is the pri- 8
mary type of content on this new medium," they wrote. "Communications over the Internet do not 'invade' an individual's home or appear
on one's computer screen unbidden." The judges found that dicey material—whether from Bianca's Smut Shack or Playboy magazine's
hugely popular site—was generally preceded by warnings admonish-
ing those under the age of 18 to keep out. Even the government's own
expert witness acknowledged that the odds were slim that a user
would come across a sexually explicit site by accident.

The contrast between the court's view of the Net and the impres- 9
sion given by the lawmakers who passed the CDA was striking. The
difference, says Bruce Ennis, lead attorney for the plaintiffs, was that
the judges "did their homework" in a way that Congress did not. "We
made a mistake," admits Republican Congressman Rick White of
Washington, who originally supported the CDA, then fought to have
the indecency language removed. "The reason we got it wrong this
time is that Congress does not understand the Internet."

Will there be a next time? That seems likely. Even if the Justice 10
Department decides to forgo a Supreme Court appeal, the Christian
Coalition, along with other "family values" groups that don't necessarily agree on other issues, has vowed to keep the heat on politicians.
And there are few of those in Washington with the courage to cast a
vote for free speech that could later be construed as a vote for pornography. The Administration, for its part, seems to be trying to have it
both ways. Two weeks ago, Vice President Al Gore told graduating seniors at M.I.T. that "fear of chaos cannot justify unwarranted censorship of free speech." Yet after the court ruling last week, the President

issued a statement reaffirming his conviction that "our Constitution allows us to help parents by enforcing this Act" and promising "to do everything I can in my Administration to give families every available tool to protect their children."

In the meantime, local prosecutors will have to grapple with how   11
to apply existing obscenity laws to the new frontier of cyberspace. As spelled out by previous Supreme Court rulings, those laws use a three-pronged standard to test for obscenity: Does the material depict sexual conduct in a patently offensive way? Does it lack artistic merit? And does it violate community standards?

That last question puts the globe-spanning Net into direct con-   12
flict with local law enforcement. A private computer bulletin-board operator in California has been successfully prosecuted in Tennessee for making obscene material available to a postal inspector in Memphis. The Memphis jury ruled that the material violated local community standards, even though it might have been found acceptable in California or in the "virtual community" of cyberspace. "The question of community standards hasn't been adequately solved in any medium," says Harvard Law School professor Laurence Tribe. Bianca, it seems, is not yet out of the woods.

Examining the Text

1. Why does Quittner mention "Bianca's Smut Shack" at the beginning of the article and throughout the text, right up to the very end? Does the author seem to be displaying a righteous indignation toward such World Wide Web sites as Bianca's Smut Shack, or does he appear to be tolerant of them? How would you characterize the editorial tone of this piece: objectively journalistic, hysterically reactive, or something in between?

2. Quittner writes, "…after being passed by an admittedly Net-illiterate Congress, the CDA (Communications Decency Act) was supposed to squelch online pornography and make the Net safe for children by banning 'indecent' content" (paragraph 1). Does it seem to you as though Quittner supports or opposes the Act? Cite specific "clues" from the text of the article as concrete evidence for your answer. What, for example, is the significance of the author's putting "indecent" in quotes? Similarly, does characterizing Congress as "admittedly Net-illiterate" reveal a certain degree of bias on the part of the author?

3. A bipartisan panel of Supreme Court justices (i.e., chosen by both Republican and Democrat presidents) concluded, "There is no evidence that sexually oriented material is the primary type of content on this new medium. Communications over the Internet do not 'invade,' an individual's home or appear on one's computer screen unbidden" (paragraph 8). What do these comments imply about the government's role in policing the Internet? Consider the hypothetical case of a twelve-year-old boy who happens to be a bit curious about the sex-oriented websites he's heard so much about. Is this hypothetical preadolescent kid the government's responsibility or his parents'?

For Group Discussion

Project yourselves into the personae of Supreme Court justices, and debate the relative merits of the Communications Decency Act. Based upon your reaction to Quittner's article, and your own experience as a browser of the World Wide Web, what is your position vis-à-vis the government's role in regulating the content of specific websites? Consider also the similarities and/or differences between cyberspace "pornography" and other types of more "traditional" pornographic fare, such as behind-the-counter magazines or X-rated videos. Would you ban one over the other, or should all these artifacts be considered equally "pornographic" and therefore deserving of similar degrees of regulation or benign neglect?

Writing Suggestion

According to Quittner's article, Vice President Al Gore asserted, "fear of chaos cannot justify unwarranted censorship of free speech." Yet. after the Court ruled against the Communications Decency Act, President Clinton said, "our Constitution allows us to help parents by enforcing this Act." He then promised " to do everything I can in my Administration to give families every available tool to protect their children"(10). What do these apparently contradictory positions reveal about our governmental leaders' stance on censoring the Net? Write an essay connecting these statements to the issue of governmental cyberporn regulation. Having completed that first step, explore beyond the issue of censorship to conclude what is really behind the decisions made by our lawmakers: are politicians really concerned with our children's protection, or are they merely out to protect their offices, as certain cynical radio talk-show hosts might suggest?

Cyberpunk—Subculture or Mainstream?

McKenzie Wark

The late 1970s and early 1980s brought us green and pink Mohawk haircuts, ripped T-shirts, safety pins used as costume jewelry, and such musical groups as the Sex Pistols. While "punk" hair and clothing styles are not as prominent today as they were a couple of decades ago, the 1990s has seen a revival in certain elements of the original punk culture, with updated versions of punk music in bands such as Green Day and Pennywise, with the proliferation of tattoos and body piercings, and with a new form of literature, coined "cyberpunk" by the media.

"Cyberpunk is a cute name for a rather motley collection of people who thought and wrote and made art about technology over the last decade," says McKenzie Wark in this article. Begun by a science fiction writer named William Gibson, cyberpunk novels, short stories, and essays all envision a world in which human interaction is drastically altered, if not eliminated altogether, by an increasing reliance on computers, digital networks, virtual reality, and by the eventual advent of robots and androids. According to Wark, this fictional world view is rapidly becoming real, as increasing numbers of people view society as hostile, gun-crazy, uncivil, and increasingly depersonalized. Internet addicts, post-apocalyptic visionaries, virtual reality faddists, net surfers, computer hackers, and Nintendo warriors all make up the emergent subculture that Wark labels as cyberpunk.

Wark believes that cyberpunk has become popular in the 1990s because "every subculture needs a fantasy place to run away from suburban life," and cyberspace provides a perfect outlet for this need: people can engage in vicarious danger, thrills, and sexual encounters while safe in their homes, in front of their computer screens.

As you read, consider Wark's statement that cyberspace "is a fantasy destination for white, middle class suburbanites who realize that rural life is even more boring than the suburbs." What does this statement imply about the direction our society is taking, as we approach the next millennium? By ascribing "cyberpunk" identification to certain individuals, is Wark denouncing the whole concept of this emergent subculture, or is he trying to sell cyberpunk to us, so that we might join an exciting new movement? Is the "lingo" of cyberpunk really "hip," as Wark says, or is it the collective product of a bunch of computer "geeks" with no social life?

A hip new lingo has infiltrated the mass media. "Cyberspace," "hypermedia" and "virtual reality" have become the techno buzz words of the '90s. After years of indifference and suspicion, the idea that technology can be fun, exciting, and sexy has surfaced again.

Two ideas in particular are now doing the rounds. One is that computers are not just for pencil-head types in lab coats and grey-suited accountants. Technology can be a tool for the imagination, opening up new terrains of images, sounds, experiences and concepts. The second idea has less to do with computers than with communications. By linking up all of the computer power languishing on desks and in basements, whole new forms of interaction are possible in a communications revolution to take us beyond the television age.

The first of these two ideas orbits somewhere around the term   3 virtual reality. The second is a vague nebula of possibilities sighted off the cyberspace cluster. Both have been around a long time, but have just recrystallized in the public's imagination. "Hypermedia" is the next phase in marketing this dream to the public. The movie Lawnmower Man has cashed in on the trend, pulping the whole lot together with some silly old Stephen King haunted house cliché. The really interesting stuff on both these current trends can be found a little off the main stream. Take a hyperspace bypass back through the cyberpunk subculture of the '80s, and you will find the creative source and force behind the present multimedia marketing push.

Cyberpunk is a cute name for a rather motley collection of people   4 who thought and wrote and made art about technology over the last decade. Some of them were harmless. Some of them were mad, bad and dangerous to know. Like many other prophetic art avant gardes in the past, they saw the future both more clearly and more crazily than their contemporaries. Like the romantic poets and the decadent artists of the 19th century; like the surrealists and futurists and constructivists of the early 20th century, they wanted to change life. So they imagined how it could be different, not only from the present, but from how the future was officially imagined to be.

Cyberpunk gathered momentum in 1984 with the publication of   5 the first of William Gibson's novels, called *Neuromancer*. Gibson has since published four novels and a collection of stories. There are half a dozen readers of cyberpunk fiction on the market, and now other writers like Bruce Sterling and Pat Cadigan have emerged. There is even a remarkable "overground" cyberpunk magazine called *Mondo 2000*, as well as a host of tiny desktop published fanzines. Cyberpunk has gone beyond a subculture and is now a full blown marketing category.

Gibson was an odd sort of person to launch an avant garde cul-   6 tural movement. He wrote pretty pulpy science fiction novels. He was a small town, white suburban kind of guy. Yet he was able to crystallize something that was in the air. He created the bleak, 'no future' landscape of punk rock and post-apocalyptic movies like *Bladerunner* and *Mad Max*, and imagined a way to escape from the street-level violence these films referred to. The way out was cyberspace.

In Gibson's world, cyberspace is a consensual hallucination cre-   7 ated within the dense matrix of computer networks. Gibson imagines a world where people can directly jack their nervous systems into the net, vastly increasing the intimacy of the connection between mind and matrix. Cyberspace is the world created by the intersection of every jacked-in consciousness, every database and installation, every form of interconnected information circuit, in short, human or in-human.

This mythology of cyberspace is interesting for two reasons.   8
Firstly, it provides an alternative to the boredom of suburbia without
having to deal with the danger of inner-city living. Every subculture
needs a fantasy place to run away from suburban life to, be it the rural
fantasy of the hippies or the urban fantasy of punk. Cyberspace is a
fantasy destination for white, middle class suburbanites who realize
that rural life is even more boring than the suburbs and the cities are
becoming far too dangerous.

The other interesting thing about cyberspace is the way it recre-   9
ates the idea of community. Every subculture needs an image of an
outsider's community to cling to, to run to. For the cyberpunk, this
community doesn't actually have a place. Its not a nightclub in New
York. It is not a street in London. It can be accessed everywhere by
modem. Of course, the bulletin boards and e-mail systems are a poor
imitation of the fully wired-up world of cyberspace, but its the nearest
thing on earth. Cyberpunk subculture is the first subculture which
doesn't have a particular place of congregation—its a suburban phenomenon made possible by the networks. There are now hundreds of
bulletin boards around the world which have a cyberpunk style,
where young cyberpunks discuss the latest hardware and software.

In a sense, subcultures are always a product of the media technol-   10
ogy of the age. The classic subcultures of the '60s and '70s, from the
mods to the punks, were a combination of the electric world of rock and
roll with a style and a place and an ethos and a certain amount of drug
abuse. The mods grew out of '50s austerity in Britain. They were the first
generation of young people to enter mass white collar employment and
acquire a disposable income at a young age. So they spent it on clothes
and music and motor scooters and weekend trips to the seaside. They
were a mobile community, growing up on television and rock and roll.
The first great pop music TV show, "Ready, Steady Go!" spread mod
style from one end of Britain to the other instantly, a fashion transformation that without television would take months or years.

The punk movements of the late '70s were where the youth sub-   11
cultures launched by the mods finally crash-landed. Punk was a subculture based on the boredom of unemployment, not the tedium of
white collar work. It lacked the excitement and innocence of the mods
who were absolute beginners in the art of living in a consumerist,
media-saturated world. Punk was a subculture created by young people in the late '70s who grew up on the media and its promises of the
good life, and were bored with all that. It had let them down: "career
opportunities, the ones that never knock" as a song from the time put
it. The punks took the media technology of the time, the music, the
fashion, the radio and video, and trashed it.

Cyberpunk grew out of this negative subcultural style, but   12
turned its back towards a positive celebration. Where the mods had

been fascinated by consumerism and the mass media, cyberpunk is fascinated by the media technologies which were hitting the mass market in the '80s. Desktop publishing, computer music and now desktop video are technologies taken up with enthusiasm by cyberpunk in the place of rock and roll. Computer networking is its alternative to the mods' pop TV or the punks' pirate radio.

Just as subcultures from mod to punk were the testing ground   13
for new styles of music and fashion, the cyberpunk crowd are the testing ground for new fashions in desktop technology. The rapid evolution from video-games to virtual reality has been helped along by the hard core of enthusiasts eager to try out each generation of simulated experience. The multimedia convergence of the publishing industry, the computer industry, the broadcasting industry and the recording industry has a spot right at its centre called cyberpunk, where these new product experiments find a critical but playful market.

Where punk was a product of unemployment and the English art   14
school, cyberpunk is a product of the huge array of technical and scientific universities created in the U.S. to service the military industrial complex. Your typical cyberpunk is white, suburban, middle class, and technically skilled. They are a new generation of white collar worker, resisting the yoke of work and suburban life for a while. They don't drop out, they jack in. They are a fabulous example of how each generation, growing up with a given level of media technology, has to discover the limits and potentials of that technology by experimenting with everyday life itself.

Subcultures are an art form. They can have their delinquent   15
edge, its true. Mods took too many amphetamines. Punks were a little prone to rioting. Cyberpunks sometimes have a romantic fascination with hacking into other peoples' computers. All this is a testing of limits, a pushing to the limit of the social norm. The enduring product of any subculture is a rapid innovation in popular style. Subcultures pioneer styles of life for the mainstream. In the case of cyberpunk, the networked world of cyberspace, the interactive world of multimedia and the new sensoria of virtual reality will all owe a little to their willingness to be the test pigs for these emergent technologies.

There is also a tension in cyberpunk between the military indus-   16
trial monster that produces technology and the sensibility of the technically skilled individual trained for the high tech machine. Like all subcultures, cyberpunk expresses a conflict. On the one side is the libertarian idea that technology can be a way of wresting a little domain of freedom for people from the necessity to work and live under the constraints of today. On the other is the fact that the technologies of virtual reality, multimedia, cyberspace would never have existed in

the first place had the Pentagon not funded them as tools of war. The pilots who bombed Baghdad flew in virtual reality.

Even the peaceful applications of these technologies can be sub-   17
ordinated to commercial imperatives abhorrent to the free thinking cyberpunk. There is a contradiction between the spirit of free enquiry and experiment and the need to keep corporate secrets and make a buck. Cyberpunk is a reflection of this contradiction. On the one hand it is a drop-out culture dedicated to pursing the dream of freedom through appropriate technology. On the other it is a ready market for new gadgets and a training ground for hip new entrepreneurs with hi-tech toys to market. Cyberpunk may be over as a subculture. It was reabsorbed into the mainstream like every other subculture before it. Yet it signals a fundamental change in the way subcultures can form and oppose themselves to the mainstream. In effect, cyberpunk was the realization that the new generation of media tools are also excellent resources for changing life, if only on the margins, and if only for a short while. Like all of the other avant gardes and subcultures before it, it has added something special to the repertoire of postmodern art.

Examining the Text

1. "Computers are not just for pencil-head types in lab coats and grey-suited accountants," says Wark (paragraph 2). "Technology can be a tool for the imagination, opening up new terrains of images, sounds, experiences and concepts." Based on your own experience, what kinds of images, sounds, experiences, and concepts are computers capable of generating? With a statement such as this one, what kinds of sentiments towards computers is Wark attempting to rally in the reader? Does his strategy work for you?

2. "In a sense, subcultures are always a product of the media technology of the age," says Wark (10). Consider this statement in light of your knowledge of history: what previous "subcultures" have been generated by the media technologies of their respective ages? Later on in the article, Wark writes, "The enduring product of a subculture is a rapid innovation in popular style. Subcultures pioneer styles of life for the mainstream" (15). How do subcultures give rise to popular styles? Cite examples of styles in art, music, fashion, entertainment that were inspired by particular subcultures.

3. Wark makes the following statement: "In effect, cyberpunk was the realization that the new generation of media tools are also excellent resources for changing life." (17). What does he mean by "media tools," and how do they serve as potent agencies for changing people's daily existences? How does cyberpunk fit into this equation: does cyberpunk merely represent a defeatist, "If you can't beat 'em, join 'em," sort of attitude in people, or is there something more positive and life-affirming about this new subculture?

For Group Discussion

In the first paragraph of this article, Wark says, "After years of indifference and suspicion, the idea that technology can be fun, exciting, and sexy has surfaced again" (1). This statement implies that there were periods in history when people considered technology sexy and fun, or at least imaginatively compelling. Based on your knowledge of history, cite instances to support this assertion. Wark's statement also overtly contends that people in our modern world love technological artifacts. Discuss the validity of such a position in light of your own tastes and preferences, and those of your friends, family, and broader community. One final question, for seven points of extra credit: based on your experience with people who participate in computer culture, do you think Wark knows what he's talking about, or is he way off base in his depiction of both punks and cyberpunks?

Writing Suggestion

Write several paragraphs discussing Wark's suggestion that cyberspace "is the world created by the intersection of every jacked-in consciousness, every database and installation, every forum of interconnected information circuit, in short human or in-human" (7). Cite as many specific examples as possible for the phenomenon he is describing. Having established an intellectual context, go on to write a comparison/contrast essay that discusses the idea of "human" versus "in-human," specifically with relation to computer culture. In what ways does the computer have the potential to enhance human potential? In what ways is it an agent of dehumanization? As a conclusion to your essay, consider your own position relative to the "human/in-human" question: what are your personal feelings about computers and cyberculture in general, and the advent of cyberpunk in particular

Virtual Communities

Cyberhood vs. Neighborhood

John Perry Barlow

We begin this section on "virtual communities," with an essay written by an unlikely expert. John Perry Barlow grew up in the small town of Pinedale, Wyoming, and ran the family cattle ranch there until he was forced to sell it in 1988. Seeing the decline of the community all around him and searching, as he explains here, for evidence "that community in America would not perish altogether," Barlow started exploring the possibilities of virtual communities—that is, communities that don't exist in a particular place but rather are formed by participants in Internet mailing lists, conferences, discussion groups, and virtual "chat rooms." In this essay, Barlow describes his initial enthusiasm for these virtual communities, as well as his subsequent disillusionment.

Barlow's strategy here is to evaluate virtual communities in terms of how closely they can reproduce the qualities of real communities, in terms of human interaction and connection as well as in terms of shared interests, diversity, and meaningfulness. In comparing real and virtual communities, Barlow defines what is essential to the concept of "community"—what makes a community thrive? Why do we form and maintain communities in the first place?

As you read, *make a list of the elements that Barlow believes are essential to a community. Which of those elements do you find in the communities you currently participate in?*

"There is no there there."

Gertrude Stein (speaking of Oakland)

"It ain't no Amish barn-raising in there..."

Bruce Sterling (speaking of cyberspace)

I am often asked how I went from pushing cows around a   1
remote Wyoming ranch to my present occupation (which *Wall Street Journal* recently described as "cyberspace cadet"). I haven't got a short answer, but I suppose I came to the virtual world looking for community.

Unlike most modern Americans, I grew up in an actual place, an   2
entire nonintentional community called Pinedale, Wyoming. As I
struggled for nearly a generation to keep my ranch in the family, I was
motivated by the belief that such places were the spiritual home of humanity. But I knew their future was not promising.

At the dawn of the 20th century, over 40 percent of the American   3
workforce lived off the land. The majority of us lived in towns like
Pinedale. Now fewer than 1 percent of us extract a living from the soil.
We just became too productive for our own good.

Of course, the population followed the jobs. Farming and ranch-   4
ing communities are now home to a demographically insignificant
percentage of Americans, the vast majority of whom live not in ranch
houses but in more or less identical split level "ranch homes" in more
or less identical suburban "communities." Generica.

In my view, these are neither communities nor homes. I believe   5
the combination of television and suburban population patterns is
simply toxic to the soul. I see much evidence in contemporary America to support this view.

Meanwhile, back at the ranch, doom impended. And, as I watched   6
the community in Pinedale growing ill from the same economic forces
that were killing my family's ranch, the Bar Cross, satellite dishes
brought the cultural infection of television. I started looking around for
evidence that community in America would not perish altogether.

I took some heart in the mysterious nomadic City of the Deadheads,   7
the virtually physical town that follows the Grateful Dead around the
country. The Deadheads lacked place, touching down briefly wherever
the band happened to be playing, and they lacked continuity in time,
since they had to suffer a new diaspora every time the band moved on or
went home. But they had many of the other necessary elements of community, including a culture, a religion of sorts (which, though it lacked
dogma, had most of the other, more nurturing aspects of spiritual practice), a sense of necessity, and most importantly, shared adversity.

I wanted to know more about the flavor of their interaction, what   8
they thought and felt, but since I wrote Dead songs (including "Estimated Prophet" and "Cassidy"), I was a minor icon to the Deadheads,
and was thus inhibited, in some socially Heisenbergian way, from getting a clear view of what really went on among them.

Then, in 1987, I heard about a "place" where Deadheads gath-   9
ered where I could move among them without distorting too much the
field of observation. Better, this was a place I could visit without leaving Wyoming. It was a shared computer in Sausalito, California, called
the Whole Earth 'Lectronic Link, or WELL. After a lot of struggling
with modems, serial cables, init strings, and other Computer arcana
that seemed utterly out of phase with such notions as Deadheads and

small towns, I found myself looking at the glowing yellow word "Login:" beyond which lay my future.

"Inside" the WELL were Deadheads in community. There were   10
thousands of them there, gossiping, complaining (mostly about the Grateful Dead), comforting and harassing each other, bartering, engaging in religion (or at least exchanging their totemic set lists), beginning and ending love affairs, praying for one another's sick kids. There was, it seemed, everything one might find going on in a small town, save dragging Main Street and making out on the back roads.

I was delighted. I felt I had found the new locale of human com-   11
munity—never mind that the whole thing was being conducted in mere words by minds from whom the bodies had been amputated. Never mind that all these people were deaf, dumb, and blind as paramecia or that their town had neither seasons nor sunsets nor smells.

Surely all these deficiencies would be remedied by richer, faster   12
communications media. The featureless log-in handles would gradually acquire video faces (and thus expressions), shaded 3-D body puppets (and thus body language). This "space" which I recognized at once to be a primitive form of the cyberspace William Gibson predicted in his sci-fi novel *Neuromancer*, was still without apparent dimensions of vistas. But virtual reality would change all that in time.

Meanwhile, the commons, or something like it, had been rediscov-   13
ered. Once again, people from the 'burbs had a place where they could encounter their friends as my fellow Pinedalians did at the post office and the Wrangler Cafe. They had a place where their hearts could remain as the companies they worked for shuffled their bodies around America. They could put down roots that could not be ripped out by forces of economic history. They had a collective stake. They had a community.

It is seven years now since I discovered the WELL. In that time, I   14
co-founded an organization, the Electronic Frontier Foundation, dedicated to protecting its interests and those of other virtual communities like it from raids by physical government. I've spent countless hours typing away at its residents, and I've watched the larger context that contains it, the Internet, grow at such an explosive rate that, by 2004, every human on the planet will have an e-mail address unless the growth curve flattens (which it will).

My enthusiasm for virtuality has cooled. In fact, unless one   15
counts interaction with the rather too large society of those with whom I exchange electronic mail, I don't spend much time engaging in virtual community, at all. Many of the near-term benefits I anticipated from it seem to remain as far in the future as they did when I first logged in. Perhaps they always will.

Pinedale works, more or less, as it is, but a lot is still missing from   16
the communities of cyberspace, whether they be places like the WELL,
the fractious newsgroups of USENET, the silent "auditoriums" of
America Online, or even enclaves on the promising World Wide Web.

What is missing? Well, to quote Ranjit Makkuni of Xerox Corpora-   17
tion's Palo Alto Research Center, "the *prāna* is missing," *prāna* being the
Hindu term for both breath and spirit. I think he is right about this and
that perhaps the central question of the virtual age is whether or not
prāna can somehow be made to fit through any disembodied medium.

Prāna is, to my mind, the literally vital element in the holy and un-   18
seen ecology of relationship, the dense mesh of invisible life, on whose
surface carbon-based life floats like a thin film. It is at the heart of the fundamental and profound difference between information and experience.
Jaron Lanier has said that "information is alienated experience," and,
that being true, *prāna* is part of what is removed when you create such
easily transmissible replicas of experience as, say, the evening news.

Obviously a great many other, less spiritual, things are also miss-   19
ing entirely, like body language, sex, death, tone of voice, clothing,
beauty (or homeliness), weather, violence, vegetation, wildlife, pets,
architecture, music, smells, sunlight, and that ol' harvest moon. In
short, most of the things that make my life real to me.

Present, but in far less abundance than in the physical world,   20
which I call "meat space," are women, children, old people, poor people, and the genuinely blind. Also mostly missing are the illiterate and
the continent of Africa. There is not much human diversity in cyberspace, which is populated, as near as I can tell, by white males under
50 with plenty of computer terminal time, great typing skills, high
math SATs, strongly held opinions on just about everything, and an
excruciating face-to-face shyness, especially with the opposite sex.

But diversity is as essential to healthy community as it is to   21
healthy ecosystems (which are, in my view, different from communities only in unimportant aspects).

I believe that the principal reason for the almost universal failure   22
of the intentional communities of the '60s and '70s was a lack of diversity in their members. It was a rare commune with any old people in it,
or people who were fundamentally out of philosophical agreement
with the majority.

Indeed, it is the usual problem when we try to build something   23
that can only be grown. Natural systems, such as human communities,
are simply too complex to design by the engineering principles we insist on applying to them. Like Dr. Frankenstein, western civilization is
now finding its rational skills inadequate to the task of creating and
caring for life. We would do better to return to a kind of agricultural
mind-set in which we humbly try to re-create the conditions from
which life has sprung before. And leave the rest to God.

Given that it has been built so far almost entirely by people with   24
engineering degrees, it is not so surprising that cyberspace has the
kind of overdesigned quality that leaves out all kinds of elements nature would have provided invisibly.

Also missing from both the communes of the '60s and from cy-   25
berspace are a couple of elements that I believe are very important, if
not essential, to the formation and preservation of a real community:
an absence of alternatives and a sense of genuine adversity, generally
shared. What about these?

It is hard to argue that anyone would find losing a modem liter-   26
ally hard to survive, while many have remained in small towns, have
tolerated their intolerances and created entertainment to enliven their
culturally arid lives simply because it seemed there was no choice but
to stay. There are many investments—spiritual, material, and temporal—one is willing to put into a home one cannot leave. Communities
are often the beneficiaries of these involuntary investments.

But when the going gets rough in cyberspace, it is even easier to   27
move than it is in the burbs, where, given the fact that the average American moves some 12 times in his or her life, moving appears to be pretty
easy. You cannot only find another bulletin board service (BBS) or newsgroup to hang out in; you can, with very little effort, start your own.

And then there is the bond of joint suffering. Most community is a   28
cultural stockade erected against a common enemy that can take many
forms. In Pinedale, we bore together, with an understanding needing little expression, the fact that Upper Green River Valley is the coldest spot,
as measured by annual mean temperature, in the lower 48 states. We
knew that if somebody was stopped on the road most winter nights, he
would probably die there, so the fact that we might loathe him was not
sufficient reason to drive on past his broken pickup.

By the same token, the Deadheads have the Drug Enforcement Ad-   29
ministration, which strives to give them 20-year prison terms without pa-
role for distributing the fairly harmless sacrament of their faith. They
have an additional bond in the fact that when their Microbuses die, as
they often do, no one but another Deadhead is likely to stop to help them.

But what are the shared adversities of cyberspace? Lousy user in-   30
terfaces? The flames of harsh invective? Dumb jokes? Surely these can
all be survived without the sanctuary provided by fellow sufferers.

One is always free to yank the jack, as I have mostly done. For   31
me, the physical world offers far more opportunity for *prāna* rich connections with my fellow creatures. Even for someone whose body is in
a state of perpetual motion, I feel I can generally find more community
among the still-embodied.

Finally, there is that shyness factor. Not only are we trying to   32
build community here among people who have never experienced any
in my sense of the term, we are trying to build community among

people who, in their lives, have rarely used the word *we* in a heartfelt way. It is a vast club, and many of the members—following Groucho Marx—wouldn't want to join a club that would have them.

And yet...   33

How quickly physical community continues to deteriorate. Even   34
Pinedale, which seems to have survived the plague of ranch failures, feels increasingly cut off from itself. Many of the ranches are now owned by corporate types who fly their Gulfstreams in to fish and are rarely around during the many months when the creeks are frozen over and neighbors are needed. They have kept the ranches alive financially, but they actively discourage their managers from the interdependence my former colleagues and I require. They keep agriculture on life support, still alive but lacking a functional heart.

And the town has been inundated with suburbanites who flee   35
here, bringing all their terrors and suspicions with them. They spend their evenings as they did in Orange County, watching television or socializing in hermetic little enclaves of fundamentalist Christianity that seem to separate them from us and even, given their sectarian animosities, from one another. The town remains. The community is largely a wraith of nostalgia.

So where else can we look for the connection we need to prevent   36
our plunging further into the condition of separateness Nietzsche called sin? What is there to do but to dive further into the bramble bush of information that, in its broadest forms, has done so much to tear us apart?

Cyberspace, for all its current deficiencies and failed promises, is   37
not without some very real solace already.

Some months ago, the great love of my life, a vivid young   38
woman with whom I intended to spend the rest of it, dropped dead of undiagnosed viral cardiomyopathy two days short of her 30th birthday. I felt as if my own heart had been as shredded as hers.

We had lived together in New York City. Except for my daughters,   39
no one from Pinedale had met her. I needed a community to wrap around myself against colder winds than fortune had ever blown at me before. And without looking, I found I had one in the virtual world.

On the WELL, there was a topic announcing her death in one of the   40
conferences to which I posted the eulogy I had read over her before burying her in her own small town of Nanaimo, British Columbia. It seemed to strike a chord among the disembodied living on the Net. People copied it and sent it to one another. Over the next several months I received almost a megabyte of electronic mail from all over the planet, mostly from folks whose faces I have never seen and probably never will.

They told me of their own tragedies and what they had done to   41
survive them. As humans have since words were first uttered, we shared the second most common human experience, death, with an

openheartedness that would have caused grave uneasiness in physical America, where the whole topic is so cloaked in denial as to be considered obscene. Those strangers, who had no arms to put around my shoulders, no eyes to weep with mine, nevertheless saw me through. As neighbors do.

42   I have no idea how far we will plunge into this strange place. Unlike previous frontiers, this one has no end. It is so dissatisfying in so many ways that I suspect we will be more restless in our search for home here than in all our previous explorations. And that is one reason why I think we may find it after all. If home is where the heart is, then there is already some part of home to be found in cyberspace.

43   So...does virtual community work or not? Should we all go off to cyberspace or should we resist it as a demonic form of symbolic abstraction? Does it supplant the real or is there, in it, reality itself?

44   Like so many true things, this one doesn't resolve itself to a black or a white. Nor is it gray. It is, along with the rest of life, black/white. Both/neither. I'm not being equivocal or whishy-washy here. We have to get over our Manichean sense that everything is either good or bad, and the border of cyberspace seems to me a good place to leave that old set of filters.

45   But really it doesn't matter. We are going there whether we want to or not. In five years, everyone who is reading these words will have an e-mail address, other than the determined Luddites who also eschew the telephone and electricity.

46   When we are all together in cyberspace we will see what the human spirit, and the basic desire to connect, can create there. I am convinced that the result will be more benign if we go there open-minded, open-hearted, and excited with the adventure than if we are dragged into exile.

47   And we must remember that going to cyberspace, unlike previous great emigrations to the frontier, hardly requires us to leave where we have been. Many will find, as I have, a much richer appreciation of physical reality for having spent so much time in virtuality.

48   Despite its current (and perhaps in some areas permanent) insufficiencies, we should go to cyberspace with hope. Groundless hope, like unconditional love, may be the only kind that counts.

In Memoriam, Dr. Cynthia Horner (1964–1994).

Examining the Text

1. What does Barlow see as the essential elements of community? How do the various physical and virtual communities Barlow discusses embody or fail to embody these elements?

2. What does Barlow mean when he suggests that the *"prāna"* is missing from cyberspace communities? Why does he nevertheless find virtual communities worthwhile?

3. Examine the organization of Barlow's essay. How does he structure his argument? Do you think that the conclusions he comes to at the end (particularly in paragraph 44) are supported by what he says in the body of the essay?

For Group Discussion

Barlow observes that when he first entered the virtual community of Deadheads and others on the WELL, he saw a place where people "could put down roots that could not be ripped out by forces of economic history." To what forces is Barlow referring? Can you think of other forces—economic, social, cultural, political, historical, religious—that have affected the sense of community in America? As a group and then as a class, make a list of these factors. Which have helped strengthen a sense of community in America and which have brought about the decline of community?

Writing Suggestion

Define the characteristics of an ideal community, using ideas from Barlow's essay as well as ideas from your own experiences and observations. Then choose one community that you inhabit or know about: for example, the college or university community to which you belong; your high school community; the community in which you grew up; communities that you've visited; or perhaps a virtual community on the Internet that you're familiar with. Describe this community and compare it with your ideal definition. How well does this particular community meet your definition of the ideal? In what ways does it fall short? What are the reasons, in your opinion, that the community you're discussing is less than ideal?

Virtuality and Its Discontents

Sherry Turkle

Sherry Turkle, a professor in MIT's Program in Science, Technology, and Society, is at the forefront of scholars studying the effects of computers and the Internet on contemporary life. She has written two books that deal with the ways in which computers and the culture of the Internet are shaping human identity: The Second Self: Computers and the Human Spirit *(1984) and* Life on the Screen: Identity in the Age of the Internet *(1995).*

In the essay that follows, which is adapted from her more recent book, Turkle discusses "MUDs" ("multi-user dungeons") as places on the Internet where people can meet and "talk" and create a virtual community. She describes her own experience in MUDs and includes interviews with other MUD partici- pants and organizers in order to assess their effects.

As a licensed clinical psychologist, Turkle is primarily concerned with ways people are using computers and computer-mediated communication to enhance (or detract from) their real-life experiences. In other words, she asks, do virtual communities enable us to live more fully and more productively in the real communities that we inhabit? What can we learn from our virtual in- teractions and relationships to help us make our real-world relationships more rewarding? Are people who spend a lot of time in virtual communities able to translate skills to the real communities in which they live?

As you read, *make note of how Turkle answers these questions. Does she, in fact, propose a single yes-or-no answer, or does she leave it to the reader to determine the relationship between virtual and real communities?*

The anthropologist Ray Oldenberg has written about the "great   1
good place"—the local bar, the bistro, the coffee shop—where mem- bers of a community can gather for easy company, conversation, and a sense of belonging. Oldenberg considers these places to be the heart of individual social integration and community vitality. Today we see a resurgence of coffee bars and bistros, but most of them do not serve, much less recreate, coherent communities and, as a result, the odor of nostalgia often seems as strong as the espresso.

Some people are trying to fill the gap with neighborhoods in cy-   2
berspace. Take Dred's Bar, for example, a watering hole on the MUD LambdaMOO. MUDS, which originally stood for "multi-user dun- geons," are destinations on the Internet where players who have logged in from computers around the world join an on-line virtual community. Through typed commands, they can converse privately or in large groups, creating and playing characters and even earning and spending imaginary funds in the MUD's virtual economy.

In many MUDS, players help build the virtual world itself. Using a   3
relatively simple programming language, they can make "rooms" in the MUD, where they can set the stage and define the rules. Dred's Bar is one such place. It is described as having a "castle decor" and a polished oak dance floor. Recently I (here represented by my character or persona "ST") visited Dred's Bar with Tony, a persona I had met on another MUD. After passing the bouncer, Tony and I encountered a man asking for a $5 cover charge, and once we paid it our hands were stamped.

> The crowd opens up momentarily to reveal one corner
> of the club. A couple is there, making out madly.
> Friendly place . . .
> You sit down at the table. The waitress sees you and
> indicates that she will be there in a minute.
> [The waitress here is a bot-short for robot-that is,
> a computer program that presents itself as a person-
> ality.]
> The waitress comes up to the table, "Can I get any-
> one anything from the bar?" she says as she puts down
> a few cocktail napkins.
> Tony says, "When the waitress comes up, type order
> name of drink.".
> Abigail [a character at the bar] dries off a spot
> where some drink spilled on her dress.
> The waitress nods to Tony and writes on her notepad.
> [I type "order margarita," following Tony's direc-
> tions.]
> You order a margarita.
> The waitress nods to ST and writes on her notepad.
> Tony sprinkles some salt on the back of his hand.
> Tony remembers he ordered a margarita, not tequila,
> and brushes the salt off.
> You say, "I like salt on my margarita too."
> The DJ makes a smooth transition from The Cure into
> a song by 10,000 Maniacs.
> The drinks arrive. You say, "L'chaim."
> Tony says, "Excuse me?"

After some explanations, Tony says, "Ah,..." smiles, and intro- 4
duces me to several of his friends. Tony and I take briefly to the dance
floor to try out some MUD features that allow us to waltz and tango,
then we go to a private booth to continue our conversation.

MAIN STREET, MALL, AND VIRTUAL CAFÉ

What changes when we move from Oldenberg's great good 5
places to something like Dred's Bar on LambdaMOO? To answer this
question, it helps to consider an intermediate step—moving from a
sidewalk café to a food court in a suburban shopping mall. Shopping
malls try to recreate the Main Streets of yesteryear, but critical elements change in the process. Main Street, though commercial, is also a
public place; the shopping mall is entirely planned to maximize purchasing. On Main Street you are a citizen; in the shopping mall, you
are customer as citizen. Main Street had a certain disarray: the town

drunk, the traveling snake-oil salesman. The mall is a more controlled space; there may be street theater, but it is planned—the appearance of serendipity is part of the simulation. If Dred's Bar seems plausible, it is because the mall and so much else in our culture, especially television, have made simulations so real.

On any given evening, nearly eighty million people in the United States are watching television. The average American household has a television turned on more than six hours a day, reducing eye contact and conversation. Computers and the virtual worlds they provide are adding another dimension of mediated experience. Perhaps computers feel so natural because of their similarity to watching TV, our dominant social experience for the past forty years. 6

The bar featured for a decade in the television series *Cheers* no doubt figures so prominently in the American imagination, at least partly because most of us don't have a neighborhood place where "everybody knows your name." Instead, we identify with the place on the screen. Bars designed to look like the one on *Cheers* have sprung up all over the country, most poignantly in airports, our most anonymous of locales. Here, no one will know your name, but you can always buy a drink or a souvenir sweatshirt. 7

In the postwar atomization of American social life, the rise of middle-class suburbs created communities of neighbors who often remained strangers. Meanwhile, as the industrial and economic base of urban life declined, downtown social spaces such as the neighborhood theater or diner were replaced by malls and cinema complexes in the outlying suburbs. In the recent past, we left our communities to commute to these distant entertainments; increasingly, we want entertainment that commutes right into our homes. In both cases, the neighborhood is bypassed. We seem to be in the process of retreating further into our homes, shopping for merchandise in catalogues or on television channels or for companionship in personals ads. 8

Technological optimists think that computers will reverse some of this social atomization; they tout virtual experience and virtual community as ways for people to widen their horizons. But is it really sensible to suggest that the way to revitalize community is to sit alone in our rooms, typing at our networked computers and filling our lives with virtual friends? 9

THE LOSS OF THE REAL

Which would you rather see—a Disney crocodile robot or a real crocodile? The Disney version rolls its eyes, moves from side to side, and disappears beneath the surface and rises again. It is designed to 10 command our attention at all times. None of these qualities is necessarily visible at a zoo where real crocodiles seem to spend most of their time sleeping. And you may have neither the means nor the inclination to observe a real crocodile in the Nile or the River Gambia.

Compare a rafting trip down the Colorado River to an adolescent girl's use of an interactive CD-ROM to explore the same territory. A real rafting trip raises the prospect of physical danger. One may need to strain one's resources to survive, and there may be a rite of passage. This is unlikely to be the experience of an adolescent girl who picks up an interactive CD-ROM called "Adventures on the Colorado." A touch-sensitive screen allows her to explore the virtual Colorado and its shoreline. Clicking a mouse brings up pictures and descriptions of local flora and fauna. She can have all the maps and literary references she wants. All this might be fun, perhaps useful. But in its uniformity and lack of risk, it is hard to imagine its marking a transition to adulthood.

But why not have both—the virtual Colorado and the real one? Not every exploration need be a rite of passage. The virtual and the real may provide different things. Why make them compete? The difficulty is that virtuality tends to skew our experience of the real in several ways. First, it makes denatured and artificial experiences seem real—let's call it the Disneyland effect. After a brunch on Disneyland's Royal Street, a cappuccino at a restaurant chain called Bonjour Café at an Anaheim shopping mall may seem real by comparison. After playing a video game in which your opponent is a computer program, the social world of MUDs may seem real as well. At least real people play most of the parts and the play space is relatively open. One player compares the roles he was able to play on video games and on MUDS. "Nintendo has a good [game] where you can play four characters. But even though they are very cool," he says, "they are written up for you." They seem artificial. In contrast, on the MUDs, he says, "There is nothing written up." He says he feels free. MUDs are "for real" because you make them up yourself.

Another effect of simulation, which might be thought of as the artificial crocodile effect, is that the fake seems more compelling than the real. In *The Future Does Not Compute: Warnings from the Internet,* Stephen L. Talbott quotes educators who say that years of exciting nature programming have compromised wildlife experiences for children. The animals in the woods are unlikely to perform as dramatically as those captured on the camera. I have a clear memory of a Brownie Scout field trip to the Brooklyn Botanical Gardens where I asked an attendant if she could make the flowers open fast. For a long while, no one understood what I was talking about. Then they figured it out: I was hoping that the attendant could make the flowers behave as they did in the time-lapse photography I had seen in Disney films.

11

12

13

Third, virtual experience may be so compelling that we believe   14
that within it we've achieved more than we have. Many of the people I
have interviewed claim that virtual gender-swapping (pretending to
be the opposite sex on the Internet) enables them to understand what
it's like to be a person of the other gender, and I have no doubt that
this is true, at least in part. But as I have listened to this boast, my
mind has often travelled to my own experiences of living in a
woman's body. These include worry about physical vulnerability,
fears of unwanted pregnancy and infertility, fine-tuned decisions
about how much make-up to wear to a job interview, and the difficulty of giving a professional seminar while doubled over with
monthly cramps. Some knowledge is inherently experiential, depending on physical sensations.

Pavel Curtis, the founder of LambdaMOO, begins his paper on   15
its social dimensions with a quote from E. M. Forster: "The Machine
did not transmit nuances of expression. It only gave a general idea of
people—an idea that was good enough for all practical purposes." But
what are practical purposes? And what about impractical purposes?
To the question, "Why must virtuality and real life compete—why
can't we have both?" the answer is of course that we will have both.
The more important question is "How can we get the best of both?"

THE POLITICS OF VIRTUALITY

When I began exploring the world of MUDs in 1992, the Internet   16
was open to a limited group, chiefly academics and researchers in affiliated commercial enterprises. The MUDders were mostly middle-class
college students. They chiefly spoke of using MUDs as places to play and
escape, though some used MUDs to address personal difficulties. By late
1993, network access could easily be purchased commercially, and the
number and diversity of people on the Internet had expanded dramatically. Conversations with MUDders began to touch on new themes. To
some young people, "RL" (real life) was a place of economic insecurity
where they had trouble finding meaningful work and holding on to middle-class status. Socially speaking, there was nowhere to go but down in
RL, whereas MUDs offered a kind of virtual social mobility.

Josh is a 23-year-old college graduate who lives in a small studio   17
apartment in Chicago. After six months of looking for a job in marketing, the field in which he recently received his college degree, Josh has
had to settle for a job working on the computer system that maintains
inventory records at a large discount store. He considers this a dead
end. When a friend told him about MUDS, he gave them a try, and
within a week stepped into a new life.

Now, eight months later, Josh spends as much time on MUDs as   18
he can. He belongs to a class of players who sometimes call themselves
Internet Hobos. They solicit time on computer accounts the way pan-
handlers go after spare change. In contrast to his life in RL, Josh's life
inside MUDs seems rich and filled with promise. It has friends, safety,
and space. "I live in a terrible part of town. I see a rat hole of an apartment, I see a dead-end job, I see AIDS. Down here [in the MUD] I see
friends, I have something to offer, I see safe sex." His programming on
MUDs is far more intellectually challenging than his day job. Josh has
worked on three MUDS, building large, elaborate living quarters in
each, and has become a specialist at building virtual cafés in which
"bots" serve as waiters and bartenders. Within MUDs, Josh serves as a
programming consultant to many less experienced players and has
even become something of an entrepreneur. He "rents" ready-built
rooms to people who are not as skilled in programming as he is. He
has been granted wizard privileges on various MUDs in exchange for
building food service software. He dreams that such virtual commerce
will someday lead to more—that someday, if MUDs become commercial enterprises, he could build them for a living. MUDs offer Josh a
sense of participating in the American Dream.

MUDs play a similar role for Thomas, 24, whom I met after giv-   19
ing a public lecture in Washington, D.C. After graduating from college, Thomas entered a training program at a large department store.
When he discovered that he didn't like retailing, he quit the program,
thinking that he would look for better opportunities. But things did
not go well for him; he couldn't find a job that would give him the
middle-class life he knew as a child. Finally, he took a job as a bellhop
in the hotel where I had just spoken. "MUDs got me back into the middle class," Thomas tells me. He has a group of MUD friends who write
well, program, and read science fiction. "I'm interested in MUD politics. Can there be democracy in cyberspace? Should MUDs be ruled by
wizards or should they be democracies? I majored in political science
in college. These are important questions for the future. I talk about
these things with my friends. On MUDs."

Thomas moves on to what has become an obvious conclusion.   20
He says, "MUDs make me more what I really am. Off the MUD, I am
not as much me." Tanya, also 24, a college graduate working as a
nanny in rural Connecticut, expresses similar aspirations. She says of
the MUD on which she has built Japanese-style rooms and a bot to
offer her guests a kimono, slippers, and tea, "I feel like I have more
stuff on the MUD than I have off it."

Josh, Thomas, and Tanya belong to a generation whose college   21
years were marked by economic recession and a deadly sexually transmitted disease. They scramble for work; finances force them to live in

neighborhoods they don't consider safe; they may end up back home living with parents. These young people are looking for a way back into the middle class. MUDs provide them with the sense of a middle-class peer group. So it is really not that surprising that it is in this virtual social life that they feel most like themselves.

Is the real self always the naturally occurring one? If a patient on   22 the antidepressant medication Prozac tells his therapist he feels more like himself with the drug than without it, what does this do to our standard notions of a real self? Where does a medication end and a person begin? Where does real life end and a game begin? Is the real self always the one in the physical world? As more and more real business gets done in cyberspace, could the real self be the one who functions in that realm? Is the real Tanya the frustrated nanny or the energetic programmer on the MUD? The stories of these MUDders point to a whole set of issues about the political and social dimension of virtual community These young people feel they have no political voice, and they look to cyberspace to help them find one.

SEX AND VIOLENCE IN CYBERSPACE

If real business increasingly gets done in cyberspace, what kinds of   23 rules will govern it? And how will those rules be made, democratically or by fiat? The issue arises starkly in connection with sex and violence.

Consider the first moments of a consensual sexual encounter be-   24 tween the characters Backslash and Targa. The player behind Back-slash, Ronald, a mathematics graduate student in Memphis, types "emote fondles Targa's breast" and "say You are beautiful Targa" and Elizabeth, Targa's player, sees on her screen:

```
Backslash fondles Targa's breasts. Backslash says,
"You are beautiful Targa."
```

Elizabeth responds with "say Touch me again, and harder.   25 Please. Now. That's how I like it." Ronald's screen shows:

```
Targa says, "Touch me again, and harder. Please. Now.
That's how I like it."
```

But consensual relationships are only one facet of virtual sex.   26 Virtual rape can occur within a MUD if one player finds a way to control the actions of another player's character and can thus "force" that character to have sex. The coercion depends on being able to direct the actions and reactions of characters, independent of the desire of their players. So if Ronald were such a culprit, he would be the only one typing, having gained control of Targa's character. In this case 15-year-old Elizabeth, who plays Targa, would sit at her computer, shocked to find herself or rather her "self" begging Backslash for more urgent caresses and ultimately violent intercourse.

Some might say that such incidents hardly deserve our concern, as they involve "only words," nothing more. But can a community that exists entirely in the realm of communication ignore sexual aggression that takes the form of words?   27

In March 1992, a character calling himself Mr. Bungle, "an oleaginous, Bisquick-faced clown dressed in cum-stained harlequin garb and girdled with a mistletoe-and-hemlock belt whose buckle bore the inscription 'KISS ME UNDER THIS, BITCH!'" appeared in the Lambda-MOO living room. Creating a phantom that masquerades as another player's character is a MUD programming trick often referred to as creating a voodoo doll. The "doll" is said to possess the character, so that the character must do whatever the doll does. Bungle used such a voodoo doll to force one and then another of the room's occupants to perform sexual acts on him. Bungle's first victim was legba, a character described as "a Haitian trickster spirit of indeterminate gender, brown-skinned and wearing an expensive pearl gray suit, top hat, and dark glasses." Even when ejected from the room, Bungle was able to continue his sexual assaults. He forced various players to have sex with each other and then forced legba to swallow his (or her?) own pubic hair and made a character called Starsinger attack herself sexually with a knife. Finally, Bungle was immobilized by a MOO wizard who "toaded" the perpetrator (erased the character from the system).   28

The next day, legba took the matter up on a widely read mailing list within LambdaMOO called *social-issues. Legba called both for "civility" and "virtual castration." A journalist chronicling this event, Julian Dibbell, contrasts the cyberspace description of the event with what was going on in real life. The woman who played the character of legba told Dibbell that she cried as she wrote those words, but he points out that her mingling of "murderous rage and eyeball-rolling annoyance was a curious amalgam." According to the conventions of virtual reality, legba and Starsinger were brutally raped, but here was the victim legba scolding Mr. Bungle only for a breach of "civility." According to the conventions of real life, the incident was confined to the realm of the symbolic—no one suffered any physical harm—but here was the player legba calling for Mr. Bungle's dismemberment. Dibbell writes: "Ludicrously excessive by RL's lights, woefully understated by VR's, the tone of legba's response made sense only in the buzzing, dissonant gap between them."   29

Virtual rape—of which the incident on LambdaMOO was only one example—raises the question of accountability for the actions of   30

virtual personae who have only words at their command. Similar issues of accountability arise in the case of virtual murder. If your MUD
character erases the computer database on which I have over many
months built up a richly described character and goes on to announce
to the community that my character is deceased, what exactly have
you, the you that exists in real life, done? What if my virtual apartment
is destroyed along with all its furniture, VCR, kitchen equipment, and
stereo system? What if you kidnap my virtual dog—my beloved bot
Rover, which I have trained to perform tricks on demand? What if you
destroy him and leave his dismembered body in the MUD?

    The problem of civil order has come up sharply in the history of   31
a MUD called Habitat, initially built to run on Commodore 64 personal computers in the early 1980s. It had a short run in the United
States before it was bought and transferred to Japan. Its designers,
Chip Morningstar and F. Randall Farmer, have written about how its
players struggled to establish the rights and responsibilities of virtual
selves. On Habitat, players were originally allowed to have guns and
other weapons. Morningstar and Farmer say that they "included these
because we felt that players should be able to 'materially' affect each
other in ways that went beyond simply talking, ways that required
real moral choices to be made by the participants." Death in Habitat,
however, had little in common with the RL variety. "When an Avatar
is killed, he or she is teleported back home, head in hands (literally),
pockets empty, and any object in hand at the time dropped on the
ground at the scene of the crime." This was more like a setback in a
game of Chutes and Ladders than real mortality, and for some players
thievery and murder became the highlights of the game. For others,
these activities were a violent intrusion on their peaceful world. An intense debate ensued.

    Some players argued that guns should be eliminated, for in a vir-   32
tual world a few lines of code can translate into an absolute gun ban.
Others argued that what was dangerous in virtual reality was not violence but its trivialization. These individuals maintained that guns
should be allowed, but their consequences should be made more serious; when you are killed, your character should cease to exist and not
simply be sent home. Still others believed that since Habitat was just a
game and playing assassin was part of the fun, there could be no harm
in a little virtual violence.

    As the debate continued, a player who was a Greek Orthodox   33
priest in real life founded the first Habitat church, the "Order of the
Holy Walnut," whose members pledged not to carry guns, steal, or engage in virtual violence of any kind. In the end, the game's designers divided the world into two parts. In town, violence was prohibited; in the
wilds outside town, it was allowed. Eventually a democratic voting

process was installed and a sheriff elected. Participants then took up discussion on the nature of Habitat laws and the proper balance between law and order and individual freedom. It was a remarkable situation. Participants in Habitat were seeing themselves as citizens; they were spending their leisure time debating pacifism, the nature of good government, and the relationship between representations and reality. In the nineteenth century, utopians built communities in which political thought could be lived out in practice. On the cusp of the twenty-first century, we are creating utopian communities in cyberspace.

Some participants have devoted much energy to the political life of   34
MUDs. LambdaMOO, like Habitat, has undergone a major change in its form of governance. Instead of the MUD wizards (or system administrators) making policy decisions, there is a complex system of grassroots petitions and collective voting. Thomas, the bellhop I met in Washington, goes on at length about the political factions with which he must contend to "do politics" on LambdaMOO. Our conversation is taking place in Fall, 1994. His home state has an upcoming race for the U.S. Senate, hotly contested, ideologically charged, but he hasn't registered to vote and doesn't plan to. I bring up the Senate race. He shrugs it off: "I'm not voting. Doesn't make a difference. Politicians are liars."

RESISTANCE OR ESCAPE?

In *Reading the Romance,* the literary scholar Janice Radaway ar-   35
gues that when women read romance novels they are not escaping but building realities less limited than their own. Romance reading becomes a form of resistance, a challenge to the stultifying categories of everyday life. If we take Radaway's perspective, we can look at MUDs and other kinds of virtual communities as places of resistance to the many forms of alienation and to the silences they impose.

But what resistance do Virtual communities really offer? Two   36
decades ago, computer hobbyists saw personal computers as a path to a new populism. They imagined how networks would allow citizens to band together to run decentralized schools and governments. Personal computers would create a more participatory political system, the hobbyists believed, because "people will get used to understanding things, to being in control of things, and they will demand more." The hobbyists I interviewed then were excited, enthusiastic, and satisfied with what they were doing with their machines. But I worried about the limits of this enthusiasm, and in my earlier book about personal computers, *The Second Self,* I wrote: "People will not change unresponsive political systems or intellectually deadening work environments by building machines that are responsive, fun, and intellectually challenging."

My misgivings today are similar. Instead of solving real prob-   37
lems—both personal and social—many of us appear to be choosing to
invest ourselves in unreal places. Women and men tell me that the
rooms and mazes on MUDS are safer than city streets, virtual sex is
safer than sex anywhere, MUD friendships are more intense than real
ones, and when things don't work out you can always leave.

To be sure, MUDs afford an outlet for some people to work   38
through personal issues in a productive way; virtual environments
provide a moratorium from RL that can be turned to constructive purpose, and not only for adolescents. One can also respect the sense in
which political activities in a MUD demonstrate resistance to what is
unsatisfying about political life more generally. And yet, it is sobering
that the personal computer revolution, once conceptualized as a tool
to rebuild community, now tends to concentrate on building community inside a machine.

If the politics of virtuality means democracy on-line and apathy   39
off-line, there is reason for concern. There is also reason for concern
when access to the new technology breaks down along traditional
class lines. Although some inner-city communities have used computer-mediated communication as a tool for real community building,
the overall trend seems to be the creation of an information elite.

Virtual environments are valuable as places where we can ac-   40
knowledge our inner diversity. But we still want an authentic experience of self. One's fear is, of course, that in the culture of simulation, a
word like authenticity can no longer apply. So even as we try to make
the most of virtual environments, a haunting question remains. For
me, that question is raised every time I use the MUD command for
taking an action. The command is "emote." If I type "emote waves"
while at Dred's café on LambdaMOO, the screens of all players in the
MUD room will flash "ST waves." If I type "emote feels a complicated
mixture of desire and expectation," all screens will flash "ST feels a
complicated mixture of desire and expectation." But what exactly do I
feel? Or, what exactly do *I* feel? When we get our MUD persona to
"emote" something and observe the effect, do we gain a better understanding of our real emotions, which can't be switched on and off so
easily, and which we may not even be able to describe? Or is the emote
command and all that it stands for a reflection of what Frederic Jame-
son has called the flattening of affect in postmodern life?

The overheated language that surrounds current discussion of   41
computer-mediated communications falls within a long tradition of
American technological optimism. The optimists today tend to represent urban decay and class polarization as out-of-date formulations of
a problem that could be solved with the right technology—for example, technology that could enable every schoolchild to experience

"being digital." Are our streets dangerous? Not to worry: The community will be "wired" so children can attend school without having to walk there! This way of thinking about cyberspace substitutes life on the screen for life in our bodies and physical communities.

But there is another way of thinking, one that stresses making the   42
virtual and the real more permeable to each other. We don't have to reject life on the screen, but we don't have to treat it as an alternative life either. Virtual personae can be a resource for self-reflection and self-transformation. Having literally written our on-line worlds into existence, we can use the communities we build inside our machines to improve the ones outside of them. Like the anthropologist returning home from a foreign culture, the voyager in virtuality can return to the real world better able to understand what about it is arbitrary and can be changed.

Examining the Text

1. Why do you think Turkle begins her essay with an example of her "virtual conversation" in Dred's Bar? What point do you think she is trying to prove with this example?

2. In what ways, according to Turkle, does the shopping mall serve as an intermediate step between the Main Streets of yesteryear and the cybercommunities of the present and future? Do you agree with Turkle's argument that shopping malls (and television) have changed the nature of communities in America? Why or why not?

3. Turkle comments on sex and violence on the Internet through her discussion of the "virtual rape" by Mr. Bungle and the gun control incident on the Habitat MUD. What point is she making through these examples? How would you summarize her position on the issues of sex and violence on the Internet?

4. What do you take to be Turkle's ultimate conclusion in this essay about the effect of virtual communities on real life communities?

For Group Discussion

Turkle uses the examples of Josh, Thomas, and Tanya, three college graduates in their twenties who are actively involved in cybercommunities, to raise questions about the relation between experiences on the Internet and "RL" (real life) experiences. She asks, "Is the real self always the one in the physical world?" Read over this section again (paragraph 22) and as a class discuss your responses to Turkle's question. How do the online personas of Josh, Thomas, and Tanya compare with their RL personas? Which do you think is more "real"? Why?

Writing Suggestion

Turkle discusses the "Disneyland effect" and the "artificial crocodile effect" (paragraphs 10–13). Choose one of these phenomena and briefly summarize what it is, drawing on Turkle's definitions and examples. Then follow your summary of Turkle with examples of your own that illustrate the effect. What influence, if any, has it had on your own understanding of real communities and real life?

Black Struggles in Cyberspace: Cyber-Segregation and Cyber-Nazis

Colin Beckles

Internet enthusiasts celebrate the possibilities for community-building and global communication offered by this new technology, along with the vast amount of information it provides in helping users make personal and professional decisions. But what if you can't afford to get on the "information superhighway," or if you lack the expertise to find your way from one destination to the next? And what if, rather than providing opportunities for interacting with others and developing new social connections, the Internet instead confronts you with hostile and hate-filled messages? According to Colin Beckles, this is the experience of some African Americans going on the Internet today. Race- and class-based factors present barriers to their access to the Internet, and once they gain access the proliferation of racist and white-supremacist discourse on the Internet present them with an unwelcoming environment, to say the least.

Beckles, a professor at Washington State University, originally published this article in The Western Journal of Black Studies *in 1997. Like other observers of the Internet, he's concerned that certain groups of people, through no fault or choice of their own, might be getting left out of the information revolution. With more and more businesses and government agencies offering services via the Internet, those who don't have access are going to be at an increasing disadvantage. Moreover, Beckles' observations about the reasons for the Internet's predominantly white, middle-class orientation might make you rethink the claims of earlier essays in this chapter about the Internet's power to create vibrant virtual communities. Does the Internet's "anything goes" approach simply make it easier to discriminate and exclude? Does the fact that interactions are virtual rather than face-to-face make it easier to insult and attack? Does the Internet actually provide a place where the civility of real communities can be disregarded?*

As you read, *think about other groups that may feel unwelcome in the Internet's virtual communities. To what extent do Beckles's observations about African-American Internet users apply, for example, to other minority groups, nonnative English speakers, women, and people with disabilities? Do* *the same kinds of problems confront individuals in these groups when they try to get on the information superhighway?*

> *"Tony Brown advocates 'a gospel of racial uplift through better computing.'"*
> —Tony Brown's Cyberspace Club. 1997.

> *"Now More Than Ever, the Mastery of Technology is Critical to Black Advancement"*
> —P. Carey, Black Enterprise Magazine. 1996.

If the phrase "knowledge is power" is to have real significance   1
for African Americans in the 21st century, it must surely be applicable
to the Internet. Computer-based communications such as the Internet
have been demonstrated to empower users by giving them "more
accurate information about matters of political, professional, and
organizational concern than peers who do not" (Anderson et al.,
3: 1995; Schuler 1996; Schwartz 1996). With the advent of relatively
easy to use Internet web browsers such as Netscape and comprehensive search engines such as Yahoo, Internet users can now benefit from
access to larger amounts of premium quality information in a faster,
user-friendly, and less expensive fashion: direct access to privileged
educational resources such as Howard University and Harvard University; access to city, state and federal politicians and their staff; access to local, national and international business and financial
information; crucial, timely reports dealing with matters of health and
science; and of course, a myriad of entertainment, travel and social
networking information (Yahoo, http://www.yahoo.com 1997; Anderson et al. 1995).

And this new knowledge base has not gone untapped. Indeed,   2
reports suggest that the Internet population, estimated to be 20 million
by the year 2000, grows by 10 to 15 percent each month while the size
of the World Wide Web, a subset of the Internet, doubles every 53
days" (Find/SVP 1997). When the information resources available on
the Internet and its rapid rate of growth are considered along with its
decentralized nature, many Internet enthusiasts are quick to characterize the Internet as a new source of democratic power for the 21st century. One of the most nationally prominent advocates of this
democratizing power is Vice President Al Gore, a relentless champion
for the Global Information Infrastructure—the G.I.I.:

> The G.I.I. will make possible a global information marketplace...It will   3
> in fact promote the functioning of democracy...(Gore, 1994)

However, despite the vice president's and others enthusiasm for   4
the G.I.I. and its U.S. counterpart, the National Information Infrastructure, many critical assessments of the Internet's democratic abilities

have come to the fore. Commonly referenced problems deal with barriers to Internet access, political and social abuses of the Internet (Anderson, 1995; Brook and Boale, 1995; Defife 1995; Dennis 1996; King and Kramer 1995; Miller 1995; Sclove 1995; Sheppard 1995; Slouka in Louv 1995; Mosco and Wasko 1988).

This paper serves to add to this growing body of literature by 5
critically examining the role of the Internet in relation to people who reside in the United States of America and are of African descent. The overall argument is that while the Internet has the potential to empower the African American community, various aspects constrain this potential. This is demonstrated in two ways. First it is argued that various socioeconomic factors continue to serve as formidable barriers blocking the majority of the Black community from access and subsequent participation on the Internet. Moreover, we argue that white racial terrorism occurring on the Internet further constrains its democratic potential. Conclusions and remarks will follow. Endnote provides a discussion of conceptual and methodological issues.

PART I: CYBER-SEGREGATION

> The 21st century will not be a century of Blacks and whites, racism and 6
> sexism. It will be a century of haves and have-nots. Haves will know how to use computer technology to create wealth and the have-nots won't. (Tony Brown, www.tonybrown.com. 1996)

As Professor and T.V. Journalist Tony Brown suggests, equal to 7
the potential democratizing benefits the Internet may bring to communities is the real danger posed by the further exclusion of already marginalized communities from this new information age. Indeed, a review of the literature on the racial and economic composition of Internet users reveals a very clear and seemingly unrefutable reality. These studies suggest that in large part, the present composition and usage of the Internet has and could continue to be the domain of historically privileged groups (Brook and Boale, 1995). Anderson et al (1995) conservatively estimated that the costs for minimum Internet services would be as follows:

Internet Costs

a) Computer with modem and Internet software $1000–3000 8
b) Internet connection costs (basic E-mail) $60/year
c) Computer and Internet training $40/year
d) User support services $140/year

(Source: Anderson et al 1995; Washington State University Instructional Services)

Examination of these sample costs suggests that there exists a   9
substantial "toll charge" for riding on the information superhighway.
Thus, it is evident that those who can afford to access the Internet are
part of a privileged class. Moreover, it is this class who will comprise
the "information elite" in the 21st century: "An information Elite still
exists, made up of those with access to and knowledge about computers and E-mail...Specifically, computer access and use is positively related to higher levels of education and income" (Anderson et al. 1995).

Statistical reports on the income and educational backgrounds of   10
Internet users bear witness to the above. 64 percent of Internet users
have at least a college degree and the average household income is approximately $60,000 (Nielsen Media Research 1995; Graphics Visual
Research, 1996 (G.V.U.); find/SVP 1). Results from the American Internet User Survey revealed that more than half of all their respondents
had incomes of $40,000 or more (Find/SVP 1995).

However, as opposed to professor Brown's suggestions, we be-   11
lieve that a privileged class of information elite will be present across
racial lines as well. Recent reports suggest that only 6 percent of
African Americans are in the $50,000 and above income bracket and
less than 25 percent had attended college as compared with 10 percent
and 33 percent of respective whites (Oliver and Shapiro, 1995; Eitzen
and Baca-Zinn, 1990). As such, the majority of the African American
community obviously cannot afford the "toll charges" for Internet access. Thus, as with the white community, the benefits of the Internet
will be restricted to a small privileged class of "Black information
elites," primarily comprised of the Black professional classes as well as
those who access the Internet through university accounts. Indeed, the
bifurcation between information haves and have nots will be even
more acute in the Black community given the fact that the economic
and educational levels are wider within the African American community than in the white community (Eitzen and Baca Zinn 1990; Oliver
and Shapiro 1996; Hacker, 1992).

Moreover, if it was solely a case of class barriers, we would expect   12
African Americans in the professional classes to be accessing and participating on the Internet on par with their economic counterparts in white
society. However, the data suggests otherwise. In fact, reports suggest
that strong support exists for independent racial effects occurring in Internet access. As such, African Americans and other minority groups are
significantly divorced from access to computers and the Internet beyond what we would expect due to economic differences alone:

>...race is independently related to computer and network access—   13
>whites being significantly more likely to have access to both than Blacks
>and Hispanics. Apparently, if current trends continue without interven-

tion, access to electronic information and communications technologies (and associated benefits) will be skewed in favor of traditionally advantaged groups. (Anderson et al, 1995:xiv)

Similar reports support these findings. The Graphic Visualiza-   14
tion Research's (1996) Fifth study of world wide web users revealed that globally, 87 percent were White, while in the U.S. 88.6% were white and only 1.3% of world wide web user were African Americans. Similarly, as Table 2 demonstrates, the American Internet User Survey reported that while African American users were the largest minority group users of the Internet, they still comprised only 5 percent of all Internet users (Find/SVP 1995). On the contrary, whites clearly dominate Internet usage:

Internet User Demographics:

Ethnic Background   15
White 83%
Black African American 5%
Hispanic 3%
Asian 3%
Other 3%
Refused 3%

(Source: Find/SVP 1995).

Thus, even among those privileged African Americans who have   16
the economic and educational qualifications for Internet access, it seems that only a small portion of those are actual computer, internet, and/or World Wide Web users. Various reasons for these independent racial effects have been put forth. One possible explanation focuses on the content of the information on the Internet. Indeed, despite the wealth of information currently available on the Internet, much of the content is probably geared toward the needs of the majority of its users—white, middle class Americans. Thus, as with other media, many African Americans and people of African descent in general may not feel that the information content on the Internet is relevant to their immediate concerns (Wilson and Gutierrez, 1995). Notes from an ongoing study of a lower income, multicultural community in Bridgeport Connecticut are telling and possibly applicable across class lines:

Providing local content that is most practical and relevant to the user is   17
the first step to providing access to a greater pool of resources. Until a critical mass of this local information is readily accessible to users it is

unlikely that many of Bridgeport's residents will want to access Bridge-
Net. (BridgeNet, 1997)

A second explanation centers upon an interrelated set of   18
processes hampering the African-American community from becoming trained effectively (Black Enterprise Editors 1997; Carey 1995;
Resnick and Russ, 1996; Anderson et al 1995). First, it is suggested that
many African Americans across class lines who may desire to use the
Internet have not had enough exposure to the Internet to overcome
hesitations about the "technological complexity" of the Internet.... But
what of those who have overcome their "techno-phobia." Are they receiving the initial training on how to become Internet Users? Even if
these initial skills are learned, is continued technical support, time,
and support needed to become fluent and effective Internet users
forthcoming? In other educational arenas, studies have demonstrated
that effective training and guidance that comes from strong culturally
based mentoring and sponsorship (Allen 1995. Frierson et al 1995,
Guyton and Hidalgo 1995; Toress-Guzman 1995; Mosco 1986). Given
the low numbers of African American Internet users, there may be a
corresponding low number of trained African American technical support staff. If these potential "black tech mentors" are absent, then the
necessary cultural mentoring would also be absent, possibly serving as
another barrier to internet usage and fluency. As such, frustration and
isolation may occur in potential African American internet users
blocking their further technological development.
        In the above section, some of the barriers posed to African Amer-
ican access and effective participation on the Internet have been
reviewed. However, in addition to the struggle against such institutionalized barriers to cyberspace, the Black information elite also has
to struggle with the overt white racial terrorism occurring on and via
the Internet. It is this issue to which we now turn.

PART II: CYBER-NAZIS:
RACIAL TERRORISM IN CYBERSPACE

... there are about 250 hate groups, 25,000 committed white supremacists   10
and 3,000 to 5,000 racist skinheads in the U.S.... They are embracing [the
'Net] more quickly than the rest of the population. (Cooper, 1996)

Historically, when African Americans have attempted to access   20
and effectively participate in so-called democratic institutions of the
U.S., various White racist groups have used overt means to discourage
and extinguish that participation. Since the 1800s, the Ku Klux Klan

has been at the forefront of those racial terrorist organizations that have attempted to block African Americans access to social power and reserve the benefits of U.S. society for the white race (Franklin and Moss 1994; Sims 1978).

Now, as the Internet rises to its potential as the newest source of   21
social power, the battle lines are drawn yet again. Reports reveal that a sub-group of the white information elite belong to historically violent white racist organizations. As the excerpt above suggests, the Ku Klux Klan, Aryan Nations, The Christian Posse Comitatus, the White Aryan Resistance and a plethora of skinhead groups are rapidly accessing the Internet (Sheppard 1995). The number of white supremacist groups utilizing the Internet is so extreme, that in 1996, the European Union established a special division to investigate and stop the spread of racism via the Internet. The European Union Commission on Racism and Xenophobia (C.R.A.X.): Reports suggest that white racists organizations are using the Internet in order to disseminate their call for white domination and violence against African American and other racial minorities (Anti-Defamation League 1996; Barney 1996; Sheppard 1995; Cooper 1996; Battle 1995). The span of white supremacists on the Internet is indeed vast, encompassing individuals, certain militia groups, academics and religious organizations: Tom Metzgers White Aryan Resistance Page—WAR; Christian Identity Links, Their web sites are filled with swastikas, skulls and other symbols of hate and violence. As Sheppard (1995) reports, they represent the objectives and themes of their "real-life" counterparts:

> A majority of the cyber-hate home pages advocate the geographical sep-   22
> aration of whites from nonwhites. Some blame Jews for the world's eco-
> nomic problems, while others blame Blacks for crime in America and
> accuse them of plotting to eliminate the white race (Sheppard, 1995).

Regardless of the particular form the white racist organizations   23
take on the Internet, the message of hate and/or violence against racial minorities in order to preserve white power is clear. As the two Internet documents below suggest, a call to armed violence in a "race war" is a commonly expressed theme:

> ...unless the white race rises up against its tormentors in a consuming   24
> fury, we will instead be consumed by them. I don't hate these people as
> individuals but only a fool would believe that we will ever live together
> in peace. Events like this, as well as Waco, Randy Weaver massacre and
> Oklahoma City portend a darkening future for America and it is
> becoming increasingly clear that unless heroic measures are taken with-
> out delay, there will be no future for our children. (Christian Posse

Comitatus of Pennsylvania, http://ww2.stormfront.org/watchman/terror.html., 1/21/1996)

The Manifesto of The CNG: 25

1. In order for these forces of darkness to triumph, it is sufficient   26
that good men do nothing. Positive and militant steps are required to
check the spread of evil in the land. Our theater of operation is Cyberspace...Conflict is the crucible from which the superior man is born.

2. We are a white nationalist organization. We represent the heart   27
and the soul of the white nation....There will be no one world government except it be a white one.

3. We represent a nation that will not sacrifice the lives of its youth   28
in the name of abstract principles like "peace" or "containment." Our
soldiers are here to KILL...

We believe that immigration must be white to preserve our culture   29
and land. All nonwhites must be either exported or segregated to prevent
further bastardization of our people, domination of our land, jobs, and position of education and employment. (CNG, http://www.io.com/
~wlp/aryan-page/ cng/ index.html. January, 1996)

If the above were isolated to disparate, individual white su-   30
premacist sites alone, that would be sufficient cause for alarm. However, as Cooper (1996) suggests, various groups are specifically
seeking out new recruits and training new members in the call for
white domination and white power via the Internet. Many utilize Internet discussion forums such as "usenet" for dual purposes of disseminating racist messages and hoping to gain new warriors to their
cause:

The CNG is a cell-based White Nationalist organization. Its battle-   31
ground is the Internet. The CNG develops propaganda, distributes
propaganda, and recruits for real world organizations. (CNG,
http://www.io.com/~wlp/aryan-page/cng/index.html. 1/21/96)

USENET offers enormous opportunity for the Aryan Resistance to   32
disseminate our message to the unaware and the ignorant. It is the
only relatively uncensored free-forum medium we have available.
Now is the time to grasp the WEAPON which is the Net. (Kleim,
http://www.io.com/~wlp/aryan-page/ cng/tac.html, 1/21/96).

However, recruitment is not restricted to white discussion 33
groups. Prominent white nationalists such as Milton Kleim advocate
recruitment in mainstream groups:

> Crucial to our USENET campaign is that our message is disseminated 34
> beyond "our" groups. We must go beyond our present domain, and
> take up positions on "mainstream" groups. (Kleim, http://www
> .io.com/~wlp/aryan-page/cng/tac.html. 1/21/96)

Alternatively, some are urged to invade usenet discussions and 35
use "hit-and-run" techniques, sending racist E-mail messages such as
the following to thousands of 'Net users (Sheppard, 1995):

> Kill that nigger he's worse than a fag 36
> Blast him in the head with a 44 mag
> Kick him punch him and crush that bro
> Douse him with gasoline and burn his fro
> Hit him with a flashlight and kick him in the head
> Just make sure that niggers dead
> Big lipped chicken eating melon stealing bast
> I can't wait to kill a nigger with a shotgun blast!

> (E-mail sent originally Nov, 1995 by DeSean Mychal-McDuffie Yarrel 37
> http://www.geocities. com/ collegepark/3571. Re-sent to Neftara Clark
> of the Anti Racist Action E-mail list, March 1997).

African-American sites also occasionally become the targets of 38
racist anger:

> White supremacists, skinheads, neo-Nazis and racists prowl through cy- 39
> berspace leaving the occasional offensive messages. A woman using the
> race-proud screen name "Ebony Queen" got flamed with a catty "Wel-
> fare Queen" response when she entered a chat room, according to the
> July issue of Newsweek. (Sheppard, 1995)

Others such as those belonging to CNG and Carolinian Lords of 40
the Caucus (C.L.O.C.) deliberately infiltrate the discussion groups and
E-mail lists frequented by marginalized groups such as African Americans and other minorities. The goal seems to be to aggressively challenge and/or attack the discussion group member and disrupt the
topics and tones of the conversations:

> One of the groups targeted by Kleim and other cyber guerrillas was 41
> alt.fan.oj-simpson, which emerged as a forum for supporters of the foot-
> ball legend during his trial for the murder of his ex-wife and her friend,
> Ronald Goldman. With input from Kleim and members of the neo-Nazi
> National Alliance, the news group became a flash point for racially

charged debate over the case, and a forum in which white nationalists sought new members, arguing that the trial showed whites, not minorities, were the victims of racism. (Sheppard, 1995)

Finally, it is predicted that by the year 2000 the total number of   42
Internet connected networks inside and outside the U.S.A. will be in the millions (Rutkowski 1994). Given this, it is also likely that the number of networks dedicated to historically violent racist groups will also climb as well. Reports suggest that networks of white supremacist are continuously being spun globally via the Internet. Therein, worldwide organizing for racial violence may occur as material and information encouraging racist violence and aggression can be exchanged globally at the click of a mouse button:

> According to EC officials, the Thule BBS's, which first appeared in 1991,   43
> started spreading the Neo-Nazi word on the Internet in late 1994, having established themselves as a means of information exchange in Germany and, to a limited extent, in France.... According to Chip magazine at the time, "The (Thule) network distributes information on demonstrations and invitations to meetings, addresses for contacting parties and groups, and it reviews and offers books and magazines. One of the mailboxes contained instructions for producing military explosives and letter bombs. (Dennis, 1996)

Today, websites such as Don Black's "Stormfront" function as   44
cyberspace organizing centers for racist networks. These sites have multi-dimensional roles, acting as information archives, resource centers, recruiters and cyberspace trainers. As major nodes in the growing networks of white supremacy, Stormfront, Thule, and the Aryan Crusaders Library facilitate the formation of new coalitions between former splinter white supremacist groups, and extend the power of larger groups such as the National Alliance (Barney, 1996). And as evidenced below, as with the rest of Internet, this network of cyber-hate is not locally confined, but instead extends across the U.S. into Canada, South America and Europe.

> The hub of the White nationalist network appears to be the Aryan Cru-   45
> sader's Library, which originates in Austin. The site provides extensive information about and links to white nationalist organizations in the U.S. and Europe.... The groups have forged links, at least electronically, to white nationalist groups in Canada, France, Germany, England, Belgium, Portugal, Denmark, Finland, Sweden, Luxembourg, Italy, Austria and the Netherlands. (Sheppard, 1995)

CONCLUSIONS AND IMPLICATONS

> Movement toward an idealized democracy...is severely constrained   46
> whenever a host of non-random factors determine that certain groups and
> individuals never achieve social and political equality. (Gandy 1988)

As opposed to the declarations of Vice President Al Gore and other   47
advocates about the democratizing power of the Internet, our preliminary
analysis has suggested that in relation to internet access, content and
usage, the Internet has not lived up to its democratic potential. Specifically, our review of specific African American issues in cyberspace has led
us to two predominant conclusions. First, despite the Internet's potential
as a source of democratic power, at present we are witnessing in cyberspace reconcentration of power along class and race lines.

African Americans remain only 5 percent of Internet users and   48
no increase has been forthcoming. The implications for the African
American community are clear. As King and Kraemer (1995) succinctly state, if African Americans "lack access to new communication
technologies, we may be at risk of exclusion from the fabric of the nation's social and economic life" (King and Kraemer, 1993).

As the benefits of Internet usage become continually re-   49
concentrated primarily in the hands of white America, a defacto state of
virtual segregation will become manifest. The majority of African Americans will remain in information ghettos outside of cyberspace, or struggle within the "gilded ghettos" of the Internet. Gilded ghettos are
characterized by a lack of resources such as of Black tech mentors. This
implies a frustrating and/or discouraging experience for many potential Black Internet users. The scarcity of such Black tech-mentors may
also hamper the technological development of those African American
children attempting to becoming fluent in the language of computers in
particular and encouraging them to pursue scientific fields of study in
general (Black Enterprise Editors 1997; Montgomery 1996; Resnick and
Russ, 1996; Anderson 1995; Carey, 1995; Chen in Mosco 1988).

The second overall conclusion is that apparently, the information   50
highway is being readily utilized by historically violent white racist individuals and organizations for the preservation of white power.
These groups are archiving and disseminating violent, racist information on the Internet, surfing cyberspace for new recruits, and verbally
attacking and threatening African Americans and other minorities in
cyberspace. Moreover, many are using the information superhighway
as an organizing device: they are connecting and consolidating with
other white supremacist organizations locally, nationally and interna-
tionally. Indeed, some are preparing for a race war both in cyberspace
and in "the real-world." Thus, in direct contrast to its democratic

ideals, the Internet is being used to specifically deny the democratic participation of African American and other people of color across the globe both on the Internet and in the "real world."

Despite the barriers served by issues of ghettoization and the   51
threat of racial violence, 5 percent of Internet participants are of African descent. Given this, various questions arise. Are those within the Black information elite attempting to empower themselves and their communities via the Internet? If so, what strategies are being employed? Are their strategies restricted to the virtual realm, or are real world events included? While an examination of these issues is beyond the scope of this paper, these and similar issues are addressed in a subsequent work (see Beckles, 1997). Therein, the role played by Black information gateways," Black Internet host providers, and black cyber-organizing centers in combating cyber-segregation and racial terrorism are assessed.

Future research needs to address the level of African American   52
ownership and control of the communication backbone—the underlying telecommunication network upon which the Internet runs. Moreover, we need to assess the effect the spread of the G.I.I. will have on African communities outside the U.S.—across the African diaspora and on the African continent itself.

Will the Black community be relegated to workers and users   53
worldwide or will we be able to own, control and design the development of the G.I.I. and thus make the Internet and its "backbone" responsive to the needs and interests of our communities?

Finally, the repressive utilization of the Internet by government   54
forces needs to be critically and rigorously monitored and investigated. Reports suggest that "left wing" cyberspace organizations such as the Institute for Global Communications are presently under surveillance by the U.S. government (Corn, 1996; U.S. Congress, Office of Technology Assessment 1995). As the call for the democratic empowerment of people of African descent via the Internet begins to be answered, we must be aware that the long shadow of "COINTELPRO" will surely continue to drape over our efforts.

REFERENCES

Allen, K., S. Jacobsen, and K. Lomotey. (1995). "American women in educational administration: Importance of mentors and sponsors." *The Journal of Education* (64) #4. 409–422.

Anderson, R., Bikson, T. K., Law, S. A. and Mitchell B. M. (1995). "Universal access to e-mail: Feasibility and societal implications." *www.rand.org/ publications/MR/MR650.*

Anderson, T. (1993). *Introduction to African American studies.* Iowa Kendall Hunt.

Barney, D. (1996). "White separatists leap on the 'net." *Network World.* (8). News Section.

Beckles, C. (1996). "Virtual resistance: A preliminary analysis of anti-racism in cyberspace." *http://www.free.net.8000/docs/ Intet96/e6_e44.htm*

Beckles, C. (1997). "Black liberation and the internet: A strategic analysis." Paper delivered at the Fourteenth Annual PanAfrican Studies Conference, Indiana State University, April 1997.

BridgeNet. (1997). "Bridgenet progress reports." *http://access.bridgenet.org/center/about/ reports/reports.html*

Brook, J., and Boale, I. (1995). *Resisting the virtual life: The culture and politics of information.* San Francisco, City Light Books.

Brown, T. (1997). "Tony Brown's Cyberspace Club." *http://www.tonybrown.com/cybclub.htm.*

Carey P. (1995). "Creating and new generation of black technocrats." *Black Enterprise.* (26) # 1. pp. 140–142.

Christian posse comitatus of PA. (1996). *http://ww2.stormfront.org/watchman/terror.html*

Clough, M. (1996). "Will global war erupt along internet?" *The Commercial Appeal.* (18), Viewpoint Section. p. 5.

CNG. 1996. *http://www.io.com/~wlp/aryan-page/cng/index.html.*

Cooper in Barney, Doug. (1996). "White separatists leap on the 'net." *Network World.* (8). News, Section, p. 5.

Corn, D. (1996). "Pentagon trolls the net." *The Nation.* (262), pp. 21–24.

Cyber Atlas. (1997). "CyberAtlas." *http://www.cyberatlas.com.*

Dennis, S. (1996). "European commission moves to stamp out racism on the internet." *Newsbytes News Network.* Information Access Company.

Drew, J. (1995). "Media activism and radical democracy." In J. Brook and I. Boale. (eds.), *Resisting the virtual life: The culture and politics of information.* San Francisco. City Light Books. pp. 71–84.

Eitzen, D. S. and Baca-Zinn M., (1993). *In conflict and order.* Boston: Allyn and Bacon.

Editors, (1997). "Black enterprise technology summit: Using technology to enhance your business." *Black Enterprise.* March. pp. 64–73.

Find/SVP. (1996). "Internet users demographic background." *http://etrg.findsvp.com/graphics/Internet/demoraphics/demo_ethnic_mr96.gif.*

Frierson, H. T., Hargrove B. and Lewis, N. "Black summer research students' perceptions and related to research mentors race and gender." *The Journal of Negro Research.* (64) #4. pp. 475–480.

Gandy, O. "Its discrimination, stupid." In J. Brook and I. Boale (eds.), *Resisting the virtual life: The culture and politics of information.* San Francisco: City Light Books. pp. 34–48.

Gore, A. (1994). "Remarks delivered at the meeting of the international telecommunications union, Buenos Aires." (21). In J. Brook and

I. Boale, (eds.), *Resisting the virtual life: The culture and politics of information.* San Francisco: City Light Books. pp. 71–80.

Graphics Visualization and Research Center. (1996). "GVU's Fifth WWW User Survey," *http://www.cc.gatech.edu/gvu/user_surveys/.*

Guyton E. and F. Hidalgo. (1995). *Characteristics, and qualities of urban school mentors, education and urban society* (28) #1. pp. 48–66.

Hacker, A. (1992). *Two nations: Black and white, separate, hostile, and unequal.* New York: Ballantine Books.

Harris, R., and Battle, S. (1995). *The african american resource guide to the internet.* Maryland: On Demand Press.

Karenga, M. (1993). *Introduction to black studies,* California: Sankore Press.

King, J. L. and Kraemer, K. (1995). "Information infrastructure, national policy, and global competitiveness." In *Information Infrastructure and Public Policy,* (4) pp. 5–28.

Kleim, M. (1996). "Usenet tactics and strategy." *http://www.io.com/ ~wlp/aryan-page/cng/tac.html.*

Louv, R. (1995). *Personal decisions ward off virtual reality.*

Lowery, M. (1995). "The rise of the black professional class." *Black Enterprise.* (26) #1. August. pp. 43–54.

Mann, B. (1995). *Politics on the net.* Indiana: Que.

Miller, L. "Women and children first: Gender and the settling of the electronic frontier." In J. Brook and I. Boale, (eds.) *Resisting the virtual life: The culture and politics of information.* San Francisco: City Light Books. pp. 59–70.

Montgomery, K. (1995). "Children in the digital age." *The American Project.* July/August. pp. 69–74.

Mosco, V. and Wasko, J. (1988). *The political economy of information.* Wisconsin: University of Wisconsin.

Nielsen Media Research Center. (1997). "Nielsen media research/commercenet." *http://www.nielsenmedia.com.*

Oliver, M. and Shapiro. (1996). *Black wealth/white wealth.* London: Routledge.

Resnick, M. and Rusk, N. (1995). "Access is not enough: Computer clubhouses in the inner city." *The American Project.* July/August. pp. 60–68.

Rutkowski, A. M. and the Internet Society. (1994). "Visions of the internet." *http://www.isoc.org-internet host counts 1990–2000. http://www.isoc.org.San Diego Union-Tribune.* (6 September). "News Editorial." pp. 1–8.

Schatzmann, J., and Strauss, A. (1973). *Field research: Strategies for a natural sociology.* New Jersey, Prentice Hall.

Sclove, R. (1996). "Making technology democratic", in J. Brook and I. Boale, (eds.), *Resisting the virtual life: The culture and politics of information.* San Francisco: City Light Books. pp. 85–104.

Sheppard. N. (1995). "Hate groups find a home in cyberspace: White nationalists spread message, seek recruits on the net." *Austin American-Statesman.* (23 December). News. p.A1.

Schwartz. E. (1996). *NetActivism: How citizens use the internet.* Songline Studios Inc. Ca.

Stormfront. (1997). "Stormfront: White nationalist resource page." *http://www/stormfront.org/Stormfront.*

Torres-Guzman, M. and Goodwin, L. (1995). *Urban bilingual teachers and mentoring for the future, education and urban society.* (28) #1. pp. 67–89.

U.S. Congress Office of Technology Assessment. (1995). "Electronic surveillance in a digital age." OTA-BP-ITC-149. Washington, D.C.: U.S. Government Printing Office. (July).

Yahoo. (1997). "Yahoo." *http://www.yahoo.com.*

Examining the Text

1. What does Beckles identify as the reasons for African Americans' low level of participation on the Internet? Are some reasons more persuasive than others? Which ones, and why?

2. According to Beckles, what advantages does an individual or group lose by not having access to the Internet? In other words, what are the costs of being among the "information have-nots"?

3. Why do you think Beckles includes so many quotations from racist and white supremacist Websites? How does this help advance his argument?

For Group Discussion

At the end of the article, Beckles offers several suggestions for increasing the number of African Americans on the Internet. Review his comments and discuss whether you think these strategies would be effective. What other suggestions can you come up with to make the Internet a more inviting place for traditionally marginalized groups? For example, do you believe that censorship or restriction of hate-speech on the Internet would be effective? Why or why not?

Writing Suggestion

Perhaps in response to the "cyber-segregation" described by Beckles, a number of sites on the World Wide Web have been created to foster a sense of community among groups that may feel marginalized or excluded by the new information technologies. Among these are the following:

Chicano/Latino Net: *http://latino.sscnet.ucla.edu/*
LatinoLink: *http://www.latinolink.com/*
NativeWeb: *http://www.nativeweb.org*
SeniorSite: *http://www.seniorsite.com/*
Family village: *http://www.familyvillage.wisc.edu/index.htmlx*
AfroNet: *http://www.afronet.com/*
MelaNet: *http://www.melanet.com/*
Estronet: *http://estronet.chickclick.com/*
Grrlspace: *http://www.grrlspace.com/*

Visit one of these Web sites (or a similar one that you know of) and write an analysis of the strategies the site uses to welcome members into its community. How does the content of the site cater to the needs and interests of its audience? How does the design of the site—its colors and images, its organization—help the audience feel welcome and "at home" at this place on the Internet? Are they any interactive components of the site that allow visitors to "talk" to each other? If so, what is the content and tone of these discussions? What other features of the site are employed to respond to its target audience? Finally, assess the overall effectiveness of the web site in creating a responsive virtual community for a particular group of people.

We Are Geeks, and We Are Not Guys: The Systers Mailing List

L. Jean Camp

Much has been written about the Internet as a place dominated by men and unfriendly to women. Statistics vary, and women are going online in increasing numbers, but it's still the case that the Internet population is predominantly male. For some observers that means that men are able to dictate the tone and content of online discussion and Web sites, and in a way that is not always welcoming to women. News media report stories of women participants on the Internet being flamed and harassed online, subject to unwanted sexual come-ons and singled out for excessively hostile treatment. In some chatrooms and MUDs participants play out violent sexual fantasies and there was even a case of "cyber-rape." (Julian Dibbell has written about this in "A Rape in Cyberspace or How an Evil Clown, a Haitian Trickster Spirit, Two Wizards, and a Cast of Dozens Turned a Database Into a Society." See http://iberia.vassar.edu/%7Emijoyce/Issues/Dibell_Reading.html.) The Web, too, has its share of misogyny and pornography, making some women find it an unwelcoming and even somewhat threatening environment.

The two related articles that follow describe an attempt to create a "safe harbor" for women on the Internet and to foster a sense of community among a particular group of women. Systers, a mailing list or virtual discussion group founded by Anita Borg in the early 1990s, is exclusively for women in the field of computer science (professionals, academics, graduate, and undergraduate students). Borg discusses the reasons why she started the list and why she wanted it to be for women only. Camp describes her experiences as a participant on the Systers mailing list, and compares this "community" to others that she's tried on the Internet. Both writers see Systers as providing an essential corrective, not only to the male-dominated Internet but also to their male-dominated profession.

As you read, *consider the differences in tone, style, and structure of Camp's and Borg's articles. Both authors explain and defend Systers, but they speak from different perspectives: Camp as a participant and Borg as founder and moderator. What are the strengths and weaknesses of each approach?*

A ship in port is safe, but that is not what ships are for. Sail out to sea and do new things.

—Admiral Grace Hopper, computer pioneer

The Internet can be rough sailing for women, buffeted by the high winds of derision, sucked down into whirlpools of contention. But in that sea of bytes there are destinations beyond compare, worlds to explore. And as we steer our craft out to sea, braving the great unknown, we know that in this world there are electronic ports where we can become refreshed, refueled and ready to sail again when we may think ourselves alone.

Systers is one of those ports of call. Systers is a mailing list of women in computer science and related disciplines. We are geeks, and we are not guys. Not guys, but geeks! How can that be? But we are, we have been and we continue to be. If it surprises you to learn that more than fifteen hundred feminist geeks are out there, imagine the surprise to each of us!

Being a geek isn't easy. It's hard, intellectually challenging work. For some people, people whose gender I won't go into here, people of less intellectual capability than some of my systers, achieving true geekdom means sacrificing their emotional development. You might have met some of these people. Technical universities and work environments tend to be full of them, and are brusque, competitive places as a result. My place of work, Carnegie Mellon University, is no exception.

1

2

3

4

So is it any wonder that I turn to the net in search of solace? But there I find that all the groups formed for women quickly become swamps of men's bile. One man told me, "I know as much about being a woman as you do." After all, he lives with women, he probably has been intimate with some women and he spends so much time thinking about our many flaws! He certainly knows all about women.

Even the discussion groups that focus primarily on parenting   5 have become arenas for men to pat themselves on their collective backs, to discuss how much more difficult it is to be a father than a mother, and to discuss the discrimination against and oppression of fathers. There is no end to the complaints of the anxious and oppressed white male on the Internet.

Consider a Usenet newsgroup specifically started to discuss is-   6 sues about women: *soc.women,* where the posts by men outnumber the women's. On the Internet, as in life, men dominate discussions about women. Many of the feminists on these newsgroups are indomitable warriors; there will always be a battle for them. But some of us chose to spend our energies elsewhere, and even indomitable warriors need a place to rest.

Too often, when women try to create spaces to define ourselves,   7 we are drowned out by the voices of men who cannot sit quietly and listen, but need to bring themselves into the discussion. Many of these men support women. But the voices of men who cannot be silent even in a space ostensibly devoted to women means that there are no public spaces for women to talk about and to other women.

So we withdraw to a room of our own—to mailing lists. Even the   8 most indomitable woman needs a port of call. Here we chatter and type in nurturing communion, knowing that the world cannot do without our unique contributions.

SYSTERS' HISTORY

A mailing list is a list of email addresses kept on one computer. A mes-   9 sage directed to the list goes to that computer and then is automatically copied to everyone on the list. Someone subscribed to a mailing list generally finds her mailbox full of an endless stream of messages full of earnest discussion, gossip, jokes and occasional discord. Each message by a mailing list member spawns its own replies, a round-robin discussion that at times resembles a support group and at other times a graduate seminar. A bad mailing list can be dull. A good one can be wonderful.

Systers, my port in times of storm, my destination of choice for   10 R&R, was begun by Anita Borg (see her account of Systers on page 401). Dr. Borg is a senior computer scientist at Digital Equipment Corporation (being senior at DEC is a big fat hairy deal in the computing world), a pilot and the benevolent matriarch of fifteen hundred systers. She is, as she has named herself, her systers' keeper. systers is an unmoderated but strongly guided mailing list open to women only. To join, you have to swear you are a woman. It if turns out otherwise, you are removed.

Moderated lists have moderators who sift and sort the stream of messages, culling here, compiling there, much as a good hostess directs the flow of traffic at a dinner party. The default is that all messages go out to everyone. If a discussion begins to dominate, posts made in reply to that discussion, called a thread, are not sent out to the list. Moderation in all things. When Dr. Borg guides mailing lists, she often posts only *Cut it out.* This usually works. She does not view every message before it goes out, as a true moderator does.

On Systers, a woman might send a question or comment to the list and then a volunteer, often the original poster, offers to summarize the results. This prevents list members' personal mailboxes from being flooded. Sometimes a post will cause a flurry of responses: Take Our Daughters to Work Day, for example, was much discussed. Pornography, needless to say, is an issue not to be mentioned under the threat of a firestorm of passionate debate and many resulting "unsubscribe" messages.

Note the discussions in *soc.men* and *soc.women* that relate to women: Threads there include discussions of why men are smarter than women, as proven by SAT math scores. Men arguing against maternity leave since women choose to be pregnant. Men who want men to be able to choose whether or not to admit paternity ("choice for men"). Why men make better parents. Abortion. Abortion. Abortion. How men take all the risks in dating since they have to ask for the dates.

The discussions about women on Usenet are just that—about women. Not by women. About.

Consider the topics that women talk about on Systers when *we* control the debate: how to recruit more women to science. How to deal with illegal questions on interviews. When/if to have children. Whether or not to go to grad school. How to deal with a coworker who harasses you. How to deal with email harassment. How to deal with a job hunt when there are two careers involved. What to do about childcare at conferences. How to select an advisor. What effect would the selection of C rather than LISP or Scheme for a first programming language have upon women in computer science? What good fellowships exists for women?

For even more specific discussions, Systers has sublists for specific affinity groups: for example, for women of color and for lesbian and bisexual women. How freeing to have a place where they don't have to deal with people very unlike them discussing "reverse discrimination" and "special rights" when they want to talk about how to just get through the week.

Systers Didn't Let Me Down

It was early in the morning and I knew it would be a very long day. I   17
had a paper to present at a conference and not one but two ear infec-
tions. The conference—The Telecommunications Policy Research Conference—is the major one in my area of research, and I had twelve
hours to finish my paper, get in the car and drive there to present it.
My advisor had stayed up until the wee hours the previous night
helping me polish. I was still editing.

My husband was actually going to do the driving, so I could   18
work on the presentation in the car. He was coming with me because
of the baby. Five months old. Still breastfeeding. Squiggly and helpless
and wonderful and everything unprofessional in the world.

Going to a conference breast-feeding a baby? There's no chapter   19
on "Dealing with Let-down in Silk" in *Dress for Success*. I didn't know
what to expect, and I didn't have anyone to clue me in. So that morning I sent out a message, a quiet cry for support to one thousand other
professional women in computer science.

They heard me. They took my virtual hand, they gave me virtual   20
hugs. I was not standing in the wilderness. Trailblazer? Hell no! So
many women had gone before me, lactating their way through dissertation defenses, conference presentations and teaching tutorials to top
management that it was no impenetrable forest I stood in, but a clear
road with a clear sign marked not "This way," but "It's Okay."

My message that morning was contained. You could hardly tell I   21
was holding my breath:

> I am going to present at a conference this weekend. Since I am breast-   22
> feeding I am taking little Addie along (4 mos.) My husband is coming
> along, too, to take care of Addie during the day (wonderful?—Yep! he is).
> If you have taken a baby to a conference I would really like to hear your ex-
> periences. I feel like a stranger going to a mostly male conference w/baby.
> How did you handle it? What problem did you have—what did you avoid
> with good judgment calls? What was most helpful/worst?

The responses flowed in. One. Two. Six. Dozens. Without Systers I   23
would have been astoundingly alone—how many lactating technical
doctoral candidates do you know? Instead, I was comforted, told that I,
a normal soul in a body leaking milk, could handle it. I felt like a pioneer,
going into the great unknown when I sent my note to Systers. When I left
for the conference, I had had dozens of responses and I knew that I was
not (and never had been) alone. I got messages from women who had
gone to conferences the previous month and women who had gone fifteen years ago! One woman told of taking her five-week-old baby to a

conference and she was preparing, seven weeks later, to take him along again. They all said, "You can do it. You will be fine."

The one message I did *not* get was: It was terrible and destroyed   24
my career. The horror stories helped there. One woman's little one did one of those massive explosive poops that violate all the laws of physics right in the middle of a session. She readjusted the baby carrier and went to the motel room and cleaned them both up. If their babies could be sick or have an ebm (e = explosive) in a session and all turned out fine, then, well, what was I so worried about!

When I returned from the conference, I reported back to all the   25
women who had reached out to me:

Knowing that there is one incredible person is not always so helpful,   26
simply because this person is so exceptional. But knowing that there are dozens of women, that I did not have to be so unique or incredible, made me feel like I, too, could pull through.

And after all those messages the one thing I was not when I left was so worried. Thank you all. Things went well for me at the conference. I ended up encumbered not by the baby—but by my ear infection!

THE LIGHTER SIDE OF SYSTERS

Systers also serves up lighter fare. Feminists often get abuse for not   27
laughing at funny jokes. Maybe it's that the jokes we're told aren't all that funny. One syster was sent a bunch of jokes about engineers, all of which assumed that engineers are male, for example: "You know you're an engineer when you have a beard because you have calculated your efficiency loss in time shaving and found it unacceptable."

This syster considered sending out a flame: "Hello! Remember   28
me? The engineer? The woman?" Instead she got onto Systers and asked for jokes that assume engineers are women. The result:

29

You know you're an engineer when...

—you have hairy legs not as a political statement but because you have calculated your efficiency loss in time shaving and found it unacceptable.

—they give you drugs during labor not because you can't take the pain but because you keep trying to rebuild your monitors.

—you try to register in the automotive department for your wedding gifts.

—you are excited about your first period because it gives you the opportunity to test the viscosity meter in your chemistry set on an interesting biological sample.

Instead of flaming the men for their sexism, she sent back a col-   30
lection of jokes from our point of view. Who says we don't have a
sense of humor?

THE BARBIE EXPERIENCE

Systers is a powerful personal resource for women, but there is an im-   31
portant public element, too. Nothing illustrates this better than the
great Barbie fracas. If you recall, Mattel introduced a Talking Barbie in
1993. This Barbie said things guaranteed to appeal to the mostly brain-
dead. Among the gems that sprang from her perfect lips was "Math is
hard."

An alert syster, possibly the appalled mother of the owner of one   32
of these dolls, sent out a message. After all the discussions we'd had of
how to keep young women and girls interested in math, this was a
broadside.

Women study math because mathematical competence leads to   33
more money, which leads to many good things, such as autonomy.
Math is fun. Math is good. Math and technical knowledge are power.
Here was Mattel saying clearly to girls: Stay away from math. You are
not interested in any quantitative professional career. Take domestic
science! Be dependent.

I read the *Washington Post* and skim the *New York Times* and the   34
Wall Street Journal regularly. I have The Associated Press and United
Press International wires available to me via Clarinet. But Systers
spoke first.

Actually, first we *screamed.* Then we discussed it. Then we got   35
down to business. Never mess with systers.

We found the number for Mattel's complaint line and started call-   36
ing. Individual systers called their professional organizations to complain, and the American Association of University Women did just that.
The mainstream media picked it up—after Systers had begun the battle.

Mattel surrendered: Barbie no longer advocates female innumer-   37
acy. Systers got women together, and we acted.

JOIN THE FRAY

Computers can give you a level of anonymity, which may give some   38
women who've never spoken up in public the courage to express themselves. But anonymity is isolation, a level of invisibility. After playing
around Web pages and lurking on Usenet groups, you want to be seen

and to define yourself. You do not want people to define you, especially not by simply looking at your name and guessing your gender.

Systers has given me comfort when I needed it, reminding me every day that I am not alone. The feeling is small, but constant. As Systers has filtered into my being over time, it has become a tremendous positive force in my life. Not being alone means not being hidden. Of course, Systers speaks to me as a technical woman in academia. But there are many other mailing lists for women—no woman needs to be alone on the net.

The very strength that Systers offers can make it a sanctuary on a hostile net. But we cannot live in a sanctuary, regardless of the temptation. It is important to go back out into the public debate and remain visible, if for no other reason than to ensure that no woman is left truly isolated. The power of connectivity to effect change is truly incredible. The Barbie experience taught me that. The far right realizes it, too, and is organizing on the net. We need to be doing the same. If not, it will be as if women were sending out missives via caravan while those who would deny women their rights were using Cruise missiles. If we're not there, the doors of electronic democracy will be closed to us.

On the Mailing List Systers, from *Computing Research News*, September 1994

Dr. Anita Borg

The existence of exclusively female forums is controversial and legitimately so. Exclusive forums such as male-only or white-only or Christian-only clubs have been used to exclude other groups from information and power sharing. As the founder of Systers, a large female-only mailing list, I have frequently been called upon to justify the exclusion of men and to explain why Systers is not discriminatory in the above sense. This article attempts such an explanation. I hope to generate discussion, but more importantly, to generate understanding and cooperation.

Increasing the number of women in computer science and making the environments in which women work more conducive to their continued participation in the field require the active development of both women and men. In particular, there must be ongoing and productive communication throughout the field concerning the unique problems that women face when they enter the field and as they progress and advance. The fact that women are a small minority in the field results in two impediments to this communication. First, women work almost exclusively with men and so have few opportunities to create and then participate in a "community of women in computer science." Second, men work almost exclusively with men and have limited opportunities to communicate with more than a few professional women. Open electronic forums can improve communication by introducing us to a larger community, but do nothing to reduce the disparity in numbers. On the other hand, exclusively female forums, such as Systers, are a particularly effective way to connect women in our field with each other. They also ultimately contribute to improved communication between women and men.

Let me first describe what Systers is and what it is not. Systers is   3
a private, unmoderated, but strongly guided, mailing list with a documented set of rules for participation. The mailing list includes female computer professionals in the commercial, academic and government worlds as well a female graduate and undergraduate computer science and computer engineering students. Systers currently has over 1,500 members in seventeen countries. We are a global community of individuals who are otherwise physically isolated from each other.

Systers is a civilized and cooperative forum in which "flaming"   4
is rare and personal attacks are actively discouraged. We ask that Systers mail not be forwarded nor its contents used outside the list without the permission of the contributors to a message. There is no rule of secrecy in Systers. This rule simply empowers our members and protects our privacy by giving each of us control over the breadth of distribution of our comments. It is based on a common courtesy that, if applied more generally, would make the net a more hospitable place for substantive group problem solving.

Systers is not analogous to a private all-male club. It is different   5
because women in computer science are a small minority of the community. It is different because Systers is not interested in secrecy or in keeping useful information from the rest of the community. In fact, useful messages are regularly made public after checking with the contributors. The likelihood that an underempowered minority will keep inaccessible information from the large empowered majority with every means of communication available to it is small indeed. I have not addressed whether a forum such as Systers would be necessary in an ideal and egalitarian world or even in a world similar to our own but with many more women in computing. When we get there, we can make that decision.

The following paragraphs enumerate the reasons for keeping   6
Systers a female-only forum. None of these benefits accrue to women in other existing open forums. Women need a place to find each other.

As a geographically dispersed and frequently individually isolated minority within computer science, women rarely have the opportunity to interact in person with other women in computer science on any subject. Women (and men) have many opportunities to interact with men. Until Systers came into existence, the notion of a global "community of women in computer science" did not exist.

Women need female role models and mentors. A primary func-   7
tion of women-only interaction is mentoring. Exposing women to the full range of significant interactions among women, without the perception of help or input from men, serves to bolster self-esteem and independence. This includes exposure to women discussing purely technical issues among themselves and shows that this makes women more rather than less able to interact professionally with men.

Women need a place to discuss our issues. Many open forums   8
whose focus is women's issues suffer from a common problem. Discussions are frequently dominated by disagreements between men and women about what the issues are rather than how to deal with them. This is not a problem with all men, but is a problem with almost all such open forums. Women more often share common ground that allows us to get beyond defining issues and on to constructing solutions.

Women need to discover our own voice. Discussion among   9
women is different from that of women together with men. Men, even when in a minority and even when well-meaning, have a different style of interaction. They often dominate discussions. Even when they don't, the style of a mixed conversation tends to be in the style of male-dominated discussions. As women understand more clearly what those differences are and what professional discourse is like on our own, we will be better able to bring our voice to open forums.

I recently received two messages that illustrate how Systers helps   10
women participate more effectively and more professionally with men.

A researcher from an industrial lab stated, "When I first joined   11
the list a few years ago, I was skeptical about the need for a list specifically devoted to issues facing women working in computer science. But since then, I have become much more aware of the differences in the ways men and women interact, and many of the experiences and views shared by others on this list have helped me to better understand how to function effectively in a male-dominated research environment." A university professor described a change in her students: "The availability of the list to our women graduate students here at [the university] has had a remarkable effect on our students. The women are becoming more self-confident and more aggressive in their dealings with our male-dominated faculty, many of whom still regard women as out of place in the program."

Systers is definitely not the only forum in which concerned   12
women participate. It is only a starting place and place of respite in

our journey to equality. It is essential that we continue to actively communicate and participate with men, that we not become isolated from professional men, and that we bring our issues to the fore at every appropriate opportunity. Since most of us work exclusively or nearly exclusively with men, it is actually impossible for us to become isolated from men even if we wish to be. Since men make up the vast majority of the field, it would be foolish to believe that real change could take place without them.

To include men in Systers would take away a vital source of mutual support from women. On the other hand, the need for serious discussion in an open forum exists. It behooves whoever runs such a forum to realize that women who have experienced conversation on Systers will be for the most part uninterested in participating in a wide-open free-for-all. The commonly applied list-management principle "if you can't take the heat, get off the list" will not work. It has been tried and has failed. The forum will need a strong leader/moderator, committed to the encouragement of productive discussion and willing to stop unproductive argument. I do this for Systers. While I do not have the desire nor the energy to run another forum, I am surely not the only person capable of it and offer my help and experience to anyone who is willing to take on the task.   13

It is not the reluctance of women nor our participation in forums like Systers that limits communication and joint problem solving with men. It is the sexism in our society, our field and our consciousness that limits us all. If men want an open forum and are seriously interested in hearing what women have to say, rather than in telling us what we need, then such a forum could be a fruitful and productive sibling for Systers.   14

Examining the Text

1. Camp begins her essay with a metaphor comparing Systers to an "electronic port of call" in the sea of the Internet. What are the implications of this metaphor? What does it suggest about both Systers and the Internet in general?

2. What problems does Camp see in other electronic forums for discussing "women's issues" (such as *soc.women*)? According to Camp, what advantages does systers have over these forums?

3. Camp provides several extended examples of the interactions she's witnessed on Systers: the discussion of bringing babies to conferences, the jokes about women engineers, the Barbie debate. What do each of these examples reveal about the character of the Systers community?

4. According to Borg, why is Systers an important virtual meeting place for women in computer science? Which of her explanations overlap with Camp's experience as a participant in Systers?

Group Discussion

Borg begins her article by recognizing that excluding men from participating in Systers is a controversial and perhaps discriminatory act. She provides a list of reasons to defend this exclusion. Review these reasons as a group and discuss which are the most and the least persuasive. Then choose a few other situations in which a marginalized minority group has created an exclusive forum for its members (think of some of the clubs on your campus or in your community). Does Borg's defense of exclusion apply to these other situations as well? Why or why not?

Writing Suggestions

Borg calls Systers a "global community of individuals who are otherwise physically isolated from each other." Working with a definition of "community" derived from other readings in this section (especially the article by Barlow) and from your own sense of what a "community" should be, write an essay in which you either agree or disagree with Borg's assessment. Based on examples from Camp's and Borg's articles, does Systers constitute a genuine community? What features does Systers share with other communities that you know about, whether on the Internet or in real life? What features are lacking?

ADDITIONAL SUGGESTIONS FOR WRITING ABOUT CYBERCULTURE

1. Recently, a movement composed of individuals who question the merits of technology in general, and computer technology specifically, has arisen in this country. Kirkpatrick Sale, considered by many to be the leader of this movement, said in a recent issue of *Wired* magazine, "Quite apart from the environmental and medical evils associated with them being produced and used, there are two moral judgments against computers. One is that computerization enables the large forces of our civilization to operate more swiftly and efficiently in their pernicious goals of making money and producing things. And, however much individuals may feel that there are industrial benefits in their lives from the use of the computer (that is to say, things are easier, swifter), these are industrial virtues that may not be virtues in another morality. And secondly, in the course of using these, these forces are destroying nature with more speed and efficiency than ever before." In an essay, respond to Sale's argument. What are the dangers inherent in our becoming increasingly dependent on computers, and what are the benefits of computer technology? After weighing the pros and cons of the computer revolution, would you consider yourself a neo-Luddite, as the adherents to Sale's philosophy are sometimes called? Are you a fierce proponent of all things high-tech? Do you fall somewhere in between the two philosophical extremes?

Internet Activities

1. Write an essay in which you compare and contrast the ways in which a topic of your choice is covered in the noncomputer-based media (such as television news, *Time* magazine, National Public Radio, your local newspaper, *The National Enquirer,* roadside billboards, a journal of your choice, and so on) and on a computer-based medium such as the World Wide Web. You may investigate any topic that arouses your curiosity: software design, tattoos and body-piercing, clinical depression, skateboard parks, contemporary Christian music, sports agents, mathematical knot theory. For each point made within this essay, be sure to include textual examples from the sources you are using, to substantiate and develop the comparison/contrast. Be sure to structure your paper so that you don't have to jump back and forth too much from point to point. You might even want to discuss *all* your observations about the non-computerized media treatment of your topic, and then go on to discuss the ways in which World Wide Web treats the same material, pointing out areas of similarity and dissimilarity. By organizing your material in this way, you can avoid choppiness in your supporting paragraphs.

2. In increasing numbers, people are using the World Wide Web to design multimedia, interactive representations of themselves in "personal homepages." These are Web sites created by individuals (rather than businesses, universities, government agencies, and so forth) that present the writer to the wide audience of Web users. Spend some time browsing the Web and looking at these personal homepages in order to get a sense of the range of possible information that can be included on such a site. You'll find several good starting points at the *Common Culture* Web site; there are links there to collections (or "webrings") of particularly good personal homepages.

As you're browsing, keep notes on the strengths and weaknesses of the different homepages, and then try designing one of your own (on paper, or using a web-authoring program if one is familiar and available to you). What information about yourself would you include?

What other Web sites would you want to link your page to? Who would be the intended audience for your personal homepage?

After you've come up with a tentaive design, write an essay in which you explain the decisions you made in creating the page. What image of yourself were you trying to present? How were your decisions influenced by your reactions to the specific homepages you looked at earlier?

3. In response to the "cyber-segregation" described by Beckles, a number of sites on the World Wide Web have been created to foster a sense of community among groups that may feel marginalized or excluded by the new information technologies. Visit one of these sites; you'll find some listed as links from this chapter at the *Common Culture* Web site. After exploring all that the site has to offer, write an analysis of the strategies it uses to welcome members into its community. How does the content of the site cater to the needs and interests of its audience? How does the design of the site—its colors and images, its organization—help the audience feel welcome and "at home" at this place on the Internet? Are there any interactive components of the site that allow visitors to communicate with each other? If so, what is the content and tone of these discussions? What other features of the site are employed to respond to its target audience? Finally, assess the overall effectiveness of the Web site in creating a responsive virtual community for a particular group of people.

4. This assignment requires that you have access to the Internet and enough know-how to join a virtual community like the ones described in the second part of this chapter. (To develop this know-how you can consult one of the many books on the Internet available in bookstores and libraries; you might also check to see if your college or university offers workshops or courses on using the Internet.) Choose a mailing list a MUD or a MOO, and participate in discussions there for a few weeks. You might begin by "lurking" or listening in on discussions without making contributions yourself. Keep notes on the general qualities of the community. What do people talk about? What tones do they adopt in their discussions? Is there any hostility or "flaming," or is the atmosphere more friendly and inviting? How would you describe the connections or relationships among the participants? After you've "lurked" for a while, you might decide to enter the discussion and ask a few questions about why the participants are involved in this particular community and how they feel about the interactions there. Finally, write an essay in which you compare the virtual community you've been monitoring with those described by Barlow and Turkle, for example. Use your experience as a way of testing the ideas of these authors on the relative benefits and drawbacks of virtual communities.

6

Sports

The United States seems to be a nation obsessed with sports, an obsession nowhere more evident than in some fans' virtual addiction to sports statistics. Somewhere there's probably a statistics maven who knows the number of foot faults in the final 1956 Davis Cup match or the most triples by a left-handed batter during Tuesday afternoon World Series games. Fans crave statistics, no matter how minute, as a way of measuring the achievements of their favorite athletes and teams—and perhaps also as a way of holding the memory of never-to-be-repeated athletic performances.

It's not difficult to find further evidence of America's preoccupation with sports. Most daily newspapers allocate an entire section to sports reports and statistics; a number of national weekly and monthly publications concentrate exclusively on sports. Special sporting events such as the Super Bowl are consistently among the most highly rated TV broadcasts, and several cable networks are devoted solely to sports twenty-four hours a day. Americans play sports trivia games, call sports telephone hotlines, and participate in a multibillion dollar sports gaming industry; they display team logos on t-shirts, sweatshirts, baseball caps, and countless other articles of clothing. Many colleges and universities capitalize on the prominence of their sports programs to increase enrollments and donations.

Sports can affect fans in surprisingly intense ways. We all probably know people whose moods fluctuate with the fortunes of their favorite team, who might "bleed Dodger blue," as they say. Indeed, entire cities rejoice when their team brings home a championship, and our national mood lifts when an American underdog takes a medal at the Olympics or when the "Dream Team" squashes an opponent. Given this obsession, it's no wonder that professional athletes are among our most revered—and highly paid—citizens.

How can we explain the popularity of professional sports? The essays in the first part of this chapter offer views about the role of sports in American life in general, including television commentator Dick Schaap's lament for the days when sportsmanship was more important to professional athletes than their next contract, and reporter Kate Rounds' analysis of the negligible status of women's athletics in a male-dominated sports culture. The essays in the second part focus on four specific sports (basketball, football, and boxing), and, by implication, the factors—physical ability, the influence of family and friends, climate and environment, even race and gender—that govern an individual's choice to participate in or follow a particular sport.

Obviously, sports can influence the way we speak and the way we feel, our notions of teamwork and individuality, success and failure, and male and female roles. From sports we learn how to deal with pressure, adversity, and physical pain and we discover models of grace, skill, and style. As you read the essays in this chapter, think of the sports you play and watch, of the athletes you admire, of the role sports play (or have played) in your life.

The Role of Sports in America

So Much of the Joy Is Gone
Dick Schaap

We begin this chapter with a sobering critique of professional sports by a long-time observer. Best known as a television sports commentator, Dick Schaap has also written extensively about sports from the position of an insider; among other publications, he coauthored football great Bo Jackson's autobiography.

In this essay, originally published in Forbes, *a magazine aimed at business executives and investors, Schaap observes that although professional athletes today are "taller, heavier, faster, stronger, smarter" than their predecessors, the joy in watching them perform is gone. According to Schaap, money and greed are at the heart of the problem. Fun, camaraderie, team loyalty, even racial equality suffer when players and owners are motivated primarily by how much they can earn, when "sports preaches green above all else."*

And, Schaap says, fans suffer, too. While there may be individual amateur and professional athletes who still lift our spirits and serve as role models, Schaap sees sports' overall influence on its fans as increasingly harmful.

***As you read,** consider the merits of Schaap's argument. To what extent do you think greed affects sports and athletes? Has the influence of sports become mostly negative? If so, would society be better off without the influence of professional sports?*

Athletes are better than ever. They are taller, heavier, faster, 1
stronger, smarter. In every sport in which achievement can be measured objectively, their progress is stunning.

A girl barely into her teens swims more swiftly than Johnny 2
Weismuller swam in the Olympics, or in his loincloth.

A high school boy jumps farther and sprints faster than Jesse 3
Owens jumped and sprinted in front of Adolf Hitler.

A 30-year-old married woman surpasses Jim Thorpe's best 4
marks in a variety of track and field events.

Even a man over 40 runs a mile faster than Paavo Nurmi ran in 5
his prime.

The performances are so much better. But so much of the joy is 6
gone.

Sports has too often been called a microcosm of society, yet its   7
present state certainly reflects the uneasy prosperity of the times, the
suspicion that, despite encouraging facts and heartening figures,
something is fundamentally wrong. The cheers may be louder than
ever, but they ring a little hollow.

It is almost impossible to overstate the pervasiveness of sports in   8
American society, the breadth and strength of its special appeal, to
bricklayers and novelists, accountants and comedians. "Have you met
Mr. Nixon yet?" the future President's press secretary once asked me.
"You'll like him. He reads the sports pages first."

Then when I did meet Richard Nixon, he phrased his political   9
thoughts in sports terms, spoke of hitting home runs and getting to
first base and striking out. Sports is a language and a diversion and
sometimes an obsession, and more than ever, it is a business.

The stakes are so high now. The *average* major league baseball   10
player earns more than a million dollars a year. Losing pitchers and
feeble hitters, men with stunningly modest statistics, demand much
more. Steve Greenberg, the deputy commissioner of baseball, used to
be an agent, negotiating players' contracts. He once told his father,
Hank Greenberg, the Hall of Famer, who was the first ballplayer to
earn $100,000 in a season, that he was representing a certain player.
"What should I ask for?" Steve said. "He hit .238."

"Ask for a uniform," Hank said.   11

Steve shook his head. "Dad," he said, "you just don't understand   12
baseball any more."

Nobody understands baseball any more. No one relates to the   13
salaries. Not even the players themselves. They earn so much more
than they ever dreamed of.

They also throw pitches Cy Young never dreamed of. (Ever see   14
Cy Young's glove? Small. Very small. Now they have big hands,
hands that can wrap around a ball and deliver a palmball.) They
swing bats with muscles Babe Ruth never dreamed of. They sprint
from home to first, or first to third, with incredible speed. That's the
biggest difference, the way they run these days. They fly.

But they don't know how to bunt. They don't know how to hit   15
and run. They don't know which base to throw to. They didn't spend
childhoods in cornfields playing baseball 10 or 12 hours a day, absorbing the nuances of the game. They may have developed terrific hand-
eye coordination playing video games, but that didn't teach them how
to hit the cutoff man.

Baseball players earn up to $7 million a season. So do basketball   16
players. Football players are embarrassed. Their ceiling is a few million dollars lower. Golfers and tennis players only go up to a million
or two a year in prize money, but they can quadruple their income by

wearing the right clothes, wielding the right clubs, advertising the right corporate logos on their visors and their sleeves.

Even athletes who are officially amateurs, runners and skaters   17
and skiers, earn hundreds of thousands of dollars a year. How can anyone afford to have fun?

Once there was a camaraderie among athletes. They competed   18
on the field, but afterward they were friends, sharing a common experience, a common attitude, bonded by their love for their game. Tennis players, for instance, traveled together, roomed together, partied together, exchanged advice and rackets. Now each has a coach, and an agent, and a father or brother, and a fistful of sponsors, walling them off, separating them. Then can face each other across the net for years and never get to know each other.

Even in team sports, team spirit is, for the most part, gone, rekin-   19
dled only occasionally by victory. "We are family," in sports terms, means: "We won." It doesn't mean we worry about each other, bolster each other, counsel each other.

How can fans relate to these athletes? How can they embrace he-   20
roes who have so much money and so little loyalty? Players change teams now as casually as they change jockstraps. Once you could fall in love with a lineup, commit it to your heart and your memory, and not have to learn more than one or two new names a year.

"The names, just to say the names, you could sing them," the   21
playwright Herb Gardner once wrote, lamenting the Dodgers' move to Los Angeles. "Sandy Amoros, Jim Gilliam, Hodges, Newcombe, Campanella, Erskine, Furillo, Podres, gone, gone... even the sound is gone. What's left? A cap, I got a cap, Dodgers, '55, and sometimes on the wind I hear a gull, and Red Barber's voice...."

Now the Dodger lineup changes every day, millionaires come   22
and go, succumbing to minor injuries, whining about imagined slights, and even the manager, Tom Lasorda, who loves the team so much he says he bleeds Dodger blue, can't call all his players by name.

Once Dodgers were Dodgers for decades, and Cardinals Cardi-   23
nals, and Red Sox Red Sox, but now they're L.A. Kings for a day, or maybe a month or a season, and if an athlete puts in a full career with one team, in one city, he isn't a hero, he's a monument.

It's easy to fault the players for earning so much money, for dis-   24
playing so little loyalty, but it isn't fair. They didn't invent greed, or ingratitude. They learned from their mentors, the owners. The baseball players of the 1950s, the football players of the 1960s, had little idea of how underpaid they were. Soon after the salaries started to soar, a baseball player named Ken Singleton told me, "The owners screwed the players for one hundred years. We've been screwing them for five. We've got ninety-five more years coming."

The owners came up with the idea of moving for the money, too.   25
The Braves went from Boston to Milwaukee to Atlanta, strip-mining
stadia along the way. The Dodgers and the Giants traveled west hand
in hand, with the other hands, of course, thrust out. They left shattered
fans behind.

"They went, and the city went with them," Herb Gardner wrote.   26
"The heart went with them, and the city started to die. Look what you
got now, look what you got without no heart. What's to root for? Duke
Snider! He went away! How many years in the stands hollering? A
lifetime in the afternoon hollering, 'I'm witcha, Duke, I'm witcha,'
never dreaming for a moment that he wasn't with *me!*"

Teams, and owners, and athletes have disappointed us in so   27
many ways. The disappointment goes beyond the greed, beyond the
selfishness. How can you put athletes up on a pedestal who flaunt fast
cars at illegal speeds, who succumb to the lures of social drugs and
performance-enhancing drugs, who maltreat women as spoils, who
lose gambling fortunes that would change most people's lives? How
can you pick a hero any more and count on him?

Sports has let us down.   28

Half a century ago, when Jackie Robinson became a Brooklyn   29
Dodger and Joe Louis was the greatest fighter in the world, sports held
out so much hope, so much promise. Equality, that elusive gift bestowed on all Americans by the Declaration of Independence, was
going to be won and secured, finally, on the playing fields.

Of course. On the playing fields, every competitor was equal.   30
The scoreboard knew no race, no religion, no nationality. Sports offered the ultimate democracy, where a man or a woman's success derived purely from his or her ability.

But, as brave as Jackie Robinson was, as good as Jimmy Brown   31
was, and Henry Aaron and Bob Gibson and O.J. Simpson and Ernie
Davis and Wilt Chamberlain and Bill Russell and Althea Gibson and
Arthur Ashe and Rod Carew and Bill White and Julius Erving and
Muhammad Ali and Sugar Ray Leonard and Magic Johnson and Oscar
Robertson and Willie Davis and Lawrence Taylor and Alan Page and
Jerry Rice and Walter Payton and so many more, the brotherhood of
man has flourished no more on the playing fields than in the streets.

Thanks to sports, there are many more black millionaires now   32
than there were a few decades ago, but there is not equality, not the
kind of equality that not so long ago seemed possible, or even likely.
Black players still tend to sit with black players on team buses and at
training tables, and white players cluster together, and so do the black
wives of black players.

For every Bill Bradley or Jack Kemp, who learned from the sports   33
experience, who gained some insight into the dreams and fears of

teammates of different color, who has sought to translate those into political action, dozens of athletes slip back into prejudice as soon as black teammates are out of sight, or out of hearing. They use privately the same cruel words that Jackie Robinson heard publicly.

Corporate America is no better, only more polite. Michael Jordan   34
and David Robinson and O.J. Simpson and Bo Jackson, men so much larger than life, have been able to transcend color and earn millions for endorsements, but below the superstar level, white athletes have an unmistakable edge, have first call on commercials and appearances and exposure.

It is ludicrous, the infinitesimally low percentage of black man-   35
agers and coaches and executives in professional and collegiate sports. They don't have "the necessities," Alex Campanis, a Los Angeles Dodgers executive, once blurted out on network television, clumsily sharing "a truth," as he, and many other management people in sports, perceived it. What necessities? Yogi Berra's IQ? Whitey Her-zog's charm? They both managed first-place teams in both big leagues; so much for necessities. There are plenty of black Berras and black Whiteys, and smarter and more charming blacks—I thought Willie Davis, the former Green Bay Packer, a Hall of Fame defensive end, an enormously successful businessman and civic leader, a warm and thoughtful man, would have been a perfect commissioner of the Na-tional Football League; he got only token consideration—but they are so often overlooked, and more often snubbed.

I share the guilt. When I was editor of a sports magazine, I was   36
frequently scolded by my employer for putting too many black ath-letes on the cover. I was told that white athletes sell more magazines, and I cycled and recycled Joe Namath and Tom Seaver and Dave DeBusschere and Pete Rose. ("I've been on the cover of *Sport* three times," Rose once cracked at a luncheon I hosted. "That's not bad for a white guy.") I've collaborated on books with many athletes—Namath, Seaver, DeBusschere, Bill Freehan, Frank Beard, Jerry Kramer and Bo Jackson—and only one was black. I accepted the publishing belief, nourished by an Ali autobiography that was a commercial disaster, that blacks did not buy books. When the Bo Jackson book became the best-selling sports autobiography ever, far outgrossing all my other works, that belief was sternly tested. Still, when I write and narrate feature stories for television, I realize, with a twinge, that I lean heavily upon white athletes as subjects and as interviewees. They certainly take up a larger portion of the screen than they do of the playing field.

Fans can be as harsh as they ever were. Once, I was on a plane to   37
Birmingham, Ala., to visit Bo Jackson's home, and a passenger across the aisle, watching me flip through Jackson clippings, leaned over and said, "You know why they call him 'Bo'?" Before I could answer, he said, "Cause they didn't know how to spell 'Bob.'"

I don't know why I was stunned.   38

Sports could be forgiven its flaws, at least some of them, if it had   39
compensating strengths, if it taught the heroic lessons that Homer
once sang of, if it emphasized positive values, if it truly rewarded per-
severance and teamwork and similar virtues.

But these days sports preaches greed above all else. Bad enough   40
that the status of all professional athletes is determined, to a considerable extent, by their income; in golf, pretense is stripped away and the
players are ranked, officially, by their earnings. Worse, the sports
world also glamorizes hypocrisy and deception and corruption.

Big-time college athletic programs are a disgrace. In almost all of   41
the major schools, the question isn't: Do the athletic departments
cheat? It's: How badly do they cheat? Even the squeaky clean programs, the Dukes and the Stanfords and the Notre Dames, the schools
that offer prestige and power and tradition instead of cash and cars
(low monthly payments? would you believe zero?), do not treat the so-
called student athletes the way they treat student nonathletes. And the
Ivy League, which preaches purity, does not always practice it. Any
good Ivy League football player, and there are more than a few every
year, who does not have a summer job on Wall Street paying an inflated salary is either remarkably passive or independently wealthy.

Colleges with winning big-time football and basketball programs   42
are making millions of dollars a year, and their coaches, with their
camps and their clinics and their TV shows, are earning hundreds of
thousands of dollars—all of that money dependent on the skills and
moods of agile and powerful teenagers. To keep all those dollars coming in, virtually all colleges and coaches to some extent are willing to
lie or distort or bribe or glorify, to stretch rules and ignore academic
deficiencies, to pamper the more gifted athletes beyond belief. (Paul
Hornung, after whom the Golden Dome at Notre Dame, his alma
mater, may have been named, once said his own epitaph should be:
"He went through life on scholarship.")

Too many college football and basketball players are treated, to   43
use the title of a book one of them wrote, like "meat on the hoof," but
surely black athletes are the most abused, fed visions of professional
sports careers that will never materialize, steered away from academic
courses that might challenge or inspire them, presented with scholarships to nowhere, free room, free board, free tuition, but not free
thought. A few years ago I visited a very talented college football
player, a likable young man, whose dormitory room was outfitted
with the latest in stereo equipment and Nike posters. There wasn't a
book in his student-athlete room, not one. He was lucky. He made it to
the National Football League. He was one of the rare ones.

In all this gloom there are glimmers of hope. In high schools and   44
colleges and even in international competition, not all sports corrupt

and demean. A pure amateur may be as rare as a whooping crane, but in such college sports as lacrosse (Princeton, of all schools, upset Syracuse for the national championship a few months ago) and field hockey (a dominion dominated by Old Dominion), to name two, sports which hold out little promise of fame or financial reward, men and women still can have fun, still can build character and self-confidence. In the Olympics, I love to wander among the winter biathletes, who couple such contradictory disciplines as shooting and skiing, and the summer pentathletes, who blend riding, shooting, fencing, swimming and running, the pursuits of an ancient courier. Their names are unknown outside the smallest circles, and their per diems are minimal, but their interests often seem to be as varied as their skills. "Our worlds are not confined by ski wax," as a biathlete once told me.

I still find individual athletes who lift my spirits: Bonny Warner,   45
America's best female luger in the 1980s, a graduate of Stanford, a reformed sportscaster, now a United Airlines pilot; Jim Abbott, one of the few baseball players ever to leap straight from college to the major leagues, a man who expects neither sympathy nor attention for the fact that he was born with only one hand, yet a man who quietly offers time and hope and encouragement to children with physical differences; Mike Reid, first an All-American football player, then an All-Pro tackle, from Altoona, Pa., a town in which it is easy to play football but takes courage to play piano, now a Grammy Award–winning songwriter and singer of sensitive ballads.

In all sports, I find stars with the ultimate saving grace, the ability   46
to laugh at themselves; stars who rose to great wealth from the meanest streets without forgetting their roots; stars whose intellect contradicts athletic stereotypes; stars whose values are the decent traditional ones that start with family and loyalty. "When I was growing up," Bo Jackson recalled, "my mom cleaned people's houses during the day and cleaned a motel at night. She also raised ten children by herself. And people try to tell me that playing two sports is hard." Bo Jackson's wife is a counseling psychologist; their three children are his most prized trophies.

Some athletes are better than ever.   47

Even off the field.   48

When I was a graduate student at Columbia, the school had a   49
very good basketball team.

The best player on the team became a degenerate gambler, a con-   50
victed criminal.

The second-best player became president of the Ford Foundation.   51

I still see both of them, on infrequent occasion, and they remind   52
me of the potential of sports, and the peril. Sports can inspire greatness, but, too often these days, it inspires only greed.

Examining the Text

1. In what ways does Schaap think sports has let fans down? What does he say fans should expect from sports? Do you share his sense that "something is fundamentally wrong" (paragraph 7) when players "have so much money and so little loyalty" (20)?

2. Schaap spends some time describing race-related problems in sports (29–40). Summarize this section of the essay. Whom does Schaap blame for racism still existing in sports? Does your own experience as a player, spectator, or reader confirm his observations?

3. In the last section of the essay, Schaap offers some positive examples of athletes he respects. What qualities do these athletes share, and why does Schaap praise them? Do you find that these qualities correspond to those you and people you know admire in professional athletes? Why or why not?

For Group Discussion

Schaap identifies a number of problems with contemporary sports, but he doesn't suggest specific solutions. As a group, make a list of recommendations Schaap and those who agree with him might offer for improving professional sports. As you construct your list, consider how easy or how difficult it might be to implement these recommendations. As a class, discuss those that are most feasible. Does everyone agree that the resulting changes would actually improve professional sports? Why or why not?

Writing Suggestion

Imagine that you own a professional sports team. Write a letter to *Forbes* magazine responding to Schaap's assertion that owners are driven by greed and are disappointing the fans. Alternatively, write a letter to *Forbes* in which you express your own responses to Schaap's argument.

Sport and the American Dream

Jeffrey Schrank

In the previous selection, Dick Schaap suggests that professional sports play a large role in the lives of many Americans. In the following essay, Jeffrey Schrank, a social commentator who often examines the interaction between the media and society, expands Schaap's analysis of sports to see how it reflects the American character and our wishes, values, and beliefs.

In detailing how sports mirrors American culture, Schrank suggests that different sports appeal to Americans for different reasons and reveal different aspects of the American character. His underlying premise is that a country can trace its national preoccupations, attitudes, and aspirations in its popular sports. For example, football, in which the goal is to gain territory against an opponent, may more accurately reflect contemporary American values than does baseball, a game in which "aggression is subservient to finesse."

*If, as Schrank suggests, sports serve as "ritualistic enactments of the American Dream," consider what the currently popular pastimes tell us about the state of this American Dream. **As you read,** think about how your own favorite sports might provide some insight into your own character, attitudes, and approach to life.*

Sports is a ritual, an acting out of a myth or series of myths. A sport that can be considered a national pastime can be expected to reflect national values and wishes. Sports that capture the national fancy are ritualistic enactments of the American Dream. Baseball is still called our national pastime but is rapidly being replaced by American football. That football should become our "national pastime" is understandable to those who can see sports as reflections of national character.

American football is passionately concerned with the gain and loss of land, of territory. The football field is measured and marked with all the care of a surveyor and the ball's progress noted to the nearest inch. Football is a precise game and its players are often trained like a military unit on a mission to gain territory for the mother country. The players are the popular heroes but the coaches and owners run the game, using the players to carry out their plans—there is comparatively little room for individual initiative. A score comes as the result of a strategic series of well-executed maneuvers and is bought on the installment plan, yard by yard.

The regulation and almost military precision of American football is a reflection of national psychology. Even the words we use to describe the game include throwing the bomb, marching downfield, game plan (which has become nearly a national phrase for any field, from selling toothpaste to covering up political scandals), guards, executions, blitz, zone, platoon, squad, drills, attack, drives, marching bands for entertainment, stars on helmets, lines that can be blasted through, and even war paint. Much of the verbal similarity comes from the fact that war was originally the ultimate game, played within the confines of certain rules agreed upon by both "teams."

Football, more than any other sport, is a game for spectators to   4
watch superhuman, mythical heroes. Football is a sport that more people watch than play. The game requires too many people, too much
space and is simply too dangerous for the weekend athlete. The size and
speed of professional players and their uniforms make them into heroic
figures capable of feats that invite admiration but not imitation. The
football spectator is in awe of the armored monsters. The viewer of a golf
match or even baseball or tennis dreams of going out the next day and
doing likewise, but football is played only by the gods who can run the
100-yard dash in ten seconds, stand six feet three and weight 260 pounds.

The demise of baseball as our national pastime reflects a change   5
in national character. The change does not mean the disappearance of
baseball, merely its relocation to a position as just another game rather
than *the* game. Professor John Finlay of the University of Manitoba,
writing in *Queen's Quarterly*, compares baseball to an acting out of the
robber baron stage of capitalism, whereas football more clearly reflects
a more mature capitalism into which we are now moving. Hence, the
rise in popularity of football and apparent decline in baseball. He
notes that Japan, still in the early stages of capitalism, has taken avidly
to baseball but not to football. It is not a question of Japanese physique
serving as a determinant since rugby has a large Asian following. He
predicts that when their capitalism moves into a higher stage, the
Japanese will move on to football, as have Americans.

Baseball is a game of a quieter age when less action was needed   6
to hold interest, when going to the park was enjoyable (baseball is still
played in ball parks while football is played in stadiums), when aggression was subservient to finesse. Baseball players did not need exposure as college players to succeed as football players do; they play a
relatively calm game almost daily instead of a bruising gladiatorial
contest weekly. Baseball has room for unique and colorful characters,
while football stresses the more anonymous but effective team member. Baseball is a game in which any team can win at any given contest
and there are no favorites; only football has real "upsets." Football's
careful concern with time adds a tension to the game that is lacking in
the more leisurely world of baseball.

Football has replaced baseball as the favorite American spectator   7
sport largely because of television. A comparison between a telecast of
a football game on one channel and a baseball game on another could
reveal baseball as a game with people standing around seemingly
with little to do but watch two men play catch. Football would appear
as twenty-two men engaged in almost constant, frenzied action. To
watch baseball requires identification with the home team; to watch
football requires only a need for action or a week of few thrills and the
need for a touch of vicarious excitement.

Baseball is a pastoral game, timeless and highly ritualized; its appeal is to nostalgia and so might enjoy periods of revitalization in comparison to football. But for now, the myth of football suits the nation better.   8

According to a 1974 Harris survey, baseball has already been statistically dethroned. In a sports survey a cross section of nearly fourteen hundred fans was asked, "Which of these sports do you follow?"   9

The decision to play or "follow" a certain sport is also the decision to live a certain myth. The team violence of football, the craftiness of basketball, the mechanistic precision of bowling, the auto racer's devotion to machinery are all subworlds within the universe of sport.   10

Golf, for example, is a unique subworld, one of the few left as a sport (unlike hunting, which does not involve scoring or teams) in which the game is played between man and nature. The winner of a match is one who has beaten the opponent, but the game itself is a person versus the environment. To understand the appeal of golf it is again necessary to consider the game as a ritual reenactment of an appealing myth.   11

Golf, perhaps more than any other sport, has to be played to be appreciated. Millions who never played football can enjoy the game on TV, but only a dedicated participant can sit through two hours of televised golf. Golf is growing in participation but still has the stigma of an upper class game. Eighty percent of the nation's golfers must play on 20 percent of the nation's courses that are open to the public. The ratio of public to private facilities hurts public participation in the game but mirrors the inequities of society and provides a convenient status symbol for those who can afford club membership. Its TV audience is not the largest of any sport but it is the most well heeled.   12

Golf is a reenactment of the pioneer spirit. It is man versus a hostile environment in search of an oasis. The goal is a series of lush "greens," each protected by natural hazards such as water, sand and unmanageably long grass. The hazards are no threat to physical life but they are to the achievement of success. Golf is a journey game with a constantly changing field. Golfers start the eighteen-hole journey, can rest at a halfway point and then resume until they return to near the point of origination.   13

The winner of the match is one who has fallen victim to the fewest hazards and overcome the terrain. Many golf courses have Indian names as if to remind the golfer of the frontier ethos. A local course called Indian Lakes invites golfers to use either one of two courses—the Iroquois trail or the Sioux trail.   14

Golf, like baseball, is a pastoral sport—with a high degree of tensions and drama but relatively little action. It is a game in which players are constantly in awe of the magic flight of the golf ball. To hit any   15 kind of ball 100 or 200 or more yards with accuracy or to hit a small target from 150 yards is an amazing feat to be appreciated only by those who have at least tried the game. Golf is very likely the most difficult game to master, yet one in which the average player occasionally hits a shot as good as the best of any professional. It is this dream of magic results that keeps the golfer on course.

Examining the Text

1. Think about the significance of Schrank's title. What is the "American Dream," and what role does Schrank give sports in defining this Dream? Do you find his observations persuasive, or do you think he makes too much of the role of sports?

2. What do you think is Schrank's purpose in writing this essay? What recommendations, if any, do you think he would make about the sports Americans should choose to play or watch? Do you believe your own favorite sports reveal anything about your values and wishes?

3. Schrank wrote this essay in 1977. Some people would suggest that in the interim basketball has overtaken football as America's national pastime. What do you think the current popularity of basketball says about the American national character, and how might this shift fit Schrank's analysis of changing American preferences for certain sports?

For Group Discussion

Schrank states that "the decision to play or 'follow' a certain sport is also the decision to live a certain myth" (paragraph 10). Reread the section on golf (11–15) and choose another "minor," but familiar sport. As a group, list some of the reasons this sport is appealing. What myths—about the environment, about teamwork and individuality, about winning and losing, for example—does this sport promote? How might it influence participants' beliefs, attitudes, or values? As a class, discuss the similarities and differences among each group's choice.

Writing Suggestion

Schrank's basic premise is that "a sport that can be considered a national pastime can be expected to reflect national values and wishes" (1). Look up information on a sport that is the national pastime of another country, such as hockey in Canada, cricket or rugby in England, or soccer in many European and South American countries.

After learning about how the sport is played, and how fans respond, what conclusions can you draw about the "values and wishes" of the players and spectators? In an essay, explain the extent to which the sport reflects the national character of those who play it.

Jockpop: Popular Sports and Politics
James Combs

The following essay is excerpted from James Combs's book, Polpop, *a study of the ways in which popular culture affects our political ideas and images. In "Jockpop," Combs looks at how playing and watching sports shapes our thoughts and actions in the realm of politics. Like Schaap and Schrank, Combs's basic premise is that "the 'lessons of sports' help orient us to the world." He argues that we are drawn to sports in large part because they teach us about "competition, teamwork, risk-taking, aggression and defense, winning and losing"; and voters and politicians alike apply these lessons to the world of politics.*

Combs identifies a number of ways in which sports and politics are interrelated. Sporting events provide a setting for political rituals and symbols, such as raising the American flag, singing the national anthem, and other expressions of patriotism. Sports provide metaphors and images politicians use in appealing to voters, explaining their policies, and promoting themselves and their programs. Sporting events, particularly international ones, may in addition take on political and national significance; Combs cites the victory of the American ice hockey team over the Soviet Union in the 1984 Olympics as an example of how a simple game can take on dramatic political overtones.

As you read, note that Combs uses specific examples to support his general theory about the influence of sports on politics. Try to identify some of the ways in which your political views and the American political system in general would be different without the influence of sports.

SPORTS AND LEARNING

In the famous opening sequence of the movie *Patton*, General   1
Patton (George C. Scott) delivered a speech to an audience of soldiers. He said in part:

> Men, all this stuff you've heard about America not wanting to fight, wanting to stay out of the war, is a lot of horsedung. Americans traditionally love to fight. All real Americans love the sting of battle. When you were kids you all admired the champion marble shooter, the fastest runner, the big league ballplayers, the toughest boxers. Americans play

to win all the time. I wouldn't give a hoot in hell for a man who lost and laughed. That's why Americans have never lost, and will never lose a war, because the very thought of losing is hateful to Americans.

Let us reflect a moment, as General Patton urges, on growing up.   2
When we were kids, we all quickly learned the importance of sports. Playing was fun, and indeed gave us a chance to prove ourselves. We discovered that organized sports at school and the Little League gave us an opportunity to play. We discovered that some could play better than others, that winning was valued, that there was a huge adult interest in sports. We found that there was a big world of sports in which adult athletes played before gigantic audiences for large amounts of money and glory. We adopted heroes among athletes in high school, or more remotely in the pro leagues. We attempted to bat, or dribble, or pass like them, even to act like them. If we hung around locker rooms or played, we heard the slogans: "Quitters never win, and winners never quit." Some of us experienced the "thrill of victory and the agony of defeat." We heard the speeches at sports banquets. We won letters, were cheerleaders and pompom girls, went to the school games. We talked about sports, followed college and pro sports, maybe even dreamed dreams of athletic glory.

And what effect did it all have on us? Specifically here, what impact does the play-world of sports have on politics? Like the other areas of the American play-world, popular sports is not "just a game." Rather, we learn much about the world from sports. Whether consciously or not, the "lessons of sports" help to orient us to the world. It is not an idle metaphor when we speak of the "game of life." For games, and what we are told about games, give us much learning about life, and even politics. Sports is a form of play which we early on learn is important, come to value, and link to "real life."   3

SPORTS AND DRAMA

The root of this may well be in the fact that sports are dramatic.   4
Games are an organized play-area, in which dramatic struggle (*agon*) occurs. The game becomes a public arena for the enactment of the more interesting aspects of human life—competition, teamwork, risk-taking, aggression and defense, winning and losing. Because sports dramatize in microcosm both eternal human truths and specific cultural truths, we are drawn in the same way we are drawn to drama. The drama "represents" life, lets us look at a heightened reality which dramatizes in the story what we want to know about life. Popular drama like soap operas dramatizes exemplary situations with which we can identify. Similarly, sports interest us because they possess such dramatic qualities. We learn from the "story" of a game because we can relate it to our lives. . . .

SPORTS AND POLITICS

The dramatization of the American Dream in sports suggests   5
that sports has important meanings for us. It is likely that we "read
into" sports a variety of messages, including political ones. So we
should expect that sports would have political meanings and realize
that these meanings have not been lost on politicians and observers of
politics. Sometimes the sports-politics connection is obvious, sometimes subtle, but it is nevertheless there. For if sports is a key part of
our cultural mythology, and is a play-setting for the dramatization of
American myths, then its relevance for the world of politics and government exists. Therefore, we can explore some of the political meanings and uses of sports: sports as a setting for political *ritual;* as a
metaphor for political *rhetoric;* as a dramatic microcosm of political
conflicts; and as a political *resource.* We will consider these in turn.

SPORTS AS A SETTING FOR POLITICAL RITUAL

Remember that we have stressed the ways that popular culture is   6
a political teacher. We learn things about ourselves as political beings
from the social messages that a popular play-form communicates. An
important part of our political socialization was through patriotic ritual at school—saluting the flag, saying the Pledge of Allegiance,
school spirit assemblies. But this is not the only setting for such symbolic dramas. We all remember the patriotic rituals attached to sporting events—the national anthem, raising the flag, color guards, and so
forth. We would feel uneasy if a high school or college football game
did not include such patriotic rituals.

These generalized rituals are more or less universal. Indeed, we   7
commonly expect sporting events to be clothed in not only political
symbolism, but also religious symbolism as well. We all recall the invo-
cations given before games, the players all praying in the huddle, and
singing "God Bless America." Patriotic and religious symbols are, of
course, closely linked in sports ritual. The presence of such ritual under-
scores that the event is not merely a game, but a play-event conducted
with proper deference by participants and audience to transcendent values. The appeal is very largely to the moral community, as when the invocation prays that the players conduct the game with respect to moral
values. Thus, the folk drama of sports comes to be imbued with patriotic
rituals which remind us not only in what country the game is being
played, but that the game occurs in the context of national values.

Now when a political crisis ensues, such patriotic ritual takes on   8
a more intensely felt meaning. During the Iranian crisis, it was com-

mon for football game rituals to recognize the hostages through moments of silence immediately before the national anthem was played, a dramatic reminder with political significance. Immediately after the release of the hostages, the 1981 Super Bowl became a festive setting for the ritual recognition of that celebrated event—everyone there wore yellow ribbons, and even the Superdome had a massive yellow ribbon on the outside.

But when the country is divided over some political issue, political rituals at sports events can become controversial and excessive. During the height of the Vietnam War, there was a clear increase in the number of college football halftime shows that involved patriotic themes and pageantry. Indeed, in 1970 ABC refused to televise a halftime show planned by the University of Buffalo band which dramatized antiwar, antiracist, and antipollution themes through music and skits on the grounds that it would be a "political demonstration." But later that season ABC did televise a halftime show at the Army-Navy game which honored Green Berets who had just conducted an unsuccessful raid on a prisoner of war camp in North Vietnam, including statements by military officers critical of antiwar activity at home. So it depends upon whose moralistic myth is to be ritualized! Such incidents do remind us that sports involve the affirmation of cultural myths, since sports "participate" in the social order. Thus, "negative" rituals which celebrate a counter-myth conflict with the traditional patriotic function that sporting rituals have served.

In the past, political rituals which celebrated the symbols of government seemed especially appropriate for sporting events, since major sports seemed to embody so nicely aspects of the American Dream. If myths of the State come to be disbelieved or doubted, then such rituals may ring hollow for many people. One may wonder what sorts of feelings playing the national anthem before a game conjures up in our breasts. But whether we still believe or not, the fact remains that sports is a major stage for the dramatization of political symbols.

SPORTS AS A METAPHOR
FOR POLITICAL RHETORIC

Politicians like to draw upon familiar symbols to illustrate some political point, and sports offer familiar and widely used metaphors. The language of the locker room permeates politics. Sports is a major repository of American mythology, so politicians can utilize the analogy, safely assuming wide familiarity with the "lessons" of sports. Since politics has many game-like aspects, reference to the dynamics of sporting games as similar to "the game of politics" is natural. Both coaches and political figures seem to believe in the necessity of inspiration, which is the most common political use of sports analogies, allegories, parables, and so on.

The "values" of sports can also be for a variety of political uses.   12
In particular, sports can illustrate the "truth" of either moralistic or materialistic myths. The American sports creed includes many tenets, most of which can be used to support or illustrate different political messages. Even though there is wide popular consensus that sports makes us "better citizens," what that means is subject to interpretation. For instance, Americans repeatedly agree on the positive lessons of sports: e.g., sports are worthwhile because they teach us "self-discipline"; sports are good because they promote "fair play" and sports are positive because they teach "respect for authority and good citizenship." However, such virtues can be variously interpreted.

Let us illustrate this by reference to two often competing aspects   13
of the sports creed: sportsmanship and winning. The ideal of sportsmanship has persisted in political rhetoric as a norm by which the game is supposed to be played, i.e., that one plays fair, enjoys the contest, and accepts victory with magnanimity and defeat with grace. Being a "good sport" was a trait admirable in all areas of life. The "truth" of sports was not whether one won or lost, but how you played the game. A "sportsman" was a gentleman committed to excellence, but within ethical bounds and without cheap tactics. Such an image smacks of the "Ivy League" pop books of an earlier age about sports heroes such as Frank Merriwell.

This venerable notion has been applied to democratic politics   14
again and again. In a classic book about democracy, we learn that sportsmanship, on the field or in politics, consists of such attitudes as tolerating and honoring the opposition; being a gracious winner and loser; and playing "the game of politics" within the bounds of rules and fair play.

This motif is complicated by a conflicting norm: winning. Winning   15
isn't everything, goes Lombardi's Law, it's the only thing. Nice guys, Durocher's Dictum has it, finish last. The winning motif is related to the idea of sports as war, in which winning takes precedence over gentlemanly traits, and indeed where sportsmanship is a hindrance to victory. The implicit locker room message is often that since winning is paramount, any means, including bending or breaking the rules, unfair play, and intimidation, are justified. At the extreme, this can justify the virtue of sheer winning in politics. Indeed, the Nixon Administration's fondness for sports metaphors was thought to have contributed to the "Watergate mentality," i.e., that the political world is a game of winners and losers locked in relentless strife, and since the "other side" are rogues and will do anything to win, we are justified in being just as nasty as them in order to win. The famous "Plumbers" office in the basement of the Nixon White House, consisting of those assigned to conduct break-

ins, dirty tricks, and the like, had a sign that paraphrased Lombardi: "Winning in politics isn't everything, it's the only thing."

The sportsmanship theme is explicitly stated in political rhetoric, but the winning theme, by emphasis, implicitly suggests to us the necessity of aggressiveness, cunning, and even violence. In areas such as business and politics, the sports metaphor reflects the tension we feel about these two values. In business, for example, we believe that pursuit of material goals all should be bound by the competitive rules of capitalism and moral rules derived from, say, religion; but we also recognize and even admire the business sharpie who makes lots of money by circumventing the rules, participating in underhanded and even illegal deals, and perhaps even using intimidation and violence. Our fascination with the super-rich, instant millionaires, and gangsters stems in part from the popular belief that one cannot make it without being a scoundrel. Similarly, it has been widely believed since Machiavelli that one cannot acquire and use power unless you are not bound by moral rules. Since politics, like sports, is a mean and competitive world, the winners have to be equal to the task. Getting the "material" of power and prestige in politics requires violating morality. Like the Godfather, you have to make people offers they can't refuse.

In American culture, our attitudes toward the conflicting values have roots in the worldview termed social Darwinism. As a metaphor drawn from the theory of evolution, the Social Darwinists argued that business and politics were hard struggles in which the fittest survived and dominated. For this viewpoint, sports offers evidence that life is like that, and thus politics is by necessity that way. Therefore, we want people in charge who use power less bound by moral restraints. But if we take the more "civilized" view of this sportsmanship motif, business and politics, like sports, should be tamed and made fair. For the political rhetorician, sports offers analogies of both motifs, although the "winning" ethic is usually not blatantly said. In any case, it is an indication of a tension in our attitude toward American politics as to which sports metaphor we think most applicable to politics.

SPORTS AS A DRAMATIC MICROCOSM OF POLITICAL CONFLICTS

The old saw has it that sports reflect society. If sports is a mirror of our conflicts, certainly when our divisions are politicized, sports become a dramatic microcosm of political conflicts. If groups experience material or moral lapses, they may be dramatized on the playing field. We have already mentioned how the post–World War II civil rights revolution was reflected in sports. Many other domestic conflicts work their way into sports. For example, it is nowadays popularly thought that America is a society of litigants eternally suing each other. Certainly this is reflected in sports, which involves a great deal of litigation over the status of players, franchises, fans, the media, and so on. If Americans think that as a people we spend a great deal of time in court, they certainly are reinforced in that view by reading the sports page.

Perhaps the most spectacular way in which sports come to be infested with politics involves international political conflicts. It is no secret that international sports—the Olympics, international track and field meets, even professional sports—often become embroiled in political controversies between nations.   19

The quadrennial Olympic games are the most important dramatic forum with political overtones. Nations are interested in "proving" the superiority of their political values by success at the Olympic games. The Nazis tried to prove the superiority of the "Aryan race" at the 1936 Olympics, but the dramatic scenario backfired somewhat by the success of American black runners. Communist countries such as the Soviet Union and East Germany invest great resources into Olympic success, since this dramatizes the alleged superiority of "socialist man." Terrorists are attracted to such games to dramatize their cause, as was the case with the Palestinian group that kidnapped the Israeli athletes at the Munich Olympics of 1972.   20

But the most memorable recent incident involving the United States occurred at the 1980 Winter Olympics. In late 1979, in an already volatile Middle East following the Iranian Revolution and the hostage crisis, the Soviet Union invaded Afghanistan. This was the culmination of a complex series of political events that signified the crisis of "detente" between the United States and the Soviet Union, and brought the world into one of those periods of international tension. Further, it was an election year in the United States, which made the role of American public opinion all the more crucial in the crisis. It became politically important for President Carter to respond to these developments, given the chauvinistic and retributive mood of the country. So he dispatched the fleet, agitated for Persian Gulf resistance to Soviet expansion, and cut off the shipment of some trade materials to the Russians.   21

But he did something else too: he called for a boycott of the 1980 Summer Olympic games in Moscow. He sent boxer Muhammad Ali to Africa to enlist support for the boycott. He advocated and arranged "alternative" games to be held somewhere other than Russia. He pressured NBC to not televise the Soviet Olympics, and stopped American companies from Olympic-related shipments to the Soviets. He sought the support of the athletes themselves, and of the international sports community. The political purpose, of course, was to symbolically (and in some measure, tangibly) "punish" the Soviets for the Afghanistan intervention.   22

In the midst of the new tension, a dramatic sports event occurred   23
which demonstrated how play can have political significance. At the
Winter Olympics in Lake Placid, New York, the American hockey
team unexpectedly upset the Soviets, 4-3. This triumph, and then later
when the Americans won the gold medal by defeating the Finns,
brought an outpouring of rejoicing and national pride. This outburst,
which included many people who knew absolutely nothing about
hockey, was clearly related to the new international tensions with the
Soviets. The defeat of the Soviet hockey team was not "just a game."
Boycotting the Olympic games for political reasons dramatized the importance accorded international sporting matches. Inviting the triumphant U.S. Winter Olympic team to the White House, including the
cowboy-hatted hockey team, became the focus for national congratulations, and gave a dramatic role to a President up for re-election.

An international sporting event conducted in the midst of a polit-   24
ical crisis, then, can take on an intensely patriotic flavor, and, if victorious, people can feel as if through play they have "won" some sort of
political victory. It focuses political emotion onto the drama of the
game, and thus gives us deep patriotic pride. Politicians and the news
media recognized the political significance of the event, and gave it
great play. The triumph gave occasion for political ritual at the White
House, associating the event formally with patriotic symbols and offering ritual thanks to the athletes. The drama did nothing to undo Soviet political intentions, but it did help people to deal with their
anxieties about international tensions and their own country's worth.
The Olympic triumph signaled a new patriotic fervor in the United
States, and helped to revive the moralistic myth about our "mission"
in the world and national superiority. The hockey match and the national outburst it caused was a dramatic microcosm of a political crisis.

SPORTS AS A POLITICAL RESOURCE

Since sports are valued popular play-activities, it is common for   25
politicians to use sports and sports figures for a wide variety of political
purposes. Like religion and show business, sports offer the politician association with something non-political that large numbers of people are
attracted to. Not only do politicians use the rhetoric of sports for political purposes, they also express their interest in sports to dramatize their
commonality. Candidates campaigning for office attend sporting
events, mention the local team, and seek the endorsement of famous athletes. Endorsement-seeking illustrates how politics seeks out popular
culture. The endorsement of a famous athlete somehow gives the aspir-
ing politician a kind of popular status and humanity he might not earn

otherwise. The athlete is an embodiment of both material and moral success on the playing-field, and the politician seems to think that with the association some of the heroic magic might rub off. All this is nothing new: both Al Smith and Herbert Hoover sought the endorsement of Babe Ruth in 1928! But it doesn't always work. Gerald Ford had an endless list of athletes who endorsed him in 1976, but he lost the election anyway. Ford and other politicians have been accused of being "jocksniffers," zealously exploiting their relationship to athletes and athletics, but the transfer of magic is not guaranteed.

President Carter did not appear to be a jocksniffer, but he was   26
aware of the political uses of participation in sports. He cultivated his Southern regional tie, including hunting, fishing, and wading in hip-boots for bait. He reigned over slow-pitch softball games between the White House staff and the press. He became the First Jogger, and was photographed jogging in long distance races with troops in Korea. President Reagan liked to ride, and professed himself a sports fan. (Many older Americans associated him with sports through his depiction of "The Gipper," since he played Notre Dame's famous George Gipp in *Knute Rockne of Notre Dame* as well as baseball pitcher Grover Cleveland Alexander in *The Winning Team*.) It is always difficult to tell the extent to which sports participation by politicians stems from their desire to stay healthy and enjoy strenuous activity, or from their awareness that such activities are popular, and by participating they communicate to the public their common human interest. In any case, most recent Presidents have cultivated some form of popular leisure activity—golf, touch-football, sailing, etc. However, if some of the recent revelations about President John Kennedy's "favorite leisure activity" are true, then it must be said that although golf and jogging have their virtues as sports, so does his, although the former type is most politically acceptable and performable in public.

Since sports figures do become popular embodiments of heroic   27
success, the celebrity status they enjoy can become a resource for successful political recruitment. Having played college football or even some professional sport seems to have helped a wide variety of political figures, ranging from Ford to Supreme Court Justice Byron "Whizzer" White (a former All-American) and former baseball pitcher and House member Wilmer "Vinegar Bend" Mizell. Former NBA star Bill Bradley became Senator from New Jersey at least partially on his sports celebrity. Congressman Jack Kemp of New York ran for Congress in the city he was an NFL quarterback, stressed how quarterbacking gave him leadership qualities, and used the rhetoric of football for political purposes. It may be the case in the future that more politicians will be drawn from the ranks of well-known sports figures.

CONCLUSION

We have not exhausted the complex relationships between popu-   28
lar sports and political culture, but the above should give the reader
the idea of some of the major linkages. As long as Americans are
sports crazy, we should expect that sports will have political relevance, and that "the game of politics" will be conducted in a culture
that includes sports as a value.

Examining the Text

1. What are some of the "eternal human truths" and "specific cultural
truths" (paragraph 4) that Combs says we learn from sports? Can you
think of others? Would everyone agree that these are "truths"?

2. Combs divides the main part of his essay (6–27) into four sections,
each dealing with a different way in which sports is connected to politics. In your opinion, which of these four seems the *most* influential?
Think of examples, other than those mentioned by Combs, to support
your opinion.

3. Apply Combs's idea that we learn values and truths through sports
to an area in our culture other than politics. For example, how does
sports affect our notions of religion, education, or work? You might
want to use Combs's four categories (for example, *as a setting for religious ritual, as a metaphor for religious rhetoric,* and so forth).

For Group Discussion

Imagine that your group is assigned to write a speech for a political candidate. Come up with a list of metaphors and images drawn
from the world of sports that your candidate could use to appeal to
voters. You can refer to Combs's essay, as well as other readings in
this chapter, for ideas. As a class, consider the effect of such metaphors
on the American political process.

Writing Suggestion

Combs gives an *objective* description of the influence of sports on
politics; he doesn't take sides or make recommendations. Using his
writing as a resource, write an essay in which you argue either that
sports should have (a) less influence on politics, or (b) greater influence on politics. To do this, you'll need to consider both the problems
and the benefits of sports' role in the political world.

Why Men Fear Women's Teams

Kate Rounds

Kate Rounds is a freelance writer and a contributor to Ms. *magazine, where this essay originally appeared. She argues here that female athletes have very few opportunities in the world of professional sports, and that women's team sports in particular are faced with what amounts to complete neglect in the media. Since professional sports are big business, if women's sports don't draw the fans and the money, then there's little hope that their professional leagues will last. College sports are similarly male-dominated, although Title IX requires colleges to devote equivalent resources to men's and women's athletic programs. Rounds' essay reminds us that when we discuss popular professional and collegiate sports, we're almost always referring to men's sports, and that sexual bias and gender stereotypes are still strong.*

Rounds contrasts the failure of a number of professional women's leagues (basketball, volleyball, and baseball) in the United States with the success of such enterprises in Europe, Japan, and elsewhere. The question, then, is why Americans fail to support talented female athletes in all but a few sports. Rounds ultimately concludes that the failure of women's professional sports reveals a "deep-rooted sexual bias and homophobia" in our culture, and that we haven't yet fully accepted a notion of femininity that incorporates power, athletic skill, and female camaraderie.

Before you read, *think back to the essays earlier in this chapter. To what extent do the ideas of Schaap, Schrank, and Combs hold true for professional women's sports? And how might these authors account for gender discrimination in professional sports? Note that Rounds' essay was written before the introduction of the WNBA in 1997; to what extent are her conclusions about gender discrimination still true today?*

Picture this. You're flipping through the channels one night, and   1
you land on a local network, let's say ABC. And there on the screen is
a basketball game. The players are sinking three-pointers, slam-
dunking, and doing the usual things basketball players do. They're
high-fiving each other, patting one another on the butt, and then saun-
tering to the locker room to talk about long-term contracts.

Now imagine that the players aren't men. They're women, big   2
sweaty ones, wearing uniforms and doing their version of what guys
thrive on—bonding. So far, this scene is a fantasy and will remain so
until women's professional team sports get corporate sponsors, television exposure, arenas, fan support, and a critical mass of well-trained
players.

While not enough fans are willing to watch women play tradi-   3
tional team sports, they love to watch women slugging it out on roller-
derby rinks and in mud-wrestling arenas. Currently popular is a
bizarre television spectacle called *American Gladiators*, in which
women stand on pastel pedestals, wearing Lycra tights and brandish-
ing weapons that look like huge Q-Tips. The attraction obviously has
something to do with the "uniforms."

The importance of what women athletes wear can't be underesti-   4
mated. Beach volleyball, which is played in the sand by bikini-clad
women, rates network coverage, while traditional court volleyball
can't marshal any of the forces that would make a women's pro league
succeed.

It took a while, but women were able to break through sexist bar-   5
riers in golf and tennis. Part of their success stemmed from the sports
themselves—high-end individual sports that were born in the British
Isles and flourished in country clubs across the U.S. The women wore
skirts, makeup, and jewelry along with their wristbands and warm-up
jackets. The corporate sponsors were hackers themselves, and the
fan—even men—could identify with these women; a guy thought that
if he hit the ball enough times against the barn door, he too could play
like Martina. And women's purses were equaling men's. In fact,
number-one-ranked Steffi Graf's prize money for 1989 was $1,963,905
and number-one-ranked Stefan Edberg's was $1,661,491.

By contrast, women's professional team sports have failed spec-   6
tacularly. Since the mid-seventies, every professional league—softball,
basketball, and volleyball—has gone belly-up. In 1981, after a four-
year struggle, the Women's Basketball League (WBL), backed by
sports promoter Bill Byrne, folded. The league was drawing fans in a
number of cities, but the sponsors weren't there. TV wasn't there, and
nobody seemed to miss the spectacle of a few good women fighting
for a basketball.

Or a volleyball, for that matter. Despite the success of bikini vol-   7
leyball, an organization called MLV (Major League Volleyball) bit the
dust in March of 1989 after nearly three years of struggling for sponsorship, fan support, and television exposure. As with pro basketball,
there was a man behind women's professional volleyball, real estate
investor Robert (Bat) Batinovich. Batinovich admits that, unlike court
volleyball, beach volleyball has a lot of "visual T&A mixed into it."

What court volleyball does have, according to former MLV execu-   8
tive director Lindy Vivas, is strong women athletes. Vivas is assistant
volleyball coach at San Jose State University. "The United States in general," she says, "has problems dealing with women athletes and strong,
aggressive females. The perception is you have to be more aggressive in
team sports than in golf and tennis, which aren't contact sports. Women
athletes are looked at as masculine and get the stigma of being gay."

One former women's basketball promoter, who insists on re-   9
maining anonymous, goes further. "You know what killed women's
sports?" he says. "Lesbians. This cost us in women's basketball. But I
know there are not as many lesbians now unless I'm really blinded.
We discourage it, you know. We put it under wraps."

People in women's sports spend a lot of time dancing around the   10
"L" word, and the word "image" pops up in a way it never does in
men's sports. Men can spit tobacco juice, smoke, and even scratch their
testicles on national television and get away with it.

Bill Byrne, former WBL promoter, knows there isn't a whole lot   11
women can get away with while they're beating each other out for a
basketball. "In the old league," he says, "my partner, Mike Connors,
from *Mannix*—his wife said, 'Let's do makeup on these kids.' And I
knew that uniforms could be more attractive. We could tailor them so
the women don't look like they're dragging a pair of boxer shorts
down the floor."

The response from the athletes to this boy talk is not always out-   12
rage. "Girls in women's basketball now are so pretty," says Nancy
Lieberman-Cline. "They're image-conscious." The former Old Dominion star, who made headlines as Martina's trainer, played with the
men's U.S. Basketball League, the Harlem Globe Trotters Tour (where
she met husband Tim Cline), and with the Dallas Diamonds of the old
WBL. "Everyone used to have short hair," she says. "Winning and
playing was everything. I wouldn't think of using a curling iron. Now
there are beautiful girls out there playing basketball."

Lieberman-Cline says she doesn't mind making the concession.   13
"It's all part of the process," she says. "You can't be defensive about
everything."

Bill Byrne is so certain that women's professional basketball can   14
work that he's organized a new league, the Women's Pro Basketball
League, Inc. (WPBL), set to open its first season shortly. Byrne talks
fast and tough, and thinks things have changed for the better since
1981 when the old league went under. "Exposure is the bottom word,"
he says. "If you get plenty of TV exposure, you'll create household
names, and you'll fill arenas. It takes the tube. But I'll get the tube this
time because the game of TV has changed. You have cable now. You
have to televise home games to show people a product."

There's no doubt that many athletes in the women's sports estab-   15
lishment are leery of fast-talking guys who try to make a buck off
women's pro sports, especially when the women themselves don't
profit from those ventures. In the old league, finances were so shaky
that some players claim they were never paid.

"We weren't getting the gate receipts," says Lieberman-Cline.   16
"They'd expect 2,000, get only 400, and then they'd have to decide to pay
the arena or pay the girls, and the girls were the last choice. There was a

lot of mismanagement in the WBL, though the intent was good." She also has her doubts about the new league: "There are not enough things in place to make it happen, not enough owners, arenas, TV coverage, or players. It's going to take more than optimism to make it work."

Given the track record of women's professional team sports in this country, it's not surprising that the national pastime is faring no better. When Little League was opened to girls by court order in 1974, one might have thought that professional women's baseball could not be far behind. Baseball is a natural for women. It's not a contact sport, it doesn't require excessive size or strength—even little guys like Phil Rizzuto and Jose Lind can play it—and it's actually an individual sport masquerading as a team sport. Still, in recent years, no one's taken a serious stab at organizing a women's professional league. 17

In 1984, there was an attempt to field a women's minor-league team. Though the Sun Sox had the support of baseball great Hank Aaron, it was denied admission to the Class A Florida State League. The team was the brainchild of a former Atlanta Braves vice president of marketing, Bob Hope. "A lot of the general managers and owners of big-league clubs were mortified," Hope says, "and some players said they wouldn't compete against women. It was male ego or something." 18

Or something, says softball hall-of-famer Donna Lopiano. "When girls suffer harassment in Little League, that's not exactly opening up opportunities for women," she says. "Girls don't have the access to coaching and weight training that boys have. Sports is a place where physiological advantages give men power, and they're afraid of losing it. Sports is the last great bastion of male chauvinism. In the last eight years, we've gone backward, not only on gender equity but on civil rights." 19

Women of color still face barriers that European American women don't, particularly in the areas of coaching and refereeing. But being a woman athlete is sometimes a bond that transcends race. "We're all at a handicap," says Ruth Lawanson, an African American who played volleyball with MLV. "It doesn't matter whether you're Asian, Mexican, black or white." 20

Historically, baseball and softball diamonds have not been very hospitable to black men and any women. Despite the fact that even men's softball is not a crowd pleaser, back in 1976, Billie Jean King and golfer Jane Blalock teamed up with ace amateur softball pitcher Joan Joyce to form the International Women's Professional Softball Association (IWPSA). Five years later, without sponsorship, money, or television, the league was history. 21

Billie Jean King has her own special attachment to the team concept. As a girl, she wanted to be a baseball player, but her father gave her a tennis racket, knowing that there wasn't much of a future for a girl in baseball. The story is especially touching since Billie Jean's 22 brother, Randy Moffitt, went on to become a pitcher with the San Francisco Giants. But even as a tennis player, Billie Jean clung to the team idea. She was the force behind World TeamTennis, which folded in 1978, and is currently the chief executive officer of TeamTennis, now entering its eleventh season with corporate sponsorship.

On the face of it, TeamTennis is a bizarre notion because it takes   23
what is a bred-in-the-bones individual sport and tries to squeeze, it into a team concept. It has the further handicap of not really being necessary when strong women's and men's professional tours are already in place.

In the TeamTennis format, all players play doubles as well as sin-   24
gles. Billie Jean loves doubles, she says, because she enjoys "sharing the victory." What also distinguishes TeamTennis from the women's and men's pro tours is fan interaction. Fans are encouraged to behave as if watching a baseball or basketball game rather than constantly being told to shut up and sit down as they are at pro tour events like the U.S. Open. The sense of team spirit among the players—the fact that they get to root for one another—is also attracting some big names. Both Martina Navratilova and Jimmy Connors have signed on to play TeamTennis during its tiny five-week season, which begins after Wimbledon and ends just before the U.S. Open.

But you have to go back almost 50 years to find a women's pro-   25
fessional sports team that was somewhat successful—though the conditions for that success were rather unusual. During World War II, when half the population was otherwise engaged, women were making their mark in the formerly male strongholds of welding, riveting—and baseball. The All-American Girls Professional Baseball League (AAGPBL) fielded such teams as the Lassies, the Belles, and the Chicks on the assumption that it was better to have "girls" playing than to let the national pastime languish. The league lasted a whopping 12 years after its inception in 1943.

The success of this sandlot venture, plagued as it was by the   26
simple-hearted sexism of the forties (the women went to charm school at night), must raise nagging doubts in the mind of the woman team player of the nineties. Can she triumph only in the absence of men?

It may be true that she can triumph only in the absence of com-   27
petition from the fiercely popular men's pro leagues, which gobble up sponsorship, U.S. network television, and the hearts and minds of male fanatics. The lack of male competition outside the United States may be partly responsible for the success of women's professional team sports in Europe, Japan, South America, and Australia. Lieberman-Cline acknowledges that Europe provides a more hospitable climate for women's pro basketball. "Over there, they don't have as many options," she says. "We have Broadway plays, movies, you name it. We're overindulged with options."

Bruce Levy is a 230-pound bespectacled accountant who escaped   28
from the Arthur Andersen accounting firm 11 years ago to market
women's basketball. "It's pretty simple," he says. "People overseas are
more realistic and enlightened. Women's basketball is not viewed as a
weak version of men's. If Americans could appreciate a less powerful,
more scientific, team-oriented game, we'd be two-thirds of the way toward having a league succeed."

Levy, who represents many women playing pro basketball   29
abroad, says 120 U.S. women are playing overseas and making up to
$70,000 in a seven-month season. They include star players like Teresa
Edwards, Katrina McClain, and Lynette Woodward. "A player like
Teresa Weatherspoon, everybody recognizes her in Italy," he says.
"No one in the U.S. knows her. If there were a pro league over here, I
wouldn't be spending all day on the phone speaking bad Italian and
making sure the women's beds are long enough. I'd just be negotiating
contracts."

Levy claims that U.S. businesswomen aren't supporting women's   30
team sports. "In Europe," he says, "the best-run and most publicized
teams are run by women who own small businesses and put their
money where their mouth is." Joy Burns, president of Sportswomen of
Colorado, Inc., pleads no contest. "Businesswomen here are too conservative and don't stick their necks out," she says. MLV's Bat Batinovich,
who says he's "disappointed" in U.S. businesswomen for not supporting women's team sports, figures an investor in MLV should have been
willing to lose $200,000 a year for five years. Would Burns have done it?
"If I'm making good financial investments, why should I?"

The prospects for women's professional team sports don't look   31
bright. The reasons for the lack of financial support go beyond simple
economics and enter the realm of deep-rooted sexual bias and homophobia. San Jose State's Lindy Vivas says men who feel intimidated by
physically strong women have to put the women down. "There's always a guy in the crowd who challenges the women when he
wouldn't think of going one-on-one with Magic Johnson or challenging Nolan Ryan to a pitching contest."

Softball's Donna Lopiano calls it little-boy stuff: "Men don't want   32
to have a collegial, even-steven relationship with women. It's like
dealing with cavemen."

Examining the Text

1. How do you respond to the title of this essay? According to
Rounds, why do men fear women's teams? What do you think of her
reasoning?

2. Rounds points out that individual sports (like tennis and golf) give female athletes more exposure and opportunities for success than team sports. How does she explain this difference? Why do you think women's professional team sports are not popular in the United States? Have you had many opportunities to watch female teams play? How do you think this affects your answer?

3. Summarize the role of television and business in the promotion of professional women's sports. How do mass media and business alter women's sports, according to Rounds? To what extent do they also alter men's sports?

For Group Discussion

Softball player Donna Lopiano is quoted as saying that "sports is the last bastion of male chauvinism." Discuss your group's reactions to Lopiano's statement. List some possible reasons that women today might have greater opportunities in other traditionally male-dominated professions than in sports. Also list any evidence that contradicts Lopiano's claim. As a class, consider whether women's situation in professional sports is likely to change.

Writing Suggestion

Assuming that Rounds' assertion that women have few opportunities in the world of professional sports is correct, do you think this is a significant problem? Determine some of the specific benefits that women miss because of gender discrimination in sports. In an essay express your opinions about what (if anything) should be done to offer women greater access to these benefits.

Analyzing Sports

Seven Points on the Game
of Football

Arthur Asa Berger

In this chapter from his book Media Analysis Techniques, *Arthur Asa Berger analyzes football from several different perspectives, treating it—he notes in his final paragraph—as "a creative effort...and a work of art that has performance aspects, aesthetic elements, and more."*

First he looks as a semiologist at the signs in and around a football game: the arena in which it is played; the clothing of players, officials, and fans; the sometimes deceptive signals players send to one another. From these and other signs, Berger suggests we can see some of the different meanings football holds for our culture, as athletic activity, entertainment, even sexual display.

Berger goes on to discuss football from a sociological perspective, noting that it teaches fans "how to get along in society, what roles to play, what life is all about...." He suggests that football "reflects our contemporary social situation," and, from an anthropological perspective, that in many ways it serves as a contemporary alternative to religion, an arena of collective and passionate interest, ritual, mystery, and heroism. Berger also offers a brief interpretation of football from Marxist and psychoanalytic perspectives.

As you read, *note Berger's "seven points" about football. Which points do you find particularly insightful, and how might you apply those insights to sports other than football?*

FOOTBALL IS A GAME OF SIGNS

Football is a very interesting subject for the semiologist because 1
the game is, at once, full of signs and also a signifier of some importance.
The stadium is itself one huge sign—a sacred space where enthusiasts
(and sometimes fanatics) gather to watch a highly organized, ritualized
contest that many have suggested functions as an alternative to war. It is
not unusual for 60,000 people or more to gather together for a game, and
with television coverage sometimes millions of people watch a game,
which means that the entire country "becomes" a football stadium.

Where one sits in the stadium—on the fifty-yard line or way up 2
behind a goalpost—is a signifier of one's wealth or power or status.

The field itself is a huge grid, a one-hundred-yard rectangle of white lines against brilliant green grass (or Astroturf). The intensity of the colors adds considerably to the excitement of the event and must not be underestimated. On this field are to be seen people in all kinds of different uniforms: the officials in their zebra strips, the players with their helmets and pads, marching bands, cheerleaders in sweaters and miniskirts, pom-pom girls, coaches with their earphones and electronic paraphernalia, drum majors and majorettes, and many other people. All of these uniforms and trappings are signifiers of the wide variety of skills, activities, and functions taking place at a game: rule enforcement, athletic activity, musical diversion, sexual display, planning and rationality, and so on. Thus a football game is not merely an athletic event but part of a much larger system of events that are connected to the game but which enlarge its significance greatly.

(I have not said anything about the people who attend the games   3
and who frequently wear the colors or emblems of their teams. Sometimes they carry signs. Frequently there are "sign sections" in stadiums and various messages are flashed during halftime, when the bands play and there are various entertainments.)

The game itself is based on signs. Signals are called in the hud-   4
dles announcing offensive plays. These signals are analogous to what we call "codes," and indicate a precise series of activities that are to be followed at a given point in time. Defensive players learn to watch their opponents for indications that a pass is to be thrown or a certain play is to be run. And a good deal of the game is based on *deception*— that is, giving opponents false signifiers so they will make mistakes. It is the capacity of signs to lie, to give false information, that creates much of the complexity in the game.

The officials also use signs—a variety of gestures that indicate the   5
various penalties to be assessed for violations of the rules. These signals are actually nonverbal, visual metaphors, which enable the officials to indicate everyone in the stadium the nature of a given transgression. The sign that is most important, the one in which an official stretches both hands over his head to indicate a score, is a signifier with two signifieds: triumph or success for the offensive team and failure for the defensive team, and at the sign, thousands and thousands of people in the stadium (and in the television audience) cheer madly or groan.

While the game progresses there is much activity on the side-   6
lines. In college games, bands play rousing songs at certain times to encourage their teams, and cheerleaders lead cheers, jump up and down (displaying their breasts and legs), and carry on, often in rather mechanical dancing and movement displays. Many professional football teams have groups of young and attractive women who "wiggle and jiggle" on the sidelines, indicating that there is a sexual dimension

to the game or, more precisely, to the spectacle in which the game is embedded.

INSTANT REPLAY AND THE MODERN SENSIBILITY

As the various subsystems that are part of the spectacle of football   7
work themselves out, there is one sign that is crucial to the understanding of what football means—in its televised form, in particular—and
that is the huge scoreboard clock. Time is of the essence in football, but,
unlike baseball and other sports, in football time can be manipulated.
And it is this manipulation of time in tightly fought games that leads to
the incredible tension generated by the sport.

In a one-sided game there is little tension, and the game often turns   8
into an exhibition of power and competence for the winning team and a
study in humiliation for the losing one. But in close games, time is everyone's enemy. The winning team fights to hold on to its advantage and
the losing one tries to use what time it has left to best advantage and to
score. Many football games are decided in the last minutes, and often
even in the last seconds of the game. A minute of playing time, because
of the rules of the game, can take many minutes of real time.

What further complicates matters, especially in televised games,   9
is the invention of the instant replay, which can show a given play
from a variety of different perspectives and which suggests, ultimately, that time doesn't pass the way it does in real life. We keep seeing the past (a given play) over and over again from a variety of
angles, so that our sense of continuity and perspective are rendered
problematic. Time doesn't pass the way we thought it did, and our
perspective on the world isn't the only one.

Televised football has become an incredibly sophisticated art form   10
and now closely resembles avant-garde films in that both now simulate
stream-of-consciousness thought, which moves backward and forward
in time, jumping around almost incoherently at times. Instant replay is
vaguely equivalent to the flashback in film, and the invention of instant
replay has dramatically altered the nature of televised football (and now
other sports as well) in particular, and the modern American sensibility,
in general. In Super Bowl XVI, between the San Francisco 49ers and the
Cincinnati Bengals, CBS used 16 cameras on the field to televise the
game and another 7 for locker room shows and other activities. It had 14
videotape machines for instant replays, which meant that an incredible
number of perspectives was possible on every play. Can anyone doubt
that a new sensibility arises out of seeing such programming? Or, at
least, that a new sensibility is made possible because of the development
of such a remarkable kind of program?

FOOTBALL SOCIALIZES US

Football does more than just entertain us. The word "entertain" 11
is like the word "interesting"—neither tells us very much. The questions we should ask about football are those such as: Why do we find
football so entertaining? What do we get out of the game? What does it
do for us (that is, what gratifications does it offer)? What might it be
doing to us? What does it tell about society?

One very important aspect of football is the way it socializes and 12
encultures us. It teaches us how to get along in society, what roles to
play, what rules to follow, what life is all about, and so on. We are not
aware that this is going on most of the time, which means that we are
all the more susceptible to the influence of what the game suggests,
teaches, and implies. Here we are looking at the game as a signifier of
values, attitudes, and beliefs and attempting to ascertain what these
signifieds are and what effects they may have upon people (admittedly, a speculative activity).

One thing we learn from examining football is that we live in a 13
highly complex society in which time is critical and communication is
important. A good deal of the game involves communication between
the coaching staff and the players. Signals are called on both sides for
every play. Nothing is done that has not been planned, rehearsed, and
prepared over and over again in practice sessions. It is only the fact
that people make mistakes, or do things that cannot be anticipated,
that messes up the plans of coaches.

In addition, we come to learn that society is highly specialized, 14
and that this specialization functions within group situations. Teams
are now made up of offensive and defensive specialists, each with particular talents and abilities. Football teams function as "models" for
modern society and we learn, from watching football, that we must be
specialists who will work in some highly structured organization, controlled from above (the coaches), and that we must pursue our specialization for the good of the group, first and foremost, and then for
ourselves. That's what it means to be a "team player." We learn from
football, without being aware of it, that we must prepare ourselves to
function in a highly bureaucratic society—most likely within a large
corporate entity. Football is "training" for working in the corporate
world, and the violence in football becomes transformed into sales
campaigns that will "smash" the public or one's competitors or both.

We also learn that specialization and ability constitute a means 15
for upward mobility, especially in professional football, where farm
boys, Blacks from working-class families, and others often earn huge
salaries. Many youngsters identify very strongly with these football
stars, whose heroics on the football field are, at times, quite incredible.

In a sense football is really about containment and breaking free,   16
about order and randomness—though it is always within the context of
the game (which is highly structured and rule-dominated). These moments of freedom are exciting and highly exhilarating, but they are fleeting and quite unpredictable. It is not too much of an oversimplification
to say that much of football is routine and boring and that what makes
the game so exciting is that there are moments when remarkable things
happen. Since we can never know when one of these great plays will
happen, we must pay attention all the time, lest we miss something.

WHY BASEBALL IS BORING

The reason we find football so exciting is that it closely approxi-   17
mates and reflects our contemporary social situation. Football is a
twentieth-century sport for people who live in a world in which time
is precious (time is money), communication is important (we live in an
"information" society), and bureaucratic entities are dominant (corporations, universities, families, and so on). Baseball, on the other hand,
is a nineteenth-century pastoral sport in which time is irrelevant, specialization is not crucial, and there is much less reliance on plays and
communication. The following list, which contrasts the two sports, is
taken from my book *The TV-Guided American:*

Football	*Baseball*
urban	pastoral
educated players	country boys
time precious	time not important
specialized	general
body contact important	body contact minimal
team effort	individualistic
upsets critical	no upsets
vicarious excitement	relaxation
weekly	daily
spectacle	austere
four quarters with intermission	nine innings, uninterrupted flow
calculation, planning	little strategy
body a weapon	bat as a weapon
small area	large playing area
twentieth century	nineteenth century
territorial	not territorial
team on offense	one player at a time on offense

This list offers a set of polar oppositions that reflect the differ-   18
ences between the two sports and their relationship to our character

and culture. Baseball is essentially a nineteenth-century sport that is no longer congruent with contemporary American cultural dynamics and thus *seems* terribly slow or "boring" to many people. Baseball games are now events at which to drink beer and relax, and the ambience at baseball games is considerably different from what one finds at football games—especially at crucial games, where ancient antagonisms or a bowl bid hang in the balance.

Our boredom with baseball is a signifier that as a society we have   19
become "hopped up" and thus baseball seems much slower and boring than it used to, years ago. Baseball doesn't offer the gratifications it once did, or, to put it somewhat differently, the gratifications baseball offers don't mean very much to most people any more. Its heroes aren't as important to us as the heroes in football are, it doesn't provide models to imitate or help us gain an appropriate identity the way football does, and it certainly doesn't have the sexual elements in the spectacle surrounding the game that football has.

Baseball still has its attractions and provides many gratifications   20
to people. Some people argue that it is a subtler game than football, which, if true, may be part of the problem. But, for a variety of reasons, it doesn't have the cultural force or resonance that football does, and thus has taken on, inadvertently I would argue, a different role from that of football.

FOOTBALL AS AN ALTERNATIVE TO RELIGION

I have suggested in my discussion of socialization in football that   21
if football's manifest function is to entertain us, its latent function is to socialize us and offer us models to imitate and notions that will help us fit into the contemporary bureaucratic corporate world. I would like to turn now to another aspect of functionalist thought, namely, the notion that some phenomena function as alternatives for other phenomena. My thesis here is that football functions for many people as an *alternative* to religion or, perhaps, that it has a religious or sacred dimension to it that we seldom recognize.

The passionate feelings people have about football (and their   22
teams) and the intensity of our collective interest in the game leads me to think that football has a dimension far beyond that of simply being a sport. Indeed, Michael R. Real in *Mass-Mediated Culture* has written convincingly about the Super Bowl as a mythic spectacle and suggested how, in secular societies, sports "fill the vacuum" left by religions. I would like to suggest here that football—and I will focus on professional football—is in many ways analogous to religion. The following list points out some interesting parallels between the two seemingly different phenomena.

Professional Football	*Religion*
superstars	saints
Sunday game	Sunday service
ticket	offering
great merger	ecumenical movement
complex plays	theology
players on the way to the Super Bowl	knights in search of the Holy Grail
coaches	clergy
stadium	church
fans	congregations

Curiously enough, as religions (especially liberal religions) become more rational and continue to *demythologize* themselves, football becomes more arcane and mysterious, with incredibly complex plays and tactics that function much the way theology does for religion. People seem to have a need for myth, ritual, mystery, and heroism, and football, perhaps more than religion in contemporary societies, is helping people satisfy these needs.   23

Whether the messages we get from football are as valuable and positive as those we get from sermons and other aspects of religion is another matter, and one that bears thinking about. Has football become "the opiate of the people"? There are some who hold that belief, and it is to their interpretation that we now turn.   24

THE MARXIST PERSPECTIVE

Football games, held in huge stadiums, with bands, cheerleaders, halftime shows, and so on, are spectacles par excellence. The function of these spectacles (that is, the latent function), it may be argued, is to divert people's attention from their real social situation, to drain them of their emotional energy (which might have been expended on political and social issues), and, ultimately, to convince them of the justness of the political order. A political system that can provide good football is worth keeping. And since football also trains us for our place in the modern, corporate, capitalist world, it is doubly valuable.   25

The great gatherings of people in America are not (generally) for political purposes, though at times this does happen. Instead we gather together to watch spectacles—of which football is of exemplary importance. It isn't hard to see a parallel between the old Roman principle of bread and circuses—to divert the mobs from their misery—and what goes on in America on Fridays (in high schools), Saturdays (in colleges), and Sundays (in the professional games), as well as Monday nights on television.   26

Is the intensity of our interest in football a measure of the alien- 27
ation we feel in our everyday lives—lives in which we sense a radical
separation from our possibilities, in which we feel hemmed in by huge
bureaucratic structures that dominate our work lives, and by the competitiveness that characterizes our social order? The less satisfying our
lives, the more bothered we are by the "rat race," the more we turn to
vicarious satisfactions like football and, curiously, the less psychic
nourishment we get from them. For, ironically, football is itself essentially routine and boring and teaches us, though we generally are not
aware of this, that we must learn how to accommodate ourselves to
the society in which we live.

Football, especially professional football, is a huge business that 28
exists for one purpose—to make money. It treats players as commodities—objects to be sold and traded, almost at whim (though unioniza-
tion has modified this a good deal). Players have little sense of loyalty,
also. They see the huge profits the owners make and now obtain huge
salaries—all that the market can bear. The ultimate irony is that it is
television that benefits most from the existence of football, and television uses football for its main purpose—as filler between commercials.
Television, as it exists in America, is a business that makes money by
selling commercial time. Football attracts large audiences and costs
relatively little to produce (compared, say, to a crime show or documentary) so it is very cost-effective.

Thus we have a situation in which everyone is exploiting or try- 29
ing to exploit everyone else, and the result of all this is that spectacles
are produced that are used by people to obtain vicarious excitement
and pleasure and that have the hidden functions of teaching people to
accept the status quo and to accommodate themselves to corporations
and the political order.

The potential for revolutionary violence in the masses is si- 30
phoned off as they watch linemen battle one another "in the trenches"
and defensive players "hit" halfbacks and cornerbacks. After a weekend of football, the heavy viewer will have participated vicariously in
enough violence to fuel a dozen revolutions.

A look at the rosters of football teams shows that Blacks are heav- 31
ily and disproportionately represented. This is an indication of the fact
that Black people suffer more from our economic system than Whites do
and thus need football (as well as boxing and other sports) as an instrument of social mobility. For poor Black kids, football is a means of escaping from poverty and achieving middle-class—at least for a while.
To be successful, however, one must learn to fit in—to adopt essentially
bourgeois values such as being a team player, not causing trouble, doing
what one is told, and so on. A player, no matter how talented, who
causes "problems" and doesn't follow the rules will not prosper in col-

lege or professional football. Thus, there is a price to be paid by play-ers—namely, "accommodation," which leads the way to "co-optation."

FOOTBALL AND THE PSYCHE

I have suggested that football functions as a means of socializing   32
people and of diverting them from paying attention to their real con-cerns. I would also like to suggest that football is vitally connected with various unconscious processes, which explain, in part, the pow-erful hold football has on people. If large numbers of people read the comics or watch football or do anything, quite likely it is because there are important psychic gratifications to be obtained, even though peo-ple may not be aware of them.

For one thing, there is the matter of violence in football. It is a   33
kind of controlled violence that may satisfy two contradictory desires we have: to be violent and, at the same time, to be controlled so our vi-olence doesn't overwhelm us. This violence is integral to the game, in which there are "blocks," "hits," "tackles," or the like on every play. It stems from a number of sources, such as the fact that we must restrain ourselves from impulsive behavior, and the fact that we are all in-volved (unconsciously) in Oedipal problems, sibling rivalries, and so on. Quite likely the matter of sexual repression is of primary impor-tance, and the violence becomes a kind of substitute gratification. (There is a connection, also, between violence and eroticism that must be kept in mind. There is a sexual dimension to violence just as there is an aggressive and violent dimension to sexuality.)

The violence in football may also help men with the matter of ob-   34
taining masculine identity. We live in an information society, in which processing data and communicating account for a dominant part of the gross national product. In such a society men find it hard to de-velop a male identity, especially since American male identity has his-torically been connected to our nineteenth-century lifestyle—cutting wood, herding cattle, doing hard physical labor. Watching violence on the football field becomes one of the few ways in which American men can help themselves form a male identity, even if this violence is vicar-ious and potentially destructive.

Football lends itself to a number of interpretations of a psychoan-   35
alytic nature. For example, we can interpret the game as mirroring the battle between id, ego, and superego forces in the human psyche:

Id	*Ego*	*Superego*
offensive team	officials	defensive team
drives	rules	prevention

In this situation, the offensive team wants to have long "drives" and to score: the defensive team wants to stop these drives and get control of the ball; and the officials function as an ego, to keep the game going.

Arnold J. Mandell, a psychiatrist who spent some time with the San   36
Diego Chargers, categorized professional football players as follows:

Position	Personality Traits
offensive linemen	ambitious, tenacious, precise, attentive to detail
wide receivers	narcissistic, vain, loners
quarterbacks	self-confident, courageous
defensive linemen	restless, peevish, irritable, intolerant of detail, uninhibited, wild
linebackers	controlled, brutal, internally conflicted

These personality traits are the ones required for people to be able to play their positions, Mandell found. The offensive players, he discovered, keep their lockers neat and orderly, but the lockers of defensive players are invariably messy.

> It became clear that offensive football players like structure and discipline. They want to maintain the status quo. They tend to be conservative as people, and as football players they take comfort in repetitious practice of well-planned and well-executed plays. The defensive players, just as clearly, can't stand structure; their attitudes, their behavior and their lifestyles bear this out.

All of this is important because more than anything else, Mandell reports, "the game is in the mind," which is probably true of all games.

CONCLUDING REMARKS

Football, though it might seem to be only a simple entertainment,   37
is actually a matter of some consequence from a number of points of view. We use language from football in our political discourse; it creates the lamentable "football widow" every fall, it is played by children, adolescents, college students, and grown men, it is an industry, it has a long history—I could go on and on, endlessly. It is a subject that attracts great attention from the general public and one that deserves attention from the media analyst.

But there is something else to be said here that every media   38
analyst must remember. When we deal with the programs carried by the media—whether we focus on the football, soap operas, news,

or any other genre—we must never forget that we are dealing with art forms. And art forms are extremely complicated phenomena. We must be careful that we do not reduce a program to nothing but a system of signs, nothing but a socializing agent, nothing but a means of manipulating people's consciousness, nothing but a subject in which drives, Oedipal problems, and the like are manifested. We must find a way, somehow, to analyze a program from a number of different points of view but also to respect it as a creative effort (perhaps not a very successful one) and a work of art that has performance aspects, aesthetic elements, and more. To be a media analyst one must know all kinds of things and, in a sense, everything at the same time.

Examining the Text

1. Berger claims that football socializes us, in part by providing an instructive model of the bureaucratic corporate world (paragraphs 11–15). What are some of the characteristics of that model, as Berger describes it? Can you think of others? Are there ways in which football offers models for rebelling *against* corporate culture?

2. Why does Berger claim that football plays a religious role in society (21–24)? Do you think he is exaggerating, or do you know people for whom football is a "religion"? How might other sports serve a similar function?

3. How does Berger explain the appeal of football's violence (33–35)? What do you think of his explanation?

4. Berger offers several interpretations of football: semiological ("a game of signs"), aesthetic ("an incredibly sophisticated art form"), sociological (it "socializes us"), comparative ("baseball is boring"), anthropological ("an alternative to religion"), marxist ("the opiate of the people"), and psychoanalytic ("vitally connected with various unconscious processes"). Do you find any of these interpretations more persuasive or revealing than others? Why do you think Berger offers several interpretations rather than just one?

Group Discussion

Choose a sport other than football and list the signs involved in that sport, using Berger's discussion of football signs as a model. Do signs function in other sports as they do in football? As a class, discuss the meanings of various signs in other sports.

Writing Suggestion

Choose one of Berger's seven interpretative perspectives or combine several of them and write an essay in which you similarly analyze another sport.

Champion of the World

Maya Angelou

Maya Angelou is a well-known poet, novelist, and performer. Born in 1928 and raised in the segregated South, Angelou persevered through countless hardships to become one of the country's most revered authors and cultural leaders. Angelou read her poem, "On the Pulse of Morning," at the 1993 inauguration of President Bill Clinton.

The selection which follows is from Angelou's first volume of autobiography, I Know Why the Caged Bird Sings *(1969). She relates an important recollection from childhood about the night in the 1930s when world heavyweight champion Joe Louis, nicknamed the "Brown Bomber," defended his boxing title against a white contender. Much of Angelou's narrative is made up of the words and feelings of the local black community gathered in her Uncle Willie's store to listen to the broadcast of that highly publicized match. Angelou shows how her neighbors' hopes and fears and their image of themselves as a people were intimately connected to the fortunes of Louis, one of a very few black heroes of the day. Her narrative reveals that a "simple" sporting event can be of intense significance for a group of people who see it as a symbol of personal victory or defeat.*

Before you read, *recall any experience you've had or heard about in which a sporting event took on an emotional power and significance far greater than the event itself would seem to warrant. Whether this event is one that you participated in, watched, or read about, think about how and why sports can have such an intense influence on people's lives.*

The last inch of space was filled, yet people continued to wedge   1
themselves along the walls of the Store. Uncle Willie had turned the
radio up to its last notch so that youngsters on the porch wouldn't
miss a word. Women sat on kitchen chairs, dining-room chairs, stools,
and upturned wooden boxes. Small children and babies perched on
every lap available and men leaned on the shelves or on each other.

The apprehensive mood was shot through with shafts of gaiety,   2
as a black sky is streaked with lightning.

"I ain't worried 'bout this fight. Joe's gonna whip that cracker   3
like it's open season."

"He gone whip him till that white boy call him Momma."   4

At last the talking finished and the string-along songs about   5
razor blades were over and the fight began.

"A quick jab to the head." In the Store the crowd grunted. "A left   6
to the head and a right and another left." One of the listeners cackled
like a hen and was quieted.

"They're in a clinch, Louis is trying to fight his way out."   7

Some bitter comedian on the porch said, "That white man don't   8
mind hugging that niggah now, I betcha."

"The referee is moving in to break them up, but Louis finally   9
pushed the contender away and it's an uppercut to the chin. The contender is hanging on, now he's backing away. Louis catches him with
a short left to the jaw."

A tide of murmuring assent poured out the door and into the   10
yard.

"Another left and another left. Louis is saving that mighty right..."   11
The mutter in the Store had grown into a baby roar and it was pierced
by the clang of a bell and the announcer's "That's the bell for round
three, ladies and gentlemen."

As I pushed my way into the Store I wondered if the announcer   12
gave any thought to the fact that he was addressing as "ladies and
gentlemen" all the Negroes around the world who sat sweating and
praying, glued to their "Master's voice."

There were only a few calls for RC Colas, Dr. Peppers, and Hires   13
root beer. The real festivities would begin after the fight. Then even
the old Christian ladies who taught their children and tried themselves to practice turning the other cheek would buy soft drinks, and if
the Brown Bomber's victory was a particularly bloody one they would
order peanut patties and Baby Ruths, also.

Bailey and I laid coins on top of the cash register. Uncle Willie   14
didn't allow us to ring up sales during a fight. It was too noisy and might
shake up the atmosphere. When the gong rang for the next round we
pushed through the near-sacred quiet to the herd of children outside.

"He's got Louis against the ropes and now it's a left to the body   15
and a right to the ribs. Another right to the body, it looks like it was
low...Yes, ladies and gentlemen, the referee is signaling but the contender keeps raining the blows on Louis. It's another to the body, and
it looks like Louis is going down."

My race groaned. It was our people falling. It was another lynch-   16
ing, yet another Black man hanging on a tree. One more woman am-
bushed and raped. A Black boy whipped and maimed. It was hounds
on the trail of a man running through slimy swamps. It was a white
woman slapping her maid for being forgetful.

The men in the Store stood away from the walls and at attention.   17
Women greedily clutched the babes on their laps while on the porch the

shufflings and smiles, flirtings and pinching of a few minutes before were gone. This might be the end of the world. If Joe lost we were back in slavery and beyond help. It would all be true, the accusations that we were lower types of human beings. Only a little higher than apes. True that we were stupid and ugly and lazy and dirty and, unlucky and worst of all, that God Himself hated us and ordained us to be hewers of wood and drawers of water, forever and ever, world without end.

We didn't breathe. We didn't hope. We waited.   18

"He's off the ropes, ladies and gentlemen. He's moving towards   19
the center of the ring." There was no time to be relieved. The worst
might still happen.

"And now it looks like Joe is mad. He's caught Carnera with a left   20
hook to the head and a right to the head. It's a left jab to the body and another left to the head. There's a left cross and a right to the head. The contender's right eye is bleeding and he can't seem to keep his block up.
Louis is penetrating every block. The referee is moving in, but Louis
sends a left to the body and it's an uppercut to the chin and the contender is dropping. He's on the canvas, ladies and gentlemen."

Babies slid to the floor as women stood up and men leaned to-   21
ward the radio.

"Here's the referee. He's counting. One, two, three, four, five, six,   22
seven...Is the contender trying to get up again?"

All the men in the store shouted, "NO."   23

"—eight, nine, ten." There were a few sounds from the audience,   24
but they seemed to be holding themselves in against tremendous pres-
sure.

"The fight is all over, ladies and gentlemen. Let's get the micro-   25
phone over to the referee...Here he is. He's got the Brown Bomber's
hand, he's holding it up...Here he is..."

Then the voice, husky and familiar, came to wash over us—"The   26
winnah, and still heavyweight champeen of the world...Joe Louis."

Champion of the world. A Black boy. Some Black mother's son.   27

He was the strongest man in the world. People drank Coca-Colas   28
like ambrosia and ate candy bars like Christmas. Some of the men
went behind the Store and poured white lightning in their soft-drink
bottles, and a few of the bigger boys followed them. Those who were
not chased away came back blowing their breath in front of themselves like proud smokers.

It would take an hour or more before people would leave the   29
Store and head home. Those who lived too far had made arrange-
ments to stay in town. It wouldn't do for a Black man and his family to
be caught on a lonely country road on a night when Joe Louis had
proved that we were the strongest people in the world.

———————————

Examining the Text

1. Unlike the other selections in this chapter which offer fairly objective, analyses of sport, Angelou relates a personal recollection. What conclusions about the influence of sports on culture, and specifically on African American culture in the 1930s, can you draw from her story? Has that influence changed significantly over the last sixty years?

2. In paragraphs 16 and 17 Angelou describes her own thoughts about the prospect of Louis losing the match. After rereading these paragraphs, what do you think they contribute to the overall meaning and drama of the story? How are they connected to the final paragraph?

3. What is the effect of the concluding paragraph in the story? How would Angelou's message be different if she had not ended it this way?

For Group Discussion

Angelou's recollection demonstrates in vivid detail how a sporting event can take on much larger significance, how people can invest a great deal of emotion in the performance of an athlete or team. In your group, list some other specific examples of sporting contests that have taken on intense emotional significance and meaning for an individual or a group of fans. As a class, discuss the advantages and disadvantages of the strong influence sports has on its fans.

Writing Suggestion

In her narrative, Angelou describes how Joe Louis was an inspiration and sign of hope for African Americans in the 1930s. Choose another athlete who you think has similarly been an inspiration to his or her fans or has served as a role model. In an essay discuss the qualities that make that person a particularly good model. At the same time, if you think that athlete has negative qualities, you may cite these as well in analyzing how he or she has influenced fans.

The Black and White Truth about Basketball

Jeff Greenfield

Jeff Greenfield, a political and media analyst for ABC News and a syndicated newspaper columnist, has written extensively about contemporary American culture, focusing on politics, sports, and the media. Originally

*published in 1975, the essay which follows has been widely anthologized since
then and was updated by the author in 1988.*

*Greenfield's thesis is that there are two different styles—"black style"
and a "white style"—of playing basketball and that these result from differences in the environments the players grow up in. So, although his analysis of
basketball focuses on the game and how it's played, Greenfield also looks
closely at broader cultural influences. This essay is notable both for its controversial thesis and for its rhetorical technique: this is an excellent example of
an essay of comparison and contrast, in which "black" and "white" basketball
are carefully contrasted in terms of their style, how they evolved, and how different players embody each style.*

*As you read, notice the form of Greenfield's essay, as well as its con-
tent. What organizational and descriptive techniques does he use to convey
his ideas clearly and persuasively? Do you find yourself agreeing with his
points? Why or why not?*

The dominance of black athletes over professional basketball is   1
beyond dispute. Two-thirds of the players are black, and the number
would be greater were it not for the continuing practice of picking
white bench warmers for the sake of balance. Over the last two
decades, no more than three white players have been among the ten
starting players on the National Basketball Association's All-Star team,
and in the last quarter century, only two white players—Dave Cowens
and Larry Bird of the Boston Celtics—have ever been chosen as the
NBA's Most Valuable Player.

And at a time when a baseball executive could lose his job for as-   2
serting that blacks lacked "the necessities" to become pro sports executives and when the National Football League still has not hired a
single black head coach, the NBA stands as a pro sports league that
hired its first black head coach in 1968 (Bill Russell) and its first black
general manager in the early 1970s (Wayne Embry of the Milwaukee
Bucks). What discrimination remains—lack of equal opportunity for
speaking engagements and product endorsements—has more to do
with society than with basketball.

This dominance reflects a natural inheritance: Basketball is the   3
pastime of the urban poor. The current generation of black athletes are
heirs to a tradition more than half a century old. In a neighborhood without the money for bats, gloves, hockey sticks and ice skates, or shoulder
pads, basketball is an eminently accessible sport. "Once it was the game
of the Irish and Italian Catholics in Rockaway and the Jews on Fordham
Road in the Bronx," writes David Wolf in his brilliant book, *Foul!* "It was
recreation, status, and a way out." But now the ethnic names have been
changed: Instead of the Red Holzimans, Red Auerbachs, and the

McGuire brothers, there are Julius Ervings and Michael Jordans, Ralph Sampsons and Kareem Abdul-Jabbars. And professional basketball is a sport with national television exposure and million-dollar salaries.

But the mark on basketball of today's players can be measured   4
by more than money or visibility. It is a question of style. For there is a clear difference between "black" and "white" styles of play that is as clear as the difference between 155th Street at Eighth Avenue and Crystal City, Missouri. Most simply (remembering we are talking about culture, not chromosomes), "black" basketball is the use of superb athletic skill to adapt to the limits of space imposed by the game. "White" ball is the pulverization of that space by sheer intensity.[1]

It takes a conscious effort to realize how constricted the space is   5
on a basketball court. Place a regulation court (ninety-four by fifty feet) on a football field, and it will reach from the back of the end zone to the twenty-one-yard line; its width will cover less than a third of the field. On a baseball diamond, a basketball court will reach from home plate to first base. Compared to its principal indoor rival, ice hockey, basketball covers about one-fourth the playing area. Moreover, during the normal flow of the game, most of the action takes place on the third of the court nearest the basket. It is in this dollhouse space that ten men, each of them half a foot taller than the average man, come together to battle each other.

There is, thus, no room; basketball is a struggle for the edge: the   6
half step with which to cut around the defender for a lay-up, the half second of freedom with which to release a jump shot, the instant a head turns allowing a pass to a teammate breaking for the basket. It is an arena for the subtlest of skills: the head fake, the shoulder fake, the shift of body weight to the right and the sudden cut to the left. Deception is crucial to success; and to young men who have learned early and painfully that life is a battle for survival, basketball is one of the few pursuits in which the weapon of deception is a legitimate tactic rather than the source of trouble.

If there is, then, the need to compete in a crowd, to battle for the   7
edge, then the surest strategy is to develop the *unexpected:* to develop a shot that is simply and fundamentally different from the usual methods of putting the ball in the basket. Drive to the hoop, but go under it and come up the other side; hold the ball at waist level and shoot from there instead of bringing the ball up to eye level; leap into the air, but fall away

---

[1]This distinction has nothing to do with the question of whether whites can play as "well" as blacks. In 1987, the Detroit Piston's Isaiah Thomas quipped that the Celtics' Larry Bird was "a pretty good player," but would be much less celebrated and wealthy if he were black. As Thomas later said, Bird is one of the greatest pro players in history. Nor is this distinction about "smart," although the Los Angeles Lakers' Magic Johnson is right in saying that too many journalists ascribe brilliant strategy by black players to be solely due to "innate" ability.

from the basket instead of toward it. All these tactics, which a fan can see embodied in the astonishing play of the Chicago Bulls' Michael Jordan, take maximum advantage of the crowding on the court. They also stamp uniqueness on young men who may feel it nowhere else.

"For many young men in the slums," David Wolf writes, "the   8
school yard is the only place they can feel true pride in what they do, where they can move free of inhibitions and where they can, by being spectacular, rise for the moment against the drabness and anonymity of their lives. Thus, when a player develops extraordinary 'school yard' moves and shots...[they] become his measure as a man."

So the moves that begin as tactics for scoring soon become calling   9
cards. You don't just lay the ball in for an uncontested basket; you take the ball in both hands, leap as high as you can, and slam the ball through the hoop. When you jump in the air, fake a shot, bring the ball back to your body, and throw up a shot, all without coming back down, you have proven your worth in uncontestable fashion.

This liquid grace is an integral part of "black" ball, almost exclu-   10
sively the province of the playground player. Some white stars like Bob Cousy, Billy Cunningham, and Doug Collins had it, and the Celtics' Kevin McHale has it now: the body control, the moves to the basket, the free-ranging mobility. Most of them also possessed the surface ease that is integral to the "black" style; an incorporation of the ethic of mean streets—to "make it" is not just to have wealth but to have it without strain. Whatever the muscles and organs are doing, the face of the "black" star almost never shows it. Magic Johnson of the Lakers can bring the ball down court with two men on him, whip a pass through an invisible opening, cut to the basket, take a return pass, and hit the shot all with no more emotion than a quick smile. So stoic was San Antonio Spurs' great George Gervin that he earned the nickname "Ice Man." (Interestingly, a black coach like Boston's K. C. Jones exhibits far less emotion on the bench than a white counterpart like Dick Motta or Jack Ramsey.)

If there is a single trait that characterizes "black" ball it is leasing   11
ability. Bob Cousy, ex-Celtic great and former pro coach, says that "when coaches get together, one is sure to say, 'I've got the one black kid in the country who can't jump.' When coaches see a white boy who can jump or who moves with extraordinary quickness, they say, 'He should have been born black, he's that good.'"

Don Nelson, now a top executive with the Golden State War-   12
riors, recalls that back in 1970, Dave Cowens, then a relatively un-known graduate of Florida State, prepared for his rookie pro season by playing the Rucker League, an outdoor competition in Harlem play-grounds that pits pros against college kids and playground stars. So ferocious was Cowens' leaping ability, Nelson says, that "when the

summer was over, everyone wanted to know who the white son of a bitch was who could jump so high." That's another way to overcome a crowd around the basket—just go over it.

Speed, mobility, quickness, acceleration, "the moves"—all of   13
these are catch-phrases that surround the "black" playground athlete, the style of play. So does the most racially tinged of attributes, "rhythm." Yet rhythm is what the black stars themselves talk about: feeling the flow of the game, finding the tempo of the dribble, the step, the shot. It is an instinctive quality (although it stems from hundreds of hours of practice), and it is one that has led to difficulty between system-oriented coaches and free-form players.

"Cats from the street have their own rhythm when they play,"   14
said college dropout Bill Spivey, onetime New York high school star. "It's not a matter of somebody setting you up and you shooting. You *feel* the shot. When a coach holds you back, you lose the feel and it isn't fun anymore."

When legendary Brooklyn playground star Connie Hawkins was   15
winding up his NBA career under Laker coach Bill Sharman, he chafed under the methodical style of play. "He's systematic to the point where it begins to be a little too much. It's such an action-reaction type of game that when you have to do everything the same way, I think you lose something."

There is another kind of basketball that has grown up in Amer-   16
ica. It is not played on asphalt playgrounds with a crowd of kids competing for the court; it is played on macadam driveways by one boy with a ball and a backboard nailed over the garage; it is played in gyms in the frigid winter of the rural Midwest and on Southern dirt courts. It is a mechanical, precise development of skills (when Don Nelson was an Iowa farm boy, his incentive to make his shots was that an errant rebound would land in the middle of chicken droppings). It is a game without frills, without flow, but with effectiveness. It is "white" basketball: jagged, sweaty, stumbling, intense. Where a "black" player overcomes an obstacle with finesse and body control, a "white" player reacts by outrunning or overpowering the obstacle.

By this definition, the Boston Celtics are a classically "white" team.   17
They rarely suit up a player with dazzling moves; indeed such a player would probably make Red Auerbach swallow his cigar. Instead, the Celtics wear you down with execution, with constant running, with the same play run again and again and again. The rebound by Robert Parrish triggers the fast break, as everyone races downcourt; the ball goes to Larry Bird, who pulls up and takes the shot or who drives and then finds Danny Ainge or Kevin McHale free for an easy basket.

Perhaps the most definitively "white" position is that of the   18
quick forward, one without great moves to the basket, without highly

developed hosts, without the height and mobility for rebounding effectiveness. So what does he do?

He runs. He runs from the opening jump to the final buzzer.   19
He runs up and down the court, from base line to base line, back and forth under the basket, looking for the opening, the pass, the chance to take a quick step, the high percentage shot. To watch San Antonio's Mark Olberding or Detroit's Bill Lambeer, players without speed or obvious moves, is to wonder what they are doing in the NBA—until you see them swing free and throw up a shot that, without demanding any apparent skill, somehow goes in the basket more frequently than the shots of many of their more skilled teammates. And to have watched the New York Knicks' (now U.S. Senator) Bill Bradley, or the Celtics' John Havlicek, is to have watched "white" ball at its best.

Havlicek or Lambeer, or the Laker's Kurt Rambis, stand in dra-   20
matic contrast to Michael Jordan or to the Philadelphia 76ers' legend, Julius Erving. Erving had the capacity to make legends come true, leaping from the foul line and slam-dunking the ball on his way down; going up for a lay-up, pulling the ball to his body, and driving under and up the other side of the rim, defying gravity and probability with impossible moves and jumps. Michael Jordan of the Chicago Bulls has been seen by thousands spinning a full 360 degrees in midair before slamming the ball through the hoop.

When John Havlicek played, by contrast, he was the living em-   21
bodiment of his small-town Ohio background. He would bring the ball down court, weaving left, then right, looking for a path. He would swing the ball to a teammate, cut behind the pick, take the pass, and release the shot in a flicker of time. It looked plain, unvarnished. But it was a blend of skills that not more than half a dozen other players in the league possessed.

To former pro Jim McMillian, a black who played quick forward   22
with "white" attributes, "it's a matter of environment. Julius Erving grew up in a different environment from Havlicek. John came from a very small town in Ohio. There everything was done the easy way, the shortest distance between two points. It's nothing fancy; very few times will he go one-on-one. He hits the lay-up, hits the jump shot, makes the free throw, and after the game you look up and say, 'How did he hurt us that much?'"

"White" ball, then, is the basketball of patience, method and   23
sometimes brute strength. "Black" ball is the basketball of electric self-expression. One player has all the time in the world to perfect his skills, the other a need to prove himself. These are slippery categories, because a poor boy who is black can play "white" and a white boy of middle-class parents can play "black." Bill Cartwright of the New

York Knicks and Steve Alford of the Dallas Mavericks are athletes who seem to defy these categories.

And what makes basketball the most intriguing of sports is how 24 these styles do not necessarily clash; how the punishing intensity of "white" players and the dazzling moves of the "blacks" can fit together, a fusion of cultures that seems more and more difficult in the world beyond the out-of-bounds line.

Examining the Text

1. What reasons does Greenfield give for the predominance of African Americans in professional basketball? Are his reasons related primarily to race, class, environment, or to a combination of all three?

2. How does the "white style" of basketball differ from the "black style," as Greenfield describes them? How does he account for these differences? Why do you think Greenfield uses quotation marks around "black" and "white" throughout his essay?

3. When this essay was first published in *Esquire* in 1975, it sparked some controversy. Do you find anything controversial or potentially offensive in Greenfield's analysis? Do you think he wanted to cause controversy? If so, why? In determining your answer, consider the author's final paragraph as well as the comparisons he makes with other professional sports in paragraph 2.

For Group Discussion

Apply Greenfield's thesis about the different styles of playing basketball to another sport. (You need not focus on "black" and "white" styles, but rather look at "male" and "female" styles or at different styles embodied by individual players.) As a group, list two or more different, yet complementary, styles in the sport you choose. Describe the styles and how they complement each other, and consider reasons the differences might exist. Report your group's analysis to the class.

Writing Suggestion

In defining "black" and "white" styles of playing basketball Greenfield vividly describes specific moves, shots, and plays made by players in general and by especially notable individuals. Using Greenfield's descriptions as a model, write your own detailed description of moves and plays in another sport. After your descriptions, try to draw some conclusions about why the sport is enjoyable for players and spectators alike.

Alternative Masculinity and
Its Effects on Gender Relations
in the Subculture of Skateboarding

Becky Beal

Certain traditional, "all-American" sports, such as football, have been criticized for being overly regimented, and even militaristic, in their underlying philosophies. For an example of football's implicit militarism, read this description of the sport from "old-school" advocates Walter Camp and Lorin Deland in their book Football:

> *After courage comes the lesson of obedience. The world has never underestimated the value of a military or naval training in teaching implicit, unquestioned obedience and a fine sense of readiness to accept discipline. Football demands obedience. An army poorly officered becomes a mob; a football team would be even worse off without strict discipline. The biting sarcasm of the coaches must be borne without a thought of rebellion; the unmerited blame must be accepted without excuse; every order must be instantly and unquestioningly obeyed.*

Many social critics contend that sports such as football, based as they are on such a martial ideology, perpetuate a culture of male dominance, competitiveness, and coercion. In the following article, author/critic Becky Beal terms this phenomenon "hegemonic masculinity," which, she contends, leads to toxic levels of "physical domination, aggression, competition, sexism, and homophobia." These qualities, she says, "are too often seen as ideals of manliness," which negatively affect male athletes' views about their relationships with other men, and their attitudes about women.

However, Beal goes on to point out that not all contemporary sports engender this kind of "hegemonic" maleness. As an example of a nonhegemonic sport she focuses on skateboarding. Skaterboarders, she says, distinguish their sport from more traditional ones "by critiquing conformity to adult authority and structured competition." Using a social-scientific research method involving observation, participation, and interviewing, Beal notes that skaters place an emphasis on cooperation and encouragement, rather than "a cut-throat form of competition." Unfortunately, Beal notes that skateboarding still excludes women to a great extent, because of certain perceived attributes of females: appearance, natural aptitude, social roles, and so forth. As you read this article, note your reaction to Beal's belief that most sports serve to promote traditional "hegemonic" male values. Consider also whether or not you agree with the reasons Beal gives to account for the small number of women who skateboard. Finally, consider whether you have observed gender inequalities changing within the sphere of sports. Have you observed the number of

females who skateboard—or who participate in other traditional and nontra-
ditional sports—increasing and/or gaining more acceptance? If so, what
would account for this change, in your opinion?

With the recent movement in men's studies there has been a   1
growing popularity of investigating different forms of masculinity and
their consequences for men, their relationships with each other, and
their relationships with women. According to Clatterbaugh (1990)
there have been several avenues of the men's movement including a
conservative, profeminist, socialist, and gay and black perspective.
Each avenue carries with it different social agendas with priorities for
addressing social problems. For example, a conservative approach can
be correlated with a profamily values orientation which asserts traditional gender norms and family relations as a way of reestablishing social order. On the other hand, a profeminist approach sees traditional
masculinity as the root of women's oppression, and therefore seeks to
change traditional gender roles as a way of promoting a more democratic society. The black and gay perspectives have demonstrated that
there is not just one form of masculinity from which all men equally
benefit. Gay men must deal with homophobia and blacks must deal
with racism, and—to more of an extent than whites—poverty. Both
these circumstances show that minority men have a different experience of masculinity.

Carrigan, Connell, and Lee (1987) effectively summarized the   2
history of research on masculinity as moving from a "sex roles" (or an
assumption of "natural" differences determining social behavior) approach to an emphasis on the social construction of gender. The latter
approach has emphasized power relations associated with different
genders. Carrigan et al. (1987) clarified that power relations are not
only between masculinity and femininity, but among different forms
of masculinity as well (e.g., gay and black perspective). The most powerful form of masculinity is called hegemonic masculinity. They stated
"what emerges from this line of argument is the very important concept of hegemonic masculinity, not as "the male role," but as a particular variety of masculinity to which others—among them young and
effeminate as well as homosexual men—are subordinated" (p. 174).

This paper will combine a profeminist and critical perspective to   3
describe how one group of young males created a nonhegemonic or alternative form of masculinity. The subculture of skateboarders I investigated chose not to live completely by the traditional and hegemonic
forms of masculinity. In doing so, they created an alternative masculinity, one which explicitly critiqued the more traditional form. This
paper will not only describe how they distinguished their subculture

from traditional sport and hegemonic masculinity, but also investigate the resulting gender relations within the subculture, particularly how the males maintained the privilege of masculinity by differentiating and elevating themselves from females and femininity.

MASCULINITY AND SPORT

The concept of masculinity is often broad and, as mentioned   4
above, does not encompass all men's experiences equally. Generally, masculinity is defined as a "social role that belongs to identifiable groups of men who exist in reasonably historical, ethnic, or religious situations" (Clatterbaugh, 1990, p. 3). Each culture and ethnicity has a masculine ideal, which may also not be the lived experiences of men, but the social expectations of the ideal can affect them nonetheless (Connell, 1990). In the United States' culture, the attributes of masculine ideal have included individualism, aggression, power, competitiveness, strength, stoicism, and protector. Two social institutions which have traditionally encouraged boys and men to live out the ideals of hegemonic masculinity have been the military and sport (Kimmel & Messner, 1989; Miedzian, 1991). As a football coach once declared, "Football is the closest thing to war you boys will ever experience. It's your chance to find out what manhood is really all about" (cited in Sabo & Panepinto, 1990, p. 124).

Several researchers have pointed to the crisis of masculinity in the   5
United States during the late nineteenth and early twentieth centuries as one of the main impetuses for the raise of modern sport (Bradley, 1989; Hantover, 1978; Kimmel, 1990; Lucas & Smith, 1978; Messner, 1992, Whitson, 1990). In this time period fewer men owned their own businesses or controlled their own labor as the factory system became more dominant. Not only were men losing control over their labor, but women were entering the job market, especially teaching, and the women's movement challenged conventional gender roles. All these threatened the traditional concepts of masculinity and men's social position. In response to the changing historical circumstances sport was promoted as one significant means of ensuring that boys became "properly" masculine. Today, sport is still a significant means of ideologically promoting hegemonic masculinity (Messner, 1988; Nelson, 1994).

HEGEMONIC MASCULINITY IN SPORT

Sport is one of the most significant institutions of male bonding   6
and male initiation rites. Sabo and Panepinto (1990) described football as a male initiation ritual which promotes hegemonic masculinity. In

their analysis they described five characteristics of male initiation rituals in patriarchal societies. The first is man–boy relationships in which the older men direct the participants through the rituals. The second characteristic is the use of a variety of means to ensure conformity to the rules of the rituals. Through this process arises the third characteristic, which is learning to defer to male authority. Sabo and Panepinto stated "the initiation rites process at once introduces boys to the wider male status hierarchy and acclimates them to male authority (p. 117). Pain is also another characteristic of these rituals, for it is the tolerance of pain that often "proves" one's manhood. In addition, these rituals take place in a segregated environment. Family members and females are not present during these rituals. These attributes illustrate many male sporting environments.

As noted by several sport sociologists (e.g., Curry, 1991; Kidd, 1987; Messner, 1992; Sabo, 1989), the paradigm of hegemonic masculinity which abounds in mainstream sport includes physical domination, aggression, competition, sexism, and homophobia. These are often seen as the ideal of manliness, which affects male athletes' views about themselves, their relationships with other men, and their attitudes about women.

7

ALTERNATIVE MASCULINITY

For profeminists an alternative masculinity gives hope that alternative values can be promoted which will decrease violence, sexism, and homophobia. In other words, alternative values which could improve the quality of life for a variety of men as well as women. It is from this perspective that I became interested in how one subculture of sport, skateboarding, redefined and lived an alternative masculinity. The following will describe how these skateboarders differentiated themselves from hegemonic sport and hegemonic masculinity, what they called the "jock" image. These skateboarders resisted many of the characteristics of the rituals of masculinity that Sabo and Panepinto (1990) described. In particular, skaters challenged a deference to adult male authority and the conformity and control fostered by that authority.

8

METHODOLOGY

I used qualitative methods of observation, participant-observation and semistructured in-depth interviews to investigate the subculture of skateboarding in northeastern Colorado. My research began in June 1989, when I started observing skateboarders in Jamestown and Welton, Colorado, at local hangouts, skateboard shops, and even a locally sponsored skateboard exhibition.

9

Most of my participants I met by stopping them while they were   10
skateboarding on the streets, and asking if I could talk with them. (They
call themselves "skaters," and the act of skateboarding they call "skating.") I met other skaters through interactions I had with their parents.
In addition, I met one female skater (a rarity) through mutual membership in a local feminist group. These initial contacts snowballed to many
others. Over a two year period (1990–1992) I talked with 41 skaters, 2
skateboard shop owners, and several parents and siblings.

Thirty-seven of the 41 participants were male and 4 were female.   11
In addition, all were anglo except two, who were Hispanic males. The
average age of those participating was 16, but ranged from 10 to 25
years. The participants had skateboarded for an average of four years,
but the range of their participation was from one to 15 years. Of the 41
skateboarders, 24 I interviewed more than once—6 of whom I had ongoing communication with, which gave me a vital source of feedback
and helped to refine my conclusions and questions. In addition, I
spent over 100 hours observing skateboarders many of whom I had
not interviewed (they were observed in public spaces).

After I finished gathering data, the information and analysis of   12
their subculture was presented to approximately one third of the participants. Their comments served to confirm and fine tune my conclusions. They especially wanted me to note that although they shared
many norms and values, they did not share all values and, therefore,
just because they were all skateboarders did not mean that they were
all good friends. This was evident in the variety of friendship groups
within skateboarding, such as "hippies," "punks," "Skinheads," and
"old-timers."

"NOT AS MILITARY MINDED"

The above heading is a statement from Craig, a 25-year-old   13
skateboarder, who described the differences between skateboarding
and more mainstream forms of sport. Craig's statement represents the
most significant departure from traditional values and structure of
mainstream sport for, overwhelmingly, the participants distinguished
their sport from more traditional ones by critiquing conformity to
adult authority and structured competition.

CONFORMITY AND SELF-EXPRESSION

The popular practice of skateboarding lacked a strict formal struc-   14
ture. In fact, the appeal for many skaters was precisely to use skate-

boarding as a means of self-expression and of challenging their own physical limits. Generally, a skating "session" (the time spent skate-boarding) involves creating and practicing certain techniques, finding fun places to skate, and trying new tricks on the obstacles found. For ex-ample, a favorite spot of skaters in Welton was a loading dock located on the backside of a grocery store. The space used for the trucks to dock was lower than the parking area which created a U-shaped ramp where the skaters did a variety of tricks. The flexibility of skateboarding was one of the main attractions. Many skaters commented on their attraction to a sport in which there are no rules, referees, set plays, nor coaches. For ex-ample, Paul claimed that to skateboard "[you] don't need uniforms, no coach to tell you what to do and how to do it." Philip added, "I quit foot-ball because I didn't like taking orders." Skaters' general disregard for conforming to an authority carried over into a criticism of those who did. Many of the skaters distinguished themselves by considering them-selves more reflective than their average peers. Philip and Jeff discussed the issue: "We might look at everything twice whereas everybody else will just go 'oh ya.'... We're not saying skating doesn't have any confor-mity, but it's more by your own choice." Jeff:

> It's not conformist conformity...I think skaters are more aware of con-   15
> formity than jocks, I think jocks just seem to deal with it and say "OK,
> well that's just the way it is," but skaters go "geez, why do I have to do
> that, man. I don't want to buy these shoes, I don't want to have to buy
> 100 dollar shoes just to fit in," you know, that kind of thing.

The flexibility within skating was a key component, for example   16
Mark claimed that there are different styles of skating and all of them are accepted, unlike football, in which he felt that a participant would be kicked off the team for having a different style of play. In a separate interview, Jeff stated a similar concern, "Skating is a lot less confined [than organized sport], people are open to new things when you skate." The lack of a formal structure allowed and encouraged the par-ticipants to control their sport; they were the ones to determine what tricks they practiced and for how long, as well as creating their own individualized standards of excellence. This environment often led to the feelings that skateboarding allowed for more freedom of expres-sion than other sports. Doug, a 25-year-old skateboarder and public school teacher, commented:

> A lot of them [skaters] are really involved with artistic endeavors, are   17
> very artistic. You can see the parallel; it's a kind of freedom of expres-
> sion that skating is. How do you express yourself playing football, play-
> ing basketball? When you're skating it's, basically skating reflects your

mood at the time and how you're skating, what you are doing, you know, it's definitely, you know, a way to express yourself.

Many athletes as well as sport sociologists would claim that one   18
can express themselves through organized sport, but the point is that
these skateboarders felt that they had more freedom to be creative in
skateboarding than in traditional organized sport. The lack of a formal
structure controlled by adult males is an essential element in this subculture, which is reflected in the lack of standardized criteria to judge
performance. As Craig commented, "There is no such thing as a perfect
'10' for a trick." What particularly stood out was the skaters' preference
not to be judged by adult authority figures. For example, Grace discussed her anxiety over skateboarding becoming a sport, "For who's to
say what trick is better? I like to do stuff that feels cool, that gives me but-
terflies in my stomach." The use of the skaters' own standards for personal worth was common as Eric's following comment reflects, "Skating
is more challenging than organized sports! You see yourself improve,
you amaze yourself." Alan, a fifth grade student and a skateboarder,
wrote an essay for his school about why he liked to skateboard:

> The reason I love to skate is because it's a challenging sport. It's the way   19
> I express myself. It's something I can do by myself and nobody's there
> to judge me.

This subculture resisted many of the tenets of organized sport   20
and of hegemonic masculinity with particular regard to the deference
to adult male authority in formal structures. Another alternative behavior encouraged in the subculture is the emphasis on participation
and cooperation as opposed to elite competition found in traditional
sport: "You never lose when you skate."

COMPETITION AND PARTICIPATION

The subculture that I investigated represents those who prefer   21
not to compete on an elite level. There are people who skateboard who
are involved in a highly structured and competitive circuit. This
bureaucratized version of skateboarding is coordinated through the
National Skateboard Association. Although skateboarding can be
practiced as a highly competitive sport, the vast majority of skaters I
interviewed described their sport as different from competition. Jeff
stated: "I don't know if I would classify it (skating) as a sport. I suppose I just find sport as competition; unless you are on the pro or amateur circuit you're not really competing against anybody." Pamela, an
18-year-old skater made this comparison:

Soccer is a lot of pressure...you have to be good if not better than every- 22
body else, you have to be otherwise you don't play at all. Skating you can't
do that, you just push yourself harder and harder...swimming is just sort
of there, you get timed, now for me you go against the clock. Now when
you skate you don't go against anything, you just skate. That's what it is.

While discussing the issue of competition with Doug, he sug- 23
gested:

Most skaters don't, you know, I don't hear, I don't hear skaters whining 24
about, you know, other people being better than them or striving to be,
or bumming out about because they're not mastering something,
whereas in other athletics they do...There's a pressure to succeed where
there isn't in skateboarding because there's not huge goals to attain.
How do you measure success in skateboarding if you're not skating in
contests, which most people don't...Skaters, even in contests, it's more
an attitude of having your best run, making all your tricks, as opposed
to beating somebody...it's not "I got to beat this guy, this is the guy I'm
going to beat."

Although there is a status hierarchy within the subculture it is 25
not determined through competition with others. The criteria for status are twofold: One must be highly skilled and creative, and one must
not use that skill to belittle others. Brian, a 13-year-old skater, elaborated on the competitive attitude.

Well, we don't, we're not like competitive, like saying, "I can ollie higher 26
than you so get away from me," and stuff like that, we're like, we just
want to do a few things people are doing, and skaters help out skaters...
and if I were to ask a good skater like some people I can skate with, like
Brad Jones, he's the best skater I know in Welton, if I asked him he
would like give me tips and stuff, you know, on how to do it, and that's
just how we do it, we want to show other people how to skate.

Jeff:

Nobody really seemed to like competitive natures. For instance, me, 27
Philip, and a couple of our friends all found that to be really a turn off. This
guy would pull a really good trick and rub it in their faces. And then
there's Hugh who can do stuff and doesn't go, "oh wow, bet you can't,"
but he's fun to be with... and he encourages you, so that's pretty cool.

From my two years of observing skaters, I found that their empha- 28
sis was placed on cooperation and encouragement as opposed to a cut-
throat form of competition. For example, I had observed skaters I did
not formally know in public spaces, and the following incident characterized the type of interaction I commonly observed: Outside a local

video store was one popular hangout in Welton because there were several parking blocks on which skaters would slide their skateboards. (That skill is termed a "rail slide.") Two teenaged skaters were practicing their rail slides on these parking blocks. Although they were on different blocks, they would check on each other by asking how the other one was doing. The interaction consisted of congratulations for achieving some goal, or encouragement to keep trying if one missed a trick. This is in marked contrast to other observations I made of more mainstream sport. At a public tennis court, I observed two preadolescent boys playing tennis. Their interaction consisted of boasting, and announcing how each was going to "kick" the other one's "ass." When I relayed this scenario to the group of skaters I knew best in Welton, and asked them what they thought, one of the skaters, Doug, commented, "That's because we don't skate against somebody, we skate with them."

CONTRADICTIONS IN THE ALTERNATIVE SUBCULTURE

The subculture of skateboarding is not solely or purely an alter- 29
native form of masculinity. It differs from traditional sport in that it demotes competition and rule-bound behavior while it promotes self-expression. Yet (to my initial surprise), it also serves as an alternative conduit for promoting an ideology of male superiority and of patriarchal relations within the subculture. This contradiction resulted because the subculture of skateboarding provided an informal structure for its participants to create their own rules, yet it simultaneously provided an avenue for the participants to create gender stratification.

As stated previously, organized sport has historically been a 30
realm in which males have bonded and created and reinforced a hegemonic masculinity which has demoted femininity, females, and homosexuals. The subculture of skateboarding I investigated had similar elements. It was male dominated (90% of the participants were male) and promoted a separation and stratification of males and females and of masculinity and femininity.

One of my formal questions addressed female participation. The 31
responses generally reflected the dominant ideology that males and females "naturally" have different social roles, and that sport, and by extension skateboarding, is a male role.

SEX-SEGREGATION

While talking with the skateboarders, I commented on the lack of 32
female participation and asked their opinion about why it occurred. Most males were taken aback and they spent time reflecting on it (as if

they had not given it much thought before), and their explanations ranged from describing "natural" differences to social preferences of males and females. All the females discussed the issue directly and with depth, and it is my interpretation that they thought about this often. For both males and females the sex-segregation of skateboarding was typically justified as a reflection of feminine and masculine behaviors. In their explanations they did not distinguish between sex (as biological behaviors) and gender (as socially expected behaviors). It appeared that the dominant ideology of "natural" differences between male and females was a fundamental assumption of these skaters.

None of the skaters I met would consciously or deliberately exclude women from skating, as reflected by Philip's statement: 33

> Well, the first time you set up boundaries it's like the first nail in the coffin, when you say well no more skating in the street or no more skating for women, that's just saying, well we can't go any further with skating, it stops as far as, you know, "only guys can skate and that's it." I really don't think anybody wants to limit it, especially skaters.   34

Even though these skaters' sexism was not intentional, it is my contention that their assumptions of "natural" differences specifically affected how this predominately male subculture related with females, and therefore, affected female participation. These males did not relate to females as equals; they commonly viewed females as significantly different and especially as an object to view and as a sexual partner. The following categories reflect the varying assumptions of male and female behavior as a means to explain the lack of female participation.   35

FEMALE APPEARANCE

One common explanation for the low number of female participants was that skateboarding does not promote the traditional feminine appearance of the immaculately groomed, petite female. The skaters' assumption is that women want to appear traditionally feminine in all realms of their lives. Part of a feminine appearance is frailness and purity. Most males could not reconcile the physical risk-taking nature of skateboarding with female behavior. For example, Craig stated that skating "is a rough sport where people get scarred, and girls don't want to have scars on their shins, it wouldn't look good." He also added that girls would get tired of wearing tennis shoes all the time. In a separate interview another skater, Stuart, a 21-year-old male stated, "Girls probably don't skate because they don't look good with bruises." Along the same line, Francis commented that in skateboarding one has to get totally hurt before one can learn, and girls don't want to get bruised to   36 learn. This type of response was very common. An 11-year-old male skater asserted, "They [girls] don't want to fall and get their butts dirty." All these comments reflect the assumption that females do not want to do anything that may disrupt appearing traditionally feminine, such as taking physical risks which may lead to bruises or to getting dirty. One female skater, Shelley, made a similar remark, "Girls don't want to do anything harsh or bruise their legs."

The bruising of one's body demonstrates a traditional masculine   37 characteristic of risking bodily injury. Most males flaunted their bruises, and often proudly told stories of past injuries. Overall, the skaters did not associate courageous injury as a feminine (and, therefore, in their assumptions, a female) attribute. It appeared that these males thought that bruises did not look good or "appropriate" on females which reflected their expectations of females as much (if not more) as females' expectations of themselves.

FEMALE NATURAL APTITUDES

A few skaters contended that women do not skate because they   38 do not have the natural abilities. Paul, an 18-year-old skater, strongly believed that "certain groups of people have innate abilities." He defended this position by stating that his dad could get on a skateboard "right now" and ride, whereas his mother could not keep her balance. When skaters made these claims, I challenged them. Paul revised his statement to, "Girls do not seem to try to skate."

Eric also believed that females are not inherently capable of skat-   39 ing as well as males: "It takes too much coordination for a girl, and it's too aggressive." When I commented that girls have traditionally been viewed as excelling in sports that require balance and coordination (e.g., gymnastics, figure skating), he modified his statement in a similar manner to Paul's: that girls do not try.

FEMALE SOCIAL ROLES

Most of the skaters presumed that males and females have differ-   40 ent social roles.

Doug replied to my question of what is a cool skater by stating,   41 "Someone who is not ashamed of it. They don't hide it in the closet around their girlfriends." The statement reflects the assumption of different social realms for males and females; skaters are male (assuming heterosexuality), and females are not typically exposed to skating. I then asked directly about female participation, and Doug responded, "there's not nearly as many, it's too bad." He seemed sincere, so I commented on the idea that it appeared to be an open sport, and he replied: "Ya, but it's also pretty aggressive, kinda, I mean, there's that end of it, it kind of looks aggressive maybe, and women don't get into it." This switch in mid-sentence from a natural difference ("but, it's also pretty aggressive") to a matter of choice ("it kind of looks aggressive, and women don't get into it") was a typical response. I interpreted him as saying: it's not that women can't be aggressive, but it's that they choose not to. Either way, women are relegated to a different social role; they could choose differently but it's not in their "nature" to do so. Males did not expect masculine behavior from women, and therefore did not interact with females in such a way as to encourage it. Tim stated that his sister wants to skate but, "she would rather spend her time doing her hair or talking on the phone." Brian commented on female interests: "No, um, I'm not too sure why girls don't like to skate, maybe because they are so interested in other things like going to the mall and hanging out with friends, their friends don't skate." Jeff, an 18-year-old skater, described the lack of female participation as a social choice of females:

> Not as many women take an interest in it, it's not intended to be a sexist   42
> point of view or anything, but I don't know if women take as much interest in it, maybe it's that, or maybe it's that women prefer to pursue other sports. Maybe it's just a male-dominated sport like football is, I don't know, I don't think it is. I don't see any reason why women shouldn't be able to skate.

Many of the skaters saw no physical or tangible barriers to females' involvement, and therefore assumed that females freely choose   43
not to be involved. Other skaters were aware of social forces that may hinder females from skating, such as lack of other female participants and lack of peer support. Rarely did the male skaters ever consider their behavior as a reason why females did not participate more regularly. Through my interviews, I became aware that males thought of the female skater as an exception. More often, they commented about females as playing a marginalized role in the subculture of skateboarding. "Skate Betties" is the name given to most females associated with skating. Skate Betties are female groupies whose intentions (according to males) are instrumental: to meet cute guys and associate with an alternative crowd. Females are not perceived as expressive or fully engaged in the values of the subculture. Doug, a 25-year-old skater, explained skate Betties in this way:

> They do it because they want to meet cute guys, or their boyfriends do   44
> it. It's the alternative crowd; it's like the girls that are kind of into alter-

native music and that stuff, and kind of skating goes along with it, not as much punk, but not mainstream, and um, they like the clothes; it's a cool look, I think it's a cool look.

Male skaters often labeled females who were attempting to skate   45 as "Betties." James was describing two women he knew that skated: "They were like skating Betties, you know, you always saw them downtown trying to skate around." The last phrase "trying to skate around" is a derogatory statement with the assumption that these females could never fully be skaters. Brian, a 13-year-old, illustrates the marginalization that many females who try to skate face. I had asked him if "girls get into skating." He replied, "Oh, sometimes, there are girls that like skaters, like they hang out, but they don't really, they aren't like, they just try to balance on the board." Female efforts were often belittled. Philip stated, "there were some girls at my school that used to skate but they weren't, I don't know, I guess they just didn't quite have the dedication for it." These comments illustrate the assumption that females are not capable or dedicated enough to be true skaters. Male skaters tend to lump all females into the marginalized role of a "skate Betty": an instrumental role, and a role that looks to the male for identity. A skate Betty's only identity is her association with, not participation in, the subculture. In addition, skate Betties are frequently seen as a reserve stock of girlfriends, similar to the cheerleader role women play in mainstream sport. As Mark stated: "some skaters think women are only there when you get done with skating." It is my contention that males act on the assumptions stated above: that males are potential skaters and females are only affiliated with male skaters. The actions derived from those assumptions affect female participation. Females do not feel as welcomed to the subculture. Some of the following comments from the female skaters illustrate this differential treatment.

DIFFERENTIAL TREATMENT OF FEMALES

Pamela, an 18-year-old skater, described her barriers with male   46 skaters. She felt that she had to be a better skater than males in order to be accepted by them.

47

With my friends they look at me as just one of the guys, that was fine, now when you go skating and meet new people you pretty much have to prove yourself and they say, "Oh, a girl skater, she probably can't do anything," so you, you got to pull off a bunch of tricks and then they say, "Oh, oh, she's pretty cool." That pretty much breaks the ice if you show your skill... If you don't prove yourself you get hassled.

She followed that statement by saying guys don't have to prove 48
themselves like girls do in order to be accepted. Once she proved herself, she did feel accepted. Acceptance based on being "one of the
guys" reinforces that females and femininity are not accepted; it is
only when females prove their masculinity ([being] one of the guys)
that they are accepted within the subculture of skateboarding.

For Shelley, this meant that she actually had to split her personal- 49
ity in two pads: masculine and feminine. When she skates she "stops
thinking like a girl" and then she can do better. While she skates she
wants to be treated like "one of the guys"; she doesn't want to "be
scammed on." Then she stated, after she skates she can get "dressed
up." While she skates she thinks in a masculine manner, and after she
skates she can be feminine. Her statement also implies that part of
being feminine is to be open to being scammed on, to being viewed as
a sexual object—to "dress up."

The perceived masculine role of skateboarding was reflected in the 50
perceived masculinization of females through participation in skating:
females become "one of the guys." Francis, an 18-year-old male skater,
portrayed another facet of this masculinization: "You don't want your
girlfriend to skate, but it's cool for others [females]." He could not explain why he felt this way, but it is my contention that these males could
not conceive of being intimate with someone else they perceived to be
masculine. Part of being treated as one of the guys means that female
masculinity is accepted (as a rare exception to the rule), but this often
meant that males would not consider being physically intimate with a
masculine female. This may partially explain why Shelley divided her
personality into a skater who would not be "scammed on," and someone who could "dress up" after she skates.

Grace, a 21-year-old skater, also stated that her acceptance was 51
based on being masculine because "skating is perceived as unfemi-
nine." Therefore, when she skates she is "one of the guys." She stated
that males "feel threatened by her," and thus treat her differently. For
example, they are more concerned when she falls, and more enthusiastic when she learns tricks which do not warrant the enthusiasm. Her
male friends tend to be overprotective, which annoyed her.

The bonding that does occur in the subculture of skateboarding 52
happens more immediately for males than females. As described
above, males unconsciously create barriers through this assumption.
These assumptions of sex difference created barriers to female participation, which effectively promoted the reification of sex difference
through the maintenance of social boundaries.

Females are accepted once they prove themselves by overcoming 53
these barriers. As noted previously, females enjoy skating for the same
reasons that males do. Yet, two of the females described feelings of iso-

lation. Grace specifically stated that she gets lonely as a female skater. Shelley indirectly addressed this when she said that she got support from males, but she really got psyched when she saw a video with a "girl" skater in it. These feelings of isolation reflect a lack of complete acceptance into the subculture.

SUMMARY AND CONCLUDING REMARKS

Whereas much of the research on masculinity and sport has fo-   54
cused on hegemonic masculinity, there is some research that has investigated alternative masculinities created through sport. With respect to
traditional sport settings, Uchacz (1994) found that male athletes in individual and noncollision sports did not fully support traditional values
of hegemonic masculinity; most notably they challenged sexism and violence. In respect to research done in nontraditional sport activities,
there are two noteworthy studies. Klein's (1993) research on the subculture of bodybuilding in Southern California found that the men exaggerated the characteristics of hegemonic masculinity, which he referred
to as "hypermasculinity" and "comic-book masculinity." Another significant work is Young's (1983) analysis of a rugby subculture. Young
found that the participants challenged some aspects of hegemonic masculinity, such as not emphasizing the outcome of competitions, but reproduced others. In particular, the social activity around rugby was
laden with sexist rituals and songs. These studies exemplify that masculinity (even in traditional settings) is socially constructed as opposed
to a fixed biological entity.

This study of skateboarding is also an example of how masculin-   55
ity is not naturally predetermined or universal, but instead a creation
of the participants which varies according to the social context. The
emphasis on participant control, self-expression, and open participation differs greatly from the hegemonic values of adult authority, conformity, and elite competition.

An interesting contradiction arises within this subculture. Even   56
though the participants' challenged mainstream masculinity, they defined skateboarding as primarily a male activity. This subculture of
skateboarding illustrates some of the incongruities that arise when
people negotiate new social relations. For on one level skateboarding
displayed resistance by redefining masculine behavior, yet on another
level it reproduced patriarchal relations similar to Young's findings
within the rugby subculture. What is essential for the maintenance of
patriarchy is creating different social roles for males and females, and
marginalizing the female role. Skaters did this by redefining masculinity, which preserved skateboarding as a male realm.

57

Because many of these male skateboarders did not participate in mainstream athletics (either by choice or size/ability), it is my contention that they created an alternative sport which met some of their specific needs, such as participant control and a deemphasis on elite competition. And skateboarding also served to meet social needs that traditional athletics have met for other males—a place where boys create friendships and differentiate themselves from girls and that which is labeled feminine.

Although the weight of this paper is on the males' attitudes and behaviors, it is evident that both the males and the females have internalized the dominant ideology of sport as a male social role. This affects how females negotiate their position within the subculture. Some of the responses are typical of females in male-dominated settings, such as feeling a need to constantly demonstrate one's ability as well as fitting into the dominant culture by being "one of the boys" (Theberge, 1993). And as Theberge (1993) noted, as long as females are judged by a standard of masculinity in a patriarchal society, they will always be marginalized.

58

REFERENCES

Bradley, H. (1989). *Men's work, women's work: A sociological history of the sexual division of labour in employment.* Minneapolis: University of Minnesota.

Carrigan, T., Connell, B., & Lee, J. (1987). "Hard and heavy: Toward a new theory of masculinity." In M. Kaufman (Ed.), *Beyond Patriarchy: Essays by men on pleasure, power, and change.* New York: Oxford University.

Clatterbaugh, K. (1990). *Contemporary perspectives on masculinity: Men, women, and politics in modern society.* Boulder, CO: Westview

Connell, R. (1990). "An iron man: The body and some contradictions of hegemonic masculinity." In M. Messner & D. Sabo (Eds.), *Sport, men, and the gender order: Critical feminist perspectives.* Champaign, IL: Human Kinetic Books.

Curry, T. J. (1991). "Fraternal bonding in the locker room: A profemininst analysis of talk about competition and women." *Sociology of Sport Journal,* 8, 119–135.

Hantover, J. (1989). "The boy scouts and the validation of masculinity." In Kimmel & Messner (Eds.), *Men's lives.* New York: Macmillan.

Kidd, B. (1987). "Sports and masculinity." In M. Kaufman (Ed.), *Beyond Patriarchy: Essays by men on pleasure, power, and change.* New York: Oxford University.

Kimmel, M. (1990). "Baseball and the reconstitution of American masculinity, 1880–1920." In M. Messner & D. Sabo (Eds.) *Sport, men, and the gender order: Critical feminist perspectives.* Champaign, IL: Human Kinetic Books.

Kimmel, M., & Messner, M. (Eds.) (1989). *Men's lives.* New York: Macmillan.

Klein, A. (1993). *Little big men and bodybuilding subculture and gender construction.* Albany: State University of New York.

Lucas, J., & Smith, R. (1978). *Saga of American sport.* Philadelphia: Lea and Febiger.

Messner, M. (1988). "Sports and male domination: The female athlete as contested ideological terrain." *Sociology of Sport Journal, 2,* 197–211.

Messner, M. (1992a). *Power at play: Sports and the problem of masculinity.* Boston: Beacon.

Messner, M. (1992b). "Like family: Power, intimacy, and sexuality in male athletes' friendships." In P. Nardi (Ed.), *Men's Friendships.* Newbury Park: Sage.

Miedzian, M. (1991). *Boys will be boys. Breaking the link between masculinity and violence.* New York: Doubleday.

Nelson, M. B. (1994). *The stronger women get, the more men love football: Sexism and the American culture of sports.* New York: Harcourt Brace & Company.

Sabo, D. (1989). "Pigskin, patriarchy, and pain." In Kimmel & Messner (Eds.), *Men's lives.* New York: Macmillan.

Sabo, D., & Panepinto, J. (1990). "Football ritual and the social reproduction of masculinity." In M. Messner & D. Sabo (Eds.), *Sport, men and the gender order: Critical feminist perspectives.* Champaign, IL: Human Kinetic Books.

Theberge, N. (1993). "The construction of gender in sport: Women coaching, and the naturalization of difference." *Social Problems, 40,* 301–313.

Uchacz, C. (1994). "Masculinities: Variations of the Hegemonic Masculine Identity by university athletes." Paper presented at the North American Society for the Sociology of Sport annual meeting, Savannah, GA, Nov. 9–12.

Whitson, D. (1990). "Sport in the social construction of masculinity." In M. Messner & D. Sabo (Eds.), *Sport, men and the gender order: Critical feminist perspectives.* Champaign, IL: Human Kinetic Books.

Young, R. (1983). "The subculture of Rugby players: A form of resistance and incorporation." Unpublished master's thesis, McMaster University.

Examining the Text

1. The term "hegemony" means predominant influence, especially when it involves coercion, as in colonialism: one country invades, takes over, and imposes its values and rules on another culture. How does this article use the concept of hegemony in relation to masculine roles? Explain the concept of "hegemonic masculinity," as presented by Beal.

2. How does the skateboarding group investigated by Beal create an "alternative masculinity, one which explicitly critiqued the more traditional form" of hegemonic masculinity, according to the author?

3. Explain the way(s) in which certain sports serve as a "male initiation ritual" for boys in our contemporary culture, according to Beal's researched sources.

4. Beal states, "For profeminists an alternative masculinity gives hope that alternative values can be promoted which will decrease violence, sexism, and homophobia." In what ways might "alternative values" improve the quality of life for a variety of men as well as women, in this author's opinion?

5. What are the specific activities and "rules" involved in skating, according to Beal? How do these activities differ from other, more traditional "masculine" sports?

For Group Discussion

1. In a full-class discussion, examine Beal's assertion that "Today, sport is still a significant means of ideologically promoting hegemonic masculinity." After summarizing her position (and perhaps explaining in some detail—and with concrete examples—what she means by hegemonic masculinity), go on to explore evidence that supports or disproves this basic thesis. What examples can you cite to support the belief that sports exist in part to ensure that boys become "properly masculine"? What examples can you cite to contradict this notion? (Hint: You might start this section of the essay by examining the recent and unprecedented popularity of the United States women's soccer team.)

2. What reasons do the skaters in Beal's article give to account for the relatively small number of women participating in the "sport"? Do you agree or disagree with these reasons? What additional reasons might account for the lack of female skaters? In your opinion, is this gender inequality changing; have you observed the number of female skaters increasing? If so, what would account for this increase, in your opinion?

Writing Suggestion

In preparing to write this article, Beal used "qualitative methods of observation, participant-observation, and semistructured in-depth interviews to investigate the subculture of skateboarding in northeastern Colorado." Following this author's model, conduct your own research on a group of sports enthusiasts, in order to discover or prove a specific hypothesis. You might, for example, decide to research Frisbee players, with the intention of proving that these individuals are attempting to create a sport that is free of competion—one hallmark of traditional hegemonic masculinity, as Beal might suggest. Whatever sport you choose—golf, soccer, water polo, rugby, surfing, or even skateboading—combine observation, perhaps some actual participation, and a number of interviews in order to support your contentions with actual evidence, as Beal does in her skateboarding article.

ADDITIONAL SUGGESTIONS
FOR WRITING ABOUT SPORTS

1. Using Maya Angelou's "Champion of the World" as a model, write a narrative in which you tell of a past experience with sports, either as a spectator or as a participant, that had a significant effect on your life. Perhaps this experience revealed something about yourself that you didn't realize, helped you to better understand someone else, taught you an important lesson, or corrected a misconception that you had. Or perhaps you're not certain what effect the experience had, and can use this assignment to speculate on its significance.

2. Attend a local sporting event, and bring a notebook and, if possible, a tape recorder or video camera. Observe and take notes about how the people around you behave, what they do and say, what they wear, how they relate to one another, what interests or bores them, when they seem satisfied or disappointed. Note also how their behavior is different from what it would likely be in other contexts. Try to be an impartial observer, simply recording what you see in as much detail as possible.

From your notes, write an extended description of one or several typical spectators, and then draw some conclusions about why people enjoy watching sports. You may also want to discuss the psychological benefits and/or harm that being a spectator might cause.

3. Choose a sport with which you're very familiar, either because you play it or watch it regularly. Reflect on your experience playing or watching this sport, and write down some of your recollections. Think about what you've learned from this sport, and how it has affected other areas of your life.

Then write an essay in which you show how this particular sport has influenced your beliefs, attitudes and values. Be as specific as possible and try to show precisely how and why the sport has influenced you.

4. Many of the writers in this chapter discuss the impact of professional sports on individuals and on society as a whole. Referring to essays in this chapter, construct your own argument about the influence of professional sports. As a prewriting exercise, make lists of the beneficial and the detrimental influences of professional sports on our society. Try to come up with specific examples to illustrate each of the items on your lists. Then working from those lists, develop a persuasive argument about the influence of sports on our society.

Internet Activities

1. Professional athletes are often role models in our society. As a prewriting exercise for this assignment, list some of the reasons why this is so, especially for young people. Also list the ways in which athletes might be good role models, as well as some of the reasons other professionals (for example, teachers or government leaders) might actually be better role models.

Then visit the links to information about professional athletes, provided at the *Common Culture* Web site, to official and unofficial homepages of individual athletes. After browsing through these links, choose an athlete who you think is either a good or a bad role model. Do further research on this athlete, looking up interviews and articles about him or her in the library. From this information, write a brief biography of the athlete, focusing on the kind of role model he or she is.

2. Professional sports teams are, as Dick Schapp points out, in the business of making money, and the World Wide Web is increasingly becoming a venue for advertising and marketing. It's no surprise then, that all of the major professional sports teams now have their own Web sites. Go to the *Common Culture* Web site for links that you can follow to visit the homepages of professional teams in baseball, football, men's basketball, women's basketball, and hockey. Choose a Web site for one team and read the site carefully and completely. Make a list of the information that the site offers, including statistics, pictures, news and "inside information," schedules, and so on. Then analyze the ways in which the information offered at the site is intended to promote or "sell" the team. Is the site addressed to current fans of the team, or is it intended to cultivate new fans? How effectively do you believe the Web site is in advertising and marketing the team it represents?

7

Movies

It's Friday night. You park in an exhaust-filled subterranean garage or a vast asphalt lot surrounding a mall. You make your way into the neon-lit mega-eight-plex, where you and a companion or two pay half a day's salary for tickets, a tub of artery-clogging popcorn, and a couple of ten-gallon sodas. You wind your way through a maze of corridors to the theater of your choice, where a psychedelic montage filling the screen is soon replaced by the first of an interminable series of quick-cutting, MTV-style previews, as you bathe in rolling quadraphonic surround-sound. You sink into your space-age plastic seat and kick back, surrendering to the waves of sound and images....

Such is moviegoing of the new millennium. Gone are the nickel matinee and the discount double-feature, newsreels, cartoons, and comic short subjects, and the drive-in, where many a pair of teenagers learned human anatomy in the back seat of a Chevy.

The external trappings of the moviegoing experience may have changed, but the reasons people go are still pretty much the same: to get out of the house and escape the routine of their daily lives; to be part of a communal group sharing an experience; to find a romantic setting where conversation is at a minimum; to indulge, for one night, in an orgy of junk food; and, above all, to be entertained and, perhaps, touched emotionally. So strong is the draw of motion pictures that Americans fork over billions of dollars a year on domestic movies alone.

As there are many reasons for going to the movies, so there are many ways of explaining their popularity and studying their influence within the fabric of contemporary culture. From a sociological perspective, movies can reflect, define, or even redefine social norms, and—in the work of politically focused filmmakers like Spike Lee— depict urgent social problems within the relative safety of the big screen. From a psychological perspective, viewers identify with the character and project their own feelings into the action, giving them a deep emotional connection to a protagonist along with feelings of tension and, ultimately release. From a literary perspective, movies can be interpreted in terms of genres—horror movies, or crime dramas or menaced-female stories—or in terms of plot, characterization, imagery, and so forth. From an economic perspective, movies may be seen primarily as a consumable product, defined solely by the marketplace. To the cultural critic, this economic influence might seem to be negative, reducing a potentially powerful artistic form to the lowest common denominator. The capitalist observer might see such forces as positive, however, because they encourage the worldwide spread of American cultural values. Finally, from a semiological perspective, movies are ripe with symbolic imagery, from the multiple associations possible in a character's name to the way images are juxtaposed in the editing.

This chapter introduces film criticism arising from several of these views. The first readings focus on the art and business of moviemaking and criticism, ending with an overview of the major critical schools. The second part looks specifically at the genre of the horror movie, interpreting horror heroes such as Frankenstein, Freddy Kreuger, and Dracula from a variety of critical perspectives. As you think and write about film and the film industry, you may find that you want to pick and choose among these various approaches, incorporating parts of any number of them into your own theoretical analyses.

Moviemaking and Criticism

The Way We Are

Sydney Pollack

If anyone knows American moviemaking, it's Sidney Pollack. A director of more than sixteen films—including The Way We Were, Tootsie, Out of Africa, *and* The Firm—*and an occasional actor (Dustin Hoffman's agent in* Tootsie*), Pollack has had an unparalleled opportunity to observe the changing tastes of the American viewing public and the movie industry's response to those changes. In the following article, a transcript of an address Pollack delivered at a conference about the influence of the popular media on American values, Pollack suggests that changes in the moral fabric of our society are responsible for the kinds of movies we see today, not vice versa.*

When he looks at contemporary America, Pollack finds a conspicuous lack of the "kind of scrupulous ethical concern for the sanctity of life" that prevailed in past decades and was reflected in motion pictures of the time, when there were less frequent and less graphic scenes of violence, when characters were esteemed for their humility and personal integrity, and when explicit sexuality was found only in "stag" films, not in mainstream theaters. Many people today, Pollack notes, are nostalgic for the "old values" and believe that movies should encourage the return of these values rather than reflecting current values. Pollack disagrees, however, pointing out that, although screenwriters and directors may want their movies to reflect some moral content, the economics of the industry require first and foremost that movies be entertaining, and therefore, they must appeal to a buying audience whose values may be very different from those of the reformers.

As you read, *consider whether you agree with Pollack's notions of artistic integrity, especially his assertions that a filmmaker's prime goal should be to entertain an audience and that movies simply reflect the surrounding society. Is it possible that, in responding to their audience's changing tastes, filmmakers also "construct" public attitudes towards violence, sexuality, and so forth by pushing their explicitness further and further?*

Six weeks ago, I thought I was going to be happy to be a part of   1
this conference, which shows you how naive I am. The agenda—for
me at least—is a mine field. Normally, I spend my time worrying
about specific problems and not reflecting, as many of you on these
panels do. So I've really thought about this, and I've talked to anyone

who would listen. My colleagues are sick and tired of it, my wife has left for the country and even my agents—and these are people I pay—don't return my phone calls. By turns, I have felt myself stupid, unethical, a philistine, unpatriotic, a panderer, a cultural polluter, and stupid. And I've completely failed to solve your problems, except in one small way. You have delayed by at least six weeks the possibility of my contributing further to the problems you see.

I know your concerns have to do with American values and 2 whether those values are being upheld or assaulted by American entertainment—by what I and others like me do. But which values exactly?

In the thirties, forties, and fifties, six men in the Valley, immi- 3 grants really, ran the movie industry. Our society was vastly different. The language of the movies was a language of shared values. If you put forward a virtuousness on the part of your hero, everybody responded to it.

When Sergeant York, played by Gary Cooper, refused to endorse 4 a breakfast cereal, knowing he'd been asked because he'd won the Medal of Honor, he said: "I ain't proud of what I've done. You don't make money off of killing people. That there is wrong." We expected him to behave that way.

But society's values have changed. That kind of scrupulous, ethical 5 concern for the sanctity of human life doesn't exist in the same way, and that fact is reflected in the movies. There's a nostalgia now for some of the old values, but so many people embrace other expressions of values that it's hard to say these other expressions aren't reality.

Their idea of love, for example, is a different idea of love. It's a 6 much less chaste, much less idealized love than was depicted in the earlier films. We are seeing some sort of return to the ideal of marriage. There was a decade or two when marriage really lost its popularity, and while young people are swinging toward it again, I don't believe one could say that values have not changed significantly since the thirties, forties, and fifties.

Morality, the definitions of virtue, justice, and injustice, the sanc- 7 tity of the individual, have been fairly fluid for American audiences in terms of what they choose to embrace or not embrace.

Take a picture like *Dances With Wolves*. You could not have made 8 it in the thirties or forties. It calls into question every value that existed in traditional Westerns. It may not reflect what everybody thinks now, but it expresses a lot of guilty re-evaluation of what happened in the West, the very things shown in the old Westerns that celebrated the frontier.

If we got the movies to assert or talk about better values, would 9 that fix our society? Well, let me quote Sam Goldwyn. When he was told by his staff how poorly his studio's new—and very expensive—

film was doing, Sam thought a minute, shrugged, and said, "Listen, if
they don't want to come, you can't stop them."

Now that's as close to a first principle of Hollywood as I can   10
come. It informs everything that we're here to discuss and it controls
every solution that we may propose.

OUT OF HOLLYWOOD

Before they can be anything else, American movies are a product.   11
This is not good or bad, this is what we've got. A very few may become art, but all of them, whatever their ambitions, are first financed
as commodities. They're the work of craftsmen and artists, but they're
soon offered for sale.

Whether we say that we're "creating a film" or merely "making a   12
movie," the enterprise itself is sufficiently expensive and risky that it
cannot be, and it will not be, undertaken without the hope of reward.
We have no Medicis here. It takes two distinct entities, the financiers
and the makers, to produce movies, and there is a tension between
them. Their goals are sometimes similar, but they do different things.
Financiers are not in the business of philanthropy. They've got to answer to stockholders.

Of course, the controlling influence in filmmaking hasn't   13
changed in 50 years: it still belongs to the consumer. That's the
dilemma and, in my view, what we're finally talking about. What do
you do about culture in a society that celebrates the common man but
doesn't always like his taste?

If you operate in a democracy and you're market-supported and   14
-driven, the spectrum of what you will get is going to be very wide indeed. It will range from trash to gems. There are 53,000 books published in this country every year. How many of them are really good?
Tired as I may be of fast-food-recipe, conscienceless, simple-minded
books, films, TV, and music, the question remains, Who is to be society's moral policeman?

Over the course of their first 30 or 40 years, the movies were a   15
cottage industry, and the morality that was reflected in them was the
morality of the early film pioneers. Now, film studios are tiny divisions of multinational corporations, and they feel the pressure for
profits that happens in any other repeatable-product business. They
look for a formula. Say you get the recipe for a soft drink and perfect
it; once customers like it, you just repeat it and it will sell. More fortunes have been lost than made in the movie business pursuing such a
formula, but unfortunately today, more junk than anything else is
being made pursuing it. And film companies are folding like crazy.

Since we are in the democracy business, we can't tell people   16
what they should or shouldn't hear, or support, or see, so they make
their choices. The market tries to cater to those choices, and we have
what we have.

MAKING FILMS

Are American films bad? A lot of them surely are, and so are a   17
lot of everybody else's, the way a lot of anything produced is bad—
breakfast cereals, music, most chairs, architecture, mail-order shirts.
There probably hasn't been a really beautiful rake since the Shakers
stopped making farm implements. But that is no excuse.

I realize that I am a prime suspect here, but I'm not sure that you   18
really understand how odd and unpredictable a business the making
of films actually is. It just doesn't conform to the logic or rules of any
other business. It's always been an uneasy merger of two antithetical
things: some form of art and sheer commerce.

If the people who make films get the money that is invested in   19
them back to the people who finance them, then they'll get to make
more. We know that the business of films is to reach as many people
as possible. That works two ways; it's not just a market discipline. You
have to remember that most of us who are doing this got into it for the
romance, the glory, the applause, the chance to tell stories, even to
learn, but rarely for the money. The more people you reach, the
greater your sense of success. Given the choice, I'd rather make the
whole world cry than 17 intellectuals in a classroom.

But, paradoxically, if you are the actual maker of the film—not the   20
financier—you can't make films and worry about whether they'll reach
a large audience or make money, first, because nobody really knows a
formula for what will make money. If they did, I promise you we would
have heard about it, and studios would not be going broke. Second, and
much more practically, if you spent your time while you were making
the film consciously thinking about what was commercial, then the real
mechanism of choice—the mechanism that is your own unconscious,
your own taste and imagination, your fantasy—would be replaced by
constant reference to this formula that we know doesn't work.

So the only practical approach a filmmaker can take is to make a   21
film that he or she would want to see. This sounds arrogant, but you
try to make a movie for yourself, and you hope that as many people as
possible will like it too. If that happens, it's because you've done something in the telling of the story that makes people care. One of the
things that makes a film distinct from other American business products is this emotional involvement of the maker. A producer of auto

parts can become pretty emotional about a sales slump, but it isn't the same thing. His product hasn't come from his history; it isn't somehow in the image of his life; and it lacks mystery. It is entirely measurable and concrete, which is certainly appropriate in the manufacture of auto parts. I wouldn't want to buy a carburetor from a neurotic, mixed-up auto manufacturer.

Fortunately for those of us in film, no such standards apply. 22 Quite the contrary, in fact. No matter what his conscious intentions are, the best part of what the filmmaker does—the part, when it works, that makes you want to see the film—doesn't come from a rational, consciously controllable process. It comes from somewhere inside the filmmaker's unconscious. It comes from making unlikely connections seem inevitable, from a kind of free association that jumps to odd or surprising places, conclusions that cause delights, something that creates goose pimples or awe.

This conference has suggested a question: While you're actually 23 making the movie, do you think about whether or not it will be doing the world any good? I can't answer it for filmmakers in general. For myself, candidly, no, I don't.

I try to discover and tell the truth and not be dull about it. In that 24 sense, the question has no significance for me. I assume that trying to discover the truth is in itself a good and virtuous aim. By truth I don't mean some grand, pretentious axiom to live by; I just mean the truth of a character from moment to moment. I try to discover and describe things like the motives that are hidden in day-to-day life. And the truth is rarely dull. If I can find it, I will have fulfilled my primary obligation as a filmmaker, which is not to bore the pants off you.

Most of us in this business have enormous sympathy for 25 Scheherazade—we're terrified we're going to be murdered if we're boring. So our first obligation is to not bore people; it isn't to teach.

Most of the time, high-mindedness just leads to pretentious or 26 well-meaning, often very bad, films. Most of the Russian films made under communism were of high quality in terms of craft, but they were soporific because their intent to do good as it was perceived by the state or an all-knowing party committee was too transparent.

I'm sure that you think the person in whose hands the process ac- 27 tually rests, the filmmaker, could exert an enormous amount of control over the film's final worthiness. The question usually goes like this: Should filmmakers pander to the public, or should they try to elevate public taste to something that many at this conference would find more acceptable? Is the job of an American filmmaker to give the public what it wants or what the filmmaker thinks the public should have? This doesn't leave much doubt as to what you think is the right answer.

But framing your question this way not only betrays a misunder- 28 standing of how the filmmaking process works but also is just plain wishful thinking about how to improve society. I share your nostalgia for some of those lost traditional values, but attempting to reinstall them by arbitrarily putting them into movies when they don't exist in everyday life will not get people to go to the movies or put those values back into life. I wish it were that simple.

ENGAGING AN AUDIENCE

This conference is concerned with something called popular cul-   29
ture and its effect on society, but I am concerned with one film at a time and its effect. You are debating whether movies corrupt our souls or elevate them, and I'm debating whether a film will touch a soul. As a filmmaker, I never set out to create popular culture, and I don't know a single other filmmaker who does.

Maybe it's tempting to think of Hollywood as some collective be-   30
hemoth grinding out the same stories and pushing the same values, but it's not that simple. Hollywood, whatever that means, is Oliver Stone castigating war in *Born on the Fourth of July* and John Milius celebrating it in *The Wind and the Lion*. It's Walt Disney and Martin Scorcese. It's Steven Spielberg and Milos Foreman. It's *Amadeus* and *Terminator* and hundreds of choices in between.

I don't want to defend Hollywood, because I don't represent   31
Hollywood—I can't, any more than one particular writer can represent literature or one painter art. For the most part, the impulse toward all art, entertainment, culture, pop culture, comes from the same place within the makers of it. The level of talent and the soul, if you'll forgive the word again, is what finally limits it.

At the risk of telling you more than you need to know about my   32
own work, I make the movies I make because there is in each film some argument that fascinates me, an issue I want to work through. I call this a spine or an armature because it functions for me like an armature in sculpture—something I can cover up and it will support the whole structure. I can test the scenes against it. For me, the film, when properly dramatized, adds up to this idea, this argument.

But there are lots of other ways to go about making a film, and   33
lots of other filmmakers who do it differently. Some filmmakers begin knowing exactly what they want to say and then craft a vehicle that contains that statement. Some are interested in pure escape. Here's the catch. The effectiveness and the success of all our films is determined by exactly the same standards—unfortunately, not by the particular validity of their message but by their ability to engage the concentration and emotions of the audience.

Citizen Kane is an attack on acquisition, but that's not why people   34
go to see it. I don't have any idea if the audience that saw *Tootsie* thought

at any conscious level that it could be about a guy who became a better man for having been a woman; or that *The Way We Were,* a film I made 20 years ago, may have been about the tension between passion, often of the moment, and wisdom, often part of a longer view; or that *Out Of Africa* might be about the inability to possess another individual and even the inability of one country to possess another. That's intellectual and stuffy. I just hope the audiences were entertained.

I may choose the movies I make because there's an issue I want to   35
explore, but the how—the framing of that issue, the process of finding the best way to explore it—is a much more mysterious, elusive, and messy process. I can't tell you that I understand it; if I did, I would have a pep talk with myself and go out and make a terrific movie every time.

I would not make a film that ethically, or morally, or politically   36
trashed what I believe is fair. But by the same token, I feel an obliga-
tion—and this is more complicated and personal—to do films about arguments. I try hard to give each side a strong argument—not because I'm a fair guy but because I believe it's more interesting. Both things are going on.

I do the same thing on every movie I make. I find an argument, a   37
couple of characters I would like to have dinner with, and try to find the most fascinating way to explore it. I work as hard as I can to tell the story in the way I'd like to have it told to me.

What is really good is also entertaining and interesting because it's   38
closer to a newer way to look at the truth. You can't do that consciously. You can't start out by saying, "I am now going to make a great film."

The virtue in making a film, if there is any, is in making it well. If   39
there's any morality that's going to come out, it will develop as you begin to construct, at every moment you have a choice to make. You can do it the honest way or you can bend it, and the collection of those moments of choice is what makes the work good or not good and is what reveals morality or the lack of it.

I've made 16 films. I've had some enormous successes and I've   40
had some colossal failures, but I can't tell you what the difference is in terms of what I did.

AN AMERICAN AESTHETIC?

In some circles, American films suffer by comparison with Euro-   41
pean films precisely because a lot of our movies seem to be the prod-
uct of little deliberation and much instinct. It's been said of European movies that essence precedes existence, which is just a fancy way of saying that European movies exist in order to say something. Cer-

tainly one never doubts with a European film that it's saying something, and often it just comes right out and says it.

American films work by indirection; they work by action and 42
movement, either internal or external, but almost always movement.
Our films are more narratively driven than others, which has a lot to
do with the American character and the way we look at our lives. We
see ourselves and our lives as being part of a story.

Most of our movies have been pro the underdog, concerned with 43
injustice, relatively anti-authority. There's usually a system—or a bu-
reaucracy—to triumph over.

More often than not, American movies have been affirmative 44
and hopeful about destiny. They're usually about individuals who
control their own lives and their fate. In Europe, the system was so
class-bound and steeped in tradition that there was no democratization of that process.

There's no prior education required to assimilate American 45
movies or American culture. American culture is general, as opposed
to the specificity of Japanese or Indian culture. America has the most
easily digestible culture.

Our movies seem artless. The best of them keep us interested 46
without seeming to engage our minds. The very thing that makes
movies so popular here and abroad is one of the primary things that
drives their critics to apoplexy, but seeming artlessness isn't necessarily mindlessness. There's a deliberate kind of artlessness in American
movies that has come from a discipline or aesthetic long ago imposed
by the marketplace. Our movies began as immigrants' dreams that
would appeal to the dreams of other immigrants, and this aesthetic
has led American films to transcend languages and cultures and communicate to every country in the world.

THE FILMMAKER'S RESPONSIBILITY

It has been suggested to some extent in this conference that I 47
ought to study my own and American filmmakers' responsibilities to
the public and to the world. I realize I have responsibilities as a filmmaker, but I don't believe that they are as a moralist, a preacher, or a
purveyor of values. I know it's tempting to use filmmaking as such,
but utility is a poor standard to use in art. It's a standard that has been
and is still used by every totalitarian state in the world.

My responsibility is to try to make good films, but "good" is a 48
subjective word. To me at any rate, "good" doesn't necessarily mean
"good for us" in the narrow sense that they must elevate our spirits

and send us out of the theater singing, or even that they must promote only those values that some think are worth promoting.

Good movies challenge us, they provoke us, they make us angry   49
sometimes. They present points of view we don't agree with. They force us to clarify our positions in opposition to them, and they do this best when they provide us with an experience and not a polemic.

Somebody gave the okay to pay for *One Flew Over the Cuckoo's*   50
Nest, Driving Miss Daisy, Stand By Me, Moonstruck, Terms of Endearment, and *Amadeus,* and despite conventional wisdom that said those films could not be successful, those decisions paid off handsomely because there are no rules. Studio executives and other financiers do exceed themselves. They take chances. They have to, and we have to hope that they'll do it more often.

What we see in movie theaters today is not a simple reflection of   51
today's economics or politics in this country but is a sense of the people who make the movies, and they vary as individuals vary. So what we really want is for this very privileged process to be in the best hands possible, but I know of no force that can regulate this except the moral climate and appetites of our society.

What we're exporting now is largely a youth culture. It's full of   52
adolescent values; it's full of adolescent rage, love, rebelliousness, and a desire to shock. If you're unhappy with their taste—and this is a free market—then an appetite has to be created for something better. How do we do that? Well, we're back to square one: the supplier or the consumer, the chicken or the egg? Let's not even ask the question; the answer is both.

Of course filmmakers ought to be encouraged toward excellence,   53
and audiences ought to be encouraged to demand it. How? That's for thinkers and social scientists to figure out. I have no idea. But if I had to play this scene out as an imaginary dialogue, I might say that you must educate the consumer first, and the best places to start are at school and at home. And then you would say that that is my job, that popular entertainment must participate in this education. And I would say, ideally, perhaps, but I do not think that will happen within a system that operates so fundamentally from an economic point of view. On an individual basis, yes, one filmmaker at a time; as an industry, no. An appetite or market will have to exist first.

That's not as bad as it sounds, because in the best of all possible   54
worlds, we do try to satisfy both needs: entertain people and be reasonably intelligent about it. It can be done, and it is done more often than you might think. It's just very difficult.

It's like the two Oxford dons who were sitting at the Boarshead.   55
They were playwrights, grousing because neither one of them could get produced, neither one could get performed. One turned to the

other and said, "Oh, the hell with it. Let's just do what Shakespeare did—give them entertainment."

Examining the Text

1. What is Pollack's point in paragraph 8? How does *Dances With Wolves* "call into question every value that existed in traditional Westerns," and how does it reflect a change in society's values? Is *Dances With Wolves* a good example of the kind of movie that critics would say contributes to the decline in American values? Why do you think Pollack mentions it so early in his speech?

2. Pollack says there "probably hasn't been a really beautiful rake since the Shakers stopped making farm implements" (paragraph 17). What does his point say in terms of questioning whether American films are "bad"? Do you find his analogy persuasive?

3. When Pollack asserts that he'd "rather make the whole world cry than 17 intellectuals in a classroom" (19), what is he implying about his—and other filmmakers'—motivations? Do you think most creative people feel this way?

4. Pollack describes his interest in making "films about arguments" and giving "each side a strong argument" (36). What does he mean? Do you think movies that balance two sides of an "argument" are "more interesting" than those with clear-cut "good guys" and "bad guys"?

For Group Discussion

Pollack himself does not make the kinds of graphically violent movies that critics claim have a negative influence on American society. Nonetheless, he argues that "scrupulous, ethical concern for the sanctity of human life doesn't exist in the same way [it did in the past], and that fact is reflected in the movies." As a group, list examples from current events and recent films that demonstrate this lack of concern for human life. As a class, consider whether, based on these examples, you agree with Pollack that movies only reflect the values of society and do not contribute to their creation.

Writing Suggestion

Rent and watch one or more of Pollack's films (titles other than those mentioned in the head note include *They Shoot Horses, Don't They?*, *Three Days of the Condor*, and *The Electric Horseman*). In an essay analyze Pollack's work as a reflection of contemporary American life. What themes or messages do you discover beyond his aim to tell a good story? Does he succeed in his stated goal of presenting an "argument"?

Do The Right Thing
Production Notes

Spike Lee

Spike Lee—film writer, director, producer, and actor—believes he has a social responsibility beyond merely making films that entertain audiences. His movies, such as Do The Right Thing *and* X, *a biographical treatment of black leader Malcolm X, frequently embody Lee's strong convictions about race relations in America—and, more specifically, about the problems facing black people in this country. Lee's commitment to social responsibility does not end with the content of his films, however; it also extends to their actual production. In the following production notes made during the filming of* Do The Right Thing, *Lee offers some unique behind-the-scenes perspectives on movie-making and illuminates some difficult issues facing minority and female film professionals.*

If you haven't already seen Do The Right Thing, *you might want to rent it. The movie is a vivid and highly controversial comedy-drama that takes place during the course of one steamy summer day in a Brooklyn ghetto. Lee himself plays Mookie, one of the neighborhood residents, and Danny Aiello and John Turturro play the Italian American owner of Sal's Pizzeria and his racist son. The movie explores the sometimes uneasy relationship between a white business owner and his customers in a black neighborhood, culminating in a riot during which the pizzeria is torched and the neighborhood left in shambles.*

As you read this piece, consider your own ideas about minority representation in the filmmaking industry, both as actors and as production personnel. Do you agree with the methods Lee used to achieve a more equitable racial balance in making Do The Right Thing? *Do you think such efforts are important?*

Do The Right Thing was my first union film. To keep our costs 1
down, Universal suggested that we shoot the film with a nonunion crew someplace outside of New York, like Philadelphia or Baltimore. I'm sorry, Philly and Baltimore are great cities, but they just aren't Brooklyn. This film had to be shot in Brooklyn, if it was to be done at all. However, there was no way we could shoot a $6.5 million film in New York City without giving the film unions a piece of the action.

On every film, I try to use as many Black people behind the cam- 2
era as possible. A major concern I had about shooting with an all-union crew was whether this would prevent me from hiring as many

Blacks as I wanted. There are few minorities in the film unions, and, historically, film unions have done little to encourage Blacks and women to join their ranks.

Originally we planned to sign a contract with the International Alliance of Theatrical State Employees (IATSE, or IA) because they have more Black members. They proved to be too expensive, so we entered into negotiations with the National Association of Broadcast Employees and Technicians (NABET). The negotiations with NABET lasted a month, but we were able to win some important concessions.

One concession was that NABET allowed us to hire a number of Blacks to work on the film who were not members of the union, including Larry Cherry, our hairstylist, my brother David Lee, the still photographer, and Darnell Martin, the second assistant cameraperson. (At the time, there were no Blacks in these union categories.) In addition, we were able to hire some nonunion people as trainees in the grip and electric departments. NABET agreed to consider granting union membership to these people if their work on the film proved satisfactory. Eventually they were admitted to the union.

We cut a similar deal with the Teamsters union, which is responsible for all the vehicles driven on a union shoot. The Teamsters have the right to determine how many drivers are assigned to a union production. At $1,500 to $2,000 per week per driver, this can eat a hole in your budget. The Teamsters allowed us to hire a small number of union drivers and use nonunion production assistants to supplement this group. Out of the five union drivers they assigned to the production, two were Black.

I wanted to film *Do The Right Thing* entirely on one block. Our location scout combed the streets of Brooklyn for two weeks and came back with a book of photos. One Saturday, Wynn Thomas, the production designer, and I visited all the locations suggested by our scout. It turned out the block that we chose was the first one he had looked at—Stuyvesant Street between Lexington and Quincy Avenues, in the heart of the Bedford-Stuyvesant section of Brooklyn.

The block had everything that we needed: brownstones which weren't too upscale or too dilapidated. And, most importantly, it had two empty lots that faced each other, where we could build sets for the Korean market and Sal's Famous Pizzeria. Once we decided on the block, Wynn went to work designing the sets and supervising construction.

I think it was Monty Ross's idea to hire the Fruit of Islam, the security force of the Nation of Islam, the Black Muslim organization, to patrol the set. Cops really have no respect in Black communities in New York, especially not in Bed-Stuy, where cops have been convicted in the past on drug trafficking charges. We knew we couldn't bring in a white security force, it had to be Black. And Black people who were respected in the community. All this led us to the Fruit of Islam.

It was obvious that crack was being sold on the block. One of the 9 first things we did was let the crack dealers know they weren't welcome. We boarded up an abandoned building that was being used as a crack house and turned another into a location site. We managed to move the dealers off the block, but we weren't able to put them out of business. They just closed up shop and moved around the corner.

During preproduction, Universal asked me to recommend a 10 filmmaker to do the electronic press kit that the studio would use to promote the film. I recommended the veteran documentary filmmaker St. Clair Bourne. When I met with St. Clair to discuss the press kit, I asked him to consider directing a film about the making of *Do The Right Thing*. We were shooting in Bed-Stuy. We were taking over an entire city block for eight weeks. And we had hired the Fruit of Islam—Farrakhan's private security force—to patrol the set and to close two crack houses. Certainly, this needed to be documented. St. Clair got to work on the project immediately.

Casting for *Do The Right Thing* was on a much smaller scale than 11 *School Daze*. Most of the major roles I had decided upon even before I completed the script. We held auditions in New York only, whereas for *School Daze*, we saw actors in Los Angeles, Atlanta, and New York. I wanted to cast white actors who feel comfortable around Black people. A white actor nervous about setting foot in Bed-Stuy wasn't gonna work for this film. The fact that Danny Aiello grew up in the South Bronx, and John Turturro in a Black neighborhood in Queens, made them ideal choices.

The first day of rehearsal the full cast met to read through the 12 script, then I opened up the floor for discussion and suggestions. Paul Benjamin, who plays ML, one of the Corner Men, is a veteran actor who I've wanted to work with for a long time. Paul was the first actor to raise a question about the script. He was worried that it showed nothing but lazy, shiftless Black people. It seemed to Paul that no one in the film had a job, and that his character and the other Corner Men just hung out all day.

It was Rosie Perez (Tina), who had never acted before in her life, 13 who answered Paul's question. Rosie grew up in Bed-Stuy and stayed with relatives there during the shoot. She went off on a ten-minute tirade about how people like the Corner Men actually exist and that Paul and everyone else should go to Bed-Stuy and take a look.

I told Paul that *Do The Right Thing* was not about Black people in 14 three-piece suits going to work, it was about Black underclass in Bed-Stuy, a community that has some of the highest unemployment, infant mortality, and drug-related homicide rates in New York City. We're talking about people who live in the bowels of the social-economic system, but still live with dignity and humor. Paul and I talked about it the next day and he understood.

We spent the rest of the rehearsal week meeting in small groups   15
to talk about characters. When the Corner Men met for their group rehearsal, they were having trouble getting their characters to mesh. I decided that we should take a trip to the location and read the dialogue there. We drove out to Stuyvesant Street and set up some chairs in the same spot where the Corner Men's scenes would be shot. Being on the set, in the community, made all the difference.

The fact this film takes on one single day was a challenge for   16
everyone involved. Continuity was a motherfucker. Especially for Ernest, who had to make two months worth of footage to look like it was shot on one day. For the most part, he had to rely on available light, since we spent most of our time outdoors.

Though this film is about young Black people in Brooklyn, Ruthe   17
Carter, the costume designer, and I wanted to downplay the gold fad. Besides the gold teeth that Mookie and Buggin' Out wear, and Radio Raheem's knuckle rings (which are really brass), you don't see much gold in this film. I think it's crazy for young Black kids to spend money they don't have on gold jewelry. The kids pick it up from the rappers. I mean no disrespect to L.L. Cool J and Eric B. & Rakim, but this gold-chains-by-the-ton shit is ridiculous.

I knew I wanted my character Mookie to wear tight bicycle   18
shorts underneath a pair of loose-fitting shorts. I got this from basketball players. Instead of wearing jock straps now, many are wearing bicycle pants beneath their uniforms. I like the look because of the contrast. So I had an idea for the bottom of my costume, but I was stumped on what to wear on top.

Cecil Holmes, one of the bigwigs in Black music at CBS Records,   19
knows I'm a baseball fan and once gave me a Jackie Robinson jersey. The night before we started shooting, I was still undecided about my costume, then I remembered the jersey.

The jersey was a good choice. I don't think Jackie Robinson has   20
gotten his due from Black people. There are young people today, even Black athletes, who don't know what Jackie Robinson did. They might know he was the first Black Major Leaguer, but they don't know what he had to bear to make it easier for those who came after him.

When you're directing a film, it takes over your life completely.   21
You get up at the crack of dawn, shoot for twelve to fourteen hours (if you're lucky), watch dailies, grab something to eat before you go to bed, then you're up again at the crack of dawn.

The first week of production went well. I felt we could have been   22
better organized in terms of communication between the assistant di-

rectors and other departments, but by the end of the week it all came together.

It rained on and off for three of the days of the first week, and we 23
were forced to shoot an interior scene, one of our precious few cover sets. There was concern about using up our cover sets so early in the shoot, since we had less than five to last us the entire shoot. But there was nothing we could do about that except pray for good weather. Depending on the size of the scene, overcast days were potential problems for us as well. Creating the effect of sunshine on a cloudy day over an area the size of a city block was something our budget didn't allow for.

We had a budget for extras on *Do The Right Thing*, which was a 24
first for me. With no money to pay extras on *School Daze*, we could never predict if we'd get the number needed for a given scene. But if you look at the film, I think we did a good job disguising how few extras we actually had.

We had two open calls for extras, one for members of the Screen 25
Actors Guild, and one for nonunion actors. We also held a community open call at a church near the location, Antioch Baptist, which graciously served as our meal hall during the shoot.

We cast a core group of extras to play block residents and they 26
worked the entire shoot. Additional extras were brought on for the big scenes. The first week of shooting we had a time coming up with a system of documenting the extras and background action scene by scene. We had to establish which core extras would be placed on various sides of the block, how long they would remain there, and how many new extras we should see in each scene. I didn't want to look at this film a year later and see the same two extras crossing through every shot. Again, this was a task made complicated by the fact that the film takes place in a 24-hour period, but was shot out of sequence.

One sequence that took forever to shoot was the johnny pump 27
sequence, where Charlie (played by Frank Vincent) and his white convertible get drenched by the kids. We allotted two days to shoot it, but we should have been more generous because it ended up taking five.

The car had to be specially rigged to withstand all the water, and 28
dried off between takes. And each time Frank got wet, he needed a wardrobe change. We used two cameras to film the kids playing in the hydrant. One was encased in underwater housing, and we used that camera to shoot the closeups of the hydrant. The camera department had a lot of fun with it. It was orange and looked like an old diver's mask.

It's a compliment to Wynn Thomas's design work that people off 29
the street were constantly wandering into Sal's Famous Pizzeria and the Korean Market, unaware they were sets. We spent almost a straight week shooting inside Sal's Famous Pizzeria. With the heat from the lights, and the crew and actors packed into one room, it really got hot in there. As soon as a take was over, people rushed to turn on

the air conditioner. During lunch break, crew members used the booths as beds and caught some shut-eye.

Despite the heat, we were able to get through these interior 30 scenes pretty quickly. John Turturro exploded one day over the prop pizza. The property master didn't have enough pies on set for John and Richard Edson to actually cut them into slices. They were told to fake it. John went off. He refused to fake it because it suspended all his belief in the scene. He was right. We saw dailies the next night and had to reshoot all the fake cutting.

I was pleased with the way we staged the conversation about 31 "niggers" vs. "Blacks" that Mookie and Pino have in the pizzeria. As it reads in the script, the scene could have been a yelling match. It works just as well as a simple conversation, and it manages to keep the same intensity. There is enough yelling and screaming in this movie as it is.

Pino and Mookie's scene sets up the racial-slur sequence. Jump- 32 cut sequences featuring a group of characters speaking toward the camera have been a staple of each of my films so far. *She's Gotta Have It* has the Dogs, *School Daze* has Half-Pint's unsuccessful attempt to pick up girls, and *Do The Right Thing* has representatives of different ethnic groups slurring each other.

In the first two films, the camera remains static while the subjects 33 talk. I wanted to vary this formula a bit in *Do The Right Thing,* so I had the camera move in quickly to the person speaking. It was Ernest's idea to have the final actor in the sequence, Mister Señor Love Daddy, come toward camera. We hooked up Love Daddy's chair to a trick wire so it looks like he's being propelled by magic.

The racial-slur sequence was meant to rouse emotions. It's funny 34 the way people react to it. They laugh at every slur except the one directed at their ethnic group. While we were watching the dailies of Pino's slur of Blacks, a woman in the Kraft Services department started hissing at John. She couldn't separate John from his character and was less than courteous to him for the rest of the shoot.

Some of the best acting in the film happens in the scene where 35 Pino asks his father to sell the pizzeria. Danny, John, and I tinkered with the dialogue while the crew was setting up for the shot. We finally got it down, but we still didn't have a clincher to end the scene. I was always on the lookout for ways to work Smiley into the film, since for the most part, he wasn't scripted. It hit me that we could end the scene by having Smiley knock on the pizzeria window and interrupt Danny and John's conversation.

Danny and John are sitting at a table in front of the pizzeria win- 36 dow. What makes that scene so great to me is that as Danny tells John about the neighborhood and why he has chosen to remain there, through the window you can see activity on the block. It lends visual support to Danny's speech.

Even if principal actors didn't have dialogue in a scene, we often   37
used them in the background, walking down the street or hanging out,
to give a sense that their characters really lived on the block. Most of the
deals we made with our principals were for eight weeks of work—the
entire shoot—so we could have them on standby for that very reason.

The climactic fight in the pizzeria was just as I envisioned it—a   38
messy street fight, complete with choking and biting. It starts inside
the pizzeria and ends up outside on the pavement. After Sal demol-
ishes Radio Raheem's box with his baseball bat, we wanted to do a
shot where Raheem would grab Sal by the neck, slam his face into the
counter, and drag him the length of the counter.

Danny refused to do the shot. He felt it was slapstick and had   39
been done a million times. Some cast members felt that Danny's refusal was a question of ego, of not wanting to be wasted that bad on
screen. I sat down with Eddie Smith, the stunt coordinator, Danny,
Danny Jr., Aiello's son and stunt double, and Bill Nunn, to hear the
opinions of all involved. I decided that Bill should pull Danny over the
counter instead of giving him a "facial." Danny was still not totally
satisfied, but we proceeded anyway.

The cast was spurred on by Danny's reluctance to cooperate with   40
what we had planned for the fight scene. As if to compensate for
Danny's lapse of team spirit, they worked extra hard to make the
scene realistic. Everyone suffered their share of bruises, including
Martin Lawrence (Cee) who took a nasty shot in the eye.

Good things come out of adversity. I think the compromise we   41
came up with made for a better shot, and I'm grateful to Danny for
standing his ground. There was no tension on my part because of our
disagreement. I think Danny felt isolated from the cast for a while. But
I noticed that in no time he was back to his usual habit of hugging on
everyone. Conflicts are bound to crop up on a film shoot. There are always differences of interpretation.

The riot scene was more involved than anything I've done on   42
film before. Just the sheer numbers of people and vehicles involved—
from extras to special-effects coordinators, from cop cars and paddy
wagons to fire trucks—made it a big deal.

In order to capture all the action in the scene, we had to burn the   43
pizzeria in stages, starting with the interior and moving outside. A big
concern was how many days the pizzeria would hold up under the
fire. If the fire got out of hand or the set caved in before we finished
shooting the riot, we'd be up shit's creek with no paddle. But things
worked out and we were able to get all the shots we wanted without
losing the pizzeria.

My most pressured moment as an actor on this film was defi-   44
nitely when I had to throw the garbage can through the pizzeria win-

dow. No one thought about this beforehand, but the window glass was almost one-quarter inch thick. Breaking glass that thick is no easy feat. I was throwing hard, but it took four or five takes before I could get the garbage can through the window. On one take it even bounced off like a rubber ball. I was on the spot: We were filming with a special crane that had to be sent back to the rental house the next day, and the sun was coming up. Finally we got the shot.

The first night we shot the firemen turning their hoses on the   45
crowd, the water pressure wasn't forceful enough. The stuntmen were overacting to compensate for it. The whole effect was fake, so we redid the shot the following evening.

The script called for a number of stunts involving characters get-   46
ting swept away by the force of the water. Ruby Dee and my sister Joie were to get hit by a blast of water and go flying down the street. I decided the scene was powerful enough without these stunts. I cut them and came up with a different way to end the scene. Ruby Dee is in the middle of the street screaming hysterically because of all the chaos around her. Da Mayor comforts her with a hug.

Sam Jackson pointed out to me that he had the honor of acting in   47
the first scene we shot of *School Daze* (he played one of the local yokels), and in the last scene we shot of *Do The Right Thing* (Mister Señor Love Daddy wakes up the Block). I hope this means luck for both of us.

Most wrap days are joyous occasions, unless your film is a real   48
bomb. I felt I had a lot to be thankful for when we wrapped *Do The Right Thing*. We had a relaxed, practically hassle-free shoot. We had shot an entire film for eight and a half weeks at one location. (What could be easier?) The block residents and the community of Bed-Stuy had given us full cooperation. And the dailies looked good.

A couple of hours before wrap, a bet was waged on the exact   49
time, down to the minute, that we would complete our last shot. One of the drivers won the bet and a pool of forty-five dollars. We broke out the champagne. And after listening to the movie unit cops grumble about permissions, we laid a plaque in front of We Love Radio Station that states that the film was shot on the block. We even put up a street sign renaming Stuyvesant Street "Do The Right Thing Avenue," but the wind blew it down, so it stays in my office now.

Examining the Text

1. Look again at veteran actor Paul Benjamin's original objections to the script of *Do The Right Thing* and at the arguments in its favor offered by Rosie Perez and Spike Lee (paragraphs 12–14). Do you think that the filmmaker's responsibility is to present positive images or to present life as it "actually exists"?

2. Why did Lee choose to "play down the gold fad" (17)? How does this decision square with the arguments he made to Paul Benjamin about showing the reality of the "Black underclass in Bed-Stuy" (14)? What other examples can you find where Lee bases his artistic decisions on his political convictions? What do you think of what he did?

3. Lee notes that during the "racial-slur sequence" of *Do The Right Thing* viewers "laugh at every slur except the one directed at their ethnic group" (34). Based on this observation, why do you suppose Lee's included the sequence in his film? If you saw the movie, how did you react to this sequence?

For Group Discussion

Lee says his goal was to use "as many Black people behind the camera as possible." Other minority and female directors have expressed similar commitments to include greater numbers of underrepresented groups in their production crews. In debating this issue, have half of your group take Lee's perspective, and the other half the perspective of a leader of a predominantly white male union. Then as a class try to reach consensus about what is "fair."

Writing Suggestion

One of the criticisms of *Do The Right Thing* is that it perpetuates racial stereotypes—Asians, police, Italians, Black militants, stutterers, Puerto Ricans, miscellaneous white bicyclists and bystanders—and ironically uses those stereotypes to condemn racism. After viewing the film, write an essay in which you agree or disagree with this criticism. Does Lee's portrayal of his secondary characters rely on stereotypes, or does he make a conscious effort to portray individuals as real people with complex personalities and motivations?

As the World Turns

David Denby

Even as American movies are charged with being "big-budget" and mindless, the United States continues to be a major supplier of movies to the rest of the world. In fact, in many countries, American films are more popular (and more profitable) than locally produced movies. What effect does this barrage of American pop imagery have on the world's cultures?

In the following piece—ostensibly a review of the American movies Back to the Future Part II *and* Harlem Nights, *film critic David Denby considers some of these effects and reports on measures foreign governments take to limit the availability and influence of American films.*

Denby credits western mass culture with having a role in revolutionary changes which saw communist governments in Central Europe topple and the Soviet Union dissolve. Pop is fun and "can be good for the soul," he says, while communist regimes are "dryly bureaucratic." Capitalist culture, as depicted in American movies, looked more appealing than the drab, regimented world under communism.

Yet Denby is not entirely comfortable with the influence the American film industry has on the world. Although he doesn't support the imposition of quotas, he doesn't want to see foreign filmmakers abandon their own cultural heritage to produce "American-style spectaculars." He would also like to see a stronger American market for foreign films, and American "indifference and self-protecting chauvinism ... vanish."

As you read, *notice that Denby digresses widely from his original task of reviewing* Back to the Future Part II *and* Harlem Nights, *and ask yourself how well he relates those films to his broader thesis about the pervasive influence of American movies on world markets.*

As I was out buying a quart of milk the other day, the leadership   1
of Czechoslovakia's Communist Party fell from power. The revolution sweeping Central Europe has come deliriously hard and fast, so fast that staying interested in new movies like *Back to the Future Part II* and *Harlem Nights* has been a little tough. Whole governments collapse between chase scenes. The possibility of a future in which America is irrelevant teases us, haunting our lockjawed president, a man frightened not only of events but of words. De Tocqueville correctly predicted 150 years ago that Russia and America would someday hold sway. But a united Europe may dominate the next century, which will change the way Americans think of themselves. It may even change the movies.

At the moment, America is supplying movies to the entire world.   2
Many Europeans resent the popularity of our films in their own markets. When people flock to American movies, less money flows back to local film industries. As a result, some countries have established quotas—restricting American movies to, say, 50 percent of the theaters. These quotas may be reinforced or expanded when the European Community becomes a single market in 1992. At the same time, many Europeans, surrounded and overwhelmed by American pop, fear the corruption of their own cultures.

I have contradictory, unresolvable feelings about this. On the one   3
hand, American mass culture is a liberator. German students threw themselves a party on top of the Berlin Wall a few weeks ago—and

what were they singing? Ray Parker Jr.'s theme from *Ghostbusters*. Bopping on the wall, they zapped the Communist phantoms. Pow, you're dead! Pop is an important element in the seduction of the East by the West, the seduction of Communism by capitalism. It's easy pleasure, quick satisfaction; it's one of the things that Communists are not very good at. For years, the longing of Eastern-bloc youth for American and British rock has amounted to a de facto aesthetic rejection of drably bureaucratic regimes. Governments trying to persuade people to give up good times in return for a future Utopia have lost their credibility. Western mass culture helped do them in.

At the same time, many educated Europeans fight American 4 movies. In 1978, I showed George Lucas's *American Graffiti* to some very serious students at the Polish state film school in Lodz, and they roared with laughter from beginning to end. But afterward, they told me that the movie was trash, completely without value. Europeans can sound awfully priggish when putting down American movies (the students weren't amused when I accused them of hypocrisy). Of course, this was a state school, and someone from the Party may have been listening. The students—all of whom would move into the government-sanctioned film apparatus if they behaved—may have been priggish out of necessity. I trust their first, spontaneous reactions.

Pop can be good for the soul. As for quotas, I'm instinctively 5 against them, since they amount to a form of censorship. People should be able to watch what they want. On the other hand, I'm also repelled by the idea of American junk playing every small town in France and Germany—and soon, presumably, every town in Hungary and Poland too. The habit of easy, violent pleasures could discourage more thoughtful kinds of local filmmaking. Some people say it already has. As a counterforce, the new European pride—the reemergent sense of Europe as the rightful center of Western civilization—may well lead to increased demands for cultural protectionism; the resistance to American pop may stiffen, which might not be such a bad idea. Americans could resist their own mass culture a little more.

Another reason the Europeans are sore is that their movies have 6 barely kept a toehold in the American market, the biggest in the world. In 1989, domestic box office (i.e., American and Canadian) may reach a record $5 billion. Yet the share of tickets sold for foreign-language films amounts to about $50 million, or one percent. As far as the United States is concerned, the German and Italian cinemas might as well not exist; the number of French films opening here has been declining, too, from 48 in 1968 to 24 last year.

The French keep trying, though. A few weeks ago, at the first 7 Sarasota French Film Festival, a group of high-powered French movie-industry types, including producers, directors, and actors, met with

American film importers and a few critics to show off some of the new French movies....My guess is that five of the thirteen new movies shown at the festival will receive American distribution, not a bad ratio at all.

At a panel of American critics, there was general agreement that 8 French films had recently fallen off in quality (this took no courage to say—the French had already flown back to Paris); everyone also agreed that the merely good French films were finding it harder to attract an audience here. If the French, as part of the new Europe, are able to amass large amounts of capital for film production, they could, of course, make American-style spectaculars and begin to claim a larger share of the world market. But then we would miss what we've always valued most in French movies—intimacy. It's not so much that French movies need to change as that American indifference and self-protecting chauvinism have to vanish. Perhaps our impending reduced standing in the world will have an effect on our moviegoing habits.

Intimacy is certainly not a quality anyone could find in Robert 9 Zemeckis's *Back to the Future Part II.* In the original, Michael J. Fox's struggle to bring his parents together so they could mate and produce *him* had a wrenching force. And with that wild man Crispin Glover giving a painfully expressive performance as the wimpy father, the comedy veered recklessly into pathos and back. But the sequel is just noise and frenzied activity. Fox and Christopher Lloyd, as the mad doctor, fly forward and then backward in time, running into other versions of themselves from the first movie's trip back in time. We get plot complexity without any point—a desperate attempt to double and redouble the central gimmick so it will explode like the grand finale of a fireworks display. The wild-eyed Lloyd, shouting gibberish, is desperately unfunny, and Fox is little more than a shuttlecock with mussed feathers. I don't care how much money it makes; the movie is a brutal setback for Zemeckis's career. As for Eddie Murphy's *Harlem Nights,* this promisingly swank fantasy of black club owners and white gangsters in thirties Harlem falls into racial and sexual taunting of frightening crudity. Eddie Murphy the mass-entertainment genius seems to be turning into Eddie Murphy the pop demagogue.

Examining the Text
1. Why, according to Denby, do many Europeans resent the popularity of American films in their own countries, and what measures have governments taken to counteract this popularity? Why does Denby say that his feelings about this are "contradictory" and "unresolvable" (paragraph 3)? What are your own feelings?

2. What does Denby mean when he claims that pop culture is an "important element in the seduction of the East by the West" (3)? What does he mean by "pop can be good for the soul" (5)? Can you give other examples of redeeming qualities of American-style pop culture?

3. How does Denby explain the poor reception for foreign films in the United States? What does he have to say about this issue? Why do you think Americans are so "chauvinistic" when it comes to foreign films?

4. How does Denby relate his central argument to his dismissive comments about *Back to the Future Part II* and *Harlem Nights*? Do you find his strategy effective?

For Group Discussion

As a group, compare several current popular American-made films with any foreign films you have seen recently, and make a list of important similarities and differences. (If no one in your group has seen a foreign film recently, you can list some reasons for that.) Then, as a class, consider what qualities a foreign film must have to succeed with American audiences. Why do American audiences tend to shun foreign films?

Writing Suggestion

Generally a fan of popular culture, Denby nonetheless contends that "Americans could resist their own mass culture a little more" (5). In an essay explain his comment and evaluate his view, drawing on specific examples from your own experience with American movies, television, and advertising.

Film Criticism

Mark J. Schaefermeyer

There's much more to criticizing a film than just deciding whether one likes it or not. This is the central point of the following essay by Mark J. Schaefermeyer. A film critic and professor of communications studies at Virginia Polytechnic Institute, Schaefermeyer begins by drawing a crucial distinction between reviewing movies and film criticism. Movie reviews, he says, are directed toward the general public, primarily to help people decide what movies to see. By contrast, film criticism is written primarily by university academics and other scholars to be published in specialized journals and read by academics and professional filmmakers.

Schaefermeyer outlines some of the main theoretical approaches critics currently use to analyze films. He breaks film criticism down into three broad subcategories—semiotic, structuralist, and contextual—and explains the premises and specific methodologies of each. Semiotic studies, as you have learned from earlier readings in this text (see especially Jack Solomon's "Masters of Desire" in Chapter 2) analyze symbolic structures and relationships. Structuralist methodology attempts "to impose its own orientation or structure"— for instance mythic, or political, or sociological—on a film. Finally, contextual critics look at a movie within a specific context, such as its directorial style, its narrative type, or its historical position.

As you read this survey of film criticism, think about which approach most closely resembles your own way of interpreting film. Are you a budding semiotician, finding symbolic meanings in Lauren Bacall's cigarette or Arnold Schwarzenegger's big gun? Are you a political structuralist, finding social and economic implications in a film's plot and characterization? Are you a contextualist, looking for the hallmarks of a director's style or for the ways the conventions of a genre are met or broken? Or are you satisfied just to "know what you like," without approaching film from a more academically critical position?

———————

The place occupied by movie critics in the popular media is perhaps stronger today than it ever has been. The success of Gene Siskel and Roger Ebert in moving from PBS to syndication with their self-described movie review program is evidence that the medium is not without those who are paid to pass judgment on it. Paperback books that describe and rate all the films available on television abound; local news programs often have a critic of their own or regularly utilize a video version of the syndicated columnist. Major news magazines and large city dailies regularly review films; even the smallest of newspapers offers a column discussing the film industry's latest releases. In some cases, movies are reviewed a second time when they are released in videocassette format. 1

And yet these instances of criticism are only part of the effort that goes into analyzing film. This reading puts into perspective the act of film criticism while providing an overview of the critical approaches currently being used. The bulk of this essay will focus on academic criticism versus the more popular media forms. The general public is aware of and utilizes criticism that is more aptly termed *movie reviewing*. Movie reviews are meant to recommend or not recommend particular films to the potential viewing public. In one sense, the popular media critic is a consumer watchdog keeping a wary eye on the film industry's attempts to obtain the viewers' dollars. 2

Distinguishing the popular media form of criticism from academic or scholarly criticism is not to suggest that the former is unscholarly or a poor cousin to the latter. Movie reviews are meant for a specific audience, and they perform a specific function: to assist consumers in choosing what films to see. For the most part, movie reviewers rely on such 3

categories as plot, characterization, or strength of the actors' performances to arrive at their assessment of the film (this is probably a
holdover from the early beginnings of such criticism when reviewers of
this new medium generally were drama critics taking on additional duties). In most cases today, reviewers' closest comments regarding purely
filmic qualities are related to a director's use of particular techniques.

In contrast, academic critical pursuits are directed toward publi-   4
cations intended for fellow academicians and/or filmmakers. Their
purpose is to foster a better understanding of film as a medium and as
an art form. Hence scholarly criticism of film invariably touches the
medium's history, functions, practitioners, techniques, or aesthetics. In
most cases, such criticism attempts to answer questions about the film's
history and other issues in order to further our knowledge about art
ourselves, and the world.

Sidney Pollack (1986), director of the critically acclaimed and   5
successful films *Out of Africa* and *Tootsie,* has stated that each film is a
revelation of the director's perceptions about how the world operates.
Each film is thus a communication of the director's overall vision of
the world. Those who seek to understand a film implicitly seek understanding of what the director has communicated. In many cases, what
is communicated is not always obvious to the viewer or the critic.
Close analysis is necessary to reveal, interpret, or merely aid the
viewer's understanding.

There are a variety of methods and critical models imposed on   6
films, all of which propose to answer specific questions about those
works of art. Indeed, the question of what the filmmaker "meant" is
not an appropriate query (many critical theorists have long ago abandoned the quest for artist's intent). Rather, the meaning of a film is just
that: what the film (or work of art) communicates. The film's meaning,
then, depends on how it is perceived, by whom, and with what particular perspective(s).

This situation appears to indicate that film meanings vary and   7
therefore criticism as a method for arriving at that meaning must be
fruitless pursuit. Quite the contrary is true. Works of art will often
hold different meanings for people because of their varied experiences
and backgrounds. Hence, each viewer approaches a film with different
sets of expectations and prejudices, as well as a distinct worldview
and knowledge base. The variety of critical perspectives allows each
individual to explore the perspective most meaningful to that person.
More important, for those of us studying the mass media, an additional gain from the variety of critical perspectives used to analyze
film is the differences that are highlighted and what those differences
tell us about ourselves, others, and the human condition in general.

The remainder of this reading will...review the various types of   8
film criticism, with examples for each type of criticism. Although no

particular perspective should be viewed as more useful or proper than any other, no doubt each reader will find one or two of those discussed to be more functional than the others. The key is that no perspective should be dismissed out of hand; each has its own merits as well as faults. Like the cinematic works of art they attempt to analyze, some critical methods work for us, and others do not. To aid us in our understanding of film as a mass medium and as an art form, it is necessary to be acquainted with the basic theory and the tools utilized by critics of film.

CRITICAL METHODS IN FILM CRITICISM

Each of the critical approaches to film discussed here falls within   9
one of three categories:

Semiotic: realist, formalist, rhetorical, mise-en-scène.
Structuralist: mythic, political, feminist, psychoanalytic, sociological, phenomenological
Contextual: auteur, genre, historical.

Grouped within the *semiotic* category are methods that tend to focus on the meaning of the filmic signs (shots and shot transitions), the relationship of these signs to other filmic signs, or the effect of the signs on the film viewer. Methods that fall under the *structuralist* category seek to define and understand the structures into which individual films and/or from where they are derived. Those under the *contextual* heading focus on aspects of film in the context of other aspects of film.

SEMIOTIC STUDIES

The most logical place to start in the review of critical approaches   10
with a semiotic impetus is with both the *realist* and *formalist traditions* within film theory. The *realist* tradition focuses on the use of film to represent reality based on the power of photography's ability to render the real world objectively (Bazin 1967). Bazin argues that long takes, depth of focus, location shooting, sunlight, and the use of nonprofessional actors all contribute to a film's realist aesthetic. In his analysis of Visconti's *La Terra Trema* (1971), Bazin discusses how the film is "real" by virtue of the manner in which the narrative is presented: without the trappings of montage (where reality is fragmented through such techniques as close-up shots and excessive editing). "If a fisherman rolls a cigarette, he [Visconti] spares us nothing: we see the whole operation; it will not be reduced to its dramatic or symbolic

meaning, as is usual with montage" (Bazin 1971, p. 43). In a review of De Sica's *Bicycle Thief*, Bazin praises the realist use of location shooting (nothing has been filmed in the studio) and actors without any previous experience in theater or film (Bazin 1971, p. 52).

Analyses using the *formalist* approach have a different focus. Because of his influence on the early history of filmmaking, the Russian filmmaker and theorist Sergei Eisenstein is most often linked (above other theorists) to film's *formalist* tradition. Eisenstein's theory of dialectical montage is influenced by the Japanese hieroglyph, as a pictorial representation of language symbols, and by Hegel's dialectic. First, Eisenstein believes that the Japanese language was built on the principle of montage. For example, the picture symbol for a *dog* plus the symbol for *mouth* means "to bark" (1949, p. 30). The combination of "two hieroglyphs of the simplest series is to be regarded not as their sum, but as their product, i.e., as a value of another dimension, another degree; each, separately, corresponds to an *object*, to a fact, but their combination corresponds to a *concept*. From separate hieroglyphs has been fused—the ideogram" (Eisenstein 1949, pp. 29–30).   11

Eisenstein theorizes that film relied on the same process: a shot combined in the editing process with another shot created a new concept. Paralleling this approach is the influence of Hegel's dialectic. *Thesis* and *antithesis* combine to form a *synthesis*—a new concept that is no longer reducible to those ideas that in combination make up the editing (as well as any other art form). Montage is the collision of independent shots (shots that are opposite to one another) (Eisenstein 1949, p. 49). Meaning in film, then, evolves from the juxtaposition of film shots that manifest conflict. The differences might be in lighting, shot composition, shot length, conflict of volumes, lines, movement of objects, or something else. Excluding Eisenstein's philosophical and political (or Marxist) orientation, the basis of his theory is film construction: shot plus shot plus shot … Hence, any critic interested in how the shots of a film are combined to "mean" would essentially be conducting formalist criticism.   12

Ted Perry's essay (1970) on Michaelangelo Antonioni's film *L'Eclisse* argues that the meaning of the film depends on certain cues given within the film. In distinguishing between what he calls *fact context* and *value context*, the author argues that the film's meaning is born of the formative forces within the film (p. 79). Perry's analysis relies heavily on the notion of combination. The value context (the attitudes, impressions, and values by which the film frames the fact context) influences the viewer's reading of the fact context (the elements that represent the actions, objects, and events of the physical world depicted in the motion picture images). This analysis reflects the formalist tradition in its focus on meaning that is built upon the combination of shots.   13

A third type of analysis within the semiotic orientation is *rhetori-*   14
cal in focus. This type of criticism examines the film as a rhetorical artifact that exhibits intentional meaning and structure. It is an approach
based on traditional notions of rhetoric as a means to persuasion.
Often relying on critical models from other disciplines, the rhetorical
criticism of film deals with the communicative potential of film.

In "Image and Ambiguity: A Rhetorical Approach to *The Exor-*   15
cist," Martin Medhurst (1978) examines the key images in six of the
film's episodes in order to define the film's central stance: a rhetoric of
choice. The author argues that certain recurring images combine in
clusters to foster the contention that people have choices to make:
"Humans must choose between the forces of good and the legions of
evil. . . . They must consciously will the good and then by a step of faith
act on that choice. This is exactly what Damien Karras does in the climax of the film. He consciously chooses to assert that Regan will not
die and then proceeds to act on the basis of that assertion" (Medhurst
1978, pp. 90–91).

Medhurst (1982) has also analyzed Alain Resnais' *Hiroshima, Mon*   16
Amour as a film about the problem of knowing reality. In essence,
Medhurst's analysis is traditionally rhetorical in his focus on the filmmaker's "cinematic statement": "Resnais has built into the film the
very paradox which forms its thesis . . . Resnais has been able to take
his thesis and transform it into a cinematic resource . . . To know reality, Resnais seems to be saying, is no easy task" (Medhurst 1982,
p. 370). Clearly in evidence is the rhetorical quest concerning what the
filmmaker means. Both of the Medhurst essays ostensibly rely on examining and interpreting the filmmaker's message.

The final type of semiotic-oriented criticism relies on *mise-en-*   17
scène—the environment of the film, which is created by its lighting,
sets, costumes, movement, and any other features that comprise the
scene as photographed by the camera. Film analysis that focuses on
these elements and on the expressive function of the individual shots
is the basis of mise-en-scène criticism (Stromgren and Norden 1984,
p. 265). Mise-en-scène criticism lies in the boundary zone between for-
malism and realism; it is "largely concerned with stylistic or expressive qualities of the single shot. . . in contrast to Bazin's perception of
the long take as a transparent realism . . . and in sharp distinction to
Eisenstein's herding of all expressive categories under the single umbrella of montage" (Nichols 1976, p. 311).

One notable example of mise-en-scène criticism is Place and Pe-   18
terson's "Some Visual Motifs of *Film Noir*" (1974). Here, the authors
define visual style by utilizing the technical terminology of Hollywood. Their analysis reveals a style reliant on low-key lighting, night-
for-night photography (versus day-for-night where the scene, shot in

the bright sunlight of day, is manipulated to create an illusion of night), depth of field (the entire shot is in focus), and anti-traditional camera setups and angles: "The 'dark mirror' of *film noir* creates a visually unstable environment in which no character has a firm moral base from which he can confidently operate. All attempts to find safety or security are undercut by the anti-traditional cinematography and mise-en-scène" (Place and Peterson, p. 338).

All of these types of criticism have semiotic underpinnings: each   19
attempts to understand and/or interpret the meaning of cinematic signs, the relationship of cinematic signs to each other, and their meaning to the viewer. There are not always clear-cut boundaries between the varying elements. However, the distinctive features of the type are clear: The primary focus is on cinematic features and the use of film theory. This is contrary to the structuralist studies, which utilize literary-cultural features. They are, in effect, extracinematic (outside of cinema).

STRUCTURALIST STUDIES

There are several types of structuralist methodology. Each   20
method attempts to impose its own orientation or structure on the film; each argues that the film exhibits particular features of the society within which it is produced.

The *mythic* approach asserts the presence of one or more specific   21
myths that, by virtue of their preeminence, are found (or likely to be found) in a society's aesthetic artifacts. Dale Williams's essay (1984) on the religious nature of Stanley Kubrick's *2001: A Space Odyssey* is an example of criticism that uncovers the meaning of the film by defining its mythic overtones. Using the theories of Kenneth Burke (1969), Williams argues that *2001* revolves around the concepts of order and redemption, sacrifice and rebirth, self-denial, and communion with God (Williams 1984, p. 321). Similarly, Martha Solomon (1983) argues that British-made *Chariots of Fire* was successful in the United States because it reflects two contradictory facets of the American dream— what Fisher (1973) calls the materialistic myth and the moralistic myth. The film's success, in part, is due to its reaffirmation of both competing myths for an audience likely to follow, individually, one or the other. *Chariots,* according to Solomon, functions both mythically and metaphorically in its depiction of a series of successful, archetypal quests by the film's mythic hero characters (p. 275).

The *political* approach to criticism is likely to focus on films and   22
their relationship to the areas of history, ideology, economics, and social criticism. Jeffrey Richards's essay (1970) on Frank Capra illustrates how the films of a single director can contain political undertones. In this case, Capra's films reflect ideals of the populist party: self-help

and individualism versus political machines and big government. Richards finds the presence of Capra's emphasis of populism in the motifs of antiintellectualism, wealth, pursuit of happiness, and the quintessential good neighbor. Capra's films in the postwar era cast aside these themes because the world had progressed, and the forces of organization had won out.

The *feminist* perspective in criticism has gained sufficient status   23
as a category, though it could be argued that its impetus is political in nature. Most of the feminist critics analyze films' treatment of women as they support or negate the role of women in contemporary society. For example, Diane Giddis (1973) explores a woman's dilemma (the fear that love represents loss of autonomy) in her analysis of *Klute.* Giddis finds that the film reflects woman's need to love and make a deep emotional commitment—a commitment unnecessary, to the same degree, for men. Constance Penley (1973) analyzes Ingmar Bergman's *Cries and Whispers* in the perspective of Bergman's other films. Penley's analysis runs counter to the majority of the film's reviews; she sees *Cries* as another example of Bergman's excessive portrayal of woman as victim, temptress, evil incarnate, and earth mother.

Psychoanalytic and *sociological* criticisms are likely to use models   24
of analysis from accepted theorists or contemporary social concerns. Rushing and Frentz (1980), for example, derive their analysis of *The Deer Hunter* from the psychological theories of Carl Jung. In a sociological critique, the critic uses sociological concepts, such as class, status, interaction, organization and culture, to analyze a film. They may also use the perspective and language of social movements.

Finally, the *phenomenological* approach to criticism is concerned   25
with the manner in which viewers perceive the film and/or its images (always, however, in relation to the whole) (see Andrew 1978). An example of this type is Janice Schuetz's analysis (1975) of *The Exorcist.* Schuetz utilizes the symbols of yin and yang from the *I Ching* as a paradigm for explaining the viewer's perceptions of the film. She argues that the film "presents reality in an organismic way, showing goodness and evil, doubt and faith, despair and hope, secular and sacred... as realistic representations of an integrated reality" (pp. 100–101). In addition, the images are sufficiently ambiguous to permit viewers to attribute meaning based on their own frame of reference (p. 101).

CONTEXTUAL STUDIES

The three types included here—auteur, genre, and historical—   26
have in common the study of film(s) within a specific context: directorial style (in its broadest sense), narrative type, and impact on or development of the film industry and/or the film as art form. Exam-

ples of each type are readily available in single texts, film periodicals, and collections of essays.

The most controversial of the three types is *auteur* criticism. Auteur theory assumes a certain amount of directorial autonomy in film production regardless of the fact that film is a product of producers, screenwriters, cinematographers, actors, musicians, film editors, and others. The film's creation and the stylistic choices made are assumed to be those of a single person—the director. Auteur criticism, then, focuses on film directors and the style manifested in two or more of their films. Directors such as Alfred Hitchcock, Charles Chaplin, John Ford, Howard Hawks, and Orson Welles have indirectly generated numerous auteur studies. No doubt, and not far off, there will be studies of George Lucas and Steven Spielberg.   27

Andrew Sarris (1968) uses auteur theory to rank various directors. Relying on three criteria—technical competence, stylistic identity, and communicability of worldview—he estimates their worth as directors. John Simon's analysis of Ingmar Bergman (1972) is an auteur study that looks at four films that Simon thinks represent Bergman's best work up to the early 1970s. Ian Cameron's two-part essay on Hitchcock (1972a) is another example of auteur criticism. It analyzes a specific feature of the director's overall style, his ability to create suspense in his films: 28

> Having arrived at such a disturbing view [everything is a potential threat], Hitchcock paradoxically relishes it and loves more than anything to torture his audiences by making them find the most innocuous thing alarming so that he can surprise and terrify them when the real threat is revealed. (Cameron 1972b, p. 34)

By examining a single film, *The Man Who Knew Too Much*, Cameron validates his auteur assumptions about Hitchcock's style. Another typical example of auteur criticism is Michael Budd's essay (1976) on visual imagery in John Ford's Westerns.   29

Genre criticism focuses on the narrative structures common to film: Westerns, war films, musicals, gangster films, and so on. This type of criticism also categorizes films according to specific characteristics. Thus, to be able to classify an object, to know where it fits, is a means toward understanding it better. We are then able to analyze a certain film based on how well it fits a particular genre and "how the director of that work used the elements of the genre—its *conventions*—to make a statement unique to that film" (Stromgren and Norden 1984). (For additional comments on genre criticism, see Kaminsky 1974; see also the extensive bibliography of genre studies in Cook 1981, pp. 691–692.)   30

Finally, *historical* studies inevitably analyze the entire scope of the film's development. Cook (1981), Ellis (1985), Giannetti and Eyman   31

(1986), and Mast (1986) are fine representatives of historical criticism. In addition, studies of particular studios (Buscombe 1975; Gomery 1976) analyze the film industry from economic, political, or corporate perspectives or the impact of new technology. A relatively new annual series edited by Bruce A. Austin, "Current Research in Film: Audiences, Economics, and Law," publishes original essays on corporate structure, film financing, legal issues, marketing and promotion strategies, and others in an attempt to provide a place for those critics whose interests and work lie outside of the scope addressed by existing film journals.

CONCLUSION

There is a danger in establishing category systems. Inevitably examples of criticism exhibit features appropriate for more than one type of critical method. Judgment as to the correct placement of each of the examples here is left up to the reader. However, no apology is made for the classification contained within; what these essays accomplish is typical of the category they exemplify. Nor are they to be considered examples of superior criticism. In some cases, they create as many questions as they answer.   32

There will continue to be a need to analyze the best, worst, and average output of the film industry. Although the ultimate arbiter for judging a film's success may be its box office receipts, those with expertise should continue to analyze film with the express purpose of better understanding it as a mass media art form. Critics of both kinds, public and scholarly, can always hope that filmmakers, and ultimately audiences, will benefit from their efforts.   33

From the opposite viewpoint, those who practice film criticism have no monopoly on perfection. Critics must continue to read other critical analyses of film in order to improve their own craft. Like the student in a public speaking course, critics benefit from witnessing the successes and blunders of other critics. New methods are tried and either validated or rejected. In a rapidly progressing world, there is comfort in the thought that our critical stance and methods also continue to progress.   34

REFERENCES

Andrew, Dudley. 1978. "The Neglected Tradition of Phenomenology in Film Theory." *Wide Angle* 2:44–49.

Bazin, André. 1967. *What Is Cinema?* Vol. 1. Translated and edited by Hugh Gray. Berkeley: University of California Press.

———. 1971. *What Is Cinema?* Vol. 2. Translated and edited by Hugh Gray. Berkeley: University of California Press.

Budd, Michael. 1976. "A Home in the Wilderness: Visual Imagery in John Ford's Westerns." *Cinema Journal* 16:62–75.

Burke, Kenneth. 1969. *A Rhetoric of Motives.* Berkeley: University of California Press.

Buscombe, Edward. 1975. "Notes on Columbia Pictures Corporation, 1926–1941." *Screen* 16. Reprinted in Nichols 1985:92–108.

Cameron, Ian. 1972a. "Hitchcock and the Mechanics of Suspense." *Movie Reader.* New York: Praeger.

———. 1972b. "Hitchcock 2: Suspense and Meaning." *Movie Reader.* New York: Praeger.

Cook, David A. 1981. *A History of Narrative Film.* New York: W. W. Norton.

Eisenstein, Sergei. 1947. *The Film Sense.* New York: Harcourt Brace Jovanovich.

———. 1949. *Film Form: Essays in Film Theory.* Translated and edited by Jay Leyda. New York: Harcourt, Brace and World.

Ellis, Jack C. 1985. *A History of Film.* 2d ed. Englewood Cliffs, N.J.: Prentice Hall.

Fisher, Walter. 1973. "Reaffirmation and Subversion of the American Dream." *Quarterly Journal of Speech* 59:160–167.

Giannetti, Louis, and Scott Eyman. 1986. *Flashback: A Brief History Film.* Englewood Cliffs, N.J.: Prentice Hall.

Giddis, Diane. 1973. "The Divided Woman: Bree Daniels in *Klute*." *Women and Film,* nos. 3–4. Reprinted in Nichols 1976:194–201.

Gomery, Douglas. 1976. "Writing the History of the American Film Industry: Warner Brothers and Sound." *Screen* 17. Reprinted in Nichols 1985:109–119.

Examining the Text

1. Why do you think Schaefermeyer begins by distinguishing between movie reviewing and movie criticism? In what ways does he suggest that the reviewer and the critic both perform important functions? Based on his examples, do you agree with his evaluation of the critic's role?

2. Briefly summarize in your own words each of the three basic critical approaches Schaefermeyer describes. How do they differ from one another? Which would you find most interesting and illuminating?

3. Schaefermeyer concludes that "the ultimate arbiter for judging a film's success may be its box office receipts" (paragraph 32). Do you think he is being entirely serious? What other ways are there to judge a film's "success"? Is any of these a better criterion than earnings?

For Group Discussion

Choose a film that each member of your group has seen and discuss how it could be analyzed using each of the three critical approaches described by Schaefermeyer. Come up with several specific examples from the film to illustrate one or more of the methods within each approach. As a class, discuss which approaches work best with which kinds of films.

Writing Suggestion

Critically analyze a specific film (or several films of the same genre, such as horror, science fiction, or romantic comedy), restricting your thematic focus to one of the structuralist approaches described by Schaefermeyer. For instance, if you consider yourself a feminist, point out instances of sexism or the objectification of women; if you're a political conservative, you might write from the perspective of a Rush Limbaugh, pointing out examples of liberal excess and misguidedness; if you are a student of mythology, you might take that approach. If possible see the movie or movies you are writing about again, preferably on video, so that your examination can be a close one.

The Horror Movie

Why We Crave Horror Movies

Stephen King

A hotel with ghosts as its guests, a downtrodden teenager whose teleki-netic powers wreak havoc at her prom, a giant dog from hell, a satanic antique store owner...all are products of the fertile (and some would say twisted) imagination of Stephen King, whose books are so widely read—and the movies made from them so popularly viewed—that his creations may well have become part of the American collective consciousness. In the following article, King takes a break from story-telling to reflect on the genre that has brought him worldwide recognition.

King begins by stating a bold and not entirely tongue-in-cheek premise: "I think that we are all mentally ill." Underneath a frequently thin veneer of civilization, he suggests, we all have fears, homicidal rages, and sexual de-sires"—baser urges which he calls "anticivilization emotions"—and the function of horror movies is to appeal to those dark elements within ourselves and therefore reduce their psychic energy. Thus purged of our negative im-pulses, we can go on to engage in positive feelings of love, friendship, loyalty and kindness. According to King, then, horror movies serve an important reg-ulating function, defusing people's destructive urges and helping to maintain a society's psychic equilibrium.

Before you read *this article, consider your own feelings about portray-als of the macabre, especially in films. If you enjoy horror movies, are you drawn to them for the reasons Stephen King suggests—that is, do you have deep-seated fears, angry urges, or inappropriate sexual drives that need defus-ing—or are there other factors involved which King has not considered? More to the point, how do you respond to King's basic premise: that everyone is in some sense mentally ill?*

I think that we're all mentally ill; those of us outside the asylums only hide it a little better—and maybe not all that much better, after all. We've all known people who talk to themselves, people who sometimes squinch their faces into horrible grimaces when they be-lieve no one is watching, people who have some hysterical fear—of snakes, the dark, the tight place, the long drop...and, of course, those final worms and grubs that are waiting so patiently underground. 1

When we pay our four or five bucks and seat ourselves at tenth-   2
row center in a theater showing a horror movie, we are daring the
nightmare.

Why? Some of the reasons are simple and obvious. To show that   3
we can, that we are not afraid, that we can ride this roller coaster.
Which is not to say that a really good horror movie may not surprise a
scream out of us at some point, the way we may scream when the
roller coaster twists through a complete 360 or plows through a lake at
the bottom of the drop. And horror movies, like roller coasters, have
always been the special province of the young; by the time one turns
40 or 50, one's appetite for double twists or 360-degree loops may be
considerably depleted.

We also go to re-establish our feelings of essential normality; the   4
horror movie is innately conservative, even reactionary. Freda Jackson
as the horrible melting woman in *Die, Monster, Die!* confirms for us that
no matter how far we may be removed from the beauty of a Robert Red-
ford or a Diana Ross, we are still light-years from true ugliness.

And we go to have fun.   5

Ah, but this is where the ground starts to slope away, isn't it? Be-   6
cause this is a very peculiar sort of fun indeed. The fun comes from
seeing others menaced—sometimes killed. One critic has suggested
that if pro football has become the voyeur's version of combat, then
the horror film has become the modern version of the public lynching.

It is true that the mythic, "fairytale" horror film intends to take   7
away the shades of gray ... It urges us to put away our more civilized
and adult penchant for analysis and to become children again, seeing
things in pure blacks and whites. It may be that horror movies provide
psychic relief on this level because this invitation to lapse into simplicity, irrationality and even outright madness is extended so rarely. We
are told we may allow our emotions a free rein...or no rein at all.

If we are all insane, then sanity becomes a matter of degree. If   8
your insanity leads you to carve up women like Jack the Ripper or the
Cleveland Torso Murderer, we clap you away in the funny farm (but
neither of those two amateur-night surgeons was ever caught, heh-
heh-heh); if, on the other hand your insanity leads you only to talk to
yourself when you're under stress or to pick your nose on the morning
bus, then you are left alone to go about your business...though it is
doubtful that you will ever be invited to the best parties.

The potential lyncher is in almost all of us (excluding saints, past   9
and present; but then, most saints have been crazy in their own ways),
and every now and then, he has to be let loose to scream and roll
around in the grass. Our emotions and our fears form their own body,
and we recognize that it demands its own exercise to maintain proper
muscle tone. Certain of these emotional muscles are accepted—even

exalted—in civilized society; they are, of course, the emotions that tend to maintain the status quo of civilization itself. Love, friendship, loyalty, kindness—these are all the emotions that we applaud, emotions that have been immortalized in the couplets of Hallmark cards and in the verses (I don't dare call it poetry) of Leonard Nimoy.

When we exhibit these emotions, society showers us with posi-   10
tive reinforcement; we learn this even before we get out of diapers. When, as children, we hug our rotten little puke of a sister and give her a kiss, all the aunts and uncles smile and twit and cry, "Isn't he the sweetest little thing?" Such coveted treats as chocolate-covered graham crackers often follow. But if we deliberately slam the rotten little puke of a sister's fingers in the door, sanctions follow—angry remonstrance from parents, aunts and uncles; instead of a chocolate-covered graham cracker, a spanking.

But anticivilization emotions don't go away, and they demand   11
periodic exercise. We have such "sick" jokes as, "What's the difference between a truckload of bowling balls and a truckload of dead babies? (You can't unload a truckload of bowling balls with a pitchfork…a joke, by the way, that I heard originally from a ten-year-old.) Such a joke may surprise a laugh or a grin out of us even as we recoil, a possibility that confirms the thesis: If we share a brotherhood of man, then we also share an insanity of man. None of which is intended as a defense of either the sick joke or insanity but merely as an explanation of why the best horror films, like the best fairy tales, manage to be reactionary, anarchistic, and revolutionary all at the same time.

The mythic horror movie, like the sick joke, has a dirty job to do. It   12
deliberately appeals to all that is worst in us. It is morbidity unchained, our most base instincts let free, our nastiest fantasies realized…and it all happens, fittingly enough, in the dark. For those reasons, good liberals often shy away from horror films. For myself, I like to see the most aggressive of them—*Dawn of the Dead*, for instance—as lifting a trap door in the civilized forebrain and throwing a basket of raw meat to the hungry alligators swimming around in that subterranean river beneath.

Why bother? Because it keeps them from getting out, man. It   13
keeps them down there and me up here. It was Lennon and McCartney who said that all you need is love, and I would agree with that.

As long as you keep the gators fed.   14

Examining the Text
1. How seriously do you think King expects readers to take his opening statement? What evidence does he offer to support his assertion? Does disagreeing with him here mean that you must automatically reject the rest of his argument about the appeal of horror movies?

2. King states that the horror movie is "innately conservative, even reactionary" (paragraph 4). Is he using these terms politically or in another sense? In what ways can horror movies be seen as "reactionary, anarchistic, and revolutionary all at the same time" (11)?

3. King basically offers three reasons for the popularity of horror movies (3, 4, and 5–14); obviously the third is his main thesis. Summarize King's three reasons. Which do you find most persuasive, and why? Can you offer any other reasons?

4. King's tone throughout this essay is quite informal (it was originally published, by the way, in *Playboy* magazine). Find several examples that illustrate his informality and describe the overall effect.

For Group Discussion

For the sake of discussion, accept King's premise that we all have "anticivilization emotions" (11). List as a group some other things besides horror movies and "sick" jokes that we use to purge these emotions and "keep the gators fed." As a class, consider the extent to which these examples are products of contemporary society and what this suggests about how our psychic behaves differ from those of people who lived a century or more ago.

Writing Suggestion

Consider several of your favorite horror movies. In an essay analyze these in light of King's theories about the horror genre's appeal. Do your examples support or disprove King's point about the daredevil, normative, and psychological function of horror movies?

Monster Movies: A Sexual Theory

Walter Evans

In an essay earlier in this chapter, Mark Schaefermeyer breaks film criticism down into three categories: semiotic critics look for signs and relationships among images in films; contextual critics examine movies in a specific context, focusing, for example, on a director's style or on a movie as a representative of a particular genre; and structuralists look at films from the perspective of a certain theory or belief system, whether mythic, political, psychological, or historical. Walter Evans, the author of the following essay, belongs to the last of these camps. In "Monster Movies: A Sexual Theory," he relies on a psychological approach to human sexual development to explain why monster movies are especially appealing to adolescents. Compared with Stephen King's explanation, Evans's is both more limited and more detailed.

Evans's central thesis is that monster movies embody many of the powerful—and sometimes socially unacceptable—impulses that preoccupy teenagers as they begin to mature, to experience unprecedented physical changes, and to be pulled by unfamiliar drives and urges. "The key to monster movies and the adolescents which understandably dote upon them," says Evans, "is the theme of horrible and mysterious psychological and physical change; the most important of these is the monstrous transformation...directly associated with secondary sexual characteristics and with the onset of aggressive erotic behavior." Since most of those aggressive, animalistic impulses cannot be acted upon in "civilized" society, Evans believes that monster movies serve as an outlet through which teenagers can ritually act out those drives.

Evans relates each of the various aspects of the movie monster's aggressive behavior to a specific adolescent erotic impulse or physical change—the onset of menstruation, the impulse to masturbate, the drive to marry and to create life. He then examines two specific film "monsters," Frankenstein and Dracula, from this perspective. The former, he says, must "give up dangerous private experiments on the human body" and learn to "deal safely and normally with the 'secret of life,'" just as adolescents must move from secretive masturbatory practices to more socially acceptable forms of sexuality: marriage and child rearing. Similarly, Dracula is like an adolescent, thrust into "a world he does not understand, torturing him with desires he cannot satisfy or even admit."

As you read *these interpretations, consider your own intellectual response to them: do you believe that Evans makes some valid points in using adolescent developmental psychology to explain the attraction of monster movies, or is he forcing his belief system on the genre?*

The key to monster movies and the adolescents which under-   1
standably dote upon them is the theme of horrible and mysterious
psychological and physical change; the most important of these is the
monstrous transformation which is directly associated with secondary
sexual characteristics and with the onset of aggressive erotic behavior.[1]
The Wolfman, for example, sprouts a heavy coat of hair, can hardly be
contained within his clothing, and when wholly a wolf is, of course,
wholly naked. Comparatively innocent and asexual females become,
after contact with a vampire (his kiss redly marked on their necks) or

---

[1]Though many critics focus on adult themes in monster movies, I believe that adolescents provide the bulk of the audience for such films, particularly the classic films shown on late night television all across America. Adolescents, of course, may be of any age.

werewolf (as in *Cry of the Werewolf*), quite sexy, aggressive, seductive—literally female "Vamps" and "wolves."[2]

As adolescence is defined as "developing from childhood to maturity,"[3] so the transformation is cinematically, defined as movement from a state of innocence and purity associated with whiteness and clarity to darkness and obscurity associated with evil and threatening physical aggression. In the words of *The Wolf Man*'s gypsy: **2**

> Even a man who is pure at heart
> And says his prayers by night
> May become a wolf when the wolfbane blooms
> And the moon is full and bright

The monsters are generally sympathetic, in large part because they themselves suffer the change as unwilling victims, all peace destroyed by the horrible physical and psychological alterations thrust upon them. Even Dracula, in a rare moment of self-revelation, is driven to comment: "To die, to be really dead. That must be glorious. . . . There are far worse things awaiting man, than death." Much suffering arises from the monster's overwhelming sense of alienation; totally an outcast, he painfully embodies the adolescent's nightmare of being hated and hunted by the society which he so desperately wishes to join. **3**

Various aspects of the monster's attack are clearly sexual. The monster invariably prefers to attack individuals of the opposite sex, to attack them at night, and to attack them in their beds. The attack itself is specifically physical; Dracula, for instance, must be in immediate bodily contact with his victim to effect his perverted kiss; Frankenstein, the Wolfman, the Mummy, King Kong, have no weapons but their bodies. The aspect of the attack most disturbing to the monster, and perhaps most clearly sexual, is the choice of victim: "The werewolf instinctively seeks to kill the thing it loves best" (Dr. Yogami in *The Werewolf of London*). *Dracula*'s Mina Seward must attack her fiance, **4**

---

[2]The transformation is less obvious, and perhaps for this reason more powerful, in *King Kong* (1933). Kong himself is safe while hidden deep in the prehistoric depths of Skull Island, but an unappeasable sexual desire (made explicit in the cuts restored in the film's most recent release) turns him into an enemy of civilization until, trapped on the world's hugest phallic symbol, he is destroyed. The psychological transformation of Ann Darrow (Fay Wray) is much more subtle. While alone immediately after exchanging vows of love with a tough sailor she closes her eyes and, as in a dream vision, above her appears the hideously savage face of a black native who takes possession of her in preparation for the riotous wedding to the great hairy ape. Significantly, only when civilization destroys the fearful, grossly physical beast is she finally able to marry the newly tuxedoed sailor.

[3]*Webster's New World Dictionary of the American Language*, 2nd College Edition (Englewood Cliffs, N.J.: Prentice Hall, 1970). Interesting, in view of the fiery death of Frankenstein's monster and others, is one of the earlier meanings of the root word: "be kindled, burn."

John. The Mummy must physically possess the body of the woman in whom his spiritual bride has been reincarnated. Even more disturbing are the random threats to children scattered throughout the formula, more disturbing largely because the attacks are so perversely sexual and addressed to beings themselves soon destined for adolescence.

The effects of the attack may be directly related to adolescent sexual experimentation. The aggressor is riddled with shame, guilt, and anguish; the victim, once initiated, is generally transformed into another aggressor.[4] Regaining innocence before death seems, in the best films, almost as inconceivable as retrieving virginity.

Many formulaic elements of the monster movies have affinities with two central features of adolescent sexuality, masturbation and menstruation. From time immemorial underground lore has asserted that masturbation leads to feeblemindedness or mental derangement; the monster's transformation is generally associated with madness; scientists are generally secretive recluses whose private experiments on the human body have driven them mad. Masturbation is also widely (and, of course, fallaciously) associated with "weakness of the spine," a fact which helps explain not only Fritz of *Frankenstein* but the army of feebleminded hunchbacks which pervades the formula. The Wolfman, and sometimes Dracula, are identifiable (as, according to underground lore, masturbating boys may be identified) by hairy palms.

Ernest Jones explains the vampire myth largely in terms of a mysterious physical and psychological development which startles many adolescents, nocturnal emissions: "A nightly visit from a beautiful or frightful being, who first exhausts the sleeper with passionate embraces and then withdraws from him a vital fluid: all this can point only to a natural and common process, namely to nocturnal emissions accompanied with dreams of a more or less erotic nature. In the unconscious mind blood is commonly an equivalent for semen...."[5] The vampire's bloodletting of women who suddenly enter full sexuality, the werewolf's bloody attacks—which occur regularly every month—are certainly related to the menstrual cycle which suddenly and mysteriously commands the body of every adolescent girl.

Monster movies characteristically involve another highly significant feature which may initially seem irrelevant to the theme of sexual change: the faintly philosophical struggle between reason and the darker emotional truths. Gypsies, superstitious peasants, and others

---

[4]It is interesting, and perhaps significant that the taint of vampirism and lycanthropy have an aura of sin and shame not unlike that of VD. The good doctor who traces the taint, communicable only through direct physical contact, back to the original carrier is not unlike a physician fighting VD.

[5]See Ernest Jones, "On the Nightmare of Bloodsucking" in *Focus on the Horror Film*, 59.

associated with the imagination eternally triumph over smugly conventional rationalists who ignorantly deny the possible existence of walking mummies, stalking vampires, and bloodthirsty werewolves. The audience clearly sympathizes with those who realize the limits of reason, of convention, of security—for the adolescent's experiences with irrational desires, fears, urges which are incomprehensible yet clearly stronger than the barriers erected by reason or by society, are deeper and more painful than adults are likely to realize. Stubborn reason vainly struggles to deny the adolescent's most private experiences, mysterious and dynamic conflicts between normal and abnormal, good and evil, known and unknown.

Two of the most important features normally associated with monster movies are the closely related searches for the "secret of life" and "that which man was not meant to know." Monster movies unconsciously exploit the fact that most adolescents already know the "secret of life" which is, indeed, the "forbidden knowledge" of sex. The driving need to master the "forbidden knowledge" of "the secret of life," a need which seems to increase in importance as the wedding day approaches, is closely related to a major theme of monster movies: marriage. 9

For the adolescent audience the marriage which looms just beyond the last reel of the finer monster movies is much more than a mindless cliche wrap-up. As the monster's death necessarily precedes marriage and a happy ending, so the adolescent realizes that a kind of peace is to be obtained only with a second transformation. Only marriage can free Henry Frankenstein from his perverted compulsion for private experimentation on the human body; only marriage can save Mina Harker after her dalliance with the count. Only upon the death of adolescence, the mysterious madness which has possessed them, can they enter into a mature state where sexuality is tamed and sanctified by marriage.[6] The 10

---

[6]In "The Child and the Book," *Only Connect*, Sheila Egoff, ed., G.T. Stubbs, and L.F. Ashley (New York: Oxford UP, 1969) noted psychiatrist Anthony Storr has discussed a precursor of monster movies, fairy tales, in a similar context.

> Why is it that the stories which children enjoy are so often full of horror? We know that from the very beginning of life the child possesses an inner world of fantasy and the fantasies of the child mind are by no means the pretty stories with which the prolific Miss Blyton regales us. They are both richer and more primitive, and the driving forces behind them are those of sexuality and the aggressive urge to power: the forces which ultimately determine the emergence of the individual as a separate entity. For, in the long process of development, the child has two main tasks to perform if he is to reach maturity. He has to prove his strength, and he has to win a mate; and in order to do this he has to overcome the obstacles of his infantile dependency upon, and his infantile erotic attachment to, his parents....The typical fairy story ends with the winning of the princess just as the typical Victorian novel ends with the marriage. It is only at this point that adult sexuality begins...It is not surprising that fairy stories should be both erotic and violent, or that they should appeal so powerfully to children. For the archetyal themes with which they deal mirror the contents of the childish psyche; and the same unconscious source gives origin to both the fairy tale and the fantasy life of the child." (93–4)

marriage theme, and the complex interrelationship of various other formulaic elements, may perhaps be best approached through a close analysis of two seminal classics, *Frankenstein and Dracula*.

Two events dominate the movie *Frankenstein* (1931), creation of   11.
the monster and celebration of the marriage of Henry Frankenstein and his fiancee Elizabeth. The fact that the first endangers the second provides for most of the conflict throughout the movie, conflict much richer and more powerful, perhaps even profound, when the key thematic relationship between the two is made clear: creation of life. As Frankenstein's perverse nightly experiments on the monstrous body hidden beneath the sheets are centered on the creation of life, so is the marriage, as the old Baron twice makes clear in a toast (once immediately after the monster struggles out of the old mill and begins wandering toward an incredible meeting with Henry's fiancee Elizabeth; again, after the monster is destroyed, in the last speech of the film): "Here's to a son to the House of Frankenstein!"[7]

Frankenstein's fatuous father, whose naive declarations are fre-   12
quently frighteningly prescient (he predicts the dancing peasants will soon be fighting; on seeing a torch in the old mill he asks if Henry is trying to burn it down), declares, when hearing of the extent to which his son's experiments are taking precedence over his fiancee: "I understand perfectly well. Must be another woman. Pretty sort of experiments they must be." Later, after receiving the burgomaster's beaming report on the village's preparations for celebration of the marriage, he again associates his son's experiments with forbidden sexuality: "There is another woman. And I'm going to find her."

There is, of course, no other woman. The movie's horror is fun-   13
damentally based on the fact that the monster's life has come without benefit of a mother's womb. At one point Frankenstein madly and pointedly gloats over his solitary, specifically manual, achievements: "the brain of a dead man, ready to live again in a body I made with my hands, my own hands!"

Significantly, a troubled search for the "secret of life" is what   14
keeps Henry Frankenstein separated from his fiancee; it literally proves impossible for Henry to provide for "a son to the House of Frankenstein" before he has discovered the "secret of life." Having discovered the "secret of life," he ironically discovers that its embodiment is a frightening monster horrible enough to threaten "normal" relations between himself and Elizabeth. Henry's attempt to lock the monster deep in the mill's nether regions are finally thwarted, and, in a wholly irrational and dramatically inexplicable (yet psychologically

---

[7]The dialogue is followed by a close-up of a painfully embarrassed Henry Frankenstein.

apt and profound) scene, the monster—a grotesque embodiment of Frankenstein's newly discovered sexuality—begins to move threateningly toward the innocent bride who is bedecked in the purest of white, then quite as irrationally, it withdraws. On his return Henry promises his wildly distracted fiancee that there will be no wedding "while this horrible creation of mine is still alive."

The monster is, of course, finally, pitilessly, destroyed,[8] and   15
Henry is only ready for marriage when his own body is horribly battered and weakened, when he is transformed from the vigorous, courageous, inspired hero he represented early in the film to an enervated figure approaching the impotent fatuity of his father and grandfather (there is plenty of fine wine for the wedding feast, Frankenstein's grandmother would never allow grandfather to drink any), prepared to renounce abnormal life as potent as the monster in favor of creating a more normal "son to the House of Frankenstein."

The message is clear. In order to lead a normal, healthy life,   16
Henry Frankenstein must—and can—give up dangerous private experiments on the human body in dark rooms hidden away from family and friends. He must learn to deal safely and normally with the "secret of life," however revolting, however evil, however it might seem to frighten and actually threaten pure, virgin womanhood; only then, in the enervated bosom of normality, is it possible to marry and to produce an acceptable "son to the House of Frankenstein."

Dracula's much more mature approach to womankind is clearly   17
aimed at psyches which have overcome Henry Frankenstein's debilitating problem. *Dracula* (1931), obviously enough, is a seduction fantasy vitally concerned with the conditions and consequences of premarital indulgence in forbidden physical relations with attractive members of the opposite sex.

---

[8]Significantly, the monster himself is pitifully sympathetic, suffering as adolescents believe only they can suffer, from unattractive physical appearance, bodies they don't understand, repulsed attempts at love, general misunderstanding. Though endowed by his single antagonistic parent with a "criminal brain," the monster is clearly guilty of little but ugliness and ignorance, and is by any terms less culpable than the normal human beings surrounding him. He does not so much murder Fritz as attempt to defend himself against completely unwarranted torchings and beatings; he kills Dr. Valdeman only after that worthy believes he has "painlessly destroyed" the monster (a euphemism for murder), and as the doctor is preparing to dissect him; the homicide which propels his destruction, the drowning of the little girl, is certainly the result of clumsiness and ignorance. She had taught him to sail flowers on the lake and, flowers failing, in a visual metaphor worthy of an Elizabethan courtier, the monster in his ignorant joy had certainly meant only for the girl, the only being who had ever shown him not only love, but even affection, to sail on the lake as had the flowers. His joyful lurch toward her after having sailed his flower is, beyond all doubt, the most pathetic and poignant lurch in the history of film.

Of all the movie monsters Dracula seems to be the most attrac-   18
tive to women, and his appeal is not difficult to understand, for he embodies the chief characteristics of the standard Gothic hero: tall, dark,
handsome, titled, wealthy, cultured, attentive, mannered, with an air
of command, an aura of sin and secret suffering; perhaps most important of all he is invariably impeccably dressed. With such a seductive
and eligible male around it is certainly no wonder that somewhere in
the translation from fiction to film Dr. Seward has become Mina's father and thus leaves Lucy, who also lost the two other suitors Bram
Stoker allowed her, free to accept the Count's attentions. Certainly any
woman can sympathize with Lucy's swift infatuation ("Laugh all you
like, I think he's fascinating.") and Mina's easy acceptance of Dracula
as her friend's suitor ("Countess, I'll leave you to your count, and your
ruined abbey.").

Having left three wives behind in Transylvania, Dracula is obvi-   19
ously not one to be sated with his second English conquest (the first
was an innocent flower girl, ravaged immediately before he meets
Lucy and Mina), and he proceeds to seduce Mina, working a change in
her which does not go unnoticed, or unappreciated, by her innocent fiance: "Mina, you're so—like a changed girl. So wonderful—." Mina
agrees that indeed she is changed, and, on the romantic terrace, alone
with her fiance beneath the moon and stars, begins, one is certain, the
first physical aggression of their courtship. John is suitably impressed.
"I'm so glad to see you like this!" Discovered and exposed by Professor Van Helsing, Mina can only admit that (having had relations with
Dracula and thus become a Vamp) she has, indeed, suffered the
proverbial fate worse than death, and shamefully alerts her innocent,
naive fiance: "John, you must go away from me."

Only when John and his older, respected helpmate foil the horri-   20
ble mock elopement—Dracula and Mina are rushing to the abbey
preparing to "sleep," he even carries her limp body across the abbey's
threshold—only when the castrating stake destroys the seducer and
with him the maid's dishonor, is Mina free to return to the honest, innocent, suitor who will accept her past, marry her in the public light of
day, and make an honest woman of her.

Lucy, who has no selfless suitor to forgive her, marry her, and   21
make an honest woman of her, is much less successful. When last seen
she has become a child molester, a woman of the night who exchanges
chocolate for horrible initiations.

The thematic importance of such innocent victims turned monster   22
as Lucy and Mina, Dr. Frankenstein's creation, King Kong, the Wolfman
and others points directly to one of the most commonly observed and
perhaps least understood phenomena of monster movies, one which
has been repeatedly noted in this paper. In those classics which are best

loved and closest to true art the audience clearly identifies with the monster. Child, adult or adolescent, in disembodied sympathetic fascination, we all watch the first Karloff Frankenstein who stumbles with adolescent clumsiness, who suffers the savage misunderstanding and rejection of both society and the creator whose name he bears, and whose fumbling and innocent attempts at love with the little girl by the lakeside turn to terrible, bitter, and mysterious tragedy.

Clearly the monster offers the sexually confused adolescent a sympathetic, and at best a tragic, imitation of his life by representing a mysterious and irreversible change which forever isolates him from what he identifies as normality, security, and goodness, a change thrusting him into a world he does not understand, torturing him with desires he cannot satisfy or even admit, a world in which dark psychological and strange physical changes seem to conspire with society to destroy him.   23

Examining the Text

1. In his first footnote, Evans states his belief that "adolescents provide the bulk of the audience" for monster movies. Do you think this is so? Why, according to Evans, are adolescents especially drawn to monster movies? In what ways do movie monsters reflect adolescent problems and concerns? Do you find Evans's evidence convincing?

2. Evans wrote this essay in 1975, drawing all his examples from classic monster movies of the 1930s and 1940s: the Wolfman, Frankenstein, Dracula, the Mummy, King Kong. What do these have in common, and what do they represent for Evans? Is his thesis generally supported by more contemporary movie monsters—Jason, Freddy Krueger, Chuckie, and others? Or might they suggest some evolution in adolescent sexuality since the 1930's and 1940's?

3. One of Evans's main points is that in classic monster movies, which, he says "are best loved and the closest to true art, the audience clearly identifies with the monster" (paragraph 22). Do you agree? Does this hold true for contemporary movie monsters? Why or why not?

For Group Discussion

Taking into account Stephen King's ideas about the appeal of horror movies as well as Evans's connection of monster movies to adolescent sexuality, broaden your scope to include both classic and contemporary examples and then, as a group, explain why adolescents seem to be particularly attracted to monster/horror movies. Bring your own knowledge of such movies and first-hand experience and observation of adolescent behavior into the discussion. As a class, see if you can agree on a ranking of your reasons.

Writing Suggestion

Apply a psychological critical model to another genre of film with which you are familiar, such as futuristic action pictures, *Airplane-* or *Naked Gun*-style satires, menaced-female thrillers, bratty-kid comedies, *Rambo*-esque revenge stories, and so on. In an essay, account for the genre's popularity by discussing its specific appeals to an audience's basic emotional needs. Like Evans, you may want to focus on a specific audience with which your genre seems most popular.

Nightmare on Elm Street:
A Review and a Cultural Analysis

As Mark J. Schaefermeyer suggested in an essay earlier in this chapter, movie reviewing and film criticism are not the same thing. Film criticism, such as the pieces in this chapter by Walter Evans and Richard Dyer, generally appears in scholarly journals whose readers are primarily academics at universities, along with serious filmmakers. Movie reviews appear in popular magazines, newspapers, and broadcast media and are aimed at the general public with the purpose of entertaining people and letting them know whether they'd enjoy a movie. Popular periodicals also may offer articles that attempt to put movies in a social or cultural context.

The first of the following newspaper pieces is a review by Stephen Hunter of the Baltimore Sun *of* A Nightmare on Elm Street 5: The Dream Child, *which discusses its plot twists, set designs, and gory sequences in an amusing ironic way. As his central thesis, Hunter states, "I'm proud to report that as professional moviegoer of many years standing, I have no idea what was going on in the movie"—and he means this as a compliment. In the second article, Douglas Heuck of the* Pittsburgh Press *goes beyond a simple review of the* Nightmare on Elm Street *films to make some serious points about their influence on the broader popular culture: Freddy Krueger—the wise-cracking, child-murdering monster in these films—has become a cult figure, and several real crimes have been "inspired" by Krueger (although Heuck is careful to avoid suggesting that the* Nightmare on Elm Street *films "caused" these crimes).*

*Heuck's article leads necessarily to a question: Do contemporary pop cultural artifacts, especially those that receive wide media dissemination, influence people's behavior to the point that they will actually commit antisocial acts? **Before you read,** consider your own position with regard to this question. Do you believe, for example, that Jeffrey Dahmer was inspired to commit his gruesome mass murders because he saw too many* Nightmare on Elm Street *films, or do you believe he would have committed those crimes without Freddy's influence?*

Review of *Nightmare on Elm Street 5*

Stephen Hunter

It turns out that all along, all you've had to do to stop Freddy   1
Krueger, the razor-digited, pizza-complexioned, fedora-crowned madman of the "Nightmare on Elm Street" series, is what you do to any
bad boy. You tell his mother.

That's the gist of *A Nightmare on Elm Street 5: The Dream Child*,   2
which opened Friday on about a zillion screens. And gist is all you're
going to get out of me, friends. If the Freddies of the past have been
dense in their narrative lines, this one is so packed it's close to critical
mass. The plot may go nuclear at any second. I'm proud to report that
as a professional moviegoer of many years standing, I have no idea
what was going on in the movie.

That's by design, actually. What has propelled the "Elm Street"   3
movies and made them consistently the most watchable—the only
watchable—entrants in the various serial slaughterfests that seem to so
beguile American teen-agers has been their high level of visual ingenu-
ity, their willingness to punch through the membrane of the literal and
to take up space in the crazed precincts of the completely surrealistic.

"The Dream Child" certainly hews to the line. It's not a story so   4
much as a pageant, a dark tapestry of horrific—but always fascinating—murders. What the Freddy films have done is restored abstract
beauty to movie mayhem, rescuing it from the utter banality into
which it had fallen in such routine atrocities as the "Fridays the 13th"
and "Halloweens"—but at the expense of coherence. The set pieces in
the film are like murder videos.

As "The Dream Child" has it, Freddy (Robert Englund) is back   5
for still a fifth time to haunt the kids of Elm Street, this time selecting
the nubile Alice (Lisa Wilcox) as his main squeeze in that he continually uses her as bait to draw her friends closer so that he can dispatch
them in spectacular ways.

But at the same time, she's flashing back (somehow) to his past   6
and origins, and comes to realize that he's the son of a nun raped by a
thousand maniacs in an asylum one very long evening, and that the
nun may still be alive in the deserted ruins of the joint, which look
more or less like the Spanish city of Seville in the year 1456.

To everybody's perpetual confusion, it now seems that Freddy   7
can kill outside of dreams as well as in them; so you never know
whether you're in dreamland or on Elm Street or at some weird fusing
of both or neither. I don't even think the director, Stephen Hopkins,
knew; but I don't think he cared much, either.

What's left is operatic mayhem, much of it spectacular. The main   8
influence on director Hopkins appears to have been M. C. Escher, the
Dutch genius of geometrical paradox and oxymoron, for Hopkins' best
tricks are to warp perspective in mind-bending ways, creating a world
where gravity is the most treacherous illusion of all. In the best of the sequences, a teen-age boy who's a comic artist is somehow sucked into the
world of his own comic books, becomes a two-dimensional picture in
black and white, and is set upon and destroyed by a two-dimensional
Freddy. In another, a motorcycle becomes some poisoned nightbloom
that actually penetrates the body of its rider and becomes one with him.

As Alice's friends keep dying, she struggles to understand the   9
riddle, and then to enlist Mother Freddy in the quest to end Freddy
and the movie. I couldn't begin to make sense of the climax; it was like
watching an Italian opera directed by an evil 12-year-old genius who
had nothing but contempt for his audience and an unlimited budget.
But I'll tell you this: If this sucker pulled in more than $8 million this
weekend, he'll be ba-ack.

Freddy Krueger: Twisted Role Model?

Douglas Heuck

"FREDDY" DEBATE LIVES ON:
POP ICON OR TWISTED ROLE MODEL?

Long, long ago, in a place called Hollywood, a relatively un-   1
known actor named Robert Englund won a role in a low-budget
slasher film. To prepare for the role of bogyman Freddy Krueger, Englund came up with this vision of his character:

"Lee Harvey Oswald smoking a cigarette, saying 'Want some   2
candy, little girl?'" he told a reporter. "Freddy has a cocky, arrogant,
sexual way of moving."

From that image of distortion, who could have guessed that   3
Freddy would become the star of six movies, have his own TV show,
gross about $460 million, and—trick-or-treat—receive civic honors?

It all happened, though, even the last part. Los Angeles Mayor   4
Tom Bradley last month declared Freddy Krueger Day, an honor reserved for entities that "benefit the people of Los Angeles or deserve
praise," Bradley's press secretary said.

From mere script character to wisecracking child-murderer to   5
American cult hero—Freddy has come a long way.

There's the Freddy board game and Nintendo video game. There   6
have been two Freddy rap songs and a couple of Freddy books. And

Freddy T-shirts, mini caskets, buttons, towels, fedoras, sweaters, sheets—you name it.

And there is the 30-minute MTV special released last month, "Slash and Burn: The Freddy Krueger Story."   7

Including the last film, "Freddy's Dead, The Final Nightmare," which opened last month, the series has had such actors as Dick Cavett, Zsa Zsa Gabor, Johnny Depp and Roseanne Barr. And aside from having teen fans across the world, the dream stalker also included Malcolm Forbes among his admirers.   8

Many people think the whole fascination with a murdering madman is sick. Many others feel it's just harmless fun.   9

But now that the Sultan of Slash and his switchblade fingers are gone, killed off for good, we're told, in the final movie, what will be the legacy of Freddy?   10

Part of it will be clear when children throughout Western Pennsylvania set out for Halloween this week, wearing $14.99 Freddy knifegloves and $29.99 masks.   11

Other parts are a matter of debate. Although Freddy attacks through dreams and is clearly a fantasy character, some fans have committed real crimes since the first Freddy movie, "Nightmare on Elm Street" debuted: 12

- In 1989 in Pittsburgh, a fast-food worker with an obsession with Krueger stabbed and bludgeoned to death Dr. Jeffrey Farkas, a promising pediatric intern.
- In 1988, a 15-year-old North Carolina boy who was obsessed with Freddy was convicted for killing his father with multiple shotgun blasts. He was wearing a Freddy costume when he was arrested.
- In 1989, a 19-year-old man from San Pedro, Calif., who dressed up as Freddy while committing crimes was convicted of murder.
- The same year, an ax-wielding man in Cedar Rapids, Iowa, shouted he was Freddy Krueger and charged two police officers, who shot him.
- Also in 1989, a Virginia girl who said she loves what Freddy Krueger does attempted to strangle a 13-year-old boy. It was the third time she attempted to strangle small boys. She said it was fun.
- And finally, People magazine reported in August that alleged Milwaukee mass murderer Jeffrey Dahmer was "fascinated" by "Nightmare on Elm Street."

The effects of television and film violence are greatly debated. Groups like the National Coalition on Television Violence see a cause and effect relationship.   13

Others dispute that claim. Among them are Michael DeLuca, 26-year-old vice president for New Line Cinemas, which made Freddy.   14

"I think most of the people making those claims have either   15
never seen the Elm Street films, or they've seen them and not understood them," said DeLuca, who wrote the script for the final movie.

"None of the films are gratuitous in their depiction of violence.   16
Most of it is fantasy-oriented—you're in a dream universe."

DeLuca said he had never heard of cases where Freddy fans   17
committed crimes. When he was made aware of a few, though, he
said, "If it wasn't Freddy, they'd dress up as something else."

"It's much easier to blame a movie or TV show than to accept the   18
blame that through child abuse or whatever, parents created this creature. "

Research contradicts DeLuca, according to Dr. Joseph Strayhorn,   19
associate professor of child psychiatry at the Medical College of Pennsylvania and director of the early childhood clinic at Allegheny General Hospital.

"The research evidence is very convincing to me that there is a   20
cause and effect relationship between exposure to violence in the
media and actual violent behavior in human beings," said Strayhorn,
who is a member of NCTV.

Strayhorn called DeLuca's claim that there is no gratuitous vio-   21
lence in the "Nightmare on Elm Street" movies "absurd."

"The whole point of the movie is gratuitous violence, at least that   22
was it in the one I saw," he said.

"And lots of younger children see them. Once movies like this   23
are on videotapes, 2½-year-old children are very capable of running
videotape machines themselves. Once the video revolution occurred,
the concept of an 'intended audience' went out the window."

The issue is not as clear-cut for Larry Cohn, motion picture editor   24
at Variety magazine in New York.

"It's a tough question. I'm not a great believer in cause and effect   25
of this stuff. I do think popular culture is important, but more as a
backdrop, as an ether in which we live."

"People want to turn on TV and have that immediate gratifica-   26
tion of seeing someone's head blown off. That's a shame, but you can't
go back. That's sensationalism. People like that, and that's a problem."

Laying the blame at the feet of Freddy Krueger, however, ignores   27
his precursors, Cohn said.

Before the 1970s, horror movies were generally the domain of the   28
horror fan, said Cohn.

"But 15 years later, everybody's into it. Horror became in some   29
way embraced and acceptable in the same way that pornography is acceptable. Horror became in the mainstream," he said, citing such other
movies as "When a Stranger Calls," "Halloween" and "Friday the
13th."

By 1984, when the first "Nightmare on Elm Street" came out, the   30
horror boom was mostly over, and, as Cohn said, "since then only the
strong have survived. Freddy is the last survivor."

The reason Freddy survived was quality, according to Anthony   31
Timpone, editor of the horror magazine *Fangoria*. "It's the first horror
film in a long time to introduce a memorable horror figure. It's one of
the most original horror films, with the dreams and nightmares."

For whatever reason, Freddy is indisputably large in the line of   32
horror creatures.

"Traditionally, you had the literary horror figures, like Dracula   33
and Frankenstein," Cohn said. "Freddy is the closest to joining that
group in years, since, perhaps 'Psycho.'"

Freddy has been more successful than Jason of "Friday the 13th"   34
and Michael Meyers of "Halloween" because he's a more full-bodied
and personal character.

"And he's more sadistic because he's more personal," Cohn said.   35

"To me, the sadism is the key to all this. The whole idea of people   36
identifying with sadists is a new phenomenon. In earlier horror, people would identify with the woman. For instance, in 'The Phantom
of the Opera,' people—including myself—would identify with the
woman when he takes his mask off. This was the old way."

James Bond, Clint Eastwood and Charles Bronson were the three   37
main breakthrough figures in making sadism in the movies more acceptable, Cohn said, because the good guys were the sadists.

"Bond was the first acceptable sadistic character" because he   38
could kill someone, or at least beat up someone, and throw in a wise-
crack while doing it. Freddy also is a master of the one-liner.

"Freddy is the spiritual heir to that. And that's sadistic, making   39
fun of the killing. Freddy is the bad guy, but he's not if people idolize
him and make him into a cultural figure."

However, to Cohn, whether Freddy Krueger has become an icon   40
is not very significant.

"These movies are a product of planned obsolescence. Their pur-   41
pose is to be consumed and to get out of the way of the next one. The horror film is almost an endangered species now. It's burned itself out."

Beverly Hills–based script consultant and media psychiatrist Dr.   42
Carole Lieberman has a different view.

"It's a sorry commentary on the state of youth and young adults   43
in America that more of them know Freddy Krueger than some of the
presidents."

"The fact that we have raised a figure like Freddy Krueger to be-   44
come an icon of society and have that be reflected in his best-selling
Halloween costumes is an indication of how our society has come to
worship violence."

Dr. Lieberman said high school youths particularly like the films   45
because high school youths are the ones who get killed—especially the
more popular and attractive students.

"To dress up like Freddy Krueger makes them feel powerful, as   46
if they could destroy their objects of envy."

Dr. Lieberman believes more Freddy movies will be made.   47

"But even if they don't make anymore movies, he's not going to   48
disappear. There are always videotapes."

Just think of the blend: Nintendo, MTV, Roseanne Barr, rap   49
music, Malcolm Forbes, TV, the movies and Freddy Krueger—a distinctly American "Nightmare."

Examining the Text

1. Stephen Hunter suggests that *Nightmare on Elm Street 5: The Dream
Child* is virtually incomprehensible, but goes on to say that the "dense
narrative line" of the movie is a quality that sets the *Nightmare* movies
apart from other "serial slaughterfests" (paragraph 3). What is Hunter
praising about these movies? If you have seen any of them, do you
find his comments justified? If you haven't, does his review make you
want to? Why or why not?

2. Like any good reporter, Douglas Heuck balances his article by including different viewpoints regarding the relationship between violent films like *Nightmare on Elm Street* and actual crime in our society.
Identify each of these. Which do you find most convincing? Why?

3. Specifically, how do these two newspaper articles define the appeal
of Freddy Krueger? If you are familiar with the *Nightmare on Elm Street*
movies, or have friends or children who are fans—how would you explain the movies' appeal, and how do your ideas compare with
Hunter's and Heuck's?

For Group Discussion

Based on your reading of Stephen King, Walter Evans, and the two
previous articles and your own viewing experiences, work together to
develop a "treatment" for the first in a series of successful new hor-
ror/monster movies. Define the prime audience for the movie; devise
one or more monsters of villains and describe him/her/it/them in detail; create a cast of non-monster characters; decide on a setting; and
roughly outline a plot. Have a recorder present your "treatment" to the
rest of the class. Be prepared to justify your choices by discussing the assumptions you made about your movie's audience.

Writing Suggestion

Choose a new film that you have seen recently or that you can see soon, and write a newspaper-style article about it. You may review it as Hunter does *Nightmare on Elm Street* (focusing directly on the merits of the film itself you work to entertain and be witty as well as informative), or you may write a discursive article, like Heuck's, that focuses more broadly on responses to the film and its potential influences.

ADDITIONAL SUGGESTIONS
FOR WRITING ABOUT MOVIES

1. In an interpretative essay, compare and contrast several movies dealing with similar themes or issues. For instance, you might compare several films about the Vietnam War, or about the lives of the current generation of "Twentysomethings," or about inner-city gangs, or about parent-child relationships. Choose movies that interest you and, ideally, that you can see again. You might want to structure your essay as an argument aimed at convincing your readers that one movie is in some way "better" than the others. Or you might use your comparison of the movies to draw some larger point about popular culture and the images it presents to us.

2. In a research or "I-search" essay, consider the complex relationship between film and social morality. Do you think films can cause people to act in antisocial ways, as do some of the critics of *Nightmare on Elm Street*, as quoted by Douglas Heuck? What do other experts say? Can you find specific current events that support your arguments?

3. Based on your reading of the essays by Mark J. Schaefermeyer and Walter Evans, and other essays by academic film critics, evaluate this kind of intellectual criticism. In your own essay, use examples which, in your opinion, show such criticism to be valid and enlightening, illustrate when it is difficult to follow the criticism, and indicate when a critic has gone too far in imposing a particular theoretical framework on a film.

4. Just as Stephen King looks at "Why We Crave Horror Movies," in an essay of your own, explore why we crave another popular genre of movies: futuristic techno-thrillers, movies based on television sitcoms and cartoons, chase movies, menaced-female dramas, psychotic-killer stories, romantic comedies, supernatural comedies, and so forth. Choose a type of movie familiar to you so that you can offer as many specific examples as possible. In approaching this assignment, try to answer some of the same questions King does: What is the "fun" of seeing this type of movie? What sort of "psychic relief" does it deliver?

Are there specific types of people who are likely to enjoy the genre more than others? Does the genre serve any function for society? In what ways do movies in this genre affect *us*, changing *our* thoughts or feelings after we've seen them?

Internet Activities

1. These days, anyone with a Web site has the power to post a movie review. Choose several online reviews—written by both professional movie critics and "regular" moviegoers such as yourself—for a movie you've seen (some options are available on the *Common Culture* Web site). Write an essay in which you note the primary differences between the reviews done by professionals and those done by the regular fan(s). What aspects of the film do the professionals focus on? Are they the same as those of the regular fan or do they vary? Does one group emphasize certain elements, such as the emotions encouraged by the film, the acting, or the cinematography? Which of the reviews most closely reflects your opinion of the movie? Why do you think these reviews are the ones with which you best identify?

2. Vist a Web site for a new film you're interested in seeing and write a review of the site (some options are available on the *Common Culture* Web site). What is offered on the Web site that a potential audience wouldn't get from any other form of media? What do you like best about the Web site? What would you change? Describe the advantages of having a Web site for a new film. Are there any disadvantages? How do you feel movie Web sites will influence which movies we want to watch?

8

Leisure

Prehistoric humans spent only 40 percent of their waking hours on the necessities of life, such as food and shelter, according to anthropologists. That left 60 percent for "leisure" pursuits—napping, grooming, storytelling, painting pictograms on cave walls, and dreaming up the wheel, the knife, and, who knows, maybe the Veg-O-Matic. Despite the proliferation of "labor-saving" devices ranging from microwave ovens to drip-irrigation systems, modern humans seem to have less leisure time than their long-lost ancestors. Visions of a twenty-hour work week, a noble idea proposed by philosopher Bertrand Russell in the 1930s, have never come to pass. In fact, as the global and domestic economy sags, many people find themselves working fifty and sixty hours a week just to get by.

In this culture, our sense of identity and even self-worth is measured largely by the work that we do, rather than by what we do with our spare time. In fact, the very adjective "spare" suggests that any time left over from work is of lesser importance. Paradoxically, however, what we do in our spare time more often defines our personalities than what we do nine to five. Certainly for some people, their professional career is congruent with personal satisfaction, but for many, work is the way to pay the bills, while leisure is an opportunity to pursue activities that truly nurture them. Juliet Schor, in her essay "Exiting the Squirrel Cage," takes this argument a step further. Drawing a distinction between "unpaid work" and "true leisure," she argues that much of what we do in our "non-working" hours, mundane activities such as house cleaning and trimming our toenails, is actually work. Therefore, when we add this unpaid work time to forty-odd hours per week on the job, we're left with almost no "true leisure" time. Yet ironically, it is this tiny fraction of "true leisure" time that plays what some would argue is the most important role in defining us as unique individuals. As Witold Rybczynski suggests, our attitude toward leisure and our leisure pursuits also serve to define us as a culture.

With so little "true leisure," the pressure to have fun and fill that time with satisfying activities becomes greater. Our weekends should be filled with great parties, hot dates, productive creativity, and meaningful spiritual activity, or we feel as though we've failed in some way. Although we look forward to the parts of our lives away from work, the pressure to occupy free time with stimulating activity can actually become as oppressive as work itself. Walt Schafer, Professor of Sociology and Social Work at Chico State University in California, calls this sense of the burden of leisure "the lifestyle trap." When the stress of work flows over into non-working hours, then leisure becomes hectic, action-packed, and anything but relaxing.

The readings in the first section of this chapter consider leisure in general: what leisure is; why our free time has declined; whether the pressure to have fun on weekends actually makes our "off" hours more stressful than working hours; and what we can do to get more meaningful, satisfying leisure in our lives. In response to the latter, Schor makes several recommendations, such as getting off the "consumption track" by redefining our values so that making money becomes less important than cultivating our talents.

The second part of the chapter focuses on specific leisure pursuits, such as playing video games, visiting amusement parks, shopping, and risk-taking. These essays approach the phenomenon of leisure from different points of view. Sharon R. Sherman, for example, looks at video games from a folklorist's perspective, while Russell Nye analyzes amusement parks from several theoretical perspectives. Still, all the essays consider questions central to leisure activity in the modern world. Why, for example, do certain activities like rollerblading or bungee-jumping suddenly become appealing to the public en masse? What satisfactions do activities like these offer to participants? Finally, what do *your* leisure activities, whether passive, like sunbathing and watching television, or active, like zipping across sand dunes in an all-terrain vehicle and performing gravity-defying skateboard tricks, reveal about you as a person and, more broadly, about the unique and sometimes quirky preoccupations of modern Americans?

Theories of Leisure

The Cult of Busyness

Barbara Ehrenreich

In this essay from her collection The Worst Years of Our Lives *(1990),
Barbara Ehrenreich describes "the cult of conspicuous busyness" that she sees
around her, particularly among professional women on the road to success.
Ehrenreich, a well-known commentator on contemporary culture and author of
many books and articles (including another in Chapter 3), observes that "busyness has become an important insignia of upper-middle-class status." According to Ehrenreich, it is now fashionable to be too busy for leisure activities
whether hobbies, conversation with friends, or inner contemplation. Indeed, the
contemporary mass media's idea of success is embodied in the image of the high-
powered professional simultaneously reading the* Wall Street Journal, *closing
a deal via one cellular phone channel and instructing his or her broker on another, all the while driving an expensive car down a busy freeway.*

*The paradox, according to Ehrenreich, is that busyness doesn't neces-
sarily lead to happiness or success; in fact, "The secret of the truly successful . . .
is that they learned very early in life how* not *to be busy." Though her essay
focuses on busyness, Ehrenreich implicitly suggests that free time is more
crucial even than success. "If it is true that success leads to more busyness
and less time for worthwhile activities . . . then who needs it?" she asks.*

*Ehrenreich's essay introduces some crucial concepts that are explored
throughout this chapter: leisure, busyness, success, happiness, work, recreation.*

Before you read, *consider how these concepts are defined, in your own
life and in the lives of those around you.*

Not too long ago a former friend and soon-to-be acquaintance   1
called me up to tell me how busy she was. A major report, upon which
her professional future depended, was due in three days; her secretary
was on strike; her housekeeper had fallen into the hands of the Immigration Department; she had two hours to prepare a dinner party for
eight; and she was late for her time-management class. Stress was taking
its toll, she told me: her children resented the fact that she sometimes got
their names mixed up, and she had taken to abusing white wine.

All this put me at a distinct disadvantage, since the only thing I   2
was doing at the time was holding the phone with one hand and attempting to touch the opposite toe with the other hand, a pastime that

I had perfected during previous telephone monologues. Not that I'm not busy too: as I listened to her, I was on the alert for the moment the dryer would shut itself off and I would have to rush to fold the clothes before they settled into a mass of incorrigible wrinkles. But if I mentioned this little deadline of mine, she might think I wasn't busy enough to need a housekeeper, so I kept on patiently saying "Hmm" until she got to her parting line: "Look, this isn't a good time for me to talk, I've got to go now."

I don't know when the cult of conspicuous busyness began, but it has swept up almost all the upwardly mobile, professional women I know. Already, it is getting hard to recall the days when, for example "Let's have lunch" meant something other than "I've got more important things to do than talk to you right now." There was even a time when people used to get together without the excuse of needing something to eat—when, in fact, it was considered rude to talk with your mouth full. In the old days, hardly anybody had an appointment book, and when people wanted to know what the day held in store for them, they consulted a horoscope.

It's not only women, of course; for both sexes, busyness has become an important insignia of upper-middle-class status. Nobody, these days, admits to having a hobby, although two or more careers—say, neurosurgery and an art dealership—is not uncommon, and I am sure we will soon be hearing more about the tribulations of the four-paycheck couple. Even those who can manage only one occupation at a time would be embarrassed to be caught doing only one *thing* at a time. Those young men who jog with their headsets on are not, as you might innocently guess, rocking out, but are absorbing the principles of international finance law or a lecture on one-minute management. Even eating, I read recently, is giving way to "grazing"—the conscious ingestion of unidentified foods while drafting a legal brief, cajoling a client on the phone, and, in ambitious cases, doing calf-toning exercises under the desk.

But for women, there's more at stake than conforming to another upscale standard. If you want to attract men, for example, it no longer helps to be a bimbo with time on your hands. Upscale young men seem to go for the kind of woman who plays with a full deck of credit cards, who won't cry when she's knocked to the ground while trying to board the six o'clock Eastern shuttle, and whose schedule doesn't allow for a sexual encounter lasting more than twelve minutes. Then there is the economic reality: any woman who doesn't want to wind up a case study in the feminization of poverty has to be successful at something more demanding than fingernail maintenance or come-hither looks. Hence all the bustle, my busy friends would explain—they want to succeed.

But if success is the goal, it seems clear to me that the fast track is   6
headed the wrong way. Think of the people who are genuinely successful—path-breaking scientists, best-selling novelists, and designers of
major new software. They are not, on the whole, the kind of people who
keep glancing shiftily at their watches or making small lists entitled "To
Do." On the contrary, many of these people appear to be in a daze, like
the distinguished professor I once had who, in the middle of a lecture on
electron spin, became so fascinated by the dispersion properties of chalk
dust that he could not go on. These truly successful people are childlike,
easily distractable, fey sorts, whose usual demeanor resembles that of a
recently fed hobo on a warm summer evening.

The secret of the truly successful, I believe, is that they learned very   7
early in life how *not* to be busy. They saw through that adage, repeated
to me so often in childhood, that anything worth doing is worth doing
well. The truth is, many things are worth doing only in the most
slovenly, halfhearted fashion possible, and many other things are not
worth doing at all. Balancing a checkbook, for example. For some reason, in our culture, this dreary exercise is regarded as the supreme test
of personal maturity, business acumen, and the ability to cope with
math anxiety. Yet it is a form of busyness which is exceeded in futility
only by going to the additional trouble of computerizing one's checking
account—and that, in turn, is only slightly less silly than taking the time
to discuss, with anyone, what brand of personal computer one owns, or
is thinking of buying, or has heard of others using.

If the truly successful manage never to be busy, it is also true that   8
many of the busiest people will never be successful. I know this first-
hand from my experience, many years ago, as a waitress. Any executive
who thinks the ultimate in busyness consists of having two important
phone calls on hold and a major deadline in twenty minutes, should try
facing six tablefuls of clients simultaneously demanding that you give
them their checks, fresh coffee, a baby seat, and a warm, spontaneous
smile. Even when she's not busy, a waitress has to look busy—refilling
the salt shakers and polishing all the chrome in sight—but the only reward is the minimum wage and any change that gets left on the tables.
Much the same is true of other high-stress jobs, like working as a telephone operator, or doing data entry on one of the new machines that
monitors your speed as you work: "success" means surviving the shift.

Although busyness does not lead to success, I am willing to be-   9
lieve that success—especially when visited on the unprepared—can
cause busyness. Anyone who has invented a better mousetrap, or the
contemporary equivalent, can expect to be harassed by strangers demanding that you read their unpublished manuscripts or undergo the
humiliation of public speaking, usually on remote Midwestern campuses. But if it is true that success leads to more busyness and less time
for worthwhile activities—like talking (and listening) to friends, read-

ing novels, or putting in some volunteer time for a good cause—then who needs it? It would be sad to have come so far—or at least to have run so hard—only to lose each other.

Examining the Text

1. Why do you think Ehrenreich begins with the anecdote about the friend who calls to say she's too busy to talk? Do you think the story is true? What do you think of this as an opening strategy?

2. What does the term "cult" imply? Why do you think Ehrenreich refers to the obsession with busyness as a "cult" (paragraph 3)? Is this a valid characterization?

3. In paragraph 8, Ehrenreich says that "many of the busiest people will never be successful." Who, according to her, are the "busiest" people, and how are they different from the participants in the "cult" of busyness? What is Ehrenreich suggesting in making this distinction?

For Group Discussion

Ehrenreich focuses on professional people in the working world. How well do her ideas apply to college students? Is there a similar "cult of conspicuous busyness" among any of your fellow students? Is busyness ever a status symbol or is the opposite more often the case? As a group, determine what most students think about the kind of busyness Ehrenreich describes. Then as a class discuss some reasons underlying the students' attitudes.

Writing Suggestion

At the end of the essay, Ehrenreich lists some activities that are more "worthwhile" than busyness. What are the differences between these activities and the "busyness" that Ehrenreich criticizes? In an essay consider your own daily activities in terms of Ehrenreich's definitions. How many of these are "worthwhile" in her sense, how many may seen as part of your own "cult of busyness," and how many are simply "surviving the shift" (8)?

Exercising the Brain

Jim Spring

The following essay offers an interesting twist on Ehrenreich's notion of the "cult of busyness." Jim Spring proposes that people aren't actually as busy as they claim to be, or rather, that the things that keep them busy are more often passive, "No-Brainer" activities than active, challenging leisure pursuits.

Spring's results are based on surveys conducted by Leisure Trends, a firm which gathers information about the leisure habits of Americans and provides it to businesses seeking customers. Thus, the purpose of this essay (which originally appeared in American Demographics*) is to offer companies advice about consumer attitudes and behaviors. However, we can also read Spring's essay as a fairly objective report on American leisure activities, and, perhaps, see ourselves reflected in the observation that "most Americans normally end up doing the things that are easiest to do and not necessarily the things they claim to enjoy the most." For instance, as Spring points out, people who say they are skiers may actually opt to spend most of their free time watching TV or reading.*

Before you read, *think of three or four activities that you say you enjoy most and ask yourself how often in the past several months you have actually done them. If your answer is a few times or not at all, what has kept you from pursuing them? How have you actually spent most of your leisure time?*

Norma Puzzle invited Charlie to a concert a month away, and Charlie said he "really wanted to go." Norma considered it a date. But when she showed up to take him, Charlie wasn't home. "Just because I said I wanted to go didn't mean we had a date," he said later. "I want to do lots of things I never do." 1

Norma wasn't happy. Aside from the costly tickets, she believed he had made a commitment. But Charlie is a typical American, according to Leisure Trends' surveys of leisure activities. Most Americans normally end up doing the things that are easiest to do and not necessarily the things they claim to enjoy the most. The result is a wide gap between the number of people who say they enjoy an activity and the much smaller number who actually do the activity regularly. 2

To understand this phenomenon, it helps to separate leisure activities into three categories; No-Brainers, Brainers, and Puzzlers. No-Brainer activities are habitual, easy to do, require a low level of decision-making, have few entry barriers, and tend to entertain. Watching television is the best example of a No-Brainer. 3

Brainer activities are less habitual, may involve other people, are more complex because they require some interaction with a person or thing, and have moderate logistical barriers. Hobbies, movie-going, and socializing at home or on the telephone are good examples of Brainers. 4

Puzzlers tend to break away from habits entirely and include the most difficult activities. The barriers to entry are higher, and the decision-making process is more complex. Puzzlers inspire questions 5 such as "Do I really like Amy?" or "Can I afford it?" Most sports activities, parties, going to the theater, or taking a weekend in the country are examples of Puzzlers. These activities involve thinking and taking inventory. To do them, people must make complex decisions. Before a party for example, many people wrestle with the following puzzler: "Do I have the right clothes, or should I go shopping first?"

NO-BRAINERS AND PUZZLERS

The difference between what people say and what they do shows   6
up clearly in eight activities that fall into the three categories described above. This article compares what people aged 16 or older did the previous day with what they say they "enjoy doing the most."

It's no surprise that the most frequent activity reported is the ul-   7
timate No-Brainer—watching television. It is simple and can be done alone. While it eats up lots of time and 77 percent of respondents did it the day before the survey, only 14 percent say they enjoy it the most.

Television viewing is such a perfect No-Brainer that many peo-   8
ple don't remember doing it at all. When asked the open-ended question, "What did you do yesterday in your leisure time?" just 31 percent of respondents spontaneously mention television. We uncovered that 77 percent of the total population actually watched television only by asking this followup question: "Did you watch television yesterday?" In this context, the small proportion of Americans who admit that television is their favorite activity starts to look suspicious. Perhaps we don't want to admit we enjoy what is offered on the tube. Or perhaps people don't count the time they spend reading, cooking, or conversing while one eye is on the television. But in any case, the gap between watching, enjoyment, and memorability is so great as to suggest that TV is a low-key form of fun.

Brainer activities such as socializing and going to the movies are   9
done less frequently than No-Brainers. But people claim to enjoy them more, so the gap between saying and doing for Brainers is smaller than for No-Brainers. Shopping for fun and do-it-yourself activities are different. People say they like these activities, and they participate in them frequently. It seems they are sufficiently motivated to overcome the barriers in getting to the store and buying materials. At the other extreme are Puzzler activities, such as fishing. People claim to enjoy them greatly, but don't do them very often.

Attitude clearly does not always predict behavior, and the data   10
offer evidence that most Americans operate on both levels. We are a combination of what we do and what we think, and the two do not necessarily go together. Which form of consumer information best pre-

dicts participation or consumption will depend on the product or service being consumed.

Behavioral data are more dependable, because past and present   11
behavior is often the best indicator of future behavior. Yet attitudinal
data can indicate new opportunities. Marketers whose products and
services fall into the No-Brainer category know that people don't need
a great deal of encouragement to participate in them, and that those
who do it today will probably do it tomorrow. They can concentrate
on broadening their market by enhancing existing products and finding new niches.

For example, snack foods are often consumed during No-Brainer   12
activities such as watching television. Mass media advertising is appropriate for these products. On the other hand, businesses with links
to Brainer or Puzzler activities may have to resort to stronger inducements. For activities people say they enjoy but don't do often, marketers can offer incentives such as discount coupons to movies or free
transportation to ski areas.

COAXING ARMCHAIR ATHLETES

The problem with predicting participation in Puzzler and   13
Brainer activities is the large difference between expectation and reality. In a two-part study for the alpine ski industry, we measured the
differences between people's intentions to ski and their actual behavior. Over a span of three years, we discovered that in any given year,
as few as 65 percent of self-defined skiers actually go skiing.

Many people who consider themselves skiers have not skied at   14
all in the last four to five years. One self-proclaimed skier had not
skied since 1947! Yet virtually all self-defined skiers who had not skied
in the last several years say they plan to ski again.

Here is a strong positive attitude that defies the facts. Anyone who   15
estimates a market's potential based on intention in this sport will be in
for a rude shock. If you're selling a skiing magazine, attitude is as important as behavior. But if you're selling lift tickets, you need a real skier.

Skiing qualifies as a true Puzzler activity because it involves spe-   16
cial equipment, can be quite costly, depends on the weather, and requires special locations and physical skill. Fishing falls into the same
category for most of the same reasons. The rule of thumb is that the
more difficult something is, the more important behavioral data are in
measuring trends in participation.

On the other hand, attitudinal information provides clues about   17
potential markets, because changes in attitudes can signal a potential
change in behavior. To understand how attitudes may predict behavior,
it is important to understand why people don't do things. People often

cite a lack of time or money as the reasons they don't pursue a Puzzler activity. For some, however, excuses disguise the true reason, which is a lack of brain power or energy. People find plenty of time for No-Brainer activities, perhaps because they provide low-energy relaxation. After a long day at work or with the kids, many people don't want to keep co-ordinating and planning. To the time-pressured adult, thinking about a weekend at a local ski area may seem like too much work.

Some people who say they enjoy an activity like skiing are perpet-   18
ual "wannabes." Even given the chance, they will not hit the slopes. But others who say they would enjoy doing something really mean it. To en-courage these people, businesses that sell Brainer and Puzzler activities should make it easy for people to translate their positive attitude into be-havior. Family ski packages that include bus transportation, rental equipment, lift tickets, and lessons for the children could persuade even weary souls to brave the slopes. For those whose biggest barrier is cost, something as simple as a free trial lift ticket could change a positive atti-tude into long-term purchasing behavior.

EACH SPORT IS DIFFERENT

Changes in attitudes and behavior do not always run parallel to   19
each other, so it is important to track both of them. A comparison of atti-tudes in 1990 and 1992 shows that interest in reading has increased, for example, while interest in watching television and socializing has de-clined slightly. A look at behavior shows that reading and socializing have increased—but that television viewing has not changed much.

Demographic trends in leisure can be surprising. Reading may   20
be a highly intellectual activity, for example. Yet this study classifies it as a No-Brainer because it is easy to do anywhere and is almost always done alone. More women than men read, and more women consider it their favorite leisure activity. Reported reading is increasing sharply among 16-to-24-year-olds and those aged 45 and older. The attitude of 25-to-34-year-olds toward reading is increasingly positive, but their behavior has not changed much. Adults aged 35 to 44 are showing a decrease in interest in reading, but are reading slightly more.

Movies in theaters, which fall into the Brainer category, are be-   21
coming more appealing to men, according to the 1990 and 1992 sur-veys. Men are also watching them more often. Americans under age 35 went to more movies in 1992 than they did in 1990, and a greater share considered them a favorite activity.

Do-it-yourself activities are Puzzlers with a twist. In particular,   22
women are more likely to participate in do-it-yourself activities than to say they enjoy them. But as the share of female do-it-yourselfers rises, so does their enjoyment level. Perhaps practice does make perfect, as

tasks done repeatedly become easier and more fun. It may also be that people are discovering that do-it-yourself activities are stress reducers. Baking bread and other activities were once necessities, but now they are usually done as a way to relax.

Another way to find clues about future trends in leisure behavior   23
is to study the attitudes of people who have just begun a new activity. In the 1990 interviews, the proportion of people who said they had gardened, camped, hiked, or backpacked for the first time had increased noticeably over 1988. Two years later, the share of regular participants in these activities had increased. Similarly, changes in attitudes often precede changes in behavior. The share of people who enjoy doing home improvement and yard work grew between 1988 and 1990, and the share who do these things grew between 1990 and 1992.

What's the leisure forecast for the 1990s? The surveys show that   24
people may be doing more shopping for fun, traveling, walking for exercise, and outside recreational activities such as camping, hiking, and alpine skiing. Organized religion also seems poised for a comeback, and interest in working on the home and yard continues to grow.

It is worth noting that all upward trends in attitudes fall into the   25
Puzzler category. Aging baby boomers may be less willing to spend time on passive activities, but only time will tell if they are ready for more challenging leisure. By the way, Norma left Charlie's house and stopped by Lance's house on the way to the concert, and he agreed to go with her. Two months later, they got married. Now they have a small Puzzle to ponder, and they don't go to concerts anymore.

Examining the Text

1. What are the differences between No-Brainer, Brainer, and Puzzler activities? Which favorite activities do you have in each of these categories? Based on the likelihood of your participating in each of these favorites, do Spring's observations hold true?

2. According to Spring, what is the relationship between what people say they do during their leisure time and what they actually do? From your own experience, do you think Spring's finding, are correct?

3. How does the purpose of Spring's article—to inform leisure-related businesses on how to attract customers—influence your response to his ideas?

For Group Discussion

Imagine that your group is asked to promote a specific Puzzler activity, such as mountain-biking, wine-tasting, or doing volunteer work. After choosing an activity, use Spring's article for ideas on how to best structure your promotional campaign and the incentives you could offer to get people to participate. Once you've developed your campaign, discuss the specific strategies with the rest of your class.

Writing Suggestion

Using the pattern of the Leisure Trends research, informally survey twenty people you know. Ask them about their leisure activities of the day before and what their three favorite leisure activities are. You might also follow up about specific interests not mentioned and about time that has elapsed since they participated in a favorite activity, In an essay, describe how your informal research corresponds to the Leisure Trends' findings.

Exiting the Squirrel Cage

Juliet Schor

The following essay considers ways to increase the quantity and quality of our leisure time. Taken from her The Overworked American, *a 1991 study of work and leisure in contemporary American culture, this essay by Juliet Schor argues for "a right to free time" that we need to protect actively for our own sake and for our families and our culture in general. For Schor, the problem of decreasing duration and quality of leisure time begins with the capitalist equation, time equals money. As she says, "The more time substitutes for money, the more difficult it is to establish an independent measure of time's value." Thus the more likely we are to spend our time in pursuit of money, even when we already have more than enough to live comfortably.*

Schor suggests how both employers and employees can make a number of changes to increase time for relaxation, contemplation, conversation, family outings, hobbies, and volunteer activities. Once we regain leisure hours, Schor advises, we'll need to learn (or relearn) how to spend those hours wisely: "If we veer too much toward work, our 'leisure skills' will atrophy."

Before you read, consider your own attitudes toward work and leisure. Schor argues that psychological (as well as social and economic) changes will be required if we are to take full advantage of leisure. What sorts of changes do you think you personally would need to make to enjoy your free time more fully?

It is often said that an economist is a person who knows the price   1
of everything and the value of nothing. On the question of time, we
may all have become economists. We are keenly aware of the price of

time—the extra income earned with a second job, the wage and a half for an hour of overtime. In the process, we may have forgotten the real worth of time.

The origins of modem time consciousness lie in the development 2 of a capitalist economy. Precapitalist Europe was largely "timeless" or, in historian Jacques Le Goff's words, "free of haste and careless of exactitude." As capitalism raised the "price" of time, people began to think of time as a scarce resource. Indeed, the ideology of the emerging market economy was filled with metaphors of time: saving time, using time wisely, admonitions against "passing" time. The work ethic itself was in some sense a time ethic. When Benjamin Franklin preached that time is money, he meant that time should be used productively. Eventually capitalism did more than make time valuable. Time and money began to substitute for each other. Franklin's aphorism took on new meaning, not only as prescription, but as an actual description. Money buys time, and time buys money. *Time itself had become a commoditiy.*

Moneylending was the first example of the sale of time, its nature 3 revealed in the colloquial "to buy on time." Then the sale of time developed in the labor market, and became, for most people, the area where the impact has been greatest. Today the principle of sale of labor time is thoroughly accepted. But this is the result of a long and contentious process. As the British historian Edward Thompson has argued, workers struggled at first from a traditional ideology of "timelessness" against the very idea of time. They resented employers' attempts to impose time and time discipline. As decades passed, they struggled over the ownership of time—how much was theirs, how much the boss's. And today, many fight for *over*time—the right to sell as much time as they can.

The unencumbered sale of time for money is now a reigning value, 4 its legitimacy so entrenched that it is no longer fully voluntary: most employees can be forced to put in overtime. The monetary equivalence to time has expanded far beyond the labor market. Patients have begun to charge doctors when they are kept waiting. The government pays jurors for each day they spend in court. The legal value of a human life is based on the future sale of working time. Every hour has a price.

The virtues of the sale of time and the equation of time and money 5 are well known: putting a price tag on each hour allows a person (or a society) to use time efficiently. But there are also vices, which are less well recognized. Many aspects of the value of time are difficult to incorporate into a purely market exchange—such as the effects of individuals' use of time on the quality of social life, or the concept of a basic human right to free time. Every society has a culture of time. Has ours perhaps gone too far in the direction of collapsing time into money?

The more time substitutes for money, the more difficult it is to es- 6 tablish an *independent* measure of time's value. And our diminishing ability to make this judgment contributes to long hours. If the market recognizes only the measure of money, then arguing that a job requires "too many hours" makes no sense: it is tantamount to saying that it pays "too much money." The inflated working hours of the Wall Street financier or the corporate lawyer are a fair trade for their inflated salaries. If low-wage employees in the nursing home industry have two full-time jobs, it is because they value money over time. In a culture where time is merely money, we risk perverse effects such as occurred after 1938 with legislation to regulate overtime. This policy was designed to install a forty-hour week, but its disincentive to companies (time and a half) turned into a powerful incentive for workers to work as many hours as they could. In the end, the legislation contracted both leisure and employment, the two things it was designed to expand.

Where time is money, it's hard to protect time for those who— 7 such as low-wage workers, children, aged parents, or community organizations—can't pay for it. And it's hard to protect time for ourselves, for relaxation, hobbies, or sleep. The pressures toward long working hours have become too powerful. But common sense tells us that working hours *can* be too long. Excessive hours are unhealthy and antisocial, and ultimately erode the quality of life.

The commensurability of time and money has other detrimental 8 social effects. It transforms a resource that is equally distributed (time) into one that is distinctly unequal (money). Both wealth and income are unequally distributed. But everyone is born with twenty-four hours in a day. And while money does skew the distribution of time to some extent (higher-income people live longer), "ownership" of time is still far more equally allocated. The sale of time undermines its egalitarianism. As time outside work becomes more precious, those with money can economize on it. And this appears to be happening. Fast-track careerists are hiring people to cook their meals, watch their children, even wait in line for them. Small companies have sprouted up, offering services from grocery shopping to changing light bulbs. The people whose time is being sold are those less economically well situated—as happened earlier, of course, in the nineteenth century when the growth of the middle class spawned a huge demand for servants. Today's scarcity of time puts us in jeopardy of producing a new servant class and undermining the egalitarianism of time.

Establishing a right to free time may sound utopian—but the 9 principle of limiting exchange has already been established. It is not legal to sell oneself into slavery. It is not legal to sell one's vote. It is not legal to sell children. Even the principle of limiting the exchange of time is well established. The state has regulated working hours since the colonial period. The right to free time has been legislated in some forms, such as legal holidays. Most important of all is the Social Security system, which assumes that workers have a right to leisure for a period at the end of their lives. What I am arguing for is the extension of this right—so that everyone can enjoy free time while they are still young and throughout their lives....

OVERCOMING CONSUMERISM

Economic feasibility is an important condition for gaining leisure. So is breaking the automatic translation of productivity into income. But for many Americans escaping the trap of overwork will also entail stepping off the consumer treadmill, which requires altering a way of life and a way of thinking. The transformation must be not only economic and social but cultural and psychological.   10

The first step is practical—to put oneself in a financial position where a fixed or smaller income is sufficient. For example, one California environmental planner spent three years preparing to cut back his work hours. He had to "grind down the charge cards," pay off his car and convince his partner that life with less money would be okay: "There are two ways to get through. You either have to make the money which will buy you the kind of life that you think you have to have or you can change those expectations and you don't need the money anymore. And that's what I've done."   11

Being able to change expectations depends on understanding the psychological and cultural functions that material goods fulfill. They can be the means to an identity or a way to create self-esteem. Things fill up empty spaces in our lives. Many couples concentrate on owning a house or filling it with nice furnishings, when what they really crave is an emotional construction—home. Some women turn to fashion to create a fantasy self that compensates for what they are consciously or unconsciously missing. Materialism can even be an altruistic vice. Men pursue the pot of gold to give it to their wives or children—to provide the "best that life can offer" or "what I never had." But in the process everyone is cheated: "I thought I was doing the right thing, making money at work all the time. But I was never home." Realization often comes too late: "Now that I'm older, I can see ... what I was missing."   12

Involuntary reductions in income caused by a company shutdown or an inability to work can be painful, often devastating. But those who willingly reject the quest for affluence can find themselves perfectly satisfied. One public employee, currently on a four-fifths schedule, swears that only a financial disaster could get her back to full-time: "The extra twenty percent just isn't worth it." Even at the California company where employees were forced to take a ten-percent reduction in pay and hours, reactions were positive: only 22 percent of the workforce rated the program negatively, and half were positive about it.   13

For many, opting out of the rat race has transformed their lives: 14
"In the last four years, I went from upper middle class to poor, but I
am a lot richer than most people, and I'm happier too." A divorced father raising three young children rejected the long hours, high-income
route. He's at home with his children in the evenings, and has learned
that "less is more." A career woman gave up her job, and along with it
designer clothes, hair and nail appointments, lunching out and a second car: "I adopted a whole new set of values and put aside pride,
envy, competitiveness and the need for recognition."

THE VALUE OF LEISURE TIME

Some people are skeptical of Americans' need for leisure time.   15
Work may be bad, but perhaps leisure isn't all it's cracked up to be either. According to economist Gary Burtless, "Most Americans who
complain they enjoy too little leisure are struggling to find a few extra
minutes to watch Oprah Winfrey and 'L.A. Law.'" Will free time be
"wasted," in front of the tube or at the mall? What will we do with all
that leisure? Won't people just acquire second jobs? These are serious
questions, embodying two main assumptions. The first is that people
prefer work or, if they don't, they should. The second is that leisure
time is wasted time that is neither valued nor valuable.

One possibility is that work is irrepressible. The Akron rubber   16
workers immediately come to mind. After they won the six-hour day,
many of the men who worked at Firestone started driving cabs, cutting
hair, and selling insurance. While no one knows exactly what percentage of the workers took on extra jobs, during the 1950s it was thought to
be between one in five and one in seven. Some observers concluded
from this experience that American workers do not want, or cannot handle, leisure time. If they are right, so be it. My aim is not to force leisure
on an unwilling population but to provide the possibility of a real
choice. If the chance to work shorter hours—when fairly presented—is
not appealing, then people will not take it. But before we take the Akron
experience as definitive, let's ask a few more questions.

Why did so many take a second job? The male rubber workers   17
were reasonably well paid by the blue-collar standards of the day, and
many of their wives worked. They did not labor out of sheer economic
necessity. I suspect that their behavior was dictated more by a cultural
imperative...that says that men with leisure are lazy. It is significant
that women rubber workers did not seek a second paycheck.

Today there are signs that this cultural imperative is becoming   18
less compelling. Perhaps most important is the transformation of sex
roles. Women have taken up responsibility for breadwinning. And
men are more at home around the house. Increasing numbers of fa-

thers want to parent. In a recent poll of men between the ages of eighteen and twenty-four, nearly half said they would like to stay home and raise their children. The ethos of "male sacrifice" is disappearing: a declining portion of the population believes that being a "real man" entails self-denial and being the family provider.

The traditional work ethic is also undergoing transformation. 19
Commitment to hard work retains its grip on the American psyche. But young people are moving away from "the frenzied work ethic of the 1980s to more traditional values." In addition, ideas of what work is, and what it is for are being altered. The late 1960s and 1970s witnessed the rise of what some have called "post-materialist values"—desires for personal fulfillment, self-expression, and meaning. Throughout the industrialized world, a culture shift occurred as young people especially began demanding satisfying work. Although there was a burst of old-style materialism during the 1980s, it did not permanently dislodge what now looks more and more like a long-term trend. People are expecting more from work than a paycheck and more from life than what 1950s culture offered.

People *will* work on their time off. They will work hard and long in 20
what is formally designated as leisure time. But where the Akron example leads us astray is the quest for the second paycheck. Americans need time for unpaid work, for work they call their own. They need the time to give to others. Much of what will be done was the regular routine in the days when married women were full-time housewives. And it is largely caring work—caring for children, caring for sick relatives and friends, caring for the house. Today many haven't got the time to care. If we could carve the time out from our jobs, we could prevent the current squeeze on caring labor. And this time around, the men should share the load. The likelihood is good that unpaid work would occupy a significant fraction of any "leisure" gained in the market. At the California company that gave its employees two days off a month, nearly as much time was devoted to household and volunteer work as to leisure itself. Predictably, women did more of this labor. But times are changing.

Other productive activities would take up uncommitted time as 21
well. Many people would like to devote more time to their churches, get involved in their children's schools, coach a sports team, or help out at a soup kitchen. But the time squeeze has taken a toll on volunteer activities, which have fallen considerably since the rise in hours began. Time out of work would also be used for schooling. Education remains a primary factor in economic success. And continual training and retraining are projected to be increasingly important in the economy of the twenty-first century, as job skills become obsolete more rapidly. A survey at two large Boston corporations found that over 20 percent of full-time employees were also enrolled in school.

The unpaid work—at home and in the community—that will fill   22
free time is vital to us as individuals and as a society—as should be
clear from the mounting social problems attendant upon its decline.
Still, if we were to gain free time only to fill it up again with work, the
battle will be only half won. There is also a pressing need for more
true leisure. For the first time in fifteen years, people have cited leisure
time as the "more important" thing in their lives than work. The nation needs to slow down, unwind, and recover from its ordeal of labor.
But can we handle leisure time?

The skeptics, who cite heavy television viewing or excessive   23
shopping, have a point. It may be, however, that work itself has been
eroding the ability to benefit from leisure time. Perhaps people are just
too tired after work to engage in active leisure. Evidence from the
Gallup Poll suggests this may be the case. Today, the most popular
ways to spend an evening are all low-energy choices: television, resting, relaxing, and reading. Although it certainly isn't proof, it is suggestive that the globe's only other rich, industrialized country with
longer hours than the United States—namely, Japan—is also the only
nation to watch more television.

The issue goes beyond the physical capacity to use free time. It   24
is also true that the ability to use leisure is not a "natural" talent, but
one that must be cultivated. If we veer too much toward work, our
"leisure skills" will atrophy. At the extremes are workaholics like
Sheila Mohammed. After sixteen-hour days—two full-time shifts—as
a drug rehabilitation counselor, Sheila finds herself adrift outside the
job: "I'm so used to...working and then when I have the time off,
what do I do, where do I go?" But even those with moderate working
habits are subject to a milder version of this syndrome. Many potentially satisfying leisure activities are off limits because they take too
much time: participating in community theater, seriously taking up a
sport or a musical instrument, getting involved with a church or community organization. In the leisure time available to us, there's less of
interest to do. To derive the full benefits of free time, we just may need
more of it.

A final impediment to using leisure is the growing connection   25
between free time and spending money. Private corporations have
dominated the leisure "market," encouraging us to think of free time
as a consumption opportunity. Vacations, hobbies, popular entertainment, eating out, and shopping itself are all costly forms of leisure.
How many of us, if asked to describe an ideal weekend, would choose
activities that cost nothing? How resourceful are we about doing
things without spending money? A successful movement to enhance
free time will have to address this dynamic head-on. Governments
and communities will need to subsidize more affordable leisure activi-

ties, from the arts to parks to adult education. We need a conscious effort to reverse "the commodification of leisure."

Whatever the potential problems associated with increasing   26
leisure time, I do not think they are insurmountable. A significant reduction in working hours will by itself alleviate some of the difficulties. And if we can take positive steps to enhance the value of leisure time, we will be well rewarded. The experience of the Kellogg workers calls for optimism: "The visitor sees…a lot of gardening and community beautification…athletics and hobbies were booming…libraries well patronized…and the mental background of these fortunate workers…becoming richer."

Examining the Text

1. What is Schor's basic point about the relationship between time and money? (Note, by the way, the pervasiveness of the metaphor that "time is money": we "spend" time, "save" time, "waste" time, and so forth.) How and why has the development of a capitalist economy influenced this relationship, according to Schor? What does she mean by "the real worth of time" (paragraph 1)?

2. Schor argues that equating time and money has several negative social effects. List them. Which do you think are the most serious and detrimental to society? Do you think Schor exaggerates any of these effects?

3. What is a "cultural imperative"? How does this concept explain why workers might take on a second job? Do you accept Schor's contention that this imperative is becoming "less compelling"?

4. What social and personal benefits does Schor argue would come from decreasing work time and increasing leisure time? Which benefits do you think are the most important?

For Group Discussion

Schor refers to "the rise of what some have called 'post-materialistic values'—desires for personal fulfillment, self-expression, and meaning" (19). Which values do you think are most prevalent in contemporary society, "materialist" or "post-materialist"? As a group, debate this question briefly, and then consider whether there is a difference in the way the mass media depicts contemporary values and the way people you know actually live their lives.

Writing Suggestion

Those who are critical of creating a greater amount of leisure time say that people will just spend it watching television, shopping, and taking part in other "No-Brainer" activities, to use Spring's term. However Schor counters that people would use the opportunity to pursue activities that are currently "off limits because they take too much time" (24). Considering yourself and people you know, which view do you think is closer to the truth?

The Problem of Leisure

Witold Rybczynski

Virtually all of us recognize the saying "TGIF." "Thank God It's Friday" means the weekend approaches, releasing us from our weekday schedules of work and school. We look forward to sleeping late, catching up on chores, socializing with family and friends, enjoying our favorite recreational activities.

But as Witold Rybczynski points out in the following chapter from his book Waiting for the Weekend *(1991), weekends present us with the interesting, sometimes anxiety-provoking question of how best to fill our free time. In his words, "The freedom to do something has become the obligation to do something....[and] the obligation to do it* well"—*to excel at whatever we take on. "For many," he says, "weekend free time has become not a chance to escape work but a chance to create work that is more meaningful," "leisure work" that offers personal satisfaction no longer found in the workplace.*

The "problem of leisure" is compounded by the decline of free time in a culture filled with fax machines, pagers, cellular phones, and portable computers that mean the work day no longer ends once we leave the office. Women may be in the workforce in record numbers but are still responsible for most housework. Economic conditions force many of us to trade leisure time for money, to work overtime or take on a second job to make ends meet. Leisure hours decrease, weekends shrink, and our decisions about how to spend our "free time" become ever more problematic: "We want leisure, but we are afraid of it too."

One of Rybczynski's interesting points is that one person's leisure activity may be a burden or even a form of work for another. Consider your own favorite leisure activities. Would everyone take pleasure in these activities? Can you think of things other people do for enjoyment that are simply chores from your perspective?

***

In 1919 the Hungarian psychiatrist Sándor Ferenczi published a   1
short paper entitled "Sunday Neuroses." He recounted that in his medical practice he had encountered several neurotics whose symptoms recurred on a regular basis. Although it's common for a repressed memory to return at the same time of year as the original

experience, the symptoms he described appeared every week. Even more novel, they appeared most frequently on one day: Sunday. Having eliminated possible physical factors associated with Sunday, such as sleeping in, special holiday foods, and overeating, he decided that his patients' hysterical symptoms were caused by the holiday character of the day. This hypothesis seemed to be borne out by one particular case, that of a Jewish boy whose symptoms appeared on Friday evening, the commencement of the Sabbath. Ferenczi speculated that the headaches and vomiting of these holiday neurotics were a reaction to the freedom that the weekly day of rest offered. Since Sunday allowed all sorts of relaxed behavior (noisy family games, playful picnics, casual dress), Ferenczi reasoned that people who were neurotically disposed might feel uncomfortable "venting their holiday wantonness," either because they had dangerous impulses to control or because they felt guilty about letting go their inhibitions.

Ferenczi described the Sunday holiday as a day when "we are our own masters and feel ourselves free from all the fetters that the duties and compulsions of circumstances impose on us; there occurs in us— parallel with this—a kind of inner liberation also." Although "Sunday neurosis" was a clinical term, the concept of a liberation of repressed instincts coupled with a greater availability of free time raised the menacing image of a whole society running amok. Throughout the 1920s there were dozens of articles and books of a more general nature, published by psychiatrists, psychologists, and social scientists in both Europe and America, on the perils of what was often called the New Leisure. There was a widespread feeling that the working class would not really know what to do with all this extra free time.

The underlying theme was an old one: less work meant more leisure, more leisure led to idleness, and idle hands, as everyone knew, were ripe for Satan's mischief. This was precisely the argument advanced by the supporters of Prohibition, who maintained that shorter hours provided workers with more free time which they would only squander on drink. Whatever the merits of this argument—and undoubtedly drinking was popular—one senses that this and other such "concerns" really masked an unwillingness to accept the personal freedom that was implicit in leisure. The pessimism of social reformers— and many intellectuals—about the abilities of ordinary people to amuse themselves has always been profound, and never more so than when popular amusements do not accord with established notions of what constitutes a good time.

In *Work Without End*, Benjamin K. Hunnicutt describes how such thinking had an important effect on reinforcing employers' opposition to the Saturday holiday in pre-Depression America. The shorter workday had eventually, and often reluctantly, been accepted by management; one reason was that studies had shown how production increased when workers had longer daily breaks and were less tired. The same did not apply, however, to the weekend. "Having Saturdays off," Hunnicutt observes, "was seen to offer the worker leisure—the opportunity to become increasingly free from the job to do other things." And if these "other things" were not good for him, then it was only proper that he should be kept in the workplace, and out of trouble.

The Depression saw this paternalistic resistance set aside, or at least modified. Although both employers and Roosevelt's administration opposed the thirty-hour week (which effectively meant a two- or three-day weekend) proposed by labor as a work-sharing measure, the Thirty-Hour Bill was passed by Congress in 1933. The law had a two-year trial period, and was watered down by the National Industrial Recovery Act, but the pressure for some sort of work sharing was too great to ignore. Many industries adopted a shorter day and reduced the length of the workweek from six days to five. 5

There were different views as to what people should do with this newfound freedom. Some economists hoped the extra free time would spur consumption of leisure goods and stimulate the stagnant economy. Middle-class social reformers saw an opportunity for a program of national physical and intellectual self-improvement. That was the message of a book called *A Guide to Civilized Loafing*, written by H. A. Overstreet in 1934. Despite the title, which in later editions was changed to the more seemly *A Guide to Civilized Leisure*, the author's view was that free time was an opportunity, and the book described a daunting array of free-time activities, from amateur drama to volunteer work. Overstreet was prescient in some of his recommendations, like bicycling and hiking, although other of his enthusiasms—playing the gong, for example—have yet to catch on. If his suggestions for "loafing" seem at times obsessive, it is because there were now so many free hours to fill. Overstreet, like earlier reformers, had a narrow idea of leisure—he neglected, for example, to list two favorite American pastimes, hunting and fishing, and, despite the repeal of Prohibition, he did not mention social drinking. 6

The two goals of filling leisure time—one economic and one cultural—appeared to many to be incompatible. Walter Lippmann's 1930 article in *Woman's Home Companion* entitled "Free Time and Extra Money" articulated "the problem of leisure." He warned that leisure offered the individual difficult choices, choices for which a work-oriented society such as America had not prepared him.[1] Lippman 7

---

[1]More than a quarter century later, in *The Human Condition,* Hannah Arendt echoed this view: "What we are confronted with is the prospect of a society of laborers without labor, that is, without the only activity left to them. Surely, nothing could be worse."

was concerned that if people didn't make creative use of their free time, it would be squandered on mass entertainments and commercial amusements. His view spawned many books and articles of popular sociology with titles such as *The Challenge of Leisure, The Threat of Leisure,* and even *The Menace of Leisure.*

Much of this concern was based on the widespread assumption   8
that the amount of available free time was greater than ever, and that the "problem of leisure" was without precedent. Before the Depression, an American working a forty-hour week spent less than half his 5,840 waking hours each year on the job—the rest was free time. By comparison, a hundred years earlier, work had accounted for as much as two thirds of one's waking hours. But as Hannah Arendt observed, this reduction is misleading, since the modern period was inevitably measured against the Industrial Revolution, which represented an all-time low as far as the number of working hours was concerned. A comparison with earlier periods of history leads to a different conclusion. The fourth-century Roman, for example, with 175 annual public holidays, spent fewer than a third of his waking hours at work; in medieval Europe, religious festivals reduced the work year to well below the modern level of two thousand hours. Indeed, until the eighteenth century, Europeans and Americans enjoyed *more* free time than they do today. The American worker of the 1930s was just catching up.

Most critics however, preferred to look to the future. What they   9
saw was further mechanization, as well as technological innovations such as automation, which promised continued gains in efficiency and productivity in the workplace. "The old world of oppressive toil is passing, and we enter now upon new freedom for ourselves...in an age of plenty, we can look forward to an increasing amount of time that is our own." Overstreet wrote this the year after the Thirty-Hour Bill was passed, and to him, as to many others, it appeared that the shortening of the working day was a trend that would continue for some time. "It would be a rash prophet who denies the possibility that this generation may live to see a two-hour day," wrote another observer.

How wrong they turned out to be. Working hours bottomed out   10
during the Depression, and then started to rise again. Job creation, not work sharing, became the goal of the New Deal. By 1938 the Thirty-Hour Bill had expired and the Fair Labor Standards Act provided for a workweek of not thirty but forty hours. As Hunnicutt observes, this marked the end of a century-long trend. On the strength of the evidence of the last fifty years, it would appear that the trend has not only stopped but reversed. In 1948, thirteen percent of Americans with full-time jobs worked more than forty-nine hours a week; by 1979 the figure had crept up to eighteen percent. Ten years later, the Bureau of Labor Statistics estimated that of 88 million Americans with full-time jobs, fully twenty-four percent worked more than forty-nine hours a week.

Ask anyone how long they spend at work and they can tell you ex-   11
actly; it is more difficult to keep track of leisure. For one thing, it is irregular; for another, it varies from person to person. For some, cutting the
lawn is a burden; for others it is a pleasurable pastime. Going to the mall
can be a casual Saturday outing, or it can be a chore. Most would count
watching television as leisure, but what about Sunday brunch? Sometimes the same activity—walking the dog—can be a pleasure, sometimes not, depending on the weather. Finally, whether an activity is part
of our leisure depends as much on our frame of mind as anything else.

Surveys of leisure habits often show diverging results. Two re-   12
cent surveys, by the University of Maryland and by Michigan's Survey
Research Center, both suggest that most Americans enjoy about thirty-
nine hours of leisure time weekly. On the other hand, a 1988 survey
conducted by the National Research Center of the Arts came to a very
different conclusion and found that "Americans report a median 16.6
hours of leisure time each week." The truth is probably somewhere in
between.

Less surprising, given the number of people working more than   13
forty-nine hours a week, was the National Research Center's conclusion that most Americans have suffered a decline in weekly leisure
time of 9.6 hours over the last fifteen years. The nineteenth-century ac-
tivists who struggled so hard for a shorter workweek and more free
time would have been taken aback by this statistic—what had happened to the "Eight Hours for What We Will"?

There are undoubtedly people who work longer hours out of per-   14
sonal ambition, to escape problems at home, or from compulsion. The
term "workaholic" (a postwar Americanism) is recent, but addiction to
work is not—Thomas Jefferson, for example, was a compulsive worker,
as was G. K. Chesterton—and there is no evidence that there are more
such people today than in the past. Of course, for many, longer hours are
not voluntary—they are obliged to work more merely to make ends
meet. This has been particularly true since the 1970s, when poverty in
America began to increase, but since the shrinking of leisure time began
during the prosperous 1960s, economic need isn't the only explanation.

Twenty years ago Staffan Linder, a Swedish sociologist, wrote a   15
book about the paradox of increasing affluence and decreasing leisure
time in the United States. Following in Lippmann's steps, Linder observed that in a prosperous consumer society there was a conflict between the market's promotion of luxury goods and the individual's
leisure time. When work hours were first shortened, there were few
luxury items available to the general public, and the extra free time
was generally devoted to leisure. With the growth of the so-called
"leisure industry," people were offered a choice: more free time or
more spending? Only the wealthy could have both. If the average person wanted to indulge in expensive recreations such as skiing or sail-

ing, or to buy expensive entertainment devices, it would be necessary to work more—to trade his or her free time for overtime or a second job. Whether because of the effectiveness of advertising or from simple acquisitiveness, most people chose spending over more free time.

Linder's thesis was that economic growth caused an increasing   16
scarcity of time, and that statistics showing an increase in personal incomes were not necessarily a sign of growing prosperity. People were earning more because they were working more. A large percentage of free time was being converted into what he called "consumption time," and mirrored a shift from "time-intensive" to "goods-intensive" leisure. According to *U.S. News & World Report*, Americans now spend more than \$13 billion annually on sports clothing; put another way, about 1.3 billion hours of potential leisure time are exchanged for leisure wear—for increasingly elaborate running shoes, certified hiking shorts, and monogrammed warm-up suits. In 1989, to pay for these indulgences, more workers than ever before—6.2 percent—held a second, part-time job; in factories, overtime work increased to an average of four hours a week, the highest number in nearly twenty years.

Probably the most dramatic change is the large-scale entry of   17
women into the labor force. In 1950 only thirty percent of American women worked outside the home, and this primarily out of economic necessity. Beginning in the 1960s middle-class women, dissatisfied with their suburban isolation and willing to trade at least some of their leisure time for purchasing power, started to look for paid employment. By 1986 more than half of all adult women—including married women with children—worked outside the home. Nor are these trends slowing down; between 1980 and 1988, the number of families with two or more wage earners rose from 19 to 21 million.

"Working outside the home" is the correct way to describe the   18
situation, for housework (three or four hours a day) still needs to be done. Whether it is shared, or, more commonly, falls on the shoulders of women as part of their "second shift," leisure time for one or both partners is drastically reduced. Moreover, homes are larger than at any time in the postwar period, and bigger houses also mean more time spent in cleaning, upkeep, and repairs.[2]

Even if one chooses to consume less and stay at home, there are   19
other things that cut into free time. Commuting to and from work takes longer than it used to. So does shopping—the weekly trip to the mall consumes more time than a stroll to the neighborhood corner store. De-

---

[2]The average size of a new American home in the 1950s was less than 1,000 square feet; by 1983 it had increased to 1,710 square feet, and in 1986 had expanded another 115 square feet.

centralized suburban life, which is to say American life, is based on the automobile. Parents become chauffeurs, ferrying their children back and forth to dance classes, hockey games, and the community pool. At home, telephone answering machines have to be played back, the household budget entered into the personal computer, the lawn mower dropped off at the repair shop, the car—or cars—serviced. All these convenient labor-saving devices relentlessly eat into our discretionary time. For many executives, administrators, and managers, the reduction of leisure time is also the result of office technology that brings work to the home. Fax machines, paging devices, and portable computers mean that taking work home at night is no longer difficult or voluntary. Even the contemplative quiet of the morning automobile commute is now disrupted by the presence of the cellular telephone.

There is no contradiction between the surveys that indicate a reversing trend, resulting in less free time, and the claim that the weekend dominates our leisure. Longer work hours and more overtime cut mainly into weekday leisure. So do longer commuting, driving the kids, and Friday-night shopping. The weekend—or what's left of it, after Saturday household chores—is when we have time to relax.   20

But the weekend has imposed a rigid schedule on our free time, which can result in a sense of urgency ("soon it will be Monday") that is at odds with relaxation. The weekly rush to the cottage is hardly leisurely, nor is the compression of various recreational activities into the two-day break. The freedom to do something has become the obligation to do something, just as Chesterton foretold, and the list of dutiful recreations includes strenuous disciplines intended for self-improvement (fitness exercises, jogging, bicycling), competitive sports (tennis, golf), and skill-testing pastimes (sailing, skiing).   21

Recreations such as tennis or sailing are hardly new, but before the arrival of the weekend, for most people, they were chiefly seasonal activities. Once a year, when vacation time came around, tennis racquets were removed from the back of the cupboard, swimwear was taken out of mothballs, skis were dusted off. The accent was less on technique than on having a good time. It was like playing Scrabble at the summer cottage: no one remembers all the rules, but everyone can still enjoy the game. Now the availability of free time every weekend has changed this casual attitude. The very frequency of weekend recreations allows continual participation and continual improvement, which encourage the development of proficiency and skill.   22

Skill is necessary since difficulty characterizes modern recreations. Many nineteenth-century amusements, such as rowing, were not particularly involved and required little instruction; mastering windsurfing, on the other hand, takes considerable practice and dexterity—which is   23 part of the attraction. Even relatively simple games are complicated by the need to excel. Hence the emphasis on professionalism, which is expressed by the need to have the proper equipment and the correct costume (especially the right shoes). The desire for mastery isn't limited to outdoor recreations; it also includes complicated hobbies such as woodworking, electronics, and automobile restoration. All this suggests that the modern weekend is characterized by not only the sense of obligation to do something but the obligation to do it *well*.

The desire to do something well, whether it is sailing a boat—or   24
building a boat—reflects a need that was previously met in the workplace. Competence was shown on the job—holidays were for messing around. Nowadays the situation is reversed. Technology has removed craft from most occupations. This is true in assembly-line jobs, where almost no training or experience, hence no skill, is required, as well as in most service positions (store clerks, fast-food attendants) where the only talent required is to learn how to smile and say "have a good day." But it's also increasingly true in such skill-dependent work as house construction, where the majority of parts come ready-made from the factory and the carpenter merely assembles them, or automobile repair, which consists largely in replacing one throwaway part with another. Nor is the reduction of skills limited to manual work. Memory, once the prerequisite skill of the white-collar worker, has been rendered superfluous by computers; teachers, who once needed dramatic skills, now depend on mechanical aids such as slide projectors and video machines; in politics, oratory has been killed by the thirty-second sound bite.

Hence an unexpected development in the history of leisure. For   25
many, weekend-free time has become not a chance to escape work but a chance to create work that is more meaningful—to work at recreation—in order to realize the personal satisfactions that the workplace no longer offers.

"Leisure" is the most misunderstood word in our vocabulary. We   26
often use the words "recreation" and "leisure" interchangeably—recreation room, rest and recreation, leisure suit, leisure industry—but they really embody two different ideas. Recreation carries with it a sense of necessity and purpose. However pleasurable this antidote to work may be, it's a form of active employment, engaged in with a specific end in mind—a refreshment of the spirit, or the body, or both. Implicit in this idea of renewal—usually organized renewal—is the notion that recreation is both a consequence of work and a preparation for more of it.

Leisure is different. That was what Lippmann was getting at when   27
he contrasted commercial recreation with individual leisure. Leisure is not tied to work the way that recreation is—leisure is self-contained. The root of the word is the Latin *licere*, which means "to be permitted," suggesting that leisure is about freedom. But freedom for what? According

to Chesterton's cheerful view, leisure was above all an opportunity to do nothing. When he said "doing nothing," however, he was describing not emptiness but an occasion for reflection and contemplation, a chance to look inward rather than outward. A chance to tend one's garden, as Voltaire put it. That is why Chesterton called this kind of leisure "the most precious, the most consoling, the most pure and holy."

Bertrand Russell placed leisure into a larger historical context in   28
his essay "In Praise of Idleness." "Leisure is essential to civilization," he wrote, "and in former times leisure for the few was only rendered possible by the labours of the many. But their labours were valuable, not because work is good, but because leisure is good." Russell, a member of the aristocracy, pointed out that it had been precisely the leisure classes, not the laborers, who had written the books, invented the philosophies, produced the sciences, and cultivated the arts. But he was not arguing for a continuation of the class system; on the contrary, he proposed extending the leisure that had previously been reserved for the few to the many. This was an explicit attack on the work ethic, which he considered a device to trick people into accepting a life without leisure. In his view, the trick hadn't succeeded; working men and women had no illusions about work—they understood it was merely a necessary means to a livelihood.

Russell's underlying argument was that we should free ourselves   29
from the guilt about leisure that modern society has imposed on us. Hence the use of terms such as "idleness" and "doing nothing," which were intended as a provocation to a society that placed the highest value on "keeping busy." Both Russell and Chesterton agreed with Aristotle, who considered leisure the aim of life. "We work," he wrote, "to have leisure."

"In Praise of Idleness" was written in 1932, at the height of the   30
Depression, and Russell's proposal of a four-hour workday now appears hopelessly utopian. But the weekend's later and sudden new popularity in so many societies suggests that leisure is beginning to make a comeback, although not as fully as Russell desired, nor in so relaxed a way as Chesterton would have wished. I cannot shake the suspicion that something more than mere functionality accounts for the widespread popularity of the weekend. Can its universal appeal be explained by a resonance with some ancient inclination, buried deep in the human psyche? Given the mythological roots of the planetary week, and the devotional nature of Sunday and the Sabbath, the answer is likely to be found in early religious attitudes.

Mircea Eliade, a historian of religion, characterized traditional   31
premodern societies as experiencing the world in two distinct ways corresponding to two discontinuous modes of being: the sacred and the profane. According to Eliade, the sacred manifested itself in vari-

ous ways—how physical space was perceived, for example. The profane, chaotic world, full of menace, was given structure and purpose by the existence of fixed, meaningful sacred places. Sacred places could occur in the landscape, beside holy trees or on certain mountains, but they could also be man-made. Hence the elaborate rituals practiced by all ancient people when they founded settlements and erected buildings, rituals not only to protect the future town or building but to delineate a sacred space.

The prime sacred space was the home, for houses were not merely shelters but consecrated places that incorporated cosmic symbolism into their very construction. The Navajo Indians, for example, affirmed that their homes—hogans—were based on a divine prototype. The conical shape of the hogan resembled a mountain in New Mexico that the Navajo called "the heart of the Earth." They believed that God had created the first forked-stick hogan using posts made of white shell, turquoise, abalone, and obsidian. When a new hogan was built, pieces of these four minerals were buried beneath the four main posts, which also corresponded to the four points of the compass. In this way the builder interrupted the continuity of the everyday world by creating a separate magical space.

A person stepping out of the desert sun into the dark, cool interior of a hogan was entering a space that was a part of the ancient past, and thus he was entering not only a sacred space but a sacred time. According to Eliade, profane time was ordinary temporal duration, but sacred time, which was also the time of festivals and holy days, was primordial and mythical, and stood apart from everyday life. During sacred time, the clock not only stopped, it was turned back. The purpose of religious rites was precisely to reintegrate this past into the present. In this way, sacred time became part of a separate, repetitive continuum, "an eternal mythical present."

Eliade characterized modern Western society as "nonreligious," in the sense that it had desacralized and demythologized the world. For nonreligious man there could be only profane space and profane time. But, he pointed out, since the roots of this society lay in a religious past, it could never divest itself completely of ancient beliefs; remnants of these remained, although in camouflaged form: for example, movies employing mythical motifs, such as the struggle between hero and monster, descent into an underworld, or the cleansing ordeal. Even in our homes, which no longer incorporate cosmic symbolism in the comprehensive way of the Navajo hogan, rituals have not altogether disappeared. Giving a housewarming party, carrying the bride over the threshold, receiving important guests at the front door instead of at the back door, decorating the exterior at festal times of year—these are all reminders that although we treat our houses as commodities, the home is still a special space, standing apart from the practical world.

Is it fanciful to propose that the repetitive cycle of week and   35
weekend is a modern paraphrase of the ancient opposition of profane
and sacred time? Obviously the weekend is not a historical remnant in
any literal sense, since it didn't even exist until the nineteenth century,
and its emergence was in response to specific social and economic conditions. Nor am I suggesting that the secular weekend is a substitute
for religious festivals, although it is obviously linked to religious ob-
servance. But there are several striking parallels.

Weekday time, like profane time, is linear. It represents an irre-   36
versible progression of days, Monday to Friday, year after year. Past
weekday time is lost time. Schooldays are followed by workdays, the
first job by the second and the third. I can never be a schoolboy again,
or a college student, or a young architect anxiously waiting to meet
my first client.[3] Not only is weekday time linear, but, like profane
time, it encompasses the unpredictable. During the week, unforeseen
things happen. People get promoted and fired. Stock markets soar or
crash. Politicians are elected or voted out of office. One has the impression that history occurs on weekdays.[4]

The weekend, on the other hand, is, in Plato's words, a time to   37
take a breather. It's a time apart from the world of mundane problems
and mundane concerns, from the world of making a living. On weekends time stands still, and not only because we take off our watches.
Just as holidays at the beach are an opportunity to re-create our childhood, to build sand castles with the kids, to paddle in the surf, to lie on
the sand and get a sunburn, many of the things we do on weekends
correspond to the things we did on weekends past. Weekend time
shares this sense of reenactment with sacred time, and just as sacred
time was characterized by ritual, the weekend, despite being an opportunity for personal freedom, is governed by convention: raking
leaves, grilling steaks on the barbecue, going to the movies, Saturday
night out, reading the Sunday paper, brunch, the afternoon opera
broadcast, weekend drives, garage sales, weekend visits. The pre-
dictability of the weekend is one of its comforts.

Although Eliade described examples of sacred time from differ-   38
ent societies and periods of history, the specific rites and rituals varied. An event could be holy in one culture and have no meaning in
another; a festival could be a taboo time because the day was consid-

---

[3]Several years ago I attended a high-school class reunion, which could be described as
an attempt to recover weekday time. Revealingly, the subject of conversation was sports
and extracurricular activities, not what we had done in the classroom.

[4]The notable exception is war, which often begins on the weekend, when it is least expected. The German blitzkrieg of 1940 was launched on a Saturday morning; the Japanese attack on Pearl Harbor occurred on a Sunday; the Egyptians started the Yom Kippur
War on the Sabbath.

ered unlucky, while elsewhere it was observed for exactly the opposite reason. The myths of their sacred histories differentiated societies.

The conventions of weekend leisure, too, vary from place to place. In Europe, for example, northerners read more books than southerners, Germans and Danes spend more than others on musical instruments, the British are the greatest gamblers, the Italians the greatest moviegoers, and every one favors tennis except the French. Canada and the United States, which have many similarities, differ in their attitude to leisure, and surveys have consistently shown that Americans believe more strongly in the work ethic than Canadians do. Probably for that reason, Canadians give personal leisure a higher importance and have been much slower to accept commercial intrusions such as Sunday shopping.

39

The differences in national attitudes toward leisure are arresting because we live in a world where the character of work is increasingly international. Around the world, in different countries, what happens between nine and five during the week is becoming standardized. Because of international competition and transnational ownership of companies, the transfer of technology from one country to another is almost instantaneous. All offices contain the same telephones, photocopiers, word processors, computers, and fax machines. The Japanese build automobile plants in the United States and Canada, the Americans build factories in Eastern Europe, the Europeans in South America. Industries are increasingly dominated by a diminishing number of extremely large and similar corporations. The reorganization of the workplace in Communist and formerly Communist countries, along more capitalist lines, is one more step in the standardization of work. And as work becomes more standardized, and international, one can expect that leisure, by contrast, will be even more national, more regional, more different.

40

Leisure has always been partly a refuge from labor. The weekend, too, is a retreat from work, but in a different way: a retreat from the abstract and the universal to the local and the particular. In that sense, leisure is likely to continue to be, as Pieper claimed, the basis of culture. Every culture chooses a different structure for its work and leisure, and in doing so it makes a profound statement about itself. It invents, adapts, and recombines old models, hence the long list of leisure days: public festivals, family celebrations, market days, taboo days, evil days, holy days, feasts, Saint Mondays and Saint Tuesdays, commemorative holidays, summer vacations—and weekends.

41

The weekend is our own contribution, another way of dealing with the ancient duality. The institution of the weekend reflects the many unresolved contradictions in modern attitudes toward leisure. We want to have our cake, and eat it too. We want the freedom to be leisurely, but we want it regularly, every week, like clockwork. The at-

42

traction of Saint Monday was that one could "go fishing" when one willed; the regularity of the weekend—every five days—is at odds with the ideas of personal freedom and spontaneity. There is something mechanical about this oscillation, which creates a sense of obligation that interferes with leisure. Like sacred time, the weekend is comfortingly repetitive, but the conventionality of weekend free time, which must exist side by side with private pastimes and idiosyncratic hobbies, often appears restrictive. "What did you do on the weekend?" "The usual," we answer, mixing dismay with relief.

We have invented the weekend, but the dark cloud of old taboos   43
still hangs over the holiday, and the combination of the secular with the holy leaves us uneasy. This tension only compounds the guilt that many of us continue to feel about not working, and leads to the nagging feeling that our free time should be used for some purpose higher than having fun. We want leisure, but we are afraid of it too.

Do we work to have leisure, or the other way around? Unsure   44
of the answer, we have decided to keep the two separate. If C. P. Snow had not already used the term in another context, it would be tempting to speak of Two Cultures. We pass weekly from one to the other—from the mundane, communal, increasingly impersonal, increasingly demanding, increasingly bureaucratic world of work to the reflective, private, controllable, consoling world of leisure. The weekend; our own, and not our own, it is what we wait for all week long.

Examining the Text

1. What is a "Sunday neurosis" (paragraphs 1–2)? Have you ever suffered any of its symptoms? Why does Rybczynski begin by describing this "clinical term"?

2. In paragraphs 2–10 and 26–29 Rybczynski traces early twentieth-century theorizing about leisure time. Why was leisure the subject of so much speculation during these years? For example, why was Walter Lippmann concerned that "free time...would be squandered on mass entertainments and commercial amusements" (7)? What does Rybczynski's survey of these ideas contribute to his own argument about the tension we feel about the weekend?

3. Rybczynski uses historian Mircea Eliade's notion of sacred and profane time to characterize the difference between weekends and weekdays (31–38). Summarize what Rybczynski names as the characteristics of weekdays that make them "profane" and the characteristics of weekends that make them "sacred." Do you find his analyses persuasive? What can you add to this discussion?

4. Rybczynski's central point is that "We want leisure, but we are afraid of it, too" (43). What reasons does he offer for our fear of leisure? Does he convince you?

For Group Discussion

Reread paragraphs 11–13. Determine how many hours a week you spend on leisure activities and what those activities are. Compare your results with other members of your group. Are there interesting divergences in the estimated amounts of leisure time; that is, do some group members suggest they have much less free time than others? If so, discuss the reasons for such differences. If not, is there also general agreement on what constitutes a "leisure activity"?

Writing Suggestion

Rybczynski asserts that "Every culture chooses a different structure for its work and leisure, and in doing so it makes a profound statement about itself" (41). Focus on some of the most popular leisure activities in the United States today and in an essay explore any "profound statements" these activities make about American culture. If you're familiar with life in another culture, you might draw some comparisons between that culture's structures of work and leisure and those in the U.S.

Leisure Activities

Perils of the Princess: Gender and Genre in Video Games[1]

Sharon R. Sherman

Video games have come under close scrutiny in the media recently, because of their suspected link to teen violence. For example, a Los Angeles Times *article, describing the 1999 Littleton incident in which 12 high school students were killed by two of their classmates, observed, "The teens cackled and shouted as though playing one of the morbid video games they loved...They ended their spree by shooting themselves in the head, the final act in the game* Postal, *and, in fact, the only way to end it." A* U.S. News and World Report *story explored this issue further, asking the question, "Did the sensibilities created by the modern video games play a role in the Littleton massacre?"*

Their answer was a resounding Yes: "Note the cool and casual cruelty, the outlandish arsenal of weapons, the cheering and laughing while hunting down victims one by one. All of this seems to reflect the style and feel of the video killing games they played so often." Video games, then, by many accounts, cause significant changes in the individuals who play them. This leads the researcher to ask some basic questions about video games: namely, what is their primal draw for children and teenagers; and what specific changes might they effect in players' behaviors and attitudes?

In the article that follows, University of Oregon English professor Sharon R. Sherman examines video games from the point of view of folkloric studies, attempting to establish a thematic connection between video games and myth. Focusing her attention mainly on the Super Mario Brothers *game, Sherman asserts that traditional mythic stories of both western and nonwestern cultures have been translated to the video environment, and this may account in large part for their appeal.*

Furthermore, Sherman notes that specific portrayals of gender roles found in folklore also exist in computer games such as Super Mario, Quake, Doom, *and* Double Dragon. *Teenage boys, to cite one telling example, rarely identify with the princess figure in* Super Mario, *because they view her as a helpless figure who must be saved—a traditionally passive view of femininity which the game helps reinforce.* **As you read** *this article, consider your own*

---

[1]An earlier version of this paper appeared in Spanish in *Revista de Investigaciones Folkloricas* 8 (December 1993): 34–41.

intellectual reaction to Sherman's thesis regarding myth and gender. Futhermore, if you agree with Sherman's thesis, do you believe these mythic indentifications are profound enough to lead chronic players to model their behavior on certain games...perhaps leading to tragedies such as the one that took place in Littleton?

Once upon a time (in 1972), computer programmers created   1
Pong, a table tennis game, often found "inside" of tables in bars and restaurants. After Pong came Pac-Man. A number of other games followed. Soon the games were sold as cartridges that plugged into game consoles hooked up to computer monitors, most of which worked on a system invented by Atari. But home computer graphics did not compare with the developing arcade game market. The video arcade became the perfect environment for the postmodern adolescent. It was a place where the loud noises, flashing colors and rapid "anything can happen now" actions of the screen world mirrored the one in which the games were located. In these ways, the games were similar to pinball. Nevertheless, by 1985, sales were waning and the video game craze seemed to be just another passing fad.

In 1986, Nintendo began marketing a video game system with hand   2
controllers that changed the action and the outcome on the screen, high quality sound, and rapid, vivid, sophisticated graphics. All one needed was a television and a few connectors. But now the player, a product of the first generation to grow up with television, could, in a sense, jump into the screen realm and control a heretofore uncontrollable television-like image and master his or her own fate. This new generation of children was waiting, ready to be, as Nintendo advertised, "playing with power." Video arcades once again flourished as places where children could try out games they did not own at home and could meet with others, learn from each other, and gain status as video game experts.

Like Tommy, who became immortalized as the "Pinball Wizard"   3
by the rock group "The Who" in the late 1960s, a young child becomes the star in a film called *The Wizard* (1989) created by Universal. In this instance, the film evokes that '60s allusion, an allusion not even known to the children whose market it was targeting, but rather an allusion thrown to the parents in a "you played this kind of game, too" message. As Marsha Kinder effectively demonstrates in *Playing with Power in Movies, Television, and Video Games* (1991), *The Wizard* introduces Nintendo's third Super Mario game directly to its intended audience of children by cleverly playing upon the power of intertextuality: the children know Mario from his first two games; they know the film's star, Fred Savage, from TV's *The Wonder Years*; and the film is about a group of children who go "on the road" (much like Dorothy who travels *to* a

wizard) to compete in playing a new game of Mario (at least that is the legend the children have heard on their journey). The National Video Championship competition is held at Universal Studios theme park, which, like video games, has multiple worlds and interactive possibilities. In yet another film, *Super Mario Bros.* (1993), produced by Jake Eberts, Nintendo creates its own cinematic version of the game.

Scholars have examined market strategies, child psychology, computer literacy, eye-hand coordination, and the intertextual nature of Nintendo. Kinder (1991), for example, masterfuly presents the transmedia aspects of the games, and how they link with Saturday morning television programs, films, commercials, and toys, to relate interactivity with consumerism and postmodernism. But another means of analyzing Nintendo lies in an unexplored corner of this intertextual picture, in the realm of folklore, particularly in folk narrative.... 4

Most Nintento Entertainment Systems or game consoles come packed with a game cartridge featuring a version of the *Super Mario Brothers.* Thus, most children learn the Mario scenario first. I believe that video games, as exemplified by Nintendo's *Super Mario Brothers* series (among others), often appeal to players because they identify as heroes in a fantasy quest. Although Kinder finds these games to be a surrogate for the father, or partriarchal authority, whom one can best in an Oedipalized drama, one also might link Jung's archetypes with Campbell's structural interpretation of the hero journey or "monomyth." Drawing upon interviews with players, I hypothesize that the appropriation of mythic...content and form ensures the success of this arena of popular culture and perpetuates gender stereotyping. Enticing players into an otherwoldly dimension, this realm, like the willful suspension of disbelief in narrating, promotes an intense liminal state. The games are captivating to males primarily because players compete with each other and with the machine to "save the princess." They know this narrative well from multiple sources and are eager to actually become the hero in the tale.... Nevertheless, as I will discuss, females subvert the male message, changing the object of the game, the gender of the main character whenever possible, and the "message." 5

STRUCTURE AND PLOT

For Joseph Campbell, in *The Hero with a Thousand Faces* (1968:30), the monomyth...is summed up as: 6

A hero ventures forth from the world of common day into a region of supernatural wonder: fabulous forces are there encountered and a decisive victory in won: the hero comes back from this mysterious adventure with the power to bestow boons on his fellow man. 7

Campbell...and others saw a structural pattern underlying the   8
mythic hero's life depicted in epics such as *Gilgamesh,* the *Illiad* and the
Odyssey, Beowulf, Chanson de Roland; biblical tales including ones about
Moses, Elijah, and Jesus; and ancient Greek and Roman myths about
Jason, Zeus, Agamemnon, Oedipus and a host of others. Each scholar
placed a slightly different emphasis on the significance of this structural
underpinning: for Raglan (1936), it could be divided into the three ritually significant stages in one's life: birth, transition from childhood and
adolescence to maturity, and death—all times at which rites of passage
occure; for Carl Jung (1968), the quest pattern is crucial to "the process of
individuation," which mirrors the stages of the psychological development of the individual. Vladimir Propp (1928) saw a similar pattern but
he limited his discussion to what Antti Aarne (1910) called "the ordinary
folktale" or *Märchen.* Propp thus analyzed the structure of what could be
called the "middle" of the pattern—the passage from childhood to
adulthood—found at the center of that suggested by those who detailed
a longer story of the hero of tradition (e.g., Campbell, de Vries, et al.). Indeed, Archer Taylor, in his "The Biographical Pattern in Traditional
Narrative" (1964), points out how similar the conclusions were which
some of these scholars reached....I believe this journey is so significant
that popular culture creators from Disney to George Lucas to Steven
Spielberg to Nintendo game producers recreate the themes most important to them from their own remembered childhood pasts and, at the
same time, create an intertextual framework instantly recognized and
reinforced by children on a global scale never dreamt of by historic-
geographic researchers.

The game of *Super Mario Brothers* has Mario and his brother   9
Luigi, who acts as the protagonist for a second player, journey to save
a princess. Mario and Luigi are Italian plumbers (which explains the
number of pipes and girders appearing in the game). Both are known
to players from earlier games. As one of my informants, a thirteen-
year-old boy, explained, Mario is Nintendo's "slogan": he appears in
Pinball to keep the ball in play and a girl from falling; for *Wrecking
Crew,* Mario and Luigi program the action, choose the monsters, and
destroy a building; in the *Original Donkey Kong,* Mario must save a girl
named Pauline amidst construction girders, ladders, and elevators; in
Donkey Kong, Jr., Mario has the player's father in a cage and the player
must free him; and in the original arcade game, *Mario Brothers,* plumb-
ing and sewer pests are central features which resurface years later in
Super Mario 3. For many children, Mario has become as familiar as
Mickey Mouse and Bugs Bunny.

Because most video game creators are children of the 1960s, drug   10
culture seems to play a subtle role in some of the games. For Mario, the
people who aid the hero are mushrooms, just as "magic" mushrooms

presumably aided Carlos Castaneda (1968), the anthropologist turned guru, whose informant, Don Carlos, taught him to see the world differently by eating mescaline mushrooms. The 1960s saw the growth of hallucinogenic drug use and psychedelic music and images. The notion of other "realities" described in J. R. R. Tolkien's popular *Lord of the Rings* trilogy (1962), and the worlds created by LSD use, became the popular culture of the creators of video games. As Mario's physical body alternately grows and shrinks back to its normal size during the games, echoes of Lewis Carroll's *Alice's Adventures in Wonderland* (1893), revived by Disney in 1951, and that enjoyed a resurgence of interest in the '60s, also emerge. The examples of such allusions seem endless.

In *Super Mario Brothers*, children learn from the game booklet that: 11

> One day the kingdom of the peaceful mushroom people was invaded by the Koopa, a tribe of turtles famous for their black magic. The quiet peace-loving mushroom people were turned into mere stones, bricks and even field horse-hair plants, and the mushroom kingdom fell into ruin. The only one who can undo the magic spell...is the Princess Toadstool, daugher of the mushroom king. Unfortunately, she is presently in the hands of the great Koopa turtle king. Mario, the hero of the story (maybe), hears about the mushroom people's plight and sets out on a quest to free [them] from the evil Koopa and restore the fallen kingdom. ...You are Mario! It's up to you to save the mushroom people from the black magic of the Koopa!

This plot outline corresponds well with Propp's functions and Camp-   12
bell's monomyth.

ARCHETYPES

In a two-player game, Mario is the hero archetype. For Jung, he   13
would be the ego consciousness which leads one forward and takes risks. His shadow figure or the negative, hidden or unclaimed, or repressed aspects of his personality are manifested by Luigi, his brother and his opponent (for whom Mario serves as the shadow). Mario (or Luigi) may appear in his regular form; he presents his mask or persona or socially adapted roles when he becomes the enlarged Super Mario by touching (perhaps, eating) a magic mushroom which enables him to reach blocks or hit bricks which are actually mushroom people turned into bricks by the magic spell (some of whom can reward Mario with coins or a power boost); when he assumes the persona of Fiery Mario by eating a fire flower, he can use fireballs to kill Turtle tribe enemies and Little Goombas (mushrooms who betrayed their

people); if he hits a star, he assumes the role or persona of Invincible Mario, a state which lasts for a brief time. When these extraordinary Mario personas are bumped into by an enemy (ogre), they don't die, but rather return to their former selves (while in this transition, they flicker [are "marked"] and are invincible as a form of protection). In *Super Mario 3*, Mario may assume the role of Froggie, a fast-swimmer; Racoon Mario, who flies and hits objects with his tail; or Tanooki, who looks like Racoon Mario, but can turn himself into a statue (as if stared upon by Medusa, and a Medusa character does appear as an object in *Super Mario 2*). The player decides which of these personas to assume depending on the skills deemed necessary for the game's action.

Mario also experiences rebirth, one of Jung's primary archetypes.   14
He is, in a sense, reborn as he moves from above ground to the under-world and is resurrected in the next level of the game. The initial Mario game has eight worlds, with four levels each. The fourth level of each of these worlds in the first *Super Mario Brothers* has a castle with a retainer of the princess who announces, "Thank you, Mario. But our Princess is in another castle." He must arrive at the end of each world within a given time after avoiding traps and enemies and tackling the terrain on his journey. The princess is in the last and most heavily guarded castle. For Freudians, the castle and the forest Mario travel through to reach it may be seen as feminine symbols. For Jungians, the castle is a place where the hero confronts the self or centering core of his psyche. In either analysis, first he must pass tests and overcome time and space through a rebirth.

CONTENT

Mario's rebirth within the span of a single life may be augmented   15
by acquiring a number of extra Marios or lives. One hundred gold coins grant another life and receiving a "1 UP" mushroom gives him an addi-tional life, as do other hidden places which can be found by accident, learning the secrets from observing friends, subscribing to *Nintendo Power Magazine,* or buying other game secrets books. In each game, the opportunities for increasing the number of Marios expand. Without these possibilities, players would have to continually begin over until they had a mastery of each increment of the game. Each game becomes progressively more difficult. As Mario performs, he becomes a partici-pant in the process of transformation and is thus a ritual figure, much like Raglan's hero of tradition. In Propp's terms, after an initial lack, he has moved from childhood to adulthood and from function XV, THE HERO IS TRANSFERRED, DELIVERED, OR LED TO THE OBJECT OF HIS SEARCH, to function XIX, THE INITIAL MISFOURTUNE OR LACK IS

LIQUIDATED. The hero provides the ultimate rebirth by eventually completing the game, and reestablishing human (or, in this case, mushroom) existence. Often marriage is implicit (funtion XXXI) and, in a Jungian sense, Mario accepts his inner feminine anima whom he, as ego, rescues to illuminate and accept his own uniqueness as an individual.

Folklorists might expland on any of the traditional elements present in the Super Mario games. The gold coins, for example, are often found in a treasury which lies behind a hidden entryway (F721.4, "Underground treasure chambers") or they may be acquired in an otherworldly heavenlike realm, reached via a beanstalk (F54.2, "Plant grows to sky"). Bowser, the Koopa turtle king, looks and breathes fire like a dragon. He must be defeated to rescue the princess (R11.1, "Princess abducted by monster"). In *Super Mario 2*, a hidden door leads to a new and dark unknown locale, and a magic potion aids the hero who encounters the egg of the world as an obstacle (T511.7.2, "Cosmic egg"). All the Super Mario games have a Grendal-like underwater place, and forests with trees that change appearance from one level to the next. In *Mario 3*, the worlds appear on a map so that players can gauge the terrain and the level of difficulty. One world, for example, is giant land. Also found in *Mario 3* are magic boxes (like that of Pandora) from which magical objects are given. One is a magic whistle: "One toot (a double entendre to drug jargon) on this whistle will take you to another land."   16

Thus, the Super Mario games and others, such as *Faxanadu* (note the blatant play on Xanadu from Samuel Taylor Coleridge's poem "Kubla Khan," the poetry of an "elite culture" which is popular with "stoner" drug culture), use a journey and magical agents which must be earned to save a kingdom or world (H1385.1, "Quest for Stolen Princess")....The appropriation of the folk narrative in both form and content elements by video games is obvious. Mario is but one example, but he is the one most children know best. Mario acts out the monomyth. He begins in an ordinary setting, travels through enchanged forests, goes to the underworld (F80, "Journey to lower world"), overcomes demons (F771.4.1, "Castle inhabited by ogres"), has supernatural helpers (the imprisoned mushroom people), is constantly reborn in new worlds, eventually saves the princess by slaying a dragon and thus breaks the spell (N711.2, "Hero finds maiden in magic castle"). Hence he brings boons to society. Campbell and Jung would undoubtedly recognize him.   17

LIMINALITY

What is not so readily apparent is the liminal nature of both Mario and the player. Mario exists in a moment of eternity in time. Players live in that moment, vicariously experiencing themselves as   18

Mario. "I died," is a common exclamation. Players tell me they did not conquer the game for months and spent many uninterrupted blocks of hours playing intently. As Loftus and Loftus comment in *Mind at Play* (1983), video games utilize reinforcement. Variable scheduled rewards make game behavior increase. Replaying allows one to correct mistakes. In some games, a password returns a player to the level at which he last played; in others such as Mario, players leave the game on "pause," or very adept players begin over and quickly reach a certain point to "warp" to a higher level, much like characters on *Star Trek* and in *Star Wars*. When the game is turned off, the character exists in limbo, ready to be reborn at the turn of a switch.

Although the player may be "playing with power," Nintendo is   19
certainly "playing" with him. Like television, the image is always there, ready to spring to life twenty-four hours a day. One player told me, "You're hooked. It's like a drug." He commented that he played throughout the winter vacation after receiving his first Nintendo set: "I probably played and slept." Two boys interviewed noted that they played almost constantly, "About half a year to a year, just trying to learn the controls and stuff....It was new when we started playing." Loftus and Loftus note that regret over what they might have done causes players to try again until that level or error is corrected; that possibility of correction combined with reward leads to addiction. What happens once a player beats the game? Once the goal is reached, one boy remarked, "fade away." In effect, the player identifies so strongly with the hero that he too "disappears" from this liminal realm (and away from the absorbing image on the screen). He or she will live again as another character in the next video land.

The image is being constantly refined. In 1991, the company   20
introduced Super Nintendo with *Super Mario World,* followed by *Yoshi's Island: Super Mario World 3.* In 1996, Nintendo 64 (a system with a 64 bit processor) appeared and added a 3D quality to the games. Each improvement required the purchase of an entirely new game set. Nevertheless, Nintendo, according to advertising on the Internet, "is proclaimed...the greatest video game of all time."[2] The music is one tie-in to the previous games. But Nintendo 64 has a Mario who takes a nonlinear journey. He can approach the castle, open doors to enter any one of the various rooms, and jump into tapestries or pictures on the wall to come to grips with a different dimension. Unlike the linear 2D Mario, the 3D Mario can look up and down and the player can see Mario's point of view by flicking a control. The media camera can also be made to appear, "reporting live"

[2]*http://n64games.com.* Sega's Genesis and Sony's Play Station are other systems built on the same technology.

and "on location," showing the player the media's point of view, and covering the action as if it were a televised competition. Similarly, the player can zoom in and out, like a camera, to see different aspects of the world he inhabits as Mario.

SOCIAL ROLES

In the world of his peers, the expert player exhibits a supremacy   21
which he may not otherwise enjoy. While playing, he may become a hero within his social group. If he knows secret moves and has dextrous skills superior to his friends, others may idolize him for his feats. His audience gazes upon him and the screen as he operates the game, only relinquishing the controls after making an error or using up a prearranged time set by the group so that someone else might play. He acquires cocial "power," earned by long hours of developing his game skill....

Video game players share their identities as Mario characters;   22
they are, at once, acting as heroes in a plot, yet also as individuals, with their self-identities shifting within the social situation. Audience members must fulfill the roles of audience members but they also wish to assume the role of storyteller. These communicative roles illuminate the similarities between gamers and storytellers, especially when seen through the frame of both individual and group behavior.

One boy said it was lucky for some players (namely, girls) that   23
they "aren't throwing their lives away with the video games. You shouldn't do it way too much...you could play too much; I used to." But a girl revealed a quite similar obsession when she first began to play at home, "like, 'til three o'clock in the morning playing Nintendo on school nights."

Like ritual, the adventure game represents a transitional state   24
which must be overcome. To see the child as a liminal person located at this adolescent, marginal stage of life, and located in the game realm via his or her identification with the actions of the game hero, is easy to accept. To see the character of Mario as a liminal passenger in the game realm takes a leap into the screen. Victor Turner, in drawing upon van Gennep's division of rites of passage into three phases—separation, transition, and incorporation—defines the midpoint as one of liminalty: "liminal entities are neither here nor there; they are betwixt and between....During the...liminal period, the characteristics of the ritual subject (the 'passenger') are ambiguous; he passes through a cultural realm that has few or none of its attributes of the past or coming state" (1969:94–95). Adolescence, with all its own attendant rituals (e.g., bar mitzvahs, female initiatory menstruation rites, Quinceñera, Sweet Sixteens, debutante balls) is also a midpoint or transitional state in the life cycle as a whole, in a puberty-induced unstable phase of the invididual's

social development. The game world provides a threshold into a temporary world of power. Mario, with whom the player so strongly identifies, is also a liminal being. "Liminal entities," Turner explains,

> may be represented as possessing nothing. They may be disguised as   25
> monsters, wear only a strip of clothing, or even go naked, to demonstrate that as liminal beings they have no status, property, insignia, secular clothing indicating rank or role, position in a kinship system—in short, nothing that may distinguish them from their fellow neophytes or initiands....It is as though they are being reduced or ground down to a uniform condition to be fashioned anew and endowed with additional powers to enable them to cope with their new station in life (1969:95).

Mario certainly fits these requirements as do characters in similar ad-   26
venture games. In *Metroid*, for example, the character is indeed naked; in *Faxanadu*, the character begins with nothing and must pass tests to acquire weapons, life energy, and information while living within a constant transformative state.

Players are similarly transformed: they become so focused on un-   27
conquered or uncompleted games that they lose all sense of where they are. Nintendo has given players more and more "power." After the game narrative concludes, players may go back and play for time or points. Boys revealed that they played for levels, but that once they had mastered the game, they wanted to "do *everything* and still pass the levels"; finding all of the hidden places one has missed on the journey becomes the new challenge for boys. The two girls I interviewed vacillated. Both initially said they played for points: "so you can get extra guys." One remarked that points were only important at the arcade because "you get to put your name on the list." Thus, for these girls, the idea of saving the princess is less important than having others know of your abilities, much like graffiti announces your moniker in yet another anonymous domain.

GENDER

The princess may be seen as the female counterpart of the   28
hero. For males, she is that which the hero lacks in all of the games. Like Propp's function VIIIa, ONE MEMBER OF A FAMILY EITHER LACKS SOMETHING OR DESIRES TO HAVE SOMETHING, this lack of a princess sets the plot in motion. In an interesting twist to increase its player base, Nintendo offered four different characters for the player of *Super Mario 2* to select as the protagonist. Every girl I asked responded instantly that she played the princess in this sequel. Boys, on the other hand, play Luigi or Toadstool.

Mario is called "primitive" by one boy. With the constant advent of   29
new games, new worlds are explored. Male interviewees told me they
prefer sports games like *Rad Racer* or role playing games such as *Final
Fantasy*, in which the player must "take care of " his character—feed
him, decide when he needs to sleep, cast spells upon him, choose his
weapons and the like. Dissimilar, both games are still perceived by boys
as having a goal. In *Rad Racer*, "you're driving to get to the goal." For
girls, driving the car and the action itself are paramount. Patricia Marks
Greenfield, in *Mind and Media: The Effects of Television, Video Games, and
Computers* (1984), has noted that action is what makes the games popular. The aggressive nature of many games may, some fear, reinforce boys
and leave girls behind in the field of computers, a field to which most
children are first exposed by video games. Parallel procesing and the
ability to deal with complex interacting dynamic variables which lead to
inductive reasoning add to the excitement, Marks notes. Girls often play
games which provide experience—*Skate or Die, Rad Racer, BMX Racing*
or *Mike Tyson's Punch-out* (created long before Tyson was convicted of
rape). A game featuring Tyson seemed like a dubious choice for a female. "If I beat him, I'd be happy," remarked one of the girls.

Boys have their connection with the computer reinforced by the   30
now common PC (personal computer) games. The University of Oregon distributes the shareware versions of a few games on the CD-ROM
it provides to all students so they can hook up to the Internet. *Quake* and
Doom, two of the most popular video games played on the computer, are
violent fantasies. In *Doom*, players are told to order the registered version: "Act like a man. Slap a few shells into your shotgun..." In *Quake*,
the enemy enters Earth from another dimension through a slipgate device (akin to the transporter room on *Star Trek*). Players pass through
levels and slipgates, combating ogres, rottweilers, zombies, and other
enemies who all serve as obstacles in the hero's attempt to complete his
"mission" to destroy Quake. The enemies are graphically torn to pieces
by some of the available weapons. For most girls, the action in *Quake* is
abhorrent and the plot nothing more than an exercise in aggression.

Both action games and adventure games are *experienced* differ-   31
ently by females and males. Boys see the option of playing the princess
in *Mario 2* as strange because "she's the one you're trying to save";
girls see her as the heroine who saves the mushroom people, much
like she does in the other Mario games but with a distinct difference—
she doesn't need Mario to release her from a spell. One boy remarked,
"In 2, you get to be the princess and that's really weird." I asked why.
He replied, "Now she's helping you instead of creating the problems,
sort of. She didn't create the problem but, you know, you were trying
to save her. And now, in *Super Mario 2*, you're supposed to save the
people that live there. Now you get to use Princess Toadstool to your
advantage (laughs)." When the female character is chosen by males it

is because she can float in the air the longest, but the notion of "using" her may also have sexual connotations. In *Mario 2*, the unexperienced part of the plot and thus the forgotten narrative element of the princess saving the people is foregrounded in the "weird" scenario of having the princess capable of action. The same boy commented further that "she's wearing some dress out in the middle of…some desert, whereas they're [the males] all wearing some sort of rugged clothes." The female doesn't quite fit as the hero and the boys tend to play other characters. Girls seize the chance to re-gender the hero, re-inforce the female's role as savior, and create a new message.

In *Metroid*, the heroic character is female, but the boys did not find 32 that strange, perhaps because she is an alien. "She has green hair, I think," said one. The other remarked, "I picture it as an it." Despite the game booklet's description of the character as female, girls thought the character was male. "He's got an astronaunt thing, a helment." Thus, the same game is discerned differently—the female becomes a green-haired monster for boys and a male action figure for girls. Girl heroines seem to be mere twins of the male in adventure games. Girls noted that the Mario games are "just an adventure for Mario." In *Mario 2*, unlike the male's "weird" goal of saving the people rather than the princess, one girl stated, "You don't save a princess or anything. You just beat the last guy and it's all a dream and then you wake up." Indeed, according to the game booklet, the game is a dream, a point not mentioned by the boys who expect Mario to continue in his role as savior of the princess.

Games in which women are purely helpless objects are not played 33 by females because the message cannot be subverted. One girl stated she would never rent *Double Dragon*. "Its never interested me. It was two guys and they were just killing things." I asked why. "I didn't know," she answered. The answer must have been suppressed because the game's narrative is obvious upon even a cursory viewing. As the boys told me, "You're tryng to save your girlfriend. You're fighting on the streets, sort of like gang warfare." The other boy interjects, "Like Detroit, downtown." I asked, "Save her from what?" "From someone that captured her," replied one. "From the big evil drug lord guy, whatever," responded the other. For boys, traditional attitudes are reinforced. In *Video Kids: Making Sense of Nintendo* (1991), Eugene F. Provenzo, Jr., analyzed the illustrations on video game covers and found most women portrayed as provocative, but submissive victims, in need of rescue. He sees the games as dangerous, reflecting gender stereotypes and under-scoring sexual discrimination against women.

My reasearch indicates that children are quite conscious of these 34 messages. In response to a question I asked about the popularity of games in which girls had to be rescued, one boy began by telling me what he thought I wanted to hear—that the games were sexist. Despite his awareness, he revealed how deep-seated his biases were: "And I can't explain it, but it's just sexism, but you play it, though, because sometimes you kinda want to be in that spot.... Because that's how life has been, that's how it used to be, really sexist; it used to be that the men would always have everything. The women couldn't do this; the men would do this [and] the women would do that. This is traditional sexism and you can't control it." Both sexes were aware of the sexism in games. I asked the girls if they wanted to add anything at the end of the interview. "The sexist thing," one stated. "Game Boy [a portable version of Nintendo] is sexist because they say only boys play because [it's called] Game *Boy*." The other remarked, "I don't know why boys always have to be on the commercials. Why can't girls?"

Because the mythic stereotypes transfer into the popular culture   35
world, females do play Nintendo less than boys. Girls see themselves as playing as much as boys, but their comments indicate less knowledge of game specifics. One noted, "On TV, *one time,* a girl played. Also in *The Wizard.*" The girl in *The Wizard,* though, does not win and she is one token female in a room of male players. Both girls, who do not have brothers, noted that, in their households, their fathers played the most. Those females who do play prefer games like *Tetris* which requires the solving of a puzzle, rather than the completion of a quest: "For girls, more stuff like *Tetris*...that doesn't involve little men or killing and stuff." Like the princess who seems to passively sit and spin gold, or Penelope who re-weaves the shroud while Odysseus has his adventures, the female provides solutions to questions, or like Psyche, Rapunzel, Cinderella, or Beauty, she breaks out of her proscribed role to experience life.

CONCLUSION

In the intertextual dimension of myth,...and video games, the   36
narrative serves as its core. The games reinforce gender roles and blur genre distinctions as the players transit through their adolescent worlds. Much like the narrating session once served up examples of how one travels on a perilous journey to become an adult, video games appropriate the monomythic folkloric kingdom creating a... rechanneling of traditional content elements and structures. Nevertheless, females re-vision the text to make the female central and powerful, akin to what Alicia Ostriker calls "revisionist mythmaking," whereby women appropriate a "tale...for altered ends" (1986:212). Like rites of passage, and areas of marginality, all these expressions of narrative transcend boundaries and have, in Turner's sense, "a multivocal character, having many meanings, and each is capable of mov-

ing people at many psychobiological levels simultaneously" (1969: 129). At the level of psychological analysis, the liminality of the folktale world moves one through the territory of the unconscious and offers wisdom about transitional stages via symbolic language. The games replicate that narrative imagery. In their appropriation of folklore, video games have created Super Myths...for the Super Mario and Princess Toadstool adolescent.

WORKS CITED

Aarne, Antti. 1910. *Verzeichnis der Märchentypen.* Helsinki: Suomalaisen Tiedeakatemien Toimituksia.

Campbell, Joseph. 1968 [1949]. *The Hero with a Thousand Faces.* Bollingen Series 17. Princeton: Princeton University Press.

Castaneda, Carlos. 1968. *The Teachings of Don Juan: a Yaqui Way of Knowledge.* Berkeley: University of California Press.

Carroll, Lewis. 1922 [1893]. *Alice's Adventures in Wonderland.* Garden City, N.Y.: Doubleday, Page.

de Lauretis, Teresa. 1984. *Alice Doesn't: Feminism, Semiotics, and Cinema.* Bloominton: Indiana University Press.

de Vries, Jan. 1963. *Heroic Song and Heroic Legend.* London: Oxford University Press.

Dundes, Alan. 1964. On Game Morphology: A Study of the Structure of Non-Verbal Folklore. *New York Folklore Quarterly* 20:276–88.

Georges, Robert A. 1969a. Toward an Understanding of Storytelling Events. *Journal of American Folklore* 82:313–28.

———. 1969b. The Relevance of Models for Analyses of Traditional Play Activities. *Southern Folklore Quarterly* 33:1–23.

———. 1970. Structure in Folktales: A Generative-Transformational Approach. *The Conch: Journal of African Cultures and Literatures* 2:4–17.

———. 1972. Recreations and Games. In *Folklore and Folklife: An Introduction,* ed. Richard M. Dorson, 173–89. Chicago: University of Chicago Press.

———.1976. From Folktale Research to the Study of Narrating. *Studia Fennica* 20:159–68.

———. 1979. Feedback and Response in Storytelling. *Western Folklore* 38:104–110.

———. 1980. Toward a Resolution of the Text/Context Controversy. *Western Folklore* 39:34–40.

———. 1981. Do Narrators Really Digress? A Reconsideration of Audience Asides in Narrating. *Western Folklore* 40:245–52.

———. 1990. Communicative Role and Social Identity in Storytelling. *Fabula* 31:4–57.

———— and Alan Dundes. 1963. Toward a Structural Definition of the Riddle. *Journal of American Folklore* 76:111–118.

Greenfield, Patricia Marks. 1984. *Mind and Media: The Effects of Television, Video Games, and Computers.* Cambridge: Harvard University Press.

Jung, C. G. 1968 [1959]. *The Archetypes and the Collective Unconscious,* trans. R. F. C. Hull. 2nd ed. Princton, N.J.: Princeton University Press.

Kinder, Marsha. 1991. *Playing with Power in Movies, Television, and Video Games: From Muppet Babies to Teenage Mutant Ninja Turtles.* Berkeley: University of California Press.

Loftus, Geoffrey R. and Elizabeth F. 1983. *Mind at Play: The Psychology of Video Games.* New York: Basic Books, Inc.

Ostriker, Alicia. 1986. *Stealing the Language.* Boston: Beacon Press.

Propp, Vladimir. 1928. *Morfologiya skazki.* Leningrad.

Provenzo, Eugene F., Jr. 1991. *Video Kids: Making Sense of Nintendo.* Cambridge: Harvard University Press.

Raglan, FitzRoy Richard Somerset. Baron. 1936. *The Hero: A Study in Tradition, Myth, and Drama.* London: Methuen & Co.

Rank, Otto. 1952. *The Myth of the Birth of the Hero: A Psychological Interpretation of Mythology,* trans. F. Robbins and Smith Ely Jelliffe. New York: R. Brunner.

Taylor, Archer. 1964. The Biographical Pattern in Traditional Narrative. *Journal of the Folklore Institute* 1:114–129.

Turner, Victor. 1969. *The Ritual Process: Structure and Anti-Structure.* Ithaca: Cornell University Press.

Von Hahn. J. G. 1864. *Griechische und albanesische Märchen.* 2 volumes. Leipzig.

Examining the Text

1. How does the language of this article's introduction ("Once upon a time…") help reinforce Sherman's theme regarding the folkloric nature of video games?

2. Explain the term "intertextuality" as employed by the author in this piece. How does this term relate to children's ability to comprehend certain video games easily?

3. Vincent A. Anfara at the University of New Orleans recently defined the term "liminality" this way: "Originally described by Van Gennep (1960) and expanded by Turner (1969), the term liminality refers to a state in which participants are stripped of their usual status and authority. All rites of passage or transitions are marked by three

phases: separation, transition or margin (limin), and reaggregation."
How does the video game player fit this description of liminality?

4. Why does Sherman bring up the drug culture of the 1960s in her
discussion of video games? Is this merely an interesting and whimsical
digression, or does it tie in somehow with the notion of liminality?

5. How do video games reinforce and/or perpetuate certain gender-
role stereotypes, according to the author?

For Group Discussion

Sherman says, "I believe that video games, as exemplified by
Nintendo's Super Mario Brothers Series (among others) often appeal
to players because they identify as heroes in a fantasy quest." In class
discussion, explain first what she means by "fantasy quest." Also explain Joseph Campbell's related term "monomyth," and cite specific
examples of well-known myths and/or fairy tales that might contain
this element of heroic quest. Next, based on your own experience with
video games, attempt to find examples of video games that either support or undermine Sherman's thesis. What video games that you have
played or seen fall into the category of the mythic quest? What games,
if any, might contradict the author's thesis?

Writing Suggestion

Write an autobiographical narrative essay in which you consider
the notion of liminality from a personal perspective. How is the developmental phase of adolescence a "liminal state," according to this
essay? In your own experince, what specific transitions did you undergo during this phase in your psychosocial development? Describe
at least one of these transitional issues in detail, arriving at some conclusions as to what specific lessons you might have learned. As a vari-
ant on this assignment, you might also consider college life a liminal
state as well. In what ways can you identify your current life as transitional? How is the liminal nature of college life challenging, and what
lessons have you derived from it thus far?

Eight Ways of Looking
at an Amusement Park

Russell B. Nye

*Whether we pose for pictures with Mickey Mouse, scream in (mock?)
terror hurtling around a 350-degree loop on a roller coaster, or pitch baseballs
at milk bottles for a stuffed animal, we go to amusement parks for any number*

of reasons. In the following article based on extensive research, Russell B. Nye offers eight possibilities to explain people's enjoyment of amusement parks.

Beginning with an overview of how the modern park developed, Nye suggests that its basic functions have remained very much the same over time: to provide excitement, adventure, and a spectacular alternative world in which to transcend inhibitions and conventional behavior, enjoy the "vicarious terror" of "riskless risks," and simply play. Moving from the parks of centuries past to World's Fairs to today's Six Flags adventurelands and Disney extravaganzas, Nye attempts to distill the amusement park's essential qualities and define our relationship to it.

Nye's essay was originally published in the Journal of Popular Culture *in 1981. As you read, test his ideas against the amusement parks you have visited recently. Do his eight categories describe the experience of an amusement park in the 1990s?*

The park is an urban phenomenon, a reaction to the crowded cities of the eighteenth century. Historically it is tied to the Romantic era, which saw nature as a curative, educational force—"God's visible smile," to quote William Cullen Bryant, on mankind. It was no accident that William Penn chose to call his colony "Penn-sylvania," with all the connotations of natural peace and beauty that the Latin word brought from the pastoral tradition.[1]   1

In 1812 Philadelphia landscaped five acres of the east bank of the Schuylkill River to create the beginnings of Fairmount Park, the birthplace of the American park system. Other city parks were founded over the next few decades in response to the demands of an emergent, prosperous middle class for access to those natural surroundings and open spaces previously available only on the estates of the rich. A third factor in the rise of the public park, particularly during the phenomenal burst of urban population in mid-century, was the desire of reformers to counteract what they believed were the dangerous social effects of city life.   2

The crowded city afforded no chance to be alone with nature or one's self, to ponder questions of life and identity, to learn from God's plants and flowers. Cities bred suspicion, selfishness, isolation; public parks could provide an effective antidote. Thus Central Park was designed by Frederick L. Olmsted and Calvert Vaux in 1858 to furnish New Yorkers a "harmonizing influence" and to "cultivate among the   3

---

[1]Penn in his Philadelphia plan of 1682 in fact set aside five squares as parks, four of which still exist. John Maass, *The Glorious Enterprise: The Centennial Exposition of 1876* (Watkins Glen, N.Y.: Association Press, 1959), pp. 16–18.

community loftier and more refined desires." It was to be a passive place, without "boisterous fun and rough sports," a contrast to as well as escape from the city. Central Park would provide a pattern for many subsequent city parks and was indeed a precursor of the philosophy that underlay the national park system.[2]

The exposition or "world's fair," a coincidental nineteenth-century development, introduced another set of factors. Instead of an escape from the city, the exposition was intended to take advantage of the urban environment for educational, cultural and especially commercial purposes, reaching as wide an audience as possible. World's Fairs at London (1851, 1862), Paris (1855, 1867, 1878, 1900) and Vienna (1873) served as models for the first major American fair, Philadelphia's Exhibition of 1876, which not only commemorated the nation's Centennial but also exhibited "the arts, manufactures, and products of soil and mine" to the country and the world. Its purposes, concluded a writer in 1812, were to[3]   4

> teach knowledge of the markets…, form, taste and judgment…, offer instructive insights into creative spheres…, and to extend the great civilizing task of educating man to be a world citizen.

Its themes were enlightenment, national pride and most of all progress. The planners of Chicago's Columbia Exposition of 1893 built their project on Philadelphia's success; chief architect Daniel Burnham envisioned a "White City" of monumental grandeur to serve as the ideal pattern of what the modern city could be. The Chicago Fair, unlike Central Park, was not an escape from the city but an idealization of it—a meeting place for art, uplift, education, social participation, the good life.[4]

Whatever Burnham's intentions, a substantial part of the Fair's success derived not from its magnificent architecture and hundreds of educational and artistic exhibits, but from the Midway Plaisance, a mile-long corridor of privately operated concessions, shops, shows,   5

---

[2]See the discussion in John F. Kasson, *Amusing the Millions* (New York: Hill and Wang, 1978), pp. 11–16. Kasson's study of Coney Island is the best treatment of an American amusement park in its socio-cultural context. One of the most handsomely designed and illustrated studies of a single park is L. Bush, E. Chukayne, R. Hehr, and R. Hersey, eds., *Euclid Beach Park Is Closed for the Season* (Mentor, Ohio: Amusement Park Books, 1978).

[3]See Maass, *op. cit.* pp. 26–72, 93. The Exhibition contained 249 buildings, 5½ miles of railroad, 153 acres of lawn and flower beds, 20,000 trees and shrubs, and three telegraph systems. It "dazzled and astounded" Ralph Waldo Emerson but depressed Henry Adams.

[4]See the discussion in Kasson, pp. 17–20.

and games that the Fair's planners included with—but kept quite separate from—the rest of the exposition. The Midway, as a contemporary account put it, was "a sideshow pure and simple of halls of entertainment, pavilions, and gardens." It featured girls—an International Beauty Show of "forty gaily dressed beauties from forty lands"; Algerian Dancers in their famous Love Dance ("the coarse animal passions of the East"); "sleek odalisques" from the Persian Palace of Eros; three lovely Samoan damsels named Lola, Mela and Feteia—in company with jugglers, sword swallowers, a Chinese joss house, the Hagenbeck Circus, glass blowers, a replica of Kilauea in eruption, and of course the huge wheel designed by George W. Ferris looming over it all.[5] Without denigrating the cultural and educational contributions of the Columbia Exposition, it is not unreasonable to say that the two sights which remained most vividly in the American imagination were the "hootchy kootchy" dance of Fatima in the Turkish Village and the profile of the great Ferris wheel which dominated the landscape.[6] The Midway was energetic, amusing, titillating and plain fun. After that no world's fair could afford to omit a "midway," though it might be called (as in St. Louis) The Pike or (in San Francisco) The Joy Zone. There, in Chicago, lay the germ of the modern amusement park.[7]

Another kind of public entertainment, the county or state fair, 6 also contributed to the creation of the amusement park, although its original purpose was commercial and educational. The first agricultural fair was probably held at Georgetown, D.C., in 1809, followed by an increasing number scattered throughout the East, particularly in New York State and New England. By the close of the century, the fair was an autumn fixture everywhere, a place to display farm machinery and farm products and to serve as an annual gathering place for the rural and small town population. Though exhibits were undoubtedly of first interest at fairs, those who attended expected entertainment—animal shows, acrobats, lectures, slide shows (later movies), horse and automobile races, and rigidly-controlled acts and games. There was almost always a section set aside for merry-go-rounds, rides and concessions that was, in effect, a pleasure park in embryo.

---

[5]For excellent photographs and descriptions see volumn IV of *The Portfolio of Photos of the World's Fair* (Chicago: Household Art Press, 1898).

[6]Chicago's Century of Progress Midway in 1933 featured Sally Rand and her famous fan dance and the Skyride, two 628-foot towers with a rocket car ride at the 200-foot level.

[7]This is not to say that the amusement park is uniquely American. European "pleasure parks" on city outskirts date certainly from the sixteenth century; London's Vauxhall Gardens (1661) and Ranelagh Gardens (1690), Paris' Ruggieri and Tivoli Gardens (later moved to Denmark) date from the eighteenth century. However, none seems to have had direct major influence on the American version.

But most certainly the Chicago Fair showed that there was a huge   7
waiting urban market for more Midways, a clientele both available and
mobile via railway, streetcar and automobile. There were literally millions of Americans eager to pay for this kind of recreation, people with
leisure and money to spend on dancehalls, vaudeville, professional
sports, movies, theaters, circuses, carnivals and much else.[8] There were
also shrewd men ready to take advantage of them. One, George C.
Tilyou, bought and transformed New York's Coney Island in 1895, setting off a wave of similar parks in New York and other urban areas—Sea
Lion Park, Steeplechase Park, Luna Park (made out of Sea Lion) and
Dreamland. Parks sprang up across the land, promoted by railroads,
inter-urbans, breweries and local entrepreneurs. The years 1900 to 1910,
in the words of a contemporary, saw "a hysteria of parks followed by
panic." Fortunes were made and lost, parks opened and closed, new
rides and concessions tried and abandoned. In 1907 the national capital-
ization of amusement parks was calculated at over $100,000,000, with
predictions of double the sum within the decade.[9]

Alert managers and designers knew what the public wanted and   8
gave it to them. The park was "pleasure to the multitude." It should
never be serious, but entertaining; it must be "different from ordinary
experience"; it must have "life, action, motion, sensation, surprise,
shock, swiftness, or else comedy." Those who paid to get in wanted innocent fun, not morality or education—as Frederic Thompson said,
they wanted "elaborated child's play." The amusement park, he continued, should be "frankly devoted to fun, the fantastic, the gay, the
grotesque."[10]

The modern American amusement park, then, was never a pas-   9
toral retreat. It was not a place of quiet self-evaluation but one for participation, noise, jostle, light, color, activity. Tilyou, Thompson and the
rest integrated the park into the city by railway, trolley, bus and automobile. It was not a flight from urban life but a journey to an intensified version of it, where one mixed with the same city crowds in a
different context, "catching," an observer commented, "the full live
sense of humanity." An early visitor described it quite accurately as
"essentially a place of merriment…, there is no other reason for going

---

[8]Dana Tatlin, "Amusing America's Millions," *World's Work* 26 (July 1913), 325–40 is an
interesting and insightful survey of the exploding market for public recreation in the period. See also Richard Henry Edwards, *Popular Amusements* (New York: Association
Press, 1915).

[9]Taitlin, pp. 335–36.

[10]Thompson explained his theories in two remarkable essays, "The Summer Show," *Independent* 62 (June 20, 1970) 1460–62; and "Amusing the Million," *Everybody's Magazine*
19 (Sept. 1908) 395–97. See also Edwin E. Slosson's classic "The Amusement Business,"
Independent 67 (July 21, 1904), pp. 134–38.

there."[11] And by enclosing the park and charging admission, operators immediately established control of who entered and what went on inside—creating an engineered environment, carefully planned to manipulate visitors into having fun but also spending money in an orderly, safe, relaxed atmosphere.

1. Thus our first view of the amusement park—as an alternative world to that of our daily lives. The amusement park provides all who come with a chance to be something other than what they are—workers, bosses, fathers, mothers, sons, daughters, anyone with responsibilities or socio-economic functions. Frederic Thompson put it succinctly: "Everything must be different from ordinary life." The park allows people the chance to operate in a different environment for purposes and rewards quite different from those of the outside workaday world. It is a place where each can set his own easily attainable goals in a known, controllable situation. In this world nothing is done for profit, nothing by necessity. We can beat the weight guesser or win the teddy bear, but in the park's insulated environment we don't have to try to do either, nor does success or failure really matter. We can live in Space World, Frontier Village or Safari Land; take chances without real risk on rides, and in games of skill or chance. In a real sense, within the park we can—for the moment—live in a way we cannot outside it, and at relatively small cost.

2. A second way of looking at an amusement park is related to the first, that is, to see it as fantasy, a stage set, a never-never land where one can walk out of his world into a much more interesting one. This, of course, is one of the oldest attractions of the amusement park and still one of its most powerful. When the visitor arrives at the park's gate, wrote Frederic Thompson,

> His eyes tell him he is in a different world—a dream world, perhaps a nightmare world—where all is bizarre and fantastic—crazier than the craziest part of Paris—gayer and more different from the everyday world....He is prepared to accept all sorts of extravagances—things that elsewhere would be impossible—in perfect faith for the time being.

O. Henry, a constant visitor to Coney Island, loved it for its "breathtaking though safeguarded dip and flight of adventure, the magic carpet that transports you to the realms of fairyland."[12] The park names themselves—Luna, Dreamland, Avalon, and the like—un-

---

[11]Lindsay Denison, "The Biggest Playground in the World," *Munsey's Magazine* 33 (August 1905), pp. 555–61.

[12]"The Summer Show," *op. cit.*, 1461. O. Henry set two of his more sentimental stories at Coney Island: "The Greater Coney," in *Sixes and Sevens* and "Brickdust Row" in *The Trimmed Lamp.*

derlined their illusory quality and encouraged the visitor's anticipation. Luna Park gave its customers a wide choice of fantasy worlds,
among them a Chinese theater, a Dutch town, a Japanese garden, an
Eskimo camp, a tour of Venice and an Indian durbar. The element of
fantasy is, of course, still a major element of the modern theme park
since Disney pioneered this reemphasis in 1955. Walt Disney World in
Florida, for example, forthrightly calls itself "A Magic Kingdom" and
offers the public six different lands which (in prose Thompson and his
era would have admired)

> capture the spirits of history, fantasy and adventure—with magic. Stroll
> beneath the soft glow of gaslights in turn-of-the-century Main Street,
> U.S.A. Sail with a crew of rowdy pirates and explore the tropical rivers
> of the world in Adventureland. Let a group of zany singing bears enter-
> tain you in the Old West atmosphere of Frontierland. Walk along Lib-
> erty Square's cobblestone streets and relive America's struggle for
> freedom. Greet your favorite childhood storybook characters amidst the
> happy aura of Fantasyland. And travel to a visionary future of rockets
> and space journeys in Tomorrowland.

This recent trend in amusement parks, the device of unifying   12
themes, is chiefly the result of the transfer of Hollywood stage-set
skills of illusion, developed over a half-century of movie making, to
the park locale. Here, out of sight of the world outside, one may cross
the boundaries of space and time to the Old West, the African jungle,
early America, or nearly any fantasy land he chooses. "Take a step
back in time and ride an authentic Iron Horse," advertises one park,
"Transport into the future when you take a voyage to another World."
Another invites the customer to an "Enchanted Voyage, an animated
journey through a world of make believe," and so do dozens more.[13]
What Tilyou and Thompson and the Midway promoters knew would
work still does. "From the moment you enter King's Island," the Ohio
park's folder says, "a whole new world of fantasy unfolds before your
eyes," just as it did at Dreamland two generations ago.[14]

---

[13]A very short list of fantasy lands would include at least six Frontier Towns, several
Ghost Towns, Storytowns, Space World, Old Town, Rivertown, several Safari Parks or
Trails, Gaslite Village, Main Street, U.S.A., Joyland, Oz City, Mother Goose Park, Dog-
patch, Silver Dollar City, Octoberfest, Alice-In-Wonderland, Lion Country, and so on.
As of 1975 there were 695 amusement parks, almost all with similar fantasy lands and
many with more than one. See *U.S. News and World Report*, July 21, 1975; Seventeen, July
1973; and *Holiday*, June–July–August 1975, for reports.

[14]Dreamland Park in Nara City, Japan, a Disneyland operation, opened in 1960. The first
theme park based on television characters seems to have been Bedrock City, Custer,
South Dakota (1960) built about the Hanna-Barbera characters The Flintstones. Other
Flintstone-theme parks appeared in Holland and Denmark in the sixties.

The theatrical element of the park, suggested by the stage set, has   13
been powerfully enhanced by the trend toward "happenings," or
playlets, acted out at intervals by employees in costume. Disneyland's
parade of story-book characters represented an early phase of this;
later theme parks elaborated the idea into what were small but full-
scale places and times. The attack on the stage coach, for example,
soon became standard fare in Western theme parks. Silver Dollar City,
an Old West theme park, had one hundred and three "happenings"
daily, staged by thirty-three "image characters," among them the
town's marshal, doctor, undertaker, mayor, various gunmen, dancehall girls and the like.[15]

The fantasy element of the park is often extended into farce and   14
foolery. Certain games and shows violate our anticipations; they reverse
what we expect, take situations and devices out of the normal world and
use them absurdly. Things that are harmless and functional in ordinary
life take on wild aspects— as in the Hall of Mirrors, the Funhouse, the
oriental Maze, Krazy Kastle and certain games which have long been
part of carnival and park attractions. One of the early rides, for example,
called The Haunted Swing, placed the visitor in a room which seemed to
turn around and upside down while he did not, leaving him with the
sensation of spinning around while standing on his head. The Tilt
Room, which does exactly that, is an old-time favorite developed
around the turn of the century. And who really wants a kewpie doll, or
needs a tasselled whip, or carries (outside the park) a pink parasol or a
balloon with a silly device? There is also a strong quality of the absurd in
some of the rides; there are little cars that don't steer right, floors that
spin, sidewalks that jiggle, gusts that blow off hats, mirrors that turn visitors into freaks, strange noises that challenge sanity. What happens is
that something that *should* do something suddenly does something
quite different; the pleasure comes from the harmless surprise which is
itself an essential component of the fantasy the park evokes. We all suspect, at times, that the world is an absurd place, and an amusement park,
for a few hours, confirms this without threatening us.

3. A third way of looking at an amusement park is to view it as   15
spectacle, as a unified, harmonious production meant to be *seen* and
heard. Park planners have always been aware of the importance of the
park as a total visual and aural experience that envelopes the visitor as
he enters and enfolds him until he leaves. The impact is more apparent
today, perhaps, than ever before because of the movie set influence.
People arrive as separate figures; once inside the gates they merge into
and become part of the spectacle. Early designers and operators recognized the necessity of maintaining spatial and architectural unity

---

[15]*Amusement Business*, January 1, 1962, 9.

within the park to emphasize this sense of unified spectacle. Thompson, for example, decided to make Luna Oriental, calling up illusions of the mysterious East; he combined towers, turrets, walls, flags, colors, lights and costumes into one big display with such success that remnants of the Oriental theme are still visible in older amusement parks of today—as in The Arcade of Cedar Point, Ohio, for example.[16]

Thus Lindsay Denison, approaching Coney, saw before him "rising to the sky a thousand glittering towers and minarets, the magically realized dream of poet or painter," a great spectacle of color, activity and excitement. Albert Bigelow Paine, Mark Twain's friend, on leaving Coney Island, looked back as its lights went out in the dusk:

> Tall towers that had grown dim suddenly broke forth in electric outlines and gay rosettes of color, as the living sparks of light travelled hither and thither, until the place was transformed into an enchanted garden, of such a sort as Aladdin never dreamed of.[17]

The contrast of this spectacle with, say, the Chicago or St. Louis fair was deliberate—the exposition style monumental, stately, disciplined; the amusement park a swirl of forms and colors. White City asked for contemplation, Luna for participation. Shapes, sounds, colors and movement combined in one great prospect that drew people into it— "it simply shouted," said one visitor, of "joyousness."

> In cupolas and minarets, in domes and flaunting finials, in myriads of gay bannerets, in the jocund motion of merry-go-rounds, circle swings and wondrous sliding follies, in laughter and shrieks, in the blare of brazen music and the throbbing of tom-toms—it speaks its various language—joyous forever.[18]

4. A fourth way of looking at an amusement park is to consider it as a release from conventional behavior, a place where some of the restraints of daily life may be relaxed. As Tilyou said, visitors can "cut loose from repressions and restrictions, and act pretty much as they feel like acting—since everyone else is doing the same thing." The amuse-

16

17

[16]See Kasson, pp. 66–67, on Luna and Dreamland.

[17]Denison, *op. cit.*, pp. 565–66; and Paine, "The New Coney Island," *Scribner's 68* (August 1904), pp. 535, 538. Chicago's "White City" was the first to capitalize on the new electric light and other parks were quick to follow. Chicago's 1933 Fair, in memory of 1893, called itself "The City of a Million Lights." On the importance of lighting, see "Painting With Light," *Amusement Business*, May 8, 1965, pp. 20–22.

[18]Rollin Lynde Hartt: "The Amusement Park," *Atlantic Monthly*, Vol. XCXIX (May 1907), p. 669.

ment park, said one analyst in 1907, "was not founded for the culture of decorum, it was founded for the culture of hilarity." "The spirit of the place," he continued, encourages the visitor "to cancel every canon of conventionality, every rubric of discretion," an overstatement but nonetheless a shrewd comment on a traditional component of the park's popularity. But though ordinary rules of behavior might be modified, they were never abandoned. The park may be "frisky," wrote Frederic Thompson, "but it knows where to draw the line."[19]

Still, one could—and can—wear funny hats, weird shirts, carry stuffed animals and fancy canes, laugh and shout, and indulge in unusual diets of

> crimson sausages, green corn in the ear, retrospective soft-shell crabs, (*and* chrome colored beverages...which once had bowing acquaintance with oranges and lemons.[20]

A variety of games and contests allowed the client to transcend his inhibitions. A booth that provided baseballs to throw at dishes advertised, "If you can't do it at home, do it here!"[21] While no man in his right mind would dare to impress his girl friend during business hours by striking a post with a maul to ring a bell, he can do it without shame in a park, a fact operators have recognized for generations.

Part of the appeal of the park's unconventionality lay in its pretense of wickedness, its illusion of letting down the bars of propriety, if only a bit. The amusement park postcard, still a standard souvenir, soon became a part of this,—"Having a H— of a Time at Lansing Park"; "Don't Bring Your Wife to Pine Point!"; "Look What I Found at Joyland!"—the pictures of girls in bathing suits or men with upraised bottles. Early amusement parks had various devices (and some still do) to blow air jets up women's skirts and rides and games intended to expose legs, thighs and whatever, all within acceptable limits of jocular deviltry. Certain rides were constructed so as to jostle people into physical contact—Love's Journey, Barrel of Fun, The Haunted House, and the traditional Tunnel of Love ("Kiss Her in the Dark!"). The proprietor of one concession called the Foolish House attributed its success to the simple fact that "the men like it because it gives them a chance to hug the girls and the girls like it because it gives them a chance to be hugged," an opinion no doubt equally fitting today.

---

[19]Tilyou is quoted by Kasson, 59. The other observer is Hartt, *op. cit.*, 669. Thompson's statement is in "The Summer Show," p. 1612.

[20]Guy Wetmore Carryl, "Marvelous Coney Island," *Munsey's Magazine* 25 (September 1901), p. 814.

[21]H. Rhodes, "City Summer," *Harper's* 131 (June 1915), p. 13.

In the easy environment of the park, the rules of etiquette tend to   20
loosen. Introductions are often dispensed with; one can be interested
in another's activities and strike up a conversation with strangers.
Families meet and share the day; people find common interests that
might extend beyond the park, but need not. Like the dancehall, just
then gaining respectability in the cities, the early amusement park provided a meeting place where the young could meet without embarrassment within the sanctioned conventionality of the midway, at the
bandstand, or as part of the camaraderie of the boardwalk. "Many
come singly,"[22] wrote an observer,

> each lad with an as yet unidentified paramour in his heart, each lass
> cherishing a shy anticipation. But how, you ask, shall these youthful
> strangers be made acquainted? Leave that to them.

One reason, no doubt, for this sense of "cutting loose" (as Thomp-   21
son called it) lies in the fact that entrance into the amusement park
makes the visitor part of the show—he becomes, in effect, both spectator
and performer. Early observers noted how easily people assumed roles
without quite realizing it.[23] A woman having her weight guessed or a
man at ring-toss is performing and knows it. The group watching is an
audience and also knows it; in fact, it may even applaud.

People-watching has long been one of the most obvious partici-   22
patory elements of park activity, and as each day progresses the
merger of spectator and performer becomes quite evident. That those
who ride the roller-coaster, for example, are playing roles has long
been known to operators and observers—the ritual screamer, the
front-seat show-off, the marathon rider, the nerveless cynic, and others. People share rides together, eat together, line up together, play
games together; one may for the moment be the center of attention by
winning (or losing) a prize or performing in some spectacular way.
Thus the park visitor becomes, in a real sense, a part of a collective
unit, a partner in the day's play; the rules of social separation are gradually relaxed, as at sporting events and traffic accidents.

5. A fifth way of understanding the amusement park is to con-   23
sider it as an extension of the backyard outing or family picnic. Early
promoters, by altering the atmosphere and character of the old
park, practically guaranteed a greatly expanded and much more
profitable middle class market. They made it attractive to "respectable
fun-seekers with their families...with decent shows, honest prices for
food and drink, and some semblance of cleanliness and public

---

[22]Hartt, p. 676.
[23]Denison, *op. cit.*, pp. 565–66.

order."[24] Frederic Thompson, in refurbishing Coney Island, got rid of "the tinhorn gambler, the short-change artist, the gamblers, swindlers, and thugs" to make it, he proudly wrote, "the place where your mother, your sister, and your sweetheart would be comfortable and safe." The change was immediately noticeable and highly profitable. "Everywhere," wrote Paine, "were clean, freshly-clad, well-groomed people and gaily-decked, brightfaced children," an impression borne out by contemporary photographs. Not only was it moral, but also good business. Businessman found[25]

> that decent people have in the aggregate more money to spend than the dissipated even though they spend it more sparingly; that eleven dimes are more than a dollar; and that a show which can take in the whole family pays better than a show to which only one would go.

Parks were shrewdly planned to provide something for everybody in the family at every age group; even those who came without family escort were made to feel somehow they were included in this excursion-like holiday venture.

Amusement parks have carefully maintained this family orientation. Walt Disney World advertises "Bring the Whole Family! We have 43 square miles for you and your family to discover, explore, and enjoy!" Cedar Point calls itself "Family Fun Capital of the Midwest..., the most exciting innovation in modern family entertainment!" Kings Island, "the perfect one-stop family vacation resort," promises "fun, adventure, and excitement for every member of the family. From the smallest toddler to the oldest grandparent." Such emphasis on family participation is a constant theme in park publicity. "Family," in this context, implies cleanliness, order, landscaping, no liquor or suggestive shows, a wide mix of attractions, cheerful and helpful young staff (like the kids next door), and plenty of free toilets.[26]

24

---

[24] *Ibid.*, p. 558. See especially his contrast of the old and new style parks. Fred F. McClure in 1911 made a survey of commercial recreation in Kansas City, rating each attraction on a "moral worth" scale from 0% to 100%. Kansas City's five amusement parks gained a 71% rating, behind shooting galleries (84% the highest), skating rinks (74%), and theaters (72%). Lowest were "stag shows" (0%), riverboat excursions (7.7%) and dancehalls (23%). Edwards, *Popular Amusements*, pp. 19–20.

[25] "Summer Show," *op. cit.*, 1467; "Amusing the Million," *op. cit.*, 386; *op. cit.*, p. 537; and Slosson, *op. cit.*, 134.

[26] Walt Disney World has a 24-hour custodial service: Cedar Point boasts that an empty cigaret pack will be picked up in five minutes or less. Disney forbids its staff to wear sunglasses since they give the impression of impersonality. Six Flags emphasizes the importance of the smile—the company song tells employees, "If you see a frown, you gotta turn it upside down." See *Fortune* (December 1977), 171–72 on staff training programs; see also "Housekeeping at Cedar Point," *Amusement Business*, February 27,1965, 18–20.

The point is to get the whole family into the park and keep it   25
there as long as possible. Operators have been notably successful at
this. About one family in five pays from $4.50 to $9.50 each for entrance to the two dozen major parks, not including admission to the
smaller operations. The big "superparks" keep customers an average
of seven and a half hours, during which time they spend about $4.50
each over the original admission fee. The reason is clear and simple—
as *U.S. News and World Report* summarized its study of amusement
parks, it is "wholesome family entertainment at reasonable prices."[27]
One might well underline *family*. A survey conducted in 1972 showed
that 58% of daily attendance at amusement parks derived from family
trade, a figure probably substantially higher today.[28]

6. A sixth way to look at an amusement park is to see it as an   26
adaptation and extension of construction and transportation technology. As Edwin Slosson perceptively pointed out seventy-five years
ago, the park of his day took clever advantage of two recent technological innovations, structural steel and electric lights, and of their application to bridge building and skyscraper construction. Not only park
architecture, but the park rides have always been directly indebted to
the kinds of transportation in common use by urban society and industry—the roller coaster and whip (railroad and streetcar); the ferris
wheel, seesaw, and its various mutations (the elevator); the towers and
buildings (bridges and office buildings).[29]

Similarly, the automobile, airplane, motor boat, and space module   27
were quickly adapted to rides in later years,—The Dodgem, the Para-
chute Drop, the Rocket Ride, The Jet Whirl, Ride the Rapids, and the like.
What park engineers have done since Slosson's time is simply to transfer—quickly, ingeniously, and with shrewd grasp of crowded psychology—the most recent technological innovations into amusement park
equivalents. The famous Switchback Railroad, for example, one of the
most popular early roller coasters, was actually a real railroad to an
abandoned mine, later run through a tunnel to complete the workday
analogy. The commercial use and social convenience of this technology
in daily life is thus transposed to the non-utilitarian purposes of pleasure, excitement, awe, and counterfeit danger. Going to work on a train,
auto, elevated car, or bus day after day is deadly dull; riding a big roller
coaster (which is simply an exaggerated version of the daily commuter

---

[27]July 2, 1975, 38–40. Also *Newsweek,* July 23, 1973, 42.

[28]*Amusement Business,* January 8, 1972. Sanlando Springs Park in Florida, in fact, experi-
mented with year-round family memberships in the style of country clubs or golf clubs.
"Funtown Atlanta" was planned on the model of a shopping mall, to make it "an integrated family recreational center." *Ibid.,* July 3, 1961. On the importance of attracting
family trade, see "Is It For You?" *Ibid.,* January 8, 1960, pp. 18–20.

[29]Slosson, *op. cit.,* pp. 135–36.

experience) is anything but. Such famous present-day coasters as Cedar Point's Gemini, Six Flags Over Georgia's Great American Scream Machine or Bob-Lo's Skystreak are actually great big trolley-car rides.[30]

In effect, the amusement park pushed technology beyond rational limits toward parody into the realm of the comic. Small wagons go uphill and downhill at great speed to nowhere; toy autos skitter about and crash without danger or destination; boat-rides down the swirling rapids hardly get the rider wet. The normal technology of transportation and construction in daily life is burlesqued into child's games—sliding on cellar doors, racing coasters down hill, riding bikes no-hands, pumping high on the backyard swing.[31]

7. The illusory or imitative aspect of the amusement park suggests a seventh way of looking at it—as what might be called the riskless risk, a place where one may take chances that are really not chances. The park's basic appeal has long been to provide a sense of imminent danger and the likelihood of disaster without the culmination of either. Early parks specialized in so-called spectacle shows that re-created famous disasters—the Johnstown Flood, the Fall of Pompeii and San Francisco Earthquake were favorites—with great theatrical verisimilitude, creating the thrill but not the tragedy. Parkgoers thus had "a chance to shudder and a chance to be scared out of their wits."[32] For the same reason many parks have featured lion tamers, balloon drops, auto races, wire-walkers, and so on. Just as simulated earthquakes, floods or train wrecks fascinated earlier patrons, so the auto "thrill show" attracted later generations conscious of the dangers of auto travel and street traffic. The original auto "thrill show" appeared in Toledo in 1923; the demolition derby, its carnival-amusement park descendant, was initiated in 1961 in Islip, New York, an interesting adaptation of changing technology to the park's attractions.[33]

A favorite feature of early amusement parks was the fire show (Coney Island's "Fire and Flame" was a pioneer) in which a building was set afire to be extinguished by park firemen with meticulous realism, including screaming women who jumped to death (into safety nets), clouds of smoke, and frequent explosions. Since fire was a con-

28

29

30

---

[30]Gemini, a double-track ride, has a lift height of 125 feet, reaches sixty or more miles per hour, and can handle 52,000 riders per day.

[31]The amusement park ride, in fact, may have developed from the public ice slides of early Russia, adapted by a Frenchman in 1804 to small wagons rolling downhill. The first modern American roller coaster seems to have appeared at Coney Island in 1884. Chicago's Columbian Exposition featured an "Ice Ride" with refrigerated tracks. One may also speculate that some amusement park games and rides may be adaptations of the dollhouse, the treehouse, and the game room.

[32]Denison, *op. cit.*, 340; Hartt, *op. cit.*, pp. 671–72.

[33]*Amusement Business,* July 24, 1961.

stant threat in the city, particularly in tenement districts, the show touched on very real urban experience. The fact that all the performers were trained acrobats and skilled showmen did not detract from the power of the illusion.[34] While disaster shows are still to be seen in some amusement parks, the movies, of course, caught on very early and did them better. Catastrophe is still big box-office; witness *The Poseidon Adventure, Airport 77, The Towering Inferno*, or the recent hit called simply *Disasters*.

The primary appeal of many park rides, like that of the spectacles, was thus predicated on the same "conspicuous joys...of vicarious terror and firsthand hair's-breadth escape." Observers of park attractions from that day to this agree on the delightful feeling of fearful anticipation, the dizzying moments of panic and the flattering sense of bravery at having dared an intimidating ride and won out, even if that risk is sham. Riders, too, often remark on the sudden feeling of camaraderie in the group at the finish at having conquered and survived. The scenic railway at Coney Island, for example, had a wooden beam that looked as if it was about to decapitate the riders but just missed—that beam seemed to have stuck in many minds for years after.[35] Designers of park rides still play heavily on this appeal. Although the actual risk is statistically quite minimal, it is a sense of danger which is ingeniously built into them. In fact, one reason that the roller-coaster structure is left unsheathed is that the latticework of open girders (usually wood) gives a false impression of fragility that heightens the prospective rider's apprehensions. Though engineers are quite capable of designing relatively noiseless cars, they know that the sound of the ride is an integral part of it, and that the rattles, squeaks and thunderous roar of the wheels impart a sense of speed and danger that adds immeasurably to the total effect. The imaginative names given to rides also tend to excite trepidation—Wildcat, Cyclone, Tornado, Blue Racer, Silver Streak, Speed Demon, The Beast—and park advertising strongly reinforces it.[36] Rides continue to constitute the amusement park's major attraction, since they seem to elicit some deep psychological response in everyone—a human need

31

---

[34]See Hartt's vivid account of such a fire show, p. 673ff., and the effect on spectators of this "coquet with death."

[35]Hartt's detailed analysis of the rides and his reactions (674–75) is worth re-reading. He rode the Scenic Railway, The Flying Airship, and a shoot-the-rapids water ride called Hell Gate.

[36]One of the more ingenious public relations tricks was that devised by Crystal Beach Park in Niagara Falls, Canada, which placed a first-aid station and a trained nurse at the unloading platform of its Cyclone roller coaster.

for "the delight of danger and the pleasure of peril," as Edwin Slosson called it. As a modern writer put it, in a superb analysis, to find out why we ride them we need to look inside ourselves:

> They go fast. It's like going over the speed limit without the danger and illegality.
> They're scary. People like to get scared.
> They're fun. They're different, a bit mysterious, almost unnatural.
> Some people need coaxing. Others giggle. Some rub their hands in anticipation. The anticipation is half the fun. There's no doubt the anxiety adds to the pleasure, both physical and mental, despite the hand-wringing, the sweaty palms.
> At the crest of the hill you open your mouth. It's hard not to. Some people gasp, others scream. You look down. Straight down.
> Your body tenses a bit. You look down at your hands and discover someone has painted them white. The car is picking up speed now. Your stomach notes that the bottom of the hill is an awfully long way down.
> Then you are up again. A mysterious force wants to lift you off your seat. There are more hills and dips up ahead. More anticipation.
> You are screaming. It is a strictly reflex action. Try to hold it in. You can't. Things are flying by awfully fast—track, trees, sky, lights—and your senses have to work overtime to keep up with it all.
> When you get out of the car your knees are likely to be weak. Like rubber. Your heart is thumping. Your hands are tingling. Your eyes are refocusing. You remark that it all happened so fast. You think back on it. The experience is a wild blur of sight, sound, feeling. It's exhilarating. Scary. Fun.[37]

8. The eighth way of looking at an amusement park is to view it as the closest approximation of the *total* play experience. It may be the only place in modern life in which all forms of play are represented in a single controlled environment.[38] All human play, as French social psychologist Roger Caillois sees it, may be grouped in four categories:

32

---

[37]Adapted from *The Coaster Enthusiast's Guide to Cedar Point* (Cedar Point, Ohio: Marketing Department, 1978). For an account of the designing and construction of a roller coaster see Jim McHugh, "Anatomy of a Roller Coaster," *Amusement Business*, August 1, 1965, dealing with Riverview Park's Jetstream, built by John Allen of the Philadelphia Toboggan Company.

[38]There are at least six modern theories of play, usefully summarized by Thomas Kando, *Leisure and Popular Culture* (St. Louis: C. V. Mosby Co., 1977), pp. 28–32. The most interesting, however, is that of Roger Caillois, *Man, Play, and Games* (New York: Free Press of Glencoe, 1961), particularly his classification system and his chapter, "Revivals in the Modern World." This portion of the paper is based on his interpretations of fairs, carnivals, parks and circuses.

Competition: contests, both individual and team.

Chance: poker, lotteries, bingo, roulette, parimutual betting, and the like.

Mimicry: theater, spectacles, movies, television, ceremonies.

Vertigo: swinging, skiing, horseback riding, racing, and other activities which distort sensory stability.[39]

The amusement park, separated by fences and guards from the   33
outside world, is itself a kind of play field, through whose gates visitors come expecting to be both spectators and participants. It is a place
of action, noise, color and confusion which people enter only to play,
filled with nothing but devices and situations to help them do so.
There are games of competition—all sorts of shooting and throwing
games, weight-guessing, strength-testing devices, and whole buildings devoted to pinball and other competitive machines. Games of
chance abound—lotteries, spinning fortune wheels, and the ubiquitous bingo hall. Mimicry, of course, is the entire purpose of the theme
park. Many parks also hire clowns, actors of book characters and animals and other masked or costumed players to wander the grounds.
Vertigo-inducing rides such as whips, ferris wheels, swings and slides
form the backbone of the park's traditional attractions. Roller coasters,
in particular, combine real speed, simulated danger and sensory disorder and relief—in two- to three-minute intervals—to produce the most
powerful vertiginous effect of all. Nowhere else in modern life may
one put together in the space of a few hours and with such minor expenditure of money and energy so complete a play experience.

Examining the Text

1. Which of Nye's eight ways of looking at amusement parks come closest to your own point of view? Why? If you enjoy amusement parks, do
you think Nye explains your reasons satisfactorily? Similarly, if you
don't enjoy these parks, do any of Nye's ideas explain why not?

2. Nye does not suggest directly that some of his eight explanations
should take precedence over others. Do you think that the order he
uses for the eight suggests anything about how he might rank them, or
does he want readers to treat them as essentially "equal"?

---

[39]See Chapter 1, "Classification of Games," in Caillois. *Vertigo* is defined as play "designed to distort, mislead, and stimulate confusion, anxiety, nausea, and momentary terror, quickly transformed back into order, at its conclusion." Slosson, *op. cit.*, pp. 136–37,
makes precisely the same point, calling it "delightful dizziness."

3. What conclusions can be drawn about Americans' interests, desires, and values based on the kinds of parks they build and visit?

For Group Discussion

Using Nye's eight viewpoints as a starting point, decide on eight to ten reasons for the popularity of amusement parks and come to some agreement about their order of importance. As a class, discuss the extent to which the most familiar parks meet these criteria and how they do so. How would you improve the modern amusement park?

Writing Suggestion

Nye essentially lumps all amusement parks together, suggesting they have the same basic appeals. Yet it could be argued that conventional amusement parks like Six Flags and Busch Gardens differ in some significant ways from the Hollywood-inspired parks like Disneyworld and Universal Studios, that these differ from exhibition parks such as Epcot Center and Sea World, and that all these differ from carnivals and fairs. If you have been to several different parks, write an essay contrasting them in terms of what they offer and the kind of patron to whom they are most likely to appeal.

Mall Culture

Steven L. Shepard

Shopping malls have been getting a ration of bad press lately, and they're frequently described by their detractors in less than glowing terms. Take a somewhat extreme example: The home page for a literary Web site uses typically dismissive language when referring to the contemporary American mall. In his opening paragraph, the site's author exhorts his reader to "exchange the phenomenal for the sublime. Leave the pasteurized, vapid shopping mall culture of suburbia . . . and travel beyond ideology, beyond orthodoxy."

This is not an isolated instance, one crackpot's ranting against the retail establishment. In recent years, cultural observers have criticized shopping malls as emblematizing a wide range of dysfunctional social and/or psychological tendencies in modern Americans. Feminist critics note that malls have attracted women because of the social discrimination that the latter have been subjected to; malls, in this view, are created specifically for women, and women are manipulated into feeling comfortable there. Meanwhile, urban social critics see shopping malls as mini-cities . . . but superficially and seductively safe and well-ordered cities, in contrast to the apparent danger and chaos of city streets, as is frighteningly displayed daily by sensationalistic news media. In the same negative vein, economic historians finger shopping malls for rapidly causing the extinction of an entire species of businessperson: the heroic small entrepreneur.

In this article Steven L. Shepard, a former writer and editor for Executive Health Report, *takes a similarly disapproving stance as he examines the suburban shopping mall from a developmental perspective, analyzing the impact of mall-based consumerism on young Americans. Further, he muses upon the way in which the idea of "wanting things" is handed down to young people through marketing and commercials for products. Shepard notes the way our contemporary culture encourages mass buying under the guise of necessity, and he labels this phenomenon as dangerous both to the individuals who buy into this ideology, and to society as a whole.* **As you read** *this piece, consider your own reactions to suburban malls: what attitudes, if any, do you have toward them? Do you think they're just harmless—and meaningless— conglomerations of clothing stores? Do you think malls do have some social function as places for people, young and old, to congregate? Or do you agree with the author that malls have a pernicious socializing influence, standing as temples to our basest material drives?*

Some time ago I had one of those thoughts so simple as to be em- 1
barrassing. Though still, it has stuck with me.

It occurred to me while driving through Los Angeles in summer- 2
time, through mile after mile of store after store. Sign after sign, mall
after mall. Perhaps it was the heat, or perhaps the idleness of mind
wrought by the relentless assault, but somewhere along the way I
thought: "What if you could do magic? What if you could suddenly
give everyone everything they wanted? What, that is, if you could do
away with the wanting? With the wanting of new cars, new clothes,
new CDs, new stereos, new appliances and amusements, new gadgets
and gizmos; with the ceaseless, endless torrent of stuff. What if you
could give everyone what they wanted?—make them content and end
the wanting. What would happen?"

The answer, of course, is simple: Life as we know it would end. 3
Without the wanting, there would be no malls, no factories or design
studios working feverishly to replace one hot item with the next. None
of the associated jobs. Except for the producers and purveyors of necessities—bulk flour and Soviet-style clothes—the economy would
stop. Which means in turn that contemporary American culture is
based on unsatisfied want. On unhappiness, really. People have to be
unhappy for our way of life to continue. For if we didn't ceaselessly
want new things, there would be little to sell or cart about.

Depressing though it is, this is not an unfamiliar concept to some 4
people. I first realized this on hearing the editor of a women's fashion
magazine interviewed on the radio. "Why," she was asked, "don't your

models look like your readers? Why not foster a definition of beauty that most women could meet? Wouldn't your readers be happier if they weren't encouraged to aspire to physiques they will never have?"

"Yes," she replied. "But then we would have no advertisers. Be-   5
cause our readers wouldn't need their help to be beautiful."

The true business of her magazine, the editor understood, was   6
the manufacture of desire—of unending discontent with one's present circumstances. If the magazine's readers were to believe they could be beautiful without the advertisers' products, the readers would have no need for the advertisers, and the advertisers none for the magazine. Therefore, the readers must be kept unhappy, always in quest of a goal that must always be kept out of reach.

I was reminded of all this when my son, then twelve, was invited   7
recently to "go to the mall." This meant joining a small group of similarly aged young people that would converge with other convening groups into an amoeboid mass that would then roam the corridors and concourses for hours. Occasionally the mass would stop before a storefront to gawk at the window display. Occasionally it would send in an emissary to make a small purchase. Occasionally it would surge into a fast food outlet. Often it would giggle. Perhaps it would visit a theatre to watch a few hours of death and disfigurement.

Recently, the trendsetting Mall of America in Minneapolis im-   8
posed a curfew on parentless teenagers. More generally, I am told that shopkeepers profess annoyance at the hordes of roving kids outside their windows. But I do not believe this. I do not believe the protestations are real. Or, if they are, I believe the mallkeepers are short-sighted in their irritation. For the malls are the temples of our culture, and "going to the mall" is in truth naught but an initiation rite. The shopkeepers should be glad of this behavior, for as the children gaze through the windows at the well-stocked shelves within, they are learning to want, learning to ache for *things*, supplied by others and of which there can never be enough.

My immediate inclination to my son's request ("Dad, can I go to   9
the mall?") was to say "no." But my wife said that she too had gone to the malls when she was young and that it had merely been a safe place she and her friends could go, a place to socialize without the tyranny of parental oversight. Other parents said it offered a benign environment for prepubescent "boy-girl stuff," our version of the *corso*—the street or square where young Italians gather and stroll for the purpose of being seen.

Certainly for social creatures such as ourselves these are impor-   10
tant functions. But why does it have to happen at the mall? There are myriad other venues and activities at which young people can meet and practice the skills of *homo teenageus*. There are sporting events, both participatory and not. There are parks and museums. There is the

beach. There are clubs and societies. There are volunteer organizations—help teach a young child to read or work to clean a littered
piece of landscape. But of course, none of these suggestions has the
lure, glitter, or ease of the mall.

   I will grant that the mall is safe, that kids need time away from   11
parents, that they need a place to be together. So why then do I object
to my son's "going to the mall?" Why does his request evoke in me
such visceral opposition?

   In part, because an activity that affords safety is not of itself in-   12
nocuous. It can, for instance, displace more valuable activities. When I
was growing up my father used to tell me and my siblings to turn off
the TV and find something to entertain ourselves—read a book, play
in the yard, play with a friend, daydream. Do anything, but do it of
your own initiative, generate it from within. Because if you provide
for yourself from within you will never be bored, never be lonely,
never need rely on the amusements of others. But now, when I say
these words to my son they sound as anachronistic as if I'd told him to
hitch up the horse. For our culture today has no use for reflection, for
solitude, for that which you can provide for yourself—for a rich inner
life. These are things that cannot be sold and they are antithetical to a
society that sees people primarily as customers or market share.

   But as important, "going to the mall" is a part of a long and   13
many-pronged courtship, a part of the relentless and powerful seduction of our children by that portion of our culture that accords human
beings no more value than the contents of their wallet. It is a part of
the initiation into a life of wanting that can never be sated, of material
desires that will never be satisfied, of slaving to buy and to have, of a
life predicated on unhappiness and discontent.

   And why would I want that for anyone? Much less my son?   14

Examining the Text

1. Explain the author's statement that "the malls are the temples of
our culture, and going to the mall is in truth an initiation rite." What is
the social function of the "temple" and "initiation rites" in societies
that hold to the precepts of certain organized religions? How might
the mall and the activities surrounding it conform to these definitions?

2. Why, according to Shepard, should mall shopkeepers not be annoyed at "the hordes of roving kids outside their windows?" Why
should the presence of these non-purchasing teens and pre-teens be
comforting to the shopkeepers, in this author's opinion?

3. What alternatives to mall-going does the author put forth in this article? How are these alternatives "healthier" for kids than going to malls, in the author's opinion?

For Group Discussion

1. Shepard describes the youthfull mall-going experience this way:

> This meant joining a small group of...young people that would converge with other convening groups into an amoeboid mass that would then roam the corridors and concourses for hours. Occasionally, the mass would stop before a storefront and gawk at the window display. Occasionally, it would send in an emissary to make a small purchase. Occasionally, it would surge into a fast food outlet. Often it would giggle. Perhaps it would visit a theater to watch a few hours of death and disfigurement.

In your experience, is this an accurate depiction of the activities of young people at the mall? Supplement or revise the author's description with more concrete examples of mall-related activitiy.

2. Critique this essay's core premise: "that contemporary American culture is based on unsatisfied want—on unhappiness, really. People have to be unhappy for our way of life to continue." In your opinion, what accounts for modern Americans' desire for the kinds of "nonessential" consumable items—handheld computing devices, fashionable clothes, rubber stamps, bath oils, portable CD players, frilly Victoria's Secret underthings, televisions—that one finds in malls? Is it truly "unhappiness" that drives the desire for these things? If so, what are the psychosocial factors underlying that unhappines; if not, then why do people want these things so much?

Writing Suggestion

In this article, the author describes a conversation with his wife. In this conversation, the author expresses a wish that his son not go to the mall ("My immediate inclination to my son's request...was to say, 'No.'"), while his wife sees some value in the mall-going experience ("...my wife said that she, too, had gone to the malls when she was young and that it had merely been a safe place she and her friends could go—a place to socialize without the tyranny of parental oversight"). Write a persuasive essay in which you argue for either of these positions: that malls serve a harmless socializing function; or that malls are evil temples to rampant consumerism. Whichever side of the issue you take, make sure that you develop your argument with at least four concrete reasons why you adhere to the opinion you express in your thesis statement.

Risk

Paul Roberts

We turn now from the relatively safe arena of the shopping mall to the steep, sheer mountain face of Icicle Canyon—one of many places where we could expect to find swarms of healthy, seemingly sane men and women risking life and limb on a Sunday afternoon climb. Why is it, Paul Roberts asks, that an increasing number of Americans are choosing "the leisure pursuit of danger," spending their free time climbing slick rocks, steep mountains, and frozen waterfalls; paragliding; whitewater rafting; or even "extreme skiing"? How can we explain the growing popularity of such high-risk activities? Whatever happened to the couch potato?

In this essay, originally published in Psychology Today, *Roberts tries to answer these questions by looking at the psychology of high-risk takers. Conventional theories of personality suggest that these people are acting on a "death-wish," and indeed, Roberts quotes one climber as saying "What we do for kicks, most people wouldn't do if you held a gun to their heads." But Roberts also discusses alternative explanations that offer a more positive view of high-risk activities. As he notes, some researchers suggest that courting peril and undertaking potentially dangerous challenges are actually essential for the progress of societies and for the development of confidence, self-awareness, and a stronger sense of identity in an individual. Although most of his examples are drawn from mountain climbing, Roberts is more broadly concerned with how a proclivity toward risky behavior affects our lives more generally, including such important areas as career choices, marital happiness, and sexual habits.*

As you read, *take note of where Roberts draws on disciplines other than psychology to account for the rise of popularity in high-risk leisure activities. How do anthropology, sociology, history, biology, and chemistry add to an understanding of risk-taking?*

In the land of seatbelts and safety helmets, the leisure pursuit of danger is a growth industry. Some experts say that courting uncertainty is the only way to protect the inner force America was founded on. Or to define the self. 1

Risky business has never been more popular. Mountain climbing is among America's fastest growing sports. Extreme skiing—in which skiers descend cliff-like runs by dropping from ledge to snow-covered ledge—is drawing wider interest. Sports like paragliding and cliff-parachuting are marching into the recreational mainstream while the adventure-travel business, which often mixes activities like climbing or river rafting with wildlife safaries, has grown into a multimillion-dollar 2 industry. "Forget the beach," declared *Newsweek* last year. "We're hot for mountain biking, river running, climbing, and bungee jumping."

> Thirty-six year-old Derek Hersey knew a thing or two about life on the edge. Where most rock climbers used ropes and other safety gear, the wiry, wise-cracking Brit usually climbed "free solo"—alone, using nothing but climbing shoes, finger chalk, and his wits. As one climbing buddy put it, Hersey went "for the adrenaline and risk," and on May 28, 1993, he got a dose of both. High on the face of Yosemite's Sentinel Rock, Hersey met with rain and, apparently, slick rock. Friends who found the battered body reckon he fell several hundred feet. In the not-too-distant past, students of human behavior might have explained Hersey's fall as death-wish fulfillment. Under conventional personality theories, normal individuals do everything possible to avoid tension and risk.

In fact, as researchers are discovering, the psychology of risk in-   3
volves far more than a simple "death wish." Studies now indicate that the inclination to take high risks may be hard-wired into the brain, intimately linked to arousal and pleasure mechanisms, and may offer such a thrill that it functions like an addiction. The tendency probably affects one in five people, mostly young males, and declines with age. It may ensure our survival, even spur our evolution as individuals and as a species. Risk taking probably bestowed a crucial evolutionary advantage, inciting the fighting and foraging of the hunter-gatherer.

In mapping out the mechanisms of risk, psychologists hope to do   4
more than explain why people climb mountains. Risk-taking, which one researcher defines as "engaging in any activity with an uncertain outcome," arises in nearly all walks of life. Asking someone on a date, accepting a challenging work assignment, raising a sensitive issue with a spouse or a friend, confronting an abusive boss—all involve uncertain outcomes, and present some level of risk. Understanding the psychology of risk, understanding why some individuals will take chances and others won't, could have important consequences in everything from career counseling to programs for juvenile delinquents.

Researchers don't yet know precisely how a risk taking impulse   5
arises from within or what role is played by environmental factors, from upbringing to the culture at large. And, while some level of risk taking is clearly necessary for survival (try crossing a busy street without it), scientists are divided as to whether, in a modern society, a "high-risk gene" is still advantageous. Some scientists, like Frank Farley, Ph.D., a University of Wisconsin psychologist and past president of the American Psychological Association, see a willingness to take big risks as essential for success. The same inner force that pushed Derek Hersey, Farley argues, may also explain why some dare to run for office, launch a corporate raid, or lead a civil-rights demonstration.

Yet research has also revealed the darker side of risk taking.   6
High-risk takers are easily bored and may suffer low job satisfaction.
Their craving for stimulation can make them more likely to abuse
drugs, gamble, commit crimes, and be promiscuous. As psychologist
Salvadore Maddi, Ph.D., of the University of California-Davis warns,
high-risk takers may have a hard time deriving meaning and purpose
from everyday life."

Indeed, this peculiar form of dissatisfaction could help explain   7
the explosion of high-risk sports in America and other post-industrial
Western nations. In unstable cultures, such as those at war or suffering
poverty, people rarely seek out additional thrills. But in a rich and
safety-obsessed country like America, land of guardrails, seat belts,
and personal-injury lawsuits, everyday life may have become too safe,
predictable, and boring for those programmed for risk-taking.

In an unsettling paradox, our culture's emphasis on security and   8
certainty—two defining elements of a "civilized" society—may not
only be fostering the current risk-taking wave, but could spawn riskier
activities in the future. "The safer we try to make life," cautions psychologist Michael Aptor, Ph.D, a visiting professor at Yale and author
of *The Dangerous Edge: The Psychology of Excitement*, "the more people
may take on risks."

UNIQUE WAVELENGTHS

In Icicle Canyon, a towering rocky corridor in the Cascade   9
Mountains of Washington State, this strange interplay between safety
and risk is a common sight. When weather permits, the canyon's formidable walls swarm with fit-looking men and women, using improb-
ably small ledges and cracks to hoist themselves upward. For novices,
risk can be kept to a minimum. Beginners' climbs are "top-roped" by a
line running from the climber to a fixed cliff-top anchor and back
down to a partner on the ground.

Even so, the novice can quickly experience a very realistic fear—   10
what veterans call "getting gripped." Halfway up one short cliff, a
first-timer in a tee shirt and shorts stabs out beneath a rock overhang.
Unable to find a foothold, the climber peels off the cliff like wet wall-
paper and dangles limply from the rope. His partner lowers him back
to safety, where he stands white-faced, like someone emerging from
an auto accident. Five minutes later, he is back on the cliff.

It's easy to see why high-risk sports receive so much academic   11
attention. Climbers, for example, score higher on risk-preference tests
than nearly all other groups. They show a strong need for intense
stimulation and seek it in environments—sheer cliffs or frozen waterfalls—that most humans seem genetically programmed to avoid.

Climbers' own explanations for why they climb illustrate the diffi-   12
culty of separating genetic, environmental, and cognitive components
of this or any other behavioral trait. Many say they climb for decidedly
conscious reasons: to test limits, to build or maintain self-esteem, to gain
self-knowledge. Some regard it as a form of meditation. "Climbing demands absolute concentration," says Barbara, a lithe, 30-ish climber
from Washington State. "It's the only time I ever feel in the moment."

Yet even the most contemplative climbers concede that their   13
minds and bodies do operate on a unique wavelength. As Forrest
Kennedy, a 32-year-old climber from Georgia, bluntly puts it, "What we
do for kicks, most people wouldn't do if you held a gun to their heads."

Many climbers recognize that their commitment to the sport bor-   14
ders on addiction, one that persists after brushes with injury and death.
Seattle attorney Jim Wickwire, for example, is probably best known for
being on the first American team to summit Pakistan's 28,250-foot K-2,
second highest peak in the world and arguably the most challenging.
(The movie K-2 was based on his story.) Yet this handsome, soft-spoken
father of five is almost as well known for his obstinacy. On K-2, Wickwire lost several toes to frostbite and half a lung to altitude sickness. A
year before, in 1977, he'd seen two climbing partners fall 4,000 feet. In
1981 on Alaska's Mount McKinley, he watched helplessly as another
partner froze to death after becoming wedged in an ice crevasse.

Wickwire vowed then never to climb again. But in 1982, he at-   15
tempted 29,028-foot Mount Everest, the world's tallest peak—and
there saw yet another partner plunge 6,000 feet to her death. In 1993,
as Wickwire, then 53, prepared for a second Everest attempt, he told a
climbing magazine that he'd "stopped questioning why" he still
climbed. Today, he seems just as uncertain. "The people who engage
in this," Wickwire says, "are probably driven to it in a psychological
fashion that they may not even understand themselves."

Until recently, researchers were equally baffled. Psychoanalytic   16
theory and learning theory relied heavily on the notion of stimulus reduction, which saw all human motivation geared toward eliminating
tension. Behaviors that created tension, such as risk taking, were
deemed dysfunctional, masking anxieties or feelings of inadequacy.

A CRAVING FOR AROUSAL

Yet as far back as the 1950s, research was hinting at alternative   17
explanations. British psychologist Hans J. Eysenck developed a scale
to measure the personality trait of extroversion, now one of the most
consistent predictors of risk taking. Other studies revealed that, contrary to Freud, the brain not only craved arousal, but somehow regulated that arousal at an optimal level. Over the next three decades,

researchers extended these early findings into a host of theories about risk-taking.

Some scientists, like UC-Davis's Maddi and Wisconsin's Farley, concentrate on risk-taking primarily as a cognitive or behavioral phenomenon. Maddi sees risk-taking as an element of a larger personality dimension he calls "hardiness," which measures individuals' sense of control over their environment and their willingness to seek out challenges. Farley regards risk-taking more as a whole personality type. Where other researchers speak of Types A and B personalities, Farley adds Type T, for thrill-seeking. He breaks Type-T behavior into four categories: T-mental and T-physical, to distinguish between intellectual and physical risk-taking; and T-negative and T-positive, to distinguish between productive and destructive risk-taking.   18

A second line of research focuses on risk's biological roots. A pioneer in these studies is psychologist Marvin Zuckerman at the University of Delaware. He produced a detailed profile of the high-sensation seeking (HSS) personality. HSS individuals, or "highs," as Zuckerman calls them, are typically impulsive, uninhibited, social, intend toward liberal political views. They like high-stimulus activities, such as loud rock music or pornographic or horror movies, yet are rarely satisfied by vicarious thrills. Some level of actual risk—whether physical, social, or legal—seems necessary. Highs tend to be heavy bettors. They may try many kinds of drugs and favor sports like skiing or mountain climbing to running or gymnastics. Highs also show a clear aversion to low-sensation situations, otherwise known as boredom.   19

High-sensation seeking plays a huge role in relationships. Highs favor friends with interesting or offbeat life-styles, and avoid boring people. They're also far more sexually permissive, particularly in the number of sex partners, than lows. Highs favor mates with similar proclivities for stimulation, while lows generally pair off with other lows. And woe, apparently, to those who break this rule. "The combination of a high- and a low-sensation seeker," says Zuckerman, "seems to put the marriage relationship at risk."   20

Indeed, one benefit of such research is that it can be applied to many areas of everyday life. Those seeking mates, the University of Wisconsin's Farley says, should focus on those who share their level of risk taking, particularly in terms of sexual habits. Likewise, thrill seekers should also look for the right level of on-the-job excitement. "If you're a Big T type working on a microchip assembly line, you're going to be miserable," Farley predicts. "But if you're Big T on a big daily newspaper or a police force, where you never know what you'll be doing next, you're probably going to thrive."   21

Many climbers fit the HSS profile. Many report difficulty keeping full-time jobs, either because the work bores them, or because it inter-   22 feres with their climbing schedule. Long-term relationships can be problematic, especially where climbers marry nonclimbers, or where one partner begins losing interest in the sport. Nonclimbing partners often complain that their spouses spend too much time away from home, or refuse to commit to projects (children, for example) that might interfere with climbing. Relationships are also strained by the ever-present threat of injury or death. As one Midwestern climber puts it, "the possibility that I might miss dinner, forever, doesn't make things any smoother."

Further, while many climbers are models of clean living, the   23
sport has its share of hard-partiers. Some even boast of making first ascents while high on marijuana or hallucinogens like LSD. Climbers say such drugs enhance or intensify the climbing experience. But studies suggest that the drugs may also mimic the process that pushes climbers in the first place.

WIRED FOR THRILLS

Researchers have long known of physiological differences between   24
high- and low-sensation seekers. According to Zuckerman, the cortical system of a high can handle higher levels of stimulation without overloading and switching to the fight-or-flight response. Psychologist Randy Larsen, Ph.D., at the University of Michigan, has even shown that high-sensation seekers not only tolerate high stimulus but crave it as well.

Larsen calls high-sensation seekers "reducers": Their brains au-   25
tomatically dampen the level of incoming stimuli, leaving them with a kind of excitement deficit. (Low-sensation seekers, by contrast, tend to "augment" stimuli, and thus desire less excitement.) Why are some brains wired for excitement? Since 1974, researchers have known that the enzyme monoamine oxidase (MAO) plays a central role in regulating arousal, inhibition, and pleasure. They also found that low levels of MAO correlate with high levels of certain behaviors, including criminality, social activity, and drug abuse. When Zuckerman began testing HSS individuals, they, too, showed unusually low MAO levels.

The enzyme's precise role isn't clear. It regulates levels of at least   26
three important neurotransmitters: norepinephrine, which arouses the brain in response to stimuli; dopamine, which is involved with the sensation of pleasure in response to arousal; and serotonin, which acts as a brake on norepinephrine and inhibits arousal. It's possible that high-sensation seekers have lower base levels of norepinephrine and thus, can tolerate more stimulation before triggering serotonin's dampening effect. High-sensation seekers may also have lower levels of dopamine and are thus in a chronic state of underarousal in the brain's pleasure centers.

Such individuals may turn to drugs, like cocaine, which mimic   27
dopamine's pleasure reaction. But they may also use intense and novel
stimulation, triggering norepinephrine's arousal reaction and getting
rewarded by the dopamine pleasure reaction. "What you get is a combination of tremendous arousal with tremendous pleasure," Zuckerman speculates. "And the faster that arousal reaches its peak, the more
intense your pleasure." Just as important, individuals may develop a
tolerance for the pleasure reaction, and thus may need ever higher levels of stimulation— of risk—to achieve the same rush.

Today such an addictive dynamic may seem largely problematic.   28
In prehistoric times it was very likely essential. Dopamine, for example, has known links to various "approach" behaviors: feeding, fighting, foraging, and exploration. Probably, the same mechanism that
gave people like Derek Hersey a rush from climbing also rewarded
their predecessors for the more necessary acts of survival.

Psychologist Aptor suggests that the willingness to take risks, even   29
if expressed by only certain individuals, would have produced benefits
for an entire group. Upon entering a new territory, a tribe would quickly
need to assess the environment's safety in terms of "which water holes
are safe to drink from, which caves are empty of dangerous animals."
Some risk takers would surely die. But, Aptor points out, "it's better for
one person to eat a poisonous fruit than for everybody."

Climbers are understandably leery of such explanations. They   30
admit that they may be more inclined to take risks than the average
human. But that inclination's ultimate expression, they argue, is largely
a matter of personal volition. "At some level, there is a reason, chemical,
mechanical, or whatever, for why we climb. But doesn't that take the
human element out of it, and make us all robots?" grouses Todd Wells,
a 40-year-old climber from Chattanooga. "I climb so I don't feel like a
robot, so I feel like I'm doing something that is motivated by the self."

Even physiologically oriented scientists like Zuckerman admit the   31
dopamine reaction is only part of the risk-taking picture. Upbringing,
personal experience, socioeconomic status, and learning are also crucial
in determining how that risk-taking impulse is ultimately expressed.

CULTURE OF ASCENT

Although many climbers report a childhood preference for   32
thrills, their interest in climbing was often shaped externally, either
through contact with older climbers or by reading about great expedi-
tions. Upon entering the sport, novices are often immersed in a tight-
knit climbing subculture, with its own lingo, rules of conduct, and
standards of excellence.

This learned aspect may be the most important element in the   33
formation of the high-sensation-seeking personality. While risk-taking
may have arisen from neuro-chemicals and environmental influences,
there is an intellectual or conscious side to it that is now not only distinct from them but is itself a powerful motivator. Working through a
challenging climbing route, for example, generates a powerful sense of
competence that can also provide climbers with a new-found confidence in their everyday life. "There is nothing more empowering than
taking a risk and succeeding," says Farley.

No wonder scaling the face of a cliff is a potent act that can pene-   34
trate to the very essence of self and help reshape it. Many climbers report using that empowering dynamic to overcome some of their own
inner obstacles. Among these, fear—of heights, of loss of control, of
death—is the most commonly cited.

Richard Gottlieb, 42-year-old climber from New York, is known for   35
climbing frozen waterfalls, one of the riskiest facets of the sport. But as a
kid, he was too scared even to go to summer camp. "Yet there was something in me that wanted to get into some swashbuckling adventure," he
says. Climbing satisfied that impulse while helping him overcome his
fearful nature. Gottlieb believes climbing has helped him cope with his
fear of death: "We open the door, see the Grim Reaper right there, but instead of just slamming the door, you push him back a few steps."

NEW OUTLETS

Traditional outlets for the risk-taking impulse have been disap-   36
pearing from everyday life. As civilization steadily minimized natural
risks, Aptor says, and as cultures have sought to maintain their hard-
won stability through repressive laws and stifling social mores, risk
takers have been forced to devise new outlets. In the 20th century, that
has brought about a rise in thrill sports. But Aptor believes the tension
between civilization and risk-taking dates back eons. Aptor wonders
how much of the British Empire "was built up by people trying to escape the desperately conformist society of Victorian England."

When channeled into sports like climbing, where skill and training   37
can minimize danger, or into starting a new business, risk-taking may
continue to be a healthy psychological outlet. It may provide a means to
cope with boredom and modern anxieties, to bolster self-esteem. Risk-
taking may provide a crucial sense of control in a period where so much
of what happens—from crime and auto accidents to environmental disasters and economic downturns—seems almost random.

Unfortunately, the risk-taking impulse doesn't always find such   38
healthy outlets. Many high-sensation seekers don't have the money or
the role models for sky-diving or rock-climbing, Zuckerman notes. "In

such groups, the main forms of sensation seeking include sex, drugs, heavy drinking, gambling, and reckless driving." Indeed, sensation-seeking may emerge as a critical factor in crime. No surprise, then, that some researchers place the risk-taking personality in the "abnormal" category and regard high-risk-takers almost as an evolutionarily obsolete subspecies. Maddi suggests that well-adjusted people are "good at turning everyday experience into something interesting. My guess is that the safecracker or the mountain climber can't do that as well. They have to do something exciting to get a sense of vitality. It's the only way they have of getting away from the sense that life sucks." Larsen is even blunter: "I think risk-takers are a little sociopathic."

Farley is more optimistic. Even civilized society, he says, holds   39
ample opportunity for constructive risk-taking: investing in a high-stakes business venture, running for political office, taking an unpopular social stand. Farley argues that history's most crucial events are shaped by Big T behavior and Big T individuals, from Boris Yeltsin to Martin Luther King, Jr. The act of emigration, he says, is an intrinsically risky endeavor that selects individuals who are high in sensation-seeking. Consequently, countries built upon immigrant population—America, Canada, Australia—probably have an above-average level of risk-takers. He warns that much of the current effort to minimize risk and risk-taking itself runs the risk of eliminating "a large part of what made this country great in the first place."

For all the societal aspects of this peculiar trait, the ultimate bene-   40
fits may continue to be purely personal. "There's a freshness to the [climbing] experience that clears away the weariness of routine and the complexity of social norms" says Seattle climber Bill Pilling. "Climbing brings you back to a primal place, where values are being created and transformed."

To push away from society's rides and protections, Farley sug-   41
gests, is the only way to get a sense of where "society" ends and "you" begin. "Taking a risk, stepping away from the guardrails, from the rules and the status quo, that's when you get a sense of who you are," he says. "If you don't stretch, try to push past the frontiers, it's very difficult to know that."

Examining the Text

1. Roberts opens his essay with a paradox that he returns to several times in the text: that America's preoccupation with safety and security seems to foster higher levels of risk-taking. Do you think that beginning an essay with a paradox—a seeming contradiciton—is a good strategy? Why or why not? Does Roberts ever "solve" this paradox?

2. In your own words, explain the psychological theory of "stimulus reduction." How does risk-taking behavior contradict and confound this theory?

3. Briefly summarize the characteristics of Farley's Type T personality and Zuckerman's HSS individual. In what ways are these models similar and different? In your opinion, which one offers a more accurate description of the personalities and motivations of high-risk-takers?

4. Consider the two "expert" sources from whom Roberts quotes: psychologists and climbers. Go back through the essay and look at the specific statements made by these experts. To what different uses does Roberts put them? How do their different kinds of expertise help Roberts construct his argument?

For Group Discussion

Roberts weighs the benefits and dangers of risk-taking activities, but he ultimately chooses to remain neutral and impartial. In groups, discuss your own opinion about whether risk-taking activities have primarily positive or negative effects on participants. Choose one side of the question and argue for it as persuasively and logically as you can, drawing on Roberts' arguments and those of the climbers and psychologists he cites in his essay. As a class, decide which arguments are the most persuasive.

Writing Suggestion

Even if you're not a high-risk-taker—one of Farley's Type T or Zuckerman's HSS personalities—you've undoubtedly taken a few risks in your life. Risking is defined in the essay as "engaging in any activity with an uncertain outcome," such as asking someone for a date or taking on a new and difficult challenge. Recall a time when you took a risk and assess both the positive and negative effects of this experience. Write an essay in which you describe your experience and evaluate its impact on you. You should draw on Roberts' assessment of the benefits and harms of risk-taking and relate them to your own experience with risk.

ADDITIONAL SUGGESTIONS FOR WRITING ABOUT LEISURE

1. For the next seven days, keep track of how you spend your time. Use a "time diary" such as the one on page 618 or some other chart to record the activity, the amount of time you spend on it, and the extent to which you enjoy it. When you've done this for seven days, look back over your charts to develop conclusions about your own habits of work and leisure. Look for patterns and contrasts in your activities. For example, you might focus on free time versus work time; or on

What You Do from 5 in the Afternoon until Midnight

Time	What did you do?	Time Began	Time Ended	Where	List Other People with You	Doing Anything Else	Enjoyment on a Scale of 1–10 Dislike = 1, Like = 10
5 P.M. →							
6 P.M. →							
7 P.M. →							
8 P.M. →							
9 P.M. →							
10 P.M. →							
11 P.M. →							

daytime versus evening activities; or on leisure activities which are social versus those which are solitary; or on the kinds of satisfaction you
receive from leisure and work activities. Based on your analysis, write
an essay explaining the place of leisure time in your life right now. In
developing this essay, draw on some of the readings in this chapter
and comment on how keeping track of how you spent your time altered your behavior, if indeed it did.

2. For a leisure activity with which you're familiar, offer a detailed
analysis modeled after the essay of Sherman, Nye, or Rose. You might
begin by describing the activity, and go on to consider some of the following questions: What satisfactions does this activity bring its participants? What are its drawbacks or detrimental effects? What sort of
people are interested in this activity? Are there differences in terms of
gender, age, class, ethnicity, or geographical location? How might this
activity influence participants? What does it teach them? In what ways
does it fit or fail to fit the criteria for leisure? Considering these and other
questions, try to develop a thorough analysis of this leisure pursuit.

3. The table on page 620, taken from *The Futurist*, identifies the number of hours per week that Americans devote to specific leisure activities and provides figures regarding gender differences and changes
over a twenty-year period.

  Imagine that you're a visitor from another country who has been
provided with this list to help introduce you to American culture.
Write an essay explaining the conclusions you can draw about Americans from this list. What values, beliefs, and attitudes does this list reveal? Be as specific as possible.

4. One of Witold Rybczynski's more striking observations is that
"Americans now spend more than $13 billion annually on sports
clothing; put another way, about 1.3 billion hours of potential leisure
time are exchanged for leisure wear—for increasingly elaborate running shoes, certified biking shorts, and monogrammed warm-up
suits." Judith Schor makes a similar point when she suggests that time
is valued only in terms of money and that if we would control our consumerism, we would have more leisure time. In an essay explore the
relationships among work, leisure, and consumerism in our society.
Use your own experience as the basis for your argument. How much
of the money you and your family members make goes to support
leisure activities? What about your friends?

Internet Activities

1. For some users, leisure activities on the World Wide Web have become preferable to real-life ones. While a umber of users prefer the ease

Spare Time: Hours per Week Adults Aged 18 to 64 Spend in Leisure Activities

	Total			Men			Women		
	1985	1975	1965	1985	1975	1965	1985	1975	1965
Total	*40.1*	*38.3*	*34.5*	*41.1*	*38.6*	*34.4*	*39.6*	*38.3*	*34.4*
TV	15.1	15.2	10.5	15.7	16.2	11.7	14.5	14.1	9.3
Visiting	4.9	5.5	6.6	5.0	5.1	5.8	4.8	5.7	7.5
Talking	4.3	2.2	2.6	3.5	1.9	1.6	5.1	2.7	3.6
Traveling	3.1	2.6	2.7	3.4	2.8	3.0	3.0	2.4	2.4
Reading	2.8	3.1	3.7	2.7	3.0	4.2	2.9	3.3	3.3
Sports/outdoors	2.2	1.5	0.9	2.9	2.3	1.4	1.5	0.8	0.5
Hobbies	2.2	2.3	2.1	1.9	1.6	1.4	2.6	3.0	2.8
Adult education	1.9	1.6	1.3	2.2	2.1	1.6	1.6	1.3	0.9
Thinking/relaxing	1.0	1.1	0.5	1.2	1.0	0.2	0.9	1.2	0.6
Religion	0.8	1.0	0.9	0.6	0.8	0.7	1.0	1.3	1.0
Cultural events	0.8	0.5	1.1	0.8	0.3	1.3	0.8	0.6	0.9
Clubs/organizations	0.7	1.2	1.0	0.8	0.9	0.9	0.6	1.5	1.2
Radio/recordings	0.3	0.5	0.6	0.4	0.6	0.7	0.3	0.4	0.4

Note: Figures may not equal total due to rounding.
Source: Americans' Use of Time Project. University of Maryland. Reprinted with permission of *American Demographics*, November 1990.

of "logging on" to going out, others are attracted by the anonymity promised by the Web. Keeping this in mind, write an essay in which you explore various Web pages that specialize in activities also available in real life (some options are available on the *Common Culture* Web site). What types of activities lend themselves more readily to the Internet? Do these Web pages offer any features unavailable in the real-life equivalent of the activity? Is the activity improved or worsened by its online counterpart? Which verson of the activity do you prefer? As an example, consider how some people prefer to shop online to avoid crowds, whereas others enjoy the experience of going out to shop.

2. The World Wide Web has made it easier than ever for Web "surfers" to partake in leisure activities. By offering e-mail, shopping, video games, chat rooms, and a host of other online activities, the Web has enabled users to participate who might not have otherwise. Write an essay describing the convenience of being a click away from a world of entertainment choices (some options are available on the *Common Culture* Web site). What are the distinct advantages of these activities? Are there any disadvantages? Consider some specific issues involving Web use, such as online addiction or the benefits of the Web to homebound disabled persons or users in remote areas.

For Further Reading: A Common Culture Bibliography

CHAPTER 2: ADVERTISING

Abernethy, Avery M. and George R. Franke. "The Information Content of Advertising: A Meta-Analysis." *Journal of Advertising* (Summer 1996): 1–18.

Affluenza. KCTS Television and Oregon Public Broadcasting. Oley, PA: Bullfrog Films, Inc., 1998. VIDEORECORDING.

Barthel, Diane. *Putting on Appearances: Gender and Advertising.* Philadelphia, PA: Temple University Press, 1988.

Benoit, William L., P. M. Pier, and Joseph R. Blaney. "A Functional Approach to Televised Political Spots: Acclaiming, Attacking, Defending." *Communication Quarterly* (Winter 1997): 1–21.

The Best Campaign Commercials, 1992. Washington, DC: *Campaign Magazine,* 1992 Videocassette.

Cortese, Anthony Joseph Paul. *Provocateur: Images of Women and Minorities in Advertising.* Lanham, MD: Rowman & Littlefield, 1999.

Craig, Steve, ed. *Men, Masculinity, and the Media.* Thousand Oaks, CA: Sage, 1992.

Ewen, Stuart and Elizabeth Ewen. *Channels of Desire: Mass Images and the Shaping of American Consciousness.* 2nd ed. Minneapolis, MN: University of Minnesota Press, 1992.

Fowles, Jib. *Advertising and Popular Culture.* Thousand Oaks, CA: Sage, 1996.

Goldman, Robert. *Reading Ads Socially.* London; New York: Routledge, 1992.

Goldman, Robert and Stephen Papson. *Nike Culture: The Sign of the Swoosh.* London: Sage, 1998.

Hine, Thomas. *The Total Package: The Evolution and Secret Meanings of Boxes, Bottles, Cans, and Tubes.* Boston, MA: Little, Brown, 1995.

Hovland, Rebecca and Gary B. Wilcox. *Advertising in Society: Classic and Contemporary Readings on Advertising's Role in Society.* Lincolnwood, IL: NTC Business Books, 1989.

Jhally, Sut. *Advertising & the End of the World.* Northampton, MA: Media Education Foundation, 1998. VIDEORECORDING.

Kilbourne, Jean, director. *Still Killing Us Softly.* Cambridge, MA: Cambridge Documentary Films, 1992. VIDEORECORDING.

Laird, Pamela Walker. *Advertising Progress: American Business and the Rise of Consumer Marketing.* Baltimore, MD: The Johns Hopkins University Press, 1998.

Manring, M. M. *Slave in a Box: The Strange Career of Aunt Jemima.* Charlottesville, VA: University Press of Virginia, 1998.

McAllister, Matthew P. *The Commercialization of American Culture: New Advertising, Control, and Democracy.* Thousand Oaks, CA: Sage, 1996.

Mitchell, Arthur. *The Nine American Lifestyles: Who We Are and Where We're Going.* New York: Warner Books, 1983.

Myers, Greg. *Words in Ads.* New York: Routledge, 1994.

O'Barr, William M. *Culture and the Ad: Exploring Otherness in the World of Advertising.* Boulder, CO: Westview Press, 1994.

Randazzo, Sal. *The Myth Makers: How Advertisers Apply the Power of Classic Myths and Symbols to Create Modern Day Legends.* Chicago, IL: Probus, 1995.

Sivulka, Juliann. *Soap, Sex, and Cigarettes: A Cultural History of American Advertising.* Belmont, CA: Wadsworth, 1998.

Stale Roles and Tight Buns. Boston: OASIS, 1991. Videocassette.

Stephenson, Theresa, William J. Stover, and Mike Villamor. "Sell Me Some Prestige! The Portrayal of Women in Business-related Ads." *Journal of Popular Culture* (Spring 1997): 255–272.

Sturges, Ingrid. "Black Images in Advertising." *Emerge* (September 1993): 21–24.

Turow, Joseph. *Breaking up America: Advertisers and the New Media World.* Chicago, IL: University of Chicago Press, 1997.

CHAPTER 3: TELEVISION

Abt, Vicki and Leonard Mustazza. *Coming After Oprah: Cultural Fallout in the Age of the TV Talk Show.* Bowling Green, OH: Bowling Green State University Popular Press, 1997.

Andersen, Robin. *Consumer Culture and TV Programming.* Boulder, CO: Westview Press, 1995.

Berger, Arthur Asa. *Television as an Instrument of Terror.* New Brunswick, NJ: Transaction Books, 1980.

Berman, Ronald. *How Television Sees Its Audience.* Thousand Oaks, CA: Sage, 1987.

Bianculli, David. *Teleliteracy: Taking Television Seriously.* New York: Simon & Schuster, 1994.

Blumenthal, Dannielle. *Women and Soap Opera: A Cultural Feminist Perspective.* Westport, CT: Praeger, 1997.

Brown, Mary Ellen, ed. *Television and Women's Culture: The Politics of the Popular.* Thousand Oaks, CA: Sage, 1994.

Day, Nancy. *Sensational TV: Trash or Journalism?* Springfield, NJ: Enslow, 1996.

Douglas, William and Beth M. Olson. "Subversion of the American Family? An Examination of Children and Parents in Television Families." *Communication Research* (February 1996): 73–100.

Douglas, Susan. "Sitcom Women: We've Come a Long Way. Maybe." *Ms. Magazine* (November–December 1995): 76–81.

Gamson, Joshua. *Freaks Talk Back: Tabloid Talk Shows and Sexual Nonconformity.* Chicago, IL: University of Chicago Press, 1998.

Gitlin, Todd. *Inside Prime Time.* 2nd ed. New York: Pantheon, 1994.

Hamamoto, Darrell Y. *Nervous Laughter: Television Situation Comedy and Liberal Democratic Ideology.* New York: Praeger, 1989.

Leonard, John. *Smoke and Mirrors: Violence, Television, and Other American Cultures.* New York: New Press, 1997.

Hartley, John. *Uses of Television.* London: Routledge, 1999.

Jones, Gerard. *Honey, I'm home!: Sitcoms, Selling the American Dream.* New York: St. Martin's Press, 1993.

Mander, Jerry. *Four Arguments for the Elimination of Television.* New York: Morrow, 1978.

Marc, David. *Comic Visions: Television Comedy and American Culture.* 2nd ed. Malden, MA: Blackwell, 1997.

Means Coleman, Robin R. *African American Viewers and the Black Situation Comedy: Situating Racial Humor.* New York: Garland, 1998.

Miller, Mark Crispin. *Boxed In: The Culture of TV.* Evanston, IL: Northwestern University Press, 1988.

Minow, Newton N. and Craig L. LaMay. *Abandoned in the Wasteland: Children, Television, and the First Amendment.* New York: Hill and Wang, 1995.

Monaco, Paul. *Understanding Society, Culture, and Television.* Westport, CT: Praeger, 1998.

Morse, Margaret. *Virtualities: Television, Media Art, and Cyberculture.* Bloomington, IN: Indiana University Press, 1998.

Newcomb, Horace. *Television: The Critical View.* 5th ed. New York: Oxford University Press, 1994.

Owen, Rob. *Gen X TV: The Brady Bunch to Melrose Place.* Syracuse, NY: Syracuse University Press, 1997.

Postman, Neil. *Amusing Ourselves to Death.* New York: Penguin Books, 1985.

Watson, Mary Ann. "The Seinfeld Doctrine—'No Hugging, No Learning'—Imprints the 1990s." *Television Quarterly* (Summer 1997): 52–55.

CHAPTER 4: MUSIC

Arnold, Gina. *Kiss This: Punk in the Present Tense.* New York: St. Martin's Press, 1997.

Baker, Houston A., Jr. *Black Studies, Rap, and the Academy.* Chicago: University of Chicago Press, 1993.

Baraka Amiri. *Blues People: Negro Music in White America*. New York: William Morrow, 1983.

Brightman, Carol. *Sweet Chaos: The Grateful Dead's American Adventure*. New York: Random House/Clarkson Potter, 1998.

Burr, Ramiro. *Tejano and Regional Mexican Music*. New York: Billboard Books, 1999.

Chang, Kevin and Wayne Chen. *Reggae Routes: The Story of Jamaican Music*. Philadelphia: Temple University Press, 1998.

Chuck D. and Yusaf Jah. *Fight the Power: Rap, Race, and Reality*. New York: Delacorte Press, 1997.

Costell, Mark and David Foster Wallace. *Signifying Rappers: Rap and Race in the Urban Present*. New York: Ecco Press, 1997.

Dickerson, James. *Women on Top: The Quite Revolution That's Rocking the American Music Industry*. New York: Billboard Books, 1999.

Fernando, S. H., Jr. *The New Beats: Exploring the Music, Culture, and Attitudes of Hip-Hop*. New York: Anchor Books, 1994.

Foster, Chuck. *Roots Rock Reggae: An Oral History of Reggae Music from Ska to Dancehall*. New York: Billboard Books, 1999.

George, Nelson. *Hip Hop America*. New York: Viking Press, 1998.

Gimarc, George. *Punk Diary: 1970–1979*. New York: St. Martin's Press, 1994.

Glasser, Ruth. *My Music Is My Flag: Puerto Rican Musicians and Their New York Communities, 1917–1940*. Berkeley: University of California Press, 1997.

Goodman, Fred. *The Mansion on the Hill: Dylan, Young, Geffen, Springsteen, and the Head-On Collision of Rock and Commerce*. New York: Vintage Books, 1998.

Heylin, Clinton, *From the Velvets to the Voidoids: A Pre-Punk History for a Post-Punk World*. New York: Penguin, 1993.

Jones, Quincey and the Editors of *Vibe* Magazine. *Tupac Amaru Shakur 1971–1996*. Pittsburgh: Three Rivers Press, 1998.

Loza, Steven. *Barrio Rhythm: Mexican American Music in Los Angeles*. Urbana-Champaign: University of Illinois Press, 1993.

Marcus, Griel. *Mystery Train: Images of America in Rock 'N' Roll Music*. New York: Plume, 1997.

Marcus, Greil. *In the Fascist Bathroom: Punk in Pop Music, 1977–1992*. Cambridge, MA: Harvard University Press, 1999.

McNeil, Legs and Gillian McCain. *Please Kill Me: The Uncensored Oral History of Punk*. New York: Penguin, 1997.

Morton, Colin B. and Chuck Death. *Great Pop Things: The Real History of Rock and Roll from Elvis to Oasis*. New York: Verse Chorus Press, 1998.

Otfinoski, Steve. *The Golden Age of Rock Instrumentals*. New York: Billboard Books, 1999.

Perkins, William Eric. *Droppin' Science: Critical Essays on Rap Music and Hip Hop Culture*. Philadelphia: Temple University Press, 1996.

Potter, Russell A. *Spectacular Vernaculars: Hip-Hop and the Politics of Postmodernism*. New York: State University of New York Press, 1995.

Queen Latifah. *Ladies First: Revelations from a Strong Woman*. New York: William Morrow, 1999.

Rettenmund, Matthew. *Encyclopedia Madonnica*. New York: St. Martin's Press, 1995.

Reynolds, Simon. *Generation Ecstasy: Into the World of Techno and Rave Culture.* New York: Little, Brown, 1998.

Rose, Tricia. *Black Noise: Rap Music and Black Culture in Contemporary America.* Middletown, CT: Wesleyan University Press, 1994.

Sicko, Dan. *Techno Rebels: The Renegades of Electronic Funk.* New York: Billboard Books, 1999.

Snowden, Don. *Make the Music Go Bang: The Early L.A. Punk Scene.* New York: St. Martin's Press, 1997.

Ward, Brian. *Just My Soul Responding: Rhythm and Blues, Black Consciousness, and Race Relations.* Berkeley: University of California Press, 1998.

Roman-Velazquez, Patria. "The Embodiment of Salsa: Musicians, Instruments and the Performance of a Latin Style and Identity." *Popular Music* v18, n1 (January 1999): 115.

Gracyk, Theodore. "Valuing and Evaluating Popular Music." *Journal of Aesthetics and Art Criticism* (Spring 1999): 205.

Wicks, Sammie Ann. "America's Popular Music Traditions as 'Canon-Fodder'." *Popular Music and Society* v22, n1 (Spring 1998): 55.

Moody, Nickianne. "Social and Temporal Geographies of the Near Future: Music, Fiction and Youth Culture." *Futures* v30, n10: 1003.

Lewis, Cynthia. "Rock 'n' Roll and Horror Stories: Students, Teachers, and Popular Culture." *Journal of Adolescent & Adult Literacy* v42, n2 (October 1998): 116.

Goodman, Fred. "La Explosion Pop Latino." *Rolling Stone*, n812 (May 13, 1999): 21.

Banks, Jack. "MTV and the Globalization of Popular Culture." *Gazette* v59, n1 (February 1997): 43.

Hemmer, Kurt. "Look Who's Listenin': Rap, Black Culture, and the Academy." *Melus* v23, n3 (Fall 1998): 232.

Wahl, Greg. "I Fought the Law: Hip-Hop in the Mainstream." *College Literature*, v26, n1 (Winter 1999): 98.

Smitherman, Geneva. "The Chain Remain the Same: Communicative Practices in the Hip-Hop Nation." *Journal of Black Studies* v29, n1 (September 1997): 3.

CHAPTER 5: CYBERCULTURE

Aronowitz, Stanley and Jonathan Cutler, eds. *Post-work: The Wages of Cybernation.* New York: Routledge, 1998.

Barrett, Neil. *Digital Crime: Policing the Cybernation.* London: Kogan Page, 1997.

Calcutt, Andrew. "Computer Porn Panic: Fear and Control in Cyberspace." *Futures* (September 1995): 749–763.

Cherny, Lynn. *Conversation and Community: Chat in a Virtual World.* Stanford, CA: CSLI, 1999.

Cherny, Lynn and Elizabeth Reba Weise, eds. *Wired Women: Gender and New Realities in Cyberspace.* Seattle, WA: Seal Press, 1996.

Dery, Mark. *Escape Velocity: Cyberculture at the End of the Century.* New York: Grove Press, 1996.

Dery, Mark ed. *Flame Wars: The Discourse of Cyberculture.* Durham, NC: Duke University Press, 1993.

Doheny-Farina, Stephen. *The Wired Neighborhood*. New Haven: Yale University Press, 1996.

Dyson, Esther. *Release 2.1: A Design for Living in the Digital Age*. New York: Broadway Books, 1998.

Ebo, Bosah, ed. *Cyberghetto or Cybertopia?: Race, Class, and Gender on the Internet*. Westport, CT: Praeger, 1998.

Grossman, Wendy. *Net.wars*. New York: New York University Press, 1997.

Harcourt, Wendy, ed. *Women@Internet: Creating New Cultures in Cyberspace*. London; New York: Zed Books, 1999.

Jones, Steven G., ed. *Virtual Culture: Identity and Communication in Cybersociety*. London; Thousand Oaks, CA: Sage, 1997.

Jordan, Tim. *Cyberpower: The Culture and Politics of Cyberspace and the Internet*. London; New York: Routledge, 1999.

Kitchin, Rob. *Cyberspace: The World in the Wires*. Chichester; New York: John Wiley & Sons, 1998.

Life on the Internet. InterNet-working. PBS Video, 1996. VIDEORECORDING.

Life on the Internet. Virtual Neighbors. PBS Video, 1997. VIDEORECORDING.

Moore, Dinty W. *The Emperor's Virtual Clothes: The Naked Truth about Internet Culture*. Chapel Hill, NC: Algonquin Books, 1995.

Porter, David, ed. *Internet Culture*. New York: Routledge, 1997.

Rheingold, Howard. *The Virtual Community: Homesteading on the Electronic Frontier*. Reading, MA: Addison-Wesley, 1993.

Seabrook, John. *Deeper: My Two-Year Odyssey in Cyberspace*. New York: Simon & Schuster, 1997.

Shields, Rob. *Cultures of Internet: Virtual Spaces, Real Histories, Living Bodies*. London; Thousand Oaks, CA: Sage, 1996.

Smith, Marc A. and Peter Kollock. *Communities in Cyberspace*. London: Routledge, 1999.

Smolan, Rick, and Jennifer Erwitt, eds. *24 Hours in Cyberspace: Photographed on One Day by 150 of the World's Leading Photojournalists*. QUE Macmillan: Against All Odds Productions, 1996.

Surratt, Carla G. *Netlife: Internet Citizens and their Communities*. Commack, NY: Nova Science, 1998.

Talbott, Steve. *The Future Does Not Compute: Transcending the Machines in our Midst*. Sebastopol, CA: O'Reilly & Associates, 1995.

CHAPTER 6: SPORTS

Baker, Aaron and Todd Boyd. *Out of Bounds: Sports, Media, and the Politics of Identity*. Bloomington, IN: Indiana University Press, 1997.

Cahn, Susan K. *Coming on Strong: Gender and Sexuality in Twentieth-Century American Sports*. New York: Macmillan, 1994.

Coakley, Jay J. *Sport in Society: Issues and Controversies*. 6th ed. Boston, MA: Irwin/McGraw-Hill, 1998.

Early, Gerald. *Tuxedo Junction: Essays on American Culture*. New York: Ecco Press, 1989.

Figler, Stephen K. and Gail Whitaker. *Sport and Play in American Life: A Textbook in the Sociology of Sport*. 3rd ed. Madison, WI: Brown & Benchmark, 1995.

Giamatti, A. Bartlett. *Take Time for Paradise: Americans and Their Games.* New York: Summit Books, 1989.

Hauser, Thomas. *The Black Lights: Inside the World of Professional Boxing.* New York: Simon & Schuster, 1991.

Hofmann, Dale and Martin J. Greenberg. *Sport$biz: An Irreverent Look at Big Business in Pro Sports.* Champaign, IL: Leisure Press, 1989.

Lee, Spike and Ralph Wiley. *Best Seat in the House: A Basketball Memoir.* New York: Crown, 1997.

Leifer, Eric Matheson. *Making the Majors: The Transformation of Team Sports in America.* Cambridge, MA: Harvard University Press, 1995.

Lupica, Mike. *Mad as Hell: How Sports Got Away From the Fans—and How We Get it Back.* New York: Putnam, 1996.

Nelson, George. *Elevating the Game: Black Men and Basketball.* New York: Harper-Collins, 1992.

Nelson, Mariah Burton. *The Stronger Women Get, The More Men Love Football: Sexism and the American Culture of Sports.* New York: Harcourt Brace, 1994.

Oleksak, Michael M., and Mary Adams Oleksak. *Beisbol: Latin Americans and the Grand Old Game.* Grand Rapids, MI: Masters Press, 1991.

Quirk, James P. and Rodney Fort. *Hard Ball: The Abuse of Power in Pro Team Sports.* Princeton, NJ: Princeton University Press, 1999.

Sailes, Gary A., ed. *African Americans in Sport: Contemporary Themes.* New Brunswick, NJ: Transaction Books, 1998.

Smith, Lissa, ed. *Nike is a Goddess: The History of Women in Sports.* New York: Atlantic Monthly Press, 1998.

Tharp, Mike. "Sports crazy!" *U.S. News & World Report* (July 15, 1996): 30–35.

Will, George. *Men at Work.* New York: Macmillan, 1992.

CHAPTER 7: MOVIES

Biskind, Peter. *Easy Riders, Raging Bulls: How the Sex-Drugs-And-Rock-'n'-Roll Generation Saved Hollywood.* New York: Simon & Schuster, 1998.

Gabler, Neal. *Life, the Movie: How Entertainment Conquered Reality.* New York: Knopf, 1998.

Scorsese, Martin. *A Personal Journey With Martin Scorsese Through American Movies.* New York: Hyperion, 1997.

Pierson, John. *Spike, Mike, Slackers & Dykes: A Guided Tour Across a Decade of American Independent Cinema.* New York: Miramax, 1997.

Williams, Linda. *Hard Core: Power, Pleasure, and the "Frenzy of the Visible."* Berkeley: University of California Press, 1999.

Lopate, Phillip. *Totally, Tenderly, Tragically: Essays and Criticism from a Lifelong Love Affair with the Movies.* New York: Anchor Books, 1998.

Martinez, Gerald. *What It Is . . . What It Was! The Black Film Explosion of the '70s in Words and Pictures.* New York: Hyperion, 1998.

Tarkovsky, Andrey. *Sculpting in Time: Reflections on the Cinema.* Austin: University of Texas Press, 1989.

Naremore, James. *More Than Night: Film Noir in Its Contexts.* Berkeley: University of California Press, 1998.

Slotkin, Richard. *Gunfighter Nation: The Myth of the Frontier in Twentieth-Century America*. Norman: University of Oklahoma Press, 1998.

Beauchamp, Cari. *Without Lying Down: Frances Marion and the Powerful Women of Early Hollywood*. Berkeley: University of California Press, 1998.

Skal, David J. *Screams of Reason: Mad Science in Modern Culture*. New York: W. W. Norton, 1998.

Ehrenstein, David. *Open Secret: Gay Hollywood 1928–1998*. New York: William Marrow, 1998.

Dunne, John Gregory. *Monster: Living Off the Big Screen*. New York: Random House, 1997.

Brown, Gene. *Movie Time: A Chronology of Hollywood and the Movie Industry from Its Beginnings*. New York: Macmillan, 1995.

May, Larry. *Screening Out the Past: The Birth of Mass Culture and the Motion Picture Industry*. Chicago: University of Chicago Press, 1983.

Gabler, Neal. *An Empire of Their Own: How the Jews Invented Hollywood*. New York: 1989.

Muller, Eddie. *Dark City: The Lost World of Film Noir*. New York: St. Martin's Press, 1998.

Morgan, Jack. "Toward an Organic Theory of the Gothic: Conceptualizing Horror." *Journal of Popular Culture* (Winter 1998): 59.

Sobchack, Vivian. "The Insistent Fringe: Moving Images and Historical Consciousness." *History and Theory* v36, n4 (Dec, 1997): 4.

Rosolowski, Tracey A. " Monsters." *Southwest Review* v84, n2 (Spring 1999): 279.

Grant, Barry Keith. "Rich and Strange: The Yuppie Horror Film." *Journal of Film and Video* v48, n1–2 (Spring–Summer 1996): 4 (13 pages).

Heba, Gary. "Everyday Nightmares: The Rhetoric of Social Horror in the Nightmare on Elm Street Series." *Journal of Popular Film and Television* v23, n3 (Fall 1995): 106.

CHAPTER 8: LEISURE

Bernstein, Carol. "The Leisure Empire." *Time* v136, n27 (December 24, 1990): 56.

Buell, John. *Democracy by Other Means: The Politics of Work, Leisure, and Environment*. Urbana-Champaign: University of Illinois Press, 1995.

Cassell, Justine and Henry Jenkins. *From Barbie to Mortal Kombat: Gender and Computer Games*. Cambridge, MA: M.I.T. Press, 1999.

Ebo, Bosah. "War as Popular Culture: The Gulf Conflict and the Technology of Illusionary Entertainment." *Journal of American Culture* v18, n3 (Fall 1995): 19.

Herz, J. C. and Michael Pietsch. *Joystick Nation: How Videogames Ate Our Quarters, Won Our Hearts, and Rewired Our Minds*. New York: Little, Brown, 1997.

Jewell, David L. *Reflections on Leisure, Play, and Recreation*. Carbondale: Southern Illinois University Press, 1997.

Kowinski, William Severini. *The Malling of America: An Inside Look at the Great Consumer Paradise*. New York: William Morrow, 1985.

Kraus, Richard. *Recreation and Leisure in Modern Society.* New York: Jones & Bartlett, 1998.

Kraus, Richard. *Leisure in a Changing America: Multicultural Perspectives.* New York: MacMillan, 1994.

Kurtti, Jeff. *Since the World Began: Walt Disney World the First 25 Years.* New York: Hyperion, 1996.

Lee, Younghill and Richard Lopez. "Talch'um: Searching for the Meaning of Play." *Journal of Physical Education, Recreation & Dance* v66, n8 (October 1995) :28.

Mannell, Roger. *Social Psychology of Leisure.* New York: Venture, 1997.

Nasaw, David. *Going Out: The Rise and Fall of Public Amusements.* Cambridge: Harvard University Press, 1999.

Nelson, Eric. *Mall of America: Reflections of a Virtual Community.* Lakeville, MI: Galde Press, 1998.

Pronovost, Gilles. "The Sociology of Leisure." *Current Sociology* v46, n3 (July 1998): 1.

Robinson, John P. and Geoffrey Godbey. *Time for Life: The Surprising Ways Americans Use Their Time.* University Park: Pennsylvania State University Press, 1997.

Ross, John F. *Polar Bear Strategy: Reflections on Risk in Modern Life.* New York: Perseus Books, 1999.

Russel, Ruth V. *Pastimes: The Context of Contemporary Leisure.* New York: Brown & Benchmark, 1995.

Rybczynski, Witold. *City Life.* New York: Touchstone Books, 1996.

Sandler, Corey. "The Game of Life: Why We Play Games and the Impacts of Computer Games." *PC World* v11, n8 (August 1993): M89.

Schor, Juliet B. *Overworked American: The Unexpected Decline of Leisure.* New York: Basic Books, 1993.

Seel, John. "Plugged In, Spaced Out, and Turned On: Electronic Entertainment and Moral Minefields." *Journal of Education* v179, n3 (Fall, 1997): 17.

Shields, Rob. *Lifestyle Shopping: The Subject of Consumption.* New York: Routledge, 1992.

Spink, John. *Leisure and the Environment.* New York: Heinemann, 1994.

Talbot, Margaret. "Le Tres Riches Heures de Martha Stewart: Money, Time, and the Surrender of American Taste." *New Republic* v214, n20 (May 13, 1996): 30.

Yates, Brock W. *Outlaw Machine: Harley-Davidson and the Search for the American Soul.* New York: Little, Brown, 1999.

Zepp, Ira G., Jr. *The New Religious Image of Urban America: The Shopping Mall As Ceremonial Center.* Boulder: University Press of Colorado, 1997.

Acknowledgments

TEXT CREDITS

Andersen, Robin, "The Talk Show's Lost Potential," from *Consumer Culture and TV Programming*. New York: Harper Collins, 1996.

Angelou, Maya, "Champion of the World," from *I Know Why the Caged Bird Sings*. Copyright © 1969 by Maya Angelou. Reprinted with the permission of Random House, Inc.

August, Melissa, Leslie Everton Brice, Laird Harrison, Todd Murphy, and David E. Thigpen, "Hip-Hop Nation: There's More to Rap than Just Rhythms and Rhymes," *Time* 153, No. 5 (February 8, 1999).

Barlow, John Perry, "Cyberhood vs. Neighborhood," from *Utne Reader* No. 58 (March–April 1995). Reprinted with the permission of the author.

Bathel, Diane, "A Gentleman and a Consumer," from *Putting on Appearances Gender and Advertising*. Copyright © 1988 by Temple University. Reprinted with the permission of Temple University Press.

Beal, Becky, "Alternative Masculinity and Its Effects on Gender Relations in the Subculture of Skateboarding," *Journal of Sport Behavior* 19, No. 3 (August 1996): 204.

Beckles, Colin, "Black Stuggles in Cyberspace: Cyber Segregation and Cyber-Nazis," *Western Journal of Black Studies* 21, No. 1 (Spring 1997): 12.

Berger, Arthur Asa, "Seven Points on the Game of Football," from *Media Analysis Techniques, Revised Edition*. Copyright © 1982, 1991 by Sage Publications, Inc. Reprinted with the permission of the publishers.

Berman, Ronald, "Soaps Day and Night," from *How Television Sees Its Audience: A Look at the Looking Glass*. Copyright © 1987 by Sage Publications, Inc. Reprinted with the permission of the publishers.

Valdes-Rodriquez, Alisa, "Crossing Pop Lines: Attention to Latinos Is Overdue, But Sometimes Off-Target," *Los Angeles Times* (June 11, 1999), Orange County Edition, Part F, p. 2, Calendar Desk.

Wark, McKenzie, "Cyberpunk: Subculture or Mainstream?" from *21*C* No. 6 (Winter 1992): 57–60. Copyright © 1992 by McKenzie Wark. Reprinted with the permission of the author.

Waters, Harry, "Life According to TV," from *Newsweek* (December 6, 1982). Copyright © 1982 by Newsweek, Inc. Reprinted with the permission of *Newsweek*. All rights reserved.

Wells, Alan, "Popular Music: Emotional Use and Management," from *Journal of Popular Culture* (Summer, 1988). Copyright © 1988. Reprinted with the permission of Popular Press.

PHOTOGRAPH AND ILLUSTRATION CREDITS

Chapter 1: Photograph courtesy of Nicole Miller/Globe Photos, Inc. 1994.

Chapter 2: Photograph courtesy of Timex, Inc.

Chapter 3: Drawing by Glen Baxter. Copyright © 1991 The New Yorker Magazine, Inc.

Chapter 4: Photograph from Lord, Dentsu & Partners/NY. Copyright © 1993 TDK Electronics Corporation.

Chapter 5: Cartoon by Randy Glasberger. Copyright © 1996 Randy Glasberger.

Chapter 6: Photography by Mimi Forsyth; courtesy of Monkmeyer Press.

Chapter 7: Photograph courtesy of Photofest.

Chapter 8: Photograph courtesy of FPG International.

Index by Rhetorical Mode

Index by Academic Discipline

Index by author and title